CORPORATE TREASURER'S
AND CONTROLLER'S
ENCYCLOPEDIA,
REVISED

CORPORATE TREASURER'S AND CONTROLLER'S ENCYCLOPEDIA, REVISED

The Prentice-Hall Editorial Staff,
Revised by Sam R. Goodman

VOLUME I

Prentice-Hall, Inc.   *Englewood Cliffs, N.J.*

Prentice-Hall International, Inc., *London*
Prentice-Hall of Australia, Pty. Ltd., *Sydney*
Prentice-Hall of Canada, Ltd., *Toronto*
Prentice-Hall of India Private Ltd., *New Delhi*
Prentice-Hall of Japan, Inc., *Tokyo*

Second Printing . . . . . April, 1976

Library of Congress Cataloging in Publication Data

Prentice-Hall, Inc.
   Corporate treasurer's and controller's encyclopedia, Revised

   Previous eds. edited by L. Doris.
   1. Corporations—United States—Finance. I. Good-
man, Sam R.   ed. II. Doris, Lillian, ed.
Corporate treasurer's and controller's encyclopedia.
III. Title
HG4061.P74   1974   658.1'5'03   74-13138
ISBN 0-13-176156-0

Printed in the United States of America

Dedicated to the memory of
Richard Prentice Ettinger,
a man who did not hesitate
to put himself out for others.

ACKNOWLEDGMENTS

Contributing authors to the earlier edition of *Corporate Treasurer's and Controller's Encyclopedia*, upon which the current *Revision* is based, were:

Sebastian A. Albrecht	George G. McConeghy
A. J. Ammon	Allen H. Ottman
Robert L. Boyd	James T. S. Porterfield
John F. Childs	P. L. Procter
W. J. Fitzsimons	George E. Rogers
R. B. Gallagher	H. H. Scaff
John W. Gladson	Charles H. Sevin
Paul J. Hamman	W. J. Shultz
Richard J. Hanwell	Mason Smith
John W. Haslett	Maurice H. Stans
Pearson Hunt	William W. Voorhees
Louis M. Kessler	Darrell H. Voorhies
William J. Madison	Frank Wallace
Joseph A. Mauriello	

I also gratefully acknowledge the assistance of John Mangini in the preparation of *Corporate Treasurer's and Controller's Encyclopedia, Revised.*

Sam R. Goodman

Contents

VOLUME I

VOLUME II

1

The Treasurer and

The Controller

CONTENTS

1

The Treasurer and
The Controller

BASIS OF THE TREASURER'S AND CONTROLLER'S FUNCTIONS

Background of financial and accounting functions. In the modern business corporation, the duties of treasurers and controllers normally relate to the financial and accounting functions. These functions are indispensable in the corporate form of organization; even the earliest corporations made provision for officers to perform them. In the movement in England to establish a company to trade in Virginia (1606), and in the organization of The Treasurer and Company of Adventurers and Planters of the City of London for the First Colony in Virginia (1609), the officers to be chosen by the company were a treasurer, deputy treasurer, husband, secretary, bookkeeper, and beadle. The principal committees were a general committee, a committee to attend to the buying and selling of commodities, and a committee for the auditing of accounts. The auditing committee, among other responsibilities, examined and passed upon all claims against the company, and caused all receipts and expenditures to be recorded in a book.[1] Even at this early date, the influences were forming for dividing business organization into its four classical parts: production, marketing, finance, and accounting. The organization arrangements in the great trading companies of the seventeenth century were founded upon their three primary functions: trading, finance, and accounting. The fourth part, production, was to begin during the industrial revolution of the following century.

In the evolution of the major elements of management—planning, coordination, and control—control was the first to emerge, its significance having been recognized in the early corporations in their provision for bookkeepers and auditors of accounts. Hence, the principles of control were developed much earlier than the principles of planning and coordination. Finance, in its modern concept, appeared later when the technical developments of the late eighteenth century were changing the structure of industry in such a manner as to require greater concentrations of capital in individual businesses, largely for the purposes of manufacturing. As production facilities increased, investment increased, and the procurement and use of funds became more and more important. Also, as facilities increased, the amount of labor, material, and

---

[1] Susan Myra Kingsbury, *The Records of the Virginia Company of London*. Washington: Government Printing Office, 1906, Vol. 1, pp. 72-73.

overhead likewise increased, and cost accounting was introduced for both the control of costs and the establishment of selling prices. Cost control was to become the basic tool of production management.[2] In this manner, finance and accounting have been long related, not only to each other, but as integral parts of production, marketing, and the business as a whole.

The title and office of treasurer. All of the titles for offices of highest rank in the modern business corporation—chairman, president, vice-president, treasurer, secretary, and controller—have had their antecedents in association with government. The title of treasurer in the first business corporations was a natural extension from its governmental association. The importance of the treasurer has been so long recognized that wherever the financial function is a necessary part of an undertaking, the organization arrangements ordinarily provide for the office and title of treasurer.

Today, the activities of the treasurer are based upon the financial functions that have arisen in modern business to carry out the objectives of the enterprise. To keep pace with corporate and financial developments, many functions have been added to the office. There has been little change, however, in the essential purpose; throughout the evolution of the office, the treasurer has retained one early and basic duty, the custody and supervision of funds. With the increase in the size and complexity of business, new techniques and procedures have been required, and new controls have been devised to cope with the new situations and new problems. Financial planning and the procurement, use, and investment of funds present problems of increasing proportions and importance. Modern developments in the use of credit as a means of expanding the volume of sales, and the evolution of the modern framework within which credits and collections are administered, have not only imposed new and essential duties upon the treasurer but have extended also the scope and importance of the office.

The addition of other responsibilities. The evolution of the office of treasurer has not been based wholly upon natural accretions. Because of their training, experience, and particular abilities, treasurers frequently serve as corporate directors, vice-presidents, and secretaries. In these and other capacities they are entrusted with many important duties and functions unrelated to finance and the office of treasurer. In New England, it has been a long-standing practice for treasurers to serve not only in financial capacities but also, at the same time, as the principal operating officer of the business. In this country, generally, the office has paralleled the offices of president and secretary from the earliest of use of corporations for business purposes.

The title and office of controller. In direct contrast with the treasurer, the office of controller is a modern development in organization and management that has had its principal growth during the present century. The title of controller, like that of treasurer, had its origin in government. In the fifteenth century, the title was used in the various offices of the English Royal Household, such as the Comptroller of Accounts in the Lord Chamberlain's office. In this country, the Continental Congress appointed a Comptroller in 1778; the Treasury Department established the office of the Comptroller in 1789; the Comptroller of the Currency was created in 1864,[3] and the title now is

---

[2] L. Urwick and E. F. L. Brech, *The Making of Scientific Management*. London: Management Publications Trust, 1946, Vol. II, Ch. II.

[3] G. Kirby Munson, "The Duties of the Controller as a Corporate Officer," *American Bar Association Journal*, Vol. XX, No. 1 (January, 1934), p. 57.

used widely in association with federal, state, and municipal offices and agencies. The title and office of controller was probably extended into the business corporation through the railroads. Prior to 1900, it had been established in The Atchison, Topeka and Santa Fe Railroad Company (1880), the Southern Pacific (1885), the New York, New Haven and Hartford (1887), the Illinois Central (1890), the Lehigh Valley (1890), and the Baltimore and Ohio (1892). Several public utility and industrial controllerships had been established before 1900, but the movement had its chief impetus after the turn of the century. Most industrial controllerships date from 1920. In the modern business corporation, the title is used ordinarily to designate the principal officer in charge of accounts. Studies show that the organization arrangements of most medium-sized and large corporations provide for the controller. The rapid adoption of the industrial controllership and the rearrangement of functions to make the controllership effective have constituted one of the most outstanding changes in the organization of the business corporation.

The president, treasurer, and secretary have long been considered as the indispensable corporate officers. In a majority of the states, the statutes governing incorporation provide that every corporation shall have a president, treasurer, and secretary, and such other officers and agents as may be deemed necessary. On the other hand, none of the state laws specifically requires a corporation to have a controller. The industrial controllership has come into existence without the aid of tradition, custom, and statutory support. Moreover, it is unlikely that the office of controller will ever be made mandatory by statute. The controllership is an organization mechanism best suited to, and most essential in, large and medium-sized companies. The office is not essential to small companies, and mandatory statutory requirements would place an undue organizational burden on the small company. For this reason, the office of controller is not likely to become universal. Its future development, as in the past, will be based upon actual need.

Controllership practice in large and medium-sized companies. In its present stage of development, the controllership is not in use in all companies where it could well serve the purposes of management. That its need is well established is borne out, first, by its adoption by most large companies, and second, by its widespread use in a majority of medium-sized companies. In a survey of 150 large, medium, and small companies, made especially for use in this encyclopedia, all of the companies include the controllership in their organization.

In companies that do not have controllers, and in the majority of smaller companies, the accounting function ordinarily comes within the jurisdiction of the treasurer or the secretary. This is the historical and traditional arrangement for the accounting function. As individual businesses grew in size and as new situations and problems arose, it became increasingly necessary to expand the use of accounting controls. This in turn, required a greater degree of specialization. The need for added control and for specialization is the basis for the separation of the accounting function from the financial and secretarial, and the addition of the controller in organization arrangements. This subject is treated more fully in the section dealing with the organization of the treasurer's and controller's departments.

The addition of other responsibilities. Like the treasurers, and for the same reasons of training, experience, and particular abilities, it is common for controllers to serve as corporate directors and vice presidents. In these and other capacities controllers are entrusted with many important duties and functions unrelated to accounting and the office of controller. From the accounting and financial standpoint, the controller comes into contact with more phases of the business than any other officer. Being called upon to interpret operations, past, present, or for the future, in terms of funds, profit, and financial conditions, the controller is in a position to know most about the company's profit and financial position and to gain the knowledge first and at first-hand. For this and other reasons, controllers frequently serve in other administrative capacities. They bring to such activities not only training and experience, but the ability to intrepret business undertakings in terms of cash, profit, and financial results.

Functions in relation to the corporate characteristics. The corporation is a creation of the law with certain attributes and characteristics that distinguish it from other forms of business organization and make it workable. The corporate attributes and characteristics constitute the foundation upon which the management and control functions are erected and maintained and give rise to the financial, accounting, and secretarial functions.[4] Hence, the present-day corporate offices of secretary, treasurer, and controller are founded upon the nature of the business corporation. An understanding of the functional and organizational arrangements under which these officers participate in the management and control of the business must therefore proceed from a review of the corporate characteristics of the business corporation.

The characteristics of the business corporation. The principal characteristics of the business corporation may be summarized as follows:

1. Creation by government sanction.
2. Separate legal entity.
3. Continuity of existence.
4. Identification by corporate name and seal.
5. Limited liability of stockholders.
6. Division of ownership into transferable shares.
7. Representative management.

With the exception of the fifth characteristic, limited liability, all of the characteristics create functional duties that must be performed through representative management. From a functional and organizational standpoint, therefore, representative management is the most important corporate characteristic. The others merely create duties peculiar to the corporate mechanism, as will be shown in the following brief discussion of each of the characteristics.

Creation by government sanction. The privilege of doing business under the corporate form of organization, the exemption of the stockholders from personal liability, and the power to pursue the corporate objectives and purposes can be obtained only by conforming to the governing statutes. As the corporation is a creature of the law, its organization and the manner of conducting its corporate affairs are prescribed by law and custom. To maintain its existence, it must conform to the prescribed requirements.

---

[4]Modern corporate practice provides for the combination of offices in one individual. The most common combination is that of secretary and treasurer. Functions of the secretary are discussed in this section as a basis for the later presentation of the principal secretarial duties when the same individual acts as both treasurer and secretary.

These requirements create two groups of procedures, each of which gives rise to important corporate functions. The first group constitutes the corporate legal functions. These embrace, in general, the proper qualification of the corporation in all states in which it does business; its maintenance in good corporate standing in each state; the establishment and maintenance of the required statutory offices and records; the protection of the corporate name; apprisement of the directors and officers of statutory changes affecting the corporate privilege; and the general conduct of the corporate affairs in conformance with the law.

The second group of procedures includes, in general, the meetings of stockholders and directors, the election of directors and officers, and the conduct of the corporate affairs within the provisions of its charter,[5] the by-laws, the resolutions of the stockholders, and the resolutions and policies of the board of directors. The duties and responsibilities incidental to this group of proceedings may be termed the corporate recording functions.

Together, the legal and recording functions include the duties and responsibilities necessary for the proper functioning of the corporate mechanism from a legal and corporate standpoint. They are at the basis of the corporate secretarial function. In many companies, responsibility for the legal functions rests in other officers than the secretary or in the company's legal counsel. The recording functions are almost universally the responsibility of the secretary. In many large companies, and some medium-sized companies, the organization includes the office of general counselor or an officer in charge of legal affairs. Such a separation of functions is clearly within the prerogatives of the corporate management. Unless, however, the legal functions are included in the duties of other offices, the secretary is basically responsible for both the recording and legal functions. He is generally provided with, or is expected to obtain, the legal assistance necessary to perform his duties properly.

The separate legal entity. The legal concept of a corporation is that of a natural person, separate and distinct from its stockholders, directors, and officers. For all practical purposes, a corporation may do any act or enter into any legal relationship, in so far as its charter will permit, with the freedom of a natural person. But since the corporation is an artificial being existing only in contemplation of the law, it cannot act for itself; it must hire natural persons as agents and employees to act for it. The corporate mechanism meets this requirement by providing for corporate offices for the representatives of highest rank and authority. The persons elected or appointed to such offices become the corporate officers. Their powers and duties are fixed by charter, by-law provision, resolution, custom, and practice.

Continuity of existence. The numerous changes that take place among the stockholders, directors, and officers do not affect the continued existence of the corporation. Continuous existence not only makes possible the pursuit of the objectives and purposes without interruption, but imparts to the corporate offices and management the degree of continuity necessary for the operation of the corporate mechanism. A majority of the states grant corporate charters in perpetuity. In the other states, the existence of the corporation is limited, but the statutes provide for the renewal or extension of

---

[5]Many statutory powers and requirements do not appear in the corporate certificate or articles of incorporation. For this reason, the charter of the corporation is deemed to include both the statutory powers and requirements and those enumerated in the articles or certificate of incorporation.

charters. For all practical purposes, this amounts to uninterrupted existence. It is also true that changes among the officers do not affect the continuity of the corporate offices, the concept of a corporate office being distinct from that of an officer. Therefore, the continuity of the corporate offices parallels the existence of the corporation and, as long as the corporation exists, the required and established corporate offices exist.

In addition to the statutory provisions for the uninterrupted existence of corporations, the laws provide also for voluntary dissolution. The extension or renewal of the corporate existence (which occurs infrequently and then only in corporations having a limited life) and the voluntary dissolution of companies are carried out under prescribed forms and conditions through certain corporate legal procedures. Basically, the duties incidental to these procedures become a part of the secretarial function but, because of their legal nature, the attendant responsibilities may be allocated to officers in charge of legal affairs or, in small companies, to counsel.

The corporate name and seal. Every corporation must have a name for purposes of identification. Because of the prestige and public confidence attaching to nationally known corporations, and to other corporations within their own spheres of activity, the protection from use by others of the corporate name and the names of subsidiary, affiliated, or even inactive companies is important. The initiation of the necessary protective action is a responsibility of the secretary. The relief to be obtained or the restraining action to be taken, however, is largely a matter of legal procedure, and, for this reason, the protection of the corporate name may be assigned as a legal rather than a secretarial function.

The use of seals, as an emblem of authority, is ancient; as an incident of incorporation, its use is likewise very old. Today, the corporation must use its seal in executing an instrument only when a seal is required by statute or charter, or when an individual executing a similar document would be required to do so under seal. In current practice, the seal is used to authenticate all formal acts and contracts, powers of attorney, deeds, mortgages, and other important agreements. Documents to be recorded in a public office are frequently unacceptable unless they are sealed, and the form of corporate acknowledgment in use in many states requires a recital that the corporate seal has been duly affixed. To afford the necessary protection against the unauthorized use of the corporate seal, the by-laws usually provide that the seal shall be in the custody of the secretary. In some companies, however, the treasurer or others have custody of the seal.

The limited liability of stockholders. Although all of the features of the business corporation are interdependent, it is generally conceded that the provision for the limited liability of stockholders is most important to the stockholders, if not to the entire corporate scheme. Historically, stockholders of corporations are not always exempted from personal liability. Before the enactment of general corporation laws in the various states, incorporation could be accomplished only by separate acts of the legislatures, and limited liability for stockholders could be secured only by special charter provision. Notwithstanding the present general rule of non-liability, in some states the certificate of incorporation must state whether the stockholders shall be subject to the payment of the corporate debts and, if so, to what extent. Hence, the feature of limited liability for stockholders presents only one duty for the secretary or other corporate officers in the incorporation of subsidiary, affiliated, or other companies. Under the laws of states requiring express stipulation in the certificate of incorporation for exemption from liability, the secretary, or other officers in charge of these matters, must make certain of this protection of the parent company or other stockholders.

The division of ownership into transferable shares. The division of ownership of the business corporation into shares as fixed by its certificate or articles of incorporation, with each share transferable from one person to another, is a basic corporate characteristic. The transferability of shares is considered second in importance only to the privilege of limited liability for the stockholders. Few forms of property can be transferred as easily. Moreover, every purchaser or other transferee is entitled to become a stockholder of record and to participate in the rights secured thereby. In general, he has the right to participate in the meetings of stockholders and to share, pro rata, in the dividends. To acquire this status, however, his ownership must be recorded on the books of the corporation. The corporation must make all required transfers of stock, and, to avoid liability, it must exercise considerable care in doing so.

This important corporate obligation and duty, whether performed within the company or through banks and trust companies acting as transfer agents and registrars, gives rise to the corporate stock transfer function and the maintenance of the corporation's basic stock records. These records not only serve the transfer function but, of equal importance, constitute the record of the corporation's stock ownership. They are the basis, therefore, for all notices to the stockholders as to meetings, the issuance and recording of proxies, admission to, and voting at, stockholders' meetings, the payment of dividends, and the preparation of income tax data required by state and federal agencies, and for corporate statistics. The responsibility for the capital stock records and the transfer function is placed, in most cases, with the secretary, and, in some companies, with the treasurer, the controller, or others.

Representative management. The provision for representative management makes possible the whole structure under which corporations are managed and controlled. Every act performed on behalf of the corporation in pursuit of its purposes and objectives, whether by the board of directors, or its officers, agents, or employees, is traceable to this feature of the corporation. The provision for representative management also causes the board of directors of the corporation to stand in a trustee relationship to the stockholders. In its arrangements for management and control, the corporate scheme provides, first, for the election of directors by the stockholders and, second, for the election or appointment of officers by the directors. The officers are accountable to the board of directors, and the directors are accountable to the stockholders, thus completing the cycle within which the corporate management and control is established and regulated.

The functions of the stockholders are exceedingly limited. It is the universal rule that the business of the corporation is within the control of its board of directors. The stockholders cannot act in relation to the ordinary business of the corporation, nor, as a general rule, can they control the board of directors in the exercise of its powers. The directors have the control of the corporate business, and hence of the property interests of the stockholders; the stockholders are the proprietors of the corporate interests, and the beneficiaries of them. This relationship between stockholders and directors gives rise to the trusteeship function of the board of directors and makes necessary the financial and accounting functions. The obligations under the trusteeship function lend further emphasis, as well, to the requirements for the secretarial function. Although the secretarial function is influenced mainly by the characteristics of the corporation, it is also necessary to the proper discharge of the obligations of the board of directors growing out of the trusteeship function.

In the conduct of the trusteeship function, the directors must discharge three primary obligations to the stockholders. They must:

1. Protect and preserve the corporate powers and assets.
2. Pursue the purposes and objectives of the business, measure and appraise results, and take the affirmative or corrective action necessary for the improvement of the profit and financial position of the company and its relationships with employees, customers, and the public.
3. Account to the stockholders for the progress of the business and, in some measure, under modern trends for large and medium-sized companies, account to the employees and the public.

It is evident that many business functions and duties must be carried out to meet the trusteeship obligations. This is accomplished, in general, through a departmentaliza-tion of the functions, under which the officers of the corporation assume both responsi-bility for, and control of, the component parts of the business under the direction and coordination of the principal corporate officer, ordinarily the president.

The functions involved in the protection and preservation of the corporate powers and assets, when broken down into component parts, become largely legal, secretarial, financial, accounting, and operating responsibilities. The functions concerned with the purposes and objectives of the business become mainly operating responsibilities, supported and aided by the use of the financial and accounting functions. The obliga-tion as to accountability is discharged largely through the accounting function. The following paragraphs summarize the financial, accounting, and secretarial functions growing out of the characteristics of the business corporation and the primary obliga-tions under representative management.

Functions concerned with the protection and preservation of the corporate powers and assets

Legal. Functions relating to the organization of the corporation, its proper qualifi-cation in all the states in which it does business, its maintenance of the proper statutory offices and records, the protection of the corporate name, appT1sement of the directors and officers of statutory changes affecting the corporate privilege, the general conduct of the corporate affairs in conformance with the law, and the protection of the corpo-rate powers.

Secretarial. Functions relating to the meetings of stockholders and directors, the election of directors and officers, minutes, notices, resolutions, proxies, and the cus-tody of the corporate seal.

Custodial. Functions relating to cash receipts, disbursements, balances, and bank-ing, and the custody of the corporate funds, securities, and financial instruments.

Protection of Properties. Functions relating to the discharge of tax liabilities on real and personal properties and to the negotiation and placement of insurance cover-age.

Credit and Collections. Functions relating to the extension of credit and the collection of accounts to prevent undue loss in the conversion of receivables to cash.

General Accounting. Functions relating to the record and protection, from a book standpoint, of the corporate assets, and the recording and discharge of liabilities within the terms thereof to protect the corporate credit, the use of properties and facilities, and to avoid defaults, liens, and lawsuits.

Tax Accounting. Functions relating to the assembling of information, the preparation of returns, and the discharge of income and excise[6] tax liabilities to avoid penalties or liens.

Auditing. Functions relating to the establishment of internal auditing controls and the audit of records and transactions to protect the corporate assets against fraud, misuse, and manipulation.

Functions concerned with purposes and objectives of the business

Legal. Functions relating to the creation and dissolution of subsidiary, affiliated, or other companies for business purposes.

Financial Planning. Functions relating to the ascertainment of needs for funds at future dates as a guide to availability for expansion of operations, expansion of fixed assets and working capital, debt retirement, and dividends.

Procurement of Funds. Functions relating to the procurement of long- and short-term funds for expansion of operations and facilities, for working capital, reimbursements to working capital, debt retirement, and the refinancing of funded or unfunded debts and liabilities.

Investment. Functions relating to the investment of surplus funds for income or other purposes, and the purchase and sale of securities.

Extension of Credit. Functions relating to the extension of credit as a means of improving the volume of sales or services and earnings.

General Accounting. Functions relating to the recording of routine transactions as a basis for determining net income, expenses, and earnings, income and excise taxes, surplus, and basic financial and statistical information.

Cost Accounting. Functions relating to the preparation of historical, predetermined, or standard costs of operations, activities, functions, services, and products, as a guide to the establishment of prices and the effective control of the various costs of doing business.

Interpretive Accounting. Functions relating to the preparation, analysis, and explanation of financial, accounting, cost, and statistical results as an aid to management·in the direction of the business, for obtaining credit or financial assistance, for reports to stockholders, or for other purposes of internal or external use.

Auditing. Functions relating to the objective verification of business, financial, and accounting transactions and their conformance with policies and procedures.

Functions necessary to accountability

Stock Transfers. Functions relating to the right of every stockholder and transferee of the common and preferred stock of the corporation to become a stockholder of record, and, in general, to become a beneficiary of the corporate interests, to participate in the meetings of stockholders and to share in dividends.

Corporate Accounting. Functions relating to the necessary accounting adjustments, and consolidation of the corporate accounts, to reflect properly the net profit or income of the business, its financial position, and the availability of surplus for dividends.

Auditing. Functions relating to the proper coordination and adjustment of the

---

[6]The term "excise tax," as used in this chapter, contemplates any tax not measured by net income, and any tax not assessed against property and not measured by the value thereof.

accounts, and the internal auditing procedures, with the requirements of the independent auditors and their certification to the earnings and financial position of the corporation.

Allocation of functions. The duties that officers and others perform may be grouped generally into two categories: (1) official functions and duties, and (2) functions assigned by the board of directors or other officers with the requisite authority.

The official functions and duties are those prescribed by statute, the certificate or articles of incorporation, the by-laws, and the resolutions of the board of directors. Of these sources, the by-laws are the most important in determining the functions to be performed, for they are ordinarily specific as to the duties of each officer. The by-laws cannot be depended upon, however, to show all of the official functions and duties; to a large extent many are based upon precedent and internal practice, which, in a majority of instances, have not been reduced to writing.

The assigned functions refer to responsibilities for particular operations or activities. In some companies, for example, secretaries may be placed in general charge of the operation of office buildings, treasurers may be in charge of purchasing, and controllers may have jurisdiction over real estate matters.

Determination of basic functions. The basic functions of corporate officers may be determined logically by combining the official functions common to each officer in a comprehensive number of companies, with the assigned or administrative functions that have become normally associated with an office through a preponderance of corporate practice. For example, the responsibility for the credit and collection function is considered as belonging basically with the treasurer because it is placed there by most companies.

The allocation of functions among officers cannot be considered as fixed and unalterable. In 1927, the leading work on this subject stated ''in respect to definitions of functions embraced in the modern offices of controller, treasurer, and auditor, the difficulty is not in outlining what may be termed ideal standards of activity, but rather in taking into account the numerous departures in practice from these general or technical characterizations. The necessity of fitting special work to the personal qualifications of executives, and the inexpediency of changing long-existing lines of authority to accord with purely logical classifications have resulted in innumerable variations of structural schemes in corporate organizations. Accordingly, any dialectical definition of these titles must be qualified by reference to the array of special conditions or exceptions which almost nullifies the validity of categorical determinations.'' In view of the past lack of uniformity in the assignment of functions to secretaries, treasurers, and controllers, it is not surprising that there are still wide and interesting dissimilarities in practices among corporations. Such differences are likely to continue, for there is always the necessity for fitting special work to the personal qualifications of individuals and the inexpediency of changing existing lines of authority. In the passage of 20 years, however, a more intensified use has been made of the principles and processes of organization, almost always with the purpose of making the corporation a more suitable mechanism for business and of meeting the problems presented by the increasing size of individual companies and the added complexity of business in general. The past decades have brought about considerable change. The influences of the corporate officers, both as individuals and through professional societies, have had a marked effect upon the nature of the functions each is to perform. This, together with the interest of business management in improved organization, has brought about practices which, in general, have become common to a large number of representative companies. Extensive studies of the allocation of functions to secretaries, treasurers, and controllers point to the emergence of leading practices.

TABLE I

ALLOCATION OF FUNCTIONS TO
TREASURERS, CONTROLLERS, SECRETARIES, AND OTHERS
(expressed in percentage of instances, 150 companies)

	Treasurer	Controller	Secretary	Others
Accounting: corporate, general, cost, and interpretive accounting, methods and systems, and the design, installation, and custody of books, records, and forms	26%	70%	—%	4%
Analyses: cost, profit, and financial analyses relating to past, present, or proposed operations	31	61	1	7
Auditing: internal	16	79	—	5
Budgets:				
expenditures:				
advertising	11	26	—	63
capital	18	27	3	52
operating	13	34	2	51
funds	37	27	—	36
Communications: telephone, telegraph, teletype, and private wires	7	20	10	63
Credits and collections	50	15	5	30
Dividends, disbursement of	35	5	43	17
Economics and statistics: development and maintenance of information	7	34	4	55
Employee benefit plans:				
pension plans	40	6	16	38
profit sharing plans	44	5	11	40
stock purchase plans	39	8	30	23
others	32	4	6	58
Filing facilities (centralized), operation of	5	19	28	48
Forecasts:				
economic	12	25	2	61
financial	35	36	2	27
profits	18	53	2	27
taxes	17	50	5	28
Funds:				
budgeting of	40	29	3	28
forecasting of	46	30	2	22
investment of	61	7	2	30
loans and advances to others	59	9	1	31
planning of	52	15	3	30
procurement of	51	7	8	34
receipts, disbursements, and balances	71	16	2	11

	Treasurer	Controller	Secretary	Others
relationships with banks	67	6	10	17
Insurance:				
fire, casualty, group, and life	29	12	22	37
surety bonds	30	13	23	34
Integrated data processing (automation):				
as applied to stock transfer	9	14	39	38
as applied to dividend payment	15	19	31	35
as applied to other administrative records	8	52	11	29
Legal (corporate): the protection of the corporate legal standing; the incorporation of new companies, state of incorporation, certificate and by-law provisions; protection of corporate names; apprisement of the directors and officers of statutory changes affecting the corporate privilege; dissolution of inactive companies; the general conduct of the corporate affairs in accordance with the law; the protection of the corporate powers	3	1	48	48
Legal (general): supervision of the legal department or staff	2	1	32	65
Office building, operation of	27	11	10	52
Office services (centralized):				
mail, receipt, distribution, and dispatch of	14	21	8	57
reception and messenger services	13	18	6	63
stenographic and duplicating services	14	22	7	57
Patents, protection of	4	—	35	61
Payrolls:				
(confidential), preparation of	56	30	2	12
(general), preparation of	44	41	—	15
Proxies:				
preparation of	5	2	81	12
review and tabulation of	10	1	75	14
Public relations	7	1	22	70
Real estate: lease or sale of properties, and the granting of rights of way or other privileges in properties	19	2	21	58
Recording (corporate): secretarial detail incidental to the meetings of stockholders and directors, the election of directors and officers, minutes, notices, resolutions, and the custody of the corporate seal	2	—	86	12
Records: custody, retention, preservation, and destruction of	12	17	50	21
Securities:				
custody of	78	4	11	7
purchase and sale of	80	2	3	15
Standard practice instructions	15	37	8	40
Stockholder reports, preparation of	19	13	40	28
Taxes:				
excise	32	47	6	15
income	31	49	6	14
property	26	38	10	26
Transfers:				
bonds and debentures	36	—	44	20
preferred and common stocks	22	1	55	22
relationships with transfer agents and registrars	26	1	66	7

SPECIFIC FUNCTIONS OF THE TREASURER AND THE CONTROLLER

Universal functions of executives. In addition to the duties that may generally pertain to an office, the incumbent has the responsibilities that are common to all supervisors. Thus, within his own segment of the enterprise, a treasurer or controller has some measure of responsibility for the plan of organization, personnel administration, and the effect of their operations upon the finances of the company. Like all supervisors, he must see that his performance of supervisory functions coordinates with the policies and procedures for the company as a whole.

The number of employees required in the conduct of the financial and accounting functions varies with the size of the business, but, in medium-sized and large companies, the number can be substantial. Hence, the control of organization, methods, and manpower is extremely important. Accounting and clerical personnel is drawn from a labor market different from that for mechanics, technicians, and operators. This brings about differences in personnel and wage and salary policies and administration. Treasurers and controllers must ordinarily take the lead in the formulation of such policies, sometimes not only for the employees within their immediate organizations, but for all other clerical personnel in the company.

Capital expenditures incidental to the financial and accounting functions are not generally as extensive in size and complexity as expenditures for operating purposes; nor does financial and accounting expense run in the same proportions as operating and maintenance expense. It is, however, both a corporate and business principle that organization and personnel administration, and the expenditure of money, shall be subject to substantially the same judicious control and accountability throughout the company. For this reason, treasurers and controllers must exercise control within their departments in the same manner as all other supervisors.

THE FUNCTIONS OF THE TREASURER

The treasurer in a business corporation is the financial executive who is essentially responsible for all the functions which are classified under the general heading of "money management." As we have noted, this means that the treasurer serves chiefly as the custodian of a corporation's funds. He retains the corporate funds in trust for the benefit of the corporation and disburses funds only when authorized.

In many companies, the treasurer serves in other corporate capacities, such as a director, or as a vice president of finance. In smaller companies he also serves as a controller. The position of controller exists primarily among larger companies. The two positions are closely related; the treasurer is responsible for money management activities, the controller serves as chief accountant and financial planner.

Duties assigned to treasurer by bylaws. An examination of the bylaws of many corporations shows a wide variety of functions delegated to the treasurer. This is due to the differences in the general organization of many corporations. The following are the duties usually assigned to the treasurer by the bylaws. This list is comprehensive; in many corporations, some of the power listed here may be delegated to the controller, secretary, or auditor, rather than to the treasurer.

1. Supervising, having custody of, and assuming responsibility for all funds and securities of the corporation.
2. Maintaining bank accounts in designated banks.
3. Making books and records available to any of the directors during business hours.
4. Preparing statements on the company's financial condition for all regular meetings of the directors, and a complete report at the annual meeting of stockholders.
5. Receiving monies due to the corporation.
6. Maintaining records giving a full account of monies personally received and paid for by the corporation.
7. Signing certificates of shares in the capital stock of the company (together with the president or vice-president).
8. Signing all checks, bills of exchange, and promissory notes, with such other officer as the board of directors may designate.
9. Advising the corporation on financial matters.
10. Maintaining custody of the stock book, and preparing the dividend payments.
11. Preparing and submitting tax reports.
12. Performing all other duties connected with the office, and any duties that the board of directors may assign.

Duties assigned to treasurer by directors, committees, and officers. Bylaw provisions are often brief, and many of the treasurer's duties are delegated to him by special action of the board of directors or of its committees, and by direction of higher executive officers, such as the president and the chairman of the board. These duties are either of a temporary character, usually terminating in a report to the board, or are of a general nature, representing permanently assigned functions.

Typical functions delegated by special authorization and assignment are investigation for the development of pension plans and group insurance plans; examination of companies in which the corporation contemplates purchasing an interest; arranging for listing the company's securities on the stock exchange; and investigation of the feasibility of stock offerings.

The treasurer's major areas of responsibility.

1. *Provision of Capital.* Establishing and executing programs for providing capital need by the business, including procurement of capital and maintaining required financial arrangements.

2. *Investor Relations.* Establishing and maintaining an adequate market for the company's securities and maintaining liaison with investment bankers, financial analysts and shareholders.

3. *Short-Term Financing.* Maintaining adequate sources for the company's current borrowing from commercial banks and other lending institutions.

4. *Banking and Custody.* Maintaining banking arrangements for receiving, holding and disbursing the company's monies and securities, plus responsibility for the financial aspects of real estate transactions.

5. *Credits and Collections.* Directing credit granting and collection of accounts and supervising arrangements for financing sales, as through time payment and leasing plans.

6. *Investments.* Investing the company's funds as required and establishing and coordinating policies to govern investment in pension funds and similar trusts.

7. *Insurance.* Providing coverage as required.

Duties assigned by treasurer to staff. Many treasurers delegate most of the details of their work to members of their staff, giving their attention to the supervision, study, and adoption of procedure consistent with the policies of the corporation.

If a treasurer is in charge of stock books and dividend payments, most of the actual work is performed by the staff. The treasurer, however, ascertains personally whether liquid funds will be available at dividend dates to meet the obligation.

Similarly, when the treasurer is in charge of group insurance plans and employees' saving and profit-sharing funds, the staff, under the direction of the treasurer, keeps the necessary records. And upon the adoption of an employee stock ownership plan, the staff performs the actual detailed work of recording installment payments and stock deliveries.

The extension of credit is usually handled by the credit manager, who has considerable responsibility, but is subject to the authority of the treasurer. In such cases, only special matters are brought to the treasurer's attention. In regard to receipts and disbursements, the responsibility is often placed on the cashier, who refers special cases to the treasurer. In many instances, the treasurer issues reports prepared by assistants under his direction.

Assistant Treasurer. The assistant treasurer is the officer of a corporation who assists the treasurer in the care, custody, receipt and disbursement of company funds.

The bylaws of large corporations sometimes provide for one or more assistant treasurers authorized to perform, in the order of their rank, all of the duties of the treasurer in the latter's absence or inability to act. Assistant treasurers perform any duties assigned to them by the treasurer or by the board of directors, and assist the treasurer at all times.

Some treasurers' departments follow the policy of assigning as much work as possible to assistants without getting out of touch with the general trend of affairs. This prevents the treasurer from becoming so burdened with detail that he loses sight of more important matters. Assistant treasurers may be delegated nearly all the details of the work of the treasurer's office to enable the treasurer to give most of his attention to outside matters.

If a growing company is financing its expansion through new issues of stocks and bonds, the treasurer's tasks may be confined to the handling of security issues, while the other duties of the office are carried out by an assistant treasurer.

In some cases, specific duties are assigned to the assistant treasurer. For example, the assistant treasurer of a parent company, with subsidiaries in many states, may be required to devote his entire time to tax matters. His full-time job will be to keep constantly informed of the tax status of all subsidiaries and branches and to follow closely all changes in the tax laws of various states. He will also keep a calendar of report dates, and see that taxes are paid within the periods prescribed by law.

In some large corporations, especially where the treasurer performs the function of controller, an assistant treasurer heads up the accounting department.

THE FUNCTIONS OF THE CONTROLLER

The controller is the financial executive of a large or medium-sized corporation who combines the responsibilities for accounting, auditing, budgeting, profit planning, performance reporting, tax control, and other corporate activities.

The control that controllers exert is based on the word "control" in the indirect sense of making decisions and controlling action toward enabling the company to make profits. The purest example of the controllership principle in common practice is in budgetary control, which includes all kinds of appraisal and measurement.

The office of controller. Although relatively new in American corporations, the office of controller, so described earlier, continues to increase in importance. Legal statutes recognize the existence of the office of controller. The Securities Act of 1933 provides that the registration statement filed with the Securities and Exchange Commission must be signed by the controller of the issuing corporation or by its principal accounting officer, as well as by its other principal officers.

In some corporations, the office of controller is not an elective one; the controller is employed like any other department head. In other corporations, the board of directors elects the controller, and his duties are outlined in the corporate bylaws. In still other corporations, the office of controller is established by act of the executive committee, and the powers and duties are prescribed by resolution of the committee. Some organizations specify the controller's duties in an order signed by the president.

Duties assigned to controller. The controller's duties, as assigned to him by the bylaws, by resolution, or by executive order, usually require him to:

1. Serve as the chief accounting officer in charge of the company's accounting books, accounting records, and forms.
2. Audit all payrolls and vouchers and have them properly certified.
3. Prepare the company's balance sheet, income accounts, and other financial statements and reports, and give the president a complete report covering results of the company's operations during the past quarter and fiscal year to date.
4. Supervise the preparation, compilation, and filing of all reports, statements, statistics, and other data that the law requires or that the company president requests.
5. Receive all reports from agents and company departments that are needed for recording the company's general operations or for directing or supervising its accounts.
6. Maintain general control over the accounting practices of all subsidiary companies.
7. Supervise the enforcement and maintenance of the classification of accounts and any other accounting rules and regulations that any regulatory body prescribes.
8. Endorse for the company any checks or promissory notes for deposit, collection, or transfer.
9. Countersign all checks that the treasurer draws against funds of the company or its subsidiaries, except as otherwise provided by the board.
10. Approve the payment of all vouchers, drafts, and other accounts payable, when required by the president or any other persons he designates.
11. Appoint the auditor and his staff and set their salaries.
13. Compose a budget showing the company's future requirements as shown by its accounts and the requisitions of the general manager and other officers.
14. Supervise all records and clerical and office procedures for departments of the company and its subsidiaries.
15. Perform any other duties and have any other powers that the board of directors may occasionally prescribe and that the president may assign.

Other responsibilities placed on controllers. The controller's office is often responsible for tax matters, insurance of corporate property, leases, and office management. In some companies, the controller has charge of all service departments such as telephone, messenger service, janitors, filing, mailing, and similar matters.

The controller frequently serves on various committees, such as the finance committee, investments committee, pension board, budget committee, insurance committee, and special committees of various kinds.

The functions of the controller cover a broad field and relate to the activities of all departments, including the treasurer's department. Primarily the controller wields a check on disbursements and receipts of the treasurer. He may approve vouchers before payment, and frequently prescribes the methods of keeping accounts in the treasurer's office.

The controller performs a quasi-official duty in supplying the president or the treasurer with statistical data drawn from the accounting records and from other sources, as a basis for current or future financing of the corporation. Included also as controllership activities are the application of electronic data processing to accounting systems and procedures, and the installation and coordination of paperwork flow.

The controller sometimes acts in an advisory capacity, with his recommendations carried out by the executives in charge of the departments concerned. The controller may recommend accounting procedures for various branches, with implementation left to each branch manager. He frequently cooperates with the sales manager in compiling data for the production budget. He usually works with the factory superintendent or sales executive, as appropriate, to see that purchases remain as low as possible, consistent with production or sales requirements.

Assistant Controller. The assistant controller is charged with assisting the controller in special areas. His qualifications should supplement those of the controller. If a controller's chief training is in accounting, his assistant should be qualified in cost standards, statistics, budgets, or other areas requiring special experience.

Many companies have more than one assistant controller. A company with two assistant controllers may put one in charge of general accounts and budgetary procedures, and the other in charge of cost accounting. A company with three assistant controllers may delegate accounts and accounting methods to one, standards and statistics to another, and budgeting and forecasting to the third.

As assistant controller, in turn, delegates responsibility to supervisors for a certain amount of the routine work. The aim is to relieve the controller of as much detail as possible by apportioning much of the work among subordinates. This leaves the controller free to concentrate on procedures and policy matters.

NEW DIRECTIONS FOR FINANCIAL MANAGEMENT

During the last ten years, profound changes have taken place which represent a basic switch in management thinking relative to the role of the financial function. Problems are becoming more and more complex and, moreover, the ramifications of these problems are so potentially severe as to tax the imagination of a conventional treasurer and controller. We find, for example, that it is extremely difficult to try any longer to discern a distinct boundary in the jobs of various executives. It is not uncommon today for controllers to participate in data processing or in management information systems design. Because finance is becoming recognized as such a major decision function in business, it is also much more common to see senior officers of companies originate from within the ranks of the financial function. One of the major reasons for this is that the financial officer has developed during his career degrees of judgment which have been tempered by discipline and objectivity. The field of accounting and finance, for example, is no longer the staid, well-defined area which it was once recognized as being. Accounting rules are changing almost daily. Financial instruments used to raise capital are being innovated almost equally as quick. Both the controller and the treasurer are being called upon to render economic judgment as well as custodial financial judgment. As an example, at the present time the Accounting Principles Board of the American Institute of Certified Public Accountants is considering making mandatory the reporting of *imputed* interest in the financial statements of an organization. Imputed interest is a cost which cannot be seen; it cannot be felt; it cannot be touched. Nevertheless, it is an opportunity cost which existed as a result of an alternative which a company has exercised. In this sense, it is not a traditional historical accounting cost. It is an economic concept of cost of funds.

Many more complexities are being generated by changes in current tax laws and these complexities are of such magnitude that they must strain the abilities of the financial officer responsible for tax procedures. Changes in Internal Revenue rulings, for example, in the areas of capitalization versus expense for capital projects, are changing almost daily and what was once an accepted rule of thumb, may no longer be valid in today's changing tax environment. For example, the revenue service is much more stringent about what portion of a capital project may be expensed for tax purposes.

New problems which have been created by the social demands of society upon the corporation can change the nature and motivations of many of our corporate actions. Pollution control, for example, may strain the credulity of a traditional prehistoric financial executive. Nonproductive, capital projects may now be required to be completed and moreover, rather than generating a positive cash flow for a corporation, they may, in fact, serve no other purpose than to satisfy a newly created social goal for corporate behavior. In addition, new forms of social legislation such as Medicare and Medicaid are increasing the complexity of the recording of social obligations of companies. In fact, the traditional profit and loss statement as we know it may someday be relegated to a historical wastebasket. It may be necessary and also desirable in the future to have a profit and loss statement based upon profit oriented operations and a separate profit and loss statement to record the expenses incurred by performing social obligations of the corporation. The two, added together, would comprise the corporate entity.

Other financial problems have been created by the multiplicity of demands on the financial area for statistical data to be reported to various services. Not only does the Federal Trade Commission require data, but the Department of Agriculture, the Department of Commerce and other various governmental functions have gotten in line for data. In addition to these purely governmental functions, quasi-governmental organizations have also assumed an inviolate role of confidant. The voluntary reporting of data to quasi-governmental and industrial agencies is becoming big business. It is not uncommon for organizations such as The National Industrial Conference Board, the Financial Executives Institute, Lionel Edie & Company and other meritorious organizations to often request information from financial executives. Because of the nature of relationships which exist between corporations and these organizations, it is often difficult to ignore requests for information, especially when anonymity is promised.

Another aspect which is changing the future direction of the financial function is the increasing involvement of the function in internal decision making affairs. These affairs may have little to do with finance, per se. They may deal with the complexities of administration of union wage negotiations, the ever present potentials for mergers and acquisitions, the explosion of internal information to various arms of the corporation, and the upset to traditional thinking which has come about as a result of the revolution that the computer and data input have brought to the corporate sphere. The financial executive is being cast more and more in the light of the executive who is to appraise the probabilities of future occurrences. By the same token, he is being required less and less to report the historical objectivity of what has happened. It is becoming increasingly true in the field of finance that yesterday is dead; the challenge is to shape tomorrow.

We are becoming increasingly confronted by esoteric concepts such as financial planning through model building, applications of operations research to aspects of accounting and to portfolio management and moreover, we are being confronted by a younger executive who has been increasingly impatient with the willingness of traditional financial management to tolerate inactivity and to perpetuate custom.

One of the most crucial decisions that is being faced by the financial manager today is the degree to which the financial area should proceed in mechanization and computerization. It is all too easy to state that the computer is a rapid multiplier, or divisor, or adder; it is more than these things. It is a giant, efficient garbage can. The difference, however, is that this particular garbage can can cost an awful lot of money, and it is the rare financial executive who calculates the financial tradeoff in transferring traditional manual functions to the garbage can. Computers, per se, create new layers of overhead. Those new layers of overhead in turn create new peripheral expenses such as the paper supplies which must support the machine operation. One should be patently convinced only after having evaluated the financial tradeoff in computerization that the movement to computer based input is necessary at all. One very large company which was instrumental in developing the entire computer concept a generation ago, has now turned full circle and is beginning to remove some of its financial programs from the computer because they have found that it is faster and in some cases, more accurate to do the job manually as it had been doing prior to the changeover.

Lastly, in the field of new directions, the financial executive is becoming increasingly needed in various other operating areas of the company. The discipline of finance as well as the objectivity form a fine base for adventurers into other decision making functions within a company. The challenge then is to create a well-rounded financial executive who is capable of taking off his blinders, of removing the rubber band from his shirt, and tossing off the green eye shade from his hairline and substituting instead the various dresses and mentalities which accompany the all-around executive required for today's environment.

THE CHANGING ROLE OF THE CONTROLLER

Traditionally, controllership is a type of staff function which in the past has been rather well defined by many organizations. Essentially the function of the position is to maintain some type of system of control and measurement of the historical operations of the business. The word "control," however, does not imply control in the literal sense, because one of the major responsibilities which controllers have in the past shied away from is the very exercise of control in decision making. For the most part they have played shy and permitted various other executive areas in line management to make major decisions. What has been lost upon the traditional controller is the very fact that because of the unique nature of his position within the corporation, he is in a very special niche to observe and moreover to influence the magnitude and direction of profit.

The controller, in exercising his responsibility as it has been traditionally defined, must be familiar with details in all facets of the business. He is the one special individual in the company who probably has, other than the chief executive officer, the best knowledge of products, manufacturing facilities, pricing, and competitive conditions. It has become increasingly important for the controller to accept responsibility in the specialty areas of data processing and communications equipment. More frequently now the controller is finding himself as a major spokesman for corporate policy in representations to governmental agencies, to unions and to interested professional organizations.

Of all individuals within the firm, the controller should be in the unique position to enjoy the mentality of appreciating profit response from various functional areas. In this manner, it is natural for the controller to be the most cost conscious individual within a firm and yet maintain the posture of constructive suggestion. Cost consciousness does not of itself imply miserly, short-term, unconstructive thinking. Cost consciousness can be a dynamic vehicle by which the chief executive officer, with the guidance of the controller, can motivate the balance of the organization to augment the profit planning routine of a company. Cost consciousness and the conservation of resources is not simply a vehicle which should be exercised during times of economic hardship; plans for long range cost reduction are as much a part of daily corporate activity as are profit planning and budgeting and the measurement and achievement for its goals. Long range cost reduction is a subject worthy of special attention and should be considered as an equal and worthy partner of profit planning. In fact, one of the most ideal circumstances would be the concurrent use of both a profit plan and a cost reduction plan for correlative periods of time and the augmentation of each of these plans by a special force appointed by the chief executive officer. Profit planning in a vacuum breeds inefficiency; long range cost reduction in a vacuum breeds negativism. A combination of constructive profit planning and cost reduction programming can bring positive results which can motivate and inspire all areas of the company.

In his new role, the controller is being increasingly cast as an internal quantitative consultant who through his various techniques, his discipline and his objectivity, can assist many other areas of the company to optimize their programs. It is the controller who is in the best position to advise the marketing area of levels of geographic and customer profitability, the efficiency or inefficiency of media and promotion policy. The controller is also in an ideal position to advise the manufacturing area relative to the efficient use of directly applied manufacturing costs as well as the utilization of manufacturing period expenses.

Controllership, in essence, is on the threshold of the next venture into specialization of that function. It is no longer enough to have a single staff controller, or, in fact, even a division controller. Decision making is largely based upon quantitative input and all areas of the company must make decisions in order to insure profitability. It is only a matter of time until we will see the creation of new forms of controllership such as a marketing controller, an advertising controller, a manufacturing controller and a distribution controller. In terms of an analogy, it is not much different from visiting your medical practitioner. It is rare today to be able to enjoy the folksiness of a general medical doctor. Most often as patients we are referred to specialists in certain areas. This same course of events is now evolving for the function of controllership. The controller will, over a period of time, become a specialist who will cross traditional corporate organizational lines and who will participate fully in the decision making function of individual areas.

THE NEW ROLE OF THE TREASURER

The other side of the financial coin is that of treasurership. The position was grounded in pure finance and the basis for the job was the concentration in procuring capital. In addition, the treasurer for the most part has been concerned with cash management and banking relations and sometimes credit and collection and insurance. In more recent times, treasurership has been augmented by increasing attention to pension fund administration.

This has become one of the more marked responsibilities of financial management in many companies. It is true whether companies are uninsured but funded or unfunded with various types of current plans. The dealings with insurance companies have come out of the pure realm of employee welfare expense, and, because of the magnitude and the size of pension plans and investments, drifted toward the sphere of financial management.

Sometimes the responsibility for the investment of the assets of the pension fund has been vested in a trustee arrangement. The trustee in most cases has been a designated lending institution. Under this type of arrangement the actions of the lending institution as trustee are reviewed by the financial executive and his main concern is the evaluation of the efficiency of the investment performance. Sometimes, even though a trustee plan may be in force, individual companies through their financial management retain the right to either advise or cancel investment decisions made by the trustee. In very large companies, it is not uncommon for the investment of pension funds to be handled entirely within the corporate staff area. In those cases company officers serve as trustees for the fund.

In the course of establishing the fund and computing liabilities of the company for invested funds, whether for past service, current or future service, it is the obligation of the financial manager in charge of pension funding to consult with independent actuarial specialists who will assist the company in measuring the degree of risk. The measurement of risk forms the basis of the periodic obligation of the company toward the fund.

In essence, if looked upon in the contrasting shadow of staff vs. line, it may be said that the treasurer is something more of an operating executive and somewhat less than a staff executive if he were to be compared to the controller. The main function of the controller is to report. This is his primary responsibility regardless of whether in the light of the foregoing discussion we agree with this description or not. The treasurer, however, is an operating executive in the sense that his main function is not to report something which happened yesterday. His obligation is day-to-day money management and as such, he is not concerned with whether a debit equals a credit. Instead, as the guardian of all capital activities, he is the designer of the capital structure of a firm and it is his mission to maintain adequate corporate/lending institution relationships which may affect sources of borrowing. One of the major decision areas confronting the treasurer in his recent involvement is the investment of corporate funds whether they be long-term or short-term. This type of investment may take the form not only of excess cash to be invested in a recognized market, but also in the granting of credit to customers. Credit is every bit as much a marketing tool as may be the media or promotion policy which is exercised by the marketing function. Through the treasurer, installment selling, financing through subsidiaries, questions of foreign exchange and possibly lease versus purchase decisions, are all funneled and evaluated.

In the exercise of his duties, it is patently clear that the treasurer is exercising some degree of a public relations function. He needs to deal frequently with the financial fraternity. He must also have immediate access to the senior levels of management of a company and must be in a position whereby he can communicate readily to the board of directors. One of the problems that has arisen to compound and confound the evolution of the position of treasurer is the changing motivation of business and the changing methodology of corporate communications. The sophistication of financial reporting and the increasing penetration into corporate activity of various interested parties also makes mandatory the attendance of the treasurer and/or the chief financial officer at such briefings. It is a reasonable question to ask whether the position of the treasurer as it is traditionally structured is sufficient to achieve all of the objectives of corporate communications and the optimization of operating capital. In the evolving status of financial management, it is also probable that corporations in the future will have two treasurers; one to deal with operating problems and the other to deal with problems of communications with interested parties.

MUTUAL PROBLEMS OF THE TREASURER AND THE CONTROLLER

If we were to look differently at financial management and examine what part of that function is involved in decision making and what part in the implementation of various decisions, it would become clear that contradictions have entered the picture. Decision making in the area of finance is, for the most part, vested in the chief executive officer of the company and through the chief financial officer and/or the treasurer. Decision implementing activities, however, may be vested in any of the foregoing but also include the controller. In more recent years the controller is being increasingly called upon to make decisions, also. It is his prerogative, within generally accepted accounting principles, to influence both the magnitude and the direction of profit, within reason. The decision as to corporate policies regarding inventories, expenses versus capitalization, research and development, advertising, and depreciation are all types of decisions which would be within the province of the controller and which may have more of an immediate effect on profit than the overt action of operating line executives.

HOW TO ORGANIZE THE CHANGE

If not properly understood, information technology has the potential of drowning the controller in his own numbers. Change is imminent; change is good, and further, change is sure to come. If the controller will not adapt to new forms of systems control and data technology, he will become remembered over a long period of time as the financial dinosaur. In order to survive, he must, in effect, assume the posture of an internal quantitative consultant who will assume the responsibility for the entire process of gathering, processing, reporting and disseminating all relevant information which is required by the various parties within a corporation. The foregoing is not meant to imply a similarity with the so-called "management information system." Distinction is made between the two by the broad scope of executive wisdom and decision making intuition found in the former; whereas the latter is a more mechanized function, more easily recognizable in the form of a computerized data output than as a process of thinking. The suggestion is made that in effect, a *corporate command post* be established to act as the headquarters for all relevant quantitative information within a firm. Further, the controller appears to be the logical candidate to serve as the chief intelligence officer who will act as the disseminator and creator of information. In effect, what is being suggested is that the controller, in particular, consider his role as that of total corporate data communications. The philosophical essence of the job should be shifted from that of traditional reporting of yesterday to the supplying of pertinent information for estimating tomorrow. In the past, leading financial writers such as Robert Beyer have stated that the controller "is closer to and understands better than perhaps anyone else the entity which is the core of the problems—a system by which information is transmitted to the various management levels." The assignment to the controller of the simple exercise of a management information system is shortchanging the magnitude of the problem. The organizational and conceptual change suggested here goes far beyond the scope of such an assignment. The solution to the reorganization problem would probably require a new approach to corporate organization. In its essence, the controller would have to make clear the fact that his responsibility is manifold. His responsibility for traditional custodial accounting, for cost accounting, for data processing, for budgeting, should all be clearly identified and supplemented by a separate unit which, for want of a better description, might be considered to be *"intelligence gathering and control."*

Rather than accepting the passive historical role which has been traditional with finance, it is suggested that the controller assume a much more vigorous posture in dealing with his fellow executives. If approached in a constructive manner, there is no reason why the controller *cannot impel* improved decisions. His world should include the design and implementation of salesmens' incentive plans, advice and counsel in pricing, timing and strategy as well as optimizing media and promotional programs.

One of the last frontiers for the investigation and improvement of cost control within corporate operation is that of physical distribution. The controller is in a unique position to take advantage and fill the void created by the information vacuum in that area. Methodology which will assist in appraising the efficiency and effectiveness of physical distribution operations will close the gap in corporate standards of performance which has existed ever since physical distribution became common a few decades ago. It is forcing a rethinking of traditional corporate organization. It has already created the position of a product manager. Hopefully, in the future it will include the creation of a specialized position which might be called the marketing controller.

BASIC FACTORS IN DEPARTMENT ORGANIZATION

The formal organizational arrangements. The same sources from which corporate officers derive their official functions and duties—the statutes, the certificate or articles of incorporation, the by-laws, and the resolutions of the board of directors-—also establish the formal organizational arrangements for corporate purposes. These arrangements, in turn, form the framework within which the balance of the organization is designed and established to provide for operations, staff, and committee activities, and for planning, coordination, and control at each level of management. Changes in the formal organizational arrangements generally require an amendment of the by-laws; changes in the balance of the organization are ordinarily within the powers of the principal executive officer.

Corporate and administrative controls. In the corporation, there are two types of controls: corporate and administrative. Corporate controls are those necessary to the proper functioning of the corporate mechanism as a framework for the business; they are largely of a legal, secretarial, and custodial nature. Recording duties as to meetings, custody of the corporate seal and corporate records, the manner of concluding corporate transactions and the execution of documents, the declaration of dividends, and similar procedures are peculiar to the corporation.

Administrative controls include all types of business controls other than corporate, such as accounting, auditing, credit, cost, financial, industrial engineering, wage and salary, and others. These types of control are common to all business enterprise and are necessary to check waste in facilities, materials, and manpower and to improve earnings and financial position. The accounting and financial functions are not only self-contained control functions within the processes of administration, but also operate in most cases to support other types of control.

The levels of control. The prerogatives with respect to both corporate and administrative controls are lodged at different levels within the corporate organization. In corporate controls, the descending levels in order of importance are the stockholders, the board of directors, the officers, and duly authorized agents or employees. In the conduct of the business, the highest level of control is in the board of directors, which consequently becomes the highest level of management. The second level of control for business purposes belongs to "top management," which consists of the officers and the department managers and assistants. Top management must conduct the affairs of the business within the general and specific policies laid down by the directors. "Supervising management," which is the lower half of the management, supervises the operating and administrative details.

All through this hierarchy, responsibility and its attendant obligations are delegated downward in the organization, from the directorate to the supervisors of lowest rank, each rank constituting a level of planning, coordination, and control.

The principal executive officer. In most corporations, the president acts as the principal executive officer, the by-laws providing in effect that the president, subject to the control of the board of directors, shall be the principal executive officer of the corporation and shall have general charge and control of all its business and affairs. In companies using the office of chairman of the board of directors, the president is ordinarily subordinate to the chairman of the board, but is still considered, subject to the control of the chairman, as the principal officer in general charge and control of the business. For this reason, all other officers are considered as subordinate to the president, particularly from the standpoint of the president's responsibility for the coordination of the component parts of the organization. All the officers may be elected or appointed by the board of directors or even the stockholders, but for the coordination of activities there must be one principal officer. This officer is ordinarily the president.

Secretaries, treasurers, and controllers. When the various officers are included in the by-laws, secretaries, treasurers, and controllers are elected or appointed normally by the board of directors. Election by the stockholders is infrequent even in those states that provide for such action by either the stockholders or the directors.[7] In theory and, in some instances, in practice, officers are considered as responsible to the source of their election or appointment. Essentially for purposes of coordination, it is customary to regard the secretary, treasurer, and controller as responsible to the board of directors through the ranking officer, ordinarily the president or chairman of the board. Some large and medium-sized companies have a vice-president in charge of finance or a chairman of the finance committee. In these companies, but not without exception, the treasurer and the controller report to such vice-president or to the chairman of the finance committee. This organizational arrangement provides for close coordination of the financial and accounting functions, the policies affecting both, and the statements and reports issued by each office.

Basic relationships of the secretary. *With the board of directors and ranking officers.* The secretary, as an elected officer of the corporation, is the recording officer of the board of directors and technically, he is responsible to the board. In practice, however, the secretary is usually responsible to the board through the president or chairman of the board. In some companies, the basic relationship is described in the by-laws.

With standing committees. The secretary's relationship with the standing committees of the board of directors is the result of his duties as the recording officer of

---

[7]Treasurers and corporate clerks are ordinarily elected by the stockholders in Massachusetts corporations.

committees. In some companies, for example, the by-laws provide that the secretary shall give notice of the meetings to the members of the executive, finance, or similar standing committees of the board and shall attend the meetings and record the proceedings. In the majority of companies so organized, this is a mandatory provision. In some instances, the requirement relates only to those committees for which a secretary shall not have been appointed, or where the by-laws provide that the duties shall be performed "when required" by the board of directors.

With the treasurer, controller, and other officers. The secretary is generally coordinate in both rank and reciprocal relationship with the treasurer, controller, and other corporate officers, other than the ranking executive officers. The actions and resolutions of the board of directors often are circulated through the secretary and, in these cases, the secretary serves as the principal source of official corporate information to the other officers, management, and staff. In some companies, to meet business needs, the secretary is also an assistant treasurer. In this capacity, the secretary is ordinarily subordinate to the treasurer. The secretary ordinarily has authority over the assistant secretaries, who are also officers of the corporation. In most cases, the by-laws provide that assistant secretaries shall act for the secretary in the latter's absence and shall perform such other duties as may be assigned to them by the board of directors, by standing committees, ranking officers with the requisite authority, or the secretary. Transfer agents and registrars are generally under the jurisdiction of the secretary in those companies where the secretary is charged with the responsibility for the transfer function.

With legal counsel. The secretary usually has a close relationship with the company's legal counsel, for the conduct of the corporate affairs is carried out generally with the assistance of counsel, and many legal matters are channeled through the secretary's office. In companies of all sizes, the secretary, in many instances, is an attorney who serves also as general counsel. In many small companies, retained counsel often acts as the secretary.

Basic relationships of the treasurer. *With the board of directors, committees, and ranking officers.* Treasurers are elected or appointed officers of the corporation, and, in the absence of a finance committee or a vice-president in charge of finance, they are responsible to the board of directors, generally through the president or the chairman of the board. In companies which place their financial affairs in charge of a finance committee of the board of directors or a vice-president in charge of finance, treasurers are ordinarily responsible to the chairman of the committee or the officer in charge of finance. In companies having finance committees of the board of directors, the treasurer is not ordinarily a member of the committee unless he is also a member of the board of directors.

With the secretary, controller, and other officers. The treasurer is generally coordinate in both rank and reciprocal relationship with the secretary, controller, and the corporate officers other than the ranking executive officers or those directly in charge of finance. In some companies, for various reasons, the treasurer is also an assistant secretary. In this capacity, the treasurer is ordinarily subordinate to the secretary. In other companies, the secretary is an assistant treasurer and the treasurer is responsible for both the secretarial and treasurer's functions. By-law provisions, or working arrangements, sometimes provide for the treasurer to report to the controller; this, however, is not a leading practice.

The treasurer is in charge of the assistant treasurers who are officers of the corporation and ordinarily provided for in the by-laws. Although the treasurer, in most cases, is superior to the assistant treasurers, the internal organizational arrangements and the board general functions of the assistant treasurers are matters generally reserved to the board of directors, a committee with the requisite authority, or to the ranking executive officer. This is particularly true of those companies organized with a finance committee, or an office in charge of finance. Transfer agents and registrars are generally under the jurisdiction of the treasurer in those companies where the treasurer is charged with the responsibility for the transfer functions.

Basic relationships of the controller. *With the board of directors, committees, and ranking officers.* Controllers are elected or appointed officers of the corporation, or hold appointive positions, according to the status of the controllership in the company. If the controller is an elected or appointed officer, he is deemed responsible to the board of directors, generally through the president or the chairman of the board. In companies which place their financial affairs in charge of a finance committee of the board of directors or a vice president in charge of finance, controllers are ordinarily responsible to the chairman of the committee or the officer in charge of finance. In companies having finance committees of the board of directors, the controller, like the treasurer, is not ordinarily a member of the committee unless he is also a member of the board of directors. When controllers hold appointive positions, they are ordinarily accountable to the officer empowered to make the appointment.

With the secretary, treasurer, and other officers. Whether the controller is an officer or an appointee, he is generally considered to be coordinate in both rank and reciprocal relationship with the secretary, treasurer, and the corporate officers, other than the ranking executive officers or those directly in charge of finance. The controller is sometimes an assistant secretary. In this capacity, he is ordinarily subordinate to the secretary. By-law provisions and working arrangements sometimes provide for the controller to report to the treasurer; this, however, is not a leading practice.

The controller is in charge of assistant controllers who may be officers or appointees to appointive positions. By-laws do not ordinarily provide for assistant controllers. There is, however, no logical reason for this omission, for the value of these positions can be easily demonstrated as equal to other assistant officers. Although the controller, in most cases, is superior to the assistant controllers, the internal organizational arrangements and the specific functions of the assistant controllers, like assistant treasurers, are matters generally reserved to the board of directors, a committee with the requisite authority, or to the ranking executive officer. This is particularly true of those companies organized with a finance committee, or those that have an officer in charge of finance.

Combination of offices in one individual. In general, the statutes governing corporate organization permit one person to hold more than one office where there is no conflict in corporate duties. State corporation laws that expressly provide for the combination of offices ordinarily exclude the combination of president and vice-president, and president and secretary, or assistant secretary. Some states, by express provision or inference, do not permit one individual to hold more than two offices. Regardless of the manner in which corporate offices may be combined in one individual, it is the universal rule that an officer shall not execute, acknowledge, or verify any instrument in more than one corporate capacity.

Unless there are by-law provisions to the contrary, the office of secretary may be combined in one individual with that of treasurer. This is the most common and probably the most effective of all combinations. It is not unusual for secretaries, treasurers, and controllers to serve as vice-presidents; for secretaries to serve as general counsel, or assistant treasurer; for treasurers to serve as assistant secretary; and for controllers to serve as secretary or assistant secretary. In some New England corporations, the president is also treasurer, but this practice is not general.

The combination of offices in one individual is most advantageous to small companies; two persons can satisfy the requirements, one as president, the other as secretary and treasurer. In a majority of large companies, the offices of secretary, treasurer, and controller are held by different persons.

It is generally agreed that the office of treasurer and the office or position of controller should not be combined, in recognition of the important principle that the power to authorize the disbursement of funds and the power to make such disbursements should not reside in the same individual.

Organizational planning. Some measure of organizational planning is necessary in companies of every size; it is a continuing responsibility of the head of any organization or any organizational component. To be effective, the arrangements must be as simple as possible, well defined, and thoroughly understood by all the individuals who must make them work. The approach to organization is the analysis and definition of functions, and their logical segregation, grouping, and assignment.

Organization is of particular importance in connection with the functions and relationships of secretaries, treasurers, and controllers, because of the traditional admixture of duties. The situation has been further complicated in some instances by the combination of two offices in one individual; officers serving as both treasurer and secretary, for example, have not always been certain as to whether particular functions were being performed as treasurer or secretary. Also, upon the establishment of some controllerships, the transfer of functions has not always been clear cut, and in some cases the transfer of duties has not been made in full contemplation of the proper controllership functions. In many instances, there has been a lack of objective planning.

The process of organizational planning for treasurers, controllers, secretaries, and other key positions in management should include (1) familiarity with the leading practices; (2) a projected plan based upon a wholly objective viewpoint; (3) creation, in chart form, of the best ultimate plan; (4) comparison of the ultimate plan with the presentation to make changes that can be undertaken at once, and to record those which must await a future date because of policies, personnel, or other elements; and (5) the preparation of specifications, an organization manual, or management guides for the key positions.

Line and staff relationships. Organizational arrangements must distinguish clearly between line and staff units of the organization and their functions. In the proper application of the line and staff principles of organization, the line management is charged with the responsibility for the accomplishment of the principal objectives of the business; it must be vested, therefore, with the right of decision, command, and control. The principal characteristic of the line organization is the manner in which the right to decide, command, and control flows downward in the organization from the principal executive officer, through intermediate management, to the lowest level of management.

The components of the staff organization are provided deliberately to assist line management in the accomplishment of its functions. The component parts of the staff organization are therefore established in accordance with the needs of the business for specialized or technical advice and service to other parts of the organization, or as adjuncts to the planning, coordination, and control functions of the line management. For example, legal and economic staff groups are provided for advisory purposes; engineering and purchasing departments are provided for purposes of service to other parts of the organization; planning agencies are for purposes of coordination; and organization, industrial engineering, standard practice, and budgetary units are for purposes of control. Financial and accounting functions include advisory and service activities also, but the essential and indispensable purpose is to aid in the control of the business. Therefore, treasurer's and controller's departments are provided for and included within the staff organization, and their relationships with the other parts of the business are governed in general by organizational practices for staff departments and agencies. Staff departments and agencies do not decide, command, or control. Their plans and recommendations are made effective through the line organization.

Designation of components. The designation of organizational components sometimes offers difficulty in organizational planning. There is no standardization in either nomenclature or practice. In companies terming their major organizational units "departments," there is considerable precedent for referring to subdivisions as "divisions," and subdivisions of divisions as "sections." This is the practice in many treasurer's and controller's departments in medium-sized and large companies. The treasurer's department, for example, may be organized as follows:

Sometimes, however, there is objection to applying the term "division" within staff components of the organization. In practice, in some medium-sized and large companies, the use of "division" is confined to operating and geographical components. The principles to be followed in the use of designations are (1) to conform closely to the organizational practice of the company, particularly if designations are standardized, and (2) to segregate and group functions along logical lines that will make designation practicable and easily understood.

In small organizations, departments may break down immediately into sections. This eliminates one layer of supervision. The number of sections reporting to one principal should not, however, exceed the span of adequate control. An excessive number imposes upon the time and efficiency of both the principal and the subordinate supervisors. To avoid this situation, closely related sections should be brought together in a divisional arrangement under an intermediate supervisor who then becomes accountable to the principal for the work to be accomplished in the sections affected.

Committee organization. Committees are used at all levels of management. In large and medium-sized companies, the by-laws may provide for an executive committee or a finance committee, or both, as well as for other committees of the board of directors. Executive, finance, and similarly constituted standing committees may be considered as formal committees. Their functions and powers are set forth in the by-laws, and some type of formal corporate procedure is ordinarily required to change them substantially. Committees of this type are empowered ordinarily to take executive action. The principal purpose of most executive committees, for example, is to act for the board of directors in all general business matters between meetings of the board. Finance committees ordinarily stand in the same relationship to the board of directors as the executive committee, but are limited in most cases to the consideration of financial matters only. As a general rule, only members of the board of directors are eligible for membership on committees of the board.

Ordinary committees, permanent or temporary, may be established by the principal executive officer or any other officer with the requisite authority. Committees of this type are used mostly for purposes of advice, reconciliation of viewpoints, or, like staff agencies, as adjuncts to the planning, coordination, and control functions of management. With the exception of the committees of the board of directors, which are executive in character, the relationships of committees with other parts of organization are governed by principles similar to those governing staff agencies. Treasurers and controllers may serve on committees of the board of directors when they are also directors, but they do so as directors and not as officers or department heads. They may serve also on ordinary committees as officers or department heads.

The following four exhibits will illustrate contemporary position descriptions for both Treasurers and Controllers in modern, large companies.

Position Description for
Treasurer
Diamond Shamrock Company

BASIC FUNCTION

Responsible to the appropriate senior officer for the performance of all the responsibilities of the treasurer as specified in the bylaws of the company; for administering and coordinating financial, credit, and tax policies and procedures of the company; for purchasing and administering property and casualty insurance; and for administering and coordinating shareowner and financial community relations programs.

GENERAL OBJECTIVES AND RESPONSIBILITIES

Responsibility is assigned and authority granted for the specific duties listed below as well as those listed under the section of the Management Guide entitled "Responsibilities, Relationships and Limits of Authority of Every Executive."

1. Formulate and recommend to the appropriate senior officer financial policies and administer approved policies, including the receiving, depositing, disbursing, and managing of all company funds plus investing any surplus funds in securities authorized by the board of directors. Have custody of and account for all company securities. Determine the company's financial requirements and see that sufficient funds are available for operating purposes.

2. Responsible for the formulation and complete administration of all tax policies and procedures, including Federal, state and local taxes.

3. Prepare and distribute all reports to shareowners in collaboration with all other departments of the company with respect to their areas of responsibility.

4. Develop and recommend the program to be followed with respect to shareowner relations and administer such approved programs.

5. Develop and recommend the program with respect to relations with the financial community and administer such approved programs.

6. Administer the necessary program to see that all property and casualty insurance risks are properly insured in accordance with approved company policies.

7. Formulate and recommend credit and collection policies and administer such approved policies.

8. Recommend a program for financing company pension plans and consult with the company trustees concerning investment policies of the pension trusts.

9. Maintain confidential incentive compensation records.

10. Recommend and administer approved programs dealing with governmental relations and political education activities.

11. Responsible for coordinating transactions involving acquisition or disposition of land.

12. Responsible for negotiating loan agreements to be entered into by the company.

RELATIONSHIP WITH OTHER UNITS IN THE ORGANIZATION

1. Serve as chairman of the contributions committee; as a member of the management advisory council, the thrift plan committee, and the appropriations committee; and as a rotating member of the employee policy committee.

LIMITS OF AUTHORITY

1. General

A. Act in accordance with limits established in the general table "Limits of Authority" and the appropriation procedure manual.

2. Bank Accounts

A. Approval of two appropriate senior officers for opening and closing general accounts in major depositories. No limitation on other accounts.

**Figure 1-1. Position Description
for Treasurer Diamond Shamrock Company**

Position Description for
Treasurer
Johns-Manville Corporation

Within the geographical limits of his own responsibility, the vice president for finance delegates responsibility to the treasurer as follows:

1. To determine the tax liabilities of the corporation and its subsidiaries.

2. To prepare and to file tax returns.

3. To deal with the appropriate agencies of governments—Federal, state, and local—regarding any problems that arise in respect of the determination of taxes.

4. To study and be familiar with tax laws and regulations, or proposed laws and regulations; to recommend and, as authorized, to take any action that will protect the interests of the enterprises.

5. To pursue such other studies or duties relating to taxes as the vice president may direct.

6. To propose principles and practices to govern receipt, banking, custody and disbursement of money and securities.

7. To receive and have custody of money and securities, except at locations at which, by authorization of the vice president, such duties may be entrusted to others.

8. To propose what banking depositories shall be employed, and the policies to govern such employment, and to conduct relationships with such depositories.

9. To disburse moneys pursuant to the prescribed authorities therefor, except at locations at which, by authorization of the vice president, this duty may be entrusted to others.

10. To recommend where the receipt and disbursement of money can best be performed by the fiscal department, and where best by others.

11. To prescribe policies to govern extension of credit to customers and collection of moneys due the enterprises and upon his initiative or when requested, to consult with and advise others concerning their problems of credits and collections.

12. To authorize extension of credit to and to collect moneys due from customers, except as any of such duties, by authorization of the vice president, may be entrusted to others.

13. To prescribe the form of evidence and the manner of collection of loans to employees.

14. Pursuant to prescribed policies, to collect all moneys due the enterprises from others if collection is the predominant interest.

15. To propose the character and extent of insurance against losses and risks.

16. Within authorized policies, to insure the corporation and its subsidiaries fully against losses and risks.

17. To administer self-insurance funds.

18. To prescribe methods for protection of the company's money and property against loss, except as to methods that have been made the responsibility of another.

19. To prepare the salary payroll and make payment thereof.

20. Where required by law, to withhold from salary payments designated amounts that apply to income taxes of salaried employees, and to pay such amounts to the appropriate government agency.

21. To advise those entrusted with the payment of hourly employees regarding the manner of withholding and the method of payment of income taxes withheld from wages.

22. To compute incentive compensation payable to salaried employees.

23. To interpret the laws and regulations that govern sales or use taxes; and to supply information regarding the invoicing of such taxes to all whose responsibility requires such information.

24. To ascertain the amounts of sales or use taxes billed to customers and to pay such amounts to the appropriate government agency.

25. To maintain the records of the retirement plan.

26. To recommend to their boards of directors the payment of dividends by subsidiary corporations.

27. To provide for loans from one affiliated corporation to another, and for the payment of inter-company accounts, in the best interests of the enterprises.

28. To observe and report upon the manner of performance of fiscal policies and methods by other departments and the divisions.

29. To pursue such other fiscal studies and duties as the vice president may direct.

**Figure 1-2. Position Description
for Treasurer Johns-Manville Corporation**

Position Description for
Controller
Johns-Manville Corporation

The Vice President for Finance delegates responsibility to the Controller as follows:

ACCOUNTING

Accounts

1. To prepare the accounts of the corporations, except such as the Vice President may entrust to other responsibilities.

2. To recommend what accounting can best be performed by the Accounting Department, and what by other responsibilities.

3. To allocate income and expenditures among classifications and responsibilities.

4. To allocate general expense among operating divisions.

Expenditures

5. To verify the propriety of disbursement to be made at Headquarters.

Statements

6. To prepare financial statements for publication in the form prescribed by the President.

7. To prepare such detailed statements of the transactions and properties of the enterprises as will assist others to improve the earnings of the enterprises.

8. To recommend the nature of the published financial statements of the corporations.

Relations with Others

9. To provide for furnishing information to guide and assist personnel engaged in accounting and cost work throughout the enterprises.

10. To observe generally the manner of performance of accounting by other responsibilities, and to make recommendations for needed improvements.

General

11. To pursue such other accounting studies and duties as the Vice President may direct.

ANALYSIS

Financial Appraisal

12. To appraise proposed expenditures, where required and not otherwise provided for, or at the request of the President, Senior Officer or Senior Operating Vice President; and to advise as to their financial desirability.

13. To appraise the financial results of operations and the benefits received from expenditures made in the enterprises and reported thereon.

Financial Methods

14. To prescribe methods of financial analysis and to maintain such manuals of practice as will be useful.

15. To observe the manner of performance of financial analysis by the operating divisions and to recommend needed improvements.

Profit Planning and Budgets

16. To prescribe the methods and procedures to be followed in profit planning and the budgetary control of expenditures.

17. To appraise proposed profit plans for the President, where not otherwise provided for, and to consolidate corporate profit, action and growth plans.

18. To prepare forecasts of earnings, cash and investment for the corporation, and to determine annually the amount of general expense to be charged to each division during the year.

Services to Others

19. To supply financial service and assistance required by the President, and by vice presidents and department managers who are not in an operating division.

Government Business

20. To develop and recommend policies and procedures that will govern the extent to which J-M divulges cost and price information to contractors or agencies of the Federal Government and to provide general assistance, appropriate to a financial responsibility, when requested by division, research and other personnel dealing with these outside parties.

General

21. In accordance with the principles prescribed by the President, to establish the prices at which one division will sell products to another division, subject to the authority of division general managers to establish such prices by agreement.

22. To pursue such other studies or duties relating to financial analysis, profit planning or budgets as the Vice President may direct.

Figure 1-3. Position Description
for Controller Johns-Manville Corporation

Position Description for
Controller
P. R. Mallory & Co. Inc.

BASIC FUNCTIONS

The duties of the Controller shall be to maintain adequate records of all assets, liabilities and transactions of the Corporation; to see that adequate audits thereof are currently and regularly made; and, in conjunction with other officers and employees, to initiate and enforce measures and procedures whereby the business of the Corporation shall be conducted with the maximum safety, efficiency and economy. His duties and powers shall extend to all subsidiary corporations, and, so far as the President may deem practicable, to all affiliated corporations.

The Controller is the chief accounting officer of the Company. In addition to his responsibility for maintaining all accounting records, the Controller's duties include the development, analysis, and interpretation of statistical and accounting information to appraise operating results in terms of costs, budgets, policies of operations, trends, and increased profit possibilities.

Has those additional responsibilities and authorities normally associated with an officer of the Corporation.

DUTIES AND RESPONSIBILITIES

1. To initiate, prepare, and issue standard practices relating to accounting policies and cost procedures as are necessary to ensure that adequate accounting records are maintained of all assets, liabilities, and transactions of the Company and that suitable systems are followed in compilation of product, manufacturing, distribution, and administrative costs.

2. To ensure that controls are adequate and current so that corrective action can be taken where necessary at the earliest possible moment.

3. To properly record financial transactions covered by minutes of the meetings of the Board of Directors.

4. Share the responsibility to see that properly qualified men occupy the positions of operating unit Controller.

5. To prepare and interpret financial statements, cost data, and management control reports of the Company. In cooperation with the Vice President–Finance, assist other executives in appraising their activities in terms of financial results, pointing out significant trends in operations as indicated by analysis of the reports; and assist the executives in determining future policies based on applying sound business judgment to the conclusions deduced from such facts.

6. To maintain a continuing internal auditing program.

7. To cooperate with public accountants appointed as auditors in the execution of their program of independent auditing.

8. To establish or approve procedures and methods for taking and costing of all inventories.

9. To review and approve procedures for handling cash and property so as to protect the Company from loss through negligence or dishonesty.

10. To maintain adequate records of authorized appropriations, and check against the appropriations the sums expended pursuant thereto.

11. In conjunction with other officers and department heads, to review and approve budgets covering all divisions and activities of the Company.

12. To coordinate clerical and office methods, records, reports, and procedures throughout the Company and its subsidiaries, and arrange for the development of standards for office and clerical activities, forms, equipment, and supplies for use throughout the Company. Develop clerical cost programs to insure that accounting and related records are maintained at lowest possible expense to the Company and its subsidiaries.

13. To supervise the activities of the Corporate Accounting, Internal Audit, Systems and the Budgetary Control departments.

ORGANIZATION RELATIONSHIPS

1. The Controller reports to the Vice President–Finance.

2. Has a functional relationship through the Vice President–Finance and President to the Presidents or General Managers of the divisions and subsidiaries and through them to the Treasurers/Controllers of those divisions and subsidiaries.

3. Maintains such relationships outside of the Company as are necessary to enhance the Company name and reputation.

**Figure 1-4. Position Description
for Controller P. R. Mallory & Co. Inc.**

ORGANIZATION OF THE TREASURER'S DEPARTMENT[8]

Practice in small companies. In small companies, only the simplest of organization arrangements can be utilized. The number of principals is ordinarily limited and, in some cases, the principals are not only the stockholders, but serve also as the directors and officers. In its most basic and simple form, the organizational arrangements for the financial, accounting, and secretarial functions in the small company can follow the organization plan shown in Figure 1-5.

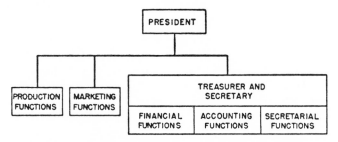

Figure 1-5. A Basic Plan for the Organization of the Financial, Accounting, and Secretarial Functions in Small Companies.

For purposes of flexibility, the small company can usually provide for a vice-president and an assistant treasurer and assistant secretary. The latter offices can be combined in one individual. The vice-president and the individual serving as both assistant treasurer and assistant secretary may be active or inactive in the business. If active, the organizational arrangements can contemplate a degree of specialization at this point. A further degree of specialization and improved control will be established through the use of two assistants to the treasurer, one as assistant treasurer, and the other as assistant secretary, as shown in Figure 1-6.

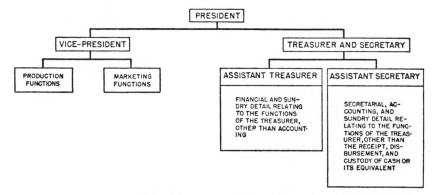

Figure 1-6. A Basic Plan of Organization for Specialization in the Financial and Accounting Functions Through the Addition of an Assistant Treasurer and an Assistant Secretary.

---

[8]The organization charts shown in the following pages are based upon leading practices. Since there is no *one* best plan of organization, the charts are presented with full recognition that other equally good basic plans might be offered.

Practice in medium-sized companies. The accounting, internal auditing, and tax functions of a company require a degree of specialization as elements of control. For this reason, it is logical to separate them from the financial functions of the treasurer, and the legal, secretarial, and recording functions of the secretary. This separation cannot always be carried out at the management level in the small business, because of an insufficient number of principals. In this case, it is customary to establish the separation at the employee level rather than at the corporate officer level. For example, the treasurer may discharge his responsibility for both the financial and accounting functions, and at the same time establish and maintain the necessary internal checks by allocating to one subordinate (a cashier) the detail of cash receipts and disbursements, and by allocating to another (an accountant), the maintenance of the control accounts. As small businesses grow in size, the separation of the accounting and financial functions can take place, and usually does in a medium-sized company.

With the transfer of the accounting functions to the controller, or elsewhere away from the treasurer, the treasurer becomes concerned largely with the financial and secretarial functions. A basic plan of organization for the separation of these functions, under the jurisdiction of a treasurer and secretary, is shown in Figure 1-7.

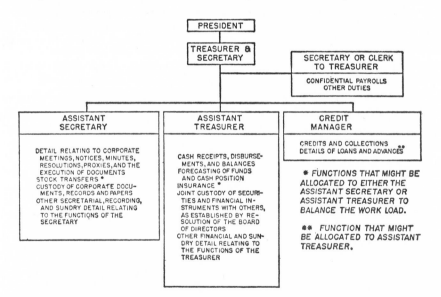

Figure 1-7. A Basic Plan of Organization for the Separation of the Secretarial and Financial Functions, When Both Must Be Maintained under the Jurisdiction of a Treasurer and Secretary.

Practice in large companies. In large companies, all functions, because of volume and complexity, require a greater degree of specialization and control. Also, the large company is in a position, normally, to provide the manpower required for separation of functions. A basic plan for the organization of the treasurer's department in large companies, where the organization arrangements may provide also for the inclusion of property taxes and bond registration and transfer in the treasurer's functions, is shown in Figure 1-8.

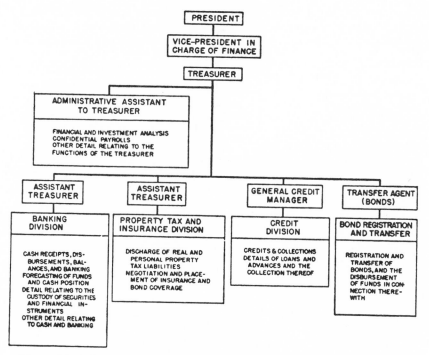

Figure 1-8. A Basic Plan for the Organization of the Treasurer's Department in Large Companies.

ORGANIZATION OF THE CONTROLLER'S DEPARTMENT

Practice in medium-sized corporations. As stated previously, the medium-sized company offers the best and sometimes the first opportunity to establish the accounting function under independent jurisdiction. The development of the industrial controllership in medium-sized companies is based not only upon the elements of internal control, but also upon the requirements of specialization within the accounting, auditing, and tax functions. A basic plan for the organization of the controller's department in medium-sized companies is shown in Figure 1-9.

With the separation of the financial and accounting functions, arrangements for organization generally have followed one of three courses:

1. The title, but not always the office of controller, was created, and the incumbent, with independent jurisdiction, was vested with the accounting function.

2. If the office or position of auditor or general auditor was one of independent jurisdiction, the incumbent assumed, or was vested with, the controllership functions over and above those of auditing. In many cases, the successive changes in title or office have been from auditor, to general auditor, to controller. As shown by various surveys, the preponderance of corporate practice in large and medium-sized companies provides for an auditor, but the responsibilities of the position are restricted normally to internal auditing. In this arrangement, the auditor is ordinarily responsible to the controller.

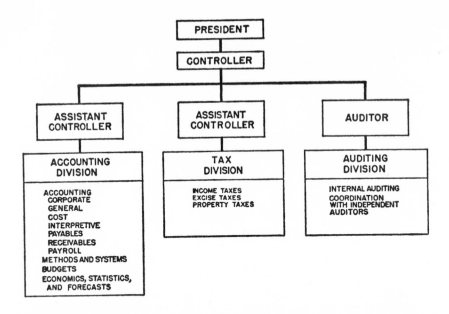

**Figure 1-9. A Basic Plan for the Organization of the Controller's Department
in Medium-Sized Companies.**

3. If the position of auditor, general auditor, or accountant was subordinate to the office of treasurer, or another officer, the details of the controller's function were performed by the auditor, or accountant, but the principal administrative duties of the controller and the natural accretions of an administrative nature remained with the treasurer or other officer. This is the organizational arrangement followed in a majority of small companies.

Practice in large companies. Whatever the situation may be in the development and use of the controllership in small and medium-sized companies, its use in large companies has become general as an independent component of the industrial business organization. The large company has the most need for, and is in the best position to make the most use of, the controllership.

In Figure 1-10, a basic plan for the organization of the controller's department of a large company is presented. The following comments, however, should be noted.

Of all of the organizational units of the industrial enterprise, the functions of the controller are probably the least fixed, even in large companies. Accounting is the only function that can be claimed as actually basic to the controllership. Both the auditing and the tax functions, generally regarded as parts of the accounting function, are to be found as duties of others in some companies. The auditing function, for example, is sometimes presented as the responsibility of some officer other than the controller. This separation is made primarily because it is inadvisable to have the same person responsible for both the function and the auditing of that function. At present, the preponderance of practice indicates the auditing function as belonging basically to the controller.

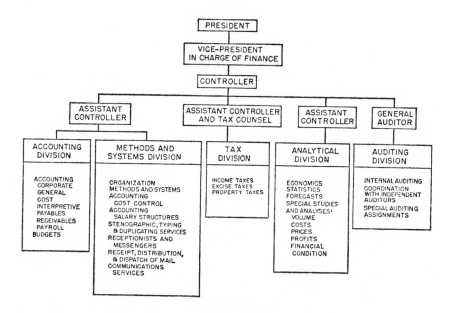

Figure 1-10. A Basic Plan for the Organization of the Controller's Department in Large Companies.

2

Taking the Guesswork Out of
Long Range Planning

CONTENTS

2

Taking the Guesswork Out of Long Range Planning

WHAT IS FINANCIAL PLANNING?

The planning process is the manifestation of a company's determination to be the master of its own fate. It is the device by which great corporations have grown and have avoided the reactive type of situation in which they merely responded to external environmental changes. Instead, an organized, integrated planning process has been the vehicle for much of American industry to penetrate the darkness of uncertainty and provide the illumination of probability. When objectives are set, the entire scope of the effort which is made to formulate plans of action, including alternatives for contingencies, gives rise to a concentration of energies within a given period toward the systematic implementation of the corporate goals to be attained.

The term "planning" has found no truly universal definition. To some it simply means a grand design of operations highlighting the development of various aspects of a company's operations and concentrating on the objectives or the work programs for the period under scrutiny. The academicians have given us some very broad definitions of planning in the literature, but they are of little value to the operating executive who does not need a professional exposition to plan for his future. A definition of planning is important because a true plan contains an immense scope of considerations and, unless the plan is complete on its face, the game plan of the corporation may be imperfect. A short workable definition of planning for our purposes is *that process which makes possible the probable*. In order to appreciate all of the ramifications of this short definition of planning, let us agree that planning is a total analytical process which:

A. Considers probable future occurrences.
B. Constantly measures the actual or probable attainment of performance against the desired goal of attainment.
C. Provides for contingent action which can be placed into being in order to achieve such goals.
D. Highlights various available courses of action.
E. Produces a clear, concise quantitative result.

F.   Considers not only the quantity aspects of money, but also the qualitative effects of various operating policies.

Financial planning is a powerful management tool and is most often subdivided into two general types—short-term planning and long range planning. The span of time covered by long range planning generally varies between three years and can stretch over a period of twenty years. Most often the selection of a time horizon for long range planning is dependent upon the confidence of the planners to anticipate the probable future occurrences and also the nature of the business in which this planning takes place. Most companies generally plan on a three to five year basis because it is a convenient time horizon for most operating managers. Beyond that time period, the temptation is simply too great to forecast the future by merely multiplying by a constant percentage increase or decrease. The end result, therefore, becomes meaningless beyond the fifth year. Some companies, however, especially in the extractive, energy, and precious metal industries do have the innate ability to forecast well into the future. The United Nuclear Corporation, for example, regularly makes long range financial plans up to twenty years ahead. Since long range planning deals with the future, it is essentially a process of information. It is important at this juncture to emphasize that the estimating process must not be merely an estimate based upon intuition but rather an estimate based upon a careful assessment of the *probability* of future occurrences.

THE ESSENTIALS OF A SOUND PLANNING PROGRAM

A successful planning program depends upon the ability and stability of an accounting system. Such an accounting system must be one which is information and decision oriented. An accounting system which is oriented mainly toward custodial reporting responsibilities is not a powerful enough device to produce a meaningful profit plan. Ideally, such a system must be able to create action-impelling data such as profitability by product line, by division, by geographic area and by customer and customer types. It is only in this manner that stipulated company goals which are to be attained can be compared with actual operating results; an unreliable accounting system does not permit a valid comparison of planned estimates or variances with actual results. The planning program also depends upon the existence of an efficient cost accounting system. Ideally, the cost accounting system is based upon standard cost but comprises the components of direct costing. It is important that the elements of manufacturing costs be identifiable by cost center, product type and commodity involved.

Another fundamental requirement for successful planning is a sound company organogram which delineates responsibilities and lines of authority. Planning is only meaningful if someone is held responsible for results. Ideally, there should be no question as to which individual is responsible for various major expenditures and various desired results. More importantly, the people given responsibility for achieving results must have all of the authority they need to accomplish that for which they are being held responsible. In practice, this is an extremely difficult thing for any company to accomplish. A simple example of a paradox in planning is the role of the product manager in profitability planning for the marketing segment. These individuals are often held responsible for profits, yet most often they cannot purchase the raw materials for their assigned products nor can they unilaterally establish the pricing policies for such products. Most often they cannot control manufacturing efficiency and finally, in more modern corporate advertising organizations, they cannot even control the advertising policy for their products. How then, even with the best of plans, can they truly be held responsible for the profits of their products? It follows then, that plans must be directed only at the people who can do something about them.

A profit plan is analogous to off-shore piloting in small boats. The directional chart for a company is the most useful document to enable the company to avoid the shoals and eddies of the forthcoming waters of experience. Before it can decide where it wants to take the company, the management must first find out where the company has been and in what position it now finds itself. This information can only be gleaned from reliable facts and data showing past performance. For example, in order to develop sales and production goals for some future period, management often must have a conception of the past performance of the organizational units concerned. In addition, information regarding past utilization of manufacturing capacity and the potential unused capacity is also necessary in order to assess the impact of higher sales forecasts on profits. The perspective with which to view future sales or production goals for individual products or product lines should be provided by past operating data for those products. This is not to say that past performance is the criteria for future planning goals and objectives. Very frequently what has happened in the past is a very poor assessment of future probabilities. Instead, as will be discussed in subsequent sections, an independent assessment of future courses of action is the essential ingredient for planning. Statistics of the past are only relics which can reinforce a perspective as to the possibility of attainment.

A most important requirement for a successful planning program is the degree to which the highest levels of management within a company endorse the effort and the goals of the planning process. There must be a complete commitment by the management to support the planning effort, and management must see to it that everyone involved in the planning process and its results adheres as closely as possible to plan. It can ensure this commitment by requiring periodic ''variation from plan'' reports with supporting analyses. A big part of the struggle to make an operating plan successful is the task of educating everyone concerned in the advantages of planning. There is a definite need for a continuing program of planning education which stresses the benefits of a formal comprehensive planning effort to all management levels. It is part of the responsibility of the financial function to demonstrate to managers exactly what can be accomplished by a firmly disciplined planning effort. It is equally important to demonstrate to other operating personnel in the company those things which a planning effort *cannot* accomplish. *Planning can never be a substitute for rational on-the-spot decision making.*

Establishing corporate objectives. Corporate planning certainly is not an art; it is more than a philosophy and moreover, it is probably a collection of techniques. These techniques, over a period of time, are modified by the strength and personality of the leader. Thus, a corporation can plan both from the ''bottom up'' or from the ''top down.'' In other words, the textbook academic approach to corporate planning says that one must plan by first going out into the lowest echelon of corporate executive structure and seeking the probabilities of attainment for next year's performance. At successively higher levels, the same questions are asked until the final compendium is put together and the presentation made to the corporate key executive who will either ratify or invalidate the plan.

The "top down" approach is probably personified by a man like Charles Mortimer, the ex-chairman of General Foods. His strength lay in his ability to say to all his key men, "You will achieve an increase of ten percent in earnings per share each year that I will be holding this office." In effect, he went to his executives and he said, "Create me the plan that will give me this objective." This is not the type of challenge which can be satisfied by drawing a line in the middle between the "bottom up" approach and the "top down" approach. Compromise here is not a virtue. My own view leans toward the "top down" approach especially if the presence of a strong, electric leader is present. It is the strength of his vision and of his persuasion which, in effect, creates the dynamics of corporate performance.

Integral to the establishment of objectives and the need for a strong leader is the question of definition of identity. Without motivation the objectives or goal attainment process is meaningless. It is the rare company that knows how to define itself. Kinney, for example, specifically states that it is a corporation which defines itself as providing services for people, whether those services imply the availability of parking garages or funeral parlors. Mohasco is another example of a company which has defined itself. That company, which is known as a maker of carpets, furniture, and interior furnishings, has stated that it regards itself as a total supplier of home furnishings. In a similar vein, Genesco admits that they are a "total apparel" organization. Other corporations specify their objectives and goals in terms of growth of earnings per share and stipulated returns on investment. The most meaningful objective from an internal operating point of view is the establishment of a corporate goal expressed in terms of *return on investment*. Moreover, that return on investment should be narrowed down to answer the question, to what type of investment is the return being applied? My leaning is toward the concept of *return on funds employed*. That concept essentially includes the result of subtracting current liabilities from total assets. Moreover, the assets included in the base should only be those tangible assets which can be productively employed in the business. Goodwill, for example, is an asset which I would exclude from the calculation. It is the rare company which can smell, touch, see, hear and, further, manipulate goodwill. There are several factors which should be taken into account in establishing profit objectives. They are the components of the return on investment equation:

A. The profit after taxes
B. Cash flow
C. Retained earnings
D. The reinvestment of earnings
E. The debt-equity ratio
F. The dividend payout to stockholders
G. The capitalization rate (the reciprocal of the price-earnings ratio for a share of stock)

A consideration of the above items can highlight a number of the supply and demand factors upon corporate resources. Desired market share, which may be part of the marketing plan component of a total plan, requires a certain rate of growth of assets to support the supply of products. The growth of assets in turn requires a growth of funding. The growth in funding gives rise to the dichotomy which can see funding taking the shape of equity or debt. Manipulation of the debt-equity ratio in turn produces the degree of leverage employed by the company in its total capitalization. That leverage is often a precursor of the price-earnings ratio. That ratio in turn is one of the elements of satisfaction for the stockholder, the true owner of the business. The other element of satisfaction for the stockholder is the dividend payout rate which is a measure of profitability resulting from the implementation of the plan.

What planning can accomplish. At best, a plan is a scientific estimate, arrived at after a study of a company's past performance. It is predicated upon management's estimate of future conditions within the company, the industry, and in the general economy. What can management possibly hope to gain from such an exercise, which is admittedly little more than "establishing" probable future company performance?

The mere fact of putting firm estimates on paper, thinking seriously about what is likely to take place in this department or that, and of what course overall company fortunes are likely to take, gives management an invaluable insight into the future. A formal planning procedure makes management more alert to conditions that might otherwise go unnoticed. Everyone is affected by the plan, and many people help prepare it. The result is concentrated thought about future plans, and how best to achieve company goals; management has the benefit of ideas and suggestions from personnel throughout the company.

Planning helps define objectives; it also helps develop policies. To properly plan such items as material purchases and expenditures, a company must have definite purchase policies, inventory control techniques, and expense control techniques. Perhaps the most valuable contribution is in the area of expense control. Expense plans are a constant check on spending. No major outlay not provided for in the plan should be made without special approval.

Planning is a tremendous aid to financial strategies. In coordinating the planning effort, finance must ask and answer many questions. The most crucial question is whether the goals and objectives put forth by top management can be financed with the firm's present resources. And if the company needs additional funds to meet its aims, how can they be raised without jeopardizing the company's long-term financial position? Will the program of activity yield a profit acceptable over both a short term and a long term? Will the foreseeable profit level make it possible to attract other investors? Will there be sufficient debt capital sources if the company follows this plan or that plan? Will one objective conflict with any other company objectives? Only a realistic planning program can answer such questions satisfactorily.

A planning program also influences price-planning. A manufacturer must know how much it costs to produce a given product before it can determine a reasonable price at which to sell the product. Manufacturing companies (and all other business enterprises, for that matter) must price their products in advance of production, on the basis of reliable plans. Without sufficient foreknowledge of costs, the business may either lose money because its products are underpriced, or lose volume because they are overpriced in relation to similar products.

What else can a comprehensive plan program do for a company? Here are a few examples of what the planning process accomplishes:

- It forces management to consider—and evaluate—basic company policies.
- It forces management to look ahead, to predict conditions likely to prevail *outside the company* during the plan period.
- It compels everyone in management positions—from the president down—to take an active part in goal-setting and planning.
- It demands a sound organization, with responsibility for each function specifically assigned.
- It requires each department to lay its plans with a view to complementing plans of other units.
- It means planning for the most effective and economical use of labor, material, facilities, and capital.
- It requires complete accounting data, showing both past and current performance.
- It forces management to put down in cold figures the capital required to achieve satisfactory results.
- It instills in all management levels the habit of giving careful consideration to all factors before reaching a final decision.
- It clears up many questions (particularly in lower management levels) on basic company policies and objectives.
- It helps eliminate inefficiency and waste.
- It promotes general understanding, throughout the company, of the problems faced in each department or unit.
- It serves as a means of checking progress—or noting the lack of progress—toward stated goals; the company always knows where it is as well as where it has been.

Personnel engaged in the planning process. The planning process is complex because it is composed of that aspect of planning which is formal and organized, and that aspect of planning which is largely intuitive and is, in fact, practiced daily. Much of the planning process in manufacturing oriented companies is done by significant individuals in the corporate management, the sales management, and the product management areas. It is less likely that marketing personnel as well as accounting personnel and field salesmen will participate as directly in the process as the managerial personnel first mentioned. In non-manufacturing oriented companies it is far more likely that the higher levels of corporate management and operations personnel will take over the planning process almost to the exclusion of all other types of operating personnel. One recent study found that manufacturing companies with their strong sales orientation include sales managers in their projection of sales twice as often as the non-manufacturing companies which generally are more service oriented. That same study showed that the corporate management group participates directly in the computation and projection of costs in over half of the companies that were surveyed in both the manufacturing and non-manufacturing categories. Department managers and sales and marketing personnel participate more frequently in manufacturing companies, although plant managers participated about equally in the two categories.

This discussion gives rise to the consideration of the role of financial personnel in the planning process. It is not uncommon in today's corporate organization to observe new positions which have been assigned major responsibilities for corporate planning. At this stage in corporate development, this position has been posted at a high level of management and the corporate planner is increasingly reporting directly to the president of the company. His is a unique job with an even more unique assignment.

Essentially, the position is that of a coordinator, a motivator who will encourage change and stimulate thought, a teacher of methodology and lastly, a salesman whose function it is to sell the worth of the planning process. His is essentially a service job and in his role he should be helping line and staff to evaluate the plans of their operations, whether they are in decentralized or centralized organizations. In addition to this role, the corporate planner frequently becomes involved in strategic planning. The concept of strategic planning is different from long range planning only in the sense that major elements of strategy are considered in strategic planning which are not necessarily a part of traditional long range planning. Questions of long-term financing, of diversification, of future avenues of operations for the company, relocation of new physical facilities—these are all considerations for strategic planning. The traditional long range planning is almost mandated to take on the mold of contemporary knowledge within the corporation.

Financial people, per se, have no direct hand in developing many aspects of the long range plan nor, in fact, do they formulate the overall specific budget such as those dealing with production considerations. Finance merely offers technical advice to sales, marketing and production people who draw up various plans. The planner then consolidates the various estimates of operating and staff groups and presents any revisions to a planning committee and to the higher levels of management for study and approval. It is the planner's additional function to prepare and disseminate copies of the final plans to the heads of all departments and divisions.

In all of their dealings with operating personnel, finance people must remember that they have no actual control over operations. Finance must be extremely careful to avoid even giving the impression of trying to assume authority that properly belongs elsewhere. Finance is a staff function; it must not attempt to exercise control over operating or line functions, although it does have an obligation to advise these functions of questionable areas of operation, and in addition, it has a further role of assisting operational areas to optimize their decision making processes.

It follows that finance must never take operating personnel to task for unfavorable budget results. Finance merely designs, directs and coordinates the administration of the planning process. It has no actual responsibility in carrying out budgeted plans and programs. The only way finance can properly influence operations is through timely follow-up reports to the right operating personnel, revealing the progress as evidenced by cost accounting data, general accounting data and other appropriate indicators of performance. Even in a carefully run planning program, knowing what to report and how takes special skills and tact. Current innovations in financial organization are permitting finance to depart from the traditional aspect of a purely service and non-control function. The concept, for instance, of a marketing controller runs slightly counter to the emphasis placed just above regarding the non-participatory role of finance in operational performance. Since it is still an innovation in corporate financial organizations, for special purposes in discussing long range planning, the position taken above is still valid.

The personnel in the financial function who administer the planning program should have a sound background in accounting theory, supported by considerable experience and an even more considerable degree of empathy into the operational problems of various functional areas. They should know the company's general cost accounting system thoroughly, they must have an intimate knowledge of company organization and in addition, they must understand how all the various functions mesh together into an integrated whole. They must also be familiar with a company's "informal" organization. They must possess an above average analytical ability and in addition must have the ability to write well and to know how to explain complex accounting concepts in simple, straightforward terms.

No one in finance, from the chief financial executive on down should ever be put in the position of having to take action to correct a line department's budget performance. To avoid such occurrences, most finance officers insist that company budget policy and organization be clearly detailed in written instructions for managers. This is one reason why a complete planning manual is of such value in the process.

SOURCES OF INFORMATION USEFUL IN
ECONOMIC FORECASTING

The federal government is the greatest collector of basic statistics and the best source of information. Statistics are gathered and dispensed by many departments, bureaus, and commissions, including the Department of Agriculture, Department of Commerce, Bureau of the Census, Department of Labor, Bureau of Labor Statistics, Department of the Interior, Bureau of Mines, Federal Trade Commission, Board of Governors of the Federal Reserve System, Interstate Commerce Commission and many others. The Economic Report to the President by the Council of Economic Advisors contains much useful data, national in scope. This report is usually made twice a year. The assembly, tabulation, and publication of much of the data collected by the government is done by many agencies, trade organizations, and trade publications.

Useful statistical tables of many types are available in the following publications:

Standard and Poor's Corporation, *Industry Surveys*. New York: Standard and Poor's Corporation (Annually).
Federal Reserve Bulletin. Board of Governors of the Federal Reserve System, Washington, D.C. (Monthly).
Survey of Current Business. U.S. Department of Commerce, Office of Business Economics, Washington, D.C. (Monthly).
Bureau of the Census, *Statistical Abstract of the United States*. Washington, D.C.: Government Printing Office (Annually).
Monthly Labor Review. United States Department of Labor, Bureau of Labor Statistics, Washington, D.C.

Current data on population trends, surveys and estimates are found in current bulletins issued in series and in special publications of the Bureau of the Census.

A number of commodity price indexes are available. The best known are the Bureau of Labor Statistics' Wholesale Price Index and Consumer Price Index.

Data on living costs and wage levels are found in the current publications of the Department of Labor.

Current statistical data are usually reported in financial journals, trade papers, and daily newspapers as soon as they are released by the collecting agencies. Indexes of industrial production, living costs, wholesale prices, car loadings, steel production, and other indications of current trends appear regularly in metropolitan dailies. If such data are collected regularly as they appear, they are useful in judging current economic trends up to the latest possible date, before they have been digested by competent economists and appear as full-blown estimates of the current economic level.

The following services discuss business in general and trends from the businessman's viewpoint:

Daily Report for Executives. Washington, D.C.: Bureau of National Affairs, Inc. (Daily).

Kiplinger Agricultural Letter. Washington, D.C.: Kiplinger Washington Agency (Bi-weekly).

Kiplinger Washington Letter. Washington, D.C.: Kiplinger Washington Agency (Weekly).

Prentice-Hall Executive Report. Englewood Cliffs, N.J.: Prentice-Hall, Inc. (Weekly).

Whaley-Eaton American Letter. Washington, D.C.: Whaley-Eaton Service (Weekly).

Whaley-Eaton Foreign Letter. Washington, D.C.: Whaley-Eaton Service (Weekly).

Executive's Tax Report. Englewood Cliffs, N.J.: Prentice-Hall, Inc. (Weekly).

SPECIFIC PLANNING FOR COMPANY OPERATION

Recent study has shown the following among the major items included in long range forecasts by manufacturing and non-manufacturing companies:

Revenues or sales
Cash flow
Capital expenditures
Operating expenses
Net earnings
Rate of return
Source and application of funds
Percent share of market
Balance sheet
Cash dividends

In addition to the above delineated components for long range forecasts, many companies go even further than the above. Some companies include further plans regarding personnel, regarding administrative measures and further, regarding organizational patterns for the future. Behind all of the planning is a formalized system for budgeting, or planning various types of operations.

Systems for planning operations vary from company to company. Some companies prepare only a rough sales forecast and an overall production plan. Such partial planning may serve some organizations, but most firms require more comprehensive programs embracing all company operations and used concurrently for planning, coordinating and controlling. Breaking a fairly typical comprehensive planning program down to reveal its component parts, we might see a result like that shown in Figure 2-1.

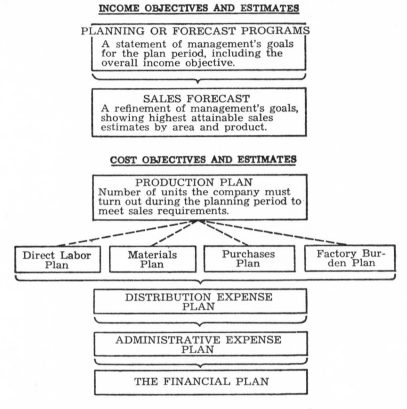

Figure 2-1.
Components of a Comprehensive Planning Program

A comprehensive program such as that illustrated by Figure 2-1, is perhaps the most dynamic planning and control tool financial management can have at its disposal. Keeping expenses below revenue means setting goals for each activity in advance, then using the proper techniques to control and coordinate efforts to reach these goals, both in individual organizational units and throughout the company. By using a number of specialized plans in an integrated control system, management can establish objectives, coordinate planning and compare actual results with objectives. And all along the line, from the beginning of the period to its end, management can bring about changes as are required to keep operations on course. Generally, such changes are made in operations to bring actual performance up to performance standards. Only occasionally are budgets revised downward—and then as a last resort—unless external conditions prove the forecast upon which the budgets were made was grossly optimistic.

The planning process and the sales forecasting process are estimates of income. The remaining forecasts are estimates of the expense required to attain the planned income; they show the costs involved in manufacturing, distribution and administration and the number of finished products called for in the sales plan. Costs may be related either to time or activity. The costs related to time are often called fixed costs or period costs. Those related to volume or activity are called variable or semi-variable costs depending upon the pattern of their behavior.

- *Period Costs*—costs or expenses that remain relatively constant and vary more over a period of time than they do with the physical activity of volume turnover. Depreciation, taxes, insurance and administrative costs are fixed costs. These costs are shown in specialized forecasts for manufacturing and administrative activities.
- *Variable Costs*—these are costs or expenses that vary in direct proportion to increases or decreases in physical output or activity in a given department or work center. Variable costs come about as a result of activity. When there is no activity there is no variable cost. Should activity increase ten times, variable costs would also increase ten times. Since direct labor and material are related to volume and activity, direct labor and material costs are variable. They may be shown in a materials forecast or in a direct labor forecast. These are costs or expenses that have some characteristics of most fixed and variable costs. They fluctuate with volume and activity, but not necessarily proportionately. In fact, they tend more often to vary with capacity. Semi-variable costs are shown primarily in long range production forecasts as well as forecasts for distribution expense and administrative expense.

Each of the above types of expenses is planned for in different forecasts and each fills a definite need. Taken together, the forecasts are a means of determining total costs, the essential factor in any planning effort. Figure 2-2 shows how the various plans go together to make up a financial forecast.

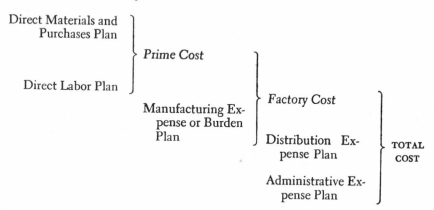

Figure 2-2. Development of the Financial Plan

Planning for revenue. The sales forecast is the beginning of the overall planning process. It is a company's best estimate of how much of each of its products it expects to sell during the planning period. It is usually broken down to show anticipated sales volume by months, weeks or even days. Anticipated sales are also classified by product, product line and are often broken down into anticipated sales for geographic or customer classifications. Most sales forecasts show anticipated sales for each product or product line in terms of both dollar volume and product units.

The sales forecast is the foundation of all company planning. The marketing executive and other sales management personnel rely heavily on past sales figures in making the sales forecasts, but they also attempt to gauge the effect of business and economic conditions, competition and other factors on future sales. In making the sales forecasts, sales management must be extremely careful to take all factors into account and come up with the most accurate forecast possible with available facts and figures. Likewise, finance must make as many facts and figures available to marketing as it possibly can. The accuracy of all other plans for profitable activity depends on the accuracy of the sales forecasts. The need for accuracy is so important in the sales forecasting phase of the overall planning process that many companies have developed simulation models to assist them in controlling the variables which enter into the forecasting picture. Sales forecasting, especially in the consumer goods industry, is one of the most complicated of all planning activities. And because forecasts of sales lead to the next evolutionary step—that of inventory management and customer service—completely new sets of variables enter upon the scene and make even more important the recognition that correct sales forecasting can minimize distribution costs. IBM has developed a data processing program called Consumer Goods System (COGS). The system is composed of two parts, one which deals with specific forecasting and the other which deals with allocations. Both of these programs are designed to overcome patterns of consumption which shift constantly, as well as external environmental factors such as seasonality of products. Used properly, the program's capability to simulate can assist the user in predicting in advance the accuracy of given forecast models. Following is a suggested table of contents for a sales plan. Major programs should be separately described in each case:

1. Projection of sales volume by product line—annually for five years
2. Price and gross margin projection by product line—annually for five years
3. Market share by product line—annually for five years
4. Total market potential by product line—annually for five years
5. Projected changes in capital required for marketing operations—by year of occurrence. (Examples would be new fleet of delivery trucks, purchase of warehouses, or the new plan of dealer financing).
6. Any major changes planned in the market operations.
7. Sales projection by new product line—annually for five years.
8. Gross margin projection by new product line—annually for five years.
9. New capital investment in support of new products by product line—annually for five years.

It is important to note that this plan projects the marketing operation only. If new products require new production facilities, then capital spending for such facilities will be shown in a capital program, even though it will then be identified with relevant marketing programs.

Figure 2-3 shows a completed sales forecast such as some companies must use in planning for revenues. Notice that the first quarter sales are broken down to show anticipated sales in each of the first three months. The forecast, sometimes called a sales plan, reveals estimated sales by product and by sales district. This overall forecast is a consolidation of sales estimates from individual sales territories.

	Totals		Northern District		Southern District		Eastern District		Western District	
	Units	Amount	Units	Amount	Units	Amount	Units	Amount	Units	Amount
Product A—$5.00 per unit										
January	3,800	$19,000	1,000	$5,000	800	$4,000	1,400	$7,000	600	$3,000
February	4,200	21,000	1,200	6,000	900	4,500	1,500	7,500	600	3,000
March	4,850	24,250	1,500	7,500	950	4,750	1,750	8,750	650	3,250
Total First Quarter	12,850	$64,250	3,700	$18,500	2,650	$13,250	4,650	$23,250	1,850	$9,250
2nd Quarter	5,450	27,250	2,000	10,000	1,000	5,000	1,750	8,750	700	3,500
3rd Quarter	5,750	28,750	2,200	11,000	1,000	5,000	1,800	9,000	750	3,750
4th Quarter	6,250	$31,250	2,500	$12,500	1,000	5,000	2,000	$10,000	750	$3,750
	30,300	$151,500	10,400	$52,000	5,650	$28,250	10,200	$51,000	4,050	$20,250
Product B—$2.00 per unit										
January	5,800	$11,600	2,000	$4,000	1,000	$2,000	2,000	$4,000	800	$1,600
February	6,900	11,800	2,500	5,000	1,200	2,400	2,200	4,400	1,000	2,000
March	7,900	15,800	3,000	6,000	1,300	2,600	2,500	5,000	1,100	2,200
Total First Quarter	20,600	$39,200	7,500	$15,000	3,500	7,000	6,700	$13,400	2,900	$5,800
2nd Quarter	8,300	$16,600	3,000	6,000	1,500	3,000	2,600	5,200	1,200	2,400
3rd Quarter	8,600	17,200	3,200	6,400	1,500	3,000	2,700	5,400	1,200	2,400
4th Quarter	9,200	$18,400	3,000	$6,000	1,700	$3,400	3,000	$6,000	1,500	$3,000
	$46,700	$91,400	16,700	$33,400	8,200	$16,400	15,000	$30,000	6,800	$13,600

Figure 2-3.
Completed Sales Forecast (Sales Plan)

The production plan. The major planning tool for production activity is the production plan which is based directly upon the sales forecast. The production plan provides a means of coordinating sales, production and inventories. It is an estimate of production quantities necessary during the planning period to satisfy sales requirements.

The production plan includes estimates for direct labor, for materials, for purchases, and for the overhead attendant to the activity contained in the forecast. The primary production plan shows only the number of finished products necessary to fill sales requirements. It ordinarily has no cost breakdowns since costs are supplied in other plans which comprise the primary production program.

A table of contents for such a plan would include the following:

1. Replacement plan listing major and minor capital projects to replace existing plant—annually for five years.
2. New plant and equipment for existing production—annually for five years.
3. New plant and equipment for new products (as specified in the marketing sales plan)—annually for five years.
4. Production costs trends by production plant or by product line—annually for five years.
5. New processes and techniques with approximate date of installation and effect on cost.

The new projects detailed in this plan should be coordinated with the new products detailed in the sales plan. The new developments should make reference to engineering feasibility studies where they exist. Care should be taken to avoid rough guesses whenever possible. Projecting five years in the future is understandably difficult, however, the plan loses its value as a management tool if the financial manager resorts to "rough estimates." Since we are dealing with somewhat uncertain forecasts, it is important that the substance of the major programs be described as fully as possible, at least in the supporting text of the report, if quantification is not feasible. Where new facilities are recommended, the justification must be stated in both absolute terms and in terms of alternative courses of action which may be available.

The actual procedures used in formulating production plans vary from company to company. In many small firms, the production executive prepares the plan himself, with little or no help from subordinates. He bases his estimates of production requirements on the sales forecast, and translates sales requirements into a balanced production program. The production plan is then approved, either by the president or by the budget committee.

But in larger companies—particularly those with decentralized production operations—division production managers and even workcenter foremen play a very important part in plan preparation. In these companies, plant accounting departments and production supervisors often work together to prepare cost estimates for each production department or workcenter. In some cases, the central finance office provides each production manager (or the production executive) with cost accounting data on production capabilities and labor and material costs, and the planning director coordinates the data as necessary.

At the same time as plans are being made for the annual operating plan, the company may be planning well beyond the period covered by the plan. In addition to a well-documented plan for the coming year's operations, divisional managers are often asked to submit a three to five year forecast of operations, showing probable volume, new product development plans, research programs, personnel needs, planned organizational changes, and inventory and facility requirements.

The cost estimates for workcenters ultimately become actual operations plans for the workcenters; when collected for all workcenters, they become divisional or departmental plans. Likewise, when these plans are combined, they comprise the overall production plan. Figure 2-4 is a simplified production plan summary, showing requirements for one product during the plan period.

Production Plan Summary—Product "A"

Required by sales forecast	$30,300
Desired ending inventory, finished goods	1,000
Total production required	$31,300
Less beginning inventory, finished goods	1,450
Planned production for year	$29,850

Figure 2-4. Simplified Production Plan Summary

More elaborate production summaries than the one shown in Figure 2-4 are used in many large production operations; they contain such supplementary information as:

- Number of operating days in each month
- Required daily production rate
- Percentage of capacity at which operations are scheduled through the plan period
- Number of factory workers involved (sometimes stated in terms of direct and indirect hours per week, month, or quarter)
- Machine capacities and machine-hours required by workcenter or production area

With information such as this, every department or unit whose work is related to production activities can plan its activities to complement the manufacturing operation.

Using the production plan summary, production prorates or allocates the required total output throughout the plan period on the basis of such considerations as these:

- Having a sufficient inventory of finished products on hand at all times to meet sales requirements
- Keeping inventory levels of raw material and components within reasonable limits.
- Manufacturing the products as economically as possible
- Maintaining a fairly stable production rate
- Attaining maximum utilization of plant capacity

This results in a detailed production plan, with quantities allocated to each month,

DETAILED PRODUCTION PLAN

PRODUCT A

	Sales Forecast R'qments	Less Finished Goods Inventory	Total Production R'qd.
January	300,000	240,000	60,000
February	225,000	10,000	215,000
March	200,000	50,000	150,000
Total 1st Quarter	725,000	300,000	425,000
2nd Quarter	600,000	200,000	400,000
3rd Quarter	550,000	100,000	450,000
4th Quarter	400,000	50,000	350,000
Total	2,275,000	650,000	1,625,000

PRODUCT B

	Sales Forecast R'qments	Less Finished Goods Inventory	Total Production R'qd.
January	150,000	75,000	75,000
February	100,000	25,000	75,000
March	90,000	20,000	70,000
Total 1st Quarter	340,000	120,000	220,000
2nd Quarter	300,000	100,000	200,000
3rd Quarter	280,000	140,000	140,000
4th Quarter	320,000	80,000	240,000
Total	1,240,000	440,000	800,000

Figure 2-5. Detailed Production Plan

quarter, etc. Figure 2-5 illustrates such a plan, broken down to show desired production quantities for two products over a plan period of one year.

Notice that neither the production summary in Figure 2-4 nor the detailed production plan show costs. Although many companies do include costs in these plans, most companies show cost figures for the first time in the more specialized expense plans that are actually components of the overall production plan. These include the material and purchases plans, the direct labor plan and the factory burden or overhead plan.

The materials plan. The materials plan is a statement of estimated quantities of material (both components and raw materials) needed to meet production requirements. The materials plan may or may not include material costs, depending on whether or not the company utilized a purchases plan in addition to the materials plan. Where both plans are used, the materials plan is likely *not* to include costs.

The materials that go into production are classed as either direct or indirect materials. Direct (or productive) materials are generally considered as all materials or parts that become integrated into the finished product and are readily identifiable with the cost of the finished item. Indirect materials are necessary to the manufacturing process, but they are not directly traceable to specific production efforts. Such items as lubricating oils, solvents, and other maintenance supplies are generally classed as indirect materials. The materials plan usually includes only direct materials, leaving maintenance supplies and other indirect materials to be included in the manufacturing expense or burden plan.

Those responsible for formulating the materials plan estimate as closely as possible the material quantities called for in the production plan, making allowances for normal spoilage, waste, and scrap. Quantities of each direct material or part are shown by month, quarter, or other convenient periods, taking such factors as normal delivery time, economic order quantities, and available storage space into consideration. Figure 2-6 shows a detailed materials plan, broken down by product and by month and quarter for a plan period of one year.

The purchases plan. If the materials plan is accurate, the company's purchasing section or department can make very accurate predictions of the prices of materials over the plan period. Purchasing submits its estimates in a purchases plan; in addition to quantities, the purchases plan may also show the timing of purchases and estimated material costs. Figure 2-7 shows a fairly typical purchases plan, revealing estimated costs of materials used in production.

The materials and purchases plans are essential for determining direct material costs. Direct material is one of the two elements of prime cost, which also includes direct labor. The direct labor plan is therefore a necessary step toward determining prime costs.

The direct labor plan. The direct labor plan is an estimate of total direct labor needed to meet planned production requirements. The direct labor plan may show direct labor costs only, or it may indicate both direct labor hours and their cost.

Like material costs, labor costs are classed as either direct or indirect. Direct labor costs are the wages paid to workers engaged directly in specific, identifiable production operations. While labor traceable to a distinct production phase is direct labor, indirect labor *supports* direct productive activity. In a sense, it is incidental to the production

Materials Plan—Unit Requirements by Product and by Time Period

Part or Material #	PRODUCT A		PRODUCT B		TOTAL UNITS MATERIAL R'QD
	Production Planned	Material R'qd	Production Planned	Material R'qd	
Part #47					
January	60,000	60,000	75,000	NONE	60,000
February	215,000	215,000	75,000	NONE	215,000
March	150,000	150,000	70,000	NONE	150,000
Total 1st Qtr	425,000	425,000	220,000	NONE	425,000
2nd Qtr	400,000	400,000	200,000	NONE	400,000
3rd Qtr	450,000	450,000	140,000	NONE	450,000
4th Qtr	350,000	350,000	240,000	NONE	350,000
GRAND TOTAL FOR YEAR	1,625,000	1,625,000	800,000	———	1,625,000
Part #58					
January	60,000	60,000	75,000	75,000	135,000
February	215,000	215,000	75,000	75,000	290,000
March	150,000	150,000	70,000	70,000	220,000
Total 1st Qtr	425,000	425,000	220,000	220,000	645,000
2nd Qtr	400,000	400,000	200,000	200,000	600,000
3rd Qtr	450,000	450,000	140,000	140,000	590,000
4th Qtr	350,000	350,000	240,000	240,000	590,000
GRAND TOTAL FOR YEAR	1,625,000	1,625,000	800,000	800,000	2,425,000
Part #19 (Note: Anticipate approximately 20,000 of this item on hand beginning January)					
January	60,000	40,000	75,000	75,000	115,000
February	215,000	215,000	75,000	75,000	290,000
March	150,000	150,000	70,000	70,000	220,000
Total 1st Qtr	425,000	405,000	220,000	220,000	625,000
2nd Qtr	400,000	400,000	200,000	200,000	600,000
3rd Qtr	450,000	450,000	140,000	140,000	590,000
4th Qtr	350,000	350,000	240,000	240,000	590,000
GRAND TOTAL FOR YEAR	1,625,000	1,605,000	800,000	800,000	2,405,000

Figure 2-6. Detailed Materials Plan

effort. Indirect labor costs include all costs other than direct labor, including such costs as supervisory salaries, wages paid to storekeepers, and maintenance labor expense. These charges are generally included (along with indirect materials costs) in the factory burden or overhead plan.

Production prepares the direct labor plan, working closely with personnel and cost accounting. Once complete, the plan becomes part of the overall production plan and is

Purchases Plan—By Product and by Time Period

Part #47	Units Required	Unit Cost	Total Cost
January	60,000	$3.00	$ 180,000
February	215,000		645,000
March	150,000		450,000
Total 1st Qtr	425,000		$1,275,000
2nd Qtr	400,000		1,200,000
3rd Qtr	450,000		1,350,000
4th Qtr	350,000		1,050,000
GRAND TOTAL FOR YEAR	1,625,000		$4,875,000
Part #58			
January	135,000	.20	$ 27,000
February	290,000		58,000
March	220,000		44,000
Total 1st Qtr	645,000		$ 129,000
2nd Qtr	600,000		120,000
3rd Qtr	590,000		118,000
4th Qtr	590,000		118,000
GRAND TOTAL FOR YEAR	2,425,000		$ 485,000
Part #19			
January	115,000	.40	$ 46,000
February	290,000		116,000
March	220,000		88,000
Total 1st Qtr	625,000		$ 250,000
2nd Qtr	600,000	.45*	270,000
3rd Qtr	590,000		265,000
4th Qtr	590,000		265,500
GRAND TOTAL FOR YEAR	2,405,000		$1,051,000

* Anticipate 5¢ price increase beginning 3rd quarter.

Figure 2-7. Purchases Plan

submitted to the plan or finance committee for approval. The direct labor plan provides finance the information it needs in determining cash requirements for direct labor. And by revealing the total cost of direct labor, it also affords a means of controlling direct labor expense.

To pinpoint responsibility for control purposes, direct labor hours are usually shown in the labor plan by product and by workcenter. If the company has a standard hour system, it can compute direct labor costs by multiplying the standard hours required for each unit of production by the total units called for in the production plan, then multiplying this figure by the average wage rate per standard hour. For example, if the production plan calls for 30,000 finished products, and each unit requires two standard hours to complete, there is obviously a direct labor demand of 60,000 standard hours. Multiplying this figure by the average wage rate of, say, $3.00 per standard hour, the company arrives at the direct labor cost to produce the desired number of finished product units—$180,000.

Direct labor costs may also be determined by relating labor cost to some other measure of production activity, such as direct machine hours or direct material costs. For example, historical ratios of direct labor hours to physical output are often used in computing direct labor costs. Many companies simply have workcenter foremen estimate the direct labor hours required to meet planned output for each workcenter, then combine workcenter estimates to arrive at a total direct labor figure. Figure 2-8 shows a direct labor plan broken down to reveal labor costs by product, time period, and workcenter.

Direct Labor Plan—First Quarter Only

Product A	Units to be Produced	Standard Hours per Unit	Total Standard Hours	Rate	Total Cost
January					
Workcenter 1	40,000	.5	20,000	$3.00	$ 60,000
Workcenter 2	10,000	.5	5,000	2.00	10,000
Workcenter 3	10,000	.5	5,000	2.00	10,000
February					
Workcenter 1	30,000	.3	9,000	$3.00	$ 27,000
Workcenter 2	42,000	.2	8,400	2.00	16,800
Workcenter 3	15,000	.8	12,000	2.00	24,000
March					
Workcenter 1	12,000	.1	1,200	$3.00	$ 3,600
Workcenter 2	34,000	1.0	34,000	2.00	68,000
Workcenter 3	18,000	2.0	36,000	2.00	72,000
TOTAL	211,000		130,600		$291,400
Product B					
January					
Workcenter 1	8,000	.5	4,000	$3.00	$ 12,000
Workcenter 2	10,000	.2	2,000	2.00	4,000
Workcenter 3	1,500	.6	900	2.00	1,800
February					
Workcenter 1	10,000	.5	5,000	$3.00	$ 15,000
Workcenter 2	8,500	.1	850	2.00	1,700
Workcenter 3	9,000	.2	4,500	2.00	9,000
March					
Workcenter 1	50,000	.3	15,000	$3.00	$ 45,000
Workcenter 2	20,000	.8	16,000	2.00	32,000
Workcenter 3	15,000	.5	7,500	2.00	15,000
TOTAL	132,000		55,750		$132,500

Figure 2-8. Direct Labor Plan

The burden or overhead plan. Prime costs (direct material and direct labor) commonly represent only about half of total costs. "Overhead" accounts for the remaining expense. Most overhead charges are fairly constant; they do not vary in direct relation to product activity. Even if the plant remains idle (or nearly so), staff salaries, many sales expenses, advertising charges, indirect labor costs, insurance premiums, taxes, the depreciation burden, and many other expenses continue to accrue.

The manufacturing expense of factory burden figure includes both indirect labor and indirect material expended in production or supporting activities. It includes such items as power, fuel, water, general supervisory expense, tool control expense, building and equipment maintenance charges, depreciation, real and personal property taxes on production facilities, and inspection and engineering costs.

Allocating these costs to specific products and workcenters is sometimes difficult. But in any effective plan and cost control effort, overhead must be charged to the particular department responsible for incurring the expense. Take the cost of power, for example; it is normally an indirect cost and therefore included in the manufacturing expense plan. As difficult as it may appear to accomplish the task, each production department must be held accountable for the power it uses in performing its function in the power (as well as the amount of other indirect items) used in the workcenter in comparison with planned amounts. Planning and cost accounting overlap when it comes to allocating factory burden.

Allocating Expense Burden

Manufacturing expense burden may be allocated in several ways. A common method is to relate burden to direct labor cost. In this method, the burden rate is found by dividing total burden by total direct labor cost for a given accounting period. The resulting rate is then applied to each workcenter according to the number of direct labor hours planned. For example, suppose a company's total direct labor cost is $180,000, with a total manufacturing expense burden of $18,000. The burden rate is 10 percent ($18,000 ÷ $180,000 = .10). Suppose there are nine workcenters, and that each of them has budgeted $20,000 in direct labor charges. By applying the burden rate of 10 percent to the planned direct labor expense, we get the manufacturing expense burden for each workcenter, which is $2,000. It is quite simple to prorate this figure throughout the plan period, or to break it down to show how much overhead should be charged to each product or product line.

The direct labor method is widely used, primarily because of its simplicity. The primary objection to this method of allocating manufacturing burden is that it introduces a variable—the hourly pay-rate—that has little connection with actual productive effort. The cost of direct labor in a given workcenter is ordinarily no indication of that unit's productivity in comparison to the output of similar units. Another method of allocating manufacturing burden—the direct labor-hours method—eliminates the variable and takes effort more into account. To use the direct labor-hours technique, the general factory burden is divided by the total direct labor-hours. The resulting rate is used in allocating burden just as the rate for total labor cost was used in the previous example.

Two other methods are in common use for allocating manufacturing expense burden: the direct materials and labor method, and the machine-hour method. The first of these is similar to the direct labor method just discussed, except that it combines direct labor and direct material costs. The machine-hour method allocates overhead according to the number of hours various machines are operated. Figure 2-9 shows a manufacturing expense plan developed under the most commonly used method for allocating burden, the direct labor method.

Partial Manufacturing Expense Plan—First Quarter Only			
	Workcenter 1	Workcenter 2	Workcenter 3
January			
Supervisory salaries	$23,000	$10,000	$ 9,200
Indirect labor	15,000	8,200	3,400
Maintenance	5,000	4,000	4,800
Depreciation	6,500	4,800	3,100
Insurance	2,000	1,400	600
TOTALS	$51,500	$29,200	$21,100
February			
Supervisory salaries	$21,000	$18,000	$11,000
Indirect labor	13,500	6,000	2,100
Maintenance	4,200	3,450	4,700
Depreciation	3,400	800	4,000
Insurance	2,100	900	2,100
TOTALS	$44,200	$29,150	$23,900
March			
Supervisory salaries	$20,800	$12,400	$ 9,400
Indirect labor	6,400	3,300	3,200
Maintenance	4,300	3,100	4,550
Depreciation	800	4,600	3,170
Insurance	700	1,250	1,130
TOTALS	$33,000	$24,650	$21,450

Figure 2-9. Manufacturing Expense Plan

The Distribution Expense Budget

Distribution expenses include all costs involved in selling, distributing, and delivering products to customers. Distribution expense is overhead, and as such may even be included in the general administrative plan instead of in a separate, specialized plan. Distribution expenses are generally allocated to individual products in much the same way that manufacturing burden is allocated for planning purposes. The allocation is likely to be done in a much more arbitrary manner, however.

While distribution expenses are determined and allocated largely as a help in product pricing, the primary objective in preparing distribution expense plans is to achieve a proper relationship between sales expense and sales volume or income. Distribution expense plans are usually broken down to show planned marketing expenses (including advertising and sales promotion costs) for sales territories and districts. Such a breakdown gives sales managers and salesmen definite expense goals and makes them personally responsible for attaining those goals. The distribution expense plan is a means of controlling sales expenses, of keeping sales costs in line with anticipated results.

Administrative Expense Plan

Administrative expenses include all costs except those incurred in manufacturing and distributing the product. They relate to the general supervision and services performed as a benefit to the total business rather than in connection with any one department or function. Administrative costs are those expenses that cannot be properly classified as either manufacturing or distributing costs.

The administrative expense plan generally includes the salaries and other compensation of officers, directors, and other executives, plus the costs of running their offices or departments; the expense of common services; and miscellaneous expenses such as dues, donations, legal fees and certain tax payments. Obviously, costs such as these are relatively fixed; they show little or no change in relation to changes in production or sales activity. This means that the administrative expense plan is likely to be based almost solely on historical cost figures. Because most administrative costs are not variable, it is fairly simple to estimate future expenditures even for cost items not included in previous plans.

The manpower plan. The rapid change of technology requires careful planning of new talents and types of experts required in future years, as well as the normal requirements for more ordinary skills. For example, data processing experts, biochemists or astrophysicists may be needed within five years. Companies often find that a nationwide shortage exists in certain fields and most plan to develop full departments and staff groups from within the firm. The objectives of this plan should be carefully coordinated with the sales and production plans.

The five-year financial plan. As the marketing, production and manpower plans take shape, the major document, the financial plan, will take form along with them. The results of careful planning will be an accurate picture of the future trends and prospects of the company. Three examples of the results of forward financial planning illustrate these benefits:

1. A computer manufacturer found that its marketing plan was so encouraging that its growth over the next five years was limited only by the capital required to match the rapidly growing sales. The financial manager recognized that the company's stock was well received by the public and carried a high price-earnings ratio. Since the sales growth was highly predictable, the risks were considered reasonable in spite of the high growth rate shown in the sales plan. The decision was made to conduct regular stock issues in future years to provide the growth capital required.
2. An airplane engine manufacturer was faced with a declining market as the military converted to missiles and rockets. The financial projection showed large quantities of cash being generated for future years as production facilities were phased out. However, the manpower plan indicated substantial risks. The firm tried to convert rapidly to the new technologies. This technical expertise was becoming obsolete. The decision was made to use the cash to buy small technically oriented firms to help make the transition.
3. A consumer goods manufacturer found that its market would continue to grow at a steady rate. Its production plan showed that the sales increase could be handled readily and that manpower and plan facilities would, in fact, outstrip the sales

growth. The financial picture looked stable and secure. The decision was made to make a major effort in new product development and new market development for existing products. A heavy market research and product planning effort was required, plus the development of an international division for sale of existing products.

PUTTING THE LONG RANGE PLAN INTO WORK

The techniques of developing balance sheets, operating statements and capital budgets are well known to most students of accounting. There is really very little difference in constructing a balance sheet or other similar financial statements specifically for a five year plan as there is for developing one for either a one or two year plan or even for a year's actual results. It should be borne in mind, however, that the five year plan does not contain so much detailed information. Examples of formats for these reports are shown in Figures 2-10, 2-11, and 2-12. In the balance sheet and operating statements, comparative data of recent actual performance are included. A capital plan shows a breakdown into three major groups. The replacement and volume expansion portion, which deals with existing product lines and new products, is shown in the third category.

Once the plans are put down on paper, they should become a tool; not merely something to file. They are first submitted to the executive committee for suggested alteration. They then go to the board of directors. Once approved, they become the basis for implementation by line department.

The five year financial plan will be developed in less detail than the annual capital budget and profit plan. This does not mean that the two are unrelated, rather that it will be necessary to establish a definite line between the first year of the financial plan and the capital budget and profit plan which is subsequently prepared covering that year. To establish this linkage without at the same time creating an inordinate burden in the planning process is a matter of some skill. However, it is an absolute necessity if we are to be certain that the same general concepts and objectives are present in the two sets of forecasts. Unless the two systems are consistent, there is no basis on which to approve the year's capital budget and profit plan, since there is no certainty that they are consistent with the long range financial plan for the company. In order to avoid the creation of unnecessary detail, it is desirable to have the operating departments comment in an affirmative fashion that their budgets and profit plans are, in fact, consistent with the approved long range financial plan for their activity.

Once the long range planning system has been installed, it is necessary to establish an orderly method of recording actual results against plan. This is desirable to provide a means of revising the company's goals and objectives and to provide insight into better means of forecasting.

It is also necessary to evaluate the performance of the various managers who are responsible for the forecasts that are built into the plan. Some managers are characteristically "target" forecasters; that is, they make a forecast which does not provide for the possibility of a normal amount of contingencies. Consequently, their forecasts are achievable only under optimum circumstances. At the other extreme, there are managers who retain too much of a "cushion" which will permit them to offset unfavorable

	Comparative Data		Projected Years				
	Two Years Ago	Last Year	1st	2nd	3rd	4th	5th

Sales
Product Line I
Product Line II
Product Line III

Direct Costs
Material
Labor
Variable Selling
Variable Overhead

Fixed Overhead
Wages & Salaries
Depreciations
Other

Corporate S & A
Salaries
Other

Profit Before Taxe

Other Income
Other Expenses

Income Taxes

Profit After Tax

Figure 2-10. Projected Operating Statement

performance. A post-audit will help to expose both types of forecasting. Suffice it to say that all planning should be on the basis of *probable attainment*.

The post-audit must be timed so as to provide a useful measure of actual performance and still be early enough to give information that can be utilized in the preparation of new plans. The post-audit will rarely be of value in correcting deficiencies in the particular project under audit, because the post-audit cannot really be undertaken until some reliable experience has been obtained from the project. By the time this experience is available, the project would generally have been so fully committed as to be irreversible. When dealing with construction projects or the purchase of equipment, the post-audit can usually take place once the facility is operating under so-called normal conditions. When dealing with the introduction of a new product, the post-audit can begin once sales have reached normal commercial levels. This may mean in general that the post-audit might take place at the end of the first third or quarter of the project's estimated life.

	Comparative Data		*Projected Data (5 years)*				
	Two Years Ago	Last Year	1st	2nd	3rd	4th	5th

Cash
Receivables External
Receivables Internal
Inventories
Other Current Assets

Internal Dept & Equity

Fixed Asset Old
Fixed Assets
Future Purchases
Less Depres. Res.

Other Assets

Payable-External
Payable-Internal
Accruals

L.T. Debt-External
L.T. Debt-Internal

Reserves
Net Worth-Bal. Forward
Plus Earnings
Less Dividends

Plus New Capital
Stock

Figure 2-11. Projected Balance Sheet

	1st. Yr.	2nd Yr.	3rd Yr.	4th Yr.	5th Yr.

Replacement Program
Machinery
Land & Building
Automotive
Marketing
Other

Volume Expansion
Machinery
Land & Building
Automotive
Marketing
Other

New Product
Machinery
Land & Building
Automotive
Marketing
Other

Figure 2-12. Projected Capital Budget

EXAMPLES OF A MODERN INTEGRATED PLANNING FORMAT

Introducing change and creativity into the planning process requires strong hearts and firm convictions. The example of an integrated planning format, which follows, is a type of format which could be used by a consumer products company finding itself in a highly competitive market situation:

A. Annual and Long Range Profit Forecast (Graph) (Figure 2-13)
B. Growth, Mature, Non-Growth, Development—by Products (Numerical Analysis (Figure 2-14)
C. Division Profit and Loss Statement (Figure 2-15)
D. Division Profit and Loss Statement—Variation Analysis (Figure 2-16)
E. Statement of Financial Position (Figure 2-17)
F. Financial Evaluations of Return on Funds Employed (Figure 2-18)
G. Profit and Loss Statement—Product Groups (Figure 2-19)
H. Profit and Loss Statement—Grocery Product Groups (Figure 2-20)
I. Profit and Loss Statements—Individual Product Highlights (Figure 2-21)
J. Product Marketing Expense Summary (Figure 2-22)
K. Market Position—by Product (Figure 2-23)

L. Indirect Expenses (Figure 2-24)
M. Research Project Expenses (Figure 2-25)
N. Graphic Analysis of Return on Funds Employed (Figure 2-26)
O. Forecasted Analysis of Return on Funds Employed (Figure 2-27)
P. Analysis of Current Assets and Total Cost of Sales (Figure 2-28)
Q. Inventory Forecast (Figure 2-29)

Wherever it has been deemed important, illustrative numbers have been inserted.

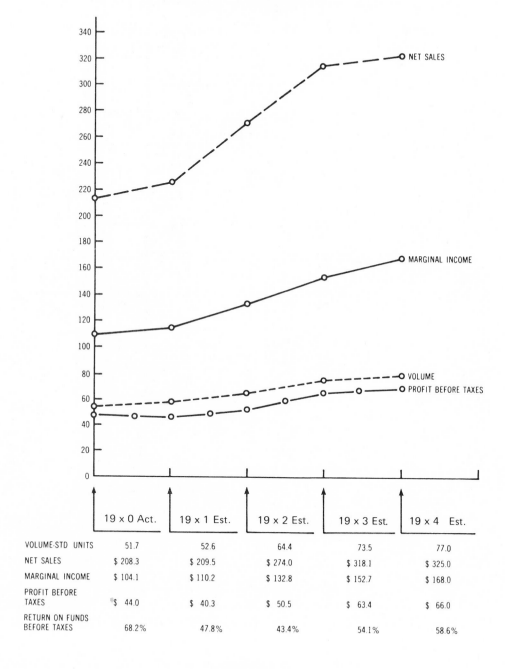

ANNUAL PROFIT FORECAST FISCAL YEAR 19 x 1
(000,000'S)

	19 x 0 Act.	19 x 1 Est.	19 x 2 Est.	19 x 3 Est.	19 x 4 Est.
VOLUME-STD UNITS	51.7	52.6	64.4	73.5	77.0
NET SALES	$ 208.3	$ 209.5	$ 274.0	$ 318.1	$ 325.0
MARGINAL INCOME	$ 104.1	$ 110.2	$ 132.8	$ 152.7	$ 168.0
PROFIT BEFORE TAXES	$ 44.0	$ 40.3	$ 50.5	$ 63.4	$ 66.0
RETURN ON FUNDS BEFORE TAXES	68.2%	47.8%	43.4%	54.1%	58.6%

**Figure 2-13.
Annual and Long Range Profit Forecast**

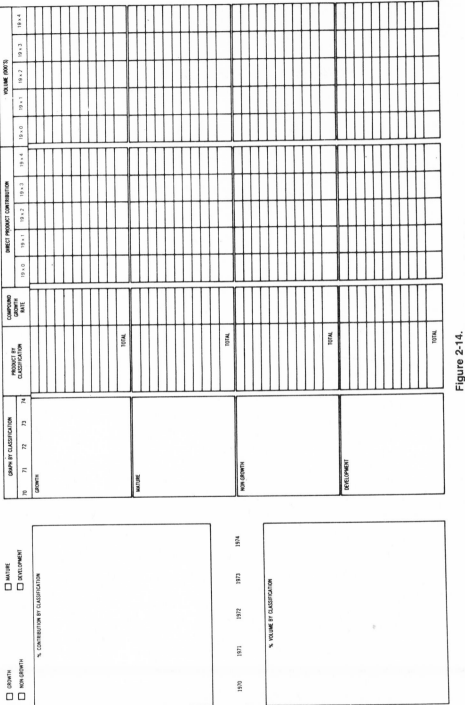

Figure 2-14.
Growth, Mature, Non-Growth, Development—by Products

	19 x 1 (LATEST ESTIMATE)		1971					LONG RANGE PLAN		
	MARCH QUARTER	YEAR	FINAL JUNE QUARTER	SEPTEMBER QUARTER	DECEMBER QUARTER	MARCH QUARTER	YEAR	19 x 2	19 x 3	19 x 4
PHYSICAL VOLUME (CUST.)										
GROCERY										
BULK										
TOTAL VOLUME										
GROSS SALES (CUST.)										
ALLOWANCES EX DEALS										
TRANSPORTATION										
WAREHOUSING										
CASH DISCOUNT										
NET SALES (CUST.)										
VARIABLE COST OF GOODS SOLD										
MARGINAL INCOME (CUST.)										
DIRECT COSTS										
MANUFACTURING OVERHEAD										
MARKETING PROMOTIONS										
MARKETING OTHER										
PRODUCT RESEARCH										
TOTAL DIRECT COSTS										
DIRECT PRODUCT CONTRIBUTION										
INDIRECT COSTS										
MANUFACTURING OVERHEAD										
MARKETING										
RESEARCH										
GEN'L & ADMINISTRATIVE										
TOTAL INDIRECT COSTS										
OPERATING PROFIT										
INTER CO GROSS PROFIT										
OTHER INCOME (EXPENSE)										
PROFIT BEFORE TAXES										
ADD INTERDIVISION PBT										
TOTAL PROFIT BEFORE TAXES										
TAXES STATE & PROVINCIAL										
FEDERAL & FOREIGN										
PROFIT AFTER TAXES										
RETURN ON FUNDS EMPLOYED										
CASH FLOW										
CAPITAL EXPENDITURES										

Figure 2-15.
Division Profit and Loss Statement

VARIATION ANALYSIS

19 x 0 — 19 x 1

DIVISION

	19 x 0	19 x 1	VARIATION	% CHANGE
PHYSICAL VOLUME (CUST.)				
GROCERY				
BULK				
TOTAL VOLUME				
GROSS SALES (CUST.)				
ALLOWANCES EX-DEALS				
TRANSPORTATION				
WAREHOUSING				
CASH DISCOUNT				
NET SALES (CUST.)				
VARIABLE COST OF GOODS SOLD				
MARGINAL INCOME (CUST.)				
DIRECT COSTS				
MANUFACTURING OVERHEAD				
MARKETING-PROMOTIONS				
MARKETING-OTHER				
PRODUCT RESEARCH				
TOTAL DIRECT COSTS				
DIRECT PRODUCT CONTRIBUTION				
INDIRECT COSTS				
MANUFACTURING OVERHEAD				
MARKETING				
RESEARCH				
GEN'L & ADMINISTRATIVE				
TOTAL INDIRECT COSTS				
OPERATING PROFIT				
INTER-CO. GROSS PROFIT				
OTHER INCOME (EXPENSE)				
PROFIT BEFORE TAXES				
ADD INTERDIVISION PBT				
TOTAL PROFIT BEFORE TAXES				
TAXES: STATE & PROVINCIAL				
FEDERAL & FOREIGN				
PROFIT AFTER TAXES				
RETURN ON FUNDS EMPLOYED				
CASH FLOW				
CAPITAL EXPENDITURES				

Figure 2-16.
Division Profit and Loss Statement—Variation Analysis

STATEMENT OF FINANCIAL POSITION -19 x 1 TO 19 x 5   DIVISION _____

CLASSIFICATION	MARCH 31, 19 x 1	JUNE 30, 19 x 1	SEPTEMBER 30, 19 x 1	DECEMBER 31, 19 x 1	DECEMBER 31, 19 x 2	DECEMBER 31, 19 x 3	DECEMBER 31, 19 x 4	DECEMBER 31, 19 x 5
CASH								
ACCOUNTS RECEIVABLE								
INVENTORIES:								
RAW MATERIALS								
PACKAGING MATERIALS								
SUPPLIES								
FINISHED GOODS — BULK								
— GROCERY								
TOTAL INVENTORIES								
PREPAID EXPENSES								
CURRENT ASSETS								
ACCOUNTS PAYABLE								
ACCRUED LIABILITIES								
INCOME TAXES								
CURRENT LIABILITIES								
WORKING CAPITAL								
(CURRENT ASSETS LESS CURRENT LIABILITIES)								
LAND, BUILDINGS, AND EQUIP. — AT COST								
LESS ACCUMULATED DEPRECIATION								
NET FIXED ASSETS								
OTHER ASSETS								
OTHER LIABILITIES								

Figure 2-17.
Statement of Financial Position

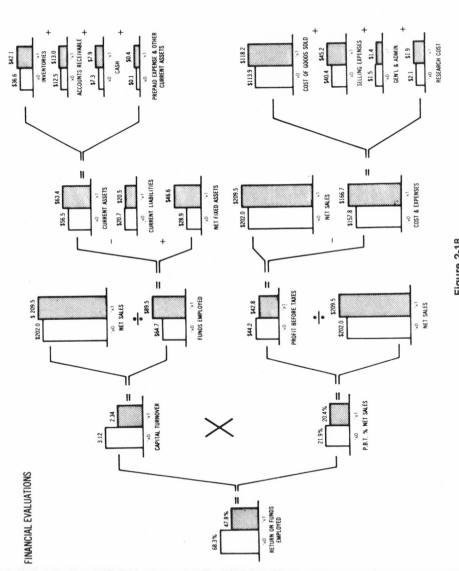

FINANCIAL EVALUATIONS

Figure 2-18.
Financial Evaluations of Return on Funds Employed

PROFIT & LOSS STATEMENTS — BY PRODUCT GROUPS

YEARS 1971 THRU 1974

_______________ DIVISION

	PRODUCT GROUP A					PRODUCT GROUP B					PRODUCT GROUP C					PRODUCT GROUP D					OTHER GROCERY				
	19 x0 ACTUAL ESTIMATED	ESTIMATED * INDEX OF CHANGE				19 x0 ACTUAL ESTIMATED	ESTIMATED * INDEX OF CHANGE				19 x0 ACTUAL ESTIMATED	ESTIMATED * INDEX OF CHANGE				19 x0 ACTUAL ESTIMATED	ESTIMATED * INDEX OF CHANGE				19 x0 ACTUAL ESTIMATED	ESTIMATED * INDEX OF CHANGE			
		x1	x2	x3	x4		x1	x2	x3	x4		x1	x2	x3	x4		x1	x2	x3	x4		x1	x2	x3	x4
VOLUME (000'S UNITS)																									
GROSS SALES																									
NET SALES																									
Variable Cost of Goods Sold																									
MARGINAL INCOME																									
LESS DIRECT COSTS EXPENSES																									
Manufacturing Overhead (CGS)																									
Marketing - Promotional																									
Marketing - Other																									
Product Research																									
TOTAL DIRECT COSTS EXPENSES																									
DIRECT PRODUCT CONTRIBUTION																									
LESS INDIRECT COSTS EXPENSES																									
Manufacturing Overhead (CGS)																									
Marketing																									
Research																									
General & Administrative																									
TOTAL INDIRECT COSTS/EXPENSES																									
OPERATING PROFIT																									
INTERCO GROSS PROFIT																									
OTHER INCOME (EXPENSES)																									
PROFIT BEFORE TAXES																									
ADD INTERDIVISIONAL PBT																									
TOTAL PROFIT BEFORE TAXES																									
PBT SUMMARY BY PRODUCT GROUPS 19x1 ___ 19x2 ___ 19x3 ___ 19x4 ___																									

* 1970 BASE = 100

Figure 2-19.
Profit and Loss Statement—Product Groups

PROFIT & LOSS STATEMENTS
1970-1974

DIVISION _____

VOLUME (000'S UNITS)	TOTAL GROCERY PRODUCTS					TOTAL BULK PRODUCTS					TOTAL DEVELOPMENT PRODUCTS				
	19 x 0	19 x 1	19 x 2	19 x 3	19 x 4	19 x 0	19 x 1	19 x 2	19 x 3	19 x 4	19 x 0	19 x 1	19 x 2	19 x 3	19 x 4
GROSS SALES															
NET SALES															
Variable Cost of Goods Sold															
MARGINAL INCOME															
LESS DIRECT COSTS EXPENSES															
Manufacturing Overhead															
Marketing - Promotional															
Marketing - Other															
Product Research															
TOTAL DIRECT COSTS EXPENSES															
DIRECT PRODUCT CONTRIBUTION															
LESS INDIRECT COSTS EXPENSES															
Manufacturing Overhead															
Marketing - Promotional															
Research															
General & Administrative															
TOTAL INDIRECT COSTS EXPENSES															
OPERATING PROFIT															
INTERCO. GROSS PROFIT															
OTHER INCOME (EXPENSE)															
PROFIT BEFORE TAXES															
ADD INTERDIVISIONAL PBT															
TOTAL PROFIT BEFORE TAXES															
TAXES State & Provincial															
Federal & Foreign															
PROFIT AFTER TAXES															
RETURN ON FUNDS EMPLOYED															
% OF PBT															

Figure 2-20.
Profit and Loss Statement—Grocery Product Groups

P & L HIGHLIGHTS BY PRODUCT

DIVISION

PRODUCT	FISCAL YEAR	GROSS SALES	NET SALES	VARIABLE MANUFACTURING	MARGINAL INCOME		DIRECT MANUFACTURING OVERHEAD	DIRECT MARKETING PROMOTION	DIRECT MARKETING OTHER	DIRECT PRODUCT RESEACH		DIRECT PRODUCT CONTRIBUTION $	DIRECT PRODUCT CONTRIBUTION P.S.U.	
PRODUCT GROUP A	19 x 0													
	19 x 1													
	19 x 2													
	19 x 3													
	19 x 4													
PRODUCT GROUP B	19 x 0													
	19 x 1													
	19 x 2													
	19 x 3													
	19 x 4													

Figure 2-21.
Profit and Loss Statements—Individual Product Highlights

PRODUCT MARKETING EXPENSE SUMMARY

DIVISION

	19 x 0	19 x 1	19 x 2	19 x 3	19 x 4
PRODUCT GROUP A					
ADVERTISING		9079			
CONSUMER DEALS		2701			
TOTAL CONSUMER PROMOTION		11780			
% OF TOTAL MARGINAL INCOME		23.5			
TRADE DEALS		999			
SALES PROMOTION		66			
TOTAL TRADE PROMOTION		1065			
% OF TOTAL MARGINAL INCOME		2.1			
TOTAL INDIRECT MARKETING		5596			
% OF TOTAL MARGINAL INCOME		11.2			
		13116			
		26.2			
PRODUCT GROUP B					
ADVERTISING		3232			
CONSUMER DEALS		234			
TOTAL CONSUMER PROMOTION		3466			
% OF TOTAL MARGINAL INCOME		21.0			

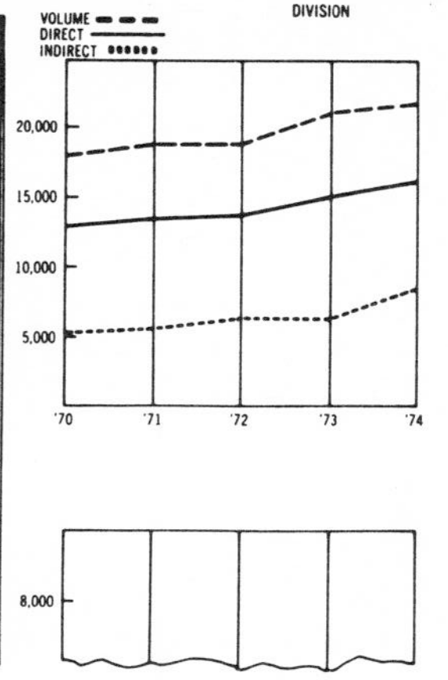

Figure 2-22.
Product Marketing Expense Summary

MARKET POSITION BY PRODUCT

PRODUCT		TOTAL MARKET (UNITS)	% SHARE MARKET	CONSUMER MOVEMENT	DIRECT MARKETING $ TOTAL $	PER UNIT CONSUMER MOVEMENT
	'x0 'x1 'x2 'x3 'x4					
	'x0 'x1 'x2 'x3 'x4					
	'x0 'x1 'x2 'x3 'x4					
	'x0 'x1 'x2 'x3 'x4					
	'x0 'x1 'x2 'x3 'x4					
	'x0 'x1 'x2 'x3 'x4					
	'x0 'x1 'x2 'x3 'x4					
	'x0 'x1 'x2 'x3 'x4					

Figure 2-23. Market Position—by Product

INDIRECT EXPENSES

DIVISION

CATEGORY	ACTUAL 19 x 0	ESTIMATED 19 x 1	ESTIMATED 19 x 2	ESTIMATED 19 x 3	ESTIMATED 19 x 4
VOLUME					
MANUFACTURING OVERHEAD					
DEPRECIATION					
SUPERVISION					
MAINTENANCE					
UTILITY					
ENGINEERING					
QUALITY CONTROL					
OTHER					
TOTAL / % M.I. / MANPOWER					
MARKETING EXPENSES					
KITCHENS					
ADMIN. MARKETING					
SALES FORCE					
SALES ACCOUNTING					
MARKET RESEARCH					
TOTAL / % M.I. / MANPOWER					
RESEARCH EXPENSES					
SALARIES					
SUPPLIES					
OTHER					
TOTAL / % M.I. / MANPOWER					
GENERAL & ADMINISTRATIVE					
TOTAL / % M.I. / MANPOWER					

Figure 2-24. Indirect Expenses

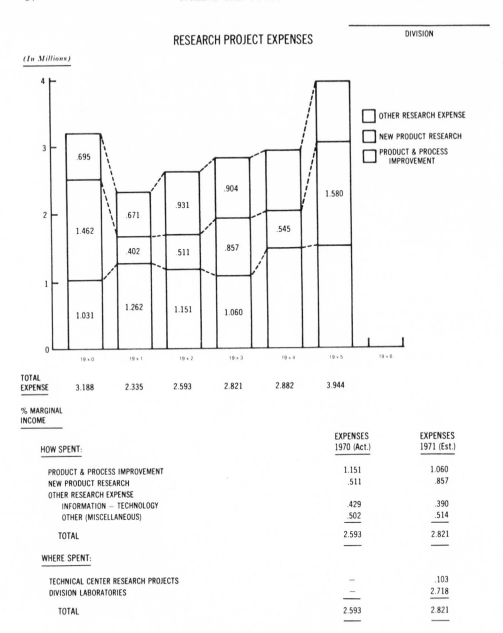

RESEARCH PROJECT EXPENSES

DIVISION

(In Millions)

OTHER RESEARCH EXPENSE

NEW PRODUCT RESEARCH

PRODUCT & PROCESS IMPROVEMENT

	19 x 0	19 x 1	19 x 2	19 x 3	19 x 4	19 x 5	19 x 6
TOTAL EXPENSE	3.188	2.335	2.593	2.821	2.882	3.944	

% MARGINAL INCOME

HOW SPENT:	EXPENSES 1970 (Act.)	EXPENSES 1971 (Est.)
PRODUCT & PROCESS IMPROVEMENT	1.151	1.060
NEW PRODUCT RESEARCH	.511	.857
OTHER RESEARCH EXPENSE		
INFORMATION — TECHNOLOGY	.429	.390
OTHER (MISCELLANEOUS)	.502	.514
TOTAL	2.593	2.821
WHERE SPENT:		
TECHNICAL CENTER RESEARCH PROJECTS	—	.103
DIVISION LABORATORIES	—	2.718
TOTAL	2.593	2.821

Figure 2-25. Research Project Expenses

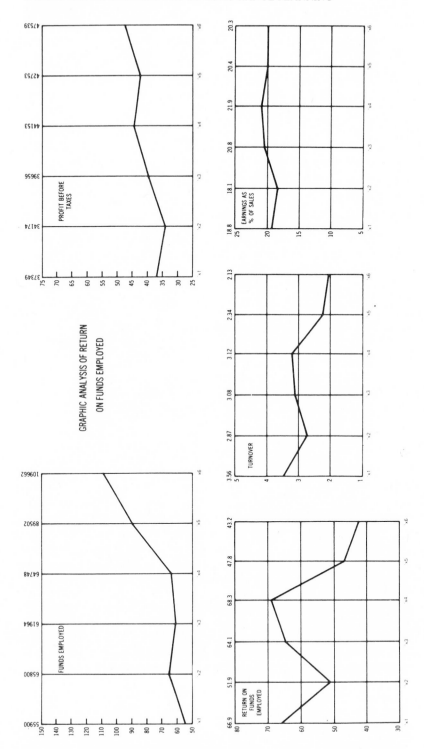

Figure 2-26.
Graphic Analysis of Return on Funds Employed

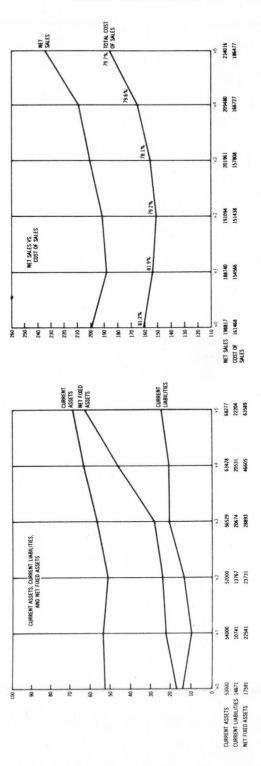

Figure 2-26. (Continued)

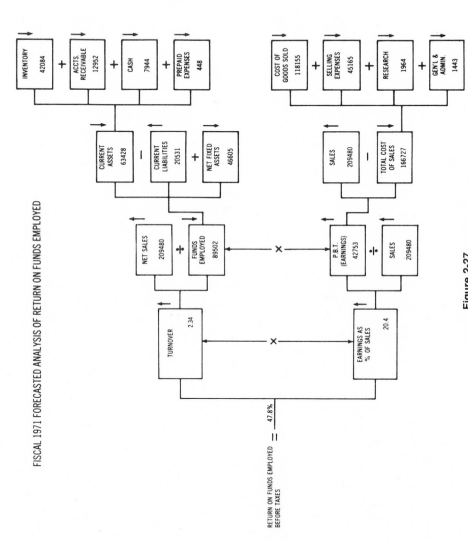

FISCAL 1971 FORECASTED ANALYSIS OF RETURN ON FUNDS EMPLOYED

Figure 2-27.
Forecasted Analysis of Return on Funds Employed

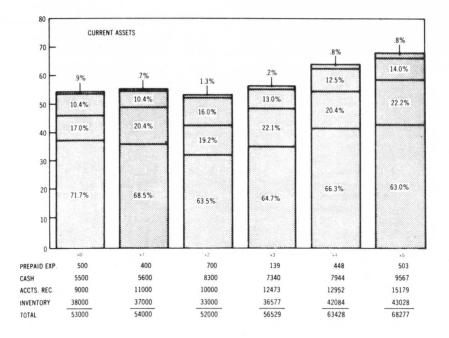

	x0	x1	x2	x3	x4	x5
PREPAID EXP.	500	400	700	139	448	503
CASH	5500	5600	8300	7340	7944	9567
ACCTS. REC.	9000	11000	10000	12473	12952	15179
INVENTORY	38000	37000	33000	36577	42084	43028
TOTAL	53000	54000	52000	56529	63428	68277

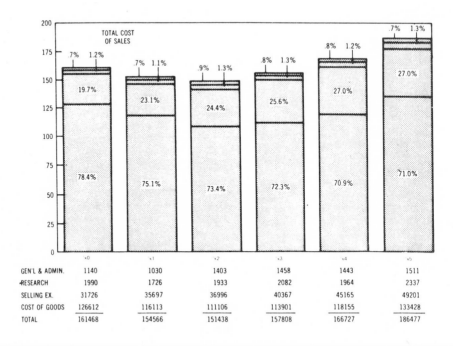

	x0	x1	x2	x3	x4	x5
GEN'L & ADMIN.	1140	1030	1403	1458	1443	1511
RESEARCH	1990	1726	1933	2082	1964	2337
SELLING EX.	31726	35697	36996	40367	45165	49201
COST OF GOODS	126612	116113	111106	113901	118155	133428
TOTAL	161468	154566	151438	157808	166727	186477

Figure 2-28.
Analysis of Current Assets and Total Cost of Sales

INVENTORY FORECAST

____
DIVISION

JUNE QUARTER FINAL						DESCRIPTION	SEPT. 30		DEC. 31		MARCH 31	
APRIL 30 $ AMOUNT	WEEKS SUPPLY	MAY 31 $ AMOUNT	WEEKS SUPPLY	JUNE 30 $ AMOUNT	WEEKS SUPPLY		$ AMOUNT	WEEKS SUPPLY	$ AMOUNT	WEEKS SUPPLY	$ AMOUNT	WEEKS SUPPLY
						GROCERY FINISHED GOODS						
						BULK FINISHED GOODS						
						RAW MATERIALS						
						PACKAGING MATERIAL & SUPPLIES						
						TOTAL INVENTORIES						
						Variations From:						
						FISCAL YEAR 1963						
						FISCAL YEAR 1962						

$ AMT.	WEEKS SUPPLY	VARIATION		$ AMT.	WEEKS SUPPLY	VARIATION		$ AMT.	WEEKS SUPPLY	VARIATION		SELECTED ITEMS	$ AMT.	WEEKS SUPPLY	VARIATION		$ AMT.	WEEKS SUPPLY	VARIATION		$ AMT.	WEEKS SUPPLY	VARIATION	
		x0	x1			x0	x1			x0	x1				x0	x1			x0	x1			x0	x1
												PRODUCT A												
												B												
												C												
												D												
												E												
												F												
												G												
												H												
												I												
												J												
												K												
												L												
												M												
												All Other Grocery												
												TOTAL GROCERY FINISHED GOODS												
												N												

Figure 2-29.
Inventory Forecast

3

Developing and Installing
a Budget Program

CONTENTS

3

Developing and Installing
a Budget Program

GENERAL ASPECTS OF BUDGETING

Basis of successful management. Many business managers do not know the professional terminology of forecasting and budgeting and are unfamiliar with the techniques of these two key elements of financial planning. Nevertheless, they operate their businesses successfully. The reason for their success is that they apply the basic principles of scientific financial planning unaware that they are doing so. Let us see how this happens by pointing out the steps in financial planning and then showing how a typical small businessman builds up a profitable, expanding business by following those steps.

The five major steps in financial planning include:

1. Establishing the goals or objectives of the business.
2. Forecasting and measuring the conditions that affect the realization of goals.
3. Budgeting and scheduling operations in terms of the forecast.
4. Controlling operations in line with the budget.
5. Appraising results, then modifying goals, the forecast, and/or the budget as may be required.

Our typical small businessman, let us say, is the successful proprietor of a men's furnishing store having an annual sales volume of $100,000 per year. He is convinced that the market he serves will permit him to double the size of his operations over a five-year period. *That is his objective.* To accomplish this goal within five years, he will have to embark on a local advertising program to cost $5,000 per year, increase his stocks of merchandise at the average rate of $5,000 per year, rent additional space at a cost of $1,200 per year, and add an additional clerk the first year and a second clerk the third year. To finance this additional cost sales must increase at the rate of $20,000 a year over the five-year period. Will business conditions be favorable enough to permit such sales increase? He knows that population in the area is increasing at the rate of 1,000 new families a year. He knows that the industries located in the area are prosperous, and he believes that they will continue to expand. He feels that the ''economic climate'' will be healthy for a number of years ahead. In other words, *the long-range forecast of conditions* that will permit the realization of his goal is favorable.

On the basis of these premises, he decides to go ahead with his plans for the first year. Using past experience and current style trends as a guide, he picks out the price lines, styles, and sizes that will sell best. He determines sufficient order quantities to maintain adequate stocks for servicing not only his present volume, but also the anticipated increase in volume. In doing so, he gives consideration to proper turnover, the time it will take vendors to supply him, and the amount of money he can afford to tie up in inventory at one time. He bases his mark-ups on competitive experience, some knowledge of his prospective selling costs, and a consideration of the amount of profit he can reasonably expect to realize from the anticipated sales volume. In fact, he has prepared a short-term forecast which, if acceptable, will become his *budgeted plan of operations* for the year in question.

As the year progresses, he watches his sales and profits by line, tries to discover the reasons for variations from expected performance, and attempts to *control his operations to meet his plan.*

If results are unfavorable, he adjusts inventories, cuts costs, and changes his prices as may be required. Should conditions so change that he is *forced to modify* his long-range goal, he will make new estimates and new plans of operation.

Thus, this storekeeper carries out essentially all of the steps of effective financial planning. But probably he would be the last man to admit that he operates his business according to the established procedures of financial planning or, as they are more narrowly applied in this chapter, to the established procedures of budgeting and budgetary control.

Functions of a budget program. A well designed budget program is an effective management mechanism for forecasting realizable results over a definite period or periods, for planning and coordinating the various operations and functions of the business to achieve realizable results, and for so controlling and limiting any variations from the approved plan of action that the desired results are realized.

Steps in budgeting and budgetary control. The steps in budgeting and budgetary control, in the order of their occurrence, follow.

1. Forecasting. The types of long-term forecasts to be made and the methods of making them were described in the preceding chapter. The short-term forecasts essential in any budgetary system will be explained in this chapter.
2. Establishing the approved budgets or plans of operation, based, in a large measure, upon the forecasts. The budget period is usually shorter than the forecast period in order to achieve greater accuracy in planning over the near term and to obviate the necessity for frequent revision of the budgets themselves.
3. Collecting data and reporting on actual performance at stated intervals during the budget period and comparing actual results with the budget allowance.
4. Measuring any variance of actual from budgeted performance and analyzing the reasons or causes for such variance.
5. Determining the necessary corrective action to be taken to reduce or eliminate the cause of the variance; delegating responsibility and authority for instituting such corrective action; and following up to see that the agreed-upon action is taken and the results achieved.

Relationship of budgets to forecasts. The forecasts determine *whether and to* *what degree* the long-range programs of the company are feasible of accomplishment. The budgets, which are based upon such forecasts, determine *exactly how* the company must operate *in detail* over a limited time period to realize that portion of the long-range program which is possible of accomplishment within the allotted time span. The forecasts may cover a period of from one to five years, or longer in the case of certain types of businesses. The budgets, however, rarely are projected for more than a year in advance, except in the case of capital additions, and often are projected for only three months.

Classification of budgets. Budgets may be broadly classified into the following two major categories.

1. Budgets that deal with sources of income, such as sales, interest and dividend income, and the like.
2. Budgets that deal with sources of expenditures, such as wages and salaries paid, material and equipment purchases, taxes, insurance, interest and dividend payments, and the like.

In addition to these general budget classifications, different types of budgets may be established to meet different requirements. The latter include fixed, variable or flexible, and combination budgets. A definition of each type and its application is described below.

Fixed budgets. The term ''fixed budget'' is generally applied to a budget established for a definite period in advance and not subject to change or alteration during the budget period. Fixed budgets are usually established by companies that can forecast with a high degree of accuracy ($\pm$ 5 per cent variation) the demand for their products and services, and hence the cost of operating to meet such demand over the budget period. A fixed or inflexible budget program should be the ultimate goal of every well run business organization that manufactures on a stock basis, because it enforces the need for accurate forecasting, accurate planning, and, most important, over-all coordination and follow-up if the budget goals are to be achieved. Such enforcement automatically brings good management, good scheduling of operations, and the highest amount of profits over the long term.

Variable or flexible budgets. This type of budget is predicated upon the variability of costs, and hence expenditures, at different levels of operation. The variable or flexible budget is used in companies where the forecasting technique has not been developed to a high degree of perfection, or where the nature of the demand for the company's products and services is especially volatile, as may be the case in a company manufacturing highly styled items or on a customer-order basis.

To a degree, certain business costs may be said to be relatively fixed or non-controllable, others semi-variable or semi-controllable, still others, fully variable or controllable. If the relatively non-controllable costs, the semi-controllable costs, and the controllable costs are segregated under the company's accounting system, it is possible to construct a ''profit-a-graph'' or ''break-even'' chart that shows, for any given volume of sales, the allowable costs of doing business and the probable profit or loss that may be expected. Similarly, charts or tables of allowable expense may be constructed by department or cost center for any given volume of activity as measured by such operating yardsticks as direct labor hours and the like. Through direct reading of the chart or table, the standard or budgeted expense allowance can be readily determined. Thus, under a variable budget program, a company that cannot forecast its sales volume over the long term with a high degree of accuracy may still achieve good budget control over its expenditures; it can plan its operations on a short-term basis to achieve satisfactory results in terms of coordination of effort and profit yield.

An example of a flexible budget is shown in figure 3-1. It is a budget originally constructed for a period of time, usually a year, which, as it is aptly named, is made flexible by breaking it up into logical pieces which may be related to seasonal patterns of time or production considerations. This type of presentation is in contrast to a "fixed" type of budget which is created in the start of a new financial period and which is not altered regardless of volume changes. The advantage of this type of presentation is that it permits greater control of manufacturing costs by allowing for the impact of volume changes on an operation which is scaled for a certain volume or production or a stipulated mix of products.

Certain generalizations are applicable to all flexible budgeting procedures:

A. The construction of a flexible budget is highly dependent upon the nature of a specific company or manufacturing facility.
B. Even variable costs which normally tend to remain stable on a per unit basis, tend to move in a "step" fashion. Variable costs, are those overhead costs which are directly related to shift production such as overtime premium and fringes.
C. The only general rule which can be applied to all plants or companies is that one must first determine what expenses shall be classified as overhead and within the classification, which are variable or semi-variable and which are truly fixed.

The flexible budget shown in Figure 3-1 is the end product.

In order to create it certain assumptions must be developed. The assumptions employed are:

A. Construct a plant.
B. Staff it with the managerial personnel required and the maintenance personnel needed in order to keep the equipment in proper condition. Further, pay taxes and insurance and buy the required supplies for the maintenance of the equipment.
C. Start production on a one-shift basis.
D. Continue producing, increasing to a second shift and a third shift over a five-day period.

By observation, it will be seen that there are overheads incurred even though the plant is not producing. These overheads comprise approximately one-quarter of the total budget required for a three-shift, five-day operation. These overheads do not increase in a gradual fashion, but rather move upwards in steps as will be seen when we go to various shifts of production.

When proceeding from a one-shift to a two-shift operation, it is necessary to acquire additional supervisory help for the various departments. The expense of these

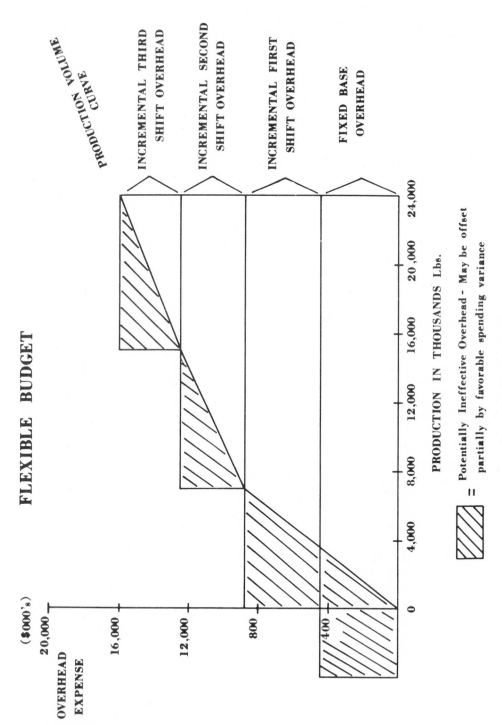

Figure 3-1. Flexible Budget

men will be incurred immediately upon their hiring, whereas, the production volume
will increase only after a period of time elapses. Further, should there be any reason for
a production facility not attaining its maximum attainable capacity, these men will still
be paid in the interim. The shaded area in the exhibit, illustrates that there are ineffective overheads when production is running at lower than capacity level for a given
shift. This shaded area helps to give some measurement to overheads which are being
incurred or which could be incurred and which are not being properly utilized.

For purposes of illustrating the step movement of overhead expense, this presentation has been oversimplified. Timing differences will change the impact of so-called
ineffective overheads. The exhibit intends only to illustrate the fact that, were everything to occur at a precise moment in time, a potential of ineffective overhead will be
incurred if we fail to meet the maximum attainable capacity of the facility. Failure to
attain this level of operation *would* result in reduced spending levels in some categories
of overhead. As an example, the maximum attainable production on a three-shift,
five-day basis, is 24 million pounds. Were we to produce only 22 million pounds or 21
or 19 during a three-shift operation, there would be a reduction in the spending levels
of some of the variable elements of overheads. One such example would be maintenance supplies as long as the production reduction is not precipitated by machine
failure and is the result of a desire to produce at lower than attainable rates, perhaps due
to a diminished marketing forecast. As a final note, it is important to remember that
fixed or base overheads make up the smallest fraction of the overall overhead picture,
but represent a considerable sum of dollars to be spent. Control of expenditures must
rest primarily in expenses which are incremental at each level of operation.

To illustrate further the movement of overheads, note Figure 3-2. Here, the
elements of expense between salaries, wages and related fringe benefits and supplies,
services, taxes and insurance, have been segregated. The shaded area represents the
labor cost portion of the overhead budget. Also displayed is the percentage of the total
expense committed to each of the two major types of expenses and the related cost per
pound at capacity level, for each shift of operation. Note that when the plant is *not* in
operation but is being staffed for operation, labor costs make up 54 percent of the total
with all other expenses comprising 46 percent. As we proceed to succeeding production levels, the labor portion of the overall budget increases. Labor costs make up the
largest proportion of so-called variable overhead expenses. Since there is no change in
taxes or insurance expense within a one-year period, these costs are fixed and tend to
bring down the portion of overhead committed to this segment of expense.

Note also, that even though the total overhead budget increases as we proceed to
various levels of production, the cost per pound is reduced. This further illustrates that
overheads do not increase in direct proportion with volume changes. If it is related to
units of production it will vary inversely because the dollars remain fixed while the
units increase. It must be noted that even though the total overhead expense increases
as we proceed through the various levels of shift operation, the cost per pound is
reduced, indicating that effective use of the dollar of expenditure has been made as we
proceed toward maximum attainable capacity. The distribution of the cost elements
indicates that when one is about to start setting flexible budgets, more emphasis should
be given to determining the variability of labor elements than should be given to
determining the variability of other elements. Further, since labor and the labor related

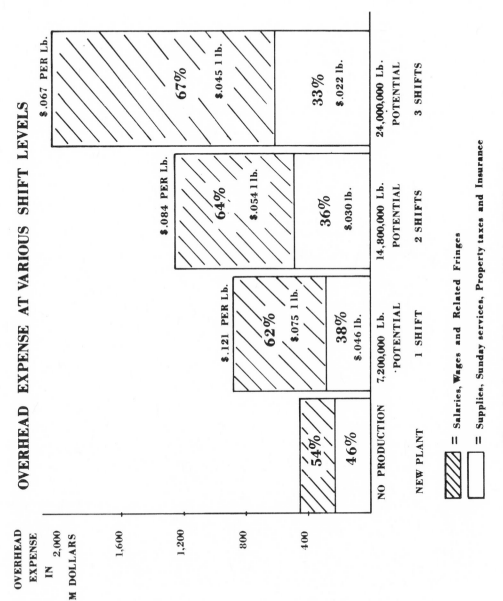

Figure 3-2. Overhead Expenses at Various Shift Levels.

costs represent about two-thirds of the total budget, they should be given the most attention because of their significance. The approach taken to determine variability of the various overhead elements, again, depends greatly on the nature of each organization or facility.

Experience plotted on scattergraphs will often indicate the movement of certain types of expense as related to volume changes. More importantly, local management, that is those people directly responsible for controlling these expenses, should be consulted with and be responsible for the preparation of realistic budget levels in relation to the volume forecasts. Ultimately, it is these people who will be responsible for reporting on the results of actual operations. To construct a budget without their involvement, means that the budget in itself is relatively ineffective since local management will claim that they had nothing to say in determining budget allowances and feel that they cannot be held responsible against such amounts. When attempting to construct flexible budgets it cannot be overemphasized that excessive detail or an attempt to make the figures extremely finite is a waste of time. Flexible budgets should only be viewed as a tool in determining fairly broad ranges of expense levels which may be incurred at various steps of operation. Over-detailing and precise determination of budgeted allowances can only lead to the generation of many reports containing data, none of which is very useful from a practical standpoint.

Most importantly, when flexible budgets are constructed, there must be understanding on the part of all parties involved from local management to top management as to the bases and assumptions employed. With such understanding, little difficulty will arise from the interpretation of the results of operation. On the other hand, action will be precipitated for those areas which have definitely gone sour. In Figure 3-1, overheads were analyzed as they are precipitated and move in relation to production volume changes. In Figure 3-2, the proportions of the various expense elements and how they change in relation to volume deviations were shown.

Figure 3-3 is a completed flexible budget for plant X. This budget has been constructed for the four operating quarters of the year. It shows the capacity level of operations employed in each quarter, the forecasting production and the percent of effective use made of available capacity. By reviewing various expense elements, we can determine which items are relatively fixed as to dollars of expenditure and which are variable. Management salaries, or the overall supervision which was originally employed as the plant was constructed, remain fixed as to dollar amounts. Property taxes and insurance behave in a similar manner.

The other major elements of cost, however, have variable segments. Note that for the three fixed elements of management salaries, taxes, and insurance the cost per pound of product goes up as volume goes down. Note also, that for the variable elements there is no precise correlation between the cost per pound change at various volume levels and the percentage of volume change. Essentially, this budget can be constructed by asking local management the question; "If you are going to be called upon to operate on three shifts, what will you have to spend?" Second, "The production program that we are calling upon you to make in the year, is below full three-shift operation but above full two-shift operation. What is the most economical means of accomplishing this program?

Overhead Budget
Year 19–
Plant X

Expense Description	Period - 1/1–3/21 Capacity Level–3 Shifts Forecasted Prod. 6,000,000 % Effective Use - 100		Period - 4/1–6/30 Capacity Level–3 Shifts Forecasted Prod. 6,000,000 % Effective Use - 100		Period - 7/1–9/30 Capacity Level–2 Shifts Forecasted Prod. 4,000,000 % Effective Use - 108		Period - 10/1–12/31 Capacity Level–2 Shifts Forecasted Prod. 4,000,000 % Effective Use - 108		Period - Year 19– Capacity Level–3-3-2-2 Forecasted Prod. 20,000,000 % Effective Use - 103	
	Amount	Per Lb.	Amount	Per Lb.	Amount	Per Lb.	Amount	Per Lb.	Amount	Per Lb.
Management Salaries	51,000	.009	51,000	.009	51,000	.009	52,000	.012	205,000	.010
Maintenance Labor	54,000	.009	54,000	.009	38,000	.009	38,000	.010	184,000	.009
All Other Labor	78,000	.013	78,000	.013	63,000	.013	63,000	.016	282,000	.014
Overtime Premium	10,000	.002	10,000	.002	15,000	.002	15,000	.004	50,000	.003
Fringes (Incl. Vac. & Hol.)	67,000	.010	67,000	.010	53,000	.010	53,000	.013	240,000	.012
Sub Total Labor	260,000	.043	260,000	.043	220,000	.043	221,000	.055	961,000	.048
Maintenance Supplies	63,000	.011	63,000	.011	46,000	.011	46,000	.012	218,000	.011
All Other Supplies	41,000	.007	41,000	.007	30,000	.007	30,000	.008	142,000	.007
Property Taxes	33,000	.005	33,000	.005	33,000	.005	33,000	.008	132,000	.006
Property Insurance	3,000	.001	4,000	.001	3,000	.001	3,000	.001	13,000	.001
Subtotal Supplies	140,000	.024	141,000	.024	112,000	.024	112,000	.029	505,000	.025
Grand Total	400,000	.067	401,000	.067	332,000	.067	333,000	.083	1466,000	.073
Effective Capacity Cost Per Lb.		.067		.067		.067		.084		.073
% of Effective Cap. Cost Per Lb.		100		100		100		99		100
Effective Volume Level	6,000,000		6,000,000		3,700,000		3,700,000		19,400,000	

Special Notes:
Last two quarters include Saturday work.

Figure 3-3. Completed Flexible Budget

Suppose that after considering the marketing needs in each of the quarters, we found that the most reasonable approach to the program is to run three shifts for the first two quarters and two shifts for the second two quarters. In the second two quarters, some Saturday production will also be called for. Running on a Saturday makes it certain that we shall have to pay overtime premium. Does this mean that we are not running on an economic basis? Not at all, as may be seen by the cost per pound during the third and fourth quarters, we are attaining a cost level of $.083 per pound as opposed to a normal plant cost of $.084 for two shift operation. This is attributed to the fact that the increment in labor for Saturday operation on a *short term basis*, is not as great as the increment in production to be derived, therefore, costs per pound tend to average down.

In the first two quarters, the plant has run at 100 percent of maximum attainable capacity for three shifts, five days. In the latter two quarters, the plant has run at 108 percent of maximum attainable capacity for two shifts, five days. The costs, however, average only 99 percent of attainable capacity costs. For the entire year, the costs average very close to costs at attainable capacity levels.

If the actual production during the year was realized at forecasted volume levels, any deviation in spending would be solely the responsibility of local management and they would be held accountable therefor. Few facilities, however, produce at budgeted levels. There is always some pressure which precipitates an under or overrun. The question may then be posed, ''How does a flexible budget assist in determining the impact of these volume changes on an actual basis?''

Two approaches may be made; one would be to utilize the established budget and evaluate the spending level against it. With this, the actual production volume would be extended by the budgeted cost per pound. The difference between the absorption at budgeted cost per pound rates and the spending allowance budgeted would constitute a *volume* deviation. The *spending* deviation would be evaluated by comparing actual levels of expense versus budgeted levels. The interpretation would then have to be made by management as to accountability and explanation for the resulting deviations.

The second approach would be to take the budgeted cost per pound for variable cost elements and multiply them by the actual production poundage, arriving at a new budgeted allowance. The actual spending level would then be evaluated against this budget allowance and accountability would then have to be interpreted as in the prior case. Both methods give effect to volume impact, and allow for increases or decreases in budgeted allowances related to volume changes. Provided that the understanding exists which was called for in our prior discussion, interpretations can be much more meaningful. Local management will feel that they are being evaluated against a budget which is adjusted in accordance with the pressures exerted on the operating facility. Top management can see the overall effect of their decisions on the economic structure of the facility.

Finally, flexible budgeting provides a tool by which management can evaluate the impact of proposed changes for the future. Flexible budgets are far more readily adjusted for changes in plans than are the fixed commitment type budget. Flexible budgets provide a meaningful, working tool in determining break-even points in profit plan preparation. One way to summarize the discussion would be to draw a simple analogy. If a man receives a yearly income of $12,000 and establishes a weekly spending budget for himself and then receives a pay cut, does he alter his weekly spending level or does he continue as originally planned? If he continues, the likely prospect is that he will go bankrupt. On the other hand, if he "flexes" his personal budget, he will probably come out in balance with whatever income he is receiving. On the other hand, if his income is increased, does he continue with the same spending level originally planned or does he perhaps re-think his position and commit additional funds on a weekly basis for savings, investment, or for normal household necessities? Fixed budgets for commitments are unrealistic and impractical. Flexible budgeting is the only rational approach to control.

Combination budgets. Many companies use a combination budget program comprising both fixed budgets and variable budgets to good advantage. For example, a company that manufactures both to a stock and on a customer-order basis, or one that is periodically subject to production delays outside of its control, may find the combination budget most appropriate. In the former case, fixed budgets are established for sales of stock items and carried forward on the same basis into manufacturing as far as practicable, whereas the variable budgets are used for controlling the sales and manufacture of items produced to customer order. In the case of a company subject to production delays outside of its control, usually the sales, selling expense, and administrative expense budgets are established on a fixed budget basis, whereas manufacturing expenditures are controlled on a variable budget basis.

Adaptability of budget programs to various types and sizes of business. From the foregoing it is apparent that an effective budget program may be developed to fit the needs of any type or size of business enterprise. A budget program, to achieve maximum results, must be tailor-made to fit the particular needs of the business to which it is applied. In developing the program, the following factors must be taken into consideration.

1. Ability to predict demand for the company's products and services and stability of demand.
2. Variety of products and services.
3. Variety of manufacturing processes used.
4. Ability to schedule and conduct manufacturing operations on a "straight-line" basis.
5. Amount of money the company can afford to spend on a budget program compared with results possible of achievement.
6. Economic intelligence of company management, including willingness to subordinate individualism to over-all coordination, planning, and control in order to achieve maximum results.

The accounting system and budgeting. Since the budget program is an instrument of organizational coordination as well as control, a company's accounting system and its chart of accounts should be designed to clearly reflect lines of functional responsibility existing in the organization. If the functional lines of responsibility are not clearly drawn in the organizational structure, it is of no avail to mirror them in the accounting system and hence in the budget program. One of the prime requisites for the operation of a successful and effective budget program is the placing of responsibility for making definite expenditures and producing definite results on certain key personnel in the organization. The more the responsibility for conducting a certain function is split, the more difficult is the problem of holding any of those who share it accountable for either the operation of the function or the results obtained. It is well to remember that a budget program is no panacea for a poor organizational structure or a poor accounting system.

A good budget program needs a good accounting system supporting it for other reasons as well. For example, to forecast and budget sales income properly, provision should be made for the statistical tabulation of unit and dollar sales not only by item but by detailed class of product, by sales territory, by salesman, and by customer. In many instances, tabulation by industry, trade class, and channel of distribution is also of value. A good accounting system will make such tabulations possible, though they can be handled outside of the accounting system on a statistical basis.

To budget and control expenditures properly, the accounting system must provide sufficient detailing of the departmental organization and of the expense accounts to permit any significant variation from budgeted cost to be readily traced to the department, to the cost center, to the particular expenditures, and to the person who was responsible for the variance. Only in this manner can control be properly exercised and immediate action instituted to correct or prevent recurrence of the mistake.

Application of standard costs to budgeting. The preparation of preliminary budgets for cost of sales, cost of production, selling expenses, administrative expenses, and other costs is facilitated if the company uses a standard cost accounting system that reflects current normal costs of operation. The use of standard costs in the costing out of the unit budgets for sales and for production affords a quick over-all picture of the probable standard profit or loss that would be realized if the projected sales and production programs were carried out. However, if the operations of the company during the budget period are estimated as varying appreciably from the level upon which the standard costs have been set, the use of such standards may be misleading.

Many companies budget on both standard and actual cost bases, for purposes of control and analysis of variations. The figures then furnish "allowable " variations from standard in advance of the time when the variations will actually occur. The availability of such budgeted allowable variations enables management to check to better advantage the reasonableness of the subsequent variations from standard developed in actual operation.

Since the principles of budgeting are the same whether or not standard costs are used, to simplify the explanation the budget program presented in this chapter has been set up only on the basis of actual costs.

Responsibility for the budget program. The responsibility for setting up an organization to coordinate and operate the details of the budget program should be entrusted only to a major corporate executive, one preferably reporting directly to the chief executive. However, as a matter of practical expediency, the chief executive may wish to delegate such responsibility to the principal accounting or financial officer. Experience conclusively demonstrates the folly of attempting to operate a budget program where the budget officer does not possess adequate organizational stature and top authority.

Duties of budget officer. The following duties are ordinarily assigned to the budget officer, referred to here as the budget director.

1. Be responsible for forecasting, developing the budget program to be followed, and preparing the manual of instruction covering the approved method and procedures that implement it.

2. Supervise the budget department personnel, and such other personnel as may be loaned to it during the budget preparation period.

3. Design the budget work sheets and issue instructions as to how, when, and by whom they should be prepared.

4. Determine the design and type of budget reports and issue instructions as to how, when and by whom they should be prepared.

5. Review all budget reports as issued, determine the reason for variances that develop, and recommend corrective action to those who will be responsible for taking such action. If corrective action is not taken, report the failure to the next higher level of organizational authority. (In a large company, this function in a plant would be delegated to the resident budget supervisor.)

6. Act as chairman of the budget committee, which should include the chief executive and the head of each primary functional division, that is, sales, manufacturing, engineering, finance accounting, and the like. It should be the function of this committee to review and finally approve all over-all company budgets before installation and to review the progress of the company toward the realization of such budgets at least once each month. (In a large company, this function in a plant would be delegated to the resident budget supervisor.)

7. Meet and counsel with the chief executive, the primary functional division heads, and, with the permission of the respective primary functional heads, with any manager, supervisor, foreman, section leader or group leader regarding the performance of his department, or section thereof, in relation to the budget.

8. Report to the chief executive the failure of any person in a position of supervisory responsibility to cooperate and coordinate his activities in line with the approved company plan of action as reflected in the budget. Such a report, however, should be made only as a final recourse after the established lines of organizational responsibility have been exhausted without resultant action.

Delegation of budget work. To avoid unnecessary duplication of work, the goal of the budget director should be to staff the budget department with the minimum personnel required to do those parts of the budget procedure that cannot be handled elsewhere in the organization. This practice serves two desirable ends: (1) maximum economy is realized, and (2) the work will largely be performed by personnel who will ultimately be accountable under the budget for the success or failure of their actions. To grant to each supervisor, as far as practical, the right to have a part in setting his own budget goals has a salutary effect in that the budget becomes a personal rather than an impersonal matter. The safeguard to the company against the establishment of loose budgets lies in the budget review and approval procedure, and, in particular, in the fine-tooth comb checking, which is the special province of the budget department.

Likewise, in the preparation of special engineering studies, economic and statistical studies, financial requirement studies, and other special investigations necessary for the establishment of sound budgets, the budget department should delegate the work as far as practical to the unit of the organization best able to handle it. If necessary, test checks may be made by the budget department to determine the validity of the studies made and the conclusions drawn.

In preparing the actual budget reports, the work ordinarily should be carried on by the accounting department, as the budget reports, in large measure, if properly designed, will replace existing accounting and financial statements.

The interpretive function. The interpretive work, including the analysis of the reasons for variations from the budget, and the corrective action necessary, cannot be delegated by the budget department, although the advice of others may be sought. The budget director must, at all times, preserve an independent viewpoint and be prepared to defend his observations and recommendations against attack from any level of company organization. In fact, the measure of his success during the formative years of the budget program may well be the number of such attacks and the number of battles won. It is axiomatic that if the budgets are to be properly set and enforced, there will be a number of preliminary skirmishes, for to err is human and no man likes to be caught in a mistake. These situations call for exceptional tact and diplomacy on the part of the budget director if the budget program is to operate with a minimum of friction and, in the final analysis, is to operate at all. It takes time and patience to "sell" the necessity of substituting coordinated company action for individual action. What is equally important, the program once "sold" must be kept sold, as there will always remain a small but aggressive minority in every company who would be glad to cut the strings that bind their personal ambitions.

The budget director must maintain an open mind and be amenable to suggestion and change. He must possess as a primary specification for the job an ingrained zest for experimentation and improvement. He must, however, keep in mind as his standard of performance, the development of a budget program that will do the job of planning and coordinating company activity toward agreed-upon goals at the lowest possible cost.

THE PREPARATION OF BUDGETS

Budgets included in a budgetary system. As previously implied, there is no one single budget program that will fit the needs of every business. The budgetary system to be explained here is representative of those used in typical, medium-sized manufacturing companies that operate under a completely coordinated budget program. The explanation illustrates one tested method of approach to the problem of installing and operating a workable budget program. Each company must experiment, pick and choose, discard and revise, until a budget program is developed that meets its individual requirements.

The budgetary system explained in this chapter comprises the preparation of the following budgets:

1. Sales budgets.
2. Cost-of-sales budgets.
3. Inventory increase or decrease budget.

4. Production budget.
5. Direct materials budgets.
6. Direct labor budgets.
7. Machine-hour budgets.
8. Direct-indirect labor budgets.
9. Utilities budgets.
10. Indirect supplies budget.
11. Other indirect labor and expense budgets (general factory overhead budgets).
12. Selling expense budgets.
13. Advertising expense budgets.
14. Administrative expense budgets.
15. Other operating income and expense budgets.
16. Nonoperating income and expense budgets.
17. Profit and loss budgets.
18. Capital expenditures budget.
19. Cash budget.

Preparation of the sales budgets. The sales budgets constitute the basic foundation upon which the budget program is constructed. Only if the sales budgets are correctly stated in terms of unit and dollar volume that can be realized during the budget period can budgets of cost and expenditures necessary to realize the budgeted sales volume be developed on an accurate and effective basis. Before an accurate sales budget can be prepared, a sales forecast must be made. When the forecasts are completed, they must be reconciled with the ability of the company to perform. Then the unit sales budget and the dollar sales budget are prepared. The methods applied in preparing the sales forecasts and the sales budgets are described below.

Responsibility for the sales forecast. Preparation of sales estimates should be primarily the responsibility of the sales organization, but those responsible directly for general budgeting and planning, and management itself, should participate sufficiently to assure complete understanding and agreement with the result. Large organizations with sales and economic research staffs will have no difficulty in undertaking the work independently. In smaller companies, the sales organization may require considerable assistance from the treasurer or controller.

Factors to be considered in making the sales forecast. Some of the significant factors to be considered in forecasting sales are:

1. *Past experience.* Analysis of previous sales experience by product lines, territories, classes of customers, and other details is generally useful as a starting point in preparing estimates. The sales forecast is prepared on the basis of past records.
2. *Company policies and limitations.* Proposed changes in products, the condition and capacity of manufacturing facilities, changes in marketing methods and policies, and condition of inventories are among the factors to be considered.
3. *Industry outlook and position of company.* An analysis of the competitive situation within the particular industry, and the company's relative position with respect to product development, customer acceptance, pricing, and the like is highly desirable. At the same time, conditions and prospects within specific industries, which may affect the principal customers of the company, should be studied.

4. *General economic conditions.* Ordinarily the appraisal of the general business outlook is the most significant factor in forecasting sales and one which presents the greatest problem. For that reason studies of the type discussed in the chapter on financial planning, are essential.

Preparing the sales forecast. The sales forecast is usually prepared by several different methods so that a cross-check may be obtained on the accuracy of the predictions. The usual methods include (1) an economic or statistical forecast based on past records, (2) a unit sales forecast, and (3) a dollar sales forecast.

The economic or statistical forecast based on past records. This forecast involves the computation of the long-range or secular trend of growth or decline in dollar sales volume by classes of products sold (referred to as product class) as shown by past records. Ten or more years are usually used, on the general premise that the greater the number of normal years included in the trend computation the more accurate the results.

If the sales data have been distorted in any particular years by major accidental factors such as a strike in a plant, war, fire, flood, or other factors affecting the ability of the company to produce or sell on a normal basis, the sales volume data in the years in question should be adjusted to compensate for such uncontrollable variation, or the abnormal years should be eliminated from the data *before the trend computation is made.* Otherwise, the slope of the trend may be distorted and therefore not truly representative of the normal performance of the company or of the demand for the company's products or services.

The computation of the statistical sales forecast involves the following steps:

1. Adjusting product class sales volume for price changes.
2. Determining the secular trend of growth or decline.
3. Finding the sales variation from the trend.
4. Finding monthly product sales trends and adjusting for seasonal variation.
5. Measuring deviation of each product sales index from its normal trend.
6. Finding an appropriate general business index that correlates with company product sales indexes.
7. Determing the relation of the magnitude of swings between the selected general business index and the company product sales index.
8. Computing probable demand.

An explanation of these steps follows.

1. *Adjusting sales volume for price changes.* Dollar sales volume for each year should be reduced to a consistent base value if significant changes in the prices of the products sold have taken place in the years for which the trend is being computed. This may be accomplished by (1) establishing an index of price variation over the years being studied, and (2) dividing the actual dollar sales volume in each year by the corresponding year's price index to arrive at a price adjusted dollar sales volume for the year for the product class.

The index of price variation is made as follows: (1) Take a representative sample of sales items for each product class; (2) select a normal or base year and consider the weighted average price of those items in the selected year as representing 100; (3) divide each year's actual unit price by the base year price. The tabulation in Figure 3-4 illustrates how the index of Product A would appear, with 1960 selected as the base year, during the period for which the trend is being studied.

PRODUCT A
ADJUSTMENT OF SALES VOLUME FOR PRICE CHANGES

Year	Actual Unit Price	Product A Actual Dollar Sales (000)	Unit Price Index 1960 – 100	Product A Price Adjusted Dollar Sales (1947 $)
1957..............	$2.33	$1,101.5	66.7	$1,651.4
1958..............	2.30	891.5	65.9	1,352.8
1959..............	2.35	1,286.3	67.3	1,911.3
1960..............	2.59	1,531.2	74.2	2,063.6
1961..............	2.74	1,674.4	78.5	2,133.0
1962..............	2.83	1,813.7	81.1	2,236.4
1963..............	2.83	1,964.5	81.1	2,422.3
1964..............	2.83	2,212.8	81.1	2,728.5
1965..............	2.83	2,322.0	81.1	2,863.1
1966..............	3.12	2,694.3	89.4	3,013.8
1967..............	3.49	3,100.2	100.0	3,100.2
1968..............	3.69	3,416.2	105.7	3,232.0
1969..............	3.62	3,364.8	103.7	3,244.7
1970..............	3.69	3,635.2	105.6	3,442.4
1971..............	3.96	3,924.3	113.5	3,457.5
1972..............	4.02	4,110.3	115.3	3,564.9
1973..............	4.08	4,341.9	116.8	3,717.4
1974..............	4.11	4,452.9	117.7	3,783.3
1975..............	4.12	4,790.6	118.1	4,056.4
1976..............	4.19	5,032.3	120.1	4,190.1
1977 Est.........	4.33 E	5,254.1 E	124.0 E	4,237.2 E

**Figure 3-4. Adjustment of Sales
Volume for Price Changes**

2. *Determining the secular trend of growth or decline.* The determination of the secular trend of growth or decline of each product class involves the fitting of a trend line to the price-adjusted dollar sales. This may be accomplished either by mathematical computation or by visual inspection. Mathematical methods include the "least-squares" method, logarithmic equations, the use of seven-and-nine-year moving averages, and other statistical techniques. The formulae for any of these techniques can be found in any standard statistical handbook. Figure 3-5 illustrates a trend line fitted to the annual price adjusted dollar sales over the years for Product A as shown above.

3. *Finding the sales variation from the trend.* Once the secular trend line has been established for each product class, the price-adjusted dollar sales for each year is divided by its respective secular trend values to obtain an index of sales variation from the trend line. The trend line is always considered normal (100). This index reflects the effect of general business or economic conditions upon the demand for the company's products over the years under study.

4. *Finding monthly product sales trends and adjusting for seasonal variation.* It is desirable for accurate measurement of turning points in company sales activity that the trends of the annual price adjusted dollar sales by product class be converted into corresponding monthly product class sales trends. It is also desirable to establish monthly sales indexes by dividing the product class sales for each month by its respective monthly trend value.

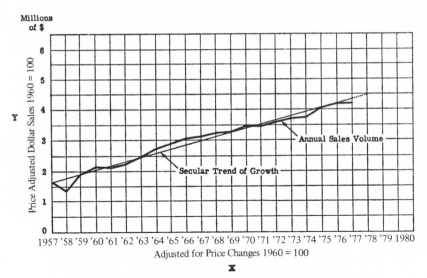

Figure 3-5. Trend Line Fitted to Annual Sales Volume

As monthly sales are normally subject to short-term or seasonal variations within each year, the effect of such seasonal influences should be eliminated from the monthly product class indexes. This may be readily accomplished by computing, for each product class, an index of monthly seasonal variation that reflects just what percentage of an average month's sales will normally be enjoyed in each month of the year. The division of each monthly index value of the seasonally unadjusted product class index by the applicable product class seasonal index for the corresponding month compensates for and removes the effect of the seasonal variation.

5. *Measuring deviation of each product class index from its normal trend.* After the annual and monthly product class indexes have been established, the next step in the forecasting procedure is to measure the standard deviation of each product class index from its trend. The purpose of this measurement is to establish the magnitude of the variation above or below the normal trend over the period of the trend study.

6. *Finding a general business index that correlates with company product class indexes.* Next follows a careful review of the available published indexes of general business activity in an effort to select one or more that show a high degree of correlation with the "swings" in the company product class indexes. If possible, a general business index whose turns precede those of the company product class indexes should be selected. Such a general business index would constitute, in effect, a barometer of the economic climate affecting the company's business and, by its movements, would anticipate and hence warn of probable turning points in the demand for the company's products and services. By plotting the company's product class indexes and selected indexes of general business activity on the same graph, it will be easy to see the degree of relationship between the indexes, the relative magnitude of the variations in each index, and the turning points of each index.

7. *Determining the relation of the magnitude of swings.* Once appropriate indexes of general business activity have been selected against which to measure company product class performances, the standard deviations of such business indexes should be

measured in order to establish the magnitude of their variations from the trend over the period of the study. It is important that the years selected for the measurement of both the company sales indexes and of the general business activity indexes be the same. By comparing the standard deviation of each product class index with the standard deviation of its corresponding index of general business activity, an exact measurement of the relation of the magnitude of swings between the two indexes is obtained. For example, if the standard deviation of the general business index is 1.5, the relation is 2 to 1. This means that, on the average, over the period of the study the variation in the demand for the company's products, as measured by the swings of its index above or below its normal trend, is twice as great as corresponding variations in the general business index.

8. *Computing probable demand.* If the approximate level of general business activity that will exist over the ensuing year can be closely forecast, the probable volume of demand for the company's products and services can be statistically computed. Figure 3-6 shows how such measurements may be made.

The illustration, Figure 3-6, assumes that when general business activity, as represented by its index, is normal, or 100, the demand for Product A, as represented by its index, will also be normal, or 100. If movements in the general business index usually precede or usually follow movements in Product A sales index, and a change from current level of business activity is predicted, then appropriate adjustment to allow for timing of swings must be made in the resultant forecast.

Experience has demonstrated in a number of companies that statistical or economic forecasts arrived at by the above procedure are, over the years, highly accurate and dependable. The principal use of the statistical forecast is to check the accuracy of other methods of sales forecasting. These methods, the unit sales forecast and the dollar sales forecast, are described below.

The unit sales forecast. The unit sales forecast is the most important of all forecasts because it is expressed in terms of the actual products or services which the company sells or renders. The unit sales forecast is usually made on an annual basis, although in certain industries such as public utilities, oils, and chemicals, where capital expenditures must be planned ahead for many years, longer-range forecasts of unit sales are not only desirable but necessary.

The sales division of the company is normally charged with the responsibility for preparing the unit sales forecast. In developing this forecast, it is usually not necessary to estimate the probable unit sales for each item the company manufactures or sells, as an analysis of sales discloses that in the average company 10 to 15 per cent of the items handled account for 85 per cent to 90 per cent of the total dollar sales.

Thus, in preparing the unit forecast worksheets, the budget or statistical department should first study each product class and segregate for listing only those items that make an important contribution to the total dollar sales of the class. However, a sufficient number should be listed to absorb 90 per cent or more of current sales. In addition to the description of the item, it is desirable to enter for the use of the sales estimator the unit sales for each item listed for each of the past three years as well as an estimate of unit sales for the current year based upon performance for the year to date. This information will provide the sales estimator with a picture of the trend of sales for each item under consideration.

FORECAST OF SALES VOLUME – PRODUCT A
At Various Levels of Business Activity

Index of Business Activity	Relation of Standard Deviation Prod. A ÷ Gen. Bus.	Resultant Index for Product A	Projection of Price Adjusted Normal Sales Trend for Product A for 1975	Price Adjusted Forecasted Sales Volume for Product A	Forecasted Product A Unit Price Index for 1975	Resultant Actual Forecasted Sales Volume for Product A
90 (or − 10 Dev.)	2 Times	80	$4,457,000	$3,566,000	125	$4,458,000
95 (or − 5 Dev.)	2 Times	90	4,457,000	4,011,000	125	5,014,000
100 (or 0 Dev.)	2 Times	100	4,457,000	4,457,000	125	5,571,000 *
105 (or + 5 Dev.)	2 Times	110	4,457,000	4,903,000	125	6,129,000
110 (or + 10 Dev.)	2 Times	120	4,457,000	5,348,000	125	6,685,000

* Level selected by Company Management.

Figure 3-6. Computation of Sales Forecast

If the estimating is done in the field by district or territorial salesmen, then, of course, the information has to be broken down for the district or territory that each salesman services. An additional refinement is the breakdown of the unit listing and supporting data by customer, for that is usually the way the salesman sells.

In preparing the original unit forecast, no information regarding price, cost, or manufacturing capacity is furnished the individual sales estimator. What the company is interested in receiving at this point is a candid opinion of the number of units of a given article that each salesman thinks he can sell during the period covered by the forecast.

A typical unit sales forecast worksheet is shown in Figure 3-7.

	UNIT SALES FORECAST WORKSHEET						
ITEM DESCRIPTION	UNITS SHIPPED				UNFILLED ORDERS	UNIT SALES FORECAST		
	19—	19—	19—	Estimated 19—	Balance- End 19—	Salesmen's Estimates	Sales Managers' Estimates	Final Estimate

Figure 3-7. Worksheet for Unit Sales Forecast

When the individual unit estimates are received from each salesman, they are totaled by the budget department to arrive at total unit estimates by item for each product class. These summary unit estimates are then reviewed by the sales managers of the various classes of products and revised upward or downward as the judgment and special knowledge of the sales manager may dictate. Significant new items that will be introduced during the forecast period should, of course, be listed and estimated.

The dollar sales forecast. Upon receipt of the summary unit estimates from the various sales managers, the budget director is in a position to price and cost out the unit sales forecast to arrive at a tentative dollar sales and cost-of-sales forecast by product class. Both the dollar sales and cost-of-sales forecasts should be increased, of course, to compensate for the items not listed on the estimate sheets. This is done by dividing the dollar sales and cost-of-sales totals by the percentage which the items estimated will absorb of the total dollar sales by product class during the current year.

Reconciliation of forecasts with ability to perform. At this point, and only at this point, should the ability of the company to produce the forecasted number of units be considered. It may be found that the available plant capacity has been oversold, automatically raising the question of possible courses of action. Such action might include subcontracting of work to outside contractors, increasing productive capacity by construction or purchase of additional plant and equipment, or scaling down of the forecasted sales to a level that can be handled by current and prospective available manufacturing facilities. In the latter course of action, the relative profitability of the various items would have an important bearing in determining which unit estimates are to be maintained and which are to be reduced.

Having prepared statistical or economic forecasts of dollar sales by product class, management has a valuable check on the reliability of the dollar sales forecasts arrived at by pricing out the unit forecasts. If there are significant differences between the two, the sales division should be required to reconcile the differences before the unit sales forecast is accepted. The sales division might appropriately attribute any excess in its forecast over the economic forecast to the introduction of new products, opening of new markets, increases in selling prices, and the like.

The unit sales budget. The unit sales budgets are the definite sales programs to which the company is committed during the budget period. They may be the same as the unit sales forecasts; more often they are not, because the unit sales forecasts are usually based on expected orders, whereas the budgets are based on shipments to be billed. It should be obvious that, if the company is to obtain the profit goals that the unit budget priced and costed out indicates, each item must be made and sold in the quantities budgeted, and all efforts must be concentrated to this end. However, too often this important fact is overlooked with the result that while the budgeted dollar sales are reached, profits are far less than expected because of the sale of greater quantities of low-margin items than are budgeted. For this reason, it is essential that unit product class budgets be broken down into district and salesmen's unit budgets and that each district sales manager and salesman be held responsible for selling his alloted unit budget quotas.

The dollar sales budget. The dollar sales budgets are arrived at by pricing out the approved unit budgets according to the item selling prices that are expected to prevail during the budget period.

The cost-of-sales budget. The dollar cost-of-sales budgets are the approved unit product class budgets costed out by the standard or actual factory manufacturing costs for the items that are expected to prevail during the budget period. The subtraction of the factory cost so determined from the dollar sales by item, establishes the margin yield by item. These figures enable management to see the following probable results by quick visual inspection: (1) the margin contribution by product class and by item; and (2) which items are yielding subnormal margins or losses.

If the budgeted product class margin is inadequate, remedial action must be taken at this time. Such remedial action would normally consist of further review of the product class unit sales, dollar sales, and cost-of-sales budgets with a view toward *(a)* improving the "product mix" by budgeting more profitable items and reducing the budgets of less profitable items, if possible; *(b)* studying loss or low-profit items from the viewpoint of increasing selling price, reducing manufacturing cost, or both; *(c)* possibly eliminating loss items from the company line, if no other remedial action can be taken. Figure 3-8 shows the effect of rebudgeting to arrive at the same total sales volume with an improved factory margin through improving product mix.

It is apparent at this stage that the product class unit sales, dollar sales, and cost-of-sales budgets must be reviewed concurrently by management before any of them may be finally approved. The approval procedure should consist of the formal affixation of the signatures of each of the reviewing functional heads to the product class budget worksheets, including the signature of the president or chief executive to denote final approval. This formal action is necessary to impress upon each functional head the commitment he has made both for himself and the members of his division to work to the agreed-upon plan of action.

	ORIGINAL BUDGET				
	Sales Budget	Cost-of-Sales Budget		Factory Margin Budget	
Product A	$1,000,000	$ 880,000	88%	$120,000	12%
Product B	500,000	280,000	56	220,000	44
Product C	2,000,000	1,840,000	92	160,000	8
Product D	750,000	600,000	80	150,000	20
Total	$4,250,000	$3,600,000	85%	$650,000	15%
	REVISED BUDGET				
Product A	$ 900,000	$ 792,000	88%	$108,000	12%
Product B	850,000	476,000	56	374,000	44
Product C	1,525,000	1,403,000	92	122,000	8
Product D	975,000	780,000	80	195,000	20
Total	$4,250,000	$3,451,000	81%	$799,000	19%

Figure 3-8. Rebudgeting for Improved Product Mix

Once the annual product class unit sales, dollar sales, and cost-of-sales budgets have been approved, the budget department can then proceed to break them down into monthly or period budgets through the application of the product class seasonal percentages previously determined.

The inventory increase or decrease budget. The units budgeted for sale will not necessarily correspond with the units budgeted for manufacture, because unit inventories necessary to service the budgeted volume of sales may have to be increased or decreased from the levels prevailing at the time the unit sales budgets are established.

The procedure in establishing the unit inventory increase or decrease budget is to list on each product class budget worksheet opposite each item budgeted, the average number of units required to service the budgeted unit sales. This is easily computed by dividing the budgeted unit sales by the normal inventory turnover ratio established for that class of product, taking into consideration the length of the manufacturing cycle, and posting the resultant average inventory requirement in the space provided. A typical worksheet for showing the unit inventory increase or decrease budget is shown in Figure 3-9. The expected inventory on hand at the beginning of the budget year is posted in the second column. In the third column is posted the expected unfilled balance of open orders on hand at the beginning of the budget year. This amount, subtracted from the inventory on hand, gives the unallocated inventory available to service sales during the ensuing budget year, to be posted in the fourth column. The subtraction of the unallocated inventory available (fourth column) from the average inventory requirement (first column) gives the unit inventory increase or decrease necessary to reach the average inventory required. The required inventory increase or decrease is posted in the fifth column.

The computation of the required unit inventory increases or decreases serves a further purpose; it brings to light excess inventories of particular items on hand and automatically raises the question of their possible disposition. In some cases the unit inventories on hand may exceed the units budgeted for sale. Where the inventories exceed one year's budgeted requirements, the units budgeted for sale cannot be increased to absorb the excess, it is recommended that the excess be written down or off the company books and that physical disposition be considered. The above procedure,

| | | UNIT INVENTORY INCREASE OR DECREASE BUDGET WORKSHEET | | | |
| | | PRODUCT A | | | |
ITEM DESCRIPTION	AVERAGE INVENTORY REQUIRED (1)	BEGINNING INVENTORY (2)	UNFILLED ORDER BALANCE (BEGINNING OF YEAR) (3)	UNALLOCATED INVENTORY AVAILABLE (4)	REQUIRED INVENTORY INCREASE OR DECREASE (5)

Figure 3-9. Worksheet for Unit Inventory Increase or Decrease Budget

if consistently followed, will insure a clean inventory consisting only of actively moving items, and will minimize any future possibility of heavy product inventory losses.

By costing out the budgeted yearly unit inventory increases or decreases required, the average amount of additional inventory investment or recovery by item and by product class is determined.

The production budget. The addition of the unit sales budget by item and the unit inventory increase (or the subtraction of the unit inventory decrease from the unit sales budget) by item, gives the net unit production budget by item. This net production budget should be increased to a gross production budget by making proper provision of the expected or normal damage. The gross production budget shows the number and amount of different articles that must be produced by the factory to service the budgeted unit sales volume.

Within the limitation of productive and storage capacity, it should be the aim of every well run company to schedule its productive operations so that an even work load is maintained as far as possible throughout the operating year. The greater the percentage of items manufactured for stock, against special customer orders, the greater the opportunity to schedule an even work load. An even work load permits maximum efficiency in the use of machinery, materials, and manpower required to manufacture the budgeted production, improves employee morale by minimizing layoffs, permits maintenance of a uniform labor force, and offers numerous other benefits. However, to accomplish this objective, it may be necessary for the company to make substantial short-term investments in product inventory, as the sales of particular items will vary considerably from month to month because of the seasonal nature of customer demand.

To discover the nature and extent of such interim monthly inventory variations, it is necessary (1) to "spread" the annual budgeted unit production *for each item* in accordance with the number of working days in each month on an equal basis by month, and (2) to subtract the resultant monthly unit production from the budgeted unit sales for each month to arrive at the monthly unit addition to or deduction from inventory on hand. The costing out of the monthly unit additions to, or deductions from, inventory indicates the growth or liquidation of product inventory investment per month. A typical computation is shown in Figure 3-10.

If the manufacture of the product involves assembly, subassembly, and parts operations, it is obvious that, for effective factory use, the unit production budget for each finished product must be "exploded" in terms of the assemblies, subassemblies,

PRODUCT A
(a typical stock item)
BUDGET OF MONTHLY INVENTORY INCREASE OR DECREASE

	Budgeted Unit Sales	Budgeted Net Unit Production*	Budgeted Unit Inventory Increase or Decrease	Budgeted Unit Inventory
Beginning Inventory —	—	—	—	3,000
January	2,000	3,721	+ 1,721	4,721
Februray	2,500	3,543	+ 1,043	5,764
March	3,000	4,075	+ 1,075	6,839
April	3,500	3,543	+ 43	6,882
May	3,000	3,898	+ 898	7,780
June	2,500	3,898	+ 1,398	9,178
July	2,500	3,543	+ 1,043	10,221
August	3,500	4,075	+ 575	10,796
September	5,000	3,543	− 1,457	9,339
October	6,000	3,897	− 2,103	7,236
November	5,500	3,721	− 1,779	5,457
December	3,000	3,543	+ 543	6,000
Year	42,000	45,000	+ 3,000	—

* Variation due to number of working days in each month.

Figure 3-10. Budget of Monthly Inventory Increase or Decrease

and individual parts of which they are composed. This is accomplished by multiplying the number of finished product units budgeted for each month by the number of component assemblies, subassemblies, and parts as listed in the product assembly bill of material.

If the manufacturing cycle involved in producing the component parts and in assembling such parts into the finished product is extensive, that is, takes more than one month, the scheduling of the manufacture of such component parts must antedate the budgeted requirement of finished product by the length of the manufacturing cycle. In many companies, the length of the manufacturing cycle may required the scheduling of parts production many months in advance of the budget inventory requirements, thus, in effect, extending factory unit production budgets over a much longer period than that encompassed by the unit sales budgets.

Where individual parts are required in the assembly of more than one finished product, the total budget requirement for each part must be obtained through the addition of the individual parts requirements for each product. At this point, the company has broken down its budgeted sales requirements to the part, the lowest physical manufacturing item with which the factory is concerned; and it has timed the production of such parts, and the subassemblies and assemblies that follow to coincide with the product requirements for sale.

The unit production budgets serve the following supplemental purposes. They aid (1) in checking adequacy of work in process and finished product storage space to meet budgeted inventory requirements, and in advance planning for additional space, if required; and (2) in checking adequacy of product handling equipment such as tote boxes, skids, conveyors, lift trucks, and the like, to meet budgeted production load, and in advance planning for additional equipment, if required.

Direct materials budget. The direct materials production budget is obtained by converting the unit parts production budgets into the component direct raw materials required to produce the budgeted production. This is accomplished by (1) multiplying the number of pieces to be produced for each part by the appropriate measure of weight, length, size, and/or type of each material of which it is composed (with due allowance for damange and scrap), and (2) by adding together the total requirements of each material.

By comparing the amount of each item of direct materials required to meet the budgeted production with the direct materials stores inventory on hand, one can obtain the amount of direct material inventory increase or decrease by item necessary to provide adequate stocks. The addition of the direct materials inventory increase or decrease by item to the corresponding item amount contained in the direct materials production budget establishes the basic requirements for the direct materials purchase budget.

The cost of the direct materials production budget, the direct materials inventory increase or decrease budget, the direct materials purchase budget may be obtained by pricing out the unit quantities shown in each. Each of these three costs is needed for proper financial planning.

The direct materials budget is also useful in (1) checking the adequacy of direct materials storage space and planning for additional space, if required; (2) checking the ability of present vendors to supply material in quantities required, and securing in advance new sources of supply, if required; (3) accurately scheduling material purchases and receipts in advance of budgeted production requirements.

Direct labor budgets. The direct labor-hour budget is obtained by converting the unit parts production budgets, the unit subassembly production budgets, and the unit assembly production budgets into the number of direct labor man-hours required to manufacture the budgeted quantity of units to be produced. This is accomplished by taking the direct labor operator's time required to process a unit through each productive operation and multiplying that time by the number of units budgeted for production.

After the original extension is made for each part, subassembly, and assembly, the total amount of direct labor time required to service the budgeted production requirements may be sorted according to the following methods.

1. *By type of operation.* This method establishes the budgeted production direct labor load on various types of machine or hand operations for the factory as a whole; for example, number of drill-press operator hours, number of punch-press operator hours, number of assembly hours, and the like and indicates the budgeted absorption of plant capacity.

2. *By direct labor classification.* This method establishes the number of operators with different skills required to service the budgeted production load; for example, the number of machinists, number of assemblers, and the like. Based on the employee requirements developed, the working force may be balanced to the budgeted production load by reducing or increasing the number of workers possessing specified skills.

3. *By cost center.* This method establishes the budgeted production load in terms of direct labor man-hours for the organizational unit of the plant against which operating costs are normally measured. If a variable expense budget has been previously established for each cost center, the amount of allowable expense by indirect expense account necessary to service the budgeted direct labor man-hours may be readily determined.

4. *By manufacturing department.* This method establishes the budgeted production load in terms of direct labor man-hours for each major organizational unit of the plant against which operating costs are to be measured. Based upon the respective departmental direct labor loads, the organizational assignment of required direct supervision and clerical time, and the allocation of required indirect supervision and clerical time, and other overhead charges may be handled with maximum effectiveness.

The conversion of direct labor-hours to direct labor-dollars, to establish the budgeted direct labor payroll by cost center, department, and for the factory as a whole, is readily accomplished by pricing out the direct labor-hours in each job classification at its job-classification hourly rate of pay.

Machine-hour budgets. The machine-hour budget is obtained by converting the unit parts production budgets into the number of machine-hours required to manufacture the budgeted quantity of units to be produced. This is accomplished by taking the machine-time required to process a unit through machine operation and multiplying that time by the number of units budgeted for production. The machine-hours thus developed will rarely agree with the number of direct labor operational hours previously developed in constructing the direct labor budget. This is because of such common situations as a single direct labor operator being able to operate two or more machines at the same time, or two or more direct labor operators being required to service one highly complicated machine.

After the original extension is made for each part, the total amount of machine-time required to service the budgeted production requirements may be sorted according to the following methods.

1. *By type of machine.* This method establishes the budgeted production machine-hour load on each type of machine for the factory as a whole; for example, number of #2 B & S Lathe hours, number of #9 Banbury hours, and the like. By checking the required machine-time against the available capacity machine-time by type of machine, any bottlenecks can be readily located. If additional capacity is required, advance provision can be made for obtaining it through scheduling of overtime operations, through the purchase and installation of new machinery, or through the subcontracting of certain work to other manufacturers. Advance knowledge like the budgeted utilization of various machine capacities is of real value to company management in balancing production loads. Management can determine whether to introduce new products or increase the budgeted sale of existing products (if possible) in order to make productive use of what would otherwise be idle equipment.

2. *By manufacturing cost center.* This method establishes the budgeted production load in terms of machine-hours for the lowest organizational manufacturing unit of the plant against which operating costs are normally measured. It aids in the establishment of accurate budgets of those expenses that are directly concerned with the opera-

tion of the machines (for example, steam, power, air, water, and gas charges), and of those expenses that are indirectly concerned with machine operation like machine repairs, machine maintenance, and the like.

Direct-indirect labor budgets. These budgets measure the number of indirect labor operators required to service *directly* the *budgeted* direct labor-hours and/or budgeted machine-hours in each manufacturing cost center and in each manufacturing department. It is expressed in terms of indirect labor-hours by job classification. Only supervision, indirect labor operators such as truckers, cleaners, maintenance men, and clerical help like dispatchers, time clerks, and the like *directly assigned* to respective manufacturing cost centers and manufacturing departments should be included in these budgets.

The conversion of direct-indirect labor-hours to direct-indirect labor-dollars is made by pricing out at the respective hourly or salary job-classification rates of pay.

Utilities budgets. The units of utilities such as kilowatt-hours, pounds of steam, cubic feet of gas, gallons of water, and the like required to service the budgeted production are based in part upon the machine-hour budgets and in part upon the normal usage in nonoperating departments. These utility units are easily converted to utility expense dollars by pricing out at the respective established cost rates. The individual utility budget should be shown in both units and dollars for each manufacturing cost center and for each manufacturing department.

Apart from their value as a measurement of probable utility costs, the utility budgets have many other important operating uses. The budgeted utility unit loads should be checked against the capacity of plant utility facilities to handle such loads. Such checking might show, for example, that the budgeted kilowatt consumption of power may be greater than the ability of the plant powerhouse to produce. In that case it would be necessary either to purchase additional power generating equipment or contract for the purchase of outside power. The checking might further show that the budgeted power requirement in a given cost center or department of the plant may overtax the capacity of the power-feed wiring supplying such cost center or department. In that case, new lines would have to be installed. The value of the utilities budget to the engineering department as a basis for effective planning cannot be overestimated.

Indirect supplies budget. The budget of indirect material and supplies (all material and supplies used by the factory except material directly entering into the product and utilities) is usually based upon historical cost relationships of the usage of such material and supplies at various levels of plant cost center and departmental operation. Because of the large variety of indirect materials and supplies used, the budget is usually expressed in terms of dollar cost only. However, the use of major supply items such as coal, lumber, lubricating oils, cartons, and the like may be advantageously estimated in units before they are converted to dollars at prevailing or prospective cost rates. These unit estimates are of additional value in checking the adequacy or inadequacy of indirect supply stocks on hand and in the revision of minimum and maximum stocks authorized.

In preparing the indirect supplies budget, the variable indirect expense budget charts by cost center and department are used to determine the probable cost of the supplies required at the level of operation (direct labor and/or machine-hours) budgeted for each cost center and department. The total of such individual cost center and departmental indirect supply costs can then be checked against the historical cost of such supplies for the factory as a whole in years of comparable productive volume. Compensation should be made in past historical cost, of course, to allow for important variations in the purchase price of indirect supplies from year to year.

The cost of indirect materials and supplies is normally an important segment of total factory cost. The usage, however, of such materials and supplies is not ordinarily subject to as close control as that exercised over direct material and direct labor. Therefore, care spent in the preparation of the indirect supplies budget and in the follow-up of actual expenditures against the budget by cost center and department will usually result in large cost savings.

Other indirect labor and expense budgets (general factory overhead budgets). These budgets cover the cost of operating all factory staff and service departments that are not directly engaged in the manufacture of the product. Typical departments include the plant manager's office, personnel department, accounting department, production control department, engineering department, inspection department, purchasing department, and the like.

Unlike the manufacturing departments, the work load of the staff and service departments will not vary directly in line with changes in the budgeted production load. Thus, it becomes necessary to estimate on an individual departmental basis the work load each staff or service department will be called upon to carry. Consideration must be given to such other factors as the number of routine and special projects each department will be required to handle during the budget year. Also, the extent of routine functions that each department must perform and its relative ability to expand or contract in line with expansion or contraction in its own work load must be considered.

Each year, in preparing the departmental operating budget for each general factory overhead department, the first step, after the ascertainment of the departmental work load, is to staff the department with a model organization embracing a sufficient number of employees with appropriate skills and training to do the job properly. The second step is to measure the existing departmental organization against the model organization and to determine what additions, reductions, or changes in personnel should be made. The third step is to determine which of the desired changes can be made within the budget period and to set up the budgeted organization accordingly. The budgeted organization should then be priced out at the appropriate job-classification salary or wage rates. The resultant departmental wage and salary budgets may or may not be the same as the current actual cost of departmental salaries and wages, depending upon how close the present organization approximates the budgeted organization. Any variance between the actual situation and the budget that develops from this initial measurement should be allowed to stand as a measure of the relative efficiency of the department and should remain as a variance until the departmental supervisor corrects his organization to coincide with the budget.

Each of the other general factory overhead departmental expenses, such as departmental office supplies, office machine rentals, and the like, should be estimated on an individual expense basis by the departmental supervisor, using past experience and his knowledge of prospective plans as a guide. These expense estimates should be checked by the resident plant budget supervisor, and revised, if necessary, in collaboration with the departmental supervisor.

The general factory overhead budgets, as well as other plant budgets, should be reviewed and tentatively approved by the plant manager before they are submitted to the budget director for subsequent handling and top management approval.

Selling expense budgets. With due consideration of sales organizational requirements (sales work loads) and the budgeted sales, allowable sales expense budgets should be developed by selling expense account classification for each sales department and section thereof. In similar manner, branch sales office expense budgets should be set up. Based on the distribution of the working time of the individual sales managers, the branch sales office managers, and each salesman, the budgeted sales departmental and branch office expenses should be directly assigned or prorated to product classes. This allocation is necessary for the subsequent preparation of the product class profit and loss budgets. The yearly selling expense budgets so determined should be broken down by month or period, care being taken to charge the proper amount of each budgeted expense to the month or period in which it will be incurred.

The individual sales departmental and branch office expense budgets should be reviewed by the sales department or branch office manager and tentatively approved by the general sales manager before they are submitted to the budget director for subsequent handling.

Advertising expense budgets. Advertising expense normally divides itself into two main classifications, (1) the cost of operating the advertising department, including the salaries and expense of the advertising personnel, and (2) the cost of the individual advertising programs, including space cost, layout and art work, printing, mailing, and the like. Accordingly, the advertising budgets should reflect both types of expense separately.

The assignment of budgeted advertising expense to product classes is usually a simple task, because the advertising programs, which constitute the major portion of the cost, are normally geared to the promotion of specific products. The budgeted expense of operating the advertising department should be prorated to product classes in accordance with the distribution of specific program expense. Institutional advertising, however, which bears no specific relationship to the promotion of a particular product class, should be split on the basis of the budgeted volume of sales in each product class.

Since advertising expense will vary considerably from month to month, based upon the timing of the specific advertising programs, in establishing the monthly or period advertising expense budgets, great care should be exercised in assigning specific costs to the exact month or period in which they will be incurred. Otherwise, the monthly budgets will be ''out of phase'' and lose much of their effectiveness as a control mechanism.

The advertising budgets, like the sales budgets, should be reviewed and tentatively approved by the general sales manager before they are submitted to the budget director.

Administrative expense budgets. The administrative expense budget for each administrative department and section thereof should be prepared by the various departmental managers, working in conjunction with the budget department. Each department budget should be constructed by individual administrative expense account classification. Careful consideration should be given to the individual departmental work loads. Some will bear a definite relation to the budgeted sales volume, for example, order-writing, billing, tabulating, accounts receivable, and the like; others, such as the executive administrative offices, will bear little or no relationship to budgeted volume sales.

As in the case of the advertising budgets, extreme care must be exercised in breaking down the annual administrative expense budgets into their monthly or period components. Many administrative expenses, such as property taxes, membership dues, donations, auditors', consultants', and legal fees, are paid only on an annual, semi-annual or quarterly basis. Although these items can be handled by an equal reserve proration of the expense to each month or period, it is generally preferable to spot the total expense in the exact month in which it is to be paid. This procedure insures that the actual and budgeted expense agree as to timing and provides a more accurate monthly measurement of how the actual administrative expenses are running in relation to the budget.

For accurate product class profit and loss budgets, it is necessary that the administrative expense budget be allocated to the various product classes. This may be done on the basis of the distribution of budgeted sales by individual product classes; for example Product A sales account for 25 per cent of the total sales budget, hence it would be charged with 25 per cent of the administrative expense budget. A better and more accurate method, however, is to study the work load of each administrative department incurred through handling the sale of each product class and resultant "paper work" and to base the allocation of administrative expense to product classes upon the results of such studies.

Other operating income and expense budgets. The budget department should estimate the probable revenue or cost to be incurred during the budget year by estimating each individual "other operating income and expense" account. Such estimates are based upon historical data as well as upon the various sales, cost and purchase budgets previously established. For example, revenue from sale of scrap materials and equipment would probably be based upon previous actual experience, unless a major plant rehabilitation program, such as the scrapping of the equipment for an entire line, was in prospect. Purchase discounts earned, however, would be computed directly from the material supplies purchase budgets. Cash discounts allowed would be computed from the sales budgets.

The budget allocation of such revenues and expense to respective months or periods should follow the allocation of the budget data on which they are based.

Nonoperating income and expense budgets. Nonoperating income and expense normally includes such items as dividends from investments, interest received on loans or mortgages, nonoperating property rental income, and the like. These items can usually be budgeted with a high degree of accuracy to the exact month in which the revenue is to be received or expense is to be incurred.

Profit and loss budgets. Profit and loss is normally budgeted by the company as a whole and by individual product classes, although, in some instances, it may be desirable to construct profit and loss budgets for major individual products. The construction of these budgets is a relatively simple matter, for it involves merely the posting of annual budget data from the various company or product class budgets —sales, cost of sales, selling, advertising, administrative expense, and other operating income and expense, and other nonoperating income and expense—to the corresponding account in the profit and loss statement and computing the residual margins and profit or loss before income taxes.

In like manner, the monthly or period profit and loss budgets are posted and computed. Figure 3-11 shows a typical company profit and loss budget for the budget year and by month.

At this point the company management can see for the first time the prospective result of the company operations for the budget year and the contribution that each product line will make to the total profit or loss. If the sales volume has been accurately forecast and the various component expense budgets carefully set, it is obvious that the budgeted result cannot be materially altered unless major changes are made in existing company sales, pricing, or operating policies. The immediate availability of the detailed budget data, however, permits the budget department to estimate quickly within close limits, the probable effect upon profit or loss of any policy change that might be contemplated and to supply the information to company management within a reasonably short time.

Capital expenditures budget. The capital expenditures budget must necessarily be geared to the long-range plans and programs of the company because of the time required to consummate the program and, more particularly, because of the ultimate effects of such expenditures on the company's progress.

In manufacturing companies, the capital expenditures budget, which is a fixed and inflexible program, is normally made for a year in advance unless the length of time necessary for the completion of individual projects extends beyond one year. The budget is developed from studies of necessary replacement of, and/or necessary additions to, present property and equipment within the ensuing budget year. The task of preparing the budget is normally assigned to company engineers who are charged with the responsibility of developing the projects to be undertaken and the estimated cost of each project. Project cost estimates should be broken down according to the portion of the cost to be capitalized, the portion to be expensed, and the portion to be inventoried, if certain equipment is to be purchased and kept in stock on a standby basis. The individual projects themselves should be segregated by general ledger capital account classification, such as buildings, building equipment, machinery, furniture and fixtures, and the like. Such segregation permits a comparison of the budgeted capital additions with the depreciation that will accrue in each account during the budget year.

In a company with more than one plant and office, the project cost estimates should be further segregated by location because the responsibility for a large share of the capital expenditures program, in many instances, will be localized.

Although the projects are initially approved in the capital expenditures budget, most companies follow the practice of instituting a "Request for the Appropriation of Funds" at the time each individual project is to be put into work. Company management is thus afforded a "second guess" before the money is actually appropriated. Unexpended balances of funds appropriated on uncompleted projects at year-end are

XYZ CO. · Form No. 128   Subject:: Company *Profit or Loss Budget* for 19___

Item	Annual Budget $	% of Net Sales	January	February	March	April	May	June	July	August	September	October	November	December
Gross Sales	12,321,620	103.0	899,480	924,120	973,400	1,035,020	998,050	948,770	911,800	1,059,650	1,195,200	1,293,770	1,185,910	936,450
Returns & Allowances	362,840	3.0	26,490	27,210	28,660	30,480	29,390	27,940	26,850	31,200	35,200	38,100	33,740	27,580
Net Sales	11,958,780	100.0	872,990	896,910	944,740	1,004,540	968,660	920,830	884,950	1,028,450	1,160,000	1,255,670	1,152,170	908,870
Direct Material	3,113,000	26.0	257,370	245,120	281,880	245,120	269,630	269,630	245,120	281,880	245,120	269,630	257,370	245,130
Direct Labor	2,569,610	21.5	212,450	202,330	232,690	202,330	222,560	222,560	202,330	232,690	202,330	222,560	212,450	202,330
Prime Overhead	2,063,090	17.3	170,570	162,440	186,820	162,440	178,690	178,690	162,440	186,820	162,440	178,690	170,570	162,440
General Overhead	1,464,400	12.2	122,030	122,030	122,040	122,030	122,030	122,040	122,030	122,030	122,040	122,030	122,030	122,040
Cost of Production	9,210,060	77.0	762,420	731,920	823,430	731,920	792,910	792,920	731,920	823,420	731,930	792,910	762,420	731,940
Product Inventory Increase or *Decrease*	183,510	1.5	103,480	*54,930*	110,330	26,310	61,760	97,880	63,960	47,140	*143,650*	*154,880*	77,050	45,920
Cost of Sales	9,026,550	75.5	658,940	676,990	713,100	758,230	731,150	695,040	667,960	776,280	875,580	947,790	839,370	686,020
Factory Margin	2,932,230	24.5	214,050	219,920	231,640	246,310	237,510	225,790	216,990	252,170	284,420	307,880	272,700	222,850
Selling Expense	849,710	7.1	67,980	67,120	68,830	72,220	70,530	71,380	73,070	71,380	70,530	71,380	72,220	73,070
Advertising Expense	327,490	2.7	18,010	19,650	21,290	22,920	24,560	26,200	29,470	36,010	42,570	39,300	31,130	16,370
Administrative Expense	706,190	5.9	61,440	59,320	57,200	60,030	59,020	58,920	59,220	58,020	57,910	55,790	59,300	60,030
Selling & Administrative Expense	1,883,390	15.7	147,430	146,090	147,320	155,170	154,110	156,500	161,760	165,410	171,010	166,470	162,650	149,470
Gross Operating *Profit or Loss*	1,048,840	8.8	66,620	73,830	84,320	91,140	83,400	69,290	55,230	86,760	113,410	141,410	110,050	73,380
Other Operating Income or *Expense* (Net)	*115,370*	1.0	*8,420*	*8,650*	*9,110*	*9,690*	*9,340*	*8,880*	*8,550*	*9,920*	*11,190*	*12,120*	*10,730*	*8,770*
Net Operating *Profit or Loss*	933,470	7.8	58,200	65,180	75,210	81,450	74,060	60,410	46,680	76,840	102,220	129,290	99,320	64,610
Other Nonoperating Income or *Expense* (Net)	29,220	.2	4,540	4,540	4,540	4,540	4,540	16,380	4,540	4,540	16,390	4,540	4,540	16,380
Net *Profit or Loss* Before Federal Income Tax	962,690	8.0	53,660	60,640	70,670	76,910	69,520	76,790	42,140	72,300	118,610	124,750	94,780	80,990
Provision for Federal Income Tax	385,080	3.2	21,460	24,260	30,760	30,760	27,810	30,720	16,860	28,920	47,440	49,900	37,910	32,400
Net *Profit or Loss*	577,610	4.8	32,200	36,380	54,960	46,150	41,710	46,070	25,280	43,380	71,170	74,850	56,870	48,520

Italicized figures appear in red.

Figure 3-11. Typical Profit and Loss Budget

carried forward, and such projects and funds automatically become part of the capital expenditures budget for the succeeding year.

Careful estimating of the cost of proposed capital expenditure projects is essential for two reasons: (1) to enable management to judge accurately the worth of each project; (2) to permit it to plan effectively the use of the cash resources of the company. Data on the average amount of capital expenditures from year to year is of little value to a management that suddenly finds itself saddled with a large capital expenditures program in a year when cash is tight. Many company managements, operating without adequate capital expenditure budgets and budgets affecting cash, have found themselves in exactly this position. Financially embarrassed, they have been forced either to borrow at premium rates or to cancel projects at a time when they were most needed. A well conceived long-range capital expenditures program, supported by detailed and accurate annual capital expenditures budgets, is insurance against such financial troubles.

Cash budget. The cash budget, as its name implies, summarizes the estimated cash income and the estimated cash disbursements of the company over the budget period and shows the resultant monthly cash position as the budget period develops. The cash budget is normally prepared by month for the budget year in advance. However, because of the acceleration or the postponement of various receipts or disbursements, it is usually reviewed for the purpose of revision once each quarter. If cash is "tight," a month-to-month short-term forecast may be warranted.

The budget of cash income principally represents the liquidation of accounts receivable through their payment. Monthly debits to accounts receivable (sales billings) are secured from the monthly budget of sales and are added to the accounts receivable beginning-of-the-month balance. The total accounts receivable is then "aged" by the company's current collection experience. The resultant amount of liquidation is the cash income from accounts receivable for each month.

Other income receipts, such as dividend income, note and interest payments received, investments sold, cash sales, and the like, which are normally of a minor nature, can be estimated closely and earmarked exactly to the month of receipt.

Budgeting cash disbursements is more difficult than budgeting receipts because of the variety of items and because many of the disbursements do not coincide with calendar months and are not uniform from one calendar month to another. To insure reasonable accuracy (± 5 per cent of actual), disbursements must be estimated in the detail in which they occur. Based upon studies of the spread between purchase and payment dates for direct material, indirect material and supplies, utility services, capital equipment, and other items, required purchases of these items by month may be translated into required payments by month. To the purchase payments are added the required payments for wages and salaries, taxes, insurance, dividends, debt retirement, and similar items, most of which can be secured directly from the corresponding monthly operating cost budgets. The total constitutes the budget of cash disbursements by months.

The net of the budgeted cash income and the budgeted cash disbursements by month is the amount of the budgeted cash gain or loss by month. This amount, added to the budgeted beginning-of-month cash balance, gives the budgeted end-of-month cash balance.

Summary. The design, installation, and operation of the type of budget program outlined in this chapter requires the continued employment of the best talent and brains available in the company, augmented, if necessary, by the retention of competent outside counsel. The design and installation period is necessarily long because of the amount of basic historical and statistical data that must be assembled or computed. In a large company, five to ten years is not an unreasonable estimate of the time required for the consummation of the program. In a smaller concern, the time would be proportionately less, but still long. Patience is required of those actively working on the program and those who authorize the expenditures required to carry on the program. The "starting-up" and construction costs of the program need not necessarily be great, but since they represent an intangible investment in the future with no immediate return during the formulative years, such costs may loom large in the eyes of the company management. For this reason, it is advocated that the program be installed a step at a time so that some of the potential benefits may be secured at the earliest possible moment.

The potential benefits of a well conceived and executed budget program in terms of cost reduction, profit enhancement, improved coordination of effort, and control of operations, even in a well run company not possessing such a program, can be tremendous. The assurance to company management that they are properly carrying out the duties and responsibilities entrusted to them to see that the affairs of the company are being managed to yield the greatest profit return over the longest period of time is, perhaps, the greatest benefit of all. Management knows through the long-range budget program what is possible of accomplishment. It knows what steps must be taken to secure the accomplishment, and when, how, and where to take corrective action, if required, to assure accomplishment. Failure to reach the budgeted objectives, if they are properly set, is not the fault of the budget, but the management itself. The budget thus becomes the yardstick against which company management may accurately measure its collective effectiveness as well as the individual effectiveness of each of its component managers. It takes courage to operate an effective budget program, but in every instance where such courage has been displayed by management the results have amply justified the price.

4

Administering a Budget Program

CONTENTS

4

Administering a Budget Program

Need for reporting system. To carry out the objectives and purposes of a budget program, actual results must be measured against budgeted figures, analyses must be made of the differences, and necessary correctives applied as the program goes forward. A system of informative reporting is therefore essential if the budget program is to be of value to management. To develop an effective reporting system, the following essentials must be considered: (1) number of reports, (2) timing, (3) type, (4) design and content, and (5) handling.

Number of reports. A basic rule in planning the number of reports is to furnish each executive with only those budget reports that concern the operation of functions and activities for which he is directly responsible. Do not flood the company primary or secondary management with a large number of budget reports, many of which may be of only academic interest to certain management executives. Obviously, if the budget-reporting system is properly conceived, all of the significant periodic reports to management will be budget reports and all duplicate reports will be eliminated.

Timing of reports. Budget reports must be current, or the corrective action which they indicate to be necessary cannot be taken in time to be effective. Weekly reports should be in the hands of operating personnel within a few days after the close of the week covered by the report; monthly reports, within ten working days following the close of the month. If budget personnel is limited, it is far better to issue a few reports promptly than many reports late.

Type of reports. Since reports are the medium of budget enforcement, the type of reports to be used must be tailored to the budget program that has been developed for the particular company. The budget reports recommended for a medium-sized manufacturing company with one or more classes of products are covered later in this chapter.

Design and content of reports. If possible, *all* budget reports within a particular company should be similar in design and size. Only standard form sizes (for example, 8½" by 11", 11" by 14", and 11" by 17") should be used. A multi-purpose form that is flexible as to subject and content is preferable to specially printed forms; it permits changes to be made quickly and economically. Lines on budget forms should be numbered to facilitate reference, and the forms should be prepunched for insertion into specified sections of budget report binders.

The form should provide space at the top for the name of the report, which should exactly describe the contents. The name should be followed by the period covered by the report, with the ending date.

Although the contents of each report varies with the subject, a standard form can be designed to cover the essentials of each report, which are usually uniform for all reports. These essentials, in the order in which they appear in columnar form, are:

1. Description of accounts or items being reported. A wide column at the left of the form, labeled "Item" is used for this purpose.
2. Annual budget. The column is so labeled.
3. Actual performance for period. The word "Actual" is sufficient as a column heading.
4. Budgeted performance for period. The word "Budget" is adequate as a column heading.
5. Variation—actual from budget. The column designation may be "Over or Under." It is important to follow a consistent method of differentiating the overs from the unders. The simplest method is to show all overs in black and all budget unders in red. The nature of the account or item itself will determine whether the variance represents a gain or loss in control.
6. Per cent variation—actual from budget. The column heading here is % Over. This computation is desirable as it helps the reader to appraise results quickly.
7. Explanation of variation—actual from budget. A column headed "Notes" is provided for this purpose. If more space is required for the explanation, reference can be made in the column to notes at the bottom of the report.
8. Percentage relation to base. On some budget reports, such as profit and loss budget reports, it is desirable to include columns showing "up and down" percentage relationships to a base or total. These figures enable management to make a rapid analysis of the results. One such column should be inserted directly after the column showing actual performance for the period and another after the column showing budgeted performance for the period.

The name of the person who prepared and issued the report and the date of issuance should appear in the lower right-hand corner of each budget report.

The budget report shown in Figure 4-1 illustrates the above points.

Handling of budget reports. A budget report binder, indexed and appropriately tabbed, should be issued to each authorized recipient of budget reports. When the reports are distributed, they should be inserted in the binders by budget personnel rather than by personnel in the office of the executive to whom the report is sent. This practice minimizes the possibility of misfiling or mislaying the information. Also, periodically someone from the budget department should audit the binders to see that the budget data and reports are properly filed.

These budget report binders should be brought to all of the budget review meetings and the reports should form the basis of the discussion.

	ITEM	LINE NO	ANNUAL BUDGET	ACTUAL	%	PERIOD BUDGET	%
	XYZ Co. Form 374			SUBJECT____ **Net Sales by Sales Class Report**			
S.C. 100	Plain Back Shovels-Round Pt.	1	408,100	36,555	7.5	34,000	7.0
110	" " " -Square Pt.	2	398,400	34,747	7.1	33,200	6.8
120	Coal Shovels - Square Pt.	3	316,700	24,965	5.1	26,300	5.4
130	Pattern Scoops	4	198,400	15,110	3.1	16,500	3.4
140	Concrete Spades	5	201,300	17,125	3.5	16,600	3.4
150	Telegraph Spoons & Shovels	6	205,700	18,078	3.7	17,200	3.5
160	Tunneling Scoops	7	98,600	8,491	1.7	8,200	1.7
170	Nursery Spades	8	103,200	8,944	1.8	8,600	1.8
180	Snow Pushers	9	78,600	5,782	1.2	6,600	1.4
190	Miscellaneous Shovels, etc.	10	244,300	21,077	4.3	20,400	4.2
	Total Shovels & Spades	11	2,253,300	190.874	39.0	187,600	38.6
		12					
S.C. 200	Forks - Hay	13	198,400	14,075	2.9	13,300	2.7
210	" - Manure	14	204,800	14,231	2.9	13,700	2.8
220	" - Spading	15	296,500	20,398	4.2	19,800	4.1
230	Potato Hooks	16	107,600	6,802	1.4	7,200	1.5
240	Cultivators	17	176,500	11,010	2.2	11,800	2.4
290	Miscellaneous Forks	18	175,040	11,936	2.4	11,700	2.4
	Total Forks	19	1,158,840	78,452	16.0	77,500	15.9
		20					
S.C. 300	Rakes - Garden	21	212,500	14,108	2.9	15,200	3.1
330	" - Steel Road	22	198,760	14,101	2.9	14,200	2.9
340	" - Fan Shape	23	102,500	7,269	1.5	7,300	1.5
350	" - Lawn Comb	24	97,600	6,345	1.3	7,000	1.4
360	" - Wire Lawn	25	78,900	5,701	1.1	5,600	1.2
390	" - Miscellaneous	26	82,300	6,408	1.3	5,900	1.2
	Total Rakes	27	772,560	53,932	11.0	55,200	11.3
		28					
S.C. 400	Hoes - Field & Garden	29	260,100	19,000	3.9	18,600	3.8
420	" - Mortar	30	185,700	13,701	2.8	13,300	2.7
430	" - Weeding	31	203,400	13,608	2.8	14,500	3.0
440	" - Socket	32	147,900	10,942	2.2	10,500	2.2
450	Socket Trowels	33	184,300	13,191	2.7	13,200	2.7
460	Turf Edgers	34	176,800	12,730	2.6	12,600	2.6
490	Miscellaneous Hoes	35	129,400	9,615	2.0	9,300	1.9
	Total Hoes	36	1,287,600	92,787	19.0	92,000	18.9
		37					
S.C. 500	Scythes - Wood	38	127,900	8,916	1.8	9,900	2.0
510	" - Bush	39	102,700	8,048	1.7	7,900	1.6
520	" - Tree	40	98,300	5,772	1.2	7,600	1.6
530	Grass Hooks	41	187,400	14,391	2.9	14,400	3.0
590	Misc. Hooks & Scythes	42	127,500	9,834	2.0	9,800	2.0
	Total Hooks & Scythes	43	643,800	46,961	9.6	49,600	10.2
		44					
S.C. 600	Pruning Shears	45	198,400	15,942	3.3	15,300	3.1
610	Grass Shears	46	97,500	8,189	1.6	7,500	1.6
690	Miscellaneous Shears	47	26,000	2,234	.5	2,000	.4
		48	321,900	26,365	5.4	24,800	5.1
		49					
		50					
	TOTAL NET SALES	51	6,438,000	489,371	100.0	486,700	100.0
		52					
	* Company operates on a 13-period	53					
	calendar	54		Italicized figures appear in red			
		55					
		56					
		57					

Figure 4-1. Sales Budget Report by Product Class.

BUDGET REPORTS FOR MEDIUM-SIZED MANUFACTURING COMPANY

Types of reports. The organization of the budget program for a typical medium-sized manufacturing company that distributes one or more classes of products was described previously. For such a company, the following budget reports are recommended:

1. Sales budget report.

OVER OR UNDER	% OVER UNDER	YEAR TO DATE						LINE NO.
		ACTUAL	%	BUDGET	%	OVER OR UNDER	% OVER UNDER	
2,555	7.5	303,021	6.1	281,600	5.9	21,421	7.6	1
1,547	4.7	280,530	5.7	274,900	5.7	5,630	2.0	2
1,335	5.1	219,109	4.4	218,500	4.5	609	.3	3
1,390	8.4	118,704	2.4	136,900	2.8	18,196	13.3	4
525	3.2	145,888	3.0	138,900	2.9	6,988	5.0	5
878	5.1	155,940	3.2	141,900	3.0	14,040	9.9	6
291	3.5	69,307	1.4	68,000	1.4	1,307	1.9	7
344	4.0	79,413	1.6	71,200	1.5	8,213	11.5	8
818	12.4	54,108	1.1	54,200	1.1	92	.2	9
677	3.3	173,561	3.5	168,600	3.5	4,961	2.9	10
3,274	1.7	1,599,581	32.4	1,554,700	32.3	44,881	2.9	11
								12
775	5.8	186,012	3.8	162,700	3.4	23,312	14.3	13
531	3.9	184,314	3.7	167,900	3.4	16,414	9.8	14
598	3.0	243,805	4.9	243,100	5.1	705	.3	15
398	5.5	84,268	1.7	88,200	1.8	3,932	4.5	16
790	6.7	130,820	2.6	144,700	3.0	13,880	9.6	17
236	2.0	150,777	3.1	143,500	3.0	7,277	5.1	18
952	1.2	979,996	19.8	950,100	19.8	29,896	3.1	19
								20
1,092	7.2	163,009	3.3	163,600	3.4	591	.4	21
99	.7	152,115	3.1	153,000	3.2	885	.6	22
.31	.4	77,807	1.6	78,900	1.7	1,093	1.4	23
655	9.4	71,275	1.5	75,200	1.5	3,925	5.2	24
101	1.8	66,480	1.3	60,800	1.3	5,680	9.3	25
508	8.6	70,432	1.4	63,400	1.3	7,032	11.1	26
1,268	2.3	601,118	12.2	594,900	12.4	6,218	1.0	27
								28
400	2.2	215,398	4.4	200,300	4.1	15,098	7.5	29
401	3.0	158,717	3.2	143,000	3.0	15,717	11.0	30
892	6.2	149,605	3.0	156,600	3.2	6,995	4.5	31
442	4.2	115,512	2.4	113,900	2.4	1,612	1.4	32
9	.1	140,213	2.8	141,900	3.0	1,687	1.2	33
130	1.0	140,030	2.8	136,100	2.8	3,930	2.9	34
315	3.4	101,014	2.1	99,600	2.1	1,414	1.4	35
787	.9	1,020,489	20.7	991,400	20.6	29,089	2.9	36
								37
984	9.9	92,716	1.9	94,600	1.9	1,884	2.0	38
148	1.9	82,431	1.7	76,000	1.6	6,431	8.5	39
1,828	24.1	70,064	1.4	72,700	1.5	2,636	3.6	40
9	.1	137,017	2.8	138,700	2.9	1,683	1.2	41
34	.3	110,754	2.2	94,400	2.0	16,354	17.3	42
2,639	5.3	492,982	10.0	476,400	9.9	16,582	3.5	43
								44
642	4.2	149,706	3.0	146,800	3.1	2,906	2.0	45
689	9.2	77,312	1.6	72,200	1.5	5,112	7.1	46
234	11.7	17,289	.3	19,200	.4	1,911	10.0	47
1,565	6.3	244,307	4.9	238,200	5.0	6,107	2.6	48
								49
								50
2,671	.5	4,938,473	100.0	4,805,700	100.0	132,773	2.8	51
								52
								53
		Prepared by:		R. Jones, Budget Supervisor				54
				September 22, 19				55
								56
								57

Figure 4-1. (Continued.)

2. Inventory budget report.
3. Cost-of-production budget report.
4. Orders received, shipments, production, inventory, and balance-order budget report.
5. Factory departmental cost budget report.
6. Selling expense budget report.
7. Advertising expense budget report.
8. Administrative expense budget report.
9. Other operating income and expense budget report.
10. Nonoperating income and expense budget report.
11. Profit and loss budget report.

12. Gain or loss in control report.
13. Capital or major expense budget report.
14. Cash budget report.

These reports are discussed on the following pages.

Sales budget reports. A period and year-to-date comparison of actual with budgeted *dollar sales* (shipments) showing variance from budget in dollars and per cent should be prepared:

1. By product class.
2. By sales territory by product class.
3. By sales territory by salesman.
4. By principal customers.

A typical sales budget report by product class is shown in Figure 4-1.

A quarterly and year-to-date comparison of actual with budgeted *unit sales* (shipments), showing variance from budget in units and per cent, should be prepared by individual products, arranged into product class groups.

Inventory budget report. This report provides a period comparison of actual with budgeted dollar inventories by product class, showing variance in dollars and per cent. It should be reviewed in conjunction with the corresponding summary dollar sales budget report by product class and the cost-of-production budget report by product class to determine whether inventory variations from budget expectancy are due to sales and/or production performance.

Cost-of-production budget report. This report provides a period and year-to-date comparison of actual with budgeted cost of production by product class showing variance in dollars and per cent. If cost of production for both actual and budget-reporting purposes is stated in terms of standard rather than actual costs, variances due to absorption of plant capacity, price of labor and material, and efficiency of operation are eliminated. Therefore, any variance from budget would be due to changes in the product mix and/or volume of products produced.

Orders received, shipments, production, inventory, and balance-order budget report. This report shows by period and year-to-date, unit orders received, unit shipments versus budget, unit production versus budget, unit inventories (finished goods) on hand, and unit balance orders on hand for each significant item carried in each of the company's product classes.

The importance and value of this report for proper coordination of sales and manufacturing activities cannot be overemphasized. It is a "must" for every well operated company.

Factory departmental cost budget reports. These reports are required for the effective control of the various costs of operating the factory. They provide for period and year-to-date comparison of actual with budgeted expense showing variance in dollars and per cent. The principal reports should include:

1. Summary of cost by factory departments and cost centers.
2. Summary of cost by expense classification.
3. Factory department cost by expense classification.
4. Factory cost-center cost by expense classification.

The factory operating expense budgets may be developed either on the basis of the budgeted production load, in which case they would be set up for the entire budget period in advance, or on the basis of predetermined expense standards for various levels of departmental operation. In the latter case the budget allowance would be computed immediately after the close of each reporting period.

Although the above budget reports are expressed in dollars of cost, unit measurement of certain expenses may provide a more effective control. Machine-hours, man-hours, kilowatt-hours, pounds of steam and air, gallons of water, and pounds of material are examples of unit measurements. Where the expense item lends itself to such measurement, the dollar budget measurements should be supplemented with appropriate unit budget measurements.

Selling expense budget reports. These reports afford a period and year-to-date comparison of actual with budgeted sales expense, showing variance in dollars and per cent. The following reports are important in controlling selling expenses:

1. Summary of sales division by sales department and sections.
2. Summary of sales division by expense classification.
3. Sales department by expense classification.
4. Sales departmental section by expense classification.

Advertising expense budget reports. The following reports should afford an effective period and year-to-date comparison of actual with budgeted advertising expense and show variance in dollars and per cent.

1. Summary of advertising department by expense classification.
2. Summary of advertising program by individual advertising projects.
3. Individual advertising projects by advertising cost breakdown; for example, layout, art work, engraving, printing, space cost, mailing, and the like.

Administrative expense budget reports. Period and year-to-date comparison of actual with budgeted administrative expense, showing variations in dollars and per cent, is provided by the following reports.

1. Summary of administrative division by administrative department and sections.
2. Summary of administrative division by expense classification.
3. Administrative department by expense classification.
4. Administrative departmental section by expense classification.

Other operating income and expense budget report. This affords a period and year-to-date comparison of actual with budgeted performance showing variations in dollars and per cent, itemized by "other operating income and expense" accounts.

Nonoperating income and expense budget report. This report provides a period and year-to-date comparison of actual with budgeted performance, showing variations in dollars and per cent, itemized by nonoperating income and expense accounts.

Profit and loss budget reports. The following profit and loss budget reports are advocated for proper control.

1. Period and year-to-date comparison of actual with budgeted performance showing variations in dollars and per cent:
   (a) Profit and loss budget statement for company.
   (b) Profit and loss budget statement by plant.
   (c) Profit and loss budget statement by product class.
   (d) Profit and loss budget statement by sales territory and/or major customers (optional).
2. Quarterly (or semi-annual) statement of actual performance showing net sales, cost of sales, gross operating margin, selling and administrative expense, and net operating margin for each individual product. These "one-line" individual product profit and loss statements ordinarily show no budget comparisons, because the primary purpose is to highlight "loss" items for consideration by management. However, it is both feasible and practical to show the corresponding budgets of net sales, cost of sales, and so on, if the number of product items is small and individual items possess sufficient volume to justify the time and expense involved.

"Gain or loss in control" report. This report, which shows a comparison of actual period and year-to-date expense variations from budget with allowable expense variations from the budget, points up the areas and elements of expense that call for better control by management. It indicates needed reductions or increases in various primary and secondary expense accounts to keep operations in line with actual sales performance. Consideration must, of course, be given to the effect of cost variations arising from a different product mix than was budgeted for sale.

Capital or major expense budget report. This report provides a period and year-to-date comparison of actual dollar expenditures made against each capital or major expense work project for which an individual budget appropriation has been approved. It also shows the unexpended dollar balance of each individual budget appropriation and the per cent of budget appropriation expended. If possible, the percentage of completion of each project should be estimated by the engineers or personnel responsible for carrying out the project. Comparison of per cent of budget expended with estimated percentage of completion affords a quick advance check on whether the budget appropriation will be sufficient to cover the probable expenditures and approximately how much the budget appropriation will be either under- or overexpended.

For purposes of proper analysis, it is desirable that the budgeted projects be segregated and summarized by location, for example, plant or office, as well as by nature of expense (capital additions or replacements, development, repairs, or inventory).

Further desirable segregations include the summarization of work projects open at the beginning of the period, authorized during the period, closed out during the period, and open at the end of the period so that open balances and performance from month to month may be watched.

Cash budget report. This report is of particular significance to a company operating on a minimum or low cash position. It provides a period comparison of actual cash income and expenditures by account or account group with budgeted cash income and expenditures, showing variance in both dollars and per cent and indicating actual versus budgeted cash balance at the end of the period. Ordinarily, a projection of the cash forecast by period covering the ensuing three or six months is included as part of this budget report. A typical cash budget report is shown in Figure 4-2.

MAKING THE BUDGET PROGRAM FUNCTION

Distribution of budget reports. The president should normally receive only summary budget reports covering all phases of company operations. The controller or chief budget officer, of course, will have access to all budget reports.

Each functional vice-president or divisional head (sales, manufacturing, engineering, purchasing, accounting, and so on) shall receive *all budget reports* directly pertaining to the operations of his respective division. In addition, he should receive such general corporate profit and loss, capital or major expense, and cash reports as are useful in appraising the operations of his particular division. In a large company, of course, such functional heads would receive only summary budget reports, but would have access as well as all detailed budget reports covering their respective divisions.

Plant managers should receive only those budget reports that pertain to the operations of their respective plants, *plus* their respective plant portion of the capital or major expense budget report.

Departmental managers and supervisors should receive only those budget reports that pertain to their respective departments or sections. Departmental sales managers, of course, should receive both their respective departmental and product class profit and loss budget statements.

Analysis and review of budget reports. The budget director or members of his staff should analyze all significant variances between actual and budgeted performance and prepare a written statement of the reasons for each such variance to accompany each budget report at the time it is issued.

At least once each period, the president and his functional vice-presidents or divisional heads should meet with the budget director to review the over-all performance of the company.

At least once each period, each functional vice-president and his respective department heads should meet with the budget director to review the performance of his division.

At least once each period, each plant manager and his departmental supervisors should meet with the vice-president or functional head of manufacturing and the budget director to review the performance of the plant as a whole and of the respective plant departments.

At least twice each period, and preferably once each week, the plant manager and the plant budget supervisor should meet with each departmental supervisor and with those foremen whose departments or sections show sufficient variation from the budget to indicate a lack of control.

XYZ CO.   Form 562   (Figures in 1,000's of dollars)   CASH BUDGET REPORT   PERIOD 9 * ENDING (SUNDAY)   September 30, 19—

ITEM	CURRENT PERIOD				PERIOD NUMBER AND DATE ENDING		BUDGET — BY PERIODS				NOTES
	ACTUAL	BUDGET	OVER OR UNDER	%	10 Oct.10	11 Nov.7	12 Dec.5	13 Jan.2	1 Jan.30	2 Feb.27	
Net Debits to Accts. Rec. (Memo)	504	522	18	3	571	591	575	573	564	553	
Collections from Accts. Rec.	492	516	24	5	506	573	625	675	503	578	
Net Hourly Payroll	203	199	4	2	208	287	235	227	222	224	
Net Salary Payroll	61	61	-	-	61	61	61	62	62	62	
Federal & State Unemployment	-	-	-	-	-	10	10	-	21	-	
Federal Old Age Tax	-	-	-	-	-	18	-	-	18	-	
Raw Material Purchases	49	57	8	14	62	24	39	32	34	28	
Direct Supplies	44	36	8	22	48	52	51	51	51	51	
Indirect Supplies	57	49	8	17	67	63	64	63	63	61	
Freight	9	10	1	10	10	10	10	10	10	10	
Selling & Administrative Expense	21	23	2	9	24	25	24	25	20	22	
Capital Equipment Purchases	9	12	3	25	35	19	6	8	8	5	
Insurance	5	4	1	25	2	24	6	3	1	7	
Taxes	2	1	1	-	56	9	2	48	1	2	
Other Operating Disbursements	4	1	2	100	2	9	2	91*	1	2	*Employee Bonus
Total Operating Disbursements	463	454	9	2	575	604	493	626	515	473	
Net Operating Cash Change	29	62	33	53	69	31	132	49	12	105	
Royalty Income	4	3	1	33	3	3	3	3	3	3	
Interest Income	-	-	-	-	4	3	3	4	3	-	
Dividend Income	-	-	-	-	35	-	-	-	25	-	
Sale of Investments, Property, etc.	-	1	1	-	-	14	1	1	-	-	Sale-Tenant Home
Other Non Operating Income	4	4	-	-	43	18	4	8	20	4	
Total Non Operating Income											
Investments Acquired	52	52	-	-	-	-	12	-	-	12	Purchase-U.S. Treas. Notes
Interest Payments	12	12	-	-	-	-	-	-	-	-	
Note & Loan Retirement	-	-	-	-	20	-	20	-	-	-	
Dividends Paid	-	-	-	-	26	-	26	-	-	-	
Other Non Operating Disbursements	2	2	1	50	2	2	2	2	2	2	
Total Non Operating Disbursements	67	66	1	2	48	2	14	48	2	14	
Net Cash Change	34	-	34	-	74	15	122	9	15	95	
Previous Cash Balance	526	526	-	-	492	418	403	525	534	549	
New Cash Balance	492	526	34	6	418	403	525	534	549	644	

* Company operates on a 13-period calendar.

Italicized figures appear in red.

Prepared by: R. Jones, Budget Supervisor
September 22, 19—

Figure 4-2. Cash Budget Report.

It is the function of the budget director to report to his superior any failure on the part of any functional vice-president, plant manager, department head, or supervisor to take corrective action agreed upon at any of the above meetings and the reason for such failure. His superior, who may be the controller, discusses the situation with other responsible functional vice-presidents or divisional heads, and if necessary action is not forthcoming, he reports the failure to the president for final adjudication.

Revision of budget program. Under the budgetary procedure previously outlined, it should not be necessary to revise most of the basic budgets more often than once each year or at the time when a new budget is established for the ensuing budget year. As pointed out, it is possible under the budgetary system outlined to calculate and grant budget allowances to one division to compensate for minor failures of another division. Only in cases where an extreme variation or change in selling prices, material, or labor costs develops within the budget year should a revision in the basic yearly budgets be necessary. Experience proves that frequent revisions of basic yearly budgets are fatal to a budgetary system. Not only are the end goals upon which the budgets were originally based forgotten and no attempt made to coordinate toward the best solution of a common task, but also even those charged with preparing and administering the budget itself grow complacent and lose interest in the program. Finally, no divisional head is held accountable for his performance, and no one particularly cares how those whom he supervises perform. When this point is reached, the usefulness of the budget, *the single most valuable and comprehensive operating tool developed to this day for the use of progressive corporate management,* is destroyed.

5

Setting Standard Costs

CONTENTS

5

Setting Standard Costs

GENERAL ASPECTS OF SETTING STANDARD COSTS

Approach to the subject. The subject of setting standard costs, as developed in this chapter, should meet the needs of any executive interested in knowing what the adoption of a standard cost system would mean for his company. It assumes he has a very limited knowledge of the subject of standard costs, but a basic knowledge of cost accounting. This chapter will answer, for him, such fundamental questions as:

1. What are standard costs?
2. Why should a company consider adopting a standard cost plan?
3. What must be done to fit a standard cost plan into an already going organization?
4. How should standards be set, and on what?
5. How is standard cost information used in the accounts?
6. What sort of records, in general, are required to support a standard cost plan?

Definitions. Those concerned with the problem must deal first with standards, second with cost standards, third with standard costs, and fourth with the standard cost system. Definition of these terms, at the outset, is essential.

Standard. An established measure of extent, quality, or value; an example for comparison; a criterion of excellence.

Cost Standard. Standard cost of any item, activity or operation, set after careful analysis and established by authority as a rule for measuring and comparing.

Standard cost. The cost of products, activities, or operations, based on computation of the unit of cost at the cost standard.

Standard cost system. A planned procedure whereby cost performance of all activities, costs of product, and end results are compared with standards (or predicted results), and variations of actual costs from standard costs, and the reasons therefor, are determined.

Need for standard costs. Lord Kelvin has been credited with this remark: ''When you can measure what you are speaking of, and express it in numbers, you know something about it. When you cannot, . . . your knowledge is of a meager and unsatisfactory kind.'' It is equally true, however, that mere knowledge of a numerical value leaves much to be desired. That value cannot be measured in terms of itself. This latter statement contains an indictment of cost accounting, and its results, prior to the introduction and use of standard costs. The answer was always: "It cost so much." There was no basis for: "It cost so much, *but*, that is more or less than it should have cost." Moreover, cost information was available only after the expenditure had been made and recorded and was seldom deliberately predetermined, as with standards.

In the last analysis, all business problems are cost problems. Decisions are made, almost without exception, on the basis of a cost determination. Of what significance is this in a discussion of standard costs? Every decision made, every course of action accepted is, whether formally acknowledged as such or not, a standard. The only step remaining is to acknowledge the real nature of these decisions and integrate them into the unified whole of a standard cost plan, thus enhancing their effectiveness. In the face of these realities the reluctance to adopt standard costs is mystifying; yet, even now, the attitude of many executives is: "It's fine for them but it won't work for us."

It is true that standard costs function more easily in some businesses than in others. The major advantages and objections which may influence a decision as to whether to adopt a standard cost plan are summarized below.

Advantages of standard costs. The following are some of the advantages to be enjoyed as soon as a standard cost plan has started to operate.

1. When performance equals or betters the standard, the achievement is noted, *but*, when it is worse than standard, the result stands out like a red lantern in an open ditch. Thus, the principal benefits are derived from taking fullest advantage of the exception principle of management.

2. The immediate appearance of off-standard conditions means the cause can be attacked in time. Data that permit this are dynamic. The figures are living and breathing.

3. Standard costs place the emphasis on performance rather than on cost of product. In the last analysis, cost of product is the sum of the cost of those activities required to make and sell that product. If the cost of the activities is under control, so is the cost of the product.

4. In view of 3 above, sales prices can be set with a greater degree of assurance. The sales department can have more faith in the cost data used to set prices.

5. Standard costs are a scientific approach to the control of costs. The inefficiencies that tend to lower plant productivity and the effectiveness of sales efforts can be nipped in the bud.

6. Recording and control of materials is greatly simplified. A standard cost plan is cheap to operate and, properly conceived, is extremely simple.

7. Since the emphasis of standard costs is laid on control of activities, and activities, in turn, are the responsibility of individuals, the entire organization tends to become "cost conscious." This psychology is fundamental to any business progress at any time. When the road is rocky, cost consciousness is essential to the very existence of the company.

Objections to standard costs. Two objections most frequently advanced against the use of standard costs follow.

1. A standard cost plan is claimed impractical for a company that manufactures and sells a large variety of products. Standards must sometimes be

changed. If there are numerous products, it is claimed, all changes cannot be made as quickly as necessary. There is, therefore, a lag in reflecting altered conditions.

2. Some executives feel that, in a business where manufacture is partially or entirely to customers' specifications, it is not possible to adopt standard costs because no two products are alike. In practice, a number of companies that manufacture numerous products, primarily to customers' specifications, have successfully used standards.

Relationship of standards and budgets. It is possible to develop and apply a practical system of budgetary control without standard costs. However, if standards already exist, the problem of establishing budgets is greatly simplified. Actually, there is no fundamental difference between a "budget" and a "standard." Both have their roots in the idea of predetermination; both operate on the "exception" principle.

When both "standards" and budgets" are in use, they are mutually supporting. Some of the uses of standard costs in the budgeting process have been indicated previously. On the other hand, budgets may be used for setting standards in the area of overhead costs. The studies required to establish the basic data for either budgets or standards in these areas are identical in approach. The application of the data to determination of standard cost of product is peculiar to this chapter. Both aspects will be treated in the necessary detail. It will be assumed that budgets do not exist.

Preparing for standard costs. Proper organization is basic to the success of a standard cost plan, but it is a preliminary most likely to be overlooked. To test whether an organization is prepared to consider adoption of a standard cost system, these questions should be answered:

1. Is there an organization chart or manual? Such a chart or manual is essential.
2. Are the duties and responsibilities of each executive, from top to bottom, clearly defined and fully understood? They should be.
3. Are there any points at which duties and responsibilities overlap, creating opportunities for "buck-passing"? If there are, they should be eliminated.

It is not necessary to tear an existing organization up by the roots in preparing for standard costs. This can often result in more harm than good. The present organization may be suitable as a starting point, or it may be made so with minor adjustments. If changes in organization are needed, they will come to light when an attempt is made to set standards for the various activities. If it does not show up then, the need will come to light in poor performance. This thought must be kept uppermost in the minds of those dealing with the problem of standard costs: No mechanism, no matter how perfect, will manage a business. Management must manage. On the other hand, a management with no goal and no definite responsibilities has difficulty making the grade.

Basic information required. The solution of any problem necessitates two separate and distinct steps: (1) analysis, or resolution of the problem into its component parts; and (2) synthesis, or assembly of the solutions to all parts into an *organized* whole.

Analysis. No complete list of everything that must be determined can be given. Such a list would range from a few items for a relatively simple business to many for the most complicated. For general guidance, however, the following can be given as the *type* of information required. Regardless of the number of products being manufactured, whether one or many, it is essential to know:

1. The kinds of material involved.
2. The manufacturing processes involved.
3. The marketing or sales methods involved.

If more than one product is manufactured, it is essential to arrive at a natural grouping of the products from the standpoint of similarity of materials, manufacturing processes, and marketing and sales methods. If the groupings by materials and manufacturing methods are not consistent with the groupings by sales methods, it may be necessary to establish one grouping for developing manufacturing cost standards and another for developing selling and administrative cost standards.

Moreover, where there are several products, it is necessary to evaluate the factor of "sales mix." This term may be defined as the percentage relationship each product manufactured and sold bears to the total of all products. Sales mix must be considered in the setting of standards for both manufacturing and selling and administration expenses.

Synthesis. This step consists of setting standards, in detail, for all cost elements. Before explaining the process, it is necessary to examine the nature of standards.

Types of standards. There are two general types of standards: (1) current or attainable standards, and (2) basic standards. Each of these is explained below.

Current or attainable standards. This type of standard reflects the performance that might be expected in the period for which the standards are set. They may be defined as the standards representing what costs should be under the prevailing circumstances. They are generally regarded as real costs, to the point of being incorporated in the books of account and carried through to the financial statements. Such standards are real costs because they are set to reflect a performance which, theoretically at least, is possible of attainment.

Several kinds of current standards have been recognized. The selection of one of them is dictated by the level of operations it is desired to reflect in the costs. These levels may be (1) expected actual, (2) normal, and (3) ideal.

Expected actual represents the costs that should be realized if prices for labor and material are as anticipated, if their use is as efficient as anticipated, and if sales and production volumes are as anticipated. From this it is obvious that performance may be better or worse than anticipated. Variations from standard, therefore, may be favorable or unfavorable.

Normal represents the costs that should be realized if prices paid for labor and material are normal, if normal efficiency in their uses is obtained, and the level of operations is normal. The not-so-obvious consideration here is: "What is normal?" An acceptable definition may be given as the average taken over a period of time sufficiently long to eliminate all seasonal and cyclical variations. Generally, such a normal is determined by statistical methods. Variations from standards set on this concept may be considered as reflecting deviations from normal material and labor prices, normal efficiency, and normal sales and production volumes.

Ideal represents the costs that should be realized if prices for labor and materials are the best possible, efficiency is the best possible, and the best possible sales and production volumes are realized. Variations from an ideal standard are always unfavorable and reflect only deviations from an ideal.

The current types of standards have this in common: They must be changed from time to time as conditions change. The frequency of change will be controlled by many factors, of which the most important are:

1. Extent of changes in conditions as revealed by size of variances caused by changed conditions rather than efficiency. How much of a given variance is really due to efficiency and how much is due to changed conditions will be revealed by analysis of the variance.
2. The clerical job involved in a change of standards, partial or complete.
3. The personal preference of the responsible executive, who will probably base his decision primarily on factors 1 and 2.

As a general rule, standards need not be changed *completely* more than once each year. This is especially true where standards for certain of the costs are changed as a matter of routine (for example, time study calls for a change in the incentive rate for a given job; obviously the new rate is paid at once). Moreover, when a complete change is made, it should be done at the close of an accounting period. This is fundamental in using current standards. Current or attainable standards must be changed occasionally, or they cease to be a reflection of what costs *should* be.

Basic standards. These may be defined as the standards that reflect what costs are at the time the standards are set. They are changed only when there is some fundamental change in product or existing methods of manufacture. They are, in essence, a statistical index number.

Consideration in selecting a type of standard. The important consideration in selecting a type of standard is not: ''What type of standard is this?'' but: ''Is it wholly realistic for the situation? Does it reflect conditions peculiar to the business and, equally important, to the organization?'' To put this point another way, orthodoxy is the poorest criterion of a good standard. The management is not attempting to measure and control the activities of a hypothetical and nonexistent organization. The tendency to create accounting fictions must be studiously avoided. Use the type of standard that accomplishes the desired end, the one that best serves as a means to measure and control the cost of doing business so that the largest net profit is realized.

Just as some companies use more than one type of current standard, others use both basic and current standards. The latter companies measure actual performance against current standards for controlling day-to-day operations and measure either actual or current standards against basic standards to develop cost trends. Data on trends are primarily of interest to higher management.

Who sets the standards? This question is of equal importance with the question: ''What kind of standards?'' Again, no hard and fast procedure can be laid down to cover each situation. Here, too, circumstances alter cases. There are, however, certain rules that cannot be overlooked in any case.

The ultimate responsibility for setting standards rests with top management, and the work must be done under its general direction. However, it may be delegated to a standards committee made up of certain executives, to the budget director, to the controller, or to whoever in the organization is best placed to carry on the work. Very large organizations often have a standards department, complete with permanent staff of experts who do all the work.

The work of setting standards in detail is carried on by those in the organization who have the most intimate knowledge of the particular activity or cost. For example, (1) standards for material usage are set by the engineering department; (2) material price standards are set by the purchasing department; (3) time standards for labor are set by the time study engineer; and (4) selling expenses by the sales manager.

The cost accountant generally does not, and in fact should not, set standards. His contribution to this work is indispensable but should be limited to furnishing information from the cost records and acting in an advisory capacity. He is the one best fitted to recommend the types of standards and procedures and to portray the company's needs for cost data. He may be the logical one to assemble and summarize the completed work.

Whoever sets the standards has an obligation that must be discharged, lest the effort expended in setting standards go for naught; he must be sure that the persons responsible for performance under the standards have something to say about how they are set. If standards are to work, the need for them and their purpose must be fully understood by those who will be affected by them.

SETTING STANDARDS FOR COST ELEMENTS

Cost elements for which standards are set. Standards for the following elements of cost are discussed in this section.

1. Direct material.[1]
2. Direct labor.
3. Variable expenses:
   (a) manufacturing.
   (b) selling (distribution).
   (c) administrative.
4. Fixed expenses:
   (a) manufacturing.
   (b) selling (distribution).
   (c) administrative.

---

[1]"Direct material" is used rather than "raw material" for several reasons. In many complex manufacturing processes, it is necessary to consider material usage at more than one point in the process. Thus, where parts are manufactured, then assembled, and, finally, the assemblies and other parts combined into the finished product, the problem of use standards arises at each point in the manufacturing process. Automobiles, typewriters, calculating machines, refrigerators, and other products of this type are examples. The same thing is true where a variety of materials are combined into a given mixture and the resultant is then used in the manufacture of end-products, as in the manufacture of rubber, plastics, steel, iron castings, brass, etc. For the foregoing reasons, "raw material" is a term too limited in connotation for use in this discussion.

Standards for all these elements must be developed with two purposes in mind: (1) the use of standards for controlling costs; and (2) the use of the same standards to develop unit product costs for establishing selling prices or other purposes. The term "unit of product," as it is used in this chapter, refers to a finished product in the form in which it is offered for sale. For example, a manufacturer of refrigerators would have a standard unit product cost for each type and size of refrigerator in the line.

The following discussion deals entirely with the development of standards for controlling costs. Standards for the unit cost of a product are derived from the control standards for material, direct labor, manufacturing expenses, selling and distribution expenses, and administrative expenses. How the unit product cost is determined is described later.

Setting standards for direct material. Three kinds of standards are established for direct material.

1. Used standard.
2. Price standard.
3. Type and quality standard.

The third, which is most fundamental, is nevertheless sometimes slighted. It is the most logical starting point for this discussion.

Type and quality standards. This is a subject not always mentioned in discussions of cost standards for direct materials, probably for two reasons: (1) standard costs are often considered to be in the field of the cost accountant, and, since type and quality do not deal directly with money values, the cost accountant, it is concluded, is not concerned with them; and (2) the work required to arrive at type and quality standards is primarily that of the production or engineering departments and it is taken for granted that someone has done it.

No reason for overlooking this aspect of setting direct material standards can be valid. The person responsible for setting standard costs *cannot* assume that anyone else has looked into type and quality standards. He must be prepared to find the answers to such questions as:

1. How many and what kinds of basic materials enter into the product?
2. How many variations (size or quality) of any given material are being used and can the number of variations in any given material be reduced?
3. It is essential that so many kinds and grades of materials be used or should there be greater concentration on certain materials?
4. Is too high a quality of material being used where a lower quality would satisfy?
5. In an assembly product, one, for example, for which there are different models of the same basic device, are all possible parts interchangeable?

In a given business, many more similar questions would need answering. However, those mentioned are the fundamental ones. They may be applied even to a business that makes everything to customers' specifications. Although, in such a business, the form or completeness of the product may vary from job to job, the basic materials are usually the same general kinds.

A number of advantages accrue from setting standards for type and quality of materials. To name a few:

1. Concentration on fewer materials or varieties of the same material may result in paying lower prices for large purchases and, possibly, getting better deliveries. Both are cost factors, the latter especially in periods of material shortages.
2. Inventories contain fewer items and are easier to control, both as to size and turnover.
3. Where interchangeable parts are a factor, more widespread use of a given part means longer production runs, with fewer setups and other costs incident to changing jobs for both machines and workers.

It is possible to set standard costs without going into the question of type and quality standards as such, but any preliminary study of the product will generally reveal the need for such standards. Furthermore, type and quality standards should be set because experience dictates that to get everything from standards, everything should be standardized.

Material use standards. Another name for this standard is "material quantity specifications." When the types of material that enter into a product are known, the next question becomes, how much?

Use standards, like type and quality standards, are in the field of the engineer. The problem may be simple or complex, depending on the type of product and the number and variety of the materials entering into it, as well as the manufacturing processes involved. By definition, a use standard is the quantity of direct material required to make a given unit of finished product.

The material use standard must take into account certain material losses which represent materials bought and paid for that do not appear as salable product. These are generally considered unavoidable losses and are usually referred to as waste or shrinkage. The exact nature and extent of these unavoidable losses is determined by the materials used and the manufacturing processes employed. Volatile liquids will disappear through evaporation, no matter how carefully stored and handled. Turning a piece of bar stock into a screw machine will inevitably result in chips. When blanks are punched from a piece of strip steel, a "skeleton" will remain. These are typical examples of unavoidable material losses. In each situation an analysis must be made to determine what can cause these unavoidable losses.

There is another form of material loss that arises simply because men and machines are not perfect. This is generally referred to as "scrap." It is not taken into the material use standard because it is generally considered avoidable. It is of most importance in the control of manufacturing costs. This can be said in passing, however: General practice in setting standards does make some allowance for such losses, but such allowances are included in the standards for variable factory overhead or burden.

Fitting material use standards to the pattern. Earlier in this chapter the different types of standards were described as basic or current, the latter having further subdivisions into ideal, normal, and expected actual. The essential difference among them, it was pointed out, lay in the degree of performance assumed for the purpose of setting standards. Once the selection of a type has been made, standards for the various elements of cost must be tailored to fit the general pattern implied by the choice as closely as possible.

In setting material use standards, the chosen type influences the allowances made for waste and shrinkage, according to the basic or current types, as follows.

Basic type. By definition, these standards reflect the conditions pertaining at the time the standards are set. Thus, whatever waste and shrinkage was taking place when the standard was set would be included in the use standard. Changes would be made only under the conditions set forth previously.

Ideal (current type). Allowances for waste and shrinkage would be made at the lowest level believed possible of attainment.

Normal (current type). Allowances for waste and shrinkage would be made at a level that usually represents an average of past experience over a long period.

Expected actual (current type). Allowances for waste and shrinkage would be made at the level of efficiency in material use expected to prevail.

Direct material price standards. Some means must be provided to translate material types, quality, and quantity into the language of all business, dollars and cents. This is the function of the direct material price standard. As the name implies, it is the monetary value assigned to the various units in which physical quantities of materials are measured—pounds, gallons, tons, feet, and so on. Like direct material use standards, these price standards are influenced by the selected pattern. Considerations are as follows:

Basic type. The prices paid for the materials at the time the standards are set, changed only under the conditions set forth previously.

Ideal (current type). At the level considered ideal for the purposes. Practically, this type of material price standard serves little useful purpose. It presumes, first, that the buyer using it is *the* major influence in the markets for the materials used. This is seldom, if ever, true under our economic system. Second, it would involve setting prices at a level usually far below the market, or, in other words, at an unrealistic level. Thus, although this type of standard may be used for other purposes, it is not practical for material prices.

Normal (current type). At the level that represents the normal price level in the markets for the materials in question. This may be established with elaborate statistical techniques, or it may be only a simple averaging process. Obviously, any techniques must be supported by sound individual judgment.

Expected actual (current type). At the prices expected to be paid for the quantities and qualities of materials purchased during the period for which the standards are set. Where a company contracts for materials over a considerable period ahead, this is an easy matter, particularly where there are no escalator clauses in the agreements. Otherwise, it becomes a matter of judging what the market will be.

Setting standards for direct labor. Basically, the problem of setting standards for direct labor is similar to that for setting material standards. There are three kinds of standards established for direct labor: (1) labor time standards—quantity; (2) labor rate standards—price; (3) working condition standards. Actually 3 should precede 1 and 2. They will, therefore, be considered in that order.

Standards for working conditions. If a type designation were assigned to these standards, it might be the ideal. That, however, would be perfection and impossible of attainment. What should be aimed at are the best possible provisions for:

1. Layout of plant.
2. Condition of equipment.
3. Location of work place.
4. Convenience of tools and materials to eliminate lost motion and increase workers' effectiveness.
5. Adequate facilities for workers' personal comfort.
6. Scheduling, routing, and control of materials to insure a steady flow of work material of the right kind, at the proper place, and on time.
7. Adequate job training or, if more appropriate, specific job instructions with each job.

Application of standards for direct labor without proper consideration of these factors is wasted effort. The variations from standard are not real measures of efficiency and cannot be analyzed to get at the underlying cause. In other words, unless working conditions are the best possible, variations from standard cannot be definitely identified as caused by either off-standard time or off-standard rates.

Time standards for direct labor. The element of time is the basis for all direct labor costs. Time is the unit of labor quantity whether expressed as "pieces per hour," "hours per piece," or in any other manner applicable to a given situation. Setting time standards involves a determination of the time required to complete each operation on each product under standard conditions of work.

Essentially such standards are "standards of labor usage." They are analogous to the "material use standards" previously described. Like those, they include allowances for losses considered unavoidable. Here, the losses are of time consumed by such factors as rest periods, material handling at the bench or machine, machine setup (unless this is considered as a separate operation), sharpening tools, or, in short, any factor inherent to the work being done.

Direct labor time standards may be set in one of several ways, or combinations of them. They may be derived from:

1. A study of past performance.
2. An advance estimate.
3. Time and motion study.

Although these methods are not equally scientific, each has its uses, as will be explained below.

Time standards based on study of past performance. This is primarily a method of averages. A study is made of past operation times shown on time tickets. If a job order cost system has been used in the past, the actual times for each operation should appear on the cost sheets. If so, these cost sheets may be used for data instead of time tickets. Such a study will usually show many instances of extreme variation in time for the same operation and product. These variations may result from a variety of causes such as machine breakdown, power failure, poor lots of material, and the like; or they may be caused by loafing on the job, lack of proper employee training or job instructions, or other purely human factors. Whatever the cause, they may be assumed to reflect unusual conditions and must be eliminated before the average is taken.

This method applies principally to a simple situation such as when (1) only one product is manufactured and the operations are not subject to frequent or radical change; or (2) there is more than one product, but the mix, or proportion of each, is fairly constant. Also, the operations are not subject to frequent or radical change.

Obviously, if a change in product or method of operation is made, past experience is not immediately available. The setting of standards by this method would have to be deferred until new experience has been accumulated.

Time standards based on estimates. As the term estimate implies, this is a forecast of the time to be taken in performing any given operation on any given product. Again, as the term implies, the exercise of judgement is assumed. In other words, the forecast has taken into account all factors that may be reasonably expected to affect the time element. This method of setting time standards has its greatest use where the product and labor operations are essentially non-repetitive. In any business of a job shop nature, where products are made to customers' specifications, no two alike in all respects, and where the order is received only after a price bid has been submitted, such estimates must be made to arrive at the selling price.

Estimated time standards should be established only after a thorough study of all relevant data. They must be based on a complete knowledge of what must be done and may be predicated, in whole or in part, on past experience with similar types of work. They will always include an allowance for the unforeseen.

Estimated time standards will always be subject to one important weakness, the interjection of the human element.

Time standards based on time and motion study. Many companies have applied time and motion study methods to the development of timing information for wage payment plans and for production planning, but for nothing else. It is, nevertheless, the best possible information on which to base time standards for establishment of standard direct labor costs.

Every complete labor operation is a composite of certain motions. Time study analyzes each operation to determine: (1) the separate and distinct motions that are fundamental to that operation under given conditions of work; and (2) the amount of time required for each of those motions. The techniques for making such studies cannot be explained here. The field of time and motion study has its own extensive writings. The end results, the by-products, and the general method, however, will be discussed.

The end results, of course, are the time standards on which all standard direct labor costs are based. Equally important are the by-products resulting from the manner in which time and motion study work is done. As each operation is resolved into its motions, the following conditions may be disclosed.

1. There are, or there are not, wasted motions. If there are, they may be caused by the factors surrounding the work location, such as improper placement of material and the like.
2. The worker has been inadequately trained or has not been given detailed instructions for his job. Accordingly, he has developed his own way of doing things and it may not be the best way.

3. The tools provided are not adequate. Perhaps there should be special-purpose wrenches, pliers, and the like.
4. There are excessive fatigue factors; for example, there may be a lack of mechanical material handling equipment, or the workers are standing instead of sitting.

This list, which is by no means complete, gives some idea of the type of inefficiencies that time and motion studies may bring to light.

The elimination of all undesirable conditions, however, is not a prerequisite for the establishment of standards by the time and motion study method. It may be possible to change some of the conditions as soon as they are discovered; others may have to wait. The standards set will take into account all the time allowances required to reflect what needs change and what cannot be changed at the moment. They will also make allowance for rest periods, time consumed in machine setup, and the like. They will, in short, be completely realistic. Thus, when variations from these standards appear, it may be determined what part of the variation is due to lack of efficiency and what part is due to other causes.

As was indicated, the operation is broken down into its component parts and the times established for these parts. The standard for the complete operation, then, is the sum of the times for all parts. The elements may be selected so that the accumulated time data may be used to construct tables of time for all operation elements likely to appear in any class of product that the company is equipped to undertake. Formulae may be derived to reflect changes in time resulting from changes in conditions surrounding the operation, changes due to size of the piece, kind of material, type of tool, type of machine, and the like. These formulae may be expressed as curves, tables, or schedules. Thus, when a new job appears, the time standard may be set by breaking it down into the elemental motions, finding the times from the standard data, and building up the standard by addition. This method is called the "standard data method," "synthetic time setting," and other names. Its application to many types of job shop manufacture is obvious. Estimates can be prepared with more assurance and standards can be applied to control direct labor cost as soon as the job is put into work.

Time and motion study has its fullest application in those industries where the manufacturing process may be broken down into a series of relatively simple, highly repetitive operations on a single product or a few basically similar products. This does not mean, however, that the method cannot be successfully applied under other conditions.

The wage payment plan in effect determines the manner in which time standards are set, if those time standards are going to be used as a basis for actual paying labor under the wage payment plan. In that case, good business judgment dictates the use of the time and motion study method for establishing time standards. If, however, labor is not to be paid on the basis of the time standards, more latitude is permitted in the choice of a method by which time standards are set. In either case, the wage payment plan must be considered as a special factor in determining the direct labor cost per unit.

Rate standards for direct labor. Direct labor rate standards are simply the means for translating time into money. It requires a combination of two standards, (1) labor quality standards and (2) labor rate standards, established in that order.

Labor quality standards. Labor quality standards are the same thing as job evaluation. It would be the unusual situation where only one grade of labor is employed. In fact, such a situation could apply only in a very small, very simple type of business. As more and more employees are required, the more diverse become the types and degrees of skill and experience required. The more complex the diversity, the greater the need for some means of classification, hence job evaluation.

Like time and motion study, job evaluation is a highly specialized field with its own extensive writings and a corps of practicing specialists. A simple description is sufficient for our needs. Job evaluation is the process of analyzing the manufacturing operations to determine the varying types and degrees of skill required, and then determining the extent of education, experience, training, physical demand, and similar factors required in the performance of each operation. It is essentially a means of providing a logical basis for wage rate differentials and for making possible a set of labor grade specifications.

It is not essential that the job evaluation be done by high-priced consultants or by a staff of employee experts as a formal program. This is expensive and the size of many companies does not justify the expenditure. It must, however, be done to some degree and, in fact, is done every day by the average businessman, as, for example, when he says: "We only need a machinist, not a toolmaker." Whoever makes such a statement has made a job evaluation, whether he is conscious of it or not.

Once the job evaluation has been set up, there is the corollary concern of fitting the individual to the job. This is the problem of personnel administration. Square pegs in round holes do not add up to standard performance.

Labor rate standards. Rates of pay must be established for each labor grade. This may involve more or less study, depending on the preference of the individual management. The essential consideration is that the rate be a fair index of the qualifications required on a given job, relative to all other jobs in the plant. Rates may be based on several factors, of which the following are typical:

1. The rates paid for comparable labor grades in the local market, particularly if there is a high degree of concentration of similar work in the locality.
2. The rates paid in a given industry over a broader area, if there is no concentration as in 1 above.
3. The average rates paid in the past, adjusted where necessary to reflect current conditions. The rates could be established by departments, or where various grades are required in a given department, further analysis by grades may be made. This method could be employed where management did not wish to make as complete a study as that implied by 1 and 2.
4. The rates written into a union contract.

Factors 1, 2, and 3 imply hiring under conditions of individual bargaining. Union contract rates usually reflect all three factors plus whatever results from labor and management negotiations.

SETTING STANDARDS FOR EXPENSES

Definition of expense. All costs necessary to run the business, but which are not made up of (1) costs of material that becomes part of the finished product (direct material) or (2) costs of labor performed directly on the product (direct labor), are included under the general classification "expenses." Expenses are referred to in various ways, typical among which are "overhead," "burden," and "loading." There is a tendency on the part of some people to think of expenses only as costs of taxes, depreciation, insurance, advertising, and similar costs. The term "expenses" actually connotes more than just these costs. It includes, in addition, all wage and salary costs and all material costs that cannot be assigned *directly* to a unit of product. Standards must be set for *all* these indirect costs.

Analysis of expense. The first step in setting standards for *any* cost is analysis, which, for expenses, must develop four major factors:

1. The functional character of the expense; that is, does it pertain to manufacturing, selling (distribution) or administration.
2. The origin of the various expenses; that is, are they wage and salary costs, material and supply costs, or other costs such as insurance, taxes and so on.
3. Responsibility for the expenses, by activity or department.
4. Degree of variability of expenses, or their tendency to move up or down, *in total*, in relation to some measure or index of the extent of effort or volume of work passing through the department or activity responsible for the expense.

The first three of these factors—classification of expenses by function, origin, and responsibility—are part of the problem of establishing a chart of accounts or accounting plan. The fourth factor, degree of variability, is a subject peculiar to the development of standard costs and is discussed in detail below.

Importance of accounting plan. The accounting plan, or chart of accounts, must be constructed to supply the information needed to satisfy requirements of taxing authorities, governmental agencies, and management. For management's purposes, the chart of accounts must be developed to show the amount spent by each responsible executive and to point out the profitable and unprofitable activities of the business. An explanation of how to set up primary and secondary accounts to accomplish these purposes is not within the scope of this chapter. However, the importance to standards of a well conceived accounting classification must be emphasized. A classification that does not permit a comparison of actual expenses with standards by individual responsibility can seriously hamper the effectiveness of standards.

The need for a clear definition of responsibility is obvious. By implication, responsibility for an activity means responsibility for cost of that activity as well as for the accomplishments. In fact, cost *versus* accomplishment is the essence of control through standards. It should cost a certain amount to accomplish certain results (a standard cost). Does it? Mr. "X" is in charge. If it costs more (unfavorable variance), he is responsible. If it costs less to accomplish those results (favorable variance), Mr. "X" gets the credit.

Degree of variability. Without a complete understanding of this subject and its implications standards for expenses cannot be properly developed or effectively applied. *All* costs have some characteristic of variability *in total* when measured against an appropriate index. This characteristic may range from complete to zero, depending on the nature of the cost. The three generally accepted classifications of variability are:

1. *Wholly variable.* The *total* cost moves up and down in exact, or "straight line" relationship to the index against which it is measured. By implication, the *cost per unit of the index* is constant.

2. *Fixed or relatively invariable.* The total cost is relatively unaffected by changes in the index against which it is measured. Although the term "fixed" cost has been used to describe these, it is better to think of them as fixed only in a relative sense, only in the sense that they are not wholly variable. The reasons for this will be more fully discussed when standards for this type of cost are explained.

3. *Partially variable or "semi-variable."* Those costs which are partially type 1 and partially type 2 are included here. For this discussion, the variable portion will be considered as part of type 1, and the "fixed" portion will be considered as part of type 2.

The analysis required to determine the index of variability and the degree of variability against that index is of major importance in the job of setting standards. It was not discussed in connection with direct material and direct labor since these are *direct* costs and the index is the unit of production. It *does* present a problem in the development of standards for expense since the costs are *indirect* in terms of units. Therefore, other indices must be used, depending on function and origin of cost.

In making the analysis of variability, reason, custom, and generally accepted practice may be used as a partial guide for determining the variable characteristics of certain expenses. Small tools, factory supplies, and defective product (scrap) costs are generally considered "wholly variable." Depreciation, taxes, and executive salaries are generally regarded as "fixed." A warning must be sounded, however, that what is wholly variable in one company may not be in another. The same expense may even show different characteristics of variability as between different departments of the same company.

COST BEHAVIOR

In order to determine the behavior of costs in given situations, one must first have an understanding of the basic distinctions between major elements of cost. When speaking of manufacturing costs, there are essentially two major segments which may be termed direct and indirect cost (Figure 5-1). Depending on the approach used in a given organization for financial reporting, direct cost is quite often interchanged with the term variable cost.

Direct cost is usually confined to elements of materials or effort necessary to the

MANUFACTURING COST BEHAVIOR—DEFINITIONS

GENERAL CLASSIFICATION	OTHER COMMON TERM	USUALLY INCLUDES	RELATIONSHIP TO PRODUCTION VALUE
Direct Cost	Variable Cost	Raw Materials. Packing Materials. Labor to Convert Raw Materials to Finished Bulk Product. Labor to Package Product. Fringe Benefits on Manufacturing Labor. Utilities Consumed in Manufacture of Product. Other Applicable Costs.	Generally may be quantitatively related to output and will usually vary in direct relation to production. Can be measured and controlled by specific reference to production. If any element is unavailable, product cannot be manufactured.
Indirect Cost	Overhead Period Expense Burden	Plant Management Salaries. Warehouse Labor. Office Labor. Maintenance Labor. Other Service Labor. Office Supplies. Maintenance Supplies. Sundry Contractual Services. Property Taxes and Insurance. Depreciation. Other Supplies and Miscellaneous Expense.	No direct relationship to production volume. Usually related to stages of operation. Generally fixed for a period of time. Product can usually be made if any one element is not available.

Figure 5-1. Manufacturing Cost Behavior—Definitions.

manufacture and availability for sale of a product in finished form. This category generally includes:

1. Raw materials from which the basic product is derived.
2. Packaging materials which are utilized to carry the product to the customers in its finished state and, very often, make the product more acceptable to the customer.
3. The labor utilized in converting the raw materials into a finished product. Within this category, are the labor time of machine operators, general factory labor used for transporting materials from department to department and labor occupied in packaging the product for movement to the market.
4. Further, since so much of direct cost results from labor time utilized, the fringe benefits associated with that labor would constitute an element of direct cost. Thus, we would have the FICA tax expense, pension expense, insurance and other related expenses.
5. In order to operate equipment and perform a manufacturing function, one must utilize sources of power, such as electricity, gas, and steam. Accordingly, the cost of utilities consumed in the manufacturing operation become a part of direct cost.
6. Finally, there may be certain specific costs not falling into the previous categories which can be treated as direct costs. One such example would be a cleaning agent which is required for use in relationship to a specific product or a specific center of production. The inclusion of this type of expense becomes, to a great extent, one of judgment on the part of management and how they feel such a cost should best be treated and will be understood in the financial reporting which results.

The justification for including the various segments described as part of direct cost, is generally that there is a direct relationship to production volume. Raw materials can always be quantitatively related to output and will usually vary in direct relation to production.

Packaging materials are relatable to production by the very nature of the packing utilized. As for example, product "Y" is packed in a case which will hold 24 tins of a given height and diameter. It is quite obvious that one case and 24 tins will be required for every "Z" number of pounds, depending on the weight filled into each tin.

Labor is relatable to production via determining the number of process hours to complete the manufacturing cycle for a product and with the knowledge of the number of personnel each has required to accomplish the manufacturing operation. Similarly, labor employed to package the product can be related to the number of cases, drums, pounds, etc., packed in a normal shift or day's operation.

Utility costs are measurable via engineering studies and have a direct correlation to machine hours of operation, which, in turn, are relatable to the production output.

Fringe benefits associated with labor, although not directly relatable to production volume, can be related to the labor costs of production and therefore follow the same pattern of activity as do the labor costs themselves.

Inasmuch as all of the *direct* cost elements can be quantitatively related to output and can be measured and controlled by reference to production, it follows that no production will occur if any of these elements is not available. Raw materials, packaging, and labor are required to start the process of moving production to the consuming market. Exceptions to the latter may be noted for such items as bulk chemicals in tank cars, or automobiles. If there is no labor force available, one cannot convert the raw materials into the finished state and without power supplies, machines cannot run. Finally, if we do not pay the going rate for fringe benefit costs, it is unlikely that the labor force will be available and it follows, no production would result.

The second major category of cost classification, is *indirect cost*. Depending upon organizational setups, financial reporting, and even how modern a financial reporting system is, indirect costs may be called overheads, period expense or burdens. Usually included in this category are such expenses as the plant management salaries, warehouse labor, office labor, maintenance labor, office supplies, maintenance supplies, outside services which are contracted for, property taxes, insurance, and depreciation. It may be said generally that none of these expenses bears direct relationship to production volume. They tend to be fixed over a period of time whether it be three months or a year and are often relatable to stages of production rather than volume of production. As an example, maintenance labor would be related to operations on a 1-, 2- or 3-shift basis. Within the shift, volume changes could occur at fairly significant levels and not alter the basic staffing requirements of the maintenance crew. In fact, production volumes could be reduced due to machine failure and this would precipitate a rise in maintenance cost, either in a total amount or in terms of cost per pound.

More often than not, overhead expenses, when stated in terms of cost per pound, tend to vary inversely with production volume changes; i.e., if production volume goes up, overhead costs per pound go down. This inverse relationship is attributable to the fixed elements contained within overhead expenses. If any given overhead expense were not incurred, we could generally still manufacture the product. For example, should the plant manager leave and no replacement be found, production would still continue, at least, on a short range basis. Individual managerial services are not fundamental to manufacture.

In the event that no warehouse crew was available, we could solicit the services of independently-owned warehouses to furnish required storage space. If a maintenance crew was not available, we could obtain the services of independent contractors. Perhaps the only exception to this general statement would be failure to pay property taxes, inasmuch as this would precipitate legal action and, perhaps, lead to closing the operating facility.

How many times have we all heard of situations such as a longshoreman's strike? In a number of instances, supervisory help performed the most necessary functions of (warehousing), loading or unloading ships. The ship's crew, which is similar to a manufacturing crew, was then able to continue with the ship's cruise.

The main points with respect to overheads are that there is no *direct* relationship to volume, and manufacturing operations can usually continue without any particular overhead burden incurred, *during a short term period*, since there are usually alternatives to supplying the services required.

In order to illustrate the movement of these two major cost elements in relationship to production, see Figure 5-2. Overhead expense is represented by the steps proceeding from left to right. Each step represents the increment in expense due to a significant change in production levels. The change in production is caused by adding an additional shift of operation to each day. The broken line indicates the movement of direct costs in relation to production changes.

It may be seen that there is no straight line relation between overhead expense and production, whereas, direct costs do tend to travel in the same line as production. It must be noted that both of these relationships are true in a *general* sense. Every facility and every company is unique and may incur expenses of a nature which would be at some variance with the general rule. So long as the treatment of these costs is understood by management, little difficulty should arise in reviewing the activities for a given period.

If the graph shown in Figure 5-2 is transcribed into the patterns of overhead expense and direct costs, the following type of statistics can be extracted:

Under the category of overhead expense, a one-shift operation, producing 7.2 million pounds, would cost $870,000. This creates a unit rate of 12¢ per pound.
A two-shift operation, producing 14.8 million pounds, would cost $1.2 million, with a unit rate of 8¢ per pound.
A three-shift operation, producing 24 million pounds, would cost $1.6 million, with a unit rate of 6¾¢ per pound.

Note, that as the number of shifts was increased and production more than trebled, the period costs only doubled. This is a characteristic of this type of cost. It tends to vary with capacity and volume of production. On the other hand, direct costs for the same production volumes increase from $.7 million on a one-shift basis to over $2 million on a three-shift basis, indicating a much closer relationship to the rate of volume increase than was shown for overhead expenses. See Figure 5-3.

This type of cost behavior is not solely limited to manufacturing costs. All costs within a company behave the same way. Advertising expense, for example, in the marketing function tends to be a fixed cost, like overhead, and whether you sell one unit or one million units, the cost is likely to be the same. On the other hand, promotion costs or even sales incentive payments, tend to vary with the number of units sold.

Even warehousing expense usually takes the form of having a fixed and variable component. Most warehouses charge a basic storage cost on a per month basis. In addition to that, they also charge a handling cost which is related to the physical turnover of products within warehouses. This pattern, then, is inherent in all expense items in varying degrees. The key to proper utilization and the maximization of cost efficiency is to recognize this and segregate costs into their behavioral patterns.

Expenses for which standards will be set. Setting standards for wholly variable and fixed expenses will be discussed separately. Under each of these headings, there will be a separate discussion of standards for the three major functional classifications, manufacturing, selling (distribution), and administrative expense. Standards for detailed expenses within the functional classifications will vary as to origin and characteristics between different types of business. Such a detailed discussion is beyond the scope of this chapter.

Fundamental differences between manufacturing, selling, and administrative expenses. Before discussing standards for expense, it is desirable to review certain

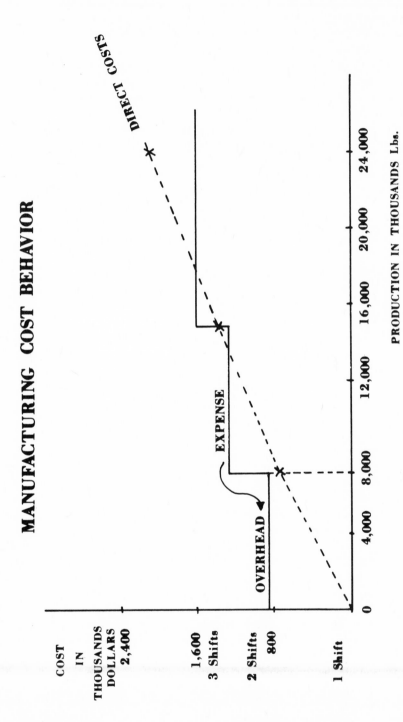

Figure 5-2. Manufacturing Cost Behavior

```
┌─────────────────────────────────────────────────────────────────┐
│                      OVERHEAD EXPENSE                             │
│                                                                   │
│  1st shift —    7,200,000 pounds @ $.121 pound — $   871,200     │
│  2nd shift — 14,800,000 pounds @ $.084 pound — $1,243,200        │
│  3rd shift — 24,000,000 pounds @ $.067 pound — $1,608,000        │
│                                                                   │
│                        DIRECT COST                                │
│  1st shift —    7,200,000 pounds @ $.100 pound — $   720,000     │
│  2nd shift — 14,800,000 pounds @ $.090 pound — $1,332,000        │
│  3rd shift — 24,000,000 pounds @ $.085 pound — $2,040,000        │
└─────────────────────────────────────────────────────────────────┘
```

Figure 5-3. Pattern of Overhead Expense and Direct Cost.

fundamental differences between manufacturing expenses, on the one hand, and selling and administrative expenses on the other.

1. The work that has been done in the field of standards for manufacturing expense far exceeds that which has been done for the others. Comparatively, the field of standards for selling and administrative expense has been unexplored. This apparent lack of interest in selling and administrative costs is no measure of their importance in the total cost of doing business. They may equal and, in many cases, exceed the cost to manufacture. It is also true that, as manufacturing costs have decreased, selling and administrative costs have increased. It is important, therefore, that they be subjected to analysis and control through standards.

2. A greater portion of selling expenses fall into the "fixed" category because of influences external to the business. These influences are: *(a)* The market for a company's products controls the conditions under which they will be sold. Customers are where they are, not where the seller would like them to be. *(b)* Factors of competition require the seller to make expenditures not otherwise necessary. Measures of effectiveness for such expenditures are those which must be used for the "fixed" category of costs. *(c)* Periods of declining business may require more, not less, sales effort and greater expenditure for the company to hold its position in a given market.

These and corollary reasons, make the amount or level of such costs primarily a matter of executive decision.

3. Administrative expenses, even more than selling expenses, are of the "fixed" type. In most cases, the level of such costs is determined almost entirely by executive decision.

There are other differences, which, however, pertain primarily to the manner in which standards for the "variable" portion of such expenses are set. These differences will be developed at the appropriate point in the discussion that follows.

Setting standards for variable expenses. Variable expenses have been defined as those which move up and down, *in total*, in relation to some measure of the extent of effort, or volume of work, passing through the department or activity responsible for the expense. These are, in other words, the expenses that would not exist were it not for the volume of work. These expenses, therefore, may be properly conceived of as *volume costs*.

It has been further stated that these costs cannot be established *directly* on a per unit basis. It follows that some expression of the volume must be established to serve as an index for measuring the degree, or rate, of variability. This index varies in form and significance for the three major functional classifications—manufacturing, selling, and administrative expenses.

Index for manufacturing variable costs. Manufacturing variable costs include all such costs associated with the operation of the factory. A distinction, however, must be made between expenses of the variable costs of (1) the producing departments, those which work directly on the product; and (2) the non-producing, or service, departments, those which do not work directly on the product, such as maintenance departments, tool room, production planning department, power department, and the like.

This is automatically done when the chart of accounts provides for the departmentalization fundamental to a determination of "Who is responsible?" It has, however, a further and equally important significance in the development of indices for manufacturing variable costs.

Index for producing department variable costs. Producing departments have been defined as those performing work directly on the product. The amount of product constitutes the volume. The index must be, therefore, a means of expressing the work done on the volume of product. The choice of an index is controlled by the type and complexity of the manufacturing processes, as well as the number of different products made. The following conditions are generally encountered.

1. There are a variety of products.
2. Each requires a different operation sequence.
3. The time on a given operation varies for each product.

Obviously, the number of units produced may not be used as an index under such conditions. An index must be found, therefore, that will (1) be a wholly natural means of expressing the product volume, (2) be readily available as a matter of routine for purposes of control, and (3) provide a suitable means for applying manufacturing expenses into units of product in building up a standard unit product cost. In practice, the final selection of such an index is based on a compromise among these three considerations. Such a compromise may result in using one of the following as an index.

1. *The direct labor-dollar.* The expense is stated as an amount per dollar of direct labor or as a percentage of direct labor cost.
2. *The direct labor-hour.* The expense is stated as an amount per hour of direct labor.
3. *The machine-hour.* The expense is stated as an amount per hour of machine time.

Some other index may appear more natural to a given situation and, at the same time, meet the basic requirements. If so, it should be used.

It is not an uncommon occurrence for the index to vary between departments, or even subdivisions of departments (cost centers). The important thing is that the index must reflect the factor that governs output. If, in one department, it is the machine, the machine-hour is generally most logical. If, in another department, handwork predominates, the direct labor-hour would be most logical.

Index for non-producing (service) department variable costs. These have been described as the departments that do not work directly on the product, hence the term "non-producing." They are, however, an integral part of the factory organization and may be said to *support* the producing departments by rendering essential services to them. The term "service departments" is more appropriate and, moreover, has special significance in setting standards for non-producing department variable costs.

There is no "volume of product" passing through the service departments. They do, however, render services to the producing departments, and the volume of product passing through the sundry producing departments gives rise to the need for such services in amounts that vary in some ratio with that product volume. In other words, although the relationship of service department variable costs to volume of production is not as close as with producing departments, without production there would be no need for the services. Thus, the service department variable costs are ultimately controlled by the production volume and the index must be some reflection, however indirect, of that volume.

In many cases the index used to measure production department variable costs can be used, with modifications, for the service departments. This would be true only where the same unit of expression (direct labor-hours, machine-hours, and the like) is used for all producing departments. The required modification would be as illustrated in the following example:

> Assume that there are three producing departments, A, B, and C. The unit used to express product volume in all three is the direct labor-hour. Assume further that there are two service departments, *S1* and *S2*. Department *S1* does work for all three producing departments. The total of their direct labor hours may, therefore, be used as an index for the volume costs of department *S1*. On the other hand, department *S2* does work only for producing departments *A* and *C*. In this case the direct labor-hours for departments *A* and *C* only might be used. Since no service is rendered to Department *B*, there would be no reason for including its direct labor-hours.

Where the indices of producing department volume are not expressed in the same terms, it is obvious that the method outlined above cannot be used, and that some other unit of expression must be found. It may also develop that, even though all producing department indices *are* expressed in the same units, another means of expression must be found for the service departments. It is impossible to give a list of conditions under which this latter situation might develop. The need for a special index and the probable character of that index will appear most clearly when detailed costs are studied. An example of this situation would appear in the case of an internal transportation department. Tonnage is a more appropriate index of transportation variable costs than, for example, machine-hours. In this example, the machine-hours would first be related to tonnage and standards for the detailed variable costs developed on a "per ton" basis.

Index for selling (distribution) variable costs. All variable costs associated with the selling or distribution function fall into this general classification. Whereas manufacturing variable costs are fundamentally related to a unit of production, selling and distribution variable costs are related to a unit of sales. This, therefore, requires development of an index related to the sales unit, which, in turn, means an index different in form and significance. In common with *all* variable cost indices, it must be an expression of effort or volume of work required to sell and/or deliver the product.

In many companies there will be a situation in the sales function roughly comparable to the producing/non-producing department relationship that exists in the manufacturing organization. There will be a home office sales department supplemented by a field organization consisting of various territories. In each territory there may be a sales office. Or the distinction in the field may be according to products rather than territories. There are countless other possibilities, depending on the particular business. The similarity to the manufacturing organization lies in the fact that the home office sales organization supports or renders services to the field group. The costs of the home office sales organization would be controlled logically by the extent of the services required to support field activity. This results in problems of index determination analogous to those previously discussed under manufacturing variable costs. Though it is true that field supervision is exercised by the home office (service) group (a basic variation from the situation found in manufacturing), this does not affect the cost relationships.

Typical indices for selling and distribution expenses are as follows:

1. The sales dollar. This is the simplest.
2. The sales unit—pounds, feet, dozens, tons, or whatever is customary in the particular business.
3. The number of orders handled.
4. The number of calls made.
5. The number of days of salesman travel.
6. Number or tonnage of deliveries.

There may be others more appropriate to a particular situation. If so, they should be used.

Where the nature of the product requires it, a separate section may be found which has the function of servicing the product after sale. The form of service organization will generally parallel the sales organization although it may not report to the sales executives. Where such a service organization exists, indices must be established for measuring and controlling its variable costs. These might be the same as the ones used for distribution or selling expenses, particularly where the service is rendered free of charge to the customer. In fact, under such conditions, service costs are generally a *part* of the selling and distribution costs. If, however, the service is "sold" to the customer after the expiration of a "free guarantee" period, as, for example, in the field of office appliances, a different means of cost measurement is required. The principles are the same as for other variable costs.

Index for administrative variable costs. It was previously stated that this class of expenses is more completely of the "fixed" type than are manufacturing or selling and distribution costs. There are, however, such things as administrative variable costs, and a discussion of standard costs that ignored this fact would be incomplete.

In general, such costs are associated with the volume of clerical effort expended primarily in support of the sales function and, secondarily, other functions. The indices used for administrative costs, therefore, would be related closely to some expression of sales volume, however indirect. A typical example would be the number of invoices written, used as an index of billing department costs. This field is wide open. There is no custom to inhibit ingenuity. The principles, however, are the same as for variable costs in the manufacturing or selling and administrative expense groups.

Relating variable costs to the index. Since this subject is being discussed separately from the determination of indices, it may appear to be a distinct problem. In practice, however, the selection of an index and relating variable costs to it are so closely related as to be inseparable and they are handled simultaneously. The two factors have been discussed separately here (1) because relating variable costs to the various indices is primarily a matter of techniques, any or all of which may be applied to any of the major expense classifications—manufacturing, selling or administrative—and (2) to insure adequate comprehension of principles involved in the selection of various indices.

The selection of an index is made on the basis of a thorough knowledge of the business and the principles previously enumerated. Relating the cost to the index determines the rate or degree of variability of the cost under consideration.

Methods of determining degree of variability. Several methods are quite commonly used. One of these is a method of averages, illustrated in Figure 5-4. It will be noted that the data for June and October have been eliminated since they appear to be

ANALYSIS OF FACTORY CLERICAL EXPENSES
(To determine expense rate per Direct Labor Hour)

Point Number on Figure 5-4	Month 19—	Direct Labor Hours	Expense Amount
1	January	11,000	$ 1,300
2	February	8,500	1,350
3	March	13,500	1,500
4	April	21,500	2,250
5	May	17,000	2,000
6	June	(24,000)	(1,750)
7	July	23,000	2,250
8	August	19,000	2,350
9	September	22,500	2,450
10	October	(21,500)	(2,950)
11	November	25,500	2,600
12	December	26,500	2,750
Adjusted Totals		188,000	$20,800

Variable rate $\dfrac{\$20,800}{188,000}$ or .1106 per hour

Note: These same date are applied to Fig. 5-4, which shows that this cost is not actually 100% variable. The above method is valid only where an expense is strictly variable, or it is felt desirable to consider it so.

Figure 5-4. Analysis of Factory Clerical Expenses, illustrating average method of determining degree of variability.

so far from the average condition that unusual, non-repetitive conditions must be suspected. These periods should not be included in the average unless the unusual conditions that account for their being out of line can be determined and the amounts adjusted. This method can suffice for costs that are felt to be perfectly variable with volume, but it has certain shortcomings that require use of other methods. Chief among these shortcomings is the fact that where a cost is partially variable and partially fixed, the degree of variability does not appear.

Another method is the simple graphic analysis shown in Figure 5-5, which overcomes the objections mentioned in the preceding paragraph. Here, the points are plotted in the sequence indicated by the numbers shown in the chart. Once this has been done, a "sight line of best fit" is drawn in such a way that the line passes as near as possible to all plotted points. Certain of these points, marked X on the chart, fall considerably away from the line and must be presumed to represent unusual conditions. These would be eliminated in a mathematical computation, and obviously must not be permitted to influence the position of a "sight line."

If it is desired to use a mathematical formula to find the line of best fit, the least-squares method may be applied. The formula for this method and the procedure may be found in any good reference book on statistical methods. In Figure 5-5, a sight line has been drawn.

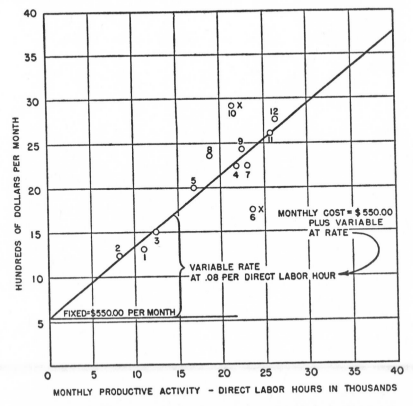

Figure 5-5. Monthly Productive Activity—Direct Labor Hours in Thousands, illustrating the graphic method of determining degree of variability.

Figure 5-5 also illustrates the so-called semi-variable expense. Note that the expense line does not intersect the vertical axis at the point representing "zero activity" but rather at a point above, $550. The difference between zero and the point of intersection represents the "fixed" or invariable portion of the cost in question, the cost that would be present in a condition of readiness to produce and sell with no actual production or sales. The distance between the fixed expense line, which is constant, and the total cost line represents the variable expense at any given level of activity. In Figure 5-5, the variable rate is 8 cents per direct labor-hour, determined as follows: Assume 20,000 hours. The chart shows the total cost at that point to be $2,150. Subtract the fixed cost of $550, leaving $1,600. Dividing by 20,000 hours gives the rate of 8 cents.

If, as a result of applying the method of simple graphic analysis or the method of least-squares, the line of total cost presents an impossible situation, the index or the data must be wrong. For example, if in Figure 5-5 the line of total cost had intersected the horizontal axis at a point to the right of zero, something obviously would be wrong because there should be a relationship between factory clerical expenses and factory activity measured in this case by direct labor-hours. Possibly the factory clerical expense had been allowed to get out of hand. In some other instance, the unrealistic position of the line might indicate that there was no relationship between the two items that were being plotted, and another index would have to be selected.

The graphic analysis illustrated above is useful for purposes described. However, the results must be applied with recognition of its limitation. Cost projections resulting are not, as might at first appear, valid for a range of activity from "zero" to "maximum." Essentially, the "straight line slope from a plateau" effect results from averaging data which would otherwise plot in the form of a curve or steps through the activity range realized in the period from which the figures were derived.

Another method of determining semi-variable expenses at varying levels of activity is frequently used. It is more time consuming, but results in a more precise standard. It is of special value in developing standards for various classes of indirect labor, clerical, material handling, janitors, maintenance men, and the like.

First, studies are made to determine the maximum practical productive capacity of each department, expressed in the units (labor hours, etc.) which comprise the index of activity. Next, the activity is stepped off in ranges of, usually, 10 per cent from zero to maximum. Then, after consultation with the concerned supervision and independent analysis, the expense level for each range of activity is established. For an indirect labor cost, the number of people in each labor grade is usually determined and translated into money by applying labor rates. This is a form of study best undertaken by industrial engineers.

A redefinition of fixed expenses. Fixed expenses have been defined as those whose *totals* are relatively unaffected by changes in any indices of volume against which they have been measured. To provide an inkling of the true nature of these expenses, the term "relatively invariable" has been used and a statement made that the term "fixed" is, in reality, a misnomer. These statements imply that there is actually no such thing as a *truly* fixed cost, one over which management has absolutely no control, one that cannot be changed, in some way, by appropriate executive action.

One cost universally classified as "fixed" is depreciation. Regardless of the method used to calculate the amount of depreciation, or the rate used, the total of the expense is based, fundamentally, on the original cost of the asset. For example, if machinery cost $100,000 and was depreciated at 10 per cent per annum, the resulting annual cost would be $10,000. Can this cost be changed? Assume, now, that the $100,000 included unused facilities having an original cost of $25,000, and that these are disposed of. The remainder is $75,000, thereby reducing the annual depreciation cost to $7,500. The decision to make such a disposition is within the power of management. So is the decision to add asset value by acquiring additional machinery and equipment, which would, in turn, increase the annual depreciation cost.

From the foregoing it is clear that the concept of "fixed" expenses will not suffice. Moreover, this fact should also be noted: Depreciation is determined on an *annual* basis, thus introducing the element of time. This time element is present without exception in all such costs. For example, the cost of fire insurance on factory buildings is predicated on two factors, amount of coverage (a management decision) and the rate per hundred dollars of such coverage, usually *per three years* (the time element). The sales manager's salary is a certain amount per year (or per month), again a combination of executive decision and time element. Numerous other examples could be cited. Those given are sufficient, however, to illustrate the important concepts, which may be summarized as follows.

1. This category of expense *is* subject to variation at the discretion of management.
2. It has no *direct* relation to volume or, in other words, presence of work to do is not the origin of the cost.
3. The total of these costs is controlled primarily by the passage of time, or, expressed in a similar manner, they pertain to a given period of time.
4. Because of 3, the cost per unit of product is a function of total cost *and* number of units produced and/or sold in a given period. Unit cost, therefore, is *not* constant and varies with the number of units.[2]
5. These are the costs associated with providing facilities with which to work and the organization required to support a given level of operations.

In view of the foregoing, it is clear that some term other than "fixed" could be used to describe these costs. They could properly be referred to as "time costs."

Setting standards for fixed costs. The logical starting point in setting these standards is the volume of sales anticipated for the period for which the standards are being set. The reasons for this approach are simple.

1. Sales are the spark plug of business. They provide the only justification for manufacturing, selling, or administrative organization and associated facilities. The anticipated volume of sales, therefore, is the controlling factor in determining what facilities are provided and what supporting organization is required for that volume.

2. The ultimate goal of business is to make a profit. That profit is the difference between sales income and cost outgo. Certain of the costs are, as has been demon-

---

[2]This is the opposite of per unit variable costs, where the *total* cost varies but the per unit cost is the same. The difference must be firmly fixed in mind.

strated, directly variable, *in total*, with the number of units produced and sold. The difference between sales income and the sum of the variable costs plus net profit[3] desired is the permissible amount of fixed costs.

The solution of the problem, therefore, has as its first step determination of the permissible amount of fixed cost. This would be in total, at first. The second step is apportionment of the total among the three major functional classifications, manufacturing, selling, and administrative. What must be provided for under each heading will be discussed in that order.

For manufacturing. To meet the sales goal certain machinery and other facilities such as buildings, power plant, and the like, must be available in readiness to operate. The costs associated with such facilities are depreciation insurance, taxes, and so on. In addition, there must be a supporting executive and clerical organization. The costs associated with this organization are principally in the form of salaries.

For selling (distribution). The costs in this classification are more completely organizational. However, facilities such as sales offices, branch warehouse space, delivery equipment, and so on may enter into the calculations.

For administration. In this classification the costs come nearest to being 100 per cent organizational, although costs of office space, depreciation on furniture, fixtures, and office equipment will enter into the determination.

The usual approach to determination of organizational costs is to consider, first, the minimum probable expenditure assuming a situation of very low sales demand and adding to this figure the *extra* costs required to support anticipated activity. These latter "extras" will be found to remain virtually constant over a wide range of activity.

The principal basis for setting fixed cost standards is generally past experience. Standards are set for each of the elements and by executive responsibility. The executives at each level of responsibility are in the best position to advise on the requirements of their respective activities and the extent to which past experience should be modified. The final result is the decision of higher management, as in the degree to which detailed study of these costs should be carried. Superficial consideration, based on the thought that nothing can be done about these costs anyhow, is to be avoided. They may be the means of making or breaking the company. The examples previously given prove they can be controlled.

The factor of sales mix was mentioned previously, and its importance to this present discussion indicated. It will be considered, now, from the standpoint of its effects on the setting of standards for fixed costs. A standard sales mix is important for two reasons. In most cases, various products have a different variable cost per unit——material, labor, and manufacturing variable costs. Moreover, it will usually be found that the spread, or difference, between total variable cost and selling price will vary for each product. Thus, in a situation where more than one product is made and sold, it becomes essential to determine how much of each is in the total. Only then can the residual available for fixed costs be determined. The following tabulation will illustrate this point more clearly.

---

[3]If federal or other income taxes are regarded as a cost element, such taxes would be added to the sum of the variable cost plus net profit to arrive at the permissible amount of fixed costs.

	Product A	Product B	Product C
1. Selling price per unit..........................	$10.00	$15.00	$20.00
2. Variable cost per unit........................	7.00	8.50	8.00
3. Desired profit—10% of price...............	1.00	1.50	2.00
4. Total of 2 and 3.............................	$ 8.00	$10.00	$10.00
5. Available for fixed costs	$ 2.00	$ 5.00	$10.00

It is obvious from the foregoing that the proportion of each product in the sales total is a determining factor in the permissible fixed cost level. It is equally obvious that, once the standard sales mix has been determined, means must be employed to check constantly to insure that the standard mix is maintained. If, for example, only 25 per cent of the total standard mix is allotted to Product A and if, for some reason, 50 per cent of total sales are in this category, the effect on the profit and loss statement can easily be imagined.

BUILDING UP STANDARD UNIT COST OF PRODUCT

Make-up of unit product cost. The approach to standard costs first involves development of standards for control. The primary purpose of standards *is* control. It automatically follows that, if costs of materials, labor, and manufacturing, selling, and administrative expenses are *under control*, so also is the cost of the units of product made and sold.

Unit product costs have their uses, however, and must be developed for many different purposes, but principally for valuation of inventories and the establishment of unit selling prices. The standards developed for control purposes, it was stated, provide the information necessary for standard unit product cost build-up. The considerations involved in determining standard unit product costs for direct material, direct labor, manufacturing expenses, and selling and administrative expenses are the subjects of the discussion that follows.

The direct material element of unit product cost. The major portion of the work was done when standards were set for direct material usage and direct material prices. The direct material element of unit product cost is a function of the use standards for all direct materials entering into a given unit of product and the price standards for those materials. It is merely a matter of multiplying one by the other, as is shown in Figure 5-6, columns (B), (C), and (D).

The direct labor element of unit product cost. The groundwork for this element of unit product cost was laid when direct labor time standards and direct labor rate standards were set. The actual determination of standard unit direct labor cost may, however, be something more than a mere multiplication of the standard time per unit by the standard direct labor rate per hour. The wage payment plan in use is the final determinant.

There are many types of wage payment plans, all varying in complexity and effect on standard direct labor unit cost. They can, however, be typed generally as follows:

STANDARD COST SHEET-PARTS
(UNIT - PER HUNDRED PIECES)

PART NAME *Accumulator Pinion*   PART NO. *BA 426X2*

MATERIALS COST

MATERIAL TYPE (A)	QUANTITY (B)	MATERIAL PRICE (C)	EXTENSION (D)
SAE #1010 CRS −.125 Thick-Shear 2½ Wide from 48" x 120" Sheet	Spacing on Strip - 1 Blank Weight 15 lbs/c Pieces	12 50 c/lbs	1 88

LABOR AND BURDEN COSTS

OPER. NO. (E)	OPERATION DECRIPTION (F)	DEPT. (G)	PIECES PER HOUR (H)	LABOR RATE (I)	LABOR COST (J)	BURDEN RATE (K)	BURDEN COST (L)	TOTAL LABOR AND BURDEN (M)
1	Blank	2	1150	90	08	180	14	22
2	First Swage	2	720	90	12	180	22	34
3	Anneal	7	NS	1 15	03	135	04	07
4	Second Swage	2	980	90	09	180	16	25
5	Anneal	7	NS	1 15	03	135	04	07
6	Drill - 2 Holes	5	360	.80	22	150	33	55
7	Ream	5	620	.80	13	150	20	33
8	Grind Face	6	900	1.10	12	205	25	37
9	Harden	7	NS	1.15	02	135	03	05
10	Inspect	10	NS	.75	15	95	14	29
11	Deliver to Stock	14	—	—	—	—	—	—

TOTAL COST PER HUNDRED (N): 4 42

Figure 5-6. Standard Cost Sheet. The letters in circles have been added to facilitate an explanation of the form.

1. *Nonincentive, day or hourly, wage plan.* Plan is computed as hours worked times the rate per day or hour. If all employees in the department receive exactly the same rate, the standard unit cost is the product of the standard unit time times that rate of pay. Any variances that may appear in comparison with actual will be efficiency variances only (standard time has been exceeded or bettered). If, however, wage rate differentials for length of service, experience, and the like appear (the more common situation), a weighted average rate must be employed as the standard direct labor rate per hour. Only by using a weighted average will the difference between actual and standard appear as a pure efficiency variance. The rate would be weighted by the number of persons in each rate-per-hour class. Thus, six employees receive $3.10 per hour, and three receive $3.00. Six times $3.10 equals $18.60; three times $3.00 equals $9.00; total $27.60 per hour, divided by nine employees equals $3.06 per hour standard labor rate.

2. *Incentive plan.* There are many types of incentive plans, and the standard unit direct labor cost is determined by the type of plan in use. For example, if a single piece rate is in effect, that piece rate *is* the standard cost, since it is the product of standard time (including unavoidable lost time and personal allowances) times the standard direct labor rate per hour. The worker is paid only for what he produces, and direct labor cost variances occur only when there is a guaranteed minimum wage and the worker has not turned out sufficient product to equal that minimum. Again, under certain types of so-called standard hour plans, where the worker is paid at a standard rate per hour for his production, which has been translated into "earned hours," based on standard time allowances, the standard unit direct labor cost is standard time per unit at standard labor rate per hour. As with the single piece work plan, guaranteed

minimums introduce the possibility of direct labor cost variances. On the other hand, if
the plan provides for a sliding scale whereby the pay for units of production increases
as the amount of production increases, unit standard direct labor cost is not constant,
but changes upward. There are many such plans, such as multiple piece rate, premium,
and bonus wage plans. The effect of each must be evaluated according to the nature of
the plan.

The manufacturing expense element of unit product cost. The direct material
and direct labor elements of standard unit product cost, as has been demonstrated, are
derived *directly* from the detailed standards. This is not true of manufacturing expense.
Control standards for expense have been set up on the basis of expense elements and,
further, along lines of responsibility. Moreover, it has been shown that manufacturing
expense is made up of costs having two different characteristics in respect to volume of
production, the variable costs and the fixed costs. It has been shown, further, that, in
relation to the "unit of product," these two costs are diametrically opposite. Variable
costs are *constant* on a per unit basis, where fixed costs are *variable* on a per unit basis.

It is the last two named characteristics that are important to this discussion. Some
means must be provided to reconcile the two. A "bond" or "composite means of
expression" must be provided for determining the manufacturing expense element of
unit product cost. This bond is found in the device known as the "standard overhead
rate" or "standard burden rate." Before the standard overhead rate can be established,
consideration must be given to the level of activity to be used. This has a more common
name, "level of plant capacity," since it is a reflection of the ability of a given factory
installation to turn out units of product.

Now, in the discussion of standards for manufacturing time costs, it was pointed
out that such costs are "facility costs." As such, they are, in effect, "capacity costs,"
and since cost per unit is controlled by the units produced (another way of saying
"capacity utilized"), predetermination of the units produced (the answer to "what
level of capacity") is an important decision. Its importance is enhanced by the fact that
total manufacturing variable cost, required to bind variable and fixed costs into the
standard overhead rate, is also controlled by the number of units, or capacity level
selected.

The decision is based on the following considerations.

1. Shall maximum capacity be used? This would effectively result in an ideal type
of standard. No plant is ever free from production interruptions caused by breakdowns,
material shortages, and other factors. Consequently, no plant can ever produce to the
maximum. Maximum capacity, then, becomes something purely theoretical. If our
standard fixed costs per unit are calculated on this basis, they cannot fail to be lower
than can reasonably be expected. Selling prices based on such costs would be unrealistic.

2. Shall practical capacity be used? Practical capacity may be defined as maximum theoretical capacity minus provisions for such factors as breakdowns, waits for
material, setups, and any other probable production delays. Standard fixed costs per
unit calculated on this basis would be somewhat higher. The difference would depend
on the extent of allowances for the above-mentioned production delays. Before this
basis is accepted, however, the question: "Can all that can be made be sold?" must be

answered. It is a matter of record that the average company's ability to make exceeds its ability to sell. The influence of existing markets, therefore, becomes a consideration in determining capacity level. This raises a further question as to the extent to which ability to sell shall be allowed to influence the decision.

3. Shall average capacity be used? This restates, in part, some of the questions raised in 2. Average capacity may be defined as that which makes due allowance for inevitable production losses and also takes into account such plant idleness as may result from lack of sales demand.

Both practical capacity and average capacity are referred to as "normal capacity." They are the usual alternatives used in setting the level of capacity. The major arguments usually advanced by the proponents of each viewpoint are as follows.

For practical capacity. It permits the segregation of fixed costs associated with plant idleness due to lack of orders from those associated with organization and facilities.

For average capacity. It results in fixed costs per unit which are safest for pricing purposes. In the long run all costs, even those that result from lack of orders, must be covered by prices if the business is to continue and show a profit.

The terms in which capacity is expressed should be the same as those used to index variable costs. This serves two major purposes. First, since this index is an expression into which units of product may be translated, it provides a convenient means of determining the total variable cost required for finding the standard overhead rate. Second, it may also be used as the means of expressing that rate. In the previous discussion of variable costs, the standard direct labor-hour, the standard direct labor-dollar and the machine-hour were cited as the most common indices found.

Calculation of standard overhead rates. Once the number of units to be used as the capacity base has been determined, the first step toward the standard overhead rate is to find the *total* variable overhead cost per unit of product. Variable overhead costs have been initially determined as a rate per hour of direct labor, per dollar of direct labor, per machine-hour, or per unit of some other index. The number of index units per unit of product is known from the data on which the variable cost standards are based. A simple calculation of capacity (units of product) times number of index units times rate per index unit gives *total* variable cost. Total fixed costs are already known. The standard overhead rate can now be calculated in accordance with the following examples in which a capacity of 10,000 units, a total manufacturing fixed cost of $5,000 and a manufacturing variable cost of $1.00 per unit are assumed.

1. *The direct labor-hour method*—3 hours per unit assumed:
   Total standard direct labor-hours 30,000
   Total standard manufacturing expense $15,000
   Standard overhead rate—per direct labor-hour .... $ .50

2. *The direct labor-dollar method*—standard direct labor rate
   of $1.50 per hour assumed:
   Total standard direct labor-hours (example 1) 30,000
   Total standard direct labor-dollars $45,000
   Total standard manufacturing expense $15,000
   Standard overhead rate—per cent of direct labor 33%

3. *The machine-hour method*—2 standard machine-hours per
    unit assumed:
    Total standard machine-hours 20,000
    Total standard manfacturing expense $15,000
    Standard overhead rate—per standard machine-hour .... $ .75

The effect of the decision as to capacity level to be used in setting the standard overhead rate can be appreciated by substituting figures based on a different number of units. The example uses 10,000 units as the base. Assume, now, that this represents practical capacity. Substitute the figure of 8,000 units, which might be considered as average capacity, (average capacity, by definition, is the lower). Higher standard overhead rates will result, meaning a higher unit cost of product. Increasing the number of base units (as for maximum capacity) would have the opposite effect.

Where conditions permit, it is much simpler to have a single, over-all, overhead rate for the entire factory, as shown by the foregoing examples. However, when indices for variable costs were discussed, it was shown that different indices might have to be used for various departments and cost centers in the same plant. Where such is the case, separate departmental or cost center standard overhead rates are also required. To put this another way, the term "where conditions permit" would automatically mean the same base—direct labor-hours, direct labor-dollars or machine-hours—in each department or cost center.

"Where conditions permit" has another, equally important, implication. It assumes a reasonably constant ratio of volume passing through each department or cost center, to the total. Shifts in the ratio can cause changes in product cost which would be effectively concealed in an over-all rate. This would be especially true where a number of products are involved and the rate, of necessity, would be predicated on a standard sales mix. The effect of shifts in sales mix would also be concealed in an over-all rate.

Total standard manufacturing cost. This is the sum of the standard per unit cost of these elements: direct material, direct labor, and manufacturing expense. It represents the point at which the factory organization ceases to be responsible for product cost. It is the standard product cost used for inventory valuation. The complete standard manufacturing cost is used for this purpose, as well as for accounting for transfers from work in process to finished goods and from finished goods to standard cost of goods sold. Obviously, for valuation of work in process inventory, only the cost to stage of completion at inventory time is used. Total standard manufacturing cost is also the base which may be used for computation of selling prices, *after* addition of factors for selling and administrative expense and profit.

The selling and administrative expense element of unit product cost. From the standpoint of individual products, these costs are the *most indirect* of all. This is especially true of the *fixed* costs in these two functional classifications. Assignment of these costs to unit of product, therefore, though done on the allocation basis similar to that used for manufacturing expense, involves even more arbitrary decisions in some cases. For this reason it would be better if this determination were not made at all. In fact, in a business where competition is not keen, and where administered prices are possible, it need not be done as a matter of routine, but only on occasions where a specific purpose is to be served. In such a business, keeping these expenses under control by element and responsibility usually suffices. If, however, the business is of the job shop type, where the product is made to customer specifications, and a cost must be determined for each job in order to place a bid prior to sale, the methods described below may be used.

The base figure, "total standard manufacturing cost per unit," has been determined as previously described. Factors for selling and administrative expenses are required. To all this is added a "profit" factor, and the sum is the selling price. Standards for selling and administrative expenses have been set by element and responsibility, for both variable and fixed costs. As stated above, the techniques are generally similar to those used for manufacturing expenses in development of the standard overhead rate.

A capacity figure must be set. In this case the number of units refers to units of sale rather than units of production. Physically, they are usually the same, but in numbers they may (probably will) differ. Sales units may be more or less than production units in number, depending on whether inventories are expected to increase or decrease. Once the number of sales units has been determined, the next steps are:

1. Determine the total variable costs for a period equal to that for which the fixed costs have already been set. This total can be developed from the indices used to measure variable costs in these functional classifications.

2. Add total variable costs to total fixed costs. The figure resulting from 2 may be used in establishing either a "rate" or a "per unit" cost.

A simple per unit cost may be obtained by dividing the total units of sales capacity into the total cost. This cost per unit is then added to the base figure, total unit standard manufacturing cost, and the resultant labeled "total cost per unit." The profit factor may be added as a lump sum or as a percentage of this total cost per unit. The final result is the selling price.

Very often it will be found that total selling and administrative costs bear a reasonably constant ratio to total manufacturing cost. This is usually mere coincidence. However, by dividing the total standard selling and administrative expense, as determined above, into total standard manufacturing cost (for the equivalent number of sales units), a rate is obtained that may be applied to individual products. This rate is expressed as a percentage of total standard manufacturing cost. Again, the profit factor may be added either as a lump sum or percentage to arrive at selling price. Even though there is no apparent relationship between total manufacturing cost and total selling and administrative expenses, this method is often used as a matter of convenience.

STANDARDS IN THE ACCOUNTS

Shall standards be used in the accounts? No discussion of setting standard costs would be complete without some general consideration of whether they shall be used in the accounts and, if so, how. The answer to this question is determined by the answer to the corollary: "Does management consider standard costs as real costs?" If not, they may feel that standard costs are to be used for statistical purposes only. There are, however, certain advantages to be gained when standard costs are incorporated in the accounts. The first major advantage is psychological. Executives are accustomed to reports drawn from the accounts. They are apt to give them more serious attention. Right or wrong, reports of a purely statistical nature are often presumed to contain an element of personal opinion. It might be said that the accounts impart a certain respectability to reports based on standard cost information. If standard costs are issued only for statistical purposes, there would be two sets of reports to read; one set or the other would, in all probability, be slighted.

Another major advantage is found in the clerical accuracy inherent because of the balancing required of double-entry bookkeeping. Data derived from records thus balanced are automatically presumed to be correct.

If standard costs are regarded as real costs, they will be taken into the accounts without question. The only question to be decided is how it will be done.

The bookkeeping of standard costs. Considerable variation exists in methods of handling standards in the accounts. Virtually all of them, however, can be typed under one of three general headings. Space does not permit a detailed consideration of any one, but a definition of each method and an outline of the relative merits of each are given.

Method 1. This is generally called the "partial" plan because actual costs are used to a certain point and standard costs beyond that. Under this plan, raw materials are charged and credited at actual cost. Work in process is charged with the actual cost of material, labor, and manufacturing expense. It is credited, however (and finished goods charged), with the standard cost of production. Finished goods are credited and cost of goods sold charged with the standard cost of units sold.

This plan is simple, requires a minimum of clerical work, and is suitable for situations where there are a minimum of operations and where frequent analyses of variations from standard are not required.

It is weak in these important respects:

1. Variances of actual from standard material usage, labor efficiency, labor rates, and manufacturing expenses must accumulate in work in process account until a physical inventory is taken.
2. When the inventory has been taken and the standard value determined, the variance represented by the difference between physical at standard cost and work in process on the books is a lump figure.
3. If detailed analysis of this lump sum is required to determine causes of variance in detail, additional work is required. Only too often the additional statistics required are not available as a matter of routine. In fact, they may at that late date not be available at all. This means that there cannot be a prompt reporting of variances for purposes of control.

Method 2. Under this plan, all inventory accounts are charged and credited at standard costs. Aside from the simplicity and economy of clerical effort with which the accounting may be done, variances appear at their source and as they occur. The cause, therefore, can be attacked and brought under control before excessive damage is done.

Method 3. Under this plan, charges and credits to inventory accounts are made at both actual and standard cost, at least up to the point of transfer from work in process to finished goods. Some organizations carry it further to the point of transfer from finished goods to cost of goods sold. This latter account is charged only with actual cost under either circumstance. The charges and credits at standard are washed out in a clearance account. This method is further characterized by general use of basic standards as the standard cost component and by the fact that variances are expressed as relative rather than as absolute amounts.

Obviously such a plan is more complex. It is harder for anyone, other than the accountant using the system, to understand. Moreover, a much finer breakdown of the cost accounts than is ordinarily made is required. On the other hand, the use of ratios to express variations shows the degree of difference. When basic standards are used, relating the variances of different periods shows trends in costs and rate, as well as direction of changes.

Variances from standard. The variance is a major product of Standard Cost Accounting procedures. It is the "exception" which facilitates control of the operation. As such, it is the item of most interest to operating management. Accordingly, the development and reporting of variances deserve special consideration in organizing the Standard Cost Accounting plan.

Variances should be developed for each element of cost, direct material, direct labor and overhead. This can be done, in total, for each element. However, this will not generally suffice for practical use. The question then arises as to the extent to which further analysis of variance in each element shall be carried. There is no generally applicable answer. The factors peculiar to each situation must be weighed and the decision made accordingly. However, a few broad principles can be set up as a guide. As a maximum, variances for the several cost elements should be provided as follows:

1. *Direct Material.* There should be a distinction between variance due to prices paid over or under standard, and those due to inefficient uses of material. This latter may include variances due to substitution of materials.
2. *Direct Labor.* There should be provision for separating variances due to changes in labor rates from those due to improper use of labor, such as operations done on a timework basis where incentive standards should be applied.
3. *Overhead Expenses.* Variances resulting from over expenditures in various expense elements should be distinguished from those resulting from a level of operations greater or lower than forecast when the standard was set.

The above can be expanded to whatever degree seems practical. It should be remembered, however, that variance analysis, like all business effort, costs money, and is an investment which must be paid out in the form of better control and reduced costs. Moreover, the degree of refinement in variance analysis cannot, as a practical matter, be carried beyond the degree of precision with which the standards were set. The results, to say the least, would be misleading. In addition, while it may be both practical and wise to refine variance analysis as far as possible at the start, it will often be found that it may be simplified once the purpose, that of reducing the cost to a reasonable level, has been achieved. Variances may be expressed as absolute amounts or as percentages. The two methods are, however, complementary and both should be used. What may be large in percentage may be small in dollars; what may be small in percentage, may be large in dollars. Either situation may call for special attention. Variances, of course, may be favorable as well as unfavorable.

Computation of variances, either absolute or relative, should always be done uniformly. Thus, the standard cost is always the base. This is essential for significant comparisons and to avoid confusion.

The treatment of variances in the financial statements will vary with each situation. Where inventories are carried at standard cost, some accountants feel that all, or a part of the variances from standard should enter into inventory valuation. Others regard variances as items of cost which should be written off to the profit and loss account of the period in which the variances are incurred. The subject of inventory valuation is a study in its own right, but a discussion of standard costs would be incomplete without at least a passing reference to this phase of it.

STANDARD COST RECORDS

The general problem. The problem of setting up the records required to support a standard cost plan can be divided into four parts:

1. What records are required?
2. Where does each record originate?
3. What activities require copies of each record?
4. What form should each record take?

This separation has been made only for the purpose of stating the problem more clearly. No such separation will be made as typical records are discussed. In practice, the first three considerations usually merge into one over-all problem.

Generally speaking, the necessary records fall into two general classes. The first might be termed "non-financial." These are the records that contain the basic physical data concerning the product, materials, processes, and so on. The second might be termed the "financial" records and are based on the first class but have monetary values added. Typical records in each class are discussed below.

Non-financial records. Some of these records are available, whether or not standards have ever been in use; for example, blueprints, bills of material (for minor assemblies, major assemblies, and final product), mixture formulae (required in foundries, rubber mills, chemical factories, and so on), tool records, process records, and the like. Very often, however, where standards have *not* been present, such records are scattered, unorganized, and, only too often, in smaller companies particularly, exist only in someone's head. Application of standards requires that all this be changed, that the records be organized and made available to all who require them. This discussion will presume, however, that *none* of the above records exists. The records described below are by no means all that can be devised to suit individual situations, but represent what might be termed the "minimum" requirements in any situation.

Blueprints and drawings are prepared by the engineering department. They show dimensions and shape of part, assembly or product, part number, description of materials, tolerances, and so on. Copies are generally distributed to production departments, inspection, purchasing, tool room and to any others requiring this information. They are not generally required by the cost department on a routine basis.

Bills of material are prepared by the engineering department, usually in the form of a descriptive list of parts required in minor assemblies, major assemblies, and the final product. See section (A) on Figure 5-7. The descriptive data tell the quantity, part number, and, if considered necessary, name of all parts entering into the assembly. Copies are generally distributed to assembly departments, production planning or scheduling department, the cost department, or any others requiring this information.

Formulae or mixture records are similar to a bill of material, except that such a record will contain a list of types and quantities of material entering into foundry mixtures, rubber compounds, chemical compounds, and the like. These are usually prepared in the laboratory and issued to production departments responsible for mixing, the production planning or scheduling department, the cost department, or any other requiring this information.

ASSEMBLY STANDARD COST SHEET
(UNIT- PER HUNDRED ASSEMBLIES)

ASSEMBLY NAME *Clutch Latch Lever Assembly* — ASSEMBLY NO. *27-4206*

PART NUMBER	PARTS DESCRIPTION	NO. PARTS PER ASS'Y.	ⒷMATERIAL		ⒸLABOR		ⒹBURDEN		ⒺTOTAL	
615X1	Hub	1		20	1	05	2	13	3	38
4206	Clutch Latch Lever	1	1	19	3	67	4	46	9	32
4575	Trip Stud	2		06		58		76	1	40
21-1327	Locating Arm Assembly	1	2	09	4	83	5	27	12	19
52136X2	Spring for Clutch Latch Lever	1		27		92	1	15	2	34
TOTAL PARTS COST- PER HUNDRED Ⓕ			3	81	11	05	13	77	28	63
ASSEMBLY COST – PER HUNDRED Ⓖ					4	57	6	23	10	80
TOTAL COST – PER HUNDRED ASS'YS. Ⓗ			3	81	15	62	20	00	39	43

(PARTS LIST Ⓐ / COSTS – HUNDRED)

Figure 5-7. Bill of Material and Assembly Standard Cost Sheet. The letters in circles have been added to facilitate an explanation of the form.

Operation sheets are prepared by the engineering department (or the laboratory). They show the type of manufacturing operations required, the sequence of operations, departments in which work is done, tools required on each operation for each part, assembly, or product, and any similar information. Copies are usually made available to production departments concerned, the production planning or scheduling department, inspection, industrial engineering (time study), and cost departments, or any others requiring the information. It is common practice to incorporate the material use standard in this record, or, in addition to the operation sequence, and the like, to show the type of material required and the standard quantity of material. In such cases, this would be shown on the operation sheets for parts only. The bill of material takes care of assemblies and assembly products.

Time standard sheets, where used, are prepared by industrial engineering (time study) and show the sequence of motions involved in performance of each direct labor operation, the tools to be used, and the standard work conditions on which the time study is based, the time standard, and other similar data. They are, in effect, condensations of the detailed time study sheets. Usually copies are distributed only at the production departments in which the work described is done and to the cost department.

Standard raw materials lists are prepared by the engineering department (or the laboratory). They show the quality and type of raw material on which the company has decided to standardize. Copies should be made available to the design engineers and purchasing department primarily, or to others requiring this information.

Financial records. The principal records required in this category follow.

Standard material price record is prepared by the department that determines material price standards. Copies should be made available to the purchasing, cost and engineering departments, the laboratory, or other departments requiring this information. The reason for furnishing this to the engineering department or laboratory may not be obvious, but is based on the idea that what is done there can appreciably affect material cost of product. It is a means of constantly reminding these departments of this fact.

Standard cost sheet (or card) is based on the operation sheet and shows production operations, their sequence, department in which performed, time allowance, labor rate for each operation, standard overhead rates, and contains computations and a summary of total direct labor and overhead. (See Figure 5-6.) The "operation description" on the standard cost sheet may include items (such as operation 11 in Figure 5-6) that are actually factory burden items and therefore not specifically costed as are the real production operations. They are included on the form to show the complete movement of the parts from raw material to finished goods. For an individual part, it may also contain material cost information (see "operation sheet") which represents an extension of standard quality and standard price. If the product itself is a single part, this sheet would then be the product standard manufacturing cost. Assemblies and assembly products are usually more conveniently handled by costing out a copy of the bill of material, using the standard cost of the individual parts, summarizing these, and adding the standard labor and overhead cost of the assembly operations. (See Figure 5-7.) These latter would be derived from costing out an operation sheet for the assembly operations. All of these records may, or may not, be prepared in the cost department. The work of pricing, extension, and summary is done there, but the basic information may be actually filled in by the engineering or other departments responsible for determining the processes and materials.

Other records may be required to suit individual situations.

The form of the records. The record described in the foregoing paragraphs must take forms to suit individual needs. Any form must show all the information required for the uses to which it will be put. However, there is such a thing as too much information on one form. No form should be so complicated as to require virtual deciphering by the user. Also, of course, basic principles of form design should be followed.

6

Controlling Production Costs

CONTENTS

6

Controlling Production Costs

GENERAL ASPECTS OF CONTROLLING PRODUCTION COSTS

Control defined. The word "control" has been used extensively for many years in the field of accounting. Control of subsidiary accounts, such as accounts receivable, accounts payable, and factory ledger, took the form of setting up an account in the general ledger suitably captioned to which totals only would be posted. Thus, to take care of the control accounts receivable, though the detail of the debits and credits would be posted into the accounts receivable ledger, only the total of such debits and the total of such credits would be posted to the accounts receivable control account in the general ledger. The schedule of accounts extracted from the accounts receivable ledger, when in agreement with the control account, was said to be in control or in balance. Only an arithmetical control is effected since the posting of a debit or credit to the wrong account is not disclosed.

The use of the word "control" was subsequently expanded to its fuller meaning through attempts to confine purchasing within the limits of managerial policy. This was achieved through perpetual inventory records, which reflected managerial policy by indicating a minimum and maximum tolerance of material in stores as a guide for the activities of the purchasing department.

Controlling production cost does not indicate either the arithmetical function of balancing the cost accounts, or the policing of the physical production of the organization. Rather, its main purpose is to enable those actively in charge of production to guide the activities of the plant along efficient, and therefore profitable, lines. This is done through the medium of proper accounting, currently maintained, and through prompt reporting.

The need for controlling production costs is evident. No matter what financial strata of the public a company is serving, its product has selling price limitations, and since the sales price is, in effect, controlled, production costs *must* also be controlled if the business is to survive competitively.

For the purpose of guiding the operations of the plant toward economical production, management lays down its policy in the form of standard costs. The differences between standard costs and actual costs are known as variances, and it is only by the prompt disclosure of such variances that effective steps may be taken to remedy the operational faults and guide the plant back to the path of managerial policy. It is evident that effective production cost control can be achieved only by the proper use of both standard costs and actual costs, together with constant and current comparisons and prompt reporting to proper authority.

After standard costs have been set, the next essential for controlling production costs is an adequate cost accounting system.

The purpose of cost accounting. The breaking down of factory costs into greater detail than is ordinarily embodied in an operating statement is not cost accounting, even though a factory cost ledger is maintained. No system of accounting, no matter how detailed it may be, has moved one step forward as a device for control of production costs if it operates only as a backing for the monthly profit and loss statement, although the cost reports will "tie in" arithmetically with the profit and loss statement and will explain that statement in greater detail.

The basic purpose of cost accounting is to help management conduct its business efficiently. It may accomplish this purpose by:

1. Disclosing the effect of inefficient operations on cost.
2. Furnishing the data on which decisions of expansion may be safely based.
3. Providing the information by which policies in regard to meeting competitive prices may be advisedly determined.
4. Distinguishing between profitable and unprofitable lines.
5. Providing the data necessary to establish standards of performance.
6. Providing the basic data necessary for the introduction of incentive plans, job evaluation, and the like.
7. Furnishing proper cost guidance in the consideration of design or engineering changes of the product.

The foregoing represents the general ways in which a cost system can serve as a tool of management. Undoubtedly there are many other ways peculiar to different enterprises.

To accomplish its purpose, a cost system must be maintained currently. That is, the system must be so devised and maintained that inefficiencies of operation (departures from standard) are promptly disclosed and reported. In many instances, monthly reports or interim reports disclosing the cost of certain products are helpful, but such reports do not disclose where the inefficiencies occur.

Selecting the proper method of ascertaining costs. The selection of the proper method of ascertaining costs is of extreme importance. Fundamentally, cost systems may be divided into two classes.

1. *Departmental or process costs methods.* These are used for continuous operations such as cotton mills, dyeing, and finishing, and so forth, or where cooperative departmental effort, instead of individual effort, is consistently necessary to one or more operations.

2. *Job cost methods.* These are used (*a*) when productive labor forms one of the chief elements of cost; (*b*) when diversified lines are manufactured; or (*c*) when the product is built to customers' specifications.

The responsibility for devising the proper system of cost accounting should not be left to the controller or treasurer alone, for although the knowledge of the fundamentals of accounting is essential, so also is a knowledge of the manufacturing operations. The management should share in the responsibility of devising the system.

Need for consistency. Chief among the weaknesses of some cost systems is the attempt to classify all of the labor and materials as direct, chargeable to specific units or jobs, without considering whether this principle can be followed consistently.

If an employee is engaged in diversified activities, some productive and some unproductive, it is essential that he understand the difference between these two classifications of labor before he is permitted to assume the responsibility of reporting the division of his time. In the absence of such understanding, the cost accounting department must introduce some method that will assure an accurate accounting.

Even though an employee who is normally engaged in unproductive work can, on occasion, charge his unproductive time against a specific job (direct), no attempt should be made to record such time as direct labor unless all of his unproductive time can be consistently charged to specific jobs. For example, suppose that, because your inspection department handles a great many components for a great many jobs, and because there is very little difference in the time allotted to each component, you have decided to classify inspection as factory overhead. Occasionally, however, a job is so large that the foregoing facts are temporarily changed and it becomes possible for inspection to measure accurately the time expended on the particular job. If this item of inspection is treated inconsistently, the costs of the particular job will be distorted not only by the inspection labor in question, but also by the application of the factory overhead attaching thereto, an overhead that will undoubtedly still contain unabsorbed inspection costs. Figure 6-1 shows the distortion that inconsistency of treatment creates.

DISTRIBUTION OF INSPECTION COSTS ON THE BASIS OF DIRECT LABOR

	Job A	Job B	Total
Material	$200.00	$150.00	$ 350.00
Direct labor	300.00	200.00	500.00
Factory overhead, including inspection costs, 100% of direct labor	300.00	200.00	500.00
Totals	$800.00	$550.00	$1,350.00

DISTRIBUTION OF PORTION OF INSPECTION COSTS AS DIRECT LABOR TO JOB A

	Job A	Job B	Total
Material	$200.00	$150.00	$ 350.00
Direct labor	550.00	200.00	750.00
Factory overhead, including unabsorbed inspection costs, 33⅓%	183.33	66.67	250.00
Totals	$933.33	$416.67	$1,350.00

DISTRIBUTION OF PORTION OF INSPECTION COSTS AS DIRECT-INDIRECT CHARGES TO JOB A

	Job A	Job B	Total
Material	$200.00	$150.00	$ 350.00
Direct labor	300.00	200.00	500.00
Inspection labor as a direct-indirect charge	250.00	—	250.00
Factory overhead, including unabsorbed inspection costs, 50% of direct labor	150.00	100.00	250.00
Totals	$900.00	$450.00	$1,350.00

Figure 6-1

Aside from the question of which treatment portrays the more accurate picture of costs, the inconsistency distorts the data from which operating comparisons may be made. It is essential that the method of treatment of the various elements of cost be determined at the outset and be consistently followed.

Simplification desirable. On the premise that complex methods are attended by excessive expense, the goal of all business is simplicity, whether it be of manufacturing, distribution, or administration. Since any cost scheme is introduced to enable management to effect economies, the controller should take care that the expense attached to the cost survey is warranted by the results obtained from it.

Selecting the unit of cost. Generally, the unit of cost such as yards, tons, or pieces is dictated by the nature of the product but where there is a choice, the selection should be made on the basis of which unit of cost permits the recording of the most direct labor because all charges other than direct must be distributed by some yardstick, which consequently affects the accuracy of the costs.

The use of machines in cost accounting. Many types of manually operated, automatic or semi-automatic machines are available for the purpose of computing, collating, and summarizing cost. Their use permits a degree of clerical accuracy and operating economy not possible with a manually operated system and, at the same time, gives greater flexibility and possibility of refinements. The capital outlay should be carefully weighed against the many advantages, and all types of equipment should be studied before a selection is made. Most machines can be adapted to any particular problem, but it is advisable to seek the advice of those familiar with the particular machine or machines selected when laying out the cost accounting system.

BASIC PROCEDURES TO ASSURE CONTROL OF PRODUCTION COSTS

The purpose of the bill of material. Before a new product or a change in the design of an old product is adopted as standard, many conferences have taken place between department heads, and, very probably, tests have been run on a pilot scale in the plant in order to anticipate the structural, mechanical, and processing difficulties that occur in all production innovations. The procedures leading up to the actual manufacture of the new or redesigned product are described below.

For each new product or each change in design of an old product, the engineering department prepares a bill of material that lists all of the materials required to complete the model or change, together with the part numbers that, in the future, will identify the material or components. The shop manager, or other designated person, will signify which materials or components shall be made within the plant and which shall be purchased from the outside. The report is then sent to the purchasing department for advice on the availability of materials, the cost, and the source. The answers to any of these questions may result in resubmitting the design to the engineering department for further changes.

Whenever the bill of material designates that a part or component is to be manufactured in the plant, that component should have its own bill of material, the purpose being to trace through this medium, the direct raw materials from which the part is made. (See Figure 6-2.)

BILL OF MATERIAL						NO. _____			

COMPLETE ASSEMBLIES RECOMMENDED _____ PAGE NO. _____ OF_____

MODEL NO. _____ PART NO. _____ SUBASSEMBLY NO. _____ PAGES _____

ENGINEERING CHANGE NO. _____ DRAWING NO _____EFFECTIVE _____

DESCRIPTION _____ AUTHORIZED BY _____

ENGINEERING DEPARTMENT PIECES FOR UNIT(S)			PURCHASING DEPARTMENT VENDOR				COST DEPARTMENT		
							TOTAL MATERIAL COST	STOCK RECOMMENDED	
PART NO.	QUANTITY	DESCRIPTION	NAME	PART NO.	DE-LIVERY	UNIT COST		MIN.	MAX.

Figure 6-2. Bill of Material.

Methods report. During the course of engineering a new product or changing products, the engineering department must work closely with the methods department in order to keep such engineering changes within the bounds of good manufacturing practice and the limits of plant facilities. It is not unusual for the methods department, because of its greater knowledge of manufacturing "know how," to suggest to the engineering department modifications of both drawings and specifications that may result in wide economies of operations.

When the proposed engineering innovations are finally adopted as standard by the technical staff, the methods department usually reduces the blueprints and specifications to manufacturing terms and practices, part by part, giving for each part the stock or raw material to be used, the operation by symbol and description, the machine or machines to be used, the tools, jigs, and fixtures necessary, including the list of new machinery and equipment necessary, the specifications of the operation, the tolerances, the estimated setup time, and, if there is no time-study department, the production time. The manufacturing operations are arranged in sequence to conform to the best possible flow with the existing or later acquired plant facilities. (See Figures 6-3 and 6-4.)

Disposition of bill of material and methods report. All data now having been assembled, the bill of material and the methods report are sent to the controller, or other responsible officer, to be summarized in terms of the fixed capital (machinery and equipment) and working capital (raw material, work in process, and finished product) necessary for the project.

The responsibility for affixing minimum and maximum quantities to the raw materials and components listed on the bill of material (Figure 6-2) usually rests with the financial department. In arriving at the minimum and maximum quantities, consideration must be given not only to sales projections and delivery time of the raw materials, but also to the economic absorption of setup time. Thus, if an operation or operations were machined on an automatic screw machine and the parts were worked to

METHODS REPORT   NO. _____

ENGINEERING CHANGE NO. _____ DWG. NO. _____ PAGE NO. _____

APPROVED BY _____ EFFECTIVE DATE _____ MODEL NO. _____

DESCRIPTION _____ SUB-ASS'Y NO. _____

                                                      PART NO. _____

                   FOR _____ UNIT(S)

	OPERATION				TIME			LABOR COST	
NO.	DESCRIPTION	TOOLS	MACHINE	SPECS.	SET-UP	RUN	RATE	SETUP	RUN

[Actual size 8½" by 11"]

Figure 6-3. Methods Report.

EQUIPMENT REQUIREMENTS   NO. _____

THE FOLLOWING MUST BE MADE OUT FOR ALL PURCHASES OF
MACHINERY, SPECIAL TOOLS, JIGS, FIXTURES RECOMMENDED AND
ALL RELOCATIONS OF PRESENT EQUIPMENT TO COMPLY WITH
ENGINEERING CHANGE NO. _____ DRAWING NO. _____
PART NO. _____ ASSEMBLY NO. { SUB _____
                                    { COMPLETE _____

EQUIPMENT		REASON	UNIT COST	TOTAL COST	COST TO INSTALL	DELIVERY
UNITS	DESCRIPTION					

[Actual size 8½" by 11"]

Figure 4. Equipment Requirements.

close tolerances, the setup time, which would include the "run-in" time, would be too costly to distribute over a few pieces. Therefore, in fixing maximum or minimum quantities to be carried in stock, recognition must be given to an economic run before the setup is broken down.

The final report to management should include not only the amount of capital necessary to effect the engineering change, but also an inventory of parts that may be made obsolete by the innovation. This inventory shows quantities and costs.

On the basis of the foregoing information, management finally approves or disapproves the proposals. If approval is given, the date on which the engineering change is to be effective is then determined, and the reports released to the departments interested.

Purpose of the planning department. The planning department becomes the backbone of the cost system by providing at the start an orderly processing of the customers' orders. Its purpose is to:

1. Transpose into shop language all customers' orders.
2. Summarize such orders by model number or other symbols.
3. Issue factory orders and intrafactory (departmental) orders.
4. Analyze factory orders in terms of raw material or component requirements and report to the purchasing department.
5. Provide information to the sales and other departments regarding the possibility of deliveries.
6. Advise management of the factory work load.

How the planning department works. At the close of each day, or other designated time, the sales department transmits either copies of all orders taken during the day, or a recapitulation of them, to the planning department. There they are summarized on a sales requirement sheet (Figure 6-5). When complete models or units are ordered, the quantity so ordered is extended in the unit column only. Provision is made for recording those parts ordered separately either as spare parts or replacements. The summary may be kept open according to the dictates of the business received. The manufacturing requirements are found by cross-totaling all columns, multiplying the total units by the number of parts for each unit, and adding thereto the extras or replacements.

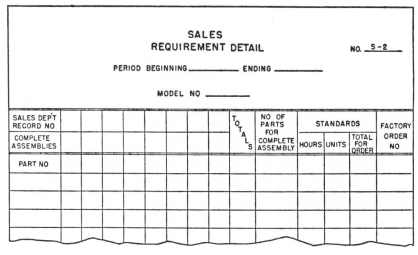

[*Actual size 8½" by 11"*]

Figure 6-5. Sales Requirements Sheet.

Figure 6-6 provides for listing as requirements those parts rejected by the inspection department and noted as unsalvageable.

Generally, the planning department does not concern itself with raw material inventories or any storeroom items, with the exception of finished goods and parts or components manufactured in its own plant. It is essential, however, that such records as receiving reports and stores requisitions having to do with finished goods or parts or components manufactured be made available to it as an aid to the timely issuance of reports of requirements.

[*Actual size 8" by 11"*]

Figure 6-6. Reject Replacement Sheet.

Factory orders may be issued against the requirements as shown in both Figures 6-5 and 6-6, but the better practice is to transfer such requirements to summary sheets (Figure 6-7) which are maintained for each part and issue the factory orders from such summaries.

Entries made to summary sheets (Figure 6-7) from reject replacement sheets (Figure 6-6) should be distinguished from other entries by the use of red ink. The detail under the headings "Requirements" and "Entered for Processing" will be entered, and the number of pieces being replaced will be entered in the column headed "Rejects." Because the amounts in the columns headed "Balance in Process" and "Work Load" are reduced only through the acceptance of good pieces taken into stock, the issuance of a factory order for replacement of rejects does not affect the figures in these columns, therefore, no entries are made.

The planning department furnishes factory orders and intra-factory orders to every department concerned in the manufacture of the unit or product. Where the operations of one or more departments are performed on material partly processed by a preceding department, the factory order may be routed first to the department performing the primary operation; it then follows, with the work, to the other departments in proper sequence. The purchasing department will receive a copy of all factory orders and,

STOCK		RUNS		LOAD	
MAXIMUM	MINIMUM	MINIMUM	RECOMMEND	HOURS	UNITS

DESCRIPTION _____ MODEL NO. _____
PART NO. _____
PRINT NO. _____

ENGINEERING CHANGES	NO.										
	DATE										

REQUIREMENTS		ENTERED FOR PROCESSING			IN STOCK			BALANCE IN PROCESS	REJECTS	WORK LOAD
REPORT	QUANTITY	FO. NO.	DATE	QUANTITY	IN	OUT	BALANCE			

[*Actual size 5½" by 8½"*]

Figure 6-7. Requirements Summary.

with the aid of the bill of material, will determine its raw material requirements. The stores department, labor cost and material cost divisions of the cost department, and, of course, the plant manager should also receive copies of all factory orders.

The result of the procedure. The foregoing procedure may be expanded or refined to meet particular situations. The framework outlined provides for an orderly presentation of the customers' orders to production, the first essential for orderly processing. The procedure described starts an even flow of material through the plant by balancing its work load; it controls the activities of the plant within the limits of orders on hand plus the tolerances allowed by management; it assures good inventory balance not only of the finished goods and work in process, but, through its reports to the purchasing department, it also maintains proper inventory balance of the raw material and components purchased from outside parties.

The storeroom. An examination of the balance sheets of many corporations will disclose that the book value of the contents of the storerooms—raw material, work in process, and finished goods—are, in the majority of cases, far in excess of the cash assets of those corporations.

The care that is exercised in the control and accountability of the cash assets is traditional. A great deal of time, thought, ingenuity, and money is expended in the constant safeguarding of these assets. Very little of this tender care is bestowed on the storeroom. Geographically divorced from the environs of the administration department, partitioned or fenced off from the manufacturing department, subject to a minimum of supervision and system, and often operated according to methods introduced by, and known only to, the storekeepers, it becomes surrounded with a self-ordained exclusiveness. It is left largely to its own devices and remains one of the unexplained paradoxes of accounting.

The operation of the storeroom is of material consequence in controlling production costs. Since this subject is discussed in detail in the chapter "Setting Up and Maintaining Inventory Control Records," control of the storeroom is not treated here.

ACCOUNTING FOR LABOR

Selecting the proper methods of accounting for labor costs. It is extremely important that the ultimate results desired from accounting for labor costs be determined at the start so that all the information necessary from the shop may be provided for. Otherwise, confusion will result from changes in the system that will have to be made to arrive at the desired results.

On the surface, accounting for labor seems to offer few difficulties, but actually a great many obstacles constantly appear or are raised that affect the value of the conclusions drawn therefrom.

Timekeeping. The basic purpose of timekeeping is to determine the individual earnings of the employees. An important collateral consideration is to determine the labor expended directly and indirectly in manufacturing the products of the company, by unit or model, component, part, operation or department, according to the cost unit adopted.

Timekeeping may run from the simple method of employing one source of information for both payroll and cost accounting purposes to the more complex method of divorcing the two. The payroll department is interested only in the total hours as shown by the time cards; the cost department is interested in time slips made out by the employee, the foreman, or departmental time clerk, showing the functional division of the total hours.

It is only in small industries that one source of information is used for both payroll and cost accounting purposes. In most cases the two are divorced because the information to be extracted for purposes of cost is often so detailed and time-consuming that it leaves insufficient time to make up the payroll before pay day comes around. If the division is not made, either the cost department hurries its analysis at the expense of accuracy, or the analysis is always deferred to the more immediate needs of the payroll department.

Timekeeping, for purposes of production cost control and payroll, must be accurate and prompt. A balance between cost and payroll departments by hours and money is, of course, desirable, but if the search for minor differences results in delaying up-to-the-minute information, the result may be the continuance of inefficient and costly production quite out of relation to the importance of arithmetical balance.

The careful application of well conceived methods of timekeeping will result in helpful information for the purpose of:

1. Price determination.
2. Design changes.
3. Technological changes of processing.
4. Spotlighting inefficiencies.
5. Comparison with standards.

6. Piece work, bonus, or profit-sharing-system.

7. Job evaluation.

8. Labor relations.

Employee responsibility for time distribution. In many industries, time distribution is a responsibility of each employee. The time slip (Figure 6-8) provides for information that cumulatively accounts for the total hours worked each day.

This method often is objectionable from the point of view of the shop supervisory staff as well as from the employees' viewpoint. It is argued with some logic that the matter is a clerical function and those not skilled in clerical work should be relieved of the necessity of doing it. It is also pointed out by the shop supervisory staff that time spent by the workman in performing this clerical function is production time lost and therefore unnecessarily expensive. To these objections of the production department the following may be added.

TIME SLIP

DATE _____ EMPLOYEE'S NAME _____
EMPLOYEE'S NUMBER_____

ORDER NO.	PART NO.	OPERATION	TIME			PIECES TO INSPECTION	IDLE TIME		
			START	FINISH	ELAPSED		REASON	HRS.	MIN.

[*Actual size 5½" by 8½"*]

Figure 6-8. Time Slip.

1. The employee usually leaves the distasteful job of filling out his time slip until the end of the day. If he has worked on different orders during one shift, his allotment of time to each is guesswork.

2. The employee is usually more concerned with showing total hours productively accounted for than with reporting idle time, on the assumption that idle time serves as a black mark against his record.

Notwithstanding the foregoing objections and deficiencies, labor accounting by the employee is often the only feasible method open. Where this is the case, the employees should be thoroughly instructed as to their responsibilities and, more important, should be made acquainted with the objectives of cost accounting in general and labor accounting in particular. It is a test of one's ingenuity and sincerity to be able to convince all the workers that the time slips are not used to compile individual efficiency records. Where two, three, or more workers are engaged on the same part number and are performing the same operation, it may be advisable to allow the total daily production of the "gang" to be prorated among the members of the gang for purposes of time slip reporting. This procedure helps to demonstrate that individual efficiency records are not a part of cost accounting.

Factory time clerks. In large organizations it is possible to delegate the responsibility of reporting time to one or more persons who have a good knowledge of shop operation coupled with a knowledge of the objectives of cost accounting. A factory time clerk may take care of one, two, or more departments according to the number of workers employed.

When a factory time clerk is responsible for distributing the time of a great many employees, he keeps making the rounds of his area and, by observation and questioning, keeps the time slips of the workers current. The element of guesswork under this method is much less than under the method of employee-made time slips.

In some large establishments, factory time clerks are located throughout the plant and are responsible for the distribution of employees' time by department or gang. They often act somewhat in the capacity of foreman's assistants by allotting work and keeping time records from a central point. In that case, a recording clock is generally used.

Factory or departmental time clerks should have sufficient knowledge of cost keeping and accounting procedures to code all time slips to proper accounts. Since they are at the source of labor activity and have a more intimate knowledge of manufacturing methods, they are in a good position to do this coding.

All factory time clerks should be responsible to the cost department and should not be allowed to forget that their duties are to serve that department.

The monotony attached to such routine positions makes it advisable to rotate factory time clerks, moving them from time to time to other departments and occasionally returning them to the main office for a refresher.

Employees' numbers. Much information may be conveyed to the cost department, the shop supervisory staff, and the payroll department by a proper system of numbering. By utilizing symbols and division, and employee's number may designate his department, employment rate, and identification. Thus, the number B-2-185-403 may designate:

B—Automatic Screw Machine Department
2—Setup man
185—Rate $1.85 per hour
403—Employee's identification

Direct and indirect labor. The terms "direct labor" and "indirect labor" are accounting terms only and have no bearing on whether that labor is productive or unproductive.

Direct labor represents that labor which may be consistently identified with the product by unit, part number, operation, or department, or by whatever unit of cost is employed in the cost system. For example, let us assume the cost system in use seeks to find costs by part numbers as a preliminary step to unit costs. The plant is arranged by departments: automatics, millers, drills, presses, grinders, polishers, and so on. Each department works on many parts or components and each department has its own inspector. If it were found impracticable consistently to keep accurate record of the time allotted to each part by the inspector, all of the inspector's time would be considered indirect labor. However, under the same conditions, if the cost system was devised for departmental costs only, the time of the inspector could consistently be charged as direct labor and would be so considered.

It is quite possible, of course, that a worker's time may include both direct and indirect labor. A person working part-time at a drilling operation and part-time in the storeroom would be able to identify the time spent on drilling with the part number or other unit of cost, and do so consistently. The distortion that may ensue from trying to classify a portion of the time of the same efforts as direct and the balance as indirect labor has already been shown.

Normal performance and idle time. No human being can, for any extended period of time, maintain a set tempo or gait of production. Proper time studies recognize the human traits that have an adverse bearing on a straight-line production performance, and production standards are drawn up accordingly. For very personal reasons the normal production of any given worker may vary from day to day, and, therefore, viewed against machine capacity—if he is a machine operator—idle time is a genuine plant ailment.

It is not the purpose of cost accounting to record under the heading of idle time all the production deficiencies measured against the possibility of machine capacity. Cost accounting recognizes the inescapable fact that normal performance is something far less, and to establish a bogey in excess of normal performance is misleading, except in the case of setting ideal standards.

Idle time, from a cost accounting point of view, represents time unproductively employed for any reason which may be obviated by the management in the future, or which has not been foreseen by it. The following represent a few of the items that the cost accounting department will record under idle time.

1. Machine breakdown may be cured by minor repair or complete overhauling, according to the gravity of the breakdown or the frequency with which it occurs.
2. Excessive grinding of production tools may be traced to faulty temper of material purchased from outside vendors and could be controlled by tightening up quality inspection of incoming material.
3. Lack of material in storeroom may result in a revision of purchasing policies.
4. Waiting for material from a preceding department may indicate an unbalanced plant condition or may uncover curable faults in preceding operations.
5. Power failures may be due to faulty generators, motor wiring, transformers, and the like.

All idle time reports should be immediately investigated by authorized executives, generally from the methods department, or at least by someone skilled in plant operation, who, because of his training and experience, can analyze the reasons for unproductive time objectively.

It is to be expected that idle time due to the fault of one department, operator or foreman will not always be correctly reported as such by the particular department, operator, or foreman. It would be stretching credulity too far to expect a foreman to report his machines idle because he failed to lay out the work, or the workman to report idle time due to his loafing on the job. The blame for such idleness could be placed on others by charging the storeroom with certain failures in the first instance, and some preceding department in the second instance. Again, even though the cause for idle time is sincerely stated by the foreman or workmen, their opinions may be restricted by a departmental perspective, when a wider range of viewpoint may indicate reasons far different. Idle time reports must be investigated.

Accounting for idle time. So seldom is it possible to identify idle time against any particular job or part that the rule of consistency invalidates its conclusion as a direct charge. Where standard costs are employed, and provision is made therein for idle time, it will be charged to that account, otherwise to the variance account.

Overtime. Overtime carries with it a wage premium that has no bearing on normal costs. It generally is a result of managerial expediency rather than policy and usually can be traced to some production irregularity or to the acceptance of orders beyond that normal capacity of the plant to produce.

It is virtually impossible to identify overtime with any particular job and often very difficult to identify it with any particular part. Even when it is possible to identify overtime with a particular operation or department, it is always advisable to charge the overtime premium to the variance account, or to an "overtime" account.

A departure may be made from this rule if a customer authorized overtime work at his expense. In that case the premium paid for the overtime is charged to some special account, to which the related income is also credited, or a special account may be used for the related income, such as "income from authorized overtime."

Costing for labor. The following steps must be observed in costing for labor.

1. Time slips must be surveyed to ascertain whether all time worked has been accounted for. If clock time cards are used for payroll purposes, time slips should be checked against them. This is one of the duties of the factory time clerk or the departmental time clerk.

2. If the employee's number does not designate the hourly pay rate, this may be entered upon the time slip or summary sheet.

3. Time slips must be arithmetically controlled for purposes of balance with the payroll department. (See Figures 6-9 and 6-10.)

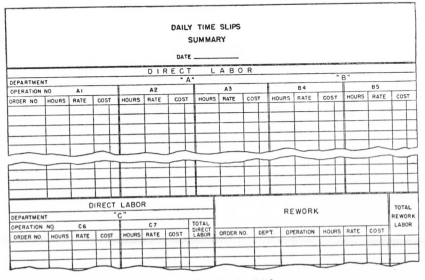

[*Actual size 11" by 14"*]

Figure 6-9. Daily Time Slips Summary, No Cross-Checking.

DAILY TIME SLIPS

SUMMARY

DATE _____

DIRECT LABOR								
EMPLOYEES NO.	ORDER NO.				ORDER NO.			
	HOURS	COST	OPERATION COST	DEPT. COST	HOURS	COST	OPERATION COST	DEPT. COST

[Actual size 8½" by 11"]

Figure 6-10. Daily Time Slips Summary Providing for Cross-Checking.

Figure 6-9 does not provide for any cross-checking between time slips and summary and should only be used where workers are employed steadily on one operation. Figure 6-10 provides for crosschecking. Entries on Figure 6-10 should be made in departmental and operational sequence. This will permit easy access to these labor costs. The scope of both Figures 6-9 and 6-10 is extended, of course, to include indirect labor and capital work such as new installations, all under proper factory ledger account numbers. The purpose is to include the cost of all labor from which balances with payroll and cost departments may be struck and proper payroll distribution may be made for factory ledger purposes.

4. Posting to the cost sheet (see Figure 6-11) is done from the summaries (Figures 6-9 and 6-10).

COST SHEET

ORDER NO _____

SHEET NO. ____ OF _____

PART NO _____ DESCRIPTION _____ QUANTITY _____

DATE STARTED _____ DATE FINISHED _____

PRODUCTION

TO INSPECTION	NOT GOOD	OPERATION NO'S	GOOD	REWORK					NET REJECTS
					LABOR			GOOD PIECES	
				DATE	HOURS	RATE	COST		

OTHER DIRECT EXPENSES			REWORK				
REQUISITION NO.	DESCRIPTION	COST	MATERIAL				
			REQUISITION NO.	PART NO.	QUANTITY	UNIT COST	TOTAL COST

MATERIAL						LABOR						
STANDARD FOR ORDER		ACTUAL				OPERATION NO.	A1	A2	A3	B4	B5	COST
PIECES	PART NO	SLIP NO.	PIECES	UNIT COST	TOTAL COST	STANDARD FOR ORDER						
						DATE	RATE	ACTUAL				

[Actual size 11" by 14"]

Figure 6-11. Cost Sheet.

ACCOUNTING FOR MATERIALS

Direct and indirect materials. In the same manner that direct labor is distinguished from indirect labor, so are direct materials distinguished from indirect materials. Those materials that may be consistently identified with the product by unit, part number, operation, or department, depending upon the type of cost system employed, are direct materials. It may be readily seen that a system devised for finding cost for each gallon, yard, or ton by department would lend itself better to a more expanded determination of direct charges—both material and labor—than one devised for the purpose of ascertaining the cost by job. It is true also that what may start out to be an indirect charge under a simple system of cost finding may well be considered and treated as a direct charge when that system becomes more refined or amplified.

Accounting for materials, particularly parts or components manufactured on the premises, is not easy. Although time slips are devised so that information as to materials may be given by the operator or the foreman (see Figure 6-8), counts made at the close of a work period, when employees are thinking more of starting for home, are not too accurate. There is the possibility of parts being counted and reported twice, as well as the danger of the inspection department's rejecting the parts or components reported as finished. The cost department must relay on the report of the storekeeper for the proper count of parts, components, and finished product taken into stock.

Inspection—in and out. In all plants, inspection of material is necessary. In small plants, the inspector or inspectors are responsible for the quality tests of inbound materials, for work in process inspection (parts-components), and for the finished product. In larger plants these responsibilities are divided into incoming inspection, process inspection, and finished goods inspection.

The inspection department is responsible for checking to quality standards. By tests, gauge, or other methods, it determines at various points of processing whether the raw material, part, component, work in process, and finished goods meet the standards shown in specifications. Generally the decision of the inspector in respect to rejects is re-examined by some person or persons having superior skill in the quality standards of the establishment as well as in the re-operational possibilities of the reject.

When the time of inspectors can be allocated consistently to the part number, department, or operator, depending on the method of cost-finding employed, such time may be considered as direct or direct-indirect.

Receiving and withdrawing materials. It is advisable that all material, whether direct, indirect, or special-purpose material, be cleared through the stores department. Such a regulation provides for an orderly flow of the paper work attached to the operation. Without this, proper control would be impossible.

Incoming material from outside vendors is generally first tested for quality by the inspection department and then transferred to the storeroom for count. A simple form of receiving report to be made out by the storekeeper is all that is necessary. Often he is provided with a copy of the purchase order (from which the number of pieces ordered is omitted in order to assure independent check) which is used as a receiving report. The storekeeper merely notes on it the number of pieces received, the good pieces, and the rejects.

Reports of material received from vendors are sent to the person or department responsible for checking and coding. Here debit slips are made out for the rejected material. The receiving report is attached to the duplicate invoice and sent to the stores record clerk. The original invoice and any debit memoranda are sent to the accounts payable clerk.

Parts, components, or subassemblies manufactured on the premises, which really represent work in process, are so reported by the storekeeper if taken into stores between operations. The report refers to good pieces only, rejects being reported by the inspection department. These receiving reports are sent directly to the cost department for proper recording and are then routed to the person responsible for maintaining work in process and finished stock records.

Requisitions for the withdrawal of materials are usually made out by the foreman, his assistant, or his clerk, who lists the number of pieces required, the part number or other description, the job number, operation or department, in accordance with the method of cost accounting employed. Withdrawal requisitions should be made out in triplicate. The triplicate remains with the foreman, the duplicate remains with the storekeeper, and the original is sent to the stores record clerk where the materials are priced and recorded. After this entry is made, the requisitions are coded to the functional accounts maintained in the factory ledger. Any requisitions coded to direct material accounts are sent to the cost clerk for entry. Finally, all requisitions are recapitulated under account numbers for factory ledger purposes.

Rejects and reworks. When the inspection department has made its final determination as to the reason for the reject and the possibilities of correction through reworking, it issues an inspection report, copies of which are sent to all departments involved (Fig. 6-12).

Generally, the extent of inspection is determined by those in charge of the inspection department and the engineering department. It is often expressed in percentage, changed from time to time to meet specific conditions. It is rarely that 100 per cent inspection is given, but if the first test indicates a high rate of rejects, a second, third, or complete test may be ordered. Sometimes an inspection of the instruments and gauges used by the inspection department is necessary.

Reworking rejected material is always expensive, especially when it necessitates breaking into the orderly tempo of a production department. Aside from getting the various departments off their gait, it unbalances the plant load and results in confusion. For this reason, a rework department may be set up to which are sent all rejects designated for corrective operations. If it is possible to keep a record of the time and material employed in the corrective treatment of rejects, such costs should be charged to the part, or other unit of cost, but distinguished from the direct labor and direct materials of straight-line processing. Should the standard costs fail to provide for reworking charges, the costs of such reworking may be charged to the variance account. In all instances they should be identified by part number, the operation number, and, if possible, analyzed further as to reason for reworking.

The proper accounting of rejects and reworks is most important for it may disclose engineering, manufacturing, or mechanical weaknesses that can be easily corrected and thus reduce this most expensive waste.

INSPECTION REPORT   NO. _____

NATURE OF TEST (1) _____ ORDER NO. _____

(2) _____ PART NO. _____

(3) _____ SUB-ASS'Y NO. _____

VENDOR _____ P.O. NO. _____ TOTAL PIECES SUBMITTED _____
(IF INCOMING MATERIAL)   FOR INSPECTION

	1st TEST		2nd TEST		3rd TEST		4th TEST		5th TEST		6th TEST		TOTAL	
	PCS.	%	PCS.	%	PCS.	%	PCS.	%	PCS.	%	PCS.	%	PCS.	%
INSPECTED	100		100		100		100		100		100		100	
ACCEPTED														
REJECTED														

REASONS FOR REJECTS

NO. PCS.	ORDER NO.	REASON	NO. PCS.	OPER. NO.	REASON

TOTAL PCS. ____	FOR FINAL INSPECTION ____	STORE ROOM ____	NEXT OPERATION ____	INSPECTORS INITIALS & DATE ____

FINAL INSPECTION   NO. PIECES SUBMITTED ____

REWORK

PART NO.	PIECES	INSTRUCTIONS	PIECES	STORES	SCRAP

NOTE: THE FOREMAN TO WHOM THIS REPORT IS SENT WILL MAKE HIS REPORT
AND SPECIFY CORRECTIVE MEASURES TAKEN ON THE REVERSE SIDE.

[*Actual size 11" by 14"*]

Figure 6-12. Inspection Report.

Accounting for scrap. The three main sources of scrap are processing, defective work, and obsolete parts. The costs and income relating to each should be maintained separately.

Processing scrap represents the surplus material cut away in profiling, turning, and the like. If raw material is ordered from the vendor in the size and shape most economical to the user, processing scrap is a controlled element of the cost of manufacture. In some manufacturing, screw machine parts, for example, the income from processing scrap may well be the total profit on the operation. Therefore, in such a case, or where processing scrap is substantial in amount, it should be properly handled. Extracting the cutting oil from turnings, separating as to metal, pressure baling, and weighing will result in added income.

Scrap from defective work is usually reported either by the inspection department or the store department. Such scrap should be mutilated so as to prevent it from being placed on the market as "second." When such defective work is reported to the cost accounting department, the cost accounts are relieved of the actual costs of the part including direct materials, direct labor, and factory overhead. The costs are charged to defective work account with some symbol that designates the operation or department responsible for the defect.

New designs or engineering changes, made for any purpose, eventually result in scrap through obsolescence. The sales department usually determines the proper time to scrap such obsolete parts, but it is the general custom to retain in stock a sufficient supply to satisfy the demand for repair parts, particularly if the old and the new part are not interchangeable.

As the demand for the obsolete part for replacements decreases, the value of such parts should be decreased so that, at the time of determination to scrap such parts, the residual value will not be greatly in excess of the amount to be derived from their sale as junk. The amount charged off from time to time by the foregoing method should be charged to obsolete parts account.

If it is possible, the record of the related income from the sale of scrap should be maintained separately. However, this will not be practicable except in large companies.

ACCOUNTING FOR OVERHEAD OR BURDEN

Overhead or burden defined. Overhead or burden in accounting means indirect costs and expenses. It represents charges for labor, material, services, and the like that cannot be consistently identified against the unit of manufacturing cost, order number, part number, operation number, or department, or that cannot economically be so identified. Were it not for the expense involved, many items generally admitted as belonging to overhead could be traced to the unit of production with as much certainty as direct labor and direct materials. For example, it is mechanically possible to equip every machine with a meter and thus accurately measure machine costs of electrical energy, but the result obtained may not justify the expenditure.

For the foregoing reason, it is impossible to adopt any definite rule in respect to the items to be properly classified as overhead.

Factory overhead. In spite of the above qualification, factory overhead, which is the only division of overhead that enters into controlling production costs, can be said to include, usually, the following items:

Indirect labor.
Indirect materials.
Power, light, fuel, water.
Departmental supervision.
General supervision.
Tool room and crib.
Maintenance of building and equipment.
Rent.

Depreciation.
Real estate and personal property taxes.
Inspection.
Engineering.
Storeroom.
Factory clerks, and so on.

Direct-indirect charges. It may often become necessary, for special purposes, to identify directly with a particular job, many items normally considered to be overhead; for example, when articles are made to a customer's specification. In such cases engineering, drafting, patterns, and the like, which normally are considered overhead charges, become direct-indirect charges. When such special jobs require special or closer tests due to narrower working tolerances allowed by the customer, inspection also may be charged directly, and so may premium rates of overtime when the overtime is authorized by and billed to, the customer.

Controlling factory overhead. Factory overhead can be controlled through two managerial devices: (1) budgets and (2) standards.

The budget is controlling factor for all expenses. Before any purchase orders are released, they must be within the financial scope of the budget or be approved by those having budget authority.

Standards, whether they be for production or for costs, represent the normals of efficiency. They serve the purpose of providing those persons who amass the figure a basis for comparison with actual. Any departure from standards is immediately reported to some person with the necessary skill and experience to diagnose the trouble accurately and cause the initiation of action to correct it.

Inasmuch as factory overhead is applied to prime cost (direct labor and direct materials) or production, through a "rate" which is reflected in standards, it follows that, if departures from standard production performances are closely followed as they occur, a secondary control of factory overhead is effected.

Distribution of factory overhead. Although distribution of direct labor and direct material costs offers some difficulties, the distribution of factory overhead to the unit of production seems to defy scientific or quasi-scientific treatment. Consequently, many factory overhead items are apportioned by some arbitrary yardstick.

Recognizing that the use of arbitrary methods for applying any portion of cost weakens the accuracy of cost determination, one has a tendency to dismiss the matter on the illogical grounds that an over-all yardstick, consistently applied, will serve adequately for comparative purposes and therefore is justified. In the majority of cases, the total factory overhead will exceed the total direct labor or the total direct material for any given accounting period; it may well exceed the total of both. If the method of application of factory overhead is dismissed too lightly because of its complexity, all the expense attached to the accounting for direct labor and direct material becomes a useless extravagance.

The ideal way to distribute factory overhead, is, of course, to track down every item of expense to its functional purpose and unit of cost, but the attendant expense is a barrier. Between this ideal and the disposition to choose the easy way out of the problem, there is an imposing area for exploration, which can yield logical methods and devices for treatment of many items of factory overhead. The number of items to be treated by some arbitrary method can thus be considerably reduced.

The items of expense chargeable to the main divisions of overhead—factory, distribution, administration, and financial— seem to fall in place quite naturally, and no accountant is long confused about their rightful disposition. Although a breakdown of factory overhead into further divisions (departments) is not so simple, yet the results achieved by an effort of this kind are decidedly worthwhile.

Through storeroom requisitions for indirect materials and through time slips for indirect labor, the accountant is already relieved of the necessity of distributing these elements of factory overhead by the medium of a common yardstick. He may seek further relief for many other items by finding a logical basis on which to apportion the item. For example, electrical energy may be departmentalized on the basis of rated horse-power; fire insurance and depreciation of machinery and equipment on the basis of values; rent on the basis of floor space, and so on. Any items that cannot be apportioned on a logical basis must be distributed by some formula. Departmental expenses may be further broken down to finer applications by the same method, if it is so desired. Here again the residue, after applying the rule of logic, must be distributed through the medium of a formula. though average methods of distributing factory overhead are not wholly eliminated by the foregoing, they are confined to rather narrow limits. The residue to be distributed by some average method is known as general factory burden.

Fixed overhead. Fixed items of expense are those that do not usually fluctuate in amount upward or downward with the production curve. Examples are rent, insurance, property taxes, depreciation, executives' salaries, and the like, and, to a limited degree, supervision, clerical, and other similar expenses. It is quite obvious that the application of this class of expense to abnormal production produces a fluctuation of unit costs that has no bearing whatsoever on the efficiency of plant operation. For this reason it is advisable to distinguish between fixed and variable overhead both in the accounts and in the "rate." The following examples illustrate this point.

EXAMPLE 1

	Standard Unit	Standard	Actual
Production	1	5,000	3.000
Cost			
Direct material	$10.00	$50,000.00	$30,000.00
Direct labor	5.00	25,000.00	15,000.00
Factory overhead	15.00	75,000.00	65,000.00
	$30.00	$150,000.00	$110,000.00

Assuming that the foregoing example shows all the facts, it may be concluded that plant operations were inefficent. Actual production being 60 percent of standard production would lead one to believe that a related reduction of factory overhead had not been accomplished. If the factory overhead is further analyzed, however, as in Example 2, it shows that lack of business is the main cause of this excess because of its failure to absorb the fixed factory overhead.

EXAMPLE 2

	Standard Unit	Standard	Actual
Production	1	5,000	3,000
Cost			
Direct material	$10.00	$50,000.00	$30,000.00
Direct labor	5.00	25,000.00	15,000.00
Factory overhead (variable)	5.00	25,000.00	15,000.00
Factory overhead (fixed)	10.00	50,000.00	50,000.00
	$30.00	$150,000.00	$110,000.00

Methods of distributing general factory burden. The methods generally employed for distributing general factory burden are:

1. Direct labor method.
2. Direct labor-hours method.
3. Direct materials and direct labor method.
4. Machine-hour method.

Direct labor method. This was one of the first methods devised for distributing factory burden to different units of production costs and it probably is used more extensively today than any other method. The direct labor method starts from the premise that all plant activity, and therefore, expense, is related to the amount of direct labor involved, expressed in monetary values. The applicable ratio of factory burden to direct labor is found by dividing the total factory burden by the total direct labor cost for any given accounting period. The rate thus found is applied to each unit of cost in accordance with the direct labor involved.

$$\frac{\text{General factory burden}}{\text{Direct labor cost}} = \text{Rate}$$

One of the objections to this method is that it introduces a variable (hourly rate of pay) that has nothing whatever to do with manufacturing effort. Its chief recommendation is that it is simple to compute. Individual rates of pay do not always indicate individual effort. It often happens that the older employees receive a higher rate of pay than those of lesser service, due to general increases, usually accompanied by a reduced production because of age. Because plant production is based on time reflected in terms of production, and rates of pay are not always related to production, the variable is created.

Direct labor-hours method. The method recognizes human effort as the basis of production but removes the objectionable variable of rate of pay. Where a product, a part of a product, operation, or department is concerned mainly with human endeavor (such as assembly may well be), the direct labor-hours method is acceptable. In such a case, the general factory burden is divided by the total direct labor-hours involved and the rate so found is used for distribution purposes.

$$\frac{\text{General factory burden}}{\text{Direct labor-hours}} = \text{Rate}$$

Direct materials and direct labor method. This method resembles the direct labor method of distributing general factory burden, except that it recognizes prime cost (direct labor and direct materials) as its base. The method was orginally devised to correct the inequities of the direct labor method where direct materials formed a major part of prime cost, but it succeeded only in adding more variables (material price changes) to a method that was already discredited because of them. Simplicity of administration is its only attraction. The rate for the distribution of general factory overhead by this method is:

$$\frac{\text{General factory burden}}{\text{Direct materials and direct labor}} = \text{Rate}$$

Machine-hour method. The advent of machinery, particularly automatic or semi-automatic machinery, changed the concept of the production base. The machine-hour method of distributing general factory burden seeks to attach to machine production hours the factory overhead that must be absorbed by the total expected normal operating hours.

EXAMPLE OF MACHINE-HOUR METHOD

Available time: 52 weeks at 40 hours		2,080
Vacations	112	
Holidays: 7 days at 8 hours	56	168
Available work time		1,912
Idle time	200	
Setup time	212	
Operating time	1,500	
	1,912	

FACTORY OVERHEAD
Department A

Department overhead	Operating	Setup
Variable	$3,500.00	
Fixed	250.00	$250.00
General factory burden		
Variable	1,000.00	
Fixed	200.00	200.00
	$4,950.00	$450.00
Variable	$4,500.00 (hour $3.00)	
Fixed	450.00 (hour $ .30)	$450.00 (hour $ .30)

MACHINE HOURS
Department A
Automatic Screw Machine

Number of machines available	5	
Number of machines necessary to full plant operation	4	
Stand-by	1	
Operating Load (4 machines, full time)	6,000	machine-hours
Setup (4 machines)	848	machine-hours

Figure 6-13.

FACTORY OVERHEAD
Machine-Hour Rate
Department A

$$\text{Operating} \qquad \frac{1,500 \times \$3.30}{6,000} = .825$$

$$\text{Setup} \qquad \frac{212 \times \$.30}{848} = .075$$

Figure 6-13 (Continued).

The normal hours of production are generally found by deducting from the available time all shutdowns such as Saturdays, Sundays, vacations, and holidays, an estimate of machine interruptions for personal reasons of the operator, and setup time.

Factory overhead is allocated to departments by a combination of those expenses properly belonging to each department, allocated by some method of logical conclusion, and the remainder, general factory burden, is allocated by some arbitrary yardstick. Setup time is usually distinguished from operating time because, during setup periods, machines are idle and therefore, it is assumed, are not incurring the usual variable factory overhead expenses.

Applying factory overhead to current costs. For the purpose of current costs, a predetermined or standard rate is set up, and applied to either direct labor costs or hours, or production units, in accordance with the method adopted.

The actual factory overhead, of course, will be reflected by the entries in the factory ledger and the difference between such actual factory overhead and the amount absorbed by costs through the rate method becomes a charge or credit to the variance account.

Variance account. The variance account is the balancing medium between actual and standard costs. Its main purpose, however, is not arithmetical. Unless this account is maintained so that it will reflect the causes of variances such as spending, or plant efficiency or deficiency, with the latter subdivided in keeping with idle time reports, it soon becomes a catch-all for all of the unanticipated and probably unwarranted expenditures of the business.

REPORTS

Examples of reports. The forms of reports to be submitted will vary materially with the type of business and the methods of cost accounting employed. Here the cost accountant has full opportunity to exercise his ingenuity and skill. To be of material advantage from an operating point of view, on-the-spot reports must be promptly made.

Foreman and shop supervisors are not primarily interested in the dollar-and-cents progress of their daily work, but are chiefly concerned with performance expressed in hours. Therefore, interim reports to these departments should be expressed in hours, which eliminates the necessity of the time-consuming process of arithmetical balancing of cost figures before they are released.

Figure 6-14 is a splendid example of a job performance report.[1] It will be noticed that on August 5th, the foreman was advised that 332.9 hours had been consumed and only 27 units submitted to test. According to the standard shown on this report, the cost clerk was confronted with a manufacturing deficiency in that 27 units at the standard time of 6.1755 hours per unit, in addition to the setup time of 10.2 hours, totals 176.9 hours, against 332.9 hours expended. He consequently notified the foreman. It is evident here, also, that, since the job was finished with 149.7 hours unused time, the report either accomplished its purpose, or on August 5th there were additional units on which time had been expended but which were not ready for test. In either event, the report was timely and the clerk undoubtedly submitted it in accordance with some definite policy.

JOB PERFORMANCE RECORD—LABOR

DESCRIPTION: Indicator-Component of Mobile-Type No. IN-23

COST DEPARTMENT					Stds. Dept.	
Date 7/xx	Est. Hrs. 6.1755	Run Quan. 100	Setup 10.2	Basic R 1.7969	Date	Std.

Type No. IN-23, J. O. No. 2110, Dept. 22

Date 19xx			Clock-Hours Worked		Labor-Hours	Units to Test	
		Explanation	Day	To Date	Unused	Today	Bal. Due
July	1	Setup			617.6		100
	18	Assemble	1.7	1.7	615.9		
	21	Assemble	52.2	53.9	563.7		
	22	Assemble	63.9	117.8	499.8		
	23	Assemble	62.2	180.0	437.6	10	90
	24	Assemble	43.5	223.5	394.1		
	25	Assemble	67.3	290.8	326.8		
Aug.	5	Assemble—foreman advised	42.1	332.9 X	284.7	17	73
	6	Assemble	13.2	346.1	271.5		
	7	Assemble	15.8	361.9	255.7		
	8	Assemble	19.6	381.5	236.1		
	11	Assemble	30.9	412.4	205.2	13	60
	12	Assemble	5.7	418.1	199.5		
	13	Assemble	12.2	430.3	187.3		
		Adjust Contacts	7.3				
	14	Assemble	15.6	453.2	164.4	25	35
	15	Assemble—foreman advised	9.1	462.3 X	155.3	35	0
		Clean-up	3.4				
	18	Trouble-shoot	2.2	467.9	149.7		
	20	Report issued	—	467.9	149.7	100	—

Figure 6-14. Job Performance Report.

[1]John G. Goette, "Daily Reports to Control Assembly Labor Time and Costs," *National Association of Cost Accountants Bulletin* (July 15, 1948), p. 1423.

EXAMPLE OF REPORT TO MANAGEMENT USING THE
DIRECT COSTING METHOD

	Total	Per cent of Sales	Product A	Per cent of Sales	Product B	Per cent of Sales
Income from net sales	$250,000.00	100	$100,000.00	100	$150,000.00	100
Direct cost of sales	100,000.00	40	45,000.00	45	55,000.00	36
Basic profit	$150,000.00	60	$ 55,000.00	55	$ 95,000.00	64
Fixed Expenses						
Factory	$ 55,000.00	22				
Selling	12,500.00	5				
Administration	15,000.00	6				
Total Fixed Expenses	$ 82,500.00	33				
Net Profit	$ 67,500.00	27				

Figure 6-15. Example of Direct Costing Method.

Reports to management. It often happens that many members of the management team are not skilled in accounting techniques and reports submitted to them based upon the absorption cost theory need explanation.

Almost every business incurs expenses which become fixed in amount, due oftentimes to company policy. These expenses are called fixed overhead, constant expenses, or period costs. The absorption of these fixed expenses by a unit of production which is variable results in unit costs wholly unrelated to the volume of production, and obviously to the unit profit factor. Any report to a management unskilled in accounting embodying these distorting factors, is bound to cause confusion.

Direct costing seeks to obviate this condition by reporting the variable costs, direct labor and direct material as separate items. (See the example in Figure 6-15.) The difference between the selling price and the direct cost is known as basic profit or gross manufacturing margin and is regarded as a contribution to the fixed expenses.

7

Controlling Distribution Costs

CONTENTS

7

Controlling Distribution Costs

Importance of distribution cost control. The control of distribution costs is receiving increasing attention by business management. More interest is being evidenced in the subject for a number of reasons.

1. Production costs are becoming increasingly affected by factors beyond the control of management, whereas distribution costs are more subject to management control.
2. Distribution costs account for a large proportion of the sales dollar for many businesses, even approaching the production costs in some lines. In the sewing machine industry, for example, marketing expenses were 36.5 per cent of sales, almost equaling the manufacturing cost ratio of 37.0 per cent.
3. A large part of the sales made by a firm may be unprofitable, even though the business as a whole shows a profit. If the distribution expenses and the revenues are analyzed to reveal the unprofitable commodities, customers, territories, and orders, management may be able to reduce costs and increase net profits substantially by taking appropriate action in regard to the unprofitable elements.
4. The use of distribution cost analysis as a management tool for cost control also presents an opportunity for more effectively achieving growth in sales volume. This growth results from the shifting of marketing effort from the unprofitable to the profitable elements of the business.

Nature of distribution cost control. There is a sharp difference between production cost control and distribution cost control. In controlling production costs, management is largely concerned with the effect of volume on unit costs. When planning distribution costs, management is concerned, at least for some of these costs, with the effect of costs on volume (for example, the effect of advertising expenditures on sales volume). With our present knowledge, management is much less certain of the effect of marketing expenditures on volume than it is about the effect of volume on unit production costs. Thus, the most profitable sales volume for any company is both "cause and effect" of the "right" amounts and kinds of selling and promotional expenditures. It follows that the control of these costs is at once a more difficult and important problem.

The objective of controlling distribution costs is, of course, to reduce them by increasing the efficiency of the marketing operations of the business. The experiences of businesses that have successfully achieved substantial reductions in their unit distribution costs show that, in reducing them, management is faced with the formulation and execution of basic marketing policies, such as:

1. How many and what kinds of customers to sell.
2. Which channels of distribution to use.
3. What territories to cover.
4. Which products to sell and at what price.

Treasurers and controllers can help management in deciding and executing these basic marketing policies by developing and using distribution cost analysis to locate the relatively unprofitable sales and the reasons for the sources of loss, in order to permit study of ways and means to makes these sales profitable.

DISTRIBUTION COST ANALYSIS

Production versus distribution costing techniques. In the present development state of distribution costing, it is more accurate to speak of distribution cost *analysis* than of distribution cost *accounting*. The results of these analyses may be classified as statistical costs. That is, the distribution cost analyses are not usually tied with the financial accounting records, but, rather, operate outside of the books of account. The analyses are made in supplementary records.

It is not generally accepted accounting practice for distribution costs to be charged to the cost of goods sold for the current period or to inventories for application against the income of future periods. A firm might allocate its distribution costs to individual products by means of statistical analyses, but the totals of such costs would be treated as expenses in the regular accounting records to be charged directly against the income of the period.

Another difference between production and distribution costing is that distribution costing is usually done on an intermittent, or even on a one-time basis, in contrast to the continuous costing in the factory.

Distribution costs are not allocated to products alone. They are also allocated to customers, territories, salesmen, order-size groups, price-discount groups, and in other ways.

Finally, distribution costing differs from production costing in the general use of historical rather than standard costs. There can be no doubt that the use of standard predetermined costs for budgetary planning and cost control is to be preferred to that of actual historical costs. However, the many difficulties of setting up standards for distribution, such as the numerous non-repetitive marketing operations, have so far proved to be too great for most firms engaged in distribution costing. Standard distribution costs probably will be developed more generally in the future, but historical cost data are useful for determining the relative profitability of different segments of the business.

In spite of the above differences, however, the basic procedures or techniques of distribution cost analysis are similar to those of production cost accounting. They are fairly simple to state, but they are difficult to apply.

Outline of distribution cost analysis techniques. A brief summarization of the basic techniques or procedures of distribution cost analysis is shown below as a frame of reference for analyzing the actual methods which are used.

1. The direct expenses are measured and assigned direct to customers, commodities, and so forth.

2. The indirect expenses are allocated or assigned to functional cost groups.

3. In some cases, only the variable marketing expenses are included in the functional cost groups, whereas in other cases, both the fixed and the variable expenses are included.

4. The factors that measure the variable activity of the various marketing functions that are performed are identified, and the amounts of these factors, in the aggregate, are determined.

5. A measurement is made of the share of the variable activity of each of these functional cost groups that is utilized by the segment of sales whose cost is being measured. This indicates the share of the cost of that function which is allocated to a particular segment of sales.

6. The excess or deficit of dollar gross margin over the sum of the direct expenses and the shares of the various functional cost groups allocated to a segment of sales indicates its relative profitability or unprofitability.

Direct distribution expenses. The separable or direct distribution expenses may constitute a significant proportion of the total costs associated with a specific segment of sales. This may be especially true of an organization engaged in extensive marketing activities, where separate sales departments are maintained for selling specific product groups and for soliciting specific customer classes.

In such an instance, if the primary expense accounts are kept in sufficient detail originally, or if provisions are made for subsequent divisions or subclassifications of the primary expense accounts, many selling expenses may be assigned direct to a product or a customer class or a territory.

For example, when a single product group is sold through a single sales department to several classes of customers, the classification of the primary accounts by sales departments will automatically assign the expense to the product, and this expense can then be allocated to customer classes and to individual customers. Likewise, when several product groups are sold through a single sales department to a single customer class, the classification of the primary expense accounts by sales department will automatically assign these selling expenses to customers and the expense can then be allocated to products.

Direct charges to primary expense accounts under each subdepartment would be made wherever possible. This applies not only to such sales solicitation expenses as salesmen's salaries, commissions, and traveling expenses, but also to such other items as advertising, transportation, packing, and shipping, which may be similarly subdivided. Also, it may be possible to divide further some or all of these sales departments into home office, district, and branch fields, so that there will be a direct charge of some expenses to territories as well as to products and customers.

Such a detailed classification of accounts and recording of expense items undoubtedly entails such additional work. It results, however, in less work in the allocation of indirect expenses and in more accurate analyses of distribution costs.

FUNCTIONAL CLASSIFICATION

Purpose of functional classification. Although the proportion of direct costs may frequently be significant, the greater part of a firm's distribution costs are likely to be indirect. To facilitate their allocation, as well as for purposes of expense control, these indirect expenses are classified into functional groups.[1]

Procedure for functional classification. The basis of the functional classification which would be used by any given firm is a study of the marketing activities performed by that company. It is important that the functional classification be sufficiently detailed so that the work performed in any one function will be of the same general kind. Such homogeneity facilitates the assignment of an entire functional cost group by the use of a single factor of allocation, as will be described hereafter.

The classification of indirect expenses by functions is in many respects similar to the process of classifying direct expenses by sales departments. The difficulties encountered in both cases are similar. It is by no means as easy to determine outlay in terms of functions as it is in terms of the so-called "natural expense" accounts. The difficulty lies in the fact that payments are often made simultaneously for the materials and equipment necessary to the performance of several functions. And when personnel performs more than one function in the regular routine of work, similar problems arise.

There can be little doubt that to aggregate the money paid out to employees under a single payroll heading and to do the same for supplies and for space and equipment charges is ordinarily simpler than a classification based on functions. But such a classification does not permit an allocation of the indirect expenses to commodities and to customers, nor does it provide an adequate basis for measuring efficiency and for controlling expenses.

Assignment of natural expenses to functions. It is usually necessary to apportion many natural expense items among several functional cost groups since they relate to more than one functional activity. They are distributed by means of time study, space measurements, counts, managerial estimates, and other methods. Table I illustrates how some of the natural expense items have been assigned to various functional cost groups. The increased cost and effort of preparing functional cost classifications may be much more than offset by the advantages of improved cost control, as well as by the advantages of cost analysis.

Most companies, especially those serving wide markets and selling a number of products, have complicated distributing organizations and engage in a wide range of marketing activities. Consequently, it is difficult to set forth a widely representative functional classification of distribution expenses. Each company would have to set up its own classification to reflect its own marketing activities.

---

[1]A functional classification puts together all the expense items that have been incurred for the same activity. A functional classification, therefore , permits the allocation of an entire cost group by means of a single factor.

TABLE I

CLASSIFICATION OF NATURAL EXPENSE ITEMS INTO FUNCTIONAL COST GROUPS

Expense Items	Means by which natural expense items are assigned to functional cost groups	Functional cost groups to which natural expense items are assigned
Sales salaries and expense	Time study	Order routine and promotion
Truck expense	Direct (to cost groups)	Handling (or delivery)
Truck wages	Ditto	Ditto
Truck depreciation	Ditto	Ditto
Outside trucking	Ditto	Ditto
Warehouse wages	Time study (or direct to cost groups)	Handling, storage and investment
Office wages	Ditto	Order routine, reimbursement, or other functions
Executive salaries	Managerial estimate	All functional groups
Rent	Space measurement	Ditto
Storage (outside)	Direct (to cost groups)	Storage
Warehouse repairs	Managerial estimate	Storage and handling
Warehouse supplies	Ditto	Ditto
Insurance:		
Property and equipment	Ditto	All functional groups
Inventory	Direct (to cost groups)	Investment
Personnel	Wages	All functional groups
Office expense	Direct (to cost groups) and managerial estimate	Order routine, reimbursement, promotion, or other functions
Utilities	Some direct (to cost groups), others to cost groups via space measurement.	All functional groups
Professional services	Managerial estimate	Functions benefited
Taxes, inventory	Direct (to cost groups)	Investment
Social security	Add to wages	All functional groups
Bad debts	Direct (to cost groups)	Reimbursement

Functional classification for wholesalers and retailers. It is, of course, impossible to set up functional classifications which will fit all wholesalers and retailers. Even those in the same trade perform different functions, and the internal organizations of those who perform the same functions vary widely. Accordingly, each wholesaler and retailer must make his own functional classification of expenses to fit his particular situation. However, the same principles and methods as those described above will apply.

Functional costs as a control device. The classification of distribution costs by functions is particularly valuable as a means of cost control. A functional analysis permits comparison of expenses in terms of the responsibilities of the executives who are charged with carrying on the distributive operations in the business. That is, the functional classification shall parallel the internal organization whereby the responsibility for marketing operations and marketing expenditures is definitely fixed.

For purposes of control of internal operations, the most useful cost comparisons are those of the budgeted and actual unit costs of each function. The bases of allocation (which will be discussed below) can be used to establish unit costs for most distributive functions. The use of unit functional costs as a control device may be made clearer by a simple illustration. In the example shown below, unit costs are figured for the personal solicitation function by dividing the total number of salesmen's calls into the total costs for this function.

	Total personal solicitation costs	Number of salesmen's calls	Unit cost
1. Previous year...................	$150,000	50,000	$3.00
2. Budget for current year.......	170,000	55,000	3.10
3. Actual results for current year....................	175,500	54,000	3.25

The next step, of course, would be a comparison of budgeted and actual unit costs with an explanation of the differences in terms of a volume factor and an efficiency factor. Unit functional costs thus reach their greatest utility for cost control purposes in connection with the preparation and administration of budgets. Budgets are generally made up on the basis of the number of units of the several kinds of services or functions required, multiplied by the expected unit costs.

ALLOCATION OF DISTRIBUTION COSTS

Basic principle of allocation. After the indirect costs have been classified by functions, they are allocated on the basis of utilization by products and customers of the variable activities giving rise to these costs. The principle followed is to charge the product or customer with the cost of its share of the variable activity of each functional cost group; that is, the cost of the portion of the variable marketing effort for which it is responsible.

Another way of starting this allocation principle is to say that the procedure is to determine, for each functional-cost group, the factor that "controls" it, tending to increase or decrease it. As used here, the term control is meant to convey the concept that under the firm's existing operating routines and policies, the dollar level of the functional cost is determined by the control factor. Or, that there is a cause-and-effect relationship between the control factor used as a basis of allocation and the dollar level of the functional-cost group.

According to this principle, functional-cost groups, in general, should not be allocated to products or customers unless there are clearly demonstrable and direct relationships between these products or customers and the basis of allocation for the expense involved. (Likewise with other segments of sales, such as territories.) Only such costs should be allocated to products where the total amount of their bases of allocation will definitely be affected over a reasonable period of time by an increase or decrease in the volume of such products. This is equally true for customers. In short, there should be a direct casual relationship in which the increase in volume causes increase in the control factor in order to make distribution cost analysis a useful tool of business management.

Variable functional activity. The identification of the variable activity that is involved in each functional cost group and the broad relationship between the functional costs and the characteristics of products and customers are often evident merely from study. Some functional activities vary according to certain characteristics of the commodity and are not greatly affected by customer characteristics. Others vary primarily according to certain customer characteristics regardless of what product is being purchased.

For example, the variable activity involved in the storage and investment functions depends almost solely on the bulk, weight, perishability, and inventory value of the product stored and is affected but little by the customer who buys the product. Similarly, the credit function will vary according to the financial integrity and other credit characteristics of customers, with little regard to the nature of the commodity on which credit was extended.

As regards still other functional cost groups, the board relationship between these costs and product and customer characteristics is more complicated, for there is every shade of combination of customer responsibility and commodity responsibility for the variable activity, hence the amount of expense, within the different functional cost groups.

Those functional activities that vary entirely with customer characteristics are not allocated to commodities, and, conversely, those related solely to commodity characteristics are not allocated to customers. Some functional cost groups would usually be allocated to both customers and commodities.

Partial allocation. In addition to the difficulty of tracing a direct connection between the variable activity of some functions and product or customer characteristics, there is another reason for not making a full allocation of distribution costs. For the control uses of distribution cost data, which we are discussing—namely, to discover the unprofitable parts of the business and to determine the appropriate action to be taken in regard to these unprofitable sales—little would be gained by making a full allocation.

A full allocation may involve the arbitrary assignment of some indirect expenses, which represent functions not being used to capacity,[2] on the basis of sales volume. This may have the effect of making some commodities, customers, and the like, with large sales volume and low percentages of gross margin, appear to be relatively unprofitable. Actually, since these functions are not being used to capacity, these indirect expenses would not be affected by substitution, elimination, or an increase of sales in the short run. For example, storage and investment costs usually would not be allocated to customers, because these activities are not usually related to customer characteristics and because they would not be affected by short-run changes in the number of customers. Likewise, credit costs usually would not be allocated to commodities since they would not be affected by addition or elimination of products "at the margin."

A desire for a full cost allocation may involve an erroneous conception of the use of distribution cost analysis in connection with pricing policy. It appears to some that if

---

[2]Such evidence as is available indicates that important facilities or marketing functions may, in normal times, be rather consistently under-utilized.

they know the total or *real* distribution cost, plus the production cost, then they can arrive at the proper price by merely adding the desired net profit. If, however, such a pricing procedure gives insufficient recognition to demand, it may be worse than one which is not based on any knowledge of costs at all. If prices determined on this cost-plus basis are too high, in the light of demand and competition, sales volume may be lower than before, so that costs per unit will be higher than calculated and may not be covered even to the higher prices. Or if cost-plus prices are not high enough, profits are sacrificed.

In short, distribution cost analysis should not be used by itself for the establishment of the most profitable prices. Distribution costing starts with prices as *given* for the purpose of determining relative profitability, and should be used in conjunction with demand analysis in setting prices.

In the discussion below, bases are suggested for assigning the principal functional cost groups which, at one time or another, would be allocated to customers and products. However, as we have seen, not all these costs would be allocated in all cases. It may be difficult to decide which costs should be allocated in a given case because of the difficulty of determining which functional activities are being used at or near capacity in the short run. Each executive needs to make such a decision in view of the particular circumstances in his business.

Allocating costs to products—manufacturers. Using the same functional cost groups that were previously set up for rubber manufacturers, bases that could be used for allocating costs to products (and to customers) are illustrated in Table II. Not all of these cost groups would be allocated in all firms. Each distributor would need to decide which functional activities were limiting factors, and, consequently, which functional costs groups should be allocated to commodities in view of the particular circumstances in his business. The bases for allocating the various functional costs are discussed below.

1. Investment. The variable activity responsible for the expense that results from carrying an inventory is largely the amount of the total average inventory value. Consequently, this expense may be allocated to each commodity on the basis of the ratio of its average inventory value to the total average inventory value.

2. Storage. The variable activity occasioning the expenses in the storage function is the number of square or cubic feet of space occupied by the merchandise (finished goods) inventory. Consequently, the measure of any commodity's portion of the storage expense is its share of the space occupied.

3. Inventory control. The function of inventory control of finished goods includes the cost of allocating stock to branch and district warehouses and of preparing orders on the factory, as well as the salary and other costs of stock record clerks. The variable activity giving rise to the expense of this function conforms most closely to the number of postings made to the perpetual inventory records, that is, to the number of invoices lines. Consequently, this cost is allocated to products or product lines or departments on the basis of the relative number of invoice lines.

4. Handling. The variable activity of this function is the amount of merchandise handled. The expense of physically handling merchandise in the distributive process is mainly the cost of the time (man-hours) involved. The size, shape, weight, perishabil-

TABLE II

BASES OF MANUFACTURER'S ALLOCATION TO COMMODITIES AND CUSTOMERS

Functional Cost Groups	Bases of Allocation	
	To Commodities	To Customers
1. Investment in finished goods	Average inventory value	Not allocated
2. Storage of finished goods	Floor space occupied	Not allocated
3. Inventory control, finished goods	Number of invoice lines	Not allocated
4. Order assembly (Handling)	Number of standard handling units	Number of invoice lines
5. Packing and shipping	Weight or number of shipping units	Weight or number of shipping units
6. Transportation	Weight or number of shipping units	Weight or number of shipping units
7. Selling	Time studies	Number of sales calls
8. Advertising	Cost of space, etc., of specific-product advertising	Cost of space, etc., of specific-customer advertising
9. Order entry	Number of invoice lines	Number of orders
10. Billing	Number of invoice lines	Number of invoice lines
11. Credit extension	Not allocated	Average amount outstanding
12. Accounts receivable	Not allocated	Number of invoices posted

ity, or nature of the package, and other factors, are handling cost determinants only because they affect the time required to handle a single piece of merchandise. Thus, by time study, a standard handling unit may be set up. If the standard handling unit is a case of goods, for example, barrels, sacks, and other packages may be expressed as multiple or fractional handling units according to their time-of-handling relationship to that of the case of goods (the standard unit).

5. Packaging and shipping. Where possible, this functional cost group should be assigned direct to each product group. Thus, the amount of shipping material used by each product group can often be determined by direct measurement. Shipping labor also can often be applied specifically to product groups and subgroups, through labor time tickets. And the overhead or indirect portion of this expense can be allocated on the direct labor-dollar basis.

Where it is not feasible to assign these costs directly, periodic tests should be made of the labor and materials cost per ton necessary to ship each product subgroup. The expense of this function can then be prorated to products by multiplying the tonnage of shipments in each product group, a shipping unit (package, crate, and the like) may be used as a basis for allocating these costs to products.

6. Transportation. Where possible, transportation charges should be analyzed from the freight bills and an average rate per cwt. or per ton computed for each product subgroup. Transportation expense can then be assigned directly to products by multiplying the tonnage of shipments in each product classification by this average rate per ton. Where weight is not available for a product group, a unit may be used similar to that set up for allocating packing and shipping expenses to product.

Where the manufacturer makes deliveries by his own trucks, the following method can be used. The wage cost of loading and unloading the truck can be allocated to commodities on the basis of the number of standard handling units or the number of pieces of merchandise delivered. The actual cost of "rolling the truck"—both truck and wage costs—can be allocated to commodities on the basis of bulk or weight. Where there are differences in the bulk or weight of the kinds of commodities that are delivered in various parts of the territory, these commodities could be weighed by delivery zones. Thus, each unit of bulk or weight in zone 2 would carry a weight of 2, and so on.

7. *Sales solicitation*. Specific product selling costs are, of course, assigned direct. Much sales promotion effort by "full line" salesmen is directed at customers rather than commodities. Promotional activities thus may vary with customer characteristics and be only partly affected by commodity characteristics. Indirect solicitation costs can be allocated to commodities on the basis of relative time or effort. The time spent by salesmen in commodity promotion can be determined by managerial estimate or by a time study. Solicitation is charged to promoted commodities on the basis of the relative amount of salesmen's time or effort spent in promoting each.

8. *Advertising*. Specific-product advertising should be assigned directly to major product groups. Further allocation should be made directly to product subgroups, or lines, or individual items advertised, on the basis of the cost of space used for each.

General institutional advertising that cannot be identified with any product (or customer) class would not be allocated. Other advertising and sales promotion expenditures, such as advertising overhead and art work, should also be assigned direct or distributed on a job-order basis, where possible. If direct assignment is not feasible, these expenses should be allocated to product (and customer) classes on the basis of relative appropriations or space and other direct advertising expenditures for each classification of sales. Otherwise, if no relationship can be traced, such items of expense should not be allocated.

9 & 10. *Order entry and billing*. These expense groups include the cost of the time spent by salesmen in routine order-taking, as distinguished from promotion, as well as the cost of the time spent by office employees in the billing process. The total expense is mainly one of time (wages). The total order routine time tends to be larger or smaller in accordance with the number of invoice lines processed. Consequently, a commodity's share in the total expense of the order routine function depends on its share of the total number of invoice lines. The office equipment and supply expenses associated with the order routine may be added to and distributed with the wages.

11 & 12. *Credit and accounts receivable*. These functions are not directly affected by commodity characteristics. That is, as far as the individual item is concerned, new products could be added or old ones dropped without affecting the total amount of the credit activity or costs. The aggregate amount of this functional activity is determined entirely by customer characteristics. Consequently, this cost is not allocated to products.

TABLE III

DETERMINATION OF RELATIVE PROFITABILITY OF A CLASS OF PRODUCTS

Functional Cost Group	(1) Total Functional Cost	(2) Total for Firm	(3) Commodity	(4) Commodity's Share (3 ÷ 2)	(5) Allocated Costs (4 × 1)
		Bases of Allocation			
				Percent	
1. Investment	$ 50,000	$500,000	$50,000	10.0	$ 5,000
2. Storage	75,000	400,000 sq. ft.	20,000 sq. ft.	5.0	3,750
3. Inventory control	25,000	$300,000	$9,000	3.0	2,500
4. Order assembly ..	100,000	$500,000	$50,000	10.0	10,000
5. Packing and shipping	60,000	$500,000	$75,000	15.0	9,000
6. Transportation ..	200,000	600,000 tons	125,000 tons	20.0	40,000
7. Selling	400,000	10,000 hrs.	2,000 hrs.	20.0	80,000
8. Advertising	150,000	———	Direct	——	33,300
9. Order entry	30,000	$400,000	$40,000	10.0	3,000
10. Billing	50,000	$400,000	$40,000	10.0	5,000
Total costs					$191,550

Sales	$850,000
Cost of goods sold	632,000
Gross margin	$218,000
Less: Direct plus allocated distribution costs (from column 5)	191,550
Excess of gross margin over costs ..	$ 26,450

Summary of procedure. There are thus certain data which must be known before the manufacturer's distribution costs by products can be ascertained. These are (1) the average inventory value of finished goods, (2) the amount of storage space occupied by these finished goods inventories, (3) the number of times the commodity is sold, that is, the number of invoice lines, (4) the number of handling units of the product that are sold, (5) the weight or number of shipping units sold, (6) the proportion of sales time consumed in promoting the product, and (7) the cost of the space or time in the various media that were used in advertising it.

These product characteristics determine the shares of the corresponding functional cost groups that are allocated to the product. The actual allocation of costs is, in effect, made by simple proportion. For example, if the average inventory value of product group X is 1/100 of the total average inventory value of all finished products, that group is charged 1/100 of the investment costs for the period. The sum of the shares of the

TABLE IV[3]

BASES OF WHOLESALER'S ALLOCATION TO COMMODITIES AND CUSTOMERS

Functional Costs	Bases of Allocation	
	To Commodity	To Customer
I. Maintenance:		
A. Investment	Average inventory value	(Not allocated)
B. Storage	Floor space occupied	ditto
II. Movement:		
A. Physical handling	Number of standard handling units	Number of invoice lines (Weighted by classes of customers)
B. Order routine ..	Number of invoice lines	Number of invoice lines
C. Delivery	1. Number of standard handling units	Number of deliveries (Weighted by delivery zones)
	2. Bulk or weight	
III. Promotion	Amount of time spent in promotion (where allocated)	Number of sales calls
IV. Reimbursement:		
A. Payments	(Not allocated)	Number of payments
B. Collections	ditto	Average amounts outstanding

various functional costs that are allocated plus any direct costs is subtracted from the dollar gross margin of the product, the difference indicating the relative profitability of the product. The results of this procedure are illustrated by the example in Table III.

This basic procedure is, of course, the same when costing major product groups, subgroups, lines, and individual items or brands. The difference lies mainly in the detail with which product sales and gross margins are classified and functional costs allocated.

Allocating costs to products—wholesalers. The bases for allocating functional cost groups to commodities for a wholesaler are generally the same as those for manufacturers. Table IV shows the functional cost groups and how they were allocated to products (and to customers) in many of the distribution cost studies made by the Department of Commerce.

Allocating costs to products—retailers. The retailer typically is concerned only with commodity cost problems, for usually he is not in a position to select his customers, his order sizes, or his territory (once he has located his store). He is, however, constantly confronted with questions concerning commodities.

The functional cost groups (or expense centers) and the bases of allocation to selling departments in department stores that are suggested in the uniform expense manual of the Controllers' Congress, National Retail Dry Goods Association, are shown in Table V.

Allocation to customers. The process of customer costing is fundamentally the same as that of commodity costing. As shown in Tables II and IV, the functional cost

[3]Charles H. Sevin, *Distribution Cost Analysis*. Washington, D.C.: Government Printing Office, 1946, p. 21.

TABLE V[4]
BASES OF RETAILER'S ALLOCATION TO SELLING DEPARTMENTS

Functional Costs (Expense Centers)	*Bases of Allocation to Departments*
110 General Management	Net Sales
121 Real Estate Costs—excluding Service and Warehouse Buildings	Weighted Floor Space
128 Real Estate Costs—Service and Warehouse Buildings	Weighted Floor Space
131 Furniture, Fixtures, and Equipment Costs—excluding Service and Warehouse Buildings	Weighted Floor Space
138 Furniture, Fixtures, and Equipment Costs—Service and Warehouse Buildings	Weighted Floor Space
140 Other Fixed and Policy Expenses	
04 Merchandise Taxes	Average Inventory
12 Merchandise Insurance	Average Inventory
Balance	Net Sales
211 Control and Office Management	Net Sales
215 Mail and Messenger Service	Net Sales
221 General Accounting and Statistical	Net Sales
225 Timekeeping and Payroll	Salary Payments
230 Accounts Payable	Number of Invoices
240 Cash Office	Net Sales
250 Sales Audit	Gross Sales Transactions
310 Credit	Gross Credit Sales Transactions
321 Pre-Billing	Gross Credit Sales Transactions
325 Billing	Gross Credit Sales Transactions
330 Bill Adjustments	Gross Credit Sales Transactions
340 Layaway	Gross Layaway Sales Transactions
410 Publicity and Display Management	Column Inches of Advertising
421 Art Work and Photography	Column Inches of Advertising
422 Copy Production	Column Inches of Advertising
423 Newspaper and Shopping News	Direct
425 Direct Mail	Direct
427 Radio and Television	Direct
429 Other Advertising and Publicity	Direct
430 Shows and Exhibits	Direct
441 Display Production	Direct
445 Sign Shop	Square Inches of Signs
511 Service and Operations Management	Net Sales
515 Supply Purchasing	Net Sales
520 General Telephone Service	Net Sales
530 Protection	Weighted Floor Space
540 Miscellaneous Customer Services	Net Sales
560 Escalators and Elevators	Net Sales
570 Cleaning	Weighted Floor Space
581 Maintenance of Properties	Weighted Floor Space
585 Utilities	Weighted Floor Space
611 Personnel	Number of Employees
613 Employment	Number of Employees
615 Training	Number of Employees

[4]From the 1957 revised edition of the *Standard Expense Center Accounting Manual*, Controllers' Congress, National Retail Dry Goods Association.

617	Training Squad	Net Sales
621	Hospital and Medical Service	Number of Employees
625	Other Employee Welfare	Number of Employees
630	Supplementary Benefits	Payroll Dollars
721	Receiving	Dollars Received
725	Returns to Vendors	Number of Returns Made
730	Checking and Marking	Number of Pieces Marked
750	Transfer Hauling	Net Sales
761	Delivery—General	Pieces Delivered (All Types)
763	Freight, Express, and Parcel Post	Pieces Delivered (Freight Express, and Parcel Post
765	Package Delivery	Pieces Delivered (Packages)
767	Furniture Delivery	Pieces Delivered (Furniture)
769	Garage	Pieces Delivered (Packages and Furniture
821	Direct Selling—Owned Retail Departments	Direct
825	Direct Selling—Owned Cost Departments	Direct
831	Other Direct and General Selling	Direct
834	Mail and Telephone Orders	Mail and Telephone Transactions
837	Personal Shopping Service	Net Sales
840	Maintenance of Stock	Direct
851	Retail Selling Supervision	Direct
855	Cost Selling Supervision	Direct
861	Merchandise Adjustment	Adjustments
863	Service Desks	Net Sales
865	Customers Returned Goods Room	Return Transactions
867	Cashiering, Inspection, Wrapping, and Light Packing	Direct
869	Crating and Heavy Packing	Tons of Merchandise Crated
910	Merchandise Management	
	05 Imputed Interest	Average Inventory
	Balance	Direct
921	Buying	Direct
924	Comparison Shopping	Net Sales
927	Testing	Net Sales
930	Domestic and Foreign Buying Offices	Net Sales

groups used in costing customers are basically the same as those used in costing products. Not all of these cost groups are allocated to customers, however, and the subdivisions and bases of allocation differ somewhat.

Customer costs for manufacturers. The basis for allocating the functional costs to customers for a manufacturer are shown in the right-hand column of Table II. These are discussed below.

1 & 2. Investment and storage. These activities are only indirectly affected by customer characteristics. It is true, of course, that maintenance costs on commodities are related to turnover rates, which depend partly on the rates at which customers purchase a specific commodity. But many other factors, such as the production policies of the manufacturer, determine merchandise turnover rates, and these are not related to customer characteristics.

Furthermore, maintenance costs would not ordinarily be allocated to customers because, so far as the individual customer is concerned, excess capacity usually exists in the investment and storage functions. That is, individual customers could be added or dropped—up to a certain point, of course—without affecting the aggregate amount of these costs.

3. Inventory control. Since the variable activity of inventory control is only remotely, if at all, affected by customer characteristics, in most cases this function would not be allocated to customers. In other words, customers could be added or eliminated—within board limits, of course—without affecting the aggregate inventory control expense.

4. Order assembly (handling). This function is affected by both customer and commodity characteristics. Weight, bulk, and perishability and product characteristics affecting the amount of movement effort or activity for which the customer is not responsible unless he purchases only certain particularly weighty, bulky, or perishable commodities. The frequency and size of his orders, however, are characteristics affecting the variable amount of movement activity for which the customer is wholly responsible. Thus, if there are no important variations in the kinds of commodities purchased by different classes of customers, that is, where all customers purchase substantially the full line, the number of his invoice lines over a period is the measure of each customer's responsibility for handling cost.

Where some classes of customers purchase only certain particularly weighty, bulky, or otherwise expensive-to-handle commodities, the number of standard handling units or the number of invoice lines weighted for different classes of customers would be a better basis for allocation.

The customer who buys less frequently and in larger quantities thus is charged with less handling cost—as a percentage of sales—than the customer in his same class who, over a period, buys the same volume but more frequently and in smaller amounts. In other words, the latter customer is assessed with a larger handling cost in proportion to the larger number of individual physical handlings of merchandise entailed in filling his numerous small-size orders.

5. Packing and shipping. The shipping rates per pound multiplied by the corresponding tonnage of shipments in each product subgroup to each customer class can be used to allocate these costs to customers. Or, if this is not feasible, an average shipping rate per pound per unit for all products combined multiplied by the tonnage of shipments to customers would give the packing and shipping costs by customer classes.

6. Transportation. Where possible, transportation charges should be analyzed from the freight bills and assigned direct to customer classes or to individual customers. If this is not feasible, the rates per ton for major product groups multiplied by the corresponding tonnages delivered to each customer class—or an average rate per ton for all products combined multiplied by tonnages delivered to customer classes—can be used to allocate transportation costs to customers.

Where the manufacturer makes deliveries by his own trucks, the following method can be used.

Truck delivery activity and expense vary according to the customer characteristics of delivered-order weight or bulk, frequency of delivery, and delivery distance. Where delivered-order weight or bulk and delivery distance differences are not as great as between customers, the cost of delivery may be charged against individual customers on the basis of number of deliveries. Where only delivery distance differences as between customers are great, the customers can be classified by zones with costs per delivery weighted by distance. Where both weight or bulk and distance differences are significant, the ton-mile basis may be used. (It is not an easy task, however, to compute ton-miles of deliveries by customers.)

7. *Selling.* Indirect selling expense is assigned to customers on the basis of the number of sales calls (whether orders are obtained or not) because customer promotion cost covers mainly that part of the salesman's effort devoted to general merchandising. In assigning this cost to customers on this basis, the view is taken that the salesman makes a promotion effort during every sales call. Where travel distances as between customers are significant, the same classification of customers by zones which is used for weighting cost per delivery by distance probably can be used to establish a similar weighting of cost per salesman's call.

8. *Advertising.* Specific customer advertising should be assigned directly to the particular customer classifications involved. General institutional advertising that cannot be identified with any customer class would not be allocated. Other advertising and sales promotion expenditures, such as advertising overhead and art work, should also be assigned direct or distributed on a job-order basis, where possible. If direct assignment is not feasible, these expenses should be allocated to customer classes on the basis of relative appropriations or space and other direct advertising expenditures for each classification of sales. Otherwise, if no relationship can be traced, such items of expense should not be allocated.

9 & 10. *Order entry and billing.* The order routine expenses, like the physical handling expense, depend on the number of orders and invoice lines, which, as an allocation basis, reflects customer characteristics of frequency and amount of purchase.

11 & 12. *Credit and accounts receivable.* This expense is the cost of the clerical effort used in recording sales and collections and the financial cost of carrying accounts and making collections. The clerical portion of this expense is allocated on the basis of the number of payments made by customers, and the financial portion varies in accordance with the average amount outstanding.

Summary of procedure. The customer data needed for allocating the functional cost groups to a customer class or customer, are, in the illustration given in Table II, (1) the number of invoice lines on all orders for the period, (2) the weight or number of shipping units of the merchandise bought by the customer, (3) the number of sales calls made on the customer, (4) the cost of the space or time in the various media used to advertise to the customer class specifically, (5) the number of orders placed by the customer, (6) the average amount outstanding, and (7) the number of invoices posted to accounts receivable.

These factors are used in allocating to the customer class a share of the functional cost groups. The total of the shares of the allocated functional cost groups plus any direct expenses gives the total customer cost. This cost deducted from the total dollar gross margin received from that customer class during the same period indicates the relative profitability of these customers.

Customer costs for wholesalers. The bases used in allocating the functional cost groups to a customer or customer class for wholesalers are generally the same as those described above for manufacturers and hence do not need to be repeated.

Related commodity and customer cost analysis.[5] In the examples that were

---

[5]The method described in this section was adapted from a procedure developed by Wroe Alderson. See Alexander, Surface, Elder, and Alderson, *Marketing* 3rd ed. (Boston: Ginn and Company, 1953.)

previously described, commodity and customer costing are distinct although parallel processes. Where, in general, all customers purchase all or similar products, this would be the most satisfactory procedure. In the case of most manufacturers, however, such a procedure would not be as satisfactory as one in which commodity and customer cost allocations were related processes. This would be true where sales of a given type of product were made only to a given class of customers. Also, the subsequent allocation of customers of expenses that could first be assigned directly to commodities, and *vice versa*, would be facilitated where commodity and customer costing were related.

Table VI shows the procedure by which the commodity and customer allocations are related. The lines on the form represent classes of commodities, and the columns represent classes of customers. The squares that result from the cross-classification represent transaction groups, that is, sales of a specific class of commodities to a specific class of customers.

One of these forms would be used for each functional cost group that is allocated.

TABLE VI
Procedure for Relating Commodity and Customer Allocation

Commodity Classes	Customer Classes						Commodity Cost Totals
	A Manu-facturers	B Dealers	C Jobbers	D Mail Order	E Chain Stores	F, G, H, etc.	
1. Pneumatic passenger tires and casings	....	....	....	....	....	....	....
2. Pneumatic truck tires and casings	....	....	....	....	....	....	
3. Tractor tires and casings	....	....	....	....	....	....	....
4. Solid tires and casings	....	....	....	....	....	....	....
5. Auto accessories	....	....	....	....	....	....	....
6. Mechanical rubber goods	....	....	....	....	....	....	....
7. Heels and soles	....	....	....		....	....	....
8. Hard rubber	....	....	....	....	....	....	
9. Footwear	....	....	....	....	....	....	
10. Tiling	....	....	....	....	....	....	....
11. Rubber thread	....	....	....	....	....	....	
12. Rubberized fabrics	....	....	....	....	....	....	....
13. Sundries	....	....	....	....	....	....	
Customer Cost Totals							(Grand total)

If the variable activity of a given function is related most closely to commodity characteristics, the first allocation would be made to commodity classes. In other words, the total amount of the cost group would be distributed as commodity class subtotals, on whatever basis of allocation is used for that functional cost group, and the amounts entered in the spaces in the column on the right. The next step is to distribute these subtotals to the cells across the form, on whatever basis is used to allocate the particular cost to customers.

A similar procedure is used if the cost group is one whose activity varies primarily with customer characteristics. The first allocation would be made to customer classes, which means the total of the functional cost group is distributed as customer class subtotals, on whatever basis of allocation is used, and these subtotals entered in the spaces along the bottom of the form. The next step is to distribute these subtotals upward into the cells which represent the classes of commodities purchased by the customer.

When all of the cost groups have been either assigned direct or allocated on separate forms, a summary form can be used to get the totals. All of the figures appearing in the corresponding cells are added together, the totals being the costs for the individual transaction groups. The next step is to add up the columns and enter the totals at the bottom, which gives the costs by classes of customers. Similarly, the totals of the amount on the lines give the costs by classes of commodities.

Finally, the dollar gross margins are entered on the summary form, and the total allocated costs by transaction groups and by customer and commodity classes are subtracted from the corresponding margins. A ranking of product groups and customer classes in the order of the amount of their excess of dollar gross margin over allocated costs discloses the relatively less profitable commodities and customers.

Allocation to order-size groups. Cost analysis by products and customers provides a powerful tool for discovering the relatively unprofitable segments of the business. In most firms, however, the investigation would not be complete without a separate analysis by order-size groups, since the size of the order is a most important factor in its effect upon costs and profits.

Manufacturers know that there are wide differences in distribution costs and profits for different-sized orders. But until they know just how the size of the order affects costs and profits, they can establish many sales policies and discount schedules only in a rough, and often wrong, way. With cost analyses available, these policies and discounts can be formulated with assurance that they will contribute to maximum profits (and also that they will conform to the requirements of the Robinson-Patman Act).

A determination of cost variations by size of order for individual products necessarily requires that attention be centered upon the line extension rather than on the order as a whole. The size of the order for the individual product can be measured either by the number of units of products per invoice-line extension, or by the dollar value per invoice-line extension.

Determination of cost variations by order size for individual customers can be found only from a study of the size of the order as a whole, measured either by the dollar value of the order, or by the number of invoice lines per order.

The process of getting costs by invoice lines, is, in general, similar to the process

TABLE VII

BASES OF ALLOCATION TO UNIT-OF-SALE GROUPS

Functional Cost Groups	Bases of Allocation	
	To sales classified by number of units of product per invoice line	To sales classified by dollar value of whole order
1. Order assembly (handling)	Number of units or time study	Number of invoice lines
2. Packing and shipping	Number of units or time and materials study	Weight or number of shipping units
3. Transportation	Number of units or time study	ditto
4. Selling	Number of invoice lines or time study	Number of invoice lines or time study
5. Order entry	Number of invoice lines	Number of orders
6. Billing	ditto	Number of invoice lines
7. Credit extension	(Not allocated)	Number of orders
8. Accounts receivable ..	ditto	ditto

of commodity costing. Functional classifications of expenses and bases of allocation are much the same as those used for product costing. The allocation of costs by total order-size groups—whether order size is measured by dollar value or by number of invoice lines—is generally similar to the process of customer costing. Table VII illustrates the functional classification of costs and the basis used in allocating costs to these two kinds of order-size groups.

Allocation to territories. Manufacturers, as well as wholesalers are also interested in analyzing distribution costs of sales by territories. In many respects, costs by territories are the simplest ones to analyze. If the manufacturer's marketing activities are organized on a territorial basis, with the geographic limits of branches and district clearly defined, a sufficiently detailed breakdown of the primary expense accounts and their classification by branches and districts results in a direct assignment of a large proportion of expenses to these territorial units.

The costs for individual salesmen's territories can be satisfactorily determined for many purposes by adding up the costs allocated to customers within the territory. This can only be done, of course, if these territories are also distinct geographic units. In other words, the sales, margins, and costs by territories can be ascertained by summarizing the corresponding figures for the customers who constitute the area. Thus, if all the customers in an area are profitable, the area itself must be profitable, and *vice versa*.

In some cases, however, it may be more satisfactory to allocate or assign directly to the territory certain branch and district expenses which are incurred jointly for several salesmen's territories. But even in such instances, there are some functional costs, difficult to allocate to commodities or customers or units of sale, which can be assigned directly to the sales territory.

The best example of the latter situation is the salesman's salary, commissions, and traveling expenses. If the salesman devotes all of his time to one territory, these, of course, are direct expenses. On the other hand, if he specializes by products or customers and divides his time between several territories, his expenses are indirect and must be allocated to territories. This is done either on a basis similar to that used in allocating selling expenses to customers or on the basis of a time study.

Other indirect selling expenses, such as salaries of district and branch managers,

TABLE VIII
BASES OF ALLOCATION TO INDIVIDUAL SALES TERRITORIES

Functional Cost Groups	Bases of Allocation
1. Order assembly (handling)	Number of invoice lines
2. Packing and shipping	Weight or number of shipping units
3. Transportation	Direct; weight or number of shipping units or ton-miles
4. Selling:	
Direct selling expenses	Direct
Overhead	Number of salesmen or estimated cost per salesman
5. Advertising	Circulation of media or direct
6. Order entry	Number of orders
7. Billing	Number of invoice lines
8. Credit extension	Average amount outstanding
9. Accounts receivable	Number of invoices posted

would also be allocated to individual sales territories. This is done by dividing the total indirect selling expense at a branch or district by the number of salesmen in that branch or district and assigning an equal share to each salesman. Or, an estimate of the indirect cost per salesman could be made by the sales managers on the basis of the relative time and effort devoted by them to each salesman.

Transportation and packing and shipping can be assigned directly to individual sales territories if the primary expense accounts are kept in sufficient detail. The remaining functional cost groups are, in general, allocated to individual territories on much the same bases that are used in allocating them to customers.

Table VIII illustrates the procedure for allocating costs to individual sales territories. The gross margin earned in each territory less its direct and allocated costs indicates its relative profitability. The territories in which the excess of gross margins over costs are the greatest are the most profitable; those in which the excess is the smallest, or those where the costs exceed the margin, are relatively unprofitable.

CONTROLLING UNPROFITABLE SALES

Cost analysis and cost control. At the beginning of this chapter it was stated that the objective of analyzing distribution costs by products, customers, order-size groups, territories, and so on, was to locate the relatively unprofitable sales and the reasons for the sources of loss, in order to permit study of ways and means to make these sales profitable. In converting unprofitable sales into profitable sales, or in eliminating unprofitable sales, management "controls" distribution costs by reducing them.

One manufacturer, for example, found that 68 per cent of the total number of his accounts, bringing in only 10 per cent of his volume, were unprofitable. Most of the unprofitable customers were gradually dropped, but nevertheless sales increased 76 per cent as a result of more effective use of selling effort. Within a period of four years, marketing expenses were cut in half, from 22.8 to 11.5 per cent of sales, and a net loss of 2.9 per cent was turned into a net profit of 15.0 per cent of sales.

Another manufacturer changed his policy of 100 per cent coverage of the market. The number of stores that he sold to directly was reduced by almost one-third, but sales increased 82 per cent, marketing expenses were reduced from 31.8 to 18.2 per cent, and operating profit rose from 4.7 to 14.8 per cent of sales. In still another case, the number of dealers was reduced from 12,000 to 5,000 in round numbers. However, sales volume doubled and the company's marketing expenses were cut from over 13 to around 7 per cent of sales.

Converting losses into profits. A large number of practical possibilities for converting losses into profits are available to the executive in the light of the knowledge of the costs accruing to the relatively unprofitable sales. Studying the functional costs, setting up standard unit costs for each function, comparing standard with actual costs, and analyzing the variances may indicate many opportunities for cost control and cost reduction.

It is the function of the controller and the treasurer to undertake the analyses of the distribution costs and the preparation and interpretation of the necessary reports. Beyond this, it is, of course, the responsibility of the marketing executives to formulate and execute the indicated changes in marketing policies that will achieve a reduction in distribution costs by changing the unprofitable sales into profitable volume.

Eliminating unprofitable sales. Sometimes, as a last resort, and after investigating all other alternatives, the decision is made by the marketing executives to eliminate the unprofitable sales.

A decision to eliminate unprofitable sales is far-reaching, affecting every aspect of the business. A decision to eliminate an unprofitable segment of sales because its *savable* distribution costs exceeds its net revenue, for example, would need to be reviewed in the light of the fact that smaller production runs and a reduced scale of production with the same amount of fixed costs might increase the unit manufacturing cost. Thus, further cost analyses are necessary if the marketing executive, after studying all of the alternative courses of action, seeks to determine the effects of eliminating those unprofitable segments of sales that cannot be turned into source of profit. These further analyses involve the following steps.

1. It is necessary to make a forecast of just what will happen to sales volume over a period of time, after the business changes from a policy of indiscriminately covering the entire market to a policy of selective distribution.

2. It is necessary to estimate the decrease in total expense that would result from eliminating the unprofitable sales. This is not an easy matter since the distribution costs that were allocated to sales to discover the unprofitable segments would not provide the answer. Some of these costs could not be saved and would continue after the sales were dropped. Therefore, it is necessary to separate the non-savable (or fixed) costs from the savable (or variable) costs. The total savable costs less the net revenue that will be

TABLE IX
Manufacturer's Analysis of Elimination of Unprofitable Commodities
(Net Sales, $415,600; Gross Margin, $75,600)

Functional Cost Groups	Allocated Costs	Savable Costs	Non-savable Costs
Investment in finished goods:			
Taxes on stock	$ 5,000	$ 5,000	———
Insurance on stock	4,500	4,500	———
Storage of finished goods	7,000	———	$ 7,000
Inventory control:			
Salaries—Stock record clerks	4,000	4,000	———
All other	1,500	———	1,500
Order assembly:			
Salaries—warehouse labor	12,000	12,000	———
Overhead	3,000	500	2,500
Packing and shipping:			
Material	5,000	5,000	———
Labor	8,000	8,000	———
Overhead	1,000	———	1,000
Transportation:			
Freight, express, and parcel post	12,000	12,000	———
Truck	3,000	300	2,500
Selling:			
Direct selling expense	35,000	35,000	———
Overhead	10,000	7,500	2,500
Advertising:			
Space and other direct costs	15,000	15,000	———
Overhead	5,000	1,000	4,000
Order entry:			
Salaries	3,000	2,000	1,000
Overhead	1,000	———	1,000
Billing:			
Salaries	6,000	5,000	1,000
Overhead	2,500	500	2,000
Total Savable Costs	$143,500	$117,500	$26,000
Less: Gross Margin Lost	———	75,600	———
Addition to Net Profits	———	$ 41,900	———

given up, shows, of course, the net savings, or the addition to the net profits of the business that will result from dropping the unprofitable sales. (Of course, if the net revenue that will be given up exceeds the expenses that will be saved, the net profits in the short run will be greater with, than without, the relatively unprofitable sales.) An example of an analysis of the savable and non-savable costs is shown in Table IX.

3. It is necessary to make definite plans to get expenses down when unprofitable sales are to be cut off. The experiences of several manufacturers have shown that projected savings in distribution costs often are never realized because of failure to make and execute definite plans for expense reduction.

When time-and-motion studies, cost accounting, and the principles of scientific management were first being developed and put in practical use in a few progressive factories, plenty of skepticism greeted the announced results of increased output and reduced unit costs. But today hardly anyone would question the very great achievements that have been made in increased output per man-hour and reduced unit factory costs since the 1880's when Frederick Taylor developed certain principles of scientific production management. And yet production men would be the first to admit that unit production costs are still very far from their irreducible minimum. The very large reductions in unit production costs which actually have been accomplished may be equaled or bettered in the future by the further development and use of management principles and techniques peculiarly adapted to the more difficult problems in the field of distribution.

8

Controlling Plant and Equipment Costs

CONTENTS

8

Controlling Plant and Equipment Costs

What is included in plant and equipment costs. Plant and equipment costs, for purposes of this discussion, include (1) expenditures covering the acquisition and disposition of plant assets, (2) expenditures covering the maintenance of plant assets while held for use in the business, and (3) expenditures charged to operating costs that represent the recovery of the original cost of plant assets. References in this chapter to capital assets or capital expenditures apply exclusively to plant assets, that is, those assets that are of permanent or semipermanent use in the company's operations, such as land, buildings, machinery, and other operating equipment.

This chapter will deal with the problems that arise in the planning and control of expenditures for plant assets, exclusive of those related to long-term forecasting and budgeting, and will present procedures and techniques that have proved effective in carrying out a capital expenditures program.

Need for controlling plant and equipment costs. Present-day manufacturing techniques call for an investment of thousands of dollars in plant and equipment assets for each employee on the payroll. It logically follows, therefore, that the supervision of these capital purchases, and the control maintained over them while they are actively producing assets of the company is a measure of the company's success in modern competitive markets. The amortization of these assets represents the fixed charges to be overcome in operations of future years. These charges, both for cost and tax determination, are of major importance in all manufacturing plants. The expenditures necessary to maintain these plant assets are even a larger portion of the final product cost. Fortunately, these costs are relatively easy to control, as will be shown in this chapter.

Responsibility for control of capital expenditures. It is the responsibility of the controller to assemble, coordinate, and, usually, interpret all data relating to proposed capital expenditures and to make a full, impartial, and intelligent presentation of the information to top management for final judgment. In this work he needs the cooperation of the plant engineers, the production manager, the sales manager, and the company economists and must draw upon his own experience in matters such as costs, sales statistics, and general business forecasting. In coordinating these data, the controller must not allow his judgment to be colored by optimistic predictions of sales and production men or by a general desire for expansion for the sake of size. Rather, he should concentrate on searching out all possible effects of the proposed acquisition upon the company's finances. He should coordinate all the submitted estimates with his own to obtain, as far as possible, the cold figures that tell the final probable results of a proposed purchase upon all phases of the business.

CONTROL OF ACQUISITION AND DISPOSITION
OF PLANT ASSETS

Classes of capital expenditures. A plan for capital expenditures control usually calls for consideration of three classes of capital expenditures.

1. Replacements of existing production facilities after useful life is terminated and additions to take care of normal and expected growth.
2. Acquisitions of cost-saving equipment.
3. Acquisitions of desirable but not necessarily cost-saving improvements.

Replacements and additions. Recommendations for replacements and additions to take care of normal and expected growth should be covered in the annual report of the production manager. Given the expected production schedule by the sales or statistical department, it is a comparatively simple task to project for a year ahead considering the existing equipment and the experience records of the past, assuming normal wear and tear, replacements, and maintenance and repair costs. The plant ledger and the plant account summaries, described later in this chapter, provide excellent experience data for such a report. If the computed output of the existing facilities does not equal the desired goal, it then becomes the duty of the plant engineers to present data covering the costs of providing for the remainder of the production. This can be done either by purchasing duplicates of existing facilities or by acquiring different or more modern equipment. In the latter case, sometimes a complete revision of producing technique is called for, thus initiating an intensive engineering study covering the entire producing functions. Generally, the plant engineers are sufficiently informed on the subject to recommend either one step or the other. In all but extreme cases, however, it is desirable to get data on both, in order to enable the men with whom the final decision rests to review all the facts in the case. In this report, the plant engineers should cover, both for existing and new equipment, and in as much detail as possible, the following points.

1. Original cost, including freight, taxes and handling charges.
2. Installation costs, including engineering, designing, and overhead charges.
3. Rate of output.
4. Operating costs.
5. Maintenance cost.
6. Useful life.
7. Obsolescence data.
8. Estimated scrap value.

Armed with this information, the controller has the basic data necessary to prepare a statement each year of the costs of providing the physical facilities necessary to attain the production desired.

Cost-saving equipment. Recommendations for the acquisition of cost-saving equipment ordinarily originate with the plant engineers. It is their function to keep abreast of all technical advances in their field, and to know at which point the acquisition of new equipment becomes or may become desirable from a cost standpoint. Not infrequently recommendations for cost-saving equipment originate with other departments, such as production or sales, but the worth of their recommendations must be tested by the plant engineers in order to give them proper standing for full consideration. Upon initiation of the recommendation, the plant engineers must prepare comparative statements containing the same information as mentioned in the preceding paragraphs on replacements and must furnish the controller with all the data necessary to prepare his presentation to top management.

The directors, or others in top management, may ask for studies to be made of expansion costs that would arise from proposals to branch out into new fields or to manufacture production units at present purchased or contracted for. The plant engineers must assemble data covering the costs of acquiring the desired production facilities, including the land, buildings, and equipment. Beyond the naked cost data, they must also assemble the information covering the effect, if any, upon the existing production facilities, as well as the ability of the contemplated acquisitions to absorb a portion of the existing overhead charges.

Desirable but not necessarily cost-saving improvements. Recommendations for the acquisition of improvements that are desirable but not necessarily cost-saving may originate with any department. The personnel department may recommend a new cafeteria, the production department may request some stand-by equipment for peak periods, the accounting department may need additional housing for records storage —all these must pass through the offices of the plant engineers to acquire the necessary cost data. This classification covers so many possibilities that it is neither possible nor advantageous to try to list them. It is sufficient to say that each one needs a detailed cost study made by the plant engineers before the data goes to the controller to be prepared for presentation to top management.

Handling of recommendations. When all proposals for the three classes of capital expenditures have been assembled for the period under consideration, the projects should then be listed in the order of their importance. Naturally, those acquisitions necessary to produce the expected necessary output will rank at the top, whether they be replacements of existing equipment or the purchase of more modern assets. The non-productive assets will normally relinquish precedence to those that are productive, although certain conditions may change this. Thus, the company executives and directors can receive for study and decision the combined opinions and recommendations of the operating heads on needed acquisitions. With knowledge of the financial position of the company, top executives and directors can then determine the relative merits of the recommendations and how many of them can be accepted.

Preparing the procedure for plant and equipment expenditures. The usual method of controlling capital expenditures is to have a written procedure outlining the steps that must be completed and information that must be obtained before approval for purchase is given. Naturally, each company must tailor its procedure to its own type of business. Generally, the procedures contain the following provisions:

1. The term "capital expenditures" is defined. As a general rule, this term is limited to the acquisitions that are of permanent or semi-permanent use in the company's operations, such as land, buildings, machinery, and manufacturing equipment. The procedure mentions the kinds of acquisitions that are treated as capital expenditures and that will therefore be subject to the rules set forth in the procedure.

2. All minor purchases of capital items are excluded from the terms of the procedure because of their large number and lack of importance. A minimum amount is usually stated above which such acquisitions are required to conform with the terms of the procedure. Authorization for expenditures below the minimum require only the approval and signature of stated authority, such as a department head, or are covered by a blanket authorization.
3. The use of a prenumbered printed form for the presentation of essential information is prescribed. Such a form is described under the heading, "Standard Practice Instruction."
4. The routine through which this form must proceed is explained in detail.
5. Responsibility for the various phases of the procedure, including final approval, is indicated.

Line of demarcation between capital and expense. In defining capital expenditures for the guidance of those initiating requests for such outlays, it is always important to be as explicit as possible in pointing out the difference between a capital and an expense item. In general, at least 80 percent of all contemplated expenditure items fall clearly within either category, but in the remaining 20 percent the resemblance can be so close that a special ruling is necessary. For example, a contemplated roof repair can be so extensive that at the completion of the job virtually a new roof has been constructed, and what started as a major repair may have become a capital addition. To provide for such contingencies, it is advisable to have a set of decisions prepared in advance covering expenditures common to the business that are normally subject to either classification. This classification should be made and approved by a member of top management, possibly the controller, and should be made only when absolutely necessary. Thus, consistency of treatment in the company's books will be assured, and comparative annual profit figures will be reliable. The list should always provide a minimum limit of expenditure under which nothing should be capitalized—say, unit expenditures of $20 or less.

In setting up a classification to determine the difference between expense and capital, there is a great temptation to lean backwards toward "charging off" to expense as much as possible in order to reduce current profit and consequently the income tax liability. Such a policy will not only understate true current profit, but also will unfairly burden the future with inadequate depreciation allowances. Also, flagrant violations of proper classifications will be adjusted by tax inspectors with consequent tax and penalty liabilities and the necessity for making complicated accounting adjustments. Therefore, a carefully considered and consistent classification, seldom modified and indicating a conscientious effort to conform with good accounting principles and tax regulations, will be most profitable and produce the best results in the long run.

Example of a capital expenditures procedure. The following is an example of a procedure governing requests for capital expenditures. This procedure is used by a company that has several manufacturing divisions. It is readily adaptable, however, by companies that operate with a single location. It is an unusually complete capital program guide.

STANDARD PRACTICE INSTRUCTION

PURPOSE

The Capital Investment Program is an integral part of corporate profit making. As such, it affects planning in various profit-making areas of the company. The purpose of the Capital Investment Program is to:

1. Identify and evaluate the most profitable opportunities for the investment of new capital funds,
2. Plan, control, and review capital outlays on authorized projects,
3. Highlight on operating statements the effect of expenses which arise out of investment in capital items, and
4. Encourage specific planning, on an intermediate term basis (six years), in order to properly evaluate future corporate capital requirements.

DEFINITIONS

Capital Asset—A tangible item which has an acquisition cost of $200 or more and a useful life of more than one year. It cannot, by definition, be consumed in the business. It includes items such as land, buildings, machinery, automotive equipment, office appliances, furniture and fixtures, etc. Within the terms of this program, leasing arrangements covering a period of more than one year shall fall under the definition above and be included in the statement of the program.

Acquisition Cost—Includes all incremental expense items such as:

    A. Invoice cost
    B. Freight cost
    C. Federal excise taxes, but not state sales taxes
    D. Assumed taxes on land and buildings
    E. Installation costs
    F. Commisions
    G. Title fees
    H. Professional fees (architect, legal, engineering, etc.)
    I. Leased property and equipment

POLICY

The Capital Budget will be submitted annually and will consist of two parts.

1. Projects for the coming plan year (original Budget year) that have progressed far enough in their engineering and cost estimates to permit reasonable evaluation, will be included in the program.
2. Intermediate term program covering a six-year period, including the plan year. Projects to be included in the intermediate portion of the program are those for

which study may not have progressed sufficiently far to identify segments but for which a conceptual identification can still be made. This program is to be completed in time for review by mid-August.

The following reports will form the basic part of the capital planning and control sequence:

Capital Budget
Finalized by mid-August for review by management by September 1st.

Carryover Budget
Finalized in time for inclusion in master plan on February 1st of the plan year.

Project Performance
Report to be completed in time for arrival in headquarters on June 10th, October 10th, and February 1st.

The Capital Budget will include all estimates of the expense portion of construction projects for the plan year and the five subsequent years.

The Financial Analysis and Planning Group, under the direction of the Controller, will ensure that all internal capital procedures meet with Corporate Requirements.The Controller will periodically review and analyze selected major capital projects after their completion and measure the results versus the objectives set forth in proposals. Such analyses will be made available to the originating parties.

A. PREPARATION OF PLANT PROPOSAL

Manufacturing   1.   Process all requests for capital funds on the Capital Investment Proposal Form 6358 (an illustration of Form 6358 and instructions concerning its use are contained in Exhibit A).

Note: Form 6358 replaces credit request forms for group I, II, III type projects previously used in the budget proposals for new jobs. On the reverse side of the form are some brief instructions. More explicit instructions regarding the data required on form 6358 are set forth in Exhibit A.

2.   Forward Forms 6358 to Financial Analysis & Planning.

Note: All requests will be initially reviewed by the Manufacturing area, then by the Financial Analysis and Planning area, for profitability evaluation and administrative purposes. In the event that profitability studies indicate a failure to meet minimum acceptable criteria,the Financial Analysis and Planning Dept. will recommend a further review of the project and a study of possible alternative approaches.

B. PREPARATION OF NON/FACTORY PROPOSALS

Financial   1.   Forward two copies of the "Non-Factory Capital Budget" Form
Analysis &   72 (Exhibit B) to department heads during the second week of
Planning   July.

Department
Heads

2. Complete and sign Form 72 (even if no items are required).

    2.1 Obtain approval of officer in charge.

    2.2 Forward original to Financial Analysis and Planning and retain duplicate in file.

Controller &
General Mgr.–
Operations

3. Review Form No. 72.

C. SUBMISSION OF PROPOSALS TO HEADQUARTERS

Financial
Analysis &
Planning

1. Collate, analyze, transcribe all approved Forms 6358 into Vevey requirements.

2. Consolidate data on Form 72 according to headquarters requirements and incorporate data with the Plant proposals.

3. Forward final budget to the Controller, Vice-President Manufacturing, and the President.

Manufacturing

4. Forward the approved budget, with appropriate correspondence, to headquarters.

D. REQUEST FOR SPECIAL OR ADDITIONAL CREDITS

Department
Heads

1. Request *Special Credits* during the year for *entirely new jobs not covered by a budget*. The proposal must be urgent, absolutely necessary and/or highly desirable; otherwise it should be included in the new jobs budget for the following year.

2. Request *Additional Credits* to cover unforeseen, excessive expenditures on jobs *already budgeted*. The request may be made during the year or when the budget proposals for brought-forward jobs are submitted.

   Note: Special Credits and Additional Credits by definition exceed $5000 and must be authorized by the officer in charge of the area requesting such credits.

3. Provide copies of the request to the President, Controller, and Treasurer.

E. APPROVAL TO SPEND

Financial
Analysis &
Planning

1. Notify originating location and affecting management personnel of headquarters approval and indicate any variations to the budget as originally submitted.

2. Forward copies of the approved programs to appropriate Marketing, Treasury, and Tax personnel.

   Note: Approval of the program by headquarters constitutes an appropriation, or setting aside of funds. It is not an authorization for expenditure.

Manufacturing   3. Prepare "Application for Expenditure" (A.F.E.) Form 825 (Exhibit C) when planning has progressed sufficiently to permit the commitment of extra funds for *Plant expenditures*.

                4. Assign sequence number to Form 825 for reporting and control purposes.

                5. Use "best estimate" available to prepare Form 825.

                6. Ensure that authority for expenditure is granted in accordance with signatory requirements.

                    Note: No funds exceeding $1000 will be expended without an approved application.

Financial   7. Compare data on Form 825 to approved Capital Program and
Analysis &   inform Vice-President Manufacturing of any increases in esti-
Planning   mated cost totalling 10% or more of the original budgeted amount.

Manufacturing   8. Forward Purchase Requisitions to the Purchasing Department when A.F.E. Approval is received.

Purchasing Dept. 9. Make necessary contractual arrangements.

Department   10. Prepare "Application for Non-Factory Expenditure"
Heads   (A.F.N.E.), Form 27 (Exhibit D) in duplicate for the following purchases:
                    A. Items budgeted in excess of $1000.
                    B. Items not budgeted that are in excess of $250.

              11. Obtain the approval of the officer in charge.

              12. Forward original Form 27 to the Financial Analysis and Planning Department. File duplicate copy.

Financial   13. Enter A.F.N.E. number, Prior Spent/Committed, total outlay,
Analysis &   and Budget amount.
Planning   14. Obtain approvals of Tax Manager, Controller, General Manager-Operations, and the Treasurer.

              15. Forward approved applications (Forms 27) to Office Services Dept. for processing.

Office Services 16. Return Forms 27 to Financial Analysis and Planning.

                    Note: Requests for expenditures not requiring an A.F.N.E. must be made directly through the Office Services Department.

F. PROGRESS REPORTS

Accounting   1. Determine actual commitments (from purchase orders) and ac-
Department   tual expenditures (from paid invoices and plant labor distribu-

tion). Post code sheets to show commitments and expenditures by budget credit for the plant or office locations.

1.1 Forward code sheets to Information Systems.

Information Systems

1.2 Prepare Accounting Tabulation on the 6th working day of each month to reflect activity through the end of the previous month. Forward report to Accounting Department.

Accounting Department

1.3 Review report and forward appropriate portions to Manager-Manufacturing and General Manager-Operations, as applicable. Forward a complete report to Financial Analysis and Planning.

Note: For capital project items, the Controller's staff will record expenditures based on the codes assigned by the Engineering Department. All expense items will be segregated from the capital items and charged to the appropriate expense accounts.

Financial Analysis & Planning

2. Prepare *Capital Expenditure, Form 6337,* (Exhibit E) each month to inform management of the status of projects within the capital program and indicate the following data:

A. *Budget*: amount of funds (current & previous totals) which headquarters has approved for each proposal,

B. *Expenditure*: amount already invoiced for each job,

C. *Outstanding Commitment*: total amount committed on the purchase order less actual expenditures,

D. *Region, District, and Warehouse Officers' Budget and Expenditures.*

3. Prepare Monthly letter regarding *Special Credits and Additional Credits* indicating all approved special credits and additional credits granted by headquarters during the previous month.

3.1 Distribute copies of letter to:
A. Vice-President, Manufacturing
B. Chief Engineer, Engineering
C. Manager, Manufacturing
D. Assistant Manager, Accounting.

4. Prepare reports of all instances where the total amount spent, or proposed, on major projects and large intermediate projects exceeds 110 percent of the budgeted amount.

4.1 Forward Over-Run Report to officer in charge.

FORM NO. 6358
/70

CAPITAL INVESTMENT PROPOSAL

DATE _____

PLANT/DIVISION _____   DEPARTMENT _____

NAME OF PROJECT _____   NUMBER OF PROJECT _____

PROJECT CATEGORY: MAJOR ☐   INTERMEDIATE ☐   BLANKET ☐   MINOR ☐

I PROJECT DESCRIPTION AND REASON FOR PROPOSAL

PROPOSED SUPPLIER: _____

TYPE: _____

CAPACITY: _____ DEGREE OF OCCUPATION _____ %

CAPACITY REQUIRED: _____ HOURS OCCUPIED _____

ESTIMATED DATE OF INITIAL OPERATION: _____

II ANALYSIS OF TOTAL CAPITAL EXPENDITURE

	BUILDINGS	MACHINES	TOOLS, FURN.	TOTAL EXPENDITURES
COST				
TRANSPORT				
DUTY				
ERECTION AND DEMOLITION				
TOTAL CREDIT TO BE GRANTED				
ESTIMATED DISTRIBUTION	19___	19___	19___	19___

III INSTALLATION TO BE REPLACED

DESCRIPTION: _____ INVENTORY NO. ____

MAKER: _____ TYPE: _____

CAPACITY: _____ YR. OF PURCHASE: ____

IV PROJECT CLASSIFICATION

SAFETY & CONVENIENCE ////	ROUTINE REPLACEMENT
SANITATION & HEALTH	OBSOLESCENCE
NON-PRODUCTIVE SPACE	OTHER

V URGENCY & RISK

SAFETY	URGENCY ////
IMPROVE PRODUCT QUALITY	NECESSARY
INCREASE PROFIT (Attach Form 1a) ////	STRONGLY RECOMMENDED
REDUCE COST	DEGREE OF RISK ////
EXPANSION · EXISTING PRODUCTS	ALMOST NONE
EXPANSION · NEW PRODUCTS	MODERATE
NECESSARY FOR OPERATION ////	SUBSTANTIAL

COMMENTS:

VI COST OF EVALUATING PROJECT

	TNCO	OUTSIDE
TOTAL COST	$	$
PAID TO DATE	$	$
PERCENT PAID TO DATE	%	%

VII START UP COST

DESCRIPTION	
a. _____	$ _____
b. _____	$ _____
c. _____	$ _____
d. OTHER _____	$ _____
TOTAL START UP COSTS	$ _____

VIII AMOUNT REQUESTED

CAPITAL PORTION	$
NON CAPITAL PORTION (before taxes)	$
TOTAL REQUEST	$
PREVIOUS REQUEST GRANTED	$
TOTAL PROJECT COSTS	$
INCLUDES CONTINGENCY OF	$

IX ESTIMATED EXPENDITURE TIMING

PERIOD ENDING · APRIL	$
PERIOD ENDING AUGUST	$
PERIOD ENDING · DECEMBER	$
YEAR END CARRYOVER	$

X FINANCIAL RETURN

RETURN ON INVESTMENT (R.O.I.)

PAYBACK _____ YRS.

XI POST AUDIT REVIEW

WHEN SHOULD THIS PROJECT BE REVIEWED RE: ACCURACY OF ESTIMATED R.O.I.

DATE: _____

XII APPROVALS   DATE

FACTORY MANAGER

CHIEF ENGINEER

TAX MANAGER

CONTROLLER

MANAGER · MANUFACTURING

VICE PRESIDENT/GENERAL MANAGER

TREASURER

Exhibit 8-A

<u>INSTRUCTIONS FOR CAPITAL INVESTMENT PROPOSAL (Form 6358)</u>

This form replaces Credit Request Forms for Group I, II and III type projects used in the Budget Proposals for New Jobs. The form is designed to furnish additional information for making investment decisions. The instructions cover only those items on the form that appear not to be self-explanatory. All the items must be completed by the personnel recommending the investment with the exception of those items which are underlined.

Project Catagory - <u>To be completed by Financial Analysis & Planning (F.A.P.) personnel located at Headquarters.</u>

I.   Project Description and Reason for proposal.

Degree of Occupation - Capacity required as a percentage of total capacity of proposed investment.

Hours Occupied - Average annual number of hours during which the investment will be used.

II.   Analysis of Total Capital Expenditure.

Estimated Distribution - Most expenditures are made in the budgeted year. However, where major projects are spread over several years, an estimate of the cash outlay should be distributed over the years involved.

III.   Installation To Be Replaced.

Year of Purchase - If the item was purchased used, indicate the date of manufacture in the comment section.

IV.   Project Classification.

Increase Profit – If any one of the three items under this category is checked, please attach a completed Form 1a, "Profitability Calculation."

V.   Urgency & Risk. (Applies only to proposals for increases in production capacity. <u>To be completed by the Marketing Department Personnel located at Headquarters.</u>

VI.   Cost of Evaluating Project.

Total Cost - Incremental Cost of evaluating the project prior to its submission as a Capital Investment Proposal, e.g. outside engineering consultation; feasibility and location studies, economic studies, operating cost studies, layouts and reports preparation, incremental traveling costs of corporate engineering and outside temporary help.

VII.   Start Up Cost

Cost of material spoilage, crew training, trial runs, and other costs in excess of planned operating standards are to be included in the profitability study.

VIII.   Amount Requested.

Capital Portion - Should equal "Total Credit To Be Granted" figure as shown in section II.

Non-Capital Portion - All expenses incurred that are applicable to the project that do not appear in the capital portion and, therefore, will not be capitalized, e.g. Evaluation Costs, Start Up Costs, Dismantling Costs etc.

Previous Requests Granted - Total funds granted for this project prior to submission of this capital investment proposal and, therefore, not included herein.

Contingency - Indicate if the outside consultants and/or suppliers have included a provision for a contingency in their estimates.

IX.   Estimated Expenditure Timing.

Period Ending - Estimate cash outlay for capital investments during the first budget year by period.

X.   Financial Return - <u>To be calculated by the F.A.P. Department at White Plains Headquarters.</u>

XI.   Post Audit Review

<u>Estimated date for an analysis of the project to determine the degree of accuracy between the forecasted R.O.I. and the calculated actual R.O.I. The Actual Post Audit will be performed by the F.A.P. Dept. at Headquarters.</u>

All capital investment proposals should be submitted to the officer in charge as soon as possible after the project evaluation is completed. The officer will determine if the urgency of the project calls for a special credit or an addition to the subsequent year's budget.

Exhibit 8-A (continued)

PROJECT CATEGORIES

For purposes of planning and control, capital projects are divided into four principal categories. It is important that all expenditures related to a particular project be brought together and considered part of the total project cost.

1. *Major Project*—That which will have a total project cost of $100,000 or more. The expense portion of individual projects should be included on a before tax basis. Incremental working capital requirements are also to be included in the estimated total project cost.

2. *Intermediate Project*—That which will have a total project cost of between $2,500 and $100,000. Related expenses and incremental working capital shall be handled as they are with major projects.

3. *Blanket Project*—Consists of a number of related individual assets or facilities. Each item is estimated to cost more than $50, but less than $2,500. However, the total cost of all the items covered by a blanket project should not exceed $10,000. Separate blanket projects could be established for each of the following categories:

   A. Plant and Equipment—Packaging and processing equipment, motor, tools, fire protection materials, etc.

   B. Office Furniture and Equipment—Desks, typewriters, calculators, and other office machinery.

   C. Laboratory Equipment—Microscopes, balances, sterilizers, ovens, and other laboratory equipment.

4. *Minor Project*—Individual items or facilities which cost over $50 but less than $2,500. Examples of minor proposals are meters, saws, storage vats, floor scrubbers, scales, pumps, etc. A minor project could be represented by any one item in the above categories for blanket projects.

PROJECT DESCRIPTION AND REASON FOR PROPOSAL

PROPOSED SUPPLIER: _____

TYPE: _____

CAPACITY:_____ DEGREE OF OCCUPATION _____%

CAPACITY REQUIRED: _____ HOURS OCCUPIED: _____

ESTIMATED DATE OF INITIAL OPERATION:_____

I.   PROJECT DESCRIPTION AND REASON FOR PROPOSAL
The description and reason should be brief but explicit enough to convey the purpose of the proposal.

A. *Proposed Supplier:* If known, the name of the manufacturer.

B. *Type:* If there is a preference, the type should be reflected (i.e. electric, propane, etc.)

C. *Capacity:* Manufacturer's capacity of the equipment.

D. *Capacity Required:* Capacity required in company operations.

E. *Degree of Occupation:* Percentage resulting from dividing the required capacity by the maker's capacity.

F. *Hours Occupied:* Number of hours in one year that the investment is expected to be utilized.

G. *Estimated Date of Initial Operations:* Month and year that the equipment is expected to be operational.

II ANALYSIS OF TOTAL CAPITAL EXPENDITURE	BUILDINGS	MACHINES	TOOLS, FURN.	TOTAL EX-PENDITURES
COST				
TRANSPORT				
DUTY				
ERECTION AND DEMOLITION				
TOTAL CREDIT TO BE GRANTED				
ESTIMATED DISTRIBUTION	19____	19____	19____	19____

II.   ANALYSIS OF TOTAL CAPITAL EXPENDITURE

A. All costs, transport, duty, erection, and demolition of the capital portion should be segregated into the three asset-type classifications provided. Any acquisition of land may be included in the building column, but the amount should be indicated separately in the comment section. The purchase of an automobile may be included in the tools and furniture column, but the cost should be noted separately in the comment section.

B. Estimated distribution of the capital investment should be shown for each year.

III INSTALLATION TO BE REPLACED	
DESCRIPTION: _____	INVENTORY NO. _____
MAKER: _____	TYPE: _____
CAPACITY: _____	YR. OF PURCHASE: _____

III.   INSTALLATION TO BE REPLACED

This section should be completed for all equipment and machinery that is being replaced. The reason for the replacement should be explained in the ''Description and Reason for Proposal'' section of this form.

IV.   PROJECT CLASSIFICATION

Capital projects will be identified for company purposes by one of the four following purpose classifications:

A.   *Regulatory, Safety, & Convenience*

Includes projects required for reasons of sanitation, health, convenience or other qualitative factors, with no reasonable alternative available.

No profitability calculations will be made by Financial Analysis and Planning but the need for immediacy and lack of alternative solutions must be clearly demonstrated in Part I of Form 6358.

B.   *Improve Product Quality*

Projects designed primarily to improve quality.

No profitability calculations will be made by Financial Analysis and Planning but the need for immediacy and lack of alternative solutions must be clearly demonstrated in Part I of Form 6358.

If possible, longer term profitability implications should be identified.

IV PROJECT CLASSIFICATION		ROUTINE REPLACEMENT	
SAFETY & CONVENIENCE	/////	OBSOLESCENCE	
SANITATION & HEALTH		OTHER	
NON-PRODUCTIVE SPACE			
SAFETY			
IMPROVE PRODUCT QUALITY			
INCREASE PROFIT (Attach Form 1a)	/////		
REDUCE COST			
EXPANSION - EXISTING PRODUCTS			
EXPANSION - NEW PRODUCTS			
NECESSARY FOR OPERATION	/////		

C.   *Increase Profit*

1. Reduced Cost: The criteria for these projects should reflect the requirement that the product involved is a reasonably long term product of the company and/or the equipment used is sufficiently flexible to be used for alternative lines.

Note: The minimum acceptable criteria (which will be calculated by Financial Analysis and Planning) are a *Payback period of not more than seven years* and an after tax Discounted Cash Flow *return on investment at least equal to the cost of capital.*

2. Expansion—Existing Products: In such cases, production capacity is increased for established lines and the risk of failure is small because the product involved is a reasonably long term product of the company and/or the equipment used is sufficiently flexible to be used for alternative lines.

   Note: Financial Analysis and Planning will verify that *payback will occur within a five-year period from the project's inception* and Discounted Cash Flow *return on investment will be at least equal to cost of capital.*

3. Expansion—New Products: In such cases, facilities are designed to manufacture and distribute a new product or product line.

   Note: Because of the greater risks involved in these projects, Financial Analysis and Planning will verify that the *payback will occur within a five-year period from the project's inception* and the Discounted Cash Flow *return on investment will be a minimum of two times the cost of capital.*

D. *Necessary for Operation*

1. Routine replacement: Includes replacing machinery, furniture, automobile tools, etc., in order to continue a normal operation.
2. Obsolescence of machinery & equipment.
3. Other is for an item that does not clearly fall in any project classification listed below. Identification of the purpose of the project should be noted in the comment section.

   Note: No profitability calculation will be made by Financial Analysis and Planning for the above except when alternative means are indicated.

$\overline{V}$ URGENCY & RISK	
URGENCY	///////
NECESSARY	
STRONGLY RECOMMENDED	
DEGREE OF RISK	///////
ALMOST NONE	
MODERATE	
SUBSTANTIAL	

V. URGENCY & RISK

This section is to be completed by the appropriate Marketing Division if the proposal is for increased production or the manufacture of new products. It is essential that the degree of Urgency & Risk be correctly stated since Financial Analysis and Planning will use these factors to form the basis for the expected payback and/or rate of return.

A. Urgency—*Necessary:* Requires immediate action to maintain the company's competitive position.

>*Strongly Recommended:* The company's competitive position will not be immediately affected.

B. Risk—Listed below are the degrees of risk and examples of each.

>*Almost None:* Volume of existing products will be increased and sales potential is known.

>*Moderate:* Equipment will be used to prepare a new product but can also be used to produce existing products.

>*Substantial:* Equipment is specialized and will be used to produce a product with an uncertain sales potential.

VI COST OF EVALUATING PROJECT	TNCO	OUTSIDE
TOTAL COST	$	$
PAID TO DATE	$	$
PERCENT PAID TO-DATE	%	%

VI.   COST OF EVALUATING PROJECT

All substantial costs directly incurred prior to the actual capital request should be tabulated. Such costs would include engineering consultation and advice, feasibility and location studies, economic studies, operating cost studies, layouts and reports preparation, travel expenses, etc. Only incremental costs of the project (i.e. out-of-pocket) should be considered in the project request.

VII START UP COST	
DESCRIPTION	
a. _____	$ _____
b. _____	$ _____
c. _____	$ _____
d. OTHER_____	$ _____
TOTAL START UP COSTS	$ _____

VII.   START-UP COST

Start-up costs are not a capital item. Therefore, funds required for start-up costs must not be included as capital in the New Jobs Capital Budget submitted to headquarters. Start-up costs will be reflected in a separate listing of the estimated expense portion of each major capital proposal. This listing accompanies the Capital Budget to headquarters. Start-up costs along with demolition and other non-recurring expenses are to be included in the total amount for the return on Investment Calculation. Some items of the start-up are as follows:

> Cost of materials spoilage
> Crew training
> Trial Runs
> Cost in excess of planned operating standards

The above should be considered as start-up costs until the project becomes operational.

VIII AMOUNT REQUESTED	
CAPITAL PORTION	$
NON CAPITAL PORTION (before taxes)	$
TOTAL REQUEST	$
PREVIOUS REQUEST GRANTED	$
TOTAL PROJECT COSTS	$
INCLUDES CONTINGENCY OF	$

VIII. AMOUNT REQUESTED

- A. *Capital Portion* —Consists of the amount of the total project cost which will be capitalized.
- B. *Non-Capital Portion*—Reflects the total of all other expenses incurred relative to the project.
- C. *Total Request*—Sum of capital portion and non-capital portion.
- D. *Previous request granted*—Indicate funds granted for this project through prior requests. Reference to these prior requests should be made in the comment section.
- E. *Total Project Costs*—Sum of total request and previous request granted.
- F. *Includes Contingency of*—Some outside consultants and/or suppliers include a provision for a contingency in their quotations. No contingency should be included by corporate personnel without the consent from headquarters management. If approved by management, reference should be made in the comment section.

```
┌─────────────────────────────────────────────────────────┐
│  IX  ESTIMATED EXPENDITURE TIMING                         │
├───────────────────────────────────────────────────────── │
│  PERIOD ENDING – APRIL              $                     │
│  PERIOD ENDING – AUGUST             $                     │
│  PERIOD ENDING – DECEMBER           $                     │
│  YEAR END CARRYOVER                 $                     │
└───────────────────────────────────────────────────────── ┘
```

IX.   ESTIMATED EXPENDITURE TIMING

The purpose of this section is to inform management as to the relative magnitude of spending by period in order to ensure that funds will be available.

```
┌─────────────────────────────────────────────────────────┐
│  X  FINANCIAL RETURN                                      │
├───────────────────────────────────────────────────────── │
│  RETURN ON INVESTMENT (R.O.I.)                            │
│  PAYBACK                                      YRS.        │
└───────────────────────────────────────────────────────── ┘
```

X.   FINANCIAL RETURN

This section will be completed by the Financial Analysis and Planning Department and has to do with profitability of the Proposed Project.

```
┌─────────────────────────────────────────────────────────┐
│  XI  POST AUDIT REVIEW                                    │
├───────────────────────────────────────────────────────── │
│  WHEN SHOULD THIS PROJECT BE REVIEWED                     │
│  RE: ACCURACY OF ESTIMATED R.O.I.                         │
│          DATE: _____                   │
└───────────────────────────────────────────────────────── ┘
```

XI.   POST AUDIT REVIEW

An estimated date for an analysis of the project to determine the degree of accuracy between the forecasted R.O.I. and the calculated actual R.O.I. The date should be as soon after the estimated date of the initial operation as is feasible.

XII APPROVALS	DATE
FACTORY MANAGER	
CHIEF ENGINEER	
TAX MANAGER	
CONTROLLER	
MANAGER - MANUFACTURING	
VICE PRESIDENT/GENERAL MANAGER	
TREASURER	

XII. APPROVALS

All capital investment proposals will require the signatures of management in the order specified in the table below.

	TOTAL CAPITAL INVESTMENT PROPOSAL		
	Less than $25,000	$25,000 to $100,000	More than $100,000
Factory Manager	X	X	X
Chief Engineer	X	X	X
Tax Manager	X	X	X
Controller	X	X	X
Manager-Manufacturing	X	X	X
Division-General Manager or Vice-President			X
Treasurer			X

Form No. 72 FINANCIAL ANALYSIS & PLANNING
7/70

NON - FACTORY CAPITAL BUDGET

None Required [ ]

Dept. Name _____

Dept. No. _____

ITEM	MONTH REQ.	QUANTITY REQUIRED			EST. UNIT PRICE	TOTAL EST. COST
		ADDITIONAL	REPLACE-MENT	TOTAL		
FURNITURE METAL - NEW						
Desk, Flat Top - 6 dwr						
Desk, Secretarial						
Chair, Swivel, Arm #900....						
Chair, Swivel #1500........						
Chair, Side						
Chair, Posture						
Files - letter 2 dwr.						
Files - letter 5 dwr.						
Files - legal 2 dwr.						
Files - legal 5 dwr.						
Credenza						
Table						
Bookcase						
Storage Cabinet (small) ...						
Storage Cabinet (large) ...						
Coat Tree						
Easels						
Tiffany Typing Stand #6000.						
Desk Typing Attachment						
Others						
(Specify)						
OFFICE MACHINES						
Typewriter, Electric						
Typewriter, Manual						
Adding Machine						
Calculator - Standard						
Calculator - Electronic ...						
Dictating Unit						
Transcribing Unit						
Others						
(Specify)						

TOTAL

Signed _____   Date _____

Approved _____   Date _____
         Officer in Charge

Exhibit 8-B

FORM NO. 625
2-66

APPLICATION FOR EXPENDITURE

A. F. E. NO._____

JOB NO._____

CLASS_____

DATE_____

LOCATION_____ _____

AMOUNT $_____

AUTHORITY IS REQUESTED TO COVER THE EXPENDITURES DESCRIBED BELOW AND IN THE PAPERS ATTACHED:

GENERAL DESCRIPTION

REASONS FOR AND RESULTS TO BE ACCOMPLISHED BY PROPOSED EXPENDITURES

ESTIMATED TIME TO COMPLETE

SUMMARY OF ESTIMATE

CLASSIFICATION	ADDITIONS & BETTERMENTS	OPERATING EXPENSE	TOTAL	STOCK	CASH	TOTAL
			DISTRIBUTION			
LAND	$	$	$	$	$	$
BUILDINGS						
EQUIPMENT						
FURNITURE AND FIXTURES						
AUTOMOBILES						
TOTAL	$	$	$	$	$	$

	RETIREMENTS	TRANSFERS
GROSS BOOK VALUE	$	$
RESERVE FOR DEPRECIATION	$	$
NET BOOK VALUE	$	$
SALVAGE OR TRANSFER VALUE	$	$
LOSS AND OBSOLESCENCE	$	$

cc: Treasurer
      Controller

DISTRIBUTION APPROVED _____

                                                        DATE
                        Manager - Taxes

APPROVED

NAME   DATE

_____

_____   AUTHORIZED

_____   _____

                                       DATE_____

Exhibit 8-C

FORM 27
1/70

APPLICATION FOR NON FACTORY EXPENDITURE

Location _____ A.F.N.E. No. _____
       Department/Office/Warehouse

                            Date _____

Location No. _____ Amount of A.F.N.E. _____

                            Prior Spent/Committed _____

                            Total Outlay _____

                            Budgeted Amount _____

Authority is requested to cover the expenditures described below and in the papers attached:

General Description

Reasons for and results to be accomplished by proposed expenditures

Classification	CHECK ONE	Requirement	CHECK ONE
Buildings		Additional	
Automobiles		Replacement	
Furniture & Fixtures		Transfer	
Machinery & Equipment			

Approvals   Authorized Date

Department Head _____ Date _____

Officer in Charge _____ Date _____

Tax Manager _____ Date _____

Controller _____ Date _____

General Manager - Operations _____ Date _____

Treasurer _____ Date _____

Exhibit 8-D

FORM NO. 8337
10/48

REPORT ON CAPITAL EXPENDITURES

BUDGET YEAR 19 _____

EXHIBIT E

PAGE _____

LOCATION: _____

STATUS AS AT _____

DESCRIPTION	PROPOSAL	GROUP	BUDGET					TOTAL PROJECT BUDGET (1)	PREVIOUS YEARS EXPENDITURES TOTAL	EXPENDITURES				TOTAL PROJECT EXPENDITURES (2)	VARIANCE			OUTSTANDING COMMITMENTS
			PREVIOUS YEARS BUDGET TOTAL	CURRENT YEAR			TOTAL PROJECT BUDGET (1)			CURRENT YEAR (Cummulative)					TOTAL PROJECT EXPENDITURES UNDER/(OVER) TOTAL PROJECT BUDGET (3)	CURRENT YEAR EXPENDITURES UNDER/(OVER) CURRENT YR. BUDGET (4)	
				PREVIOUS YEAR CARRYOVER	CURRENT YEAR PROPOSALS	TOTAL				1ST PERIOD	2ND PERIOD	3RD PERIOD					
1	2	3	4	5	6	7	8	9	10	11	12	13	14	15	16

1 - TOTAL PROJECT BUDGET - COLUMN 4 + 6
2 - TOTAL PROJECT EXPENDITURE - COLUMN 9 + LATEST EXPENDITURE FIGURE RECORDED IN COLUMNS 10-12
3 - VARIANCE FOR TOTAL PROJECT - COLUMN 8 LESS COLUMN 13
4 - VARIANCE FOR CURRENT YEAR - COLUMN 7 LESS LATEST EXPENDITURE FIGURE RECORDED IN COLUMNS 10-12

Exhibit 8-E

Estimating maintenance costs in studies of proposed expenditures. In assembling the data for proposed expenditures, close study must be given to maintenance costs, since these, over the life of the asset, usually exceed original cost. The engineers or production men should be required to show, in as much detail as possible, all information that can be obtained as to the amount of replacements and repairs necessary to keep the asset in good operating or useful condition over the span of its estimated life. Past experience of engineering data will generally provide the bulk of these figures, but allowance must be made for price fluctuations in maintenance materials and labor. These figures are best presented by estimating the cost cyclically over the proposed life of the asset, showing for each year the proposed repair and maintenance work necessary to keep the asset in its most efficient condition. An excellent and simple example is seen in estimating maintenance on an airplane motor. Experience has shown that a check on certain parts of the motor must be made every 25 hours of operation. Certain other additional items are checked after 50 hours of operation, and others at the 100-hour mark. Then the entire motor is overhauled at some point near 1,200 hours of operation. Past records show the normal number of hours and replacement parts needed in each inspection. Since experience has shown this method of maintaining the motor to be the most efficient, a simple and effective method of predicting maintenance expenditures is assured.

Factors in evaluating a suggested capital purchase. Three important factors to consider when attempting to evaluate a proposed capital purchase are (1) Alternative procedures and their measurement, (2) the effect of intangibles, and (3) the method of measuring the effect of the proposed purchase upon earnings.

Alternative procedures. In assembling the data covering a proposed acquisition for presentation to top management, the controller must keep in mind that all practicable alternative procedures must be considered. If any reasonable doubt exists concerning the superiority of the contemplated purchase, full data on the alternative method must be included. In most cases, the alternative to acquisition of a new machine is simply to continue with the equipment to be replaced, if that is possible. There are many cases, however, where a new or different type of machine can be substituted, different techniques for processing materials can be proposed, or even a complete reorganization of existing production facilities can be considered. Also, the possibility of contracting for work to be done outside at lower rates must never be overlooked. The individual case will provide its own alternatives. It is the duty of the controller to present fairly those alternatives that merit consideration. The method of arriving at a cost of alternative methods should be left to independent engineering surveys, because, as a general rule, the controller is not equipped to make such estimates.

Effect of intangibles. Many intangible factors enter into a contemplated capital purchase, any of which may be sufficient to determine the final decision, and all of which should be presented for top management's consideration. One way of arriving at the effect of these intangibles is to discuss the proposed expenditure with the heads of all departments to be affected and to record the views expressed. Some ways in which various departments might be affected follow.

Financial department. An expensive acquisition might place a dangerous strain on the financial structure of the company, enough to prevent other and equally desirable capital purchases. If working capital should be dangerously depleted, a very expensive chain reaction could start, completely nullifying all advantages of the acquisition. If the factor of early obsolescence is present or inherent, future large expenditures may be necessary and must be provided for. In any event, the planning of plant expenditures must be integrated with the company's long-term financial planning.

Production department. If the proposed expenditure leads to faster production, facilities to handle this extra production must be fully provided for. Care should be taken to prove the necessity of the acquisition; many purchases are made merely because up-to-date equipment is desired or because original cost has been fully amortized. Personal dislike of a machine has sometimes been a factor in its abandonment; personnel changes might be less expensive.

Personnel department. Calculated labor savings may not be realized if "made" work is found to accommodate displaced personnel. If labor relations are poor, passive or even active resistance may be encountered with new equipment or procedures. Conversely, new acquisitions can be a source of pride to labor, and improved or well maintained labor relations may justify a purchase. Top management too takes pride in the progress indicated by improvements due to capital expenditures, though that factor alone should not be dominant in any decision.

Sales department. A competitive position in the market must be maintained, and any extra production must have a ready market. Quality must be maintained, and even a small improvement in quality with no compensating profit increase may justify a new acquisition. A new process or new equipment may be a valuable advertising and selling point, even though it cannot be justified on a straight cost basis.

Measuring effects of capital expenditures upon earnings. Several methods may be used for measuring the effect upon the earnings statement of the purchase of new equipment. The two most commonly used are (1) the comparison of annual costs and (2) the rate of return on the average net investment.

The comparison of annual costs method. This method is the more common one and is usually used in comparing costs of using existing facilities with those that would result from using proposed new equipment. In both cases only direct costs should be used; estimates must be obtained from the best sources available. Following is an example of such comparison.

Net investment required on proposed installation $50,000
Estimated life of proposed installation .... 10 years
Estimated tax rate.. 48 per cent

Costs based on an equal number of units produced annually.

	FIRST YEAR		SECOND YEAR		THIRD YEAR	
	Pres-ent	Pro-posed	Pres-ent	Pro-posed	Pres-ent	Pro-posed
Annual direct costs						
Labor	$10,000	$5,000	$11,000	$5,000	$12,000	$5,500
Power and supplies	3,000	2,500	3,800	2,600	4,100	2,700
Other direct costs	1,500	1,000	1,700	1,100	1,900	1,200
Total direct costs	$14,500	$8,500	$16,500	$8,700	$18,000	$9,400

	FIRST YEAR		SECOND YEAR		THIRD YEAR	
	Present	Proposed	Present	Proposed	Present	Proposed
Annual savings in direct costs	$6,000		$7,800		$8,600	
Less amortization of new investment	5,000		5,000		5,000	
Annual savings	$1,000		$2,800		$3,600	
Less income tax at 52%	520		1,456		1,872	
Net annual savings	$ 480		$1,344		$1,728	

The point at which the purchase can profitably be made can be determined from such a comparison of annual costs. It should be noted that only direct costs plus depreciation on the proposed purchase and an allowance for income tax are used in this calculation. No provision is made for depreciation on discarded equipment since this is a cost already assumed and cannot be avoided beyond the effect of the value realized upon disposition. Interest costs may be added where financing is a factor, or if there is an appreciable difference in the new investment required. In that case interest on the original cost would be added at the rate to be paid in acquiring the capital.

The rate of return on the average net investment method. This method is best used to evaluate a piece of property with long life, such as a building. By formula, the rate of return on the average net investment is the net annual saving divided by the average net investment. As a simple example, let us assume a building is erected at a net cost of $100,000. The estimated life is 50 years, the annual depreciation $2,000, and the annual savings in direct costs over the previous building is $16,000. The average net investment is $51,000, computed by totaling the annual decreasing net investment and dividing by the number of life years. ($100,000 + 98,000 + 96,000 etc. ÷ 50) or by formula,

$$\frac{(\$100,000 + 2,000)}{2}$$

The net annual savings is computed by deducting the depreciation figure of $2,000 from the annual direct savings of $16,000 and reducing the result by 48 per cent to allow for income tax. The net annual savings thus becomes $7,280 ($14,000 × 48%) and, by formula, the rate of return on the average net investment is then 14.27 per cent ($7,280 ÷ $51,000).

The income tax rate is a very important factor in testing the worth of a proposed purchase. A period of high or excess-profits taxes can completely remove the desirability of most acquisitions and is probably the most discouraging factor in growth or expansion plans. In the preceding example, an income tax rate of 85 per cent would reduce the rate of return from 14.27 per cent to 4.11 per cent.

The interest factor has long been injected into calculations attempting to measure the effects of capital expenditure. The trend, however, has been to eliminate this factor in all but major acquisitions because of the relative unimportance of the total interest amount and the variation possible in the estimated figures. Academically, the return for use of money is a guiding factor, but, in actual practice, the determination of the

```
                                                    DIVISION _____
                                                    DATE _____

                              CAPITAL ASSET

                          DISMANTLEMENT REPORT

         REPORT NO.

         DESCRIPTION·



         Reasons and authorization for dismantlement or disposition:



         HISTORY:  Acquisition date        Depreciation record:  Charged to date
                   Asset No.                                      Remaining
                   Original cost                                  Book value
                   Replaced by Asset No.



         DISPOSITION DATA:  To whom sold
                            Value received
                            Date of receipt



         DISPOSITION COSTS (itemize)




         Accounting for disposition costs and salvage value:
              Acct No.
              Acct No.
              Acct No.
              Net Total

                  Accountant                      Division Administrator
```

Figure 8-1. Capital Asset Dismantlement Report.

economic value of a capital acquisition is broad enough so that the omission of the interest factor will not sway management in its decision one way or the other.

Authorization for disposal and transfers. Although primary emphasis is naturally placed upon the acquisition of capital assets, the importance of their transfer or disposition should not be overlooked. Top management has the responsibility over these assets during the entire period of ownership and their disposition requires sound executive judgement. The procedure method described for acquisitions is normally followed here, and a standard form, to be initiated when any asset purchased under the acquisition procedure is transferred, sold, or dismantled, is provided. This standard form should cover the reasons, costs, salvage value, accounting history, and disposition of the asset and should require authorization of top management. This form is often used to satisfy requirement 7 in the capital purchase authorization form mentioned previously. An example of such a form is shown in Figure 8-1.

		AUTHORIZED CAPITAL EXPENDITURE REPORT								
Division _____								Month _____		
Auth. No.	Description	Authorized Amounts				Expended to Date				Estimated to Complete
		Labor	Mat'ls	Other	Total	Labor	Mat'ls	Other	Total	

[*Actual size 10″ by 8½″*]

Figure 8-2. Authorized Capital Expenditures Report.

Control of authorized expenditures. The most common way of controlling capital expenditures as they accumulate is through individual project reports. As material is purchased and labor is performed, the amounts so accumulated should be shown on some type of running record, which also shows the amounts authorized. If it should appear that the project will exceed the approved amount, a revision of the expected costs should be made and immediately forwarded to top management with all possible explanation of the causes. Approval for further expenditures up to the required amount should be requested. A limit should be set under which this procedure is necessary, for minor overages are to be expected. The procedure described already specifies the amount of $1,000 or 10 per cent of the approved total, whichever is the lower.

These accumulations should be watched by departmental accountants, and periodic reports should be sent by them to the controller or treasurer, whichever has been named as the authority responsible for controlling the disposition of the authorized amounts.

An example of this report is shown in Figure 8-2.

Recording of capital assets. The recording of capital assets by a manufacturing company is normally effected by entries in a plant ledger, the total of which agrees with the general ledger total of capital assets. The plant ledger is usually a loose-leaf record, although there is a trend toward the use of visible card files. Whatever the type of record, however, the following are the important data necessary.

1. Asset's assigned company number.
2. Description.
3. Classification.
4. Date of acquisition, with purchase authorization reference.
5. Maker's name and number.
6. Total cost price, including freight and delivery charges, with title paper and accounting reference.
7. Periodic physical existence verification

PROPERTY RECORD

MACHINE OR ARTICLE NO.		CLASSIFICATION		

MAKE		MAKER'S NO.		LOCATION

BOUGHT OF

P.O.	DATE	COST	FREIGHT	

| FINAL DISPOSITION | | DATE | | VOUCHER NO. |

ACCRUED DEPRECIATION RELIEVED DATE   VOUCHER NO

DESCRIPTION

[*Actual size 4" by 8"*]

Figure 8-3. Property Record.

ORIGINAL COST.

	DEPRECIATION				DEPRECIATION	
DATE	ANNUAL DEPRECIATION	TOTAL DEPRECIATION	DATE		ANNUAL DEPRECIATION	TOTAL DEPRECIATION

Figure 8-4. Property Record, Reverse Side.

8. Building and floor location.
9. Annual depreciation rate.
10. Depreciation record.
11. Disposition date, including authorization, reference, value received.

An example of a card record is shown in Figures 8-3 and 8-4, that of a loose-leaf record is illustrated in Figure 8-5. It will be noted that the reverse side of Figure 8-5 (Figure 8-5a) contains a record of maintenance and repairs as well as a record of periodic revaluations.

The importance of maintaining an accurate plant ledger cannot be overemphasized. This record, properly and accurately maintained, furnishes management with detailed and current information concerning its most important assets—those which produce its income. It also gives a sound basis for (1) insurance valuations and claims,

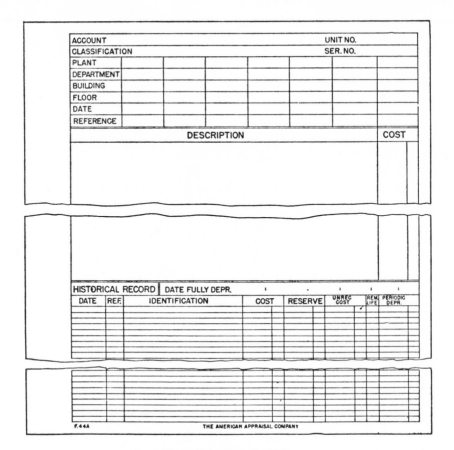

[*Actual size 8½" by 11"*]

Figure 8-5. Property Record in Plant Ledger.

(2) verification of personal property assessments, (3) allocations of departmental costs, and (4) the planning and budgeting of replacement equipment.

In assembling a plant ledger, a great deal of detail can be eliminated by grouping together under one asset total a homogeneous group of low-cost assets, such as office desks, and equipment whose detailed recording would be cumbersome and inefficient. The usual procedure when such assets are grouped is to record additions and disposals as made, with no identification other than the number of units in the group so affected. One depreciation total is then taken on the average value of the group during the course of the fiscal period. A single property record sheet is maintained for each year's additions in each group.

The plant ledger sheets are classified by location, according to building and floors, and further segregated according to functions, by accounts, departments, and production or cost centers. The records thus are arranged to assist in cost accounting, and in determining and allocating depreciation and other property charges to cost centers.

New plant ledger pages are made out for all new items that are to be capitalized on

Figure 8-5a. Reverse Side of Figure 8-5.

the accounts. The information for posting such new property is obtained from vendors' invoices, where the item was acquired through purchase, or from a job order, where the item was constructed in whole or in part with plant labor and material. After expenditures pertaining to buildings, machinery, and equipment have been recorded on the general books, the invoices and job orders are sent to the plant ledger clerk for entry on the proper sheets.

As retirements take place or items become fully depreciated in accordance with the life indicated on the ledger sheets and in the controls, the pages pertaining to the particular items are removed and held in a separate file.

The upkeep of the plant ledger does not entail a great deal of work because the cost, depreciation reserve, and annual depreciation provision shown on the plant ledger pages are accumulated by departments and accounts and set up on control summaries. One control is set up for each department and subaccounts (see Figure 8-6). With this type of control it is not necessary to make individual postings on the detailed ledger pages except in those instances where there is a change in the physical status of an item, or where changed conditions require that the remaining lives be revised. The periodic depreciation is not posted on each ledger page, but is handled through the control. This represents a saving of time in entries.

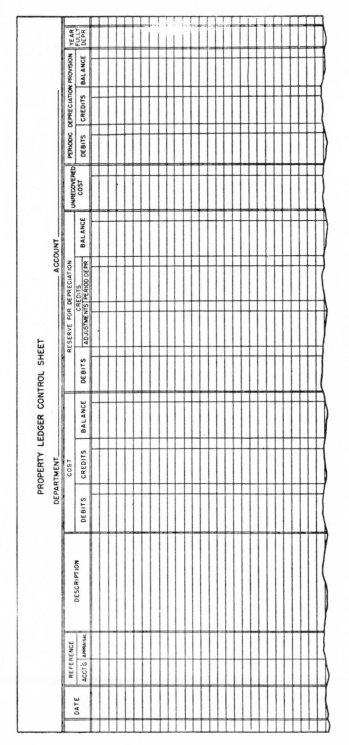

[Actual size 5½" by 8"]

Figure 8-6. Property Ledger Control Sheet.

Many companies have recognized the adaptability of the plant ledger to punch card systems. Wherever tabulating facilities are available, therefore, careful study should be made of the advantages of its use in producing the plant ledger as well as in computing the annual depreciation allowance.

In companies with a high percentage of fixed assets, a separate property record, which does not tie in with the books of account may be maintained for each asset item showing estimated replacement cost, so that insurance coverage will be adequate. This is done in order to keep appraisal and insured amounts comparable and expressed in current dollar values. Savings on insurance premiums will usually more than compensate for this additional record-keeping and appraisal cost.

CONTROL OF MAINTENANCE COSTS

Essentials of maintenance control. The control of maintenance expenditures is usually considered as one of the most difficult tasks confronting a plant manager. This belief arises chiefly from the fact that maintenance has usually been considered as an appendage of the operating program. As such, it has sometimes been regarded as a necessary evil. Since maintenance costs comprise an appreciable portion of the total product cost, such an attitude is both dangerous and costly. The only answer is a controlled maintenance program.

The four main essentials of a controlled maintenance program are (1) centralized maintenance control, (2) an efficient inspection staff, (3) reliable maintenance and repair cost records, and (4) first-rate property records.

Procedure for effective control. Let us suppose that a company having the four essentials just mentioned wishes to know what its maintenance needs are, how many of these needs are absolutely essential, how many are deferrable, and how such costs, after authorization, can be controlled. A logical approach to the problem calls for the following procedure:

1. *Preparation of a basic maintenance estimate, covering only the productive assets that are necessary to the operation of the plant.* The maintenance and repair cost records will show the cost history of each machine. From this record, the costs for the fiscal period under consideration must be projected. The maintenance staff can inform the maintenance supervisor which of the machines are subject to extraordinary repair. Allowances must be made for fluctuation in material costs, and any unusual cost or saving must be calculated. If cost records do not give adequate experience data, an engineering department or manufacturer's estimate must be included. To these direct costs must be added the cost of maintaining adequate inspection of these assets to insure that the equipment is maintained at an efficient point and will not be subject to unforeseen and costly breakdowns.

When all of the items have been assembled, they should be individually tested for economy between self and contract servicing. If repair services are inadequate, if trained personnel are not available, or if repair work will be concentrated within a limited period, estimates of the cost of contracting for this work from outside sources must be obtained. Also, methods of maintaining and servicing equipment should be examined. More frequent inspections, improved efficiency of spare parts, or better familiarity with operations may have improved the performance of a machine and deferred the major overhaul period. An increased or decreased rate of production can also greatly affect the cost of maintenance, and the production estimate must be consulted to cover this contingency.

When all of these factors have been taken into consideration, the maintenance supervisor has the basic cost of maintaining the plant's operating assets. This is the irreducible minimum below which the plant cannot attain the scheduled production.

2. *Examination of all of the remaining plant assets, such as buildings, auxiliary equipment, and nonoperating assets.* A careful inspection should be made to each item shown in the property records to determine the amount of maintenance necessary. The cost of this maintenance should then be carefully estimated and classified as urgent, deferrable within the fiscal period, and deferrable beyond the fiscal period.

3. *Presentation of maintenance cost program to management.* When the entire maintenance cost program of the plant has been assembled, it is presented to top management for its consideration. After management has selected the non-productive assets that are to be scheduled for maintenance and has indicated the extent of its authorization for maintenance costs, the program is ready for budgeting and scheduling.

4. *Budgeting and scheduling.* In budgeting and scheduling the amortized portions of the program, attention must be given to the following important points:

(a) The authorized tasks should be converted into time units in order to schedule an even flow of work.

(b) Production department heads should be consulted before scheduling major repair work.

(c) All routine work should be done by the same individual or crew, wherever possible.

(d) Schedule sheets should be made up for each machine or group of machines to aid in controlling the amount of work planned and completed.

(e) The items of deferrable maintenance should be evenly spread over the entire schedules so that, when the inevitable variations occur, the slack or overload can be adjusted.

(f) If a peak repair period is to be scheduled during an anticipated shutdown, services of competent personnel should be secured well in advance to insure no delay in reopening.

(g) Material requisitions should be scheduled to cause no delay in any portion of the program.

(h) Correct accounting and cost distribution must be assured to evaluate properly the progress of the program and to furnish dependable figures for future programs.

When the scheduling is completed, it may be translated into work orders, limiting to the scheduled amount the labor and material costs budgeted. In this way, the maintenance supervisor is able to follow the development of the program and to watch closely the variations from the planned schedule. At stated periods, he must then report to top management how the work that was authorized is being completed, both in respect to maintenance tasks completed and budgeted funds disbursed.

CHARGES TO OPERATING COSTS FOR USE OF ASSETS

Depreciation—a definition. It is dangerous and incorrect to assume, as most laymen do, that depreciation amounts cover a reasonably accurate charge to operations for the use of the capital assets employed in the production of the company's output, and that the reserves built up over the years will enable the company at any time to replace the exhausted assets. Describing the depreciation as an "Annual Allocation of Basic Plant Cost," and the reserves as "Accumulated Allocations Charged to Operations" brings out more accurately the function of depreciation and the depreciation reserves.

The Committee on Accounting Procedure of the American Institute of Accountants has approved the following definition: "Depreciation accounting is a system of accounting which aims to distribute the cost or other basic value of tangible capital assets over the estimated useful life of the unit (which may be a group of assets) in a systematic and rational manner. It is a process of allocation, not of valuation. Depreciation for the year is the portion of the total charge under such a system that is allocated to the year. Although the allocation may properly take into account occurrences during the year, it is not intended to be a measurement of the effect of all such occurrences."

Depreciation charges and replacement costs. Such a definition as is given above and correct terminology tend to overcome the periodic attempts to correlate depreciation charges with replacement cost. Those who argue this question overlook the fact that the theory of depreciation covers only the recapture of original or basic cost. It does not provide for any difference between the original and basic cost and the cost of replacing the asset. The problem of providing for replacement cost, therefore, is not relevant in a discussion of depreciation. It seems appropriate, however, to mention that many business executives, secure behind their annual depreciation allocations, continue to overlook the fact that their profits may be seriously overstated as a result of ignoring replacement costs. This overstatement of profit could be followed by overpayment of dividends, and consequent serious impairment of the company's financial position when the time comes for replacing exhausted and outmoded production facilities.

No reliable method has been developed for measuring this replacement cost. A lump sum appropriation from earned surplus is generally used and, seems the most practicable method of handling the problem. Other methods involving index numbers, annual appraisal of plant values, or application of a fixed percentage to cost of sales have been attempted, but no real pattern for arriving at an accepted figure has yet been reached.[1] Until such a pattern gains widespread acceptance, all such charges will go unrecognized by the Treasury Department as equitable charges to operations subject to deduction in computing taxable income.

Computation of depreciation. Many systems have been devised to apportion

---

[1] See *Journal of Accounting,* Vol. LXXXIV, No. 6, pp. 453-459, for a number of divergent views on the problem of depreciation and replacement cost.

depreciation in the manner that will most closely approach reality, but the five basic methods are:

1. Straight-line method.
2. Production method.
3. Diminishing-balance method.
4. Sum of the years-digit method.
5. Sinking fund method.

In all but the third of the above methods, original cost may be reduced by a declared salvage value and then depreciated. This practice is usually followed in cases where the scrap value will be a substantial percentage of the original cost, and in cases where removal costs will not be large enough to offset residual value.

The straight-line method, by far the most widely used, and attractive because of its simplicity, charges equal amounts during equal periods of time to liquidate completely original cost over the estimated life of the asset. For example: An asset costing $6,000 with an estimated life of 120 months would be depreciated at $50 per month. The basic assumption in the straight-line method is that an asset depreciates at a constant rate over an estimated life period. Although this is obviously purely theoretical, alternatives may lead to complicated accounting procedures.

The principal theoretical objection to this straight-line method is that it distorts costs when productivity is maintained at an uneven rate.

The production method consists in allocating depreciation either by units produced, hours of operation, or, in the case of assets purchased for a single project, by the jobs undertaken. This unit production method is used in those industries where potential production can be easily measured, such as depletion of a stand of timber or the output of a machine whose past performances indicate, within reasonable limits, its productive capacity. The ''hours of operating'' method is used when production is best measured by operating time, such as with airplane motors whose output is measured in hours of operation. The ''jobs undertaken'' method can best be illustrated by the case of a shipyard which receives an order for a certain type of ship, the construction of which requires the purchase of a new crane that will be disposed of after the completion of the order since it cannot be used in the shipyard's normal business. Disregarding the time element, the cost of the crane will then be allocated directly to the order and, at its completion, will have only scrap value on the company's books. The latter is very similar to a leasehold amortization.

The diminishing-balance method applies a fixed percentage of depreciation to the net value of the asset at the end of each fiscal period. For example: An asset with an original cost of $10,000 might be depreciated on the diminishing-balance method at a 20 per cent rate. As a result, the depreciation charges by years would then be $2,000 in the first year, $1,600 in the second year, $1,280 in the third year, $1,024 in the fourth year, and so on, so that, in slightly more than 10 years, the net value would equal $1,000, if that be the estimated residual value. It is obvious in this method that a residual value must always be set, since theoretically a true zero balance can never be reached. The chief value of this method is that it assigns greatest depreciation to the early years of the asset when maximum loss of resale value normally occurs.

The sum of the years-digits method applies a changing fraction to the taxpayer's cost for the property. In the fraction used for any particular year, the numerator is the number of years of useful life left to property, and the denominator is the sum of the numbers representing the years of life of the property. For example: An asset has a 5 year life. The fraction used in computing the depreciation allowance for the first year would be 5/15, 5 being the number of remaining years of life, and 15 being the sum of 1 + 2 + 3 + 4 + 5. For the second year, the fraction would be 4/15, and so on. The chief value of this method is that it assigns a greater depreciation to the early years of life when the greatest decrease in value is likely to occur.

The sinking fund or interest method consists in the payment of a fixed sum annually for a given period of years to a trustee for investment at a fixed rate of interest, so that the fixed sum plus all interest earned will equal, at the end of the stated time, the original cost or depreciable amount of the capital asset. Therefore, the depreciation charge against the asset each year will equal the fixed payment plus interest earned on the fund that year, and the reserve depreciation will always equal the value of the fund.

In some cases, such as amortization of patents where actual recovery of funds is not required but the interest-earned principle is desired, a theoretical fund is used with an estimated interest rate in order to arrive at an increasing depreciation rate. The complexity of the accounting in this method has restricted its use in almost all fields, except the public utility field, where it is generally used to satisfy legal requirements. Its only obvious advantage is to guarantee the replacement of funds originally expended for a capital asset. Its disadvanatages include the fact that the depreciation charges are higher in the later years when repairs and maintenance costs are also high, thus tending to distort profits in those years.

Importance of correct depreciation. By far the most common method of computing depreciation is the straight-line method using the rates approved for tax purposes. This system has the advantage of simplicity, but in competitive industry it can be very dangerous. Where pricing in a competitive market is important, and a larger capital investment is present, the amounts allocated to depreciation can determine the economic health of the company, Overdepreciation, or attempting to amortize the asset cost too quickly, results in a higher product cost which may result in losing a profitable market. On the other hand, underdepreciation, or insufficient amortization, can result in too low a product cost and corresponding capital depletion. Therefore, it is very important that, whenever competitive pricing is a factor, amortization of capital assets be carefully studied and periodically revised in order to reflect current values (replacement or reproduction) rather than book values.

Depreciation and federal tax regulations. The recognition of depreciation as a deduction from taxable income is contained in the Internal Revenue Code, Section 167, which states that, in computing taxable income, there shall be allowed as a deduction "a reasonable allowance for the exhaustion, wear and tear (including a reasonable allowance for obsolescence) (1) of property used in the trade or business or (2) of property held for the production of income."

The taxpayer may also enter into written agreements with the Treasury Department as to the useful life and proper depreciation rate for any particular asset. Such agreements are binding on both parties. They are particularly useful with respect to assets about which some doubt or special problems may exist, or which are not adequately covered by the Code.

Treasury regulations likewise do not discriminate directly against any particular method of computing depreciation. All five methods which have been outlined in this chapter have been accepted; and, generally speaking, any method that is customary in a particular industry will be accepted.

The 1958 tax law contains a provision for faster depreciation in that it permits, in the year of acquisition, an additional writeoff to corporations of up to 20 percent of the first $10,000 paid for new or used operating equipment or other tangible property (excluding buildings) having a useful life of six years or more, and which was purchased after December 31, 1957. This provision was designed to help the small business man, but it can be utilized by all corporations. In computing the new initial allowance, salvage is not to be considered. No provision for using the new allowance has been made in any of the preceding examples of depreciation calculations, because it is available only in the year the property is acquired.

Recognition of obsolescence is also granted for tax purposes. Experience has shown, however, that care should be taken in claiming income tax deduction under this ruling, because only cases of extraordinary obsolescence will qualify. It is necessary to substantiate a sudden change in style or demand or radical departures in manufacturing methods to justify such a deduction. If it can reasonably be determined in advance that equipment will become obsolete prior to the end of its original estimated useful life, obsolescence may be the reason for increasing the depreciation rate to recover original cost by the time obsolescence arrives, but in every case, the burden of proof of obsolescence is on the taxpayer.

ADR AND DEPRECIATION POLICY

The ADR rules set forth in Regulation 1.167(a)-11 were issued by the Treasury on April 20, 1973 and covered the *Asset Depreciation Range System*. Essentially the system introduces three major areas of substantial tax savings to business and eliminates some potential areas of controversy with the Internal Revenue Service.

The three areas are:

A. Making shorter useful lives available for certain eligible property.
B. Providing for an annual repair allowance without question as to whether items should have been capitalized.
C. Liberalizing salvage value rules.

Generally speaking, "eligible" property is depreciable tangible property, used in the United States, and placed into service after 1970. Overall ADR permits a 25 per cent increase in the annual depreciation expense over that currently available under the guidelines . . . a boon for low liquidity companies. The effect that ADR has on salvage value determination is that whereas formerly salvage values were deducted at the outset, under the new ADR rulings depreciation is figured on the full basis. Taxpayers who elect the ADR system will be permitted an "annual repair allowance" deduction without question as to whether any part of the deduction should have been capitalized. This can eliminate the annual spirited dialogue with IRS agents.

Treatment of fully amortized assets still in use. Normally, the number of fully depreciated assets still in use is very small, and the subsequent understatement of normal amortization cost is negligible. Under certain circumstances, however, it is possible to have a large increase in fully amortized assets, continuing in use and giving rise to the need for special accounting treatment in order to record fairly a true operating cost. Two examples of this condition may be cited. One is the case of wartime emergency facilities which have been granted a high amortization rate by the government and which continue into useful production life after the emergency period during which they were fully amortized. The other is the case of aircraft which, through unforeseen circumstances are required to continue to operate far past the period when they originally were thought to have become obsolete.

The usual method of handling this situation is to charge normal depreciation to costs as long as the assets are in use but to offset these charges with a well defined credit to the profit and loss account.[2] The value of this method can be seen by the fact that it insures more uniform operating costs and, at the same time, gives management a measure by which it may gauge the advantage in cost provided by these full amortized assets. Some firms prefer to give no such accounting recognition to the situation but to outline the situation in a balance sheet note. The important thing, however, is the recognition of the effect that fully amortized assets can have upon the earnings statement. Therefore, when a company or any department thereof retains in use an applicable amount of fully amortized assets, some type of accounting treatment is necessary to provide for the lack of amortization charges.

Whatever recognition is given to this condition, there must always be borne in mind that no federal income tax deduction can be allowed for further amortization of once fully amortized facilities, and any attempt to account for the use of these facilities must reflect this fact.

Appraisals. The use of appraisal figures covering capital assets is becoming increasingly popular as the variety of their uses becomes known. Although such figures can never be reliably introduced into the books of account without serious complications, their application in the determination of capital acquisitions and disposal values, insurance values, tax assessment values, and replacement costs is very valuable. In addition, where the industry is competitive, amortization costs based on the opinions of competent apprasiers can be of extreme importance in fixing product costs.

There are many different degrees of values on a current balance sheet. The cash and receivables are reflected in present-day dollars, machinery and equipment may be reflected in dollars of a decade ago, and land values may be stated in dollars of still another decade preceding that. It is almost impossible, therefore, for executives to know accurately the actual worth of all company assets, and as long as the world economy moves in cycles of varying purchasing power, only competent and frequent appraisals can disclose their true values.

---

[2]Where asset group depreciation rather than unit depreciation is used, the lives of individual units may be much shorter or much longer than the average life of the group. With continuing groups, occasional actuarial checks should be made.

9

How to Compute and Use
the Break-Even Point

CONTENTS

9

How to Compute and Use the Break-Even Point

What is the break-even point? A statement of income, profit, and loss indicates the amount of net gain or loss for the period covered. However, when such a statement shows a loss, it does not show what additional amount of sales would have been needed to eliminate the loss. When it shows a profit, it does not show what amount of reduction in sales would have wiped out the profit. The point in dollars of sales volume at which neither loss nor gain is made is known as the break-even point.

The break-even point is not an invariable figure for all time for a particular enterprise. It may change from time to time as the factors affecting it undergo change. Some of these factors are:

1. Changes in the total of periodical expenditures for such costs and expenses as are relatively fixed in amount regardless of variations in the activity of the business. (Examples: rent, taxes on real property, and the like.)
2. Changes in price levels.
3. Changes in the percentage distribution of sales (''sales mix'') among more profitable and less profitable classes of business.
4. Changes in the productivity of labor.
5. Changes in unit costs of materials.
6. Changes in unit rates of any expenditure, such as changes in wage rates, electric utility charges, social security taxes, unemployment insurance, and so on.
7. Changes in the mark-up percentage for profit added to normal costs in pricing.
8. Changes in the ratio of materials consumed to direct labor.
9. Changes in physical conditions within or surrounding the enterprise and affecting expenditures, such as variations from a mean average external temperature.

Uses of the break-even point. Despite the variability of the break-even point, its ascertainment yields information useful for guidance in making business decisions and in forecasting. This will be evident from the illustrations used in this chapter to show:

1. How to determine the break-even point (Example 1).

2. How to determine the increase in sales needed to break even when there has been a loss (Example 2).
3. How to determine the amount of sales needed to produce a certain amount of profit before taxes (Example 3).
4. How to determine the amount of sales needed to produce a certain amount of profit before taxes if direct labor costs are reduced by the additional volume (Example 4).
5. How to determine the amount of sales needed to produce a certain profit before taxes if there has been a loss, labor costs are reduced, and fixed costs are reduced (Example 5).
6. How to use the break-even point in determining questions of business policy concerning price and volume changes (Example 6).
7. How to determine the price level needed to produce a certain amount of profit when sales volume declines (Example 7).

The principles brought out in the illustrations, and the mathematical operations explained, can be applied to numerous situations beyond those presented. For example, data can be obtained on variable costs for individual products and product lines for purposes of comparisons of profitability. This can be extended for use in studies of compensation of sales personnel, profitability of advertising expenditures and increases therein, and the like. (Variable costs are those that vary directly with the volume of sales or output.)

Limitations of illustrations. The examples that follow have, of necessity, been based on hypothetical statements of income, profit, and loss. They show what could or should have been done during a period in the past. The computations would be mere useless mathematical speculations if they could be applied only to past operations. They can be, and frequently are, used in connection with planning future operations. The data for computations in connection with such planning can be derived from data on operations of the past. Success in applying break-even point principles to future operations is approximately in direct proportion to (1) the accuracy of the analysis of past operations and (2) the accuracy of the estimates of future changes and of the effects of such changes on all items entering into the computations. These computations, as will be evident, can become a major tool in forecasting the effects of changes in business policy, changes in costs, productivity, sales volume, pricing, and other factors.

The examples that follow make the following assumptions, for purposes of keeping the explanation simple.

1. That estimates of normal cost used in quoting prices are accurate.
2. That all prices include a uniform percentage of mark-up over normal costs, and that the sales mix remains constant.
3. That there is no variation in labor productivity, except as noted.
4. That changes in variable costs are compensated for in price changes to the exact extent necessary to preserve variable costs at the same *percentage* of the sales dollar as obtained prior to any changes in variable costs and selling prices.

In any actual situation these assumptions would not hold. Each factor would have to be taken into account in applying the principles to estimates relating to future operations. One of the major factors to be considered is sales mix.

The figures used are taken at random and are not intended as factual or representative of actual facts in any way. Rates used for federal and state taxes on income are merely illustrative and are not actual rates. The computations have not been carried out to exact figures and the last two digits may not be exact.

EXAMPLES ILLUSTRATING PRINCIPLES OF COMPUTING AND USING THE BREAK-EVEN POINT

Example 1. How to determine the break-even point. Assume the following simplified statement of income, profit, and loss of a manufacturing corporation, disregarding conventional grouping of costs and expenses and applying the designation "expenses," without distinction, to items conventionally described as "costs" or "other deductions" as well as those ordinarily classified as "expense."

Assume further that all sales are priced at a uniform mark-up over normal cost and that accurate normal costs are used in preparing price quotations.

Question: At what point in sales volume might there have been no profit and no loss?

To obtain the answer to this question, first analyze all the costs and expenses into two groups:

1. Those costs and expenses that might not have been more or less than those indicated if sales had been more or less ("fixed expenses").

Sales		$100,000.00
Cash discount on sales	$ 1,200.00	
Materials consumed	20,000.00	
Direct labor	30,000.00	
Rent	5,000.00	
Light and power	2,000.00	
Repairs and maintenance	4,000.00	
Depreciation	3,000.00	
Indirect labor	4,800.00	
Manufacturing supplies	3,000.00	
Fire and sprinkler leakage insurance	500.00	
Compensation insurance:		
On direct labor	400.00	
On indirect labor and all salaries	65.00	
Unemployment insurance:		
On direct labor	870.00	
On indirect labor and all salaries	440.00	
Social security taxes:		
On direct labor	300.00	
On indirect labor and all salaries	145.00	
Other insurance expense	100.00	
Office supplies	1,000.00	
Office salaries	8,000.00	
Salaries of officers	1,000.00	
Sales commissions	2,000.00	
Selling expenses	1,000.00	
Interest expense	200.00	
Total expenses		$89,020.00
Deduct:		
Cash discount on purchases	$350.00	
Interest income from bonds	100.00	

Total deductions from expenses	$ 450.00	
Net expenses	$88,570.00	
Net profit before taxes		$ 11,430.00

2. Those costs and expenses that vary directly with the sales volume, or are a fixed *percentage* of the sales dollar ("variable expenses").

Some items will be known to contain elements of both classes: that is, some items will consist partly of "fixed" and partly of "variable" costs or expenses. These are referred to in this explanation as "mixed costs," but, for purposes of the present illustration, each item of cost or expense will be treated as either entirely fixed or entirely variable. The separation of the fixed from the variable element of mixed costs involves a special technique which will be explained later.

Analysis of the items into fixed and variable costs and expenses on the above basis results in the following:

	Fixed in amount regardless of sales volume	Variable directly with sales
Cash discount on sales		$ 1,200.00
Materials consumed		20,000.00
Direct labor		30,000.00
Rent	$ 5,000.00	
Light and power		2,000.00
Repairs and maintenance		4,000.00
Depreciation	3,000.00	
Indirect labor	4,800.00	
Manufacturing supplies		3,000.00
Fire and sprinkler leakage insurance	500.00	
Compensation insurance:		
On direct labor		400.00
On indirect labor and all salaries	65.00	
Unemployment insurance:		
On direct labor		870.00
On indirect labor and all salaries	440.00	
Social security taxes:		
On direct labor		300.00
On indirect labor and all salaries	145.00	
Other insurance expense	100.00	
Office supplies	1,000.00	
Office salaries	8,000.00	
Salaries of officers	1,000.00	
Sales commissions		2,000.00
Selling expenses	1,000.00	
Interest expense	200.00	
	$25,250.00	$63,770.00
Deduct:		
Cash discount on purchases		$ 350.00
Interest income from bonds	$ 100.00	
	$25,150.00	$63,420.00

Solution: The variable costs and expenses of $63,420 represent 63.42 per cent of the sales of $100,000. The difference between 63.42 per cent and 100 per cent is 36.58 per cent and represents the average contribution of each sales dollar toward defraying the fixed costs of $25,150. To find what approximate total sales will absorb the fixed cost of $25,150 divide this amount by 36.58 per cent. The result is $68,700. This is the approximate sales volume (at the same price level, labor productivity, and so on) at which there would have been neither gain nor loss (the break-even point). Every dollar of sales beyond that volume contributed on the average about 36.58¢ to net profit. Had sales been less than $68,700, the net loss would have been approximately 36.58 per cent of the difference between $68,700, and the (lower) actual sales. (The break-even point and the exact percentage of profit differential could be ascertained more precisely if "mixed costs and expenses" were analyzed to obtain their fixed and variable components, by the method explained later.)

Proof of computation:

If sales had been		$68,700
Variable costs would have been about		
63.42% of $68,700	$43,550	
Fixed costs would have remained at		
about	25,150	
Total costs would have been about		68,700
Net profit or loss would have been about		None

Example 2. How to determine the increase in sales needed to break even when there has been a loss. Using the facts given in Example 1, assume that the sales, because of lower prices (20 per cent average), had been only $80,000 instead of $100,000 and that all costs and expenses (including cash discount on sales) had remained in the same amount as stated. The statement would have shown a net loss of $8,570.

Question: What approximate amount of additional sales (over $80,000) would have been needed at the same price to eliminate the loss?

Solution: Variable costs of $63,420 were 79.275 per cent of the $80,000 of sales. Deducting 79.275 per cent from 100 per cent leaves 20.725 per cent as the contribution of differential sales towards defraying the fixed costs of $25,150.

To find the sales needed at the same price level, same labor productivity, and so on as the $80,000 of sales to break even, divide $25,150 by 20.725 per cent. The answer is $121,500 of sales.

Proof of computation:

Sales at breakeven point		$121,500
Costs and expenses:		
Variable (79.275% of $121,500)	$96,350	
Fixed	25,150	
Total costs and expenses		121,500
Net profit or loss		None

Thus, additional sales of $41,500 (52 per cent increase) would have been needed at the same price level, and so on, to wipe out the loss incurred when total sales were $80,000 or prices were an average of 20 per cent lower than in Example 1.

Example 3. How to determine the amount of sales needed to produce a certain profit before taxes.

Question: Using the facts given in Example 2, suppose further that it is desired to learn what amount of sales beyond $80,000 would have been needed to produce an $8,000 net profit before taxes. (The additional sales would have to be at the same price level and labor productivity, and other variable cost factors would have to remain unchanged as percentages on sales.)

Solution: Treat the desired profit of $8,000 as if it were a fixed cost. Adding $8,000 of desired profit (before taxes) to $25,150 of fixed costs makes an amount of $33,150 to be absorbed out of total sales. Since differential sales yield 20.725 per cent, divide $33,150 by 20.725 per cent. The result of $160,000 is the total sales needed to meet fixed costs and produce a net profit of $8,000. This is an increase in sales of $80,000 or 100 per cent over the actual sales of $80,000 (or, $8,570 loss plus $8,000 desired profit = $16,570 to be absorbed by added sales. $16,570 ÷ .20725 = $80,000 added sales needed).

Proof of computation:

Sales:		
Originally	$ 80,000	
Increase needed	80,000	
Total sales needed		$160,000
Costs and expenses:		
Variable: 79.275% of $160,000	$126,850	
Fixed costs	25,150	
Total costs and expenses		152,000
Net profit before taxes		$ 8,000

Example 4. How to determine the amount of sales needed to produce a certain net profit before taxes if direct labor costs are reduced by the additional volume. Using the facts given in Examples 1 and 2, assume that sales were $80,000 as in Example 3, and that it has been *definitely established* that, if the volume of sales had been very substantially higher and at the same price level, the cost of all direct labor per unit of production and sale would have been reduced by 8 per cent because of more intensive utilization of the labor force or for other reasons.

Question: What sales would then have been needed to produce an $8,000 net profit before taxes?

Solution:

Variable costs on sales of $80,000 were		$63,420
(for details see Example 1)		
This included $30,000 of direct labor. 8% of		
$30,000 is to be deducted from variable costs	$2,400	

It is assumed that three items of variable expense will vary in cost in direct proportion to
variations in cost of direct labor. These are
compensation insurance, $400; unemployment
insurance, $870; and social security taxes,
$300; total, $1570.

8% of $1570 is......................................	125
Total deductions	2,525
Revised variable costs	$60,895

$60,895 is 76.12 per cent of sales of $80,000 as the revised percentage of variable
costs on sales. Subtracting 76.12 per cent from 100 per cent leaves 23.88 per cent as
the average contribution of all sales to the payment of fixed costs and the production of
net profit.

Fixed costs are	$25,150
Profit desired is	8,000
Total	$33,150

Divide $33,150 by 23.88 per cent. The result of $138,819 or an increase of $58,819
(73.5 per cent) over the basic $80,000 of sales, is the total of sales needed to produce a
net profit of $8,000.

An 8 per cent reduction in direct labor unit cost in this example makes it possible
to make the same net profit with a 73.5 per cent increase in sales as against a 100 per
cent needed sales increase in the absence of the benefit of this labor productivity
increase. (An 8 per cent reduction in labor unit costs is the result of an 8.7 per cent
increase in hourly labor productivity.)

Proof of computation:

Sales		
Originally	$ 80,000	
Added sales needed	58,819	
Total sales needed		$138,819
Costs and expenses:		
Variable costs		
$63,420 less $2,525 = $60,895 ÷ $80,000 =		
76.12% × $138,819	$105,699	
Fixed costs	25,150	
Total costs		130,819
Net profit as desired (before taxes)		$ 8,000

**Example 5. How to determine amount of sales needed to produce a certain
profit before taxes if there has been a loss, if prices are lowered,and if labor costs
and fixed costs are lowered.** Assume the following:

1. Sales are $80,000 as in Example 2 with costs as stated in Example 1.
2. There has been a loss of $8,570.
3. Productivity of labor is increased to the extent necessary to reduce labor costs per unit by percent of labor costs.
4. Sales can be increased only by a uniform price reduction of 5 per cent on all of the additional business.
5. Fixed costs are reduced by $1,150.
6. A net profit of $4,000 (before taxes) is desired.

Question: What total sales are needed to produce the profit desired?
Solution:

Fixed costs are $25,150 less $1,150	$24,000
Desired profit is	4,000
Total of fixed costs and desired profit is	$28,000

We know from Example 4 that the margin over variable cost on the first $80,000 of sales is 23.88 per cent or $19,105. Therefore the additional sales (at 5 per cent price reduction) must absorb $8,895 ($28,000 less $19,105). The margin on the additional sales is 19.88 per cent. (Variable cost is $76.12 on $95 of sales, or 80.12 per cent of additional sales. 100% less 80.12 per cent = 19.88 per cent.)

Divide $8,895 by 19.88 per cent. The result is $44,750.

To absorb $8,895 at 19.88 per cent margin will require $44,750 of added sales (56 per cent increase over $80,000), or total sales of $124,750.

Proof of computation:
Sales:

At full price	$80,000	
At 5% reduction	44,750	
Total sales		$124,750

Costs and expenses:
Variable costs:

76.12% of $80,000 =	$60,895	
[1]76.12% of $44,750 =	35,855	
95%		
($35,855 is 80.12% of $44,750)		
Total variable costs	$96.750	
Fixed costs	$25,150	
Less reduction	1,150	

---

[1]Explanation of line reading: 76.12% of $\frac{\$44.750}{95\%}$ = $35.855

Since the additional sales are the equivalent of $.95 for each $1.00 of sales contained in the basic $80,000 of sales, and since the variable cost of 76.12% must be taken on the basic sales dollar, the equivalent basic sales dollars are found by treating the $44,750 as having a value of only 95% and therefore representing $47,105 of sales at full price ($44,750 ÷ 95%).

Fixed costs—balance	$24,000	
Total costs and expenses		$120,750
Net profit (before taxes) as desired		$ 4,000

Example 6. How to use the break-even point in determining questions of business policy concerning price and volume changes. A new set of facts will now be presented to show how the break-even point can be used in determining such questions of business policy as:

1. What will be the break-even point and net profit or loss if current prices are maintained and sales rise or fall by various percentages?
2. What will be the break-even point and net profit or loss if current prices fall 5 per cent and sales rise or fall by various percentages?
3. What will be the break-even point and net profit or loss if current prices rise 10 per cent and sales rise or fall by various percentages?
4. What will be the break-even point and net profit or loss if current prices rise 15 per cent and sales rise or fall by various percentages?

Basic data for finding the break-even points in situations 1, 2, 3, and 4. Assume that statement of income, profit and loss shows the data appearing in the column of figures headed "At actual level of sales and prices."

The computations in 1 through 4 indicate the type of "thinking in figures" that is made possible by the use of the break-even principles and mathematics in trying to forecast the future effect of present pricing policies on profits in the future when volume of business may be greater or less than the present.

On the basis of 10 per cent net profit (before taxes) on sales of $5,000,000 per year:

	At actual level of sales and prices	Same volume of business at actual price level less 5% price reduction
Sales per year	$5,000,000	$4,750,000
Net profits		
Before taxes: 10% at present level of sales	500,000 10% on sales	250,000 5.3% on sales
After federal income and state taxes of		
about 40.7%,† net profit is	296,500 5.9% on sales	148,250 3.1% on sales
Costs:		
Sales	5,000,000	4,750,000
Profit before taxes	500,000	250,000
Total costs (sales less profit)	$4,500,000	$4,500,000

Costs consist of:		
*Variable costs	3,300,000*	*69.5% on
(66.0% on sales of $5,000,000)		sales of
*Fixed costs (fixed in amount)	1,200,000	$4,750,000
	$4,500,000	
Breakeven point is:		
Sales per year of	$3,540,000	$3,940,000
Breakeven point will be reached if present		
sales volume should decline by	29.2%	17%
Proof of computation:		
Sales at breakeven point	3,540,000	3,940,000
Fixed costs	$1,200,000	$1,200,000
Variable costs		
(66% of $3,540,000; 69.5% of $3,940,000)	2,340,000	2,740,000
Total costs	$3,540,000	$3,940,000
Profit or loss	None	None
Loss per sales dollar if sales fall below		
breakeven point		
($1.00 − 66% = 34¢; $1.00 − 69.5% = 30½¢)	34¢	30½¢

† This tax rate may be lower or higher at any particular time depending upon the laws then in effect.

* Assume that these figures result from complete analysis of all "mixed" costs into their fixed and variable elements.

1. AT PRESENT PRICES

Sales	$5,500,000	$5,000,000	$4,500,000	$4,000,000	$3,500,000	$3,000,000
% Above or Below Present Volume:	10% Up	Present Volume	10% down	20% down	30% down	40% down
Costs:						
Fixed	$1,200,000	$1,200,000	$1,200,000	$1,200,000	$1,200,000	$1,200,000
Variable (66%)	3,630,000	3,300,000	2,970,000	2,640,000	2,310,000	1,980,000
Total costs	$4,830,000	$4,500,000	$4,170,000	$3,840,000	$3,510,000	$3,180,000
Net profit or *loss*					Loss	Loss
Before taxes	$ 670,000	$ 500,000	$ 330,000	$ 160,000	$ 10,000	$ 180,000
After taxes	397,000	296,500	196,000	95,000	*	*
Per cent Net profit or *loss* on sales						
Before taxes	12.2%	10.0%	7.4%	4.0%	*	6.0%
After taxes	7.2%	5.9%	4.4%	2.4%	*	*
Per cent decline in net earnings before and after taxes	Base Gain	25.3% Base	50.6% 34%	76% 68%	all all	

* Net losses after taxes may be less than those stated before taxes if company is entitled to federal tax refunds by reason of operation of loss carry-back provisions of tax law.

Break-even Point is $3,540,000 in sales per year

2. AT 5% REDUCTION IN PRICES

% Above or Below Present Volume:	10% up	Present Volume	10% down	20% down	30% down	40% down
Sales:						
Present prices	$5,500,000	$5,000,000	$4,500,000	$4,000,000	$3,500,000	$3,000,000
Reduce 5%	275,000	250,000	225,000	200,000	175,000	150,000
Revised sales	$5,225,000	$4,750,000	$4,275,000	$3,800,000	$3,325,000	$2,850,000
Total costs	4,830,000	4,500.000	4,170,000	3,840,000	3,510,000	3,180,000
Net profit or *loss*:				Loss	Loss	Loss
Before taxes	$ 395,000	$ 250,000	$ 105,000	$ 40,000	$ 185,000	$ 330,000
After taxes	234,000	148,250	62,200			
Per cent profit or *loss* on sales:						
Before taxes	7.6%	5.3%	2.5%	1.0%	5.6%	11.5%
After taxes	4.5%	3.1%	1.5%			

Break-even Point is $3,940,000 in sales per year at prices 5% lower than present level

3. AT 10% INCREASE OVER PRESENT PRICE LEVEL

% Above or Below Present Volume:	10% up	Present Volume	10% down	20% down	30% down	40% down
Sales:						
Present prices	$5,500,000	$5,000,000	$4,500,000	$4,000,000	$3,500,000	$3,000,000
Add 10%	550,000	500,000	450,000	400,000	350,000	300,000
Revised sales	$6,050,000	$5,500,000	$4,950,000	$4,400,000	$3,850,000	$3,300,000
Total costs	4,830,000	4,500,000	4,170,000	3,840,000	3,510,000	3,180,000
Net profit:						
Before taxes	$1,220,000	$1,000,000	$ 780,000	$ 560,000	$ 340,000	$ 120,000
After taxes	723,000	593,000	462,000	332,000	201,600	71,160
Per cent profit on sales:						
Before taxes	20.2%	18.2%	15.8%	12.7%	8.9%	3.6%
After taxes	11.9%	10.8%	9.4%	7.5%	5.2%	2.1%

Break-even Point is $3,000,000 in sales per year at prices 10% higher than present level

4. AT 15% INCREASE OVER PRESENT PRICE LEVEL

% Above or Below Present Volume:	10% up	Present Volume	10% down	20% down	30% down	40% down
Sales:						
Present prices	$5,500,000	$5,000,000	$4,500,000	$4,000,000	$3,500,000	$3,000,000
Add 15%	825,000	750,000	675,000	600,000	525,000	450,000
Revised sales	$6,325,000	$5,750,000	$5,175,000	$4,600,000	$4,025,000	$3,450,000
Total costs	4,830,000	4,500,000	4,170,000	3,840,000	3,510,000	3,180,000

% Above or Below Present Volume:	10% up	Present Volume	10% down	20% down	30% down	40% down
Net profit:						
Before taxes	$1,495,000	$1,250,000	$1,005,000	$ 760,000	$ 515,000	$ 270,000
After taxes	886,000	741,000	596,000	450,000	305,000	160,000
Per cent profit on sales:						
Before taxes	23.6%	21.7%	19.4%	16.5%	12.8%	7.8%
After taxes	14.0%	12.9%	11.5%	9.8%	7.6%	4.6%

Break-even Point is $2,825,000 in sales per year at prices 15% higher than present level

Example 7. How to determine the price level needed to produce a certain profit when sales volume declines. Assume the following facts:

Present annual sales volume	$5,000,000

Present costs:

Fixed	$1,200,000
Variable	3,300,000 (66% of sales)
Total costs	$4,500,000
Present net profit before taxes	$ 500,000 (10% on sales = 11.11% above cost)

On the basis of the above assumptions as to present facts:
Break-even point is $3,540,000 of annual sales.
(Margin of 29.2% from sales of $5,000,000.)

Question: What price level is needed to produce 10 per cent profit (before taxes) on sales when volume is one-third lower than at present (10 per cent before taxes = 5.9 per cent after taxes)?

Solution:

If volume should decline by 33.33%, with no changes in price levels or costs, sales would be	$3,333,333
Required profit of 10% (before taxes) would be	333,333
Leaving allowable total cost of	$3,000,000
Of this cost, fixed cost is	1,200,000
Leaving variable cost *to be allowed* of	$1,800,000
But variable costs are 66% of sales and would, therefore, be	$2,200,000
(66% of $3,333,333)	
Add fixed costs	1,200,000
Total costs	$3,400,000

10% profit on sales = 11.11% above cost 377,777

Sales would have to be $3,777,777

This new sales figure of $3,777,777
is 444,444
more than $3,333,333 (sales at present prices and
   indicates need of an increase in pricing *over*
   present price levels of 13.33%
Therefore, instead of pricing at 11.11% over cost, pricing should be at 25.89% above
cost. (111.11% of cost = present price; 111.11% + 13.33% price increase = 111.11
× 1.13-1/3 = new price level of 125.89% of cost or 25.89% above cost.)

Proof of computation

Sales at present volume and present prices (and present
   mark-up of 11.11% above cost) $5,000,000
Total costs of same 4,500,000
Add 25.89% to cents 1,165,050

Sales at present volume with 25.89% mark-up above cost 5,665,050
If volume should decline 33.33% at same prices (25.89%
   mark-up) sales would be reduced by 1,888,350

Sales at lower volume 3,776,700

Costs at lower volume (assuming no change in costs)
   Fixed $1,200,000
   Variable (2/3 of $3,300,000) 2,200,000

   Total costs at lower volume 3,400,000
Profit before taxes at lower volume 376,700

This profit is roughly 10% on the $3,777,777 of sales when volume declines by
33.33% and prices are 25.89% over cost.

Other solutions (rather than price increase) should be considered, namely: (a)
What reductions in fixed and variable costs are needed to avoid a price increase? (b) If
cost reductions indicated by (a) are beyond the range of possibility, what combinations
of possible cost decrease and price increase will accomplish the same end as a price
increase alone?

Additional uses for data obtainable by break-even point techniques. 1. Comparison of profitability of products. This can be achieved by means of a breakdown of
all costs by product for each plant in which manufactured, into fixed and variable
elements, being certain to include in the variable costs all costs that can be assessed as
direct costs, such as promotion, advertising, selling, warehousing, packaging, delivery, servicing, order-processing, correspondence, invoicing, credits and collections,
maintenance of accounts receivable records, and other costs not always conceived as
direct costs. This is not intended to imply that for this purpose all selling, administrative and accounting costs should be arbitrarily allocated over all products but rather that

those portions of these costs that are definitely traceable to particular products should be treated as variable costs of such products. The reason for the necessity for including costs beyond manufacturing costs when presenting data on variable costs is that the use of direct manufacturing costs alone can lead to grossly erroneous estimates of marginal income that will produce some deceitful results in pricing and may also lead to erroneous decisions in such matters as expansion or contraction of operations, sales efforts, and advertising appropriations. Data on variable costs should include data as to the range of quality or dollar-volume to which the variable cost stated is applicable. Costs should also be stated for quantities and dollar-values above and below this range in whatever stages or ranges are appropriate in view of the effects on variable and total costs of increases in volume to and between "lowest unit-cost plateaus."

For each product, there can be ascertained the quantity which must be sold at various price-levels at and between "lowest unit-cost plateaus" to "break even," that is, to absorb the product's fair burden of all fixed overhead costs, including adequate allowances for depreciation and obsolescence of equipment and pro-rated costs of any selling and administration which have been arbitrarily allocated.

2. To ascertain the separate effects on net profits attributable to price changes, sales mix, wage rate changes, changes in productivity per dollar of wages, changes in unit costs of materials and so on.

3. Historical records of product profitability. Experience indicates that almost every product has an individual market and profit history. A product may be introduced by one company and be quite profitable for a considerable time. Quickly or gradually, others produce and market the same or a substitutable product. Eventually the supply of the original product and its new competitors may increase to and beyond the point where full demand is present at the original price. Increasing competition for the existing demand leads to progressive price deterioration, sometimes without an offsetting widening of the market. From this point on, a number of developments may occur. Unit margins and total gross profits may begin and continue to decline; or unit margins may decline and total gross profit may remain constant due to increments in the total number of units sold; or unit costs may be reduced in the same or a lesser or greater amount per unit than the reduction in unit price; or unit costs may rise from inflationary or other causes while unit prices remain static or decline; or uneconomical additional services may be required to maintain sales; or sales may be made in smaller individual quantities without adequate compensatory price adjustments; or other combinations of such factors as cost changes, price changes and changes in the volume of units sold may occur.

The accounting records should reflect the history of each product throughout these various changes. Such records may indicate need for remedial action, sometimes extending to abandonment of the product. It is often just as important to know when to get out of the market for a particular product as when to get into it. In this way the operation of the law of diminishing returns should be kept under constant observation by the controller and should be reflected in his records and reports for every product. This should help to maintain flexibility in the organization's total output and sales-mix to the end of maintaining and improving over-all profits, assuming the exercise by responsible authority of the requisite watchfulness and the courage to make loss-terminating decisions without procrastination and to introduce new products.

The accounting records and reports should make it possible to know the sources, by product, of the net profits of the enterprise and what improvement or deterioration there has been in the net profit from each such source by comparison with prior periods.

Break-even point techniques can be utilized to substantial advantage in these areas.

How to estimate the break-even point when only limited data are available. It is possible to estimate the approximate break-even point in sales when only the following data can be obtained for one full year and for the next preceding full year:

(a) Dollars of sales.
(b) Dollars of net profit.

Example:

	This Year	*Last Year*	*Increase This Year Over Last Year*
Sales	$1,000,000	$900,000	$100,000
Net profit	100,000	75,000	25,000

Since the increase of $25,000 in profit accompanies an increase of $100,000 in sales, the differential profit is 25% of sales.

The break-even point on which there would be no profit or loss is estimated as follows:

As 25 per cent is the profit on added sales, then the above profit of $100,000 was earned on added sales of $400,000 ($100,000 divided by 25%). Deduct this $400,000 from the sales of $1,000,000 to arrive at the approximate break-even point of $600,000 of sales.

Test this by applying the data to the data for the preceding year as follows:

Sales	$900,000
Break-even point	$600,000
Sales in excess of break-even sales	$300,000
Profit on this should be on 25%, namely	$ 75,000

Data from actual experience will rarely work out so readily. For this situation, a simple formula can be applied to any array of such data as follows:

Let:

B.E.P. equal breakdown point in dollars of sales.

S-1 equals sales of this year.

S-2 equals sales of preceding year.

S-d equals S-1 minus S-2.

That is the increase (or decrease) in sales this year as against last year.

S-ABP equals sales beyond break-even sales.

P-1 equals net profit this year.

P-2 equals net profit of preceding year.

P-d equals P-1 minus P-2.

That is the increase (or decrease) in profit of this year as compared with last year.

Using the above notation, compute the approximate break-even point as follows:

Step 1: Start with sales of this year (S-1) $1,000,000

Step 2: Divide P-d by S-d = 25% = .25
Step 3: Divide P-1 by the .25 ($100,000 divided
         by .25) which will produce the result of
         $400,000. S-ABP = $400,000, namely the
         sales beyond the break-even sales.
Step 4: Deduct S-ABP from S-1   400,000

         to find BEP of .... $ 600,000

SEPARATION OF MIXED COSTS

Method of separating mixed costs into fixed and variable elements. To develop the fullest usefulness of the break-even point principles in connection with future operations, it is necessary to master the technique used to separate "mixed" costs into their two component elements, namely the fixed and the variable. This technique is based on the use of the "method of least-squares," a well known mathematical operation. It can also be used to test whether a cost assumed to be entirely variable or entirely fixed is so in fact.

A mixed cost may be represented graphically as in Figure 9-1.

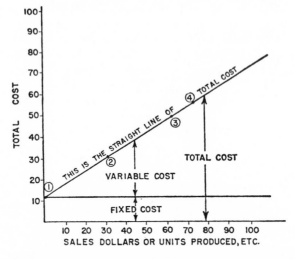

Figure 9-1. Separation of Mixed Costs into Fixed and Variable Elements.

Mixed costs may behave in any one of a number of ways other than that represented by this graph but if, without too great a sacrifice of accuracy, we can make the behavior conform to such a straight-line graph we will have a very useful analytical instrument.

Some of the ways in which costs actually behave (in relation to sales or volume of output, units of output, or other base) are shown in graphs (a), (b), and (c) of Figure 9-2.

If enough data were available in each of these cases, a mathematical formula could be found for each, but these formulae would have the disadvantage of being quite complicated.

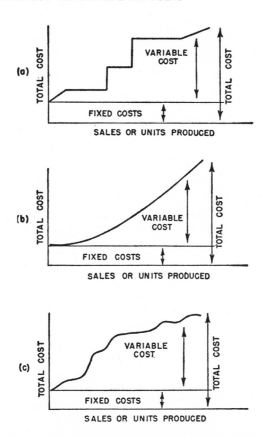

Figure 9-2. Behavior of Costs in Relation to Sales, or Volume of Output, Units of Output, or Other Base.

The general formula for Figure 9-2 is simple. It is:

Total Cost = Fixed Cost plus a percentage of sales

Method of least squares. The mathematical derivation of the necessary final formulae is omitted here. The final formulae to be applied to a succession of periodic monthly, and so on) data are:

Let y = total cost

Let a = fixed element of total cost

Let x = sales (or units of output or volume or any other base)

Let b = the factor by which sales (or other base) must be multiplied to find the variable element of total cost

Then $y = a + bx$

This is a formula for a straight line (the line of total cost in Figure 9-2).

To find a and b for the formula ($y = a + bx$) above, use the following two formulae. First find

$$b = \frac{n\,(\Sigma xy - \Sigma x\Sigma y)}{n\Sigma y^2 - (\Sigma x)^2}$$

Then use the value found for b to find

$$a = \frac{\Sigma y - b\Sigma y}{n}$$

NOTE: n means the number of periods used.

The symbol Σ (sigma) means "the sum of."

Σxy means the grand total of all the products of each pair of x's and y's.

$\Sigma x \Sigma y$ means that the total sum of all the x's is multiplied by the total sum of all the y's.

Σx^2 means that all the x's are squared (each multiplied once by itself) and then added to get a grand sum.

$(\Sigma x)^2$ means that the grand total of all the x's is squared (multiplied by itself).

x = sales (or units of output for each of the periods used.

y = total cost for each of the periods used.

Σy = aggregate total of the y's.

Σx = aggregate total of the x's.

a = average amount *per period* for fixed costs.

Rough proof to check accuracy of computations:

Formula: $na + b\Sigma x$ = an amount very close to Σy

Example of proof. Assume that computations resulted in:

a = \$360 (fixed costs per month)

b = .0509 (5.09% of sales)

and number of periods (n) used was 9 months. Then n = 9.

Assume Σx = \$717,762

Assume Σy = \$ 39,772

Substituting these data in the verifying formula ($na + b\Sigma x$ = an amount very close to Σy):

(9 × \$360) + (.0509 × \$717,762 = \$3,240 + \$36,534

= \$39,774

Caution in using the method of least-squares. In analyzing any item of cost or expense by the above method, the purpose is to obtain a picture of the fixed and variable elements at prices and cost levels prevailing at a particular time. Therefore, it is necessary first to adjust any dollar figures used to the same price levels. For instance, if a period of 12 months is being studied in connection with cost of power related to dollars of sales, assume that, starting with the fifth month and going through the twelfth month, the rates of the company furnishing the power were increased by 15 per cent. Increase the figures for cost of power for each of the first four months by this same percentage. If, in addition to this change, your own selling prices were increased, say, during the last three months of the year, add the same percentage to the sales figures for each of the preceding nine months. Of course, if the base, instead of being sales dollars, is units of production, a change in your own selling price will not affect the monthly figures of units of production used as the base.

Despite the possibility of obtaining needed data by the method of least-squares, it is important that, wherever possible, direct analysis be made of each item of cost and expense to approximate the amount of probable expenditure at each level of productive activity. The data obtained by such direct analysis should be placed in "picture" form by charting them. This should yield useful information as to the amounts of the fixed elements in costs and the behavior of the variable elements for comparison with data obtained by means of the application of the method of least-squares.

It is important never to assume that any item of cost or expense is entirely variable or entirely fixed. For example, in a given situation, labor cost might readily be assumed to be a completely and directly variable cost, or rent (or equivalent) cost might be assumed to be entirely fixed. Both should be put to the test of analysis by the method of least-squares to detect any fixed element in the labor cost and any variable element in the rent cost.

EXPLANATIONS FOR PUZZLING ANSWERS

Perplexing answers. In the course of using these break-even techniques, perplexing answers sometimes occur. Most of these will fall into one of three classes:
1. Where break-even points are computed from the same data for
     (a)   the enterprise as a whole, and
     (b)   for each of the subdivisions making up the entire enterprise, and the grand total of the break-even points for the subdivisions will be found to be not exactly equal to the break-even point computed for the enterprise as a whole.

This will be puzzling because both (a) and (b) were computed from the same data. It can be demonstrated by mathematical proof beyond the scope of this book that this puzzling result is natural and need cause no concern, assuming, of course, that there are no errors in the computations.

2. A negative answer for the element of fixed cost. Computations usually result in a plus ($+$) sign preceding the dollars of fixed cost per accounting period (fixed cost is a in the formula $y = a + bx$). On rare occasions, this sign preceding the dollars of fixed cost may be found to be negative, that is, it will be a minus ($-$) sign. This would mean that an item of total cost would consist, not of a fixed cost amount plus a variable cost, but of a variable cost *less* a net fixed amount of periodical income. Usually this does not make sense. The first step would be a verification of the computations. If that develops no change, then it is possible that the data in the ledger accounts used for the computations may have contained credit entries for income of regular occurrence, probably in uniform amounts, in excess of the fixed costs in these accounts. Examples of such income would be royalties, rent from subleases, and the like. These accounts should be examined and analyzed. If such income is found, its effects on the data should be eliminated, new computations should be made from the corrected data, and the income should be handled separately. This should result in the normal positive ($+$) result for the amount of fixed cost per accounting period.

3. A negative answer for the variable cost, that is, a minus ($-$) sign preceding the variable cost (b in the formula $y = a + bx$). The interpretation of such a negative result would be: As total dollar volume of sales (or total units of output) rises, the total cost is falling.

In the absence of any error in computation, this unexpected result might have issued from an unfortunate choice of basic data. The data chosen for the purpose of separating the fixed from variable elements of cost may have been taken for a series of periods during which important cost reductions (including cost reductions from drastic declines in the cost of materials, from the introduction of new equipment, and the like) occurred after the passage of a few of the earlier periods in the series. Another cause of a falling total cost per dollar of sales might lie in any radical increases in selling prices, especially during periods of rising total volume. Any such factors should be eliminated from the basic data and new computations made from the corrected data.

How accurate are the results? It can be observed from Figure 9-1 that the straight line of total cost will overstate total costs at some points of volume and understate them at others. If it were possible to establish the maximum extent of such overstatement or understatement, then the usefulness of the method of least-squares would be greatly enhanced, especially if it could be done by means of simple procedures. How this can be accomplished is next shown. To clarify the exposition of the procedure, the data are shown in tabular form in Figure 9-3.

It is necessary to start with some *definitions*.

1. "Line of Best Fit"—Assume that data for 12 periods of one month each have been used to compute (by the method of least-squares) the straight line representing total cost. (See Figure 9-2.) This line is the "Line of Best Fit" to the 12 separate items of total cost.

2. "Line of Regression"—This is the same as the "Line of Best Fit."

3. "Numerical Formula"—This is the formula in numbers which was found to express the value of y. Example: $y = a + bx$. When this is solved for the particular set of figures used in the table (Figure 9-3), it produces the "Numerical Formula," $y =$ \$11,227 per month plus 59.3% of monthly sales dollars.

4. "Actual Values of Y"—In the table (Figure 9-3), the actual values of y ($y =$ Total Cost) for each month appear in column 4. Most of these "actual values of y" will lie above or below the straight line of total cost.

5. "Computed Values of Y"—After finding the numerical formula for y, we can use it to compute new values for the total cost of each of the 12 months, using the actual values of x (sales) for each month. Each of these "computed values of y" will lie exactly on the straight line of total cost. In the table, Figure 9-3, these computed values appear in column 7. This is done by making 12 calculations, one for each month, substituting in the formula the values already determined for a and b and the actual value for x for each month and computing a value for y for that month.

This series of 12 operations will produce for each of the 12 months new values for y (total cost) which will be found in column 7, in the table in Figure 9-3, for each of the 12 months. These values of y are described as the "computed values of y." In most instances, these computed values will be different numerically from the "actual values of y."

This difference between the "computed values" and the "actual values" raises an interesting question, namely:

Inasmuch as the "actual values of y" are almost always more or less than the

	Column 1 Item No.	Column 2 Month	Column 3 Sales (Dollars)	Column 4 Actual Total Cost	Column 5 Sales x Actual Total Cost	Column 6 Sales x Sales	Column 7 Computed Total Cost	Column 8 Difference between Actual Total Cost and Computed Total Cost (Col.4 less Col.7)	Column 9 Data in Column 8 Squared
Definition or Description				"actual values of y"			"computed values of y"		
Symbol (Notation)			x	y	xy	x²		d	d²
Formula							$y = a + bx$ $a = -\$11{,}227$ $b = 59.3\%$		
	1	Dec.	$8,000	$15,900	$127,200,000	$64,000,000	$15,972	$ - 72	$ 5,041
	2	Oct.	12,000	18,600	223,200,000	144,000,000	18,344	+ 256	65,536
	3	June	18,000	21,600	388,800,000	324,000,000	21,900	- 300	90,000
	4	Feb.	20,000	23,300	466,000,000	400,000,000	23,088	+ 212	44,944
	5	March	27,000	26,900	726,300,000	729,000,000	27,237	- 337	113,569
	6	Nov.	28,000	27,400	767,200,000	784,000,000	27,832	- 432	186,624
	7	April	38,000	34,500	1,311,000,000	1,444,000,000	33,762	+ 738	544,644
	8	Jan.	44,000	37,200	1,636,800,000	1,936,000,000	37,320	- 120	14,400
	9	May	58,000	45,300	2,627,400,000	3,364,000,000	45,620	- 320	102,400
	10	Sept.	60,000	46,800	2,808,000,000	3,600,000,000	46,807	- 7	49
	11	July	74,000	55,900	4,136,600,000	5,476,000,000	55,110	+ 790	624,100
	12	Aug.	103,000	71,900	7,405,700,000	10,609,000,000	72,308	- 408	166,464
Total			490,000	425,300	22,624,200,000	28,874,000,000	425,300		1,957,771
Symbol for total			Σx	Σy	Σxy	Σx^2			Σd^2

$$\frac{d^2}{n} =$$

$1,957,771÷12 = $163,147.58 of which the square root is $403.91 — one standard error of estimate. ($404.00)

Figure 9-3. Total Cost Computation

"computed values," is it possible to find a formula to give a range between a maximum and minimum for each "computed value of y" so that every actual value of y will fall within such a range? If this formula can be found, it will afford these advantages:

1. For purposes of budgetary control, enabling a statement of the maximum acceptable variation above and below the stated "Line of Best Fit" (the line of total cost), and

2. Making possible a graphical representation of y with a surrounding band consisting of two lines parallel to the line y, one above it and one below it, which will show the limits of accuracy for any computed value of y. This can be done by using the usual statistical procedure for finding the "Standard Error of Estimate." The "Standard Error of Estimate" measures the extent of the variation of actual values from the "Line of Best Fit" (the Line for $y = a + bx$). This is accomplished through the application of the standard formula for the standard error which is as follows: $\dfrac{\sqrt{\Sigma\, d^2}}{N}$

The symbol $\sqrt{\ }$ indicates the square root of the data enclosed within it.

N represents the number of periods (12 in this example). The total (Σd^2) called for by the formula appears at the foot of column 9. This is now divided by 12 and the square root of the result is found from a table of square roots[2] to produce the answer, $404.00 (see foot of column 9 of table Figure 9-3).

This procedure may appear to be quite complex but if the reader will perform the operations described, he will find that they are not difficult.

We now use the value found for the standard error ($\pm$ $404) to supplement the numerical formula already computed for the line $y = a + bx$ as follows:

The original line of total cost was found to be $y = $11,227 + 59.3\%$ of sales dollars.[3]

Adding the "Standard Error of Estimate" to this will produce the following numerical formula:

$$y = \$11,227 + 59.3\% \text{ of sales dollars}[4] \pm \$404$$

From this we find, for example, that when sales are $60,000, the total computed cost (y) will be $46,807 with the possibility of being as much as $404 more or less, that is, the computed total cost might vary to become as much as $47,211 or as little as $46,403.

But this information is of doubtful assistance if we do not know whether all the actual values will fall within the range indicated by the numerical formula for the present set of facts. Statistical science has determined that this solution will include very close to 67½% of the actual values.

The statistical method for finding by simple means a set of limits that will include very close to 95% of the actual values is as follows:

Use double the amount of the standard error, that is, use two standard errors

---

[2] Or by means of logarithms, utilizing the principle that the logarithm of the square root of a number is half of the logarithm of the number.

[3] Where units of output are used instead of dollars of sales, the expression "Percent of Sales Dollars" becomes "Dollars per Unit of Output," and "sales dollars" becomes number of units of output.

[4] The symbol $\pm$ means "plus or minus."

instead of one (as the means of finding the range). Here is how it is applied in this example.

The standard error in this instance is ± $404

Twice that = two standard errors = ± $808

Using this latter value in the formula changes it to the following:

y (total cost) = $11,227 + 59.3% of sales dollars ± $808

This will include very close to 95% of the actual values and ought to be sufficient for most practical purposes.

If still greater refinement is considered necessary, the use of three standard errors will give a coverage of very close to 99.7%.

In this example, the formula including three standard errors would be (where one standard error is ± $404):

y = $11,227 + 59.3% of sales dollars ± $1212

Whether "two standard errors" or "three standard errors" is used, computations can be made to show for each value of y both the maximum and minimum which an actual value may take. The computation will indicate the maximum and minimum cost totals for each individual cost or expense and for all costs and expenses in total.

In using this in budgeting and control, if subsequent experience indicates that actual costs tend to remain in or above the upper band, it may be taken as an indication that costs are tending to rise or profit margins are tending to decline in comparison with the period from which the basic data were taken. If such later actual costs tend to remain in or fall below the lower band[5] (below the "Line of Best Fit") favorable tendencies are indicated.

As to terminology, the "Standard Error of Estimate" as here used may sometimes be referred to as the "Standard Deviation." The following distinction is made between the two terms:

The "Standard Error of Estimate" is the measure of the extent of the scattering of variations above and below the "Line of Best Fit" (Line of Regression), but the "Standard Deviation" is the measure of the extent of the scattering of variations above and below the arithmetic average of all the actual values.

The arithmetic average of the actual values is not synonymous with the values on the "Line of Best Fit."

---

[5]The upper band is the area between the line of the computed values and the line showing computed values plus two (or three) standard errors of estimate. The lower band is the area between the line of the computed values and the line showing computed values minus two (or three) standard errors of estimate.

10

Financing Needs for Current Operations

CONTENTS

10

Financing Needs for
Current Operations

Changes in the standards of short-term financing. The following pages are intended primarily for the financial manager who expects to obtain credit in order to supply some of his company's short-term needs. They should also be useful to the financial manager of a company that is more generously financed. All financial officers need to understand the behavior of current capital, the reasons why it is desirable to plan in advance, and in detail, the effects of operations upon the cash fund of a business.

In the early 1930's, loan officers of commercial banks were just beginning to break away from long-established standards. The standards that had been general until then, and which had been reinforced by the attitude of bank examiners in the depression years, required that many loan applications of the sort now receiving approval should be denied because of "insufficient capital," or because the loan was not "self-liquidating," or for some similar reason. A principal reason why this was the case is that loan decisions were usually made on the basis of annual figures, as submitted by the applicant. As a result, loan officers were not fully informed about the operations of the business in the period between the dates of statements and so were forced to reject many applications when more complete data would have justified the loan.

In the same period, however, good loans that did not meet bankers' standards were being made by other lenders, especially by the group usually referred to as "the finance companies." These lenders took the trouble to go beyond periodic financial statements into the reality of the day-to-day needs of the business. By the 1940's, most bankers had learned the same lesson: that the working out of a scheme to provide funds to finance current operations requires imaginative work on the part of both the prospective borrower and the prospective lender. The task is not unlike that of putting together a jigsaw puzzle, for the special characteristics of a particular borrower's needs must be matched to the type of loan arrangement that best fits those needs and also suits the particular aspects of the lender's types of business.

The deepening understanding of the field of short-term financing that has occurred in the last three decades has created both an opportunity and a challenge to financial executives. Many more types of arrangements are being used. Consequently, the job of

311

the corporate treasurer now requires that he be conversant with the various types. Most important, the treasurer must be able to visualize what assurances the lender really needs. On the other side of the negotiation, the lending officer must have real insight into the affairs of the prospective borrower.

Of course, it is clear that the maximum success in achieving mutual understanding will occur when each side trusts the other to the extent of furnishing detailed information when it is needed. Many businesses still reduce their credit standing by unnecessary reticence in furnishing this information.

THE FINANCIAL CYCLE OF CURRENT OPERATIONS

Current capital defined. At any moment, the current operations of a business determine the make-up of its current capital. The *current capital* of a business, also referred to as its *circulating capital* or *gross working capital*, consists, first, of those goods that are obtained and worked on to produce the product to be sold. These are commonly referred to as the *inventories* of the business. The working capital also includes, the *receivables*, resulting from sales, and the *cash* funds, which are needed to bridge the gaps between expenditures and receipts. In contrast, such business property as buildings or machines is not expected to produce funds directly by its sale and is not considered as part of the circulating capital. Briefly, current capital may be defined as the capital invested in those assets that, in the ordinary course of business, can be or will be turned into cash within a brief period (not exceeding a year, normally), without undergoing diminution in value and without disrupting the organization.

Those who have studied accounting will recognize that the above definition of current capital is one that follows the usual distinction between the "current assets" as shown on a balance sheet, and the "non-current" or "fixed" assets. In fact, many balance sheets can be found on which the current assets as listed are the working capital of the business. Exceptions exist in cases where the company has an excess of liquid funds that is not needed for current operations. There can be more current assets than are being used for circulating capital at a certain time, but the opposite cannot be true.

Most of this chapter will deal with the way in which needed current capital can be obtained by borrowing. But, paradoxically, some of the current capital of a business must be regarded as requiring a permanent investment of funds, for it is clearly apparent that not all the funds needed to provide the circulating capital should be borrowed. A retail store gives an adequate example of this important fact. Each item of the inventory of such a store is for sale; it will be "marked down" if necessary to move it. Yet there must be an inventory of goods on hand at all times. Thus, although the *physical* inventory is truly circulating capital, there must always be an *investment* in goods on hand.

The same is true of receivables and cash, or of any other part of circulating capital. Although the physical things flow through the business, funds are permanently tied up. The amount of needed funds varies from time to time, but some permanent investment of funds in circulating capital is necessary in any business. For this reason it is impossible to finance all of a firm's needs for current capital by short-term loans. Perhaps this important fact can be made clearer by an analogy. Circulating capital is not unlike a river. The river is there from day to day, yet the water in it is constantly changing. So in a business, there must always be an investment of funds in circulating capital though the physical items are constantly changing.

Net working capital. An individual item on one side of a balance sheet cannot be associated with some particular item on the other side, but the items classed as *current assets* can be regarded as the principal source of the funds for paying the current liabilities. This fact lends significance to the *net working capital*, which is defined as the difference between the dollar totals of the current assets and the current liabilities. Net working capital represents the excess of values in the current assets over the liabilities due within a year. Though this sum cannot be realized in full, a large amount of net working capital gives some assurance to an analyst that debts can be paid at maturity.[1]

The financial cycle of current operations. A variation in the amount of funds that is needed from time to time to provide current capital normally occurs in every business. The demand for short-term financing arises out of such variations, which will be explained by an example of a concern that manufactures fireworks for display purposes. It has been named the Fourth of July Company because the company has but a single selling season. Figure 10-1 presents a series of statements of current assets and current liabilities taken from the company's records of a typical year at significant dates.

The affairs of the Fourth of July Company are shown at their seasonal low in the December 31 figures. An accumulation of materials and supplies (powder, fusing, wrapping, etc.) is on hand; the accounts receivable have been worked down to a group of difficult collection problems, and the cash fund is ample. It may even seem excessive. December, then, sees the Fourth of July Company in relatively liquid condition, with a good stock of raw materials on hand.

By March 31, the production season is well under way. More raw materials have been purchased, yet the flow of production has converted the new purchases and much of the December stock into goods in process, and then into finished goods. Little progress has been made with the slow receivables. Cash has fallen greatly, due to the increased investment in inventory, especially the finished goods. But so far the company has not exceeded its capacity to supply its own current capital. Accounts payable have grown, but the dollar amount of growth is small.

By the end of May, the production program is substantially completed. More funds have been invested in labor and materials, and most of the goods are finished and ready for sale. Some goods have already moved into customers' hands, as the growth in receivables shows. The cash account is at the lowest figure of the year. Furthermore, the large investment in finished goods has more than exhausted the company's own cash fund, so $11,250 has been added to the circulating capital by borrowing. June is to be the big month of sales, and the May 31 statement reflects the company's readiness to meet the demand.

At the end of September, the plant has been shut down. There is a small stock of unsold goods, and the raw material inventory is as low as it can get. Receivables, on

---

[1]Some people in financial circles identify the term *"working capital"* with the sum of the current assets; others, with the excess of current assets over current liabilitites. The precise term of *net working capital* eliminates any confusion.

	December 31	March 31	May 31	September 30
Current Assets				
Cash	$19,488	$ 1,877	$ 904	$ 8,266
Accounts receivable	8,388	8,189	10,017	62,968
Inventories				
Raw material, supplies	20,118	6,863	783	619
In process	——	6,211	4,233	——
Finished goods	3,451	29,456	50,931	5,520
Total	$51,445	$52,596	$66,868	$77,373
Current Liabilities				
Accounts payable	$ 173	$ 472	$ 740	$ 295
Notes payable	——	——	11,250	6,800
Total	$ 173	$ 472	$11,990	$ 7,095
Net Working Capital	$51,272	$52,124	$54,878	$70,278

Figure 10-1. Selected Statements of Current Position of the Fourth of July Company, Illustrating the Financial Cycle of Current Operations.

the other hand, are very high. They reflect the transfer of the funds invested in inventory *with the addition of profit* into the obligations of customers. Cash has been built up from collections already made, and the loan has been paid off in part.

The cycle of funds for the Fourth of July Company will end in the ensuing December, with a condition similar to that at the end of the preceding year end. It will be observed that some of the high earnings that are shown by the growth of net working capital to September 30 will have been eaten away by salaries and other expenses before the next season begins.

The case of the Fourth of July Company is, of course, extreme, but it serves to show the nature of the changes to be studied in any business. In particular, and this is of the greatest importance, the example shows that the cycle of funds is accomplished by shifts in the nature of current assets on hand. That is, the funds are needed consecutively for raw materials, for goods in process, for finished goods, and for receivables. As will appear below, the most desirable type of loan arrangement will probably change as the need changes.

Changing risks in the cycle of operations. Since a transmutation takes place as the funds move from one use to another, there is a significant change in the risk of operation as the cycle progresses, which in turn means that the availability of credit changes.

The Fourth of July Company can also serve as an example of this important fact. This time, however, the cycle will be traced in reverse order.

In September, this company's major problem is: "Can the receivables be collected?"

In May, the question was: "Can the finished goods be sold?"

In March, another question was added: "Can the goods be processed into finished form in time for sale?"

And in December, there was also the question: "Can we acquire the needed materials?"

Each of these questions represents a separate business risk. Therefore, from a credit point of view, the risk of making a loan to a business varies with the stage of the current cycle that exists at the time the loan is wanted. For this reason, a financial manager finds it easiest to borrow in order to finance receivables, and hardest to borrow in order to finance purchases of material that must be processed before sale.

ESTIMATING SHORT-TERM FINANCIAL REQUIREMENTS

Importance of estimating short-term financial requirements. Effective working capital management depends upon careful estimating of short-term financial requirements. The financial manager needs to know the amount, timing, and duration of these requirements. He can then plan to raise the funds needed in the most appropriate way; he can have confidence in his ability to meet future outlays as they fall due; and he can avoid holding large amounts of excess cash. Furthermore, evidence of careful planning of financial requirements makes a favorable impression upon lending agencies and thus makes easier the task of raising needed funds.

Forecasts of future cash needs are customarily made by one of two methods: (1) the cash-budget method or (2) the projected balance-sheet method. These two techniques are described in turn below.

The cash budget. The cash budget is an estimate by periods of future cash receipts and disbursements. Figure 10-2 shows a simple example of a cash budget. For each period, the anticipated cash receipts and disbursements are listed, and the difference between the respective totals is computed. These differences between total receipts and disbursements for each period are next made cumulative from period to period to show the running effect upon cash. If disbursements exceed receipts, the cumulative cash deficiency will give a measure of borrowing needs. Of course, if at the beginning of the forecast, the company holds cash or highly liquid assets in excess of normal requirements, this will serve to reduce indicated borrowing needs. Similarly, if cash and its equivalent are judged to be too low for ordinary operations at the start, borrowing needs will be higher than the cumulative excess of disbursements over receipts.

In constructing a cash budget, it is essential to differentiate between the accrual of income and expense, in an accounting sense, and receipts and disbursements of cash. It is the latter that are entered in the cash budget. For example, credit sales anticipated in January and expected to be collected in February would appear as income for January in a projected profit and loss statement. However, they would not be reflected in the cash budget until February, when it is expected that the cash would actually be received. Similarly, purchase payments entered in the cash budget would lag behind scheduled purchases if deferred payments were made in accordance with the terms of sale. Certain items of expense that appear in a profit-and-loss statement would not be reflected in the cash budget at all. These are non-cash expenses, with which no outlay of cash is associated. A prominent example is depreciation.

(Thousands of Dollars)

	Jan.	Feb.	March	April	May	June	July	Aug.	Sept.	Oct.	Nov.	Dec.
CASH RECEIPTS												
Collections of Accounts Receivable	310	1070	1030	1560	2390	2550	3280	2690	1850	1110	620	540
Sale of Machinery						900				1200		
Interest on Marketable Securities						90						90
Total	310	1070	1030	1560	2390	3540	3280	2690	1850	2310	620	630
CASH DISBURSEMENTS												
Payments for Materials	780	750	850	920	1060	1040	910	830	800	690	660	710
Payroll	520	540	590	620	680	610	580	550	520	490	470	500
Overhead Disbursements	110	130	130	150	160	170	160	140	130	120	120	110
Operating Expense Disbursements	60	70	90	90	110	100	100	90	80	80	70	70
Tax Payments			400			400						
Payments for Machinery				100	100	100	100					
Payments on Mortgage			210						210			
Dividend Payments						250						250
Total	1470	1490	2270	1880	2110	2670	1850	1610	1740	1380	1320	1640
Receipts Less Disbursements	(1160)	(420)	(1240)	(320)	280	870	1430	1080	110	930	(700)	(1010)
Cumulative Change *	(1160)	(1580)	(2820)	(3140)	(2860)	(1990)	(560)	520	630	1560	860	(150)

* Bracketed figures show indicated borrowing need. Unbracketed figures show additional cash generated. Assumes beginning cash balance is normal.

Figure 10-2. Cash Budget for XYZ Company

One problem encountered in making a cash budget is to decide upon the frequency of the periods to be employed. Should the budget be constructed on a daily, weekly, monthly, or other basis? The answer to this question lies in the periodicity of the cash flows of the particular company for which the forecast is made. The periods should be selected so as to reveal the peaks and valleys of borrowing needs. It is especially important to choose periods short enough to indicate the maximum cash strain. It would be unwise to project a cash budget by months if the bulk of the company's disbursements came early in the month (possibly as a result of E.O.M. discount datings on purchases) while receipts were spread relatively evenly throughout the month. The result would be an intra-month, cash-need peak that would not be revealed by a monthly budget. On the other hand there would be little need for a more frequent budget period if the company's cash flows were such that intra-month peaks did not occur. Usually, monthly budget periods prove to be satisfactory.

The making of a cash budget involves translating the forecasted operations of the business into the effects of these operations upon the cash balance of the company. Hence, before the specific items of cash receipts and disbursements can be estimated, it is essential that there exist realistic and detailed forecasts of sales, production, purchases of materials, purchases and sales of capital assets, and other operating plans. Useful financial projections cannot be made without reliable forecasts of operations.

In order to estimate cash receipts, the forecast of sales must be converted into collections of accounts receivable. This may be accomplished by applying a projected collection period to the sales forecast. For example, if the projected collection period were 30 days, the estimated collections for April would be equal to the planned sales for March. The past collection experience of the company is a useful guide in estimating the future collection period. Of course, it should be modified for any foreseeable changes in the conditions affecting collections.

In addition to collections, cash sales and other projected inflows of cash must be entered in the receipt section of the cash budget. Examples include dividends from stock holdings, payments received on the sale of capital assets, and repayments of advances made to officers and employees.

Some disbursements can be estimated with considerable certainty, since they will be payable regardless of the level of operations achieved. However, it should not be overlooked that there are major classes of disbursements (including purchase payments and wage payments) that will depend, at least in part, upon the accuracy of the sales forecast insofar as the latter affects production plans.

An important class of cash disbursements is payments for purchases of materials and supplies. These payments may be calculated from the purchases budget by applying a payment period based upon the terms of sale. Purchase payments will tend to lag behind scheduled purchases by an interval equal to the payment period. Otherwise, payments ordinarily will be scheduled to comply with the net credit terms offered. Hence, if purchases are made on terms of net 30 days, the purchase payments of one month will tend to be equivalent to the planned purchases of the previous month.

Payments for wages and other manufacturing costs may be derived from the production schedule. It should be remembered that these payments are customarily made at weekly, semi-monthly, or monthly intervals rather than concurrently with the accrual of manufacturing costs. For example, it is possible for a company with level production to have uneven wage payments in certain months when the number of weekly pay-days varies.

Payments for salaries, rents, and utilities can often be scheduled with considerable certainty and regularity. There are frequently other significant disbursements, such as dividend payments, tax payments, and the repayment on retirement of loans and securities that can be inserted individually in the cash budget at the times when they fall due.

The projected balance sheet. A second principal method of estimating short-term financial requirements is by means of the projected balance sheet. Under this method, the various assets and liabilities (here defined to include net worth) of a business are estimated at some future date. Any excess of estimated assets over liabilities measures the borrowing need that must be supplied from one source or another. On the other hand, an excess of estimated liabilities over assets indicates additional cash that will be generated over and above the amount of cash used in the estimate of assets.

The rationale of the projected balance sheet method of estimating short-term financial requirements is simple. The anticipated level of operations of the company on the future date considered will require the commitment of funds to the various assets. These operations may be expected also to generate certain sources of funds in the form of liabilities normally found on the balance sheet. If the required investment in assets exceeds the funds generated in customary liabilities, the deficiency must be made up by additional borrowing or equity investment or by reducing the investment in assets.

Like the cash budget, the projected balance sheet depends upon accurate and detailed forecasts of the operations of the business. The forecasts are normally provided by means of estimates of sales, production, purchases, capital investments, and other operating plans.

The actual construction of the projected balance sheet involves estimating the dollar investment in the various assets and liabilities as at a future date or dates. It should prove helpful to consider some of these accounts specifically.

Cash is usually estimated at the level normally deemed necessary to support the projected level of operations. Accounts receivable will be a result of forecasted sales and collection experience. Frequently, the level of receivables is estimated by applying a given collection period to anticipated sales. The collection period used may be the same as that presently experienced by the company, or it may be modified for expected changes in collection experience. As one example, increased sales may involve the addition of more poorly financed customers, thus slowing the anticipated collection period.

This level of inventory may be estimated by adding beginning inventory to planned purchases and subtracting planned sales at cost. In the absence of more precise information, it is frequently sufficient to project a change in inventory proportional to the expected change in sales.

Accounts payable are usually estimated with the expectation that the company will pay invoices when due and will take cash discounts when offered. The level of accounts payable can therefore be derived from the schedule of purchases. Income taxes payable may be forecast by applying the tax rate likely to be in effect on expected profits.

Estimating the level of surplus also requires projecting profits for the company to the date of the projected balance sheet. Hence, in order to construct the balance sheet, it is necessary to make at least an abbreviated projected income statement. Estimated earnings are then reduced by planned dividends to arrive at the addition to surplus.

When the projected balance sheet is completed, comparing total assets with total liabilities will indicate whether additional sources of funds must be found and, if so, in what amount. The alternative to additional borrowing or equity investment, when estimated assets exceed liabilities, is to reduce the planned investment in assets by one means or another.

It will be noted that, unlike the cash budget, this method provides an estimate of financial requirements for one date only—the date of the projected balance sheet. In order to obtain the same information with respect to financial requirements that the cash budget supplies, it is necessary to make a balance sheet for each cash budget period.

If the projected balance sheet method is used, it is essential to make sufficient balance sheets to show the peaks and valleys of financial requirements. In particular, it is vitally necessary that the maximum cash need be revealed by an accurate choice of balance sheet dates. As explained above, a monthly cash budget will not disclose intra-month peak needs, if such exist. It is even more likely that a single year-end balance sheet will not show the maximum cash need during the year. Hence, the frequency of each of these tools must be fitted to the ebb and flow of the company's financial requirements.[2]

The tentative nature of financial projections. In making and using financial projections, such as the cash budget and the projected balance sheet, it is sometimes easy to forget that they are only estimates. The use of precise amounts and the systematic construction of future schedules may unconsciously lead the financial manager to place more confidence in the precision of these estimates than is justified.

Financial projections, such as those described in this section, cannot be more accurate than the forecasts of operations upon which they rest. Even if these forecasts are carefully made, they can, of course, go seriously awry, and the associated financial projections will prove to be correspondingly inaccurate. Therefore, it is wise to interpret these projections with caution, bearing constantly in mind the possibility of error. It is for this reason that astute financial managers frequently make two sets of projections, one representing the likely maximum, and one representing the likely minimum, of financial requirements.

The need for liquid reserves. To the degree that a company's resources permit, the wise financial officer will plan to have a liquid reserve fund, which is considered separately from the budgetary calculation for current operations. If the reserve fund is large, only part of it will be carried as a minimum cash balance. The remainder can be invested in high-grade short-term obligations, usually United States bonds or certificates of indebtedness. As an alternative, where the position of the company is very strong, the financial officer may consider as a substitute for cash the certainty that loans from banks or other sources will be available in emergencies.

---

[2] A form providing for the simultaneous preparation of pro forma cash budgets and balance sheets has been designed by the Chicago Chapter of the Robert Morris Associates. It may be obtained from Cadwallader & Johnson, Inc., 225 W. Huron Street, Chicago 60610, Illinois. Form No. C117.

The uses of a liquid reserve fund or minimum cash balance will be described below.

Normal fluctuations between budget dates. Anyone who has gone through the experience of preparing a cash budget is aware of the numerous assumptions that must be made, all the way from the sales forecast to the division of expected capital expenditures among the budget periods. Even if a budget were to prove exactly accurate in its forecast of conditions at the end of a budget period, cash flows probably would not work out to even proportions on a day-to-day basis. For this reason, the minimum cash balance should provide for *normal fluctuations of income and outgo within the budget periods.*

The cash records of many firms will show that there is usually an excess of payments over receipts in the first days of any month, because the firm takes discounts for prompt payment of receivables. Collections, on the other hand, are seldom so promptly converted into cash. If the intervals within the budgets are monthly, the financial manager usually can get a fairly accurate idea of the monthly swing of cash (associated with the terms of trade) from the daily information in the cash ledger. Few companies figure so closely, however, preferring to follow a rule of thumb such as "begin a month with cash enough to make all planned disbursements without any receipts."

Provision for contingencies. Such a rule of thumb does more than provide for the normal day-to-day fluctuations. It also makes up part of the second element of a cash reserve. The financial manager should study the history of the business he manages and should attempt to measure likely contingencies in terms of their effect upon cash receipts and disbursements. Such events as floods in plants located near large rivers, or freight-car shortages for companies with little storage capacity, or strikes within or outside the company can be foreseen (though not the date of their occurrence), and plans can be made to adjust the company's disbursements accordingly. But the commitments of a concern to pay cash can seldom be revised as quickly as its receipts may be cut down, and a cash reserve is therefore necessary.

Two warnings should be introduced here. (1) The reserve funds for contingencies need not be cumulative. Strikes, floods, freight-car shortages and other contingencies do not happen simultaneously. Thus, the sum needed can be much less than the total of the contingencies that the financial manager has listed. Also, the amounts of contingency reserves can overlap the uses of the cash funds still to be described, as bank balances can be drawn down below "compensatory" levels in emergencies. (2) Nothing that has been said above justifies the holding of a large sum against "contingencies," if this means merely a vague fear that something may happen some day. What is recommended is a listing of possible events, and a careful evaluation of their effect on receipts and disbursements, leading to the selection of a sum that will be held against the day the event occurs.

Bank balances to support activity. A third sum that makes up a part of the cash fund of a properly financed concern is *an amount to compensate for banking services in handling deposits and withdrawals.* It is now an almost universal practice of commercial banks in the United States to impose "service charges" on customers, unless the average balances are large enough to make a charge unnecessary. The maintenance of a balance large enough to cover activity costs in any bank that is used actively in connection with receipts and withdrawals is usually less costly than the service charges that the balance avoids. Just how much this balance should be can be determined by an interview at the bank. However, this element of the cash fund need not be added to the contingency fund, as it is reasonable to plan on incurring a service charge in a period of emergency.

Closely related to the activity-supporting balance is the matter of "float." Checks that are deposited by a customer are not collected instantaneously, but in a period of one to three days.[3] A depositor should not draw his own checks against deposits until after they have been collected, as the checks deposited but uncollected may prove to be bad.

The amount of funds credited to an account but uncollected is referred to as "float." Bankers figure activity-supporting balances in terms of collected funds, and financial managers should keep their deposits large enough to cover float and activity.

Compensating balances at lending banks. Another element of a static cash reserve fund is the "compensating balance" that banks may require a borrower to keep on deposit. This requirement may also extend to companies not currently borrowing but having arranged credit lines with their banks. Compensating balances are believed to promote closer relationships between customer and bank and to discourage borrowing from multiple sources. If the compensating balance exceeds the customer's normal cash-fund needs, its effect is to raise the cost of borrowing.

A survey conducted by the Federal Reserve System indicated that many banks required business borrowers to maintain minimum deposit balances. Large banks are especially apt to impose these requirements, and the balances required are also usually higher in relation to the amount borrowed in the case of large banks. Ninety per cent of banks with over $500 million in deposits required minimum deposit balances. These typically ranged from 16 to 20 per cent of the loan outstanding. Only 5 per cent of the sample of banks having deposits under 20 million required minimum deposit balances. Some banks based the deposit requirement on a percentage of the credit line.

Some companies that have neither borrowed from a bank nor arranged credit lines make a practice of maintaining substantial deposit balances in the hope of influencing a favorable decision by the bank whenever a loan may be requested. This practice is more logical in periods of tight credit than during the easy money conditions that characterized our economy until relatively recently. The Federal Reserve Survey indicated that a number of banks took a customer's usual deposit balance into account in setting interest rates on loans.

If a company's customary cash reserve is large enough, compensating balance requirements may not, of course, necessitate an increase in the total cash reserve.

OBTAINING CREDIT—TYPES OF LOAN ARRANGEMENTS

Fundamentals of a credit negotiation. Three factors must be considered as basic in any discussion of the fundamentals of a credit negotiation: (1) presenting the request, (2) anticipating questions, and (3) the lender's needs.

---

[3]Using the Federal Reserve schedule of times, as is the practice of most banks.

Presenting the request. The person who negotiates a credit arrangement for his company usually finds that it is desirable to present the facts about his company in a form that emphasizes the most important circumstances in the particular case. By so doing, he will save the time of the lending officer who considers the matter. He will also further the cause of his company by demonstrating that he knows what the important things are.

Nothing that is said here should be construed as suggesting the suppression of an inconvenient fact or of a pessimistic estimate. The candid statement of the problem, if accompanied by an explanation of the proposal to meet it, is more productive of a credit than the suppression of inconvenient information. It also avoids the damaging long-run results that would follow the discovery of the true situation.

Anticipating questions. Not infrequently, loan officers ask applicants to fill out forms that have been prepared in order to obtain financial statements and supporting detail. A typical example of a long form is reproduced in Figure 10-3[4]. As will be seen, this form makes a searching examination of the balance sheet position of the applicant and calls for a detailed statement of profit and loss. Notice particularly the questions relating to contingent liabilities (page 2, Figure 10-3), receivables (page 3, Figure 10-3), and merchandise (page 3, Figure 10-3). Any financial officer should be able to answer questions of the type shown. But it is clear that this form is merely a starting point. "Where are you?" as asked by this form, is but a preliminary to "Where are you going?" For example, the loan form of one well managed institution places in a prominent place the questions:

Amount and Purpose of loan? (Describe proposed expenditures.)

Program for Liquidation of loan? (Indicate sources of funds.)

The evidence supplied by loan forms reinforces the conclusion that the man who presents a loan application should have made a forecast of his company's future at least in sufficient detail to permit making pro forma statements that show the likely range of possibilities.

---

[4]American Bankers Association, Bank Management Commission, *Corporation Financial Statement* (Long Form).

PAGE 1 OF FINANCIAL STATEMENT

FORM NO. 3

FORM DESIGNED AND APPROVED BY BANK MANAGEMENT COMMISSION AMERICAN BANKERS ASSOCIATION

CORPORATION FINANCIAL STATEMENT

(LONG FORM)

NAME ______________________ (DATE) __________

BUSINESS ______________________ ADDRESS ______________________

TO ______________________ (NAME OF BANK)

FOR THE PURPOSE OF OBTAINING ADVANCES FROM TIME TO TIME ON BILLS, NOTES AND OTHER COMMERCIAL PAPER SIGNED OR ENDORSED BY THE UNDERSIGNED, AND OF OBTAINING CREDIT GENERALLY, THE UNDERSIGNED MAKES THE FOLLOWING STATEMENT OF ________ FINANCIAL CONDITION AS OF THE CLOSE OF BUSINESS ON THE ______ DAY OF ____________ 19___, AND CERTIFIES TO THE ABOVE-NAMED BANK THAT THE INFORMATION HEREINAFTER SET FORTH IS IN ALL RESPECTS TRUE, ACCURATE AND COMPLETE AND CORRECTLY REFLECTS THE FINANCIAL CONDITION OF THE UNDERSIGNED ON THE DATE AFOREMENTIONED.

(FILL ALL BLANKS, WRITING "NO" OR "NONE" WHERE NECESSARY TO COMPLETE INFORMATION.)

ASSETS

- CASH—ON HAND $ ________ ; IN BANK $ ________
- NOTES RECEIVABLE OF CUSTOMERS (SEE SCHEDULE)
- ACCOUNTS RECEIVABLE OF CUSTOMERS (SEE SCHEDULE)
- MERCHANDISE—FINISHED (SEE SCHEDULE)
- —IN PROCESS
- —RAW
- SECURITIES OWNED (OTHER THAN IN SUBSIDIARIES AND AFFILIATES) (SEE SCHEDULE)
- OTHER CURRENT ASSETS (ITEMIZE)
- TOTAL CURRENT ASSETS
- INVESTMENTS IN SUBSIDIARIES AND AFFILIATES (EXCLUDING LOANS, ADVANCES, ETC.) (SEE SCHEDULE)
- DUE FROM SUBSIDIARIES AND AFFILIATES (SEE SCHEDULE)
- DUE FROM STOCKHOLDERS, DIRECTORS, OFFICERS, AND EMPLOYEES
- LIFE INSURANCE—CASH SURRENDER VALUE (DO NOT DEDUCT LOANS) (SEE SCHEDULE)
- GOODWILL, PATENTS, TRADEMARKS, COPYRIGHTS, DIES, PATTERNS, ETC.
- LAND—USED IN BUSINESS (SEE SCHEDULE)
- BUILDINGS—USED IN BUSINESS } BEFORE DEPRECIATION RESERVES
- MACHINERY AND EQUIPMENT } BEFORE DEPRECIATION RESERVES
- FURNITURE AND FIXTURES } BEFORE DEPRECIATION RESERVES
- TRUCKS AUTOS HORSES, WAGONS, ETC. } BEFORE DEPRECIATION RESERVES
- LAND AND BUILDINGS—NOT USED IN BUSINESS (SEE SCHEDULE)
- PREPAID EXPENSES—INTEREST, INSURANCE, ETC.
- OTHER ASSETS (ITEMIZE)
- TOTAL

LIABILITIES

- NOTES PAYABLE
  - TO BANKS
  - FOR MERCHANDISE
  - FOR MACHINERY, EQUIPMENT, ETC.
  - TO OTHERS FOR BORROWED MONEY
- TRADE OR BANK ACCEPTANCES PAYABLE
- ACCOUNTS PAYABLE—NOT DUE
- —PAST DUE
- DUE TO SUBSIDIARIES AND AFFILIATES
- DUE TO STOCKHOLDERS, DIRECTORS, OFFICERS, AND EMPLOYEES
- DIVIDENDS DECLARED BUT UNPAID
- RESERVED FOR, AND ACCRUED TAXES
- ACCRUED EXPENSES—WAGES, INTEREST, INSURANCE
- CHATTEL MORTGAGES } DUE WITHIN 1 YEAR
- MORTGAGES } DUE WITHIN 1 YEAR
- BONDED DEBT } DUE WITHIN 1 YEAR
- OTHER CURRENT LIABILITIES (ITEMIZE)
- TOTAL CURRENT LIABILITIES
- CHATTEL MORTGAGES } DUE AFTER 1 YEAR
- MORTGAGES } DUE AFTER 1 YEAR
- BONDED DEBT (SEE SCHEDULE) } DUE AFTER 1 YEAR
- LOANS ON LIFE INSURANCE
- OTHER LIABILITIES (ITEMIZE)
- TOTAL LIABILITIES
- RESERVES FOR DEPRECIATION
  - BUILDINGS
  - MACHINERY AND EQUIPMENT
  - FURNITURE AND FIXTURES
  - TRUCKS, AUTOS, ETC.
- RESERVE FOR CONTINGENCIES
- OTHER RESERVES (ITEMIZE)
- TOTAL RESERVES
- CAPITAL AND SURPLUS
  - PREFERRED STOCK } (SEE SCHEDULE)
  - COMMON STOCK } (SEE SCHEDULE)
  - EARNED SURPLUS
  - CAPITAL SURPLUS
- TOTAL

(BE SURE ALL SCHEDULES ARE FILLED OUT)

Figure 10-3. Long Form of Financial Statement.

PAGE 2 OF FINANCIAL STATEMENT

CONTINGENT LIABILITIES

NOTES RECEIVABLE, TRADE ACCEPTANCES, OR DRAFTS DISCOUNTED OR SOLD
NOTES RECEIVABLE OR TRADE ACCEPTANCES PLEDGED OR ASSIGNED
CUSTOMERS' ACCOUNTS DISCOUNTED OR SOLD
CUSTOMERS' ACCOUNTS ASSIGNED OR PLEDGED
ACCOMMODATION PAPER, ENDORSEMENTS OR NOTES EXCHANGED WITH OTHERS

GUARANTOR FOR OTHERS ON NOTES, ACCOUNTS OR CONTRACTS
MAXIMUM LIABILITY FOR PROPOSED ADDITIONAL INCOME TAXES
BONDS OR UNFINISHED CONTRACTS
PURCHASE COMMITMENTS OUTSTANDING
LITIGATION IN PROCESS OR THREATENED
OTHER CONTINGENT LIABILITIES

STATEMENT OF PROFIT AND LOSS

FOR THE PERIOD BEGINNING _____ 19___ AND ENDING _____ 19___

GROSS SALES
LESS: RETURNS AND ALLOWANCES
NET SALES
COST OF GOODS SOLD:
 TOTAL INVENTORIES AT BEGINNING OF PERIOD
 ADD: PURCHASES DURING PERIOD
 FOR MANUFACTURER ONLY { DIRECT LABOR / DEPRECIATION / OTHER FACTORY OVERHEAD }
 TOTAL
 DEDUCT: TOTAL INVENTORIES AT CLOSE OF PERIOD
GROSS PROFIT
SELLING EXPENSES
 SALARIES
 COMMISSIONS
 TRAVELING
 ADVERTISING
 TOTAL
ADMINISTRATIVE AND GENERAL EXPENSES
 OFFICERS' SALARIES
 OTHER SALARIES
 RENT
 NOTES AND ACCOUNTS CHARGED OFF
 DEPRECIATION (NOT APPLICABLE ELSEWHERE)
 TOTAL

TOTAL ADMINISTRATIVE, GENERAL AND SELLING EXPENSES
OPERATING PROFIT
OTHER INCOME
 INVESTMENTS
 CASH DISCOUNTS RECEIVED
 RECOVERIES FROM NOTES AND ACCOUNTS PREVIOUSLY CHARGED OFF
 OTHER
 TOTAL
OTHER EXPENSES
 INTEREST
 CASH DISCOUNTS GIVEN
 OTHER
 TOTAL
NET PROFIT OR LOSS BEFORE INCOME TAXES
ACCRUED FEDERAL INCOME TAXES
ACCRUED STATE INCOME TAXES
 TOTAL
NET PROFIT OR LOSS CARRIED TO SURPLUS

AMOUNT OF DIVIDENDS DECLARED AND/OR PAID SINCE STATEMENT DATE $_____

RECONCILIATION OF EARNED SURPLUS

EARNED SURPLUS AT CLOSE OF PREVIOUS FISCAL YEAR
ADD: NET PROFITS (FROM PROFIT & LOSS STATEMENT)
 OTHER ADDITIONS (ITEMIZE)

 TOTAL ADDITIONS
LESS: DIVIDENDS PAID
 CASH—PREFERRED, RATE ___%
     —COMMON, RATE ___%
 STOCK—PREFERRED ___ RATE
     —COMMON ___ RATE
 OTHER DEDUCTIONS (ITEMIZE)
 TOTAL DEDUCTIONS
EARNED SURPLUS AT END OF PERIOD (SEE BALANCE SHEET)

RECONCILIATION OF CAPITAL SURPLUS

CAPITAL SURPLUS AT CLOSE OF PREVIOUS FISCAL YEAR
ADDITIONS (ITEMIZE)

 TOTAL ADDITIONS
DEDUCTIONS (ITEMIZE)

 TOTAL DEDUCTIONS
CAPITAL SURPLUS AT END OF PERIOD (SEE BALANCE SHEET)

WAS AN AUDIT MADE? _____ NAME OF INDEPENDENT ACCOUNTANTS? _____
THE FISCAL PERIOD OF THIS CORPORATION CLOSES ON THE _____ DAY OF _____

BANK ACCOUNTS

NAME AND LOCATION OF BANKS	CASH BALANCE	CREDIT LINES	AMOUNT OF LOANS	ON WHAT BASIS? (ENDORSEMENTS, RECEIVABLES, COLLATERAL, ETC.)
	$	$	$	

Figure 10-3. (Continued)

PAGE 3 OF FINANCIAL STATEMENT

NOTES AND TRADE ACCEPTANCES RECEIVABLE
—Customers Only (excluding those from affiliates)

NOT DUE		
RENEWED		
PAST DUE AND PROTESTED		
TOTAL NOTES AND TRADE ACCEPTANCES RECEIVABLE		
LESS: RESERVE FOR DOUBTFUL		
NOTES AND TRADE ACCEPTANCES RECEIVABLE—NET		
AMOUNT CONSIDERED OF SLOW COLLECTION		
AMOUNT CONSIDERED OF DOUBTFUL COLLECTION		

ACCOUNTS RECEIVABLE
—Customers Only (excluding those from affiliates)

ACCOUNTS CHARGED WITHIN:		
30 DAYS		
31 TO 60 DAYS		
61 TO 90 DAYS		
3 TO 6 MONTHS		
OVER 6 MONTHS		
TOTAL ACCOUNTS RECEIVABLE		
LESS: RESERVE FOR DOUBTFUL ACCOUNTS		
ACCOUNTS RECEIVABLE—NET		
AMOUNT OF ACCOUNTS CONSIDERED DOUBTFUL		
SELLING TERMS:		

MERCHANDISE

MERCHANDISE ON HAND		
" CONSIGNED TO OTHERS		
" IN TRANSIT		
TOTAL		
LESS: RESERVES (IF ANY)		
TOTAL AS PER STATEMENT		

1. AMOUNT OF MERCHANDISE PLEDGED
2. IS MERCHANDISE CONSIGNED TO YOU INCLUDED IN ASSETS?
3. AT WHAT TIME OF YEAR IS INVENTORY HIGHEST? _____ LOWEST?
4. AVERAGE AMOUNT OF INVENTORY
5. DOES INVENTORY REPRESENT PHYSICAL COUNT? _____ WHEN TAKEN?
6. DESCRIBE IN DETAIL THE BASIS OF VALUATION
7. STATE THE EXTENT OF ACCOUNTANTS' VERIFICATION, IF ANY
8. GIVE DATE (OR DATES) ON WHICH INVENTORY IS TAKEN AND BOOKS ARE CLOSED

SECURITIES OWNED

FACE VALUE (BONDS) NUMBER OF SHARES (STOCKS)	PERCENT OF TOTAL ISSUE	DESCRIPTION OF SECURITY	COST	PRESENT BOOK VALUE	MARKET VALUE	INCOME RECEIVED LAST YEAR	TO WHOM PLEDGED
			$	$	$	$	

ARE ALL SECURITIES OWNED REGISTERED IN THE NAME OF THE CORPORATION?

DUE FROM SUBSIDIARIES AND AFFILIATES

NAME OF CONCERN	LOCATION	FOR ADVANCES	WHEN DUE	FOR MERCHANDISE	TERMS
		$		$	

REAL ESTATE

	LOCATION AND DESCRIPTION	AGE	CONDITION	COST WITH IMPROVEMENTS	ASSESSED VALUE
1				$	$
2					
3					
4					
5					

	FIRE INSURANCE	ESTIMATED PRESENT VALUE	MORTGAGE AMOUNT	MORTGAGE MATURITY	MORTGAGEE	USED IN BUSINESS?	YEARLY GROSS RENTAL INCOME
1	$	$	$				$
2							
3							
4							
5							

THE LEGAL AND EQUITABLE TITLE TO ALL THE REAL ESTATE LISTED ABOVE IS SOLELY IN THE CORPORATION'S NAME, EXCEPT AS FOLLOWS:

IF BOOK VALUE (BEFORE DEPRECIATION RESERVES) HAS DECREASED DURING THE YEAR, STATE REASON

LIFE INSURANCE

NAME OF PERSON INSURED	TYPE OF POLICY	FACE AMOUNT OF POLICY	TOTAL CASH SURRENDER VALUE	TOTAL LOANS AGAINST POLICY	TO WHOM POLICY IS ASSIGNED
		$	$	$	

Figure 10-3. (Continued)

PAGE 4 OF FINANCIAL STATEMENT

BOND ISSUES (describe each issue separately)

DESCRIPTION OF ASSETS (INCLUDING CURRENT ASSETS, IF ANY) PLEDGED TO SECURE BOND ISSUES: _____

SUMMARY OF INDENTURE PROVISIONS, INCLUDING SINKING FUND REQUIREMENTS: _____

THERE ARE NO DEFAULTS IN CONNECTION WITH ANY OF THE PROVISIONS OF THE INDENTURE(S), EXCEPT AS FOLLOWS: _____

NAME AND ADDRESS OF TRUSTEE(S): _____

CAPITAL STOCK

PREFERRED _____ % PAR VALUE $_____ CUMULATIVE? _____	SUMMARY OF PREFERRED STOCK PROVISIONS: _____
AUTHORIZED $_____	
UNISSUED $_____	
OUTSTANDING $_____	
COMMON PAR VALUE $_____	VOTING POWERS OF PREFERRED STOCKHOLDERS: _____
AUTHORIZED $_____	
UNISSUED $_____	
OUTSTANDING $_____	AMOUNT OF PREFERRED STOCK DIVIDENDS ACCUMULATED AND UNPAID
COMMON: NO PAR VALUE—SHARES OUTSTANDING _____	$_____ , REPRESENTING A PERIOD OF _____

LIABILITY INSURANCE (automobile, truck, general public liability, etc.)

NAME AND ADDRESS OF INSURANCE COMPANY	TYPE OF POLICY	AMOUNT OF COVERAGE PERSONAL INJURY, ETC.	PROPERTY DAMAGE	EXPIRATION DATE
		$	$	

OTHER INSURANCE

FORM	CARRIED ON	NATURE	ASSIGNEE	AMOUNT
FIRE _____	MERCHANDISE _____			
" _____	BUILDINGS _____			
" _____	MACHINERY AND EQUIPMENT _____			
" _____	FURNITURE AND FIXTURES _____			
" _____	TRUCKS, AUTOS, WAGONS, ETC. _____			
CREDIT, USE AND OCCUPANCY, FIDELITY BONDS _____	ACCOUNTS AND NOTES RECEIVABLE _____			
OTHER _____				

OFFICERS

	NAMES IN FULL	NUMBER OF SHARES HELD PREFERRED	COMMON	ANNUAL COMPENSATION	ADDRESS
PRESIDENT _____					
VICE-PRES. _____					
VICE-PRES. _____					
SECRETARY _____					
TREASURER _____					

DIRECTORS

NAMES IN FULL	NUMBER OF SHARES HELD PREFERRED	COMMON	ANNUAL COMPENSATION	ADDRESS

IN SUBMITTING THE FOREGOING STATEMENT THE UNDERSIGNED GUARANTEES ITS ACCURACY WITH THE INTENT THAT IT BE RELIED UPON BY THE AFORESAID BANK IN EXTENDING CREDIT TO THE UNDERSIGNED AND WARRANTS THAT_____HAS NOT KNOWINGLY WITHHELD ANY INFORMATION THAT MIGHT AFFECT_____ CREDIT RISK; AND THE UNDERSIGNED EXPRESSLY AGREES TO NOTIFY IMMEDIATELY SAID BANK IN WRITING OF ANY MATERIAL CHANGE IN_____FINANCIAL CONDITION WHETHER APPLICATION FOR FURTHER CREDIT IS MADE OR NOT AND IN THE ABSENCE OF SUCH WRITTEN NOTICE IT IS EXPRESSLY AGREED THAT SAID BANK IN GRANTING NEW OR CONTINUING CREDIT MAY RELY ON THIS STATEMENT AS HAVING THE SAME FORCE AND EFFECT AS IF DELIVERED UPON THE DATE ADDITIONAL CREDIT IS REQUESTED OR EXISTING CREDIT EXTENDED OR CONTINUED.

SIGNED AT_____

THIS_____DAY OF_____19___

SIGNATURE OF CORPORATION

_____
OFFICER

TITLE
GHC 141-7-1940

Figure 10-3. (Continued)

What the lender needs. The principal differences among types of loans are discussed on the following pages. The central problem in any credit negotiation is the question of *assurance of repayment*. The ways of giving the assurance can be grouped under five headings. If the first is satisfied, the others are unnecessary. If the first is in doubt, the second is needed also, and so on.

1. *Conviction that the proposed operation will succeed.* If the lender is sure that the loan will be used for an operation that is certain to work out substantially as planned, a simple unsecured promise to pay is all that is required. It is useful to remember that such a loan on a plain note is the goal that is desirable to both parties in a loan transaction.

2. *Demonstration that the borrower's financial strength is such that the loan can be paid even if the proposed operation should fail.* This is the type of assurance sought by credit analysis that is based on financial statements. A record of sustained earning power, the history of periodic "clean up" by payment of all short-term loans, and a large margin of net working capital are examples of the factors that are studied for this aspect of the establishment of credit. This type of credit status also fits the pattern of the plain note.

3. *Specific agreements limiting financial policy.* Whenever the margins of financial strength are slim, or there is some doubt of the judgment of the management, loan agreements may be proposed. These are enforceable contracts, in which the borrower promises to do, or not to do, certain things. The purpose of such provisions, often called "protective provisions," is to add to the certainty that financial strength will not be dissipated. Loan arrangements of this character still use the unsecured note, as far as the legal position against other creditors is concerned, but the protective provisions represent agreed guides to, or limits of, policy.

The variety of protective provisions is great, but promises limiting the amounts of dividends or salaries are not infrequent. Other frequently encountered provisions include promises not to give any preference to other creditors, promises to maintain a certain net working capital, and promises to keep inventories below a specified sum. Some typical protective provisions are explained later in this chapter.

4. *Giving collateral.* If the outlook for the borrower is not clear enough to assure certainty of payment and justify use of one of the above devices, it may be desirable to resort to the segregation of specified assets, over which the lender will receive domination in preference to other creditors in case of default. As will appear below, loans of this type require attention to legal and other details greatly in excess of that attending a plain note. Yet it is the availability of collateral that makes many loans possible.

In a few businesses, notably those dealing in securities or in great quantities of raw materials where the inventories are large relative to the owner's capital, the use of collateral loans is almost universal. In most other businesses, collateral loans are less desired than unsecured ones.

5. *Addition of a promise to pay by somone of financial strength.* In cases where the applicant cannot, by any combination of the above factors, supply the assurance that the lender needs, he may be able to obtain the aid of a person or firm that will supply the need by adding its promise to pay. This may be done by guarantee, endorsement, or co-marker procedure. As will appear below, many such loans are arranged, but it is beyond the scope of this chapter to describe the inducements leading to them.

Trade credit. The greatest source of credit for financing short-term needs is the normal "open account" relationship between buyer and seller. Since no source of credit is more frequently used, it is of the first importance that a financial manager establish and maintain good relationships with suppliers. No single policy does more to create trade credit than the exercise of care in settling all accounts according to their terms, and if possible during the discount period. It is far better to arrange a loan with a financial institution than to let accounts payable become overdue. The business should never be permitted to drift into the latter condition.

Most credit men periodically appraise their company's accounts. In doing this, they often use the services of the credit agencies (Dun & Bradstreet, National Credit Office, and so on) for the information they give in addition to the customer's financial statement. These agencies follow the policy of questioning the principal suppliers of the companies they study, and the results are tabulated in the reports that are sent to clients. This record of actual experience is often more important for the establishment of trade relationships than any quantity of talk. Another frequently used method of appraising accounts is the interchange of information directly with some firms that do business with the same purchaser.

The means chosen to obtain funds by loans also affects the volume of trade credit available. Since the accounts payable are current liabilities, the pledging of current assets to other classes of creditors often seems to credit men to reduce their chance of collection. This attitude seems especially prevalent when accounts receivable are pledged. This disadvantage, however, is seldom so great as to prevent the arrangement of a collateral loan. Nevertheless, some tightening of trade credit may result when suppliers learn of a loan program involving a pledge of receivables.

After a credit relationship is well established, exceptions to the usual terms of trade may be negotiated for short periods when the circumstances warrant. The principles of negotiation already referred to, frankness, assurance of payment, and the like, can be applied in this type of case also.

The subject of establishing trade credit is covered in the chapter, "Credit and Collections," where the viewpoint of a credit manager is taken. This is a reverse side of the coin, but the principles are the same.

Unsecured loans. As has been pointed out, the use of the plain, unsecured note is desired by all parties when the nature of the transaction permits it. Such a note is a simple promise to pay a definite sum of money at a specified place and time ("90 days after date," "on demand," and so on). Interest for such a loan may be collected by discount in advance, or at maturity. In the latter case, the rate of interest will be stated on the note.

Priority of notes. Many persons think that an unsecured note payable has a priority in cases of insolvency over other unsecured debts of the firm, such as accounts payable. This is not the case. Only the giving of collateral can confer a priority over general claimants. Nevertheless, there is an advantage to the holder of the note in the fact that it is evidence of a debt that cannot be challenged since its terms are definite and it bears an authorized signature of the debtor.

Borrowing procedure. A variety of practices exist in connection with the creation of notes that are executed to finance circulating capital needs. The most rational is to divide the need into parts expressed in round numbers, and to execute a series of notes that mature at intervals to reduce the loan as the budget shows declining need. This procedure is seldom followed closely as to maturity, for few budgets are sufficiently accurate, but it is customary to execute notes in series as the need for funds builds up. However, the practice of signing demand notes is to be questioned even in cases where the essence of the promise to pay "on demand" is understood by all the parties to be a promise to pay "when convenient." The maturity of a note, or the possibility that it may be called, always furnishes an occasion for reexamination of the credit. If the future is foreboding, renewal may be difficult.

The most convenient method is that of signing notes for the desired sums to run until after the budgeted need is past, with an understanding that the amount of the note may be reduced by partial payments in advance of maturity as funds become available. This scheme provides the desired flexibility for the borrower, without holding the lender to more than he agreed to when the loan was approved. Few banks refuse the privilege of repayment, unless it is misused to gain a few days' interest.

Line of credit. After approving a loan proposal to finance circulating capital expansion, a bank often states that it has made a "credit line of $.........," to be used for the agreed purposes. This statement, however, is not a contractual obligation that can be enforced. The established law on the matter is that the bank can change its opinion at any time, so far as the unused portion of the line of credit is concerned. In practice, however, bankers find it unwise to change their stand unless circumstances have altered greatly, for customer good will suffers major damage. While the line is open, the corporation must keep the bank informed of its operations and financial condition and must continue to maintain its deposit there. The bank usually requires all loans made within the line of credit to be paid off within the period of a year and that the borrower remain free of debt for at least a 30-day period.

Commitment. The availability of credit can be assured by making a contract with the lender and by paying a fee, usually a fraction of 1 per cent of the amount committed. Experience indicates that there is little to be gained by this step except in periods of tight money. A commitment agreement usually contains conditions which mean that the company's credit, at the time of need, would be good enough for a loan without the commitment. The advantages gained by such a contract in periods of tight credit are predetermination of the rate of interest to be charged on the possible loan and assurance of the supply of credit. Also, the commitment may avoid the effect of a general shift in the loan policy of the bank.

Loans with restrictive agreements but without collateral. Many credit situations are uncertain enough to cause the lender to define certain policies of the borrower during the period of the loan but not to ask for collateral. These agreements are most common in connection with term loans, which run for a period of years. Typically, such promises are obtained in a loan agreement, which is separate from the note evidencing the debt. The two instruments are interrelated, however, so that the whole arrangement is to be found in the two instruments together. In some instances, the note and the other promises are combined into one contract.

The general purpose of restrictive convenants or protective provisions is to give added assurance that the borrower will manage his affairs within limits deemed desirable at the time the agreement is made. The usual effect of any breach of the terms is the

immediate maturity ("acceleration") of the whole amount loaned. A typical acceleration clause reads:

> In the event that default shall be made in the due performance or observance of
> any of the covenants, agreements, or conditions on the part of the Company to be kept,
> observed, or performed in this agreement contained . . . and such default shall con-
> tinue for a period of thirty (30) days after written or telegraphic notice to the Company
> from the Bank, then and in each and every such case the unpaid principal of the
> outstanding Notes, together with all accrued and unpaid interest thereon, shall, . . . be
> and become due and payable immediately, anything herein or in the Notes contained to
> the contrary notwithstanding, and thereupon the holder of each and any of the Notes
> may institute such proceedings for its collection as it may deem proper. The Bank may
> from time to time by written or telegraphic notice to the Company extend said period of
> thirty (30) days indefinitely or for such periods of successive periods as the Bank may
> in its discretion deem advisable.

The variety of clauses can be as great as the imagination of the draftsmen, but
those frequently encountered in short-term lending can be classified as follows:

Maintenance of desired degree of liquidity. The agreement may be that the current
ratio is not to fall below a stated figure, or that the net working capital shall not be less
than an agreed sum. Such over-all tests are usually less desirable than ones that reflect
more thought about the particular business, such as a limitation upon the amounts of
purchases, inventory, or accounts payable when the risk is felt to be that goods on hand
may become excessive. Similarly, the amount of accounts receivable may be limited if
it is feared that a company may be too liberal in its own credit management.

Protection against "waste" of funds. Again, a borrower may be required to limit
salaries, dividends, or investments in fixed assets. Such expenditures tend to reduce the
liquidity of a concern when the lender would prefer to have it maintained against the
maturities of the loan.

Protection against giving priority to other creditors, or against overborrowing.
Sometimes the lender may require that no borrowing shall be arranged elsewhere,
except for trade credits in the usual course of business. Usually this requirement is
resisted by the borrowers. More frequently one finds a promise that no other lender will
receive collateral, or otherwise obtain a stronger claim in the event of insolvency than
that held by the present lender.

Policy in negotiating restrictive provisions. The financial managers of borrowing firms too frequently accept the provisions proposed by lenders without studying
them sufficiently. It is of the essence of all such agreements that they should be
adjusted to suit the circumstances. This means not only that the clause should be
examined as to its general effect but also that the proposal should be read with reference to its relationship to the borrower's accounting system, to assure that the desired
measures can be computed and sent to the lender at the intervals specified. Each clause
should be considered with reference to possible developments during the period it is in
force in order to avoid all foreseeable conflict. Finally, the representative of the
borrower should insist upon a clause allowing the alteration of any restriction by
mutual consent during the life of the agreement. For example, a well drafted clause
with reference to capitalization reads:

> . . . *without the written consent of the Bank first obtained*, the Company . . . shall not

issue any additional stock or retire or purchase any outstanding stock of the Company . . ., effect any change in its capital structure, merge or consolidate with or into any other corporation, amend its corporate objects or purposes, or sell, lease, or exchange all or the major portion of its assets or properties. . . .

The unstated terms of unsecured loans. Since restrictive agreements are arranged where the condition of the borrower does not justify a loan on a plain note, it is to be remembered that most of the matters that have explicit form in such agreements are implicit in a loan that is evidenced in writing only by a note. A financial officer should therefore manage his company's affairs with care to such matters, even if credit standing is the highest. Liquidity, conservation of funds, the creation of priorities, and so on are matters that are looked into in every credit situation.

Endorsement or co-maker. An accommodation endorser guarantees payment of the debt and is looked to after the principal defaults. A co-maker makes a direct promise to pay with the signer of the obligation and may be proceeded against at the same time as the signer. In either situation, the essence is that a third party puts his credit standing at risk to induce the making of an advance to one whose own credit position is weak. The maker of the note who defaults does not avoid liability, for the rights of the payee are transferred to the third party who made good for him.

It is necessary to state here only the chief legal requirements for a binding endorsement or guarantee. (1) The promise must be in writing, and based upon a consideration (such as the extension of credit) given at the time of the writing. The supplementary promise must be connected with the original loan, a renewal, or increase. It cannot be made effective if given when a loan is running according to previously agreed terms. (2) The obligation of the third party is terminated by any significant alteration in the terms of the credit, unless his consent, in writing, is obtained at the time the terms are changed. This rule must be remembered at the time of renewal or of any other change in the loan arrangement.

Subordination. A debt may be subordinated to another by agreement with the first creditor. In general, such an agreement has the effect of deferring the subordinated claim until the satisfaction of the promises made on another debt. The enforceability of such agreements depends upon the rules stated in the preceding paragraph.

Although often encountered in the financial arrangements of new firms, this procedure is seldom entered into by an established business until it is in an extremely weak credit position. Usually the only creditors who will consent to subordination are persons extremely close to the debtors, for example, the officers or owners who have made loans to it. The extent of subordination can be varied and will depend upon the wording of the agreement used.

Collateral loans. The giving of collateral does not create a loan; the obligation is the promise to pay. Collateral is given when a lender's doubts about the credit can be satisfied only by giving him first claim upon certain assets, to be used in case of default.

Most collateral loans work out according to their terms, so that the lender does not have to use the supplementary assurance which he has received. But when collateral must be used, the rights given to the holder of the collateral turn out to be rights against other creditors of the debtor in default. The preference gives a certain creditor superior rights over the other creditors, who are highly motivated to challenge the rights of the secured claimants. Therefore, the rules surrounding collateral arrangements have been established to provide adequate notice of the taking of security, so that a general credit advance will not be made in ignorance. The legal rules are supplemented by the standards of auditors and others, to the end that all diligent persons can be advised of the true credit situation. Thus, with but one exception, a secured creditor must either (1) have *possession* of the collateral, or (2) have *recorded* the transaction at an office of record, or (3) have *notified* the other creditors of the nature of the security held. In succeeding paragraphs, these general rules will be detailed as they apply.

The status of collateral, so long as the loan contract is being executed according to its terms, is that it is the property (by legal or equitable title) of the borrower, who receives any incomes or right that may accrue thereon. Upon default, the property is taken by the secured creditor, who may use its value against the debt due to him. If the value exceeds the debt, the excess is returned for the benefit of the other creditors. If the value is insufficient, the balance due is joined with the unsecured claims. It is completely inaccurate to say of collateral, as many do say, for instance, "the holder of a mortgage has a first claim on all the fixed assets of the mortgagor." His prior claim is against the specific collateral only.

The procedure for the sale of collateral is specified by statute in the case of mortgages. In cases where public sale at auction after advertising is required by law, there is usually a clause in the collateral agreement between the borrower and the lender which gives the lender greater freedom, subject only to his good faith in carrying out the sale. A typical clause reads:

> . . . with full power and authority in the holder of this note on the failure of the undersigned to pay this note, and so long as said Bank shall be the holder hereof, on the non-payment of any of the liabilities above mentioned, or at any time or times [after default] to sell, assign, and deliver the whole of said property or any part thereof or any substitutes therefor or any additions thereto at any Brokers' Board or at public or private sale at the option of the holder hereof without advertisement or any notice to the undersigned or to any other person; and said Bank, its officers or assigns, or the holders hereof, may become purchasers at any such sale, if public or at Brokers' Board.

Pledge of assets as collateral. The term "pledge" refers to an arrangement under which the collateral is actually put into the possession of the lender. It is the simplest type of collateral arrangement, but is suitable only when the use of the property is not needed by the borrower during the life of the loan. Stock or bond holdings, life insurance policies, and similar property are the usual items pledged. As stated above, the right to dividends, interest, and the like remain the borrower's. The holder of the collateral is obligated to turn over promptly any such receipts.

Although the law does not require that a pledge be recorded in an office of record, most auditors will not certify a financial statement that does not indicate the existence of such pledges as may have been made. Certainly a borrower has an ethical obligation to disclose fully the existence of such pledges.

A variant of the usual pledge is known as a "general collateral agreement." Under this agreement, which looks forward to loans from time to time as necessary, the collateral arrangement continues in force to be used as necessary. It is a convenient device for those who expect to be borrowers from time to time. One form for such an agreement begins:

> KNOW ALL MEN BY THESE PRESENTS, that the undersigned, in consideration of financial accommodations heretofore given or which may be given, or continued, to the undersigned, by or through [Name of Bank] (herein called the bank), and for other valuable considerations, hereby agrees with respect to any liability or liabilities, direct or contingent, of the undersigned now or hereafter existing, due or to become due to, or held or to be held by, the bank, whether created directly or acquired by assignment or otherwise, that the bank shall have the following rights, in addition to those otherwise created or existing, against the undersigned, or the executors, administrators, successors, and assigns of the undersigned, namely:
>
> 1. All property now or hereafter given unto, or left in the possession or custody of said bank for any purpose (including safekeeping or pledge for any liability of the undersigned), by or for account of the undersigned, or as to which the undersigned may have any interest or power, including power of hypothecation or disposition, (all remittances and property to be deemed left with said bank, as soon as put in transit to it, by mail or carrier) shall be held by said bank subject to a lien and as security for any and all such liabilities. The balance of any deposit account (whether general or special or for any special purpose) of the undersigned with, or any claim of the undersigned against, said bank, existing from time to time, shall be subject to a lien as security for and also shall be a setoff to any and all such liabilities. The bank may at any time transfer into its own name or that of its nominee any or all property held as security.
>
> The bank may, but is not obligated to demand, sue for, collect and/or receive any money or property at any time due, payable, or receivable on account of, or in exchange for, any obligation securing said liabilities of the undersigned to the bank, and may compromise and settle, with any person liable on such obligation, and may extend the time of payment of or otherwise change the terms thereof, as to any party liable thereon, all without incurring responsibility to, or affecting any liability of, the undersigned. . . .

Real estate mortgage. Despite its frequent use, the mortgage of real estate is one of the least satisfactory types of collateral loan arrangements for any short-term purpose. The procedure is too cumbersome. Nevertheless, its use indicates its serviceability where other types of collateral provide insufficient protection. The placing of a mortgage requires search of title, to give assurance that no other liens exist on the property. Records of search must be brought up to date each time the mortgage is altered. All of this procedure is costly and requires time.

As mortgaged property remains in the possession of the borrower, the statutes require that no mortgage shall be effective against another creditor unless it is recorded in a specified office, often called "Registry of Deeds."

Chattel mortgage—conditional sales. Property of other types than real estate may be mortgaged under chattel mortgage procedure, or the use of the property may be obtained under a conditional sale agreement. Though dissimilar in theory, the two procedures have the same effect, and the choice between them depends upon the details of the law in the state where the arrangement is made. In each case, recording at the designated public office is usually required.

Although such agreements have been found to be very useful for financing the purchase of such items as machines, store fixtures, autos, and trucks, they do not lend themselves to the financing of the purchase of goods or other property that turns over in the normal course of business.

Current assets as collateral—revolving credit. Since short-term financial needs arise from changes in the amounts of funds absorbed by current assets, the most satisfactory type of collateral arrangements uses the current assets themselves. A revolving credit is usually the most suitable. By this arrangement, a borrower may obtain a loan that varies in amount as his needs change. Revolving credits may be regarded as a series of loans made under an overriding contract. Thus, a revolving credit for inventory can be set up to provide an agreed fraction, say 75 per cent, of the invoice price of goods received into stock. Each invoice is the source of a loan, and as goods are withdrawn from stock there is a loan repayment. Thus, the total sum of the separate loans outstanding at any time is based upon the inventory on hand. The loan is said to "revolve" in the same sense as current capital is said to "circulate." All of the types of collateral arrangements dealt with below are of this revolving type.

Goods in warehouses as collateral. If it is to be effective against other creditors, the pledge of inventory must be made effective. This is most easily done by placing the goods in an independent public warehouse under a warehouse receipt. Possession of this receipt assures the lender's control of the collateral.

In recent years the method of field warehousing has grown in importance, when the use of a warehouse separate from the borrower's property would cause inconvenience, extra expense, or additional investment in goods. Under this scheme, an independent public warehouseman leases a portion of the borrower's storage space, posts notices, and places the area under lock and key. Warehouse receipts are then used with reference to this area just as they would be for a separate storage space. Sometimes the custodian is jointly the employee of the borrower and the warehousing company. A standard agreement for setting up a field warehouse appears in Figure 10-4.

Although this arrangement may seem to attenuate the idea of possession almost to the breaking point, it does serve the essential functions of segregating the property used as collateral, and of giving notice to other creditors that collateral has been given. Looked at from this point of view, a field warehouse may give better notice to creditors than a separate storage building.

FIELD WAREHOUSE STORAGE AGREEMENT

THIS AGREEMENT, made and entered into at .... , ... , this .... day of .... 19......, by and between —— WARE-HOUSE COMPANY, a .... corporation, party of the first part, hereinafter called "_____" and ....

....

.... , a .... party of the second part, hereinafter called "The Depositor," in consideration of the mutual covenants and agreements hereinafter contained,

WITNESSETH:

1. The depositor hereby employs _____ to establish and operate all field warehouses required in the depositor's business upon the following terms and conditions:

2. The depositor agrees to lease, or cause to be leased, to _____, upon its form of Field Warehouse Lease, adequate warehouse storage space for all commodities to be warehoused so located and constructed as to secure the proper storing and safety of commodities to be warehoused.

Figure 10-4. Field Warehouse Storage Agreement. *(Courtesy, Lawrence Warehouse Company, New York.)*

3. The depositor agrees to pay to _____ for conducting such field warehouse or warehouses, and for storing commodities therein, the following:

Commodities:

Location charge (each location): $............... per year or fraction thereof, payable on receipt of invoice, covering regular examinations and premium on Fidelity Bonds for not to exceed two employees. Additional employees, $25 each, per year or fraction thereof.

Storage charges:

The storage charges above set forth are subject to an annual minimum payment of .... per year or fraction thereof, per location, payable on the date of this agreement and annually thereafter on the same day of each succeeding year during the term of this agreement. Storage charges accruing in excess of minimum payable on receipt of invoice.

The actual cost incurred by _____ (plus ten per cent (10%) if not paid within ten (10) days) for all employees required by _____ in the conduct of said warehouse or warehouses, and in the storing and handling of commodities therein. As of the date of this agreement, it is estimated that such actual cost will be $............................ per month, plus Workmen's Compensation Insurance and contributions for Unemployment and Old Age Benefit Insurance. Costs are subject to adjustment in accordance with the actual number of employees required and their rates of pay. Depositor agrees to pay actual costs as adjusted, plus Workmen's Compensation Insurance and contributions for Unemployment and Old Age Benefit Insurance, plus ten per cent (10%) of the total, monthly in advance upon receipt of invoice, such ten per cent (10%) to be deducted if invoice is paid within ten days from the date thereof.

All license fees, taxes or charges levied or imposed by Federal, State, County or Municipal Governments or governmental agencies upon the operation of said warehouses, payable upon presentation of invoice.

$............................. for installation, non-recurring, payable in advance.

Special examinations, special travel expenses, etc., at cost, payable upon presentation of invoice.

All expenses including attorneys' fees incurred by _____ incident to conducting any warehouse under this agreement, maintaining possession of the warehoused commodities for the benefit of warehouse receipt holders and the depositor, and in connection with any litigation in which _____ or the depositor is a party, payable upon presentation of invoice.

4. _____ hereby accepts the employment on the terms hereinbefore set forth, and agrees to extend to the depositor the full benefit of its facilities and experience as field warehouseman.

5. It is mutually agreed that all commodities of like description stored pursuant to this agreement may each be warehoused as one general lot of fungible goods, and that the holder of a warehouse receipt shall be entitled to such portion of each such general lot as the amount of each commodity represented by such receipt bears to the whole of such general lot of such commodity.

6. This agreement shall continue in full force and effect for three (3) years from the date hereof, and thereafter for successive three (3) year terms unless either party gives to the other written notice of intention to terminate at least ninety (90) days prior to the expiration of the then current three (3) year term, provided, that no such notice of intention to terminate given by the depositor shall become effective unless all warehouse receipts, or other evidence of the storage of commodities, issued by _____ shall have been surrendered to _____ and cancelled and all charges of _____ shall have been paid prior to the expiration of said term, and provided further, that

Figure 10-4. (Continued)

_____ shall have the right to cancel this agreement at any time upon giving thirty (30) days written notice to the depositor if the depositor is in arrears in payment of charges or is interfering with the operation of any warehouse established pursuant to this agreement.

7. It is mutually agreed that in the event no warehouse receipts are outstanding at the beginning of or issued during any contract year, and field warehouse storage is not required during such contract year, the obligaiton of the depositor to pay the minimum storage charges hereinbefore provided for, shall be suspended, and thereafter the term of this agreement shall be extended one year for each year of such suspension. Contract year as used herein shall mean the twelve (12) successive months immediately following the date of this agreement, and each successive twelve (12) month period.

IN WITNESS WHEREOF, _____ has caused this agreement to be executed by its proper corporate officers and its corporate seal to be hereunto affixed, and the depositor has

{ caused this agreement to be executed by its proper corporate officers and its corporate seal to be hereunto affixed,

{ caused this instrument to be executed by a partner thereunto duly authorized,

(set his hand and seal,

the day and year first above written.

ATTEST: _____ WAREHOUSE COMPANY

....   By ....
            Assistant Secretary   Vice-President

ATTEST: ....

....   By ....

Figure 10-4. (Continued)

Goods in transit as collateral. Quite similar to the warehouse receipt, and suitable as a means of providing collateral in the form of goods in transit, is the bill of lading, issued by a common carrier. When issued in "order-notify" form, these bills serve to limit the delivery of the goods in transit to authorized persons and thus are a means of using shipments as collateral. For instance, a shipment may be made, and a draft on the purchaser, with bill of lading attached, discounted with a lender. The lender forwards the papers to a correspondent in the city where delivery is to be made. This correspondent collects the invoiced amount before releasing the bill of lading, thus protecting the loan until payment, because the bill of lading must be presented to obtain delivery.

Goods on display or in process as collateral. The trust receipt procedure came into use to supplement the segregation of inventory in a warehouse. Before this procedure was available, goods in the possession of the borrower (for display or processing) could not be pledged. Now, in states where trust receipt legislation has been passed, the property can be released to the borrower, but only in trust to be used in the manner specified, and then the goods or the proceeds of their sale must be returned to the lender's "possession."

The trust receipt is also used to cover the temporary release of pledged customer paper so that the buyer can transfer title to the goods in connection with a sale, thereby obtaining the funds to clear the loan.

The position of the lender in relation to other creditors is established by the recording of the basic trust receipt arrangement in an office of record, and by the careful marking of the goods while they are in the borrower's hands. Considerable doubt still exists over the significance of a trust receipt when goods are being worked on, but the procedure is quite often used to permit dealers to display goods.

Every collateral arrangement can be misused by a fraudulent borrower, but trust receipt procedure is especially open to misuse. It has been aptly said that the trust receipts act proceeds upon the theory that the lender is entitled to protection only against honest insolvency of the trustee, and that any dishonest action of the trustee is a credit risk.

Receivables as collateral. Accounts receivable can be used as the basis for loans. As has been pointed out, receivables represent goods sold, so the business risks of their conversion into cash are less than the risks associated with other types of circulating capital. As a committee of the American Bar Association said a number of years ago:

> It is now generally recognized by bankers and other loaning institutions that accounts receivable constitute prime and not ''bottom of the barrel'' collateral security for commercial loans for the reason that they represent current indebtedness and are in effect self-liquidating. Accounts receivable financing is no longer looked upon as a sign of financial distress on the part of borrowers. Moreover, it is not unlikely that in the coming . . . period accounts receivable will be more widely used than ever as collateral for loans, particularly by the smaller business firms.

Despite this growing use, there is still some prejudice among mercantile credit men against firms that pledge their receivables. In their view, receivables should be used as a general fund for meeting current debt. They regard the pledge as a sign of ''last-ditch'' financing, and tend to restrict trade credit accordingly. Although this feeling is on the wane, it still exists, and the financial manager who uses receivables as collateral should provide for enough funds to take care of some shrinkage in trade credits when the arrangement becomes known, as it may eventually if the auditor's report is published.

Receivables financing is available on a ''notification'' and ''non-notification'' basis. In the latter case, which is the more frequent, the customer who owes the account is not notified that his account has been assigned. It has been found that customer goodwill is shaken when a lending agency is the collector.

The usual procedures for receivables financing appear in the agreement, Figure 10-5, and may be outlined as follows: The lender studies the condition of the accounts, and the credit of the firms on the books. The loan agreement will specify the margins to be used, and a separate letter will name the customers to be excluded, if any. Advances are obtained by filing a list of current charges to accounts, and the proper ledger sheets are stamped to indicate the fact of pledge. All items received in payment of the accounts are deposited in a separate bank account and used to reduce the loan.

This type of financing, like the trust receipt procedure, is subject to fraudulent misuse by borrowers. The agreement is not intended to be a protection against such activity, this being, as in the other case, a credit risk undertaken by the lender.

AGREEMENT made this .... day of ...., 19 ...., at ....,
by and between _____ (hereinafter called the "Borrower"), and _____ BANK
(hereinafter called the "Bank").

1. Definitions—Unless the context otherwise requires:

"Accounts" as used herein and in the below form of Assignment means accounts
receivable, including sums owing (though not yet payable) under existing contracts but not sums to become due for goods not yet completed and invoiced or
services not yet rendered, and excluding any sums due an assignor for his personal
services as an employee and judgments, notes, drafts, acceptances, conditional
sale contracts and other instruments for the payment of money, the assignment
of which is usually made by endorsement on or delivery of the instrument.

"Assigned Accounts" means Accounts assigned by an Assignment duly executed
and delivered by the Borrower to the Bank pursuant to this agreement.

"Loan Percentage," until changed by an agreement of the parties in writing, shall
be   % of the net value of Accounts, that is, the face value of Accounts less
all discounts and credits to which the debtors thereon may be entitled.

"Assignment" means an instrument in the following form, together with the
schedules, and invoices therein referred to, by which all Accounts shall be
assigned to the Bank, viz:—

"ASSIGNMENT

For value received, the undersigned Borrower hereby pledges, sells, assigns and
transfers to The .... Bank the Accounts identified on the
schedule or represented by the invoices attached hereto, all guarantees and
security therefore, and all right, title and interest of the Borrower in the property,
if any, giving rise thereto, including the right of stoppage in transit.

This Assignment is made pursuant to, and for the purposes set forth in, an
agreement between the undersigned Borrower and
.... Bank,   dated ...., 19......., and the
covenants, terms and provisions of said agreement are expressly incorporated
herein.

Dated:

                    , 19   .

                                        ....

                                        By...

                                                        Authorized Official

"Borrower's Loan Account" means the account upon the books of the Bank, in
which will be recorded all loans by the Bank to the Borrower pursuant to this
agreement, payments on such loans and other appropriate debits and credits.

2. *Original Loan*. Contemporaneously with the execution and delivery of this
agreement, the Bank has loaned to the Borrower, by crediting the deposit account of
the Borrower and charging the Borrower's Loan Account with, an amount equal to
the Loan Percentage of Accounts assigned to the Bank by the Borrower. The Accounts so assigned and all Accounts hereafter assigned by the Borrower to the Bank
shall, together with the general credit of the Borrower, secure the Borrower's indebtedness to the Bank as evidenced by the Borrower's Loan Account, and all other
indebtedness and liabilities of the Borrower to the Bank, absolute or contingent, due
or to become due, and now existing or hereafter arising.

Figure 10-5. Agreement for Financing Accounts Receivable

3. *Borrower's Representations and Covenants re Assigned Accounts.* The Borrower represents and covenants with the Bank:

(a) That each account purported to be assigned under and identified in an Assignment or schedule or invoice attached thereto will be a valid Account of the type above defined for an existing, undisputed indebtedness and will be promptly paid when due; that there are and will be no offsets or counterclaims of any nature against it; that no agreement under which any adjustment, deduction or discount (other than the discounts indicated in the Assignment thereof) may be claimed, has been or will be made with any debtor on any Assigned Account without the approval of the Bank; that at the time of assignment of each Assigned Account the Borrower will have full title thereto and full right to sell, assign and transfer the same and that it has not and will not be assigned to any other person or in any way encumbered except to the Bank;

(b) That the Borrower will immediately notify the Bank of any return, rejection or repossession of, or loss or damage to, property giving rise to Assigned Accounts and any negotiation or dispute with respect thereto or any event affecting the amount or collectibility of Assigned Accounts; that on any return to or repossession by the Borrower of property giving rise to an Assigned Account, the Borrower will, until a new Account is assigned or cash is paid to the Bank in substitution therefor in the manner provided by paragraph 4 hereof, set aside and mark such property as the property of the Bank, and the Bank may at any time without notice or demand enter upon any premises and take possession of and remove such property with or without process of law;

(c) That the Borrower will, upon each assignment of Accounts to the Bank, promptly make entries, the form of which the Bank may prescribe, on its books of record and account relating to such Accounts to indicate the assignment thereof to the Bank; that it will, when and in the manner requested by the Bank, promptly notify the respective debtors on all Assigned Accounts that such accounts have been assigned and are payable to the Bank and that the Bank may itself, at any time or times, give such notification and require the payment of Assigned Accounts directly to it;

(d) That the Borrower will at all reasonable times and from time to time allow the Bank, through any person designated by it, to examine, audit and make extracts from the Borrower's books, accounts, records, audits, correspondence and other papers relating to Assigned Accounts and will furnish to the Bank such statements or information as to its financial condition as the Bank may reasonably request;

(e) That the Borrower will at all times and from time to time at the request of the Bank do, make, execute and deliver any and all additional and further acts, things and instruments which the Bank may deem necessary in order more completely to vest in and assure to the Bank and make available for it the Accounts assigned to it pursuant to this agreement, and to carry into effect the provisions and intent of this agreement;

(f) That while this agreement is in force and effect, the Borrower will not borrow on the security of accounts receivable from any source other than the Bank or sell any accounts receivable without first offering the same to the Bank on at least as favorable terms.

4. *Substitutions and Adjustments of Assigned Accounts.* The debit balance in the Borrower's Loan Account shall at no time exceed the Loan Percentage of Assigned Accounts and the Borrower shall assign new Accounts to the Bank or shall

Figure 10-5. Agreement for Financing Accounts Receivable (Continued).

pay cash to the Bank in an amount at least equal to all adjustments or credits required or made on Assigned Accounts and in an amount at least equal to and in substitution for each Assigned Account with respect to which, and if and when, any of the following events occur:

(i) Any property, the sale of which gave rise to such Assigned Account, is returned, rejected, repossessed, lost or damaged;

(ii) Any merchandise or other dispute arises with respect to such Assigned Account and the Bank requests that substitution be made therefor;

(iii) Such Assigned Account becomes past due under the original terms of sale and the Bank requests that substitution be made therefor;

(iv) Death, termination of existence, business failure, appointment of a receiver of any part of the property, of, assignment for the benefit of creditors by, or the filing of a petition in bankruptcy, or the commencement of any proceedings under any bankruptcy or insolvency laws or any laws relating to the relief of debtors, readjustment of indebtedness, reorganization, composition or extension, by or against the debtor on such Assigned Account.

Upon the assignment of new accounts or the payment of cash in substitution for Assigned Accounts pursuant to the provisions of this paragraph 4, the Bank shall be deemed to have reassigned to the Borrower the Assigned Accounts for which substitution has been so made and to have released to the Borrower all interest in the property giving rise thereto and the Bank shall, at the request of the Borrower, execute and deliver to the Borrower a reassignment of such accounts and a release of such property.

5. *Collections.* If and so long as the Bank does not notify or request the Borrower to notify debtors on Assigned Accounts of the assignment thereof to the Bank, the Borrower shall, as agent for and on behalf of the Bank, collect all Assigned Accounts. The Borrower agrees that it will hold all proceeds of collections received by it in trust for the Bank and will pay and deliver to the Bank, on the day of receipt thereof and in the form received, but properly endorsed where necessary, all cash, checks, drafts or other media of payment received by it in payment of, or as security for, Assigned Accounts. The Bank shall credit to the Borrower's Loan Account proceeds of Assigned Accounts received or collected by it, such credit to be made as of the following the date on which payment is received by the Bank in cash or solvent credits or, if said day be a holiday, then as of the next following business day. Credits are conditional upon final payment to the Bank as its own office of all items giving rise to the credits and if any item is not so paid, any credit for it shall be reversed, whether or not the item is returned.

6. *Additional Loans.* The Bank may, but shall not be obligated to, make additional loans to the Borrower upon Assignment by the Borrower to the Bank of new Accounts as security therefor. When such Accounts are assigned the Bank shall credit the Borrower's deposit account and charge the Borrower's Loan Account with an amount equal to the Loan Percentage of the Accounts assigned to the Bank by the Borrower.

7. *Interest—Charges—Expenses—Monthly Statement of Account.* The Borrower shall pay

(a) to the Bank, on demand, the amount of the debit balance in the Borrower's Loan Account and interest at the rate of   % per annum computed on the daily debit balances in the Borrower's Loan Account;

(b) to the Bank as a handling or service charge, such amount as shall from time to time be agreed upon by the Borrower and the Bank;

Figure 10-5. Agreement for Financing Accounts Receivable (Continued)

(c) all expenses, including attorney's fees, expenses of litigation or otherwise, reasonably incurred by the Bank in the collection or attempted collection of Assigned Accounts.

The Borrower hereby authorizes the Bank to charge such interest, charges and expenses, if not otherwise paid by the Borrower, to any Deposit Account of the Borrower with the Bank or to the Borrower's Loan Account, as the Bank may elect.

On or before the tenth day of each month, the Bank shall render to the Borrower a statement of account, which statement shall be considered correct and accepted by the Borrower and conclusively binding upon the Borrower unless the Borrower notifies the Bank to the contrary within twenty days after receipt of such statement.

8. *Appointment of Bank as Attorney.* The Borrower hereby irrevocably appoints the Bank its true and lawful attorney, with power of substitution, for the Borrower and in the Borrower's name or in the name of the Bank or otherwise, for the use and benefit of the Bank, but at the cost and expense of the Borrower, (1) to demand, collect, receive payment of, receipt for and give discharges and releases of the Assigned Accounts or any of them and any moneys due or to become due in respect thereof; (2) to settle, compromise or adjust the Assigned Accounts or any of them; (3) to commence and prosecute any suits, actions or proceedings at law or in equity, in any court of competent jurisdiction, to collect the Assigned Accounts or any of them, or enforce any rights in respect thereof; (4) to settle, compromise, adjust or defend any such action, suit or proceeding; and (5) generally to sell, assign, transfer, pledge, make any agreement with respect to or otherwise deal with any of the Assigned Accounts and any returned or repossessed property as fully and completely as though the Bank were the absolute owner thereof for all purposes. Until all Assigned Accounts have been paid in full, the Bank, or any representative designated by it, may receive, open and dispose of all mail addressed to the Borrower and may endorse notes, acceptances, checks, drafts, money orders, bills of lading, warehouse receipts or other evidences of payment, shipment or storage, or any form of collateral for Assigned Accounts, on behalf of and in the name of the Borrower. The powers conferred on the Bank by this paragraph are solely to protect its own interests and shall not impose any duty upon the bank to exercise any such powers.

9. *Enforcement of Security.* In addition to the right on the part of the Bank to receive the proceeds of Assigned Accounts as herein provided, the Borrower hereby fully authorizes and empowers the Bank, on the non-performance of any promise made herein or the non-payment when due of any liability of the Borrower to the Bank, or at any time or times thereafter, to sell, assign and deliver all of the security therefor or any part thereof or any substitute therefor or any additions thereto at any broker's board or at public or private sale, at the option of the Bank or any officer or anyone acting in behalf of the Bank, without advertisement or any notice to the Borrower or any other person, and the Bank, its officers or assigns, may bid and become purchasers at any such sale if public or at any broker's board.

Any deposits or other sums at any time credited by or due from the Bank to the Borrower or to any guarantor or surety for any liabilities of the Borrower to the Bank hereunder and any securities or other property of the Borrower or of any such guarantor or surety which at any time are in the possession of the Bank may at all times be held and treated as collateral security for the payment of the liabilities of the Borrower to the Bank hereunder and any and all other liabilities, direct or indirect, absolute or contingent, due or to become due, now existing or hereafter arising, of said respective Borrower, guarantor or surety to the Bank. The Bank may apply or set off such deposits or other sums against such liability at any time in the case of the Borrower, but only with respect to matured liabilities in the case of guarantors or sureties.

Figure 10-5. Agreement for Financing Accounts Receivable (Continued)

10. *Waivers.* The Borrower waives presentment, demand, protest, notice of default, non-payment, partial payments and all other notices and formalities and consents to and waives notice of the granting of indulgence or extension of time payment, the taking or releasing of security, the addition or release of persons primarily or secondarily liable on or with respect to liabilities of the Borrower to the Bank or any of the Assigned Accounts, the acceptance of partial payments thereon and/or the settlement or compromising of any thereof, all in such manner and at such time or times as the Bank may deem advisable. The Bank shall not be required to prosecute collection or other remedies against the makers of or other persons liable on any of the Assigned Accounts, or to enforce or resort to any security, liens, collateral or other remedies appertaining to Assigned Accounts, before calling on the Borrower for payment or otherwise, nor shall any such aot or omission of the Bank in any way impair or affect any of the indebtedness or liabilities of the Borrower to the Bank or rights of the Bank in any security. No delay or omission by the Bank to exercise any right, power or remedy hereunder and no indulgence given to the Borrower in case of any default shall impair any such right, power or remedy, or be construed as a waiver of any default by the Borrower or an acquiescence therein, or as a variation or waiver of any of the terms or provisions of this agreement.

11. *Return to Borrower of Security.* If and when all indebtedness and liabilities of the Borrower to the Bank have been paid in full, the Bank shall retransfer to the Borrower all uncollected Assigned Accounts and other security, if any, then held by it.

12. *General.* Each account offered as security for the Borrower's indebtedness under this agreement is subject to approval by the Bank at is uncontrolled discretion. This agreement and all rights hereunder shall be governed by the law of .... This agreement shall bind and inure to the benefit of, and the terms "Borrower" and "Bank" respectively as used in this agreement shall include, the respective parties and their respective executors, administrators, successors and assigns. Either party may terminate this agreement at any time, by giving notice in writing to the other party of such termination, PROVIDED HOWEVER, that such termination shall in no way affect any transactions entered into or rights created or obligations incurred prior to the receipt of such notice by the other party, as to which transactions, rights and obligations this agreement shall be fully operative until the same are fully disposed of, concluded and/or liquidated.

IN WITNESS WHEREOF the parties have hereunto set their hands and seals. Executed in duplicate.

....

By...
                     BANK

By...
              Authorized Signature

Figure 10-5. Agreement for Financing Accounts Receivable

This plan for the assignment of a receivable without notice to the customer is the most frequent procedure. In a growing number of trades, but still chiefly in the textile and shoe industries, the procedure of "factoring" is found. A factor usually buys the accounts "without recourse"; that is, he accepts the risks of bad debts. Ordinarily, too, the factor takes over all his customers' credit functions, and bills the account directly in his own name. It is the existence of factoring as an accepted procedure that leads to the expectation that the buyer's prejudice against the assignment of receivables, where it exists, will wane as time goes by.

Margin requirements. It is to be expected that lenders will not lend the whole book value of the collateral taken. The only time they would try to sell the collateral would be in case of default, probably when business conditions are poor, and under circumstances that force prompt sale. On the other hand, a borrower should ask for an appraisal of the specific collateral offered, rather than the automatic application of some accepted ratio.

The margins on receivable loans are usually small. A few lenders may advance 100 per cent of the net amounts billed, but a range of 80 to 95 per cent is common. Even when the accounts are of the best quality, lenders hesitate to risk loss from adjustments to customers. Margins on inventories are always based on an appraisal, rather than on book value. They vary greatly, depending on the anticipated difficulty of sale. Raw materials in frequent demand produce the largest loans against their book value, with 60 to 75 per cent being common. Finished goods of specialized nature and goods in process seldom produce more than junk values, although finished goods of general acceptability rank with the raw materials already mentioned.

Property pledged under chattel mortgages and conditional sale agreements is valued by similar tests. Real estate seldom has a loan value in excess of 66 per cent of its current appraisal, although if a loan is known to be for a short term, the loan may be greater.

Loans on guarantees by governmental agencies. This chapter does not cover governmental loan arrangements of specialized interest, such as loans available in the agricultural industries.

The Small Business Administration does make loans and provides other assistance to small businesses generally. It is authorized to make loans for the following purposes to independently owned and operated businesses which are not dominant in their fields of endeavor: (1) to finance plant construction, conversion, or expansion; (2) to finance the acquisition of equipment, machinery or supplies; or (3) to supply working capital to be used in war, defense or essential civilian production. These loans can be made directly by the SBA only when no private lenders will advance funds, in participation with the SBA.

Under the law, the Small Business Administration is restricted as to the amount it may lend any one borrower and as to the maximum maturity of any loan. All loans or loan participations made by the SBA must be of such sound value or so secured as to give reasonable assurance of repayment. Strict provisions with reference to salaries, dividends, and similar matters are often included.

The Small Business Investment Act of 1958 provides for SBA financing of private small business investment companies that will provide long-term loans and equity capital for small businesses.

The cost of borrowed money. The nominal rates of interest named in loan agreements often do not state even approximately the true cost of borrowing. Consequently, brief treatment will be given to the means of making closer cost estimates.

The basic arithmetic is simple. Find the cost of the loan in dollars, divide it by the principal of the loan, and state the result as the interest rate for the period the loan is outstanding.

Elements of cost. All payments that would be unnecessary if the loan were not obtained are to be regarded as part of the cost of borrowing. This will include the "interest" paid the lender, and all other costs associated with the loan arrangement, such as extra clerical work in processing receivables, fees to field or other warehousemen, recording fees as paid, costs of title search, and so on.

The principal of the loan. This is the actual amount that the borrower has to use. It is often less than the amount stated in a loan arrangement, because of prepayment of interest or because an agreed amount must be left on deposit, unused. Installment loans should be scheduled to show the amounts actually available in the various periods, with a weighted average taken as the principal in calculating the cost of borrowing. Amounts available in revolving loan arrangements change frequently, and it is almost impossible to be accurate in advance. Historical records should be based on weighted averages as in the case of installment loans.

Example of computaton of cost of borrowed money. An example of the calculation of a weighted average and the determination of the cost of borrowing is presented below.

Assume a loan of $550,000 made July 1, 19x1, with payments scheduled as shown in Figure 10-6.

Date	Payment	Balance of Loan
On January 1, 19x2	$ 30,000	$520,000
On January 1, 19x3	75,000	445,000
On January 1, 19x4	75,000	370,000
On January 1, 19x5	110,000	260,000
On July 1, 19x5	260,000	0

The amounts made available by this loan should be tabulated against the respective periods of availability, and a weighted average made as follows:

From	To	Period (months)	Amount	Product
July 1, 19x1	January 1, 19x2	6	$550,000	3,300,000
January 1, 19x2	January 1, 19x3	12	520,000	6,240,000
January 1, 19x3	January 1, 19x4	12	445,000	5,340,000
January 1, 19x4	January 1, 19x5	12	370,000	4,440,000
January 1, 19x5	July 1, 19x5	6	260,000	1,560,000

Total Weight 48
Total Product 20,880,000
Weighted Average ....20,880,000 ÷ 48 = $435,000

The results of the calculations almost always show that borrowing is an expensive procedure whenever a revolving credit is set up. Simple pledges of security or long-term loans against real estate sometimes serve to reduce the cost as compared with unsecured credit, but otherwise the plain note is the least costly, for it is the simplest loan arrangement.

Bargaining for rates. The establishment of the rate which the lender will charge for his funds is ordinarily a somewhat onesided process, because the lender is better informed on the subject and the borrower is usually not inclined to question. On the other hand, financial managers should have some idea of going rates at the time that they enter loan negotiations.

The levels of customer rates vary considerably even at one time, with higher rates to be expected on small loans by small lenders in small communities. A single national average figure is therefore of little help but financial managers can get information on going rates from the *Federal Reserve Bulletin*. Each month the *Bulletin* carries a table showing annual and quarterly averages of bank rates on short-term business loans. The quarterly averages are broken down into averages for 19 large cities, New York City, 7 Northern and Eastern cities, and 11 Southern and Eastern cities. The averages are also broken down into rates on loans of various sizes.

Statistics that may serve as a guide can be found not only in the *Federal Reserve Bulletin* but also in several of the monthly reviews published by the Federal Reserve Bank of each district. Some trade associations also have confidential information on the subject. For more detailed local information on the subject, the financial manager must usually inform himself as best he can.

Types of lending agencies. Although the traditional source of credit for current needs is the commercial bank, the growing activities of the finance companies, both national and regional, have made their services available as alternate sources of credit in most communities. It can be stated as a generalization that finance companies usually are ready to take more risks, but that the banks are usually less costly sources of funds. Also, finance companies have in the past been more ready to finance receivables on a non-recourse basis. Beyond this little can be said, because the two types of institutions compete for all types of loans. Often the choice of a lending agency will be influenced by the impression that the loan officer makes upon the financial manager of the borrowing company who is negotiating the loan.

Since the financial officers of a corporation are most likely to apply for loans at the bank or banks in which the company maintains accounts for regular operations, special consideration should be given in choosing a depository to the bank's lending policy and the size of the loans it is accustomed to make. These and other factors in the selection of a bank are discussed in the chapter, "Cash Management."

11

Long-Term Financing

CONTENTS

11

Long-Term Financing

Importance of making a record to aid financing. If a company anticipates having to raise new capital some time in the future, it should keep in mind that today's operations will be part of the record that investors will examine critically in deciding whether or not to purchase the company's securities. When the time for long-term financing arrives, the past record cannot be changed. The Securities Act of 1933 makes it necessary for a company to tell a complete and accurate story.

The officials of the company must realize that the policies they follow will be reflected in the record. The balance sheets and income statements over a period of years may reveal to investors unsound financial policies causing overextended bank borrowing, inadequate depreciation, or a milking of the company through too high salaries and dividends. A company that today does not come under the public eye because it is closely owned cannot afford to follow policies that will be criticized in the future when new financing is sought. A good record makes financing easy; a bad one may make it costly, unsatisfactory to the original owners, or utterly impossible.

Sources of advice on long-term financing. Long-term financing calls for a comprehensive understanding of the financial needs of corporations, types of securities, the various markets for different securities, the mechanics of finance, and an up-to-date appraisal of the market. Only by handling many security deals involving different types of companies, under changing market and business conditions, is this knowledge acquired. Generally executives of small and medium-sized industrial companies do not have the specialized training needed for solving their long-term financing problem. Therefore, they must usually seek outside advice. They may turn for this advice to:

1. *Investment bankers.* Investment bankers are the specialized merchants in long-term securities. They are constantly buying and selling them and have a broad background of experience with long-term financial policy. They know what type of security and special features buyers are interested in at a particular time. Many of the innovations in financing are developed by the investment banking fraternity. The bankers are in a good position to formulate new financing ideas to meet a company's individual requirements. Choosing an investment banking firm is discussed later.

2. *Commercial banks.* Although commercial bankers are primarily concerned with short-term credit, they generally have a broad knowledge of long-term financing. They know that the issuance of a certain type of security might affect their interest in making a loan. It is therefore advisable for a company to discuss its new long-term

financing with its commercial banker and to keep him informed of its plans and of what it is going to do with the money.

A small company in need of funds for expansion purposes may turn to its commercial bank first to suggest the names of investment bankers who might be helpful. If a company is located in a small community and does business with a bank that is not qualified to advise on long-term financing, the local banker may be willing to refer the question to a correspondent bank in one of the principal cities like New York, Chicago, or San Francisco.

3. *Large institutional investors.* A company that has access to some insurance company, investment trust, charitable organization, or other institution with a sizable investment portfolio, may find the experts in charge of the investments ready and helpful advisers. They are thoroughly familiar with sound principles of long-term financing. Furthermore, their advice may be of particular interest, because it will give the buyer's point of view.

4. *Management consultants.* Some management consultants supply financial advice as part of their service. However, except in specialized fields, they do not generally offer very comprehensive services.

A word of caution should be mentioned here about sources of financial advice in general. Some people may give the impression of being well versed in finance, but actually know very little about sound financial policy. If their advice is followed, it will almost certainly lead to difficulties. When a company seeks financial advice, it should be most careful to choose reliable sources. It is well not to depend entirely upon one source. Many times there is no one answer as to the correct securities to use; the views of a number of experts will be added assurance that the correct decision is reached.

CHOOSING THE TYPE OF SECURITY

How to view the long-term financing problem. Once a company's needs for permanent capital are known, the next step is to determine the type of securities to be used. However, in order to make this decision, executives should understand the following basic factors:

1. What constitutes sound financing.
2. The importance of market demands.
3. The timing element—keeping the best type of security to the last.
4. Pricing of securities.

What constitutes sound financing. Sound financing mainly involves the building of a proper capital structure. This may be complicated by many factors, such as the difficulty in raising money for a new enterprise, or the desire of some group to keep the controlling interest.

The tests to be applied in deciding what securities to use are: (1) What will be the lowest cost of money over the long run, obtained from both equity and debt financing? (2) How much debt can the company stand during adverse conditions without becoming financially embarrassed? In other words, if a bond issue should mature during bad business conditions, will the company be able to meet that maturity without a strain?

How much debt and preferred stock a company can use will depend upon all of the surrounding circumstances. A study of the capital structure and the past earnings records, especially during depression periods, of companies in the same and similar industries may reveal what is a sound relationship between various classes of securities that make up capital structure.

Arguments in favor of conservative capitalization. The arguments in favor of a conservative capitalization, made up of high-grade securities, follow.

1. Financing can generally be accomplished on the cheapest basis over the long run if capitalization consists of high-grade securities. Around 1946 there was little difference in yield in top-quality bonds and those of lower grade. The yield on bonds rated Aaa was only about 1½ of 1 per cent lower than the yields on bonds rated Baa. At that time it did not matter substantially what a company's bonds were rated when a new issue was sold. In 1957, the yield was approximately 1 per cent. But the spread between the various grades may be substantial, as it was in 1938 when the average yield on Baa bonds exceeded 4 per cent, whereas the Aaa's were on about a 3 per cent basis. In the years 1931, 1932, and 1933, the spread was even greater, as Figure 11-1 shows. When the spread widens, a company that is able to sell the highest bonds will be able to benefit by the change.

There are no similar types of indexes to show the action of the various grades of preferred and common stocks in the past. However, it is known that good stocks hold up in bad times, and that investors are eager to purchase poorer issues on a low-yield basis only in boom times.

The question may be asked, will not the over-all financing cost be lower if a large amount of debt is used rather than preferred or common stock? Under certain market conditions this might be true. However, over the long run, if the debt of a company is allowed to increase past a certain point in relation to its equity securities, an element of risk is added that increases its cost and correspondingly increases the cost of equity money. This results in paying a higher combined financing rate.

2. The company can generally raise funds even in bad times. The chart in Figure 11-1, shows that the Aaa bonds never yielded more than 5½ per cent in the 28-year period covered. Except in most unusual conditions a top-grade company can always find a market for its bonds. The same chart shows that the yields on the lower-grade bonds were so high at times as to almost prevent any bond financing.

3. The company will be able to sell whatever type of security is best suited to the market at a particular time. In other words, if the common stock market is poor, it can choose between the sale of preferred stock or bonds, and if the preferred stock market is also weak, bond financing can be used.

4. Unforeseen difficulties in the industry can be met without disaster. The railroad industry is a good example of what happens to an industry that is topheavy with debt when it experiences unforeseen difficulties. Years ago, such factors as the adverse effect of truck and pipeline competition could hardly have been foreseen.

5. Good relations are maintained with security holders. This is espcially important in some industries. The many small investors who are the owners of common stock

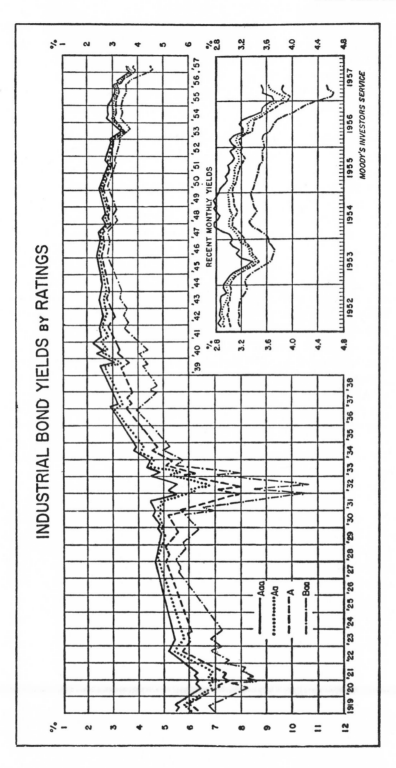

Figure 11-1. Industrial Bond Yields.

are usually uninformed about financing and care only about the dividends they receive and the price quotations for their stocks. They may be easily angered and show their resentment if their dividend is reduced or the price of their stock falls, regardless of whether the company is to blame.

Applicability of conservative policy to new companies. At times even an established company must use a medium of financing that it does not prefer. A new and unseasoned company may find it difficult to do any financing, no matter what type of securities are considered. It may take the best brains in finance to figure out ways to induce investors to put their money into a new enterprise.

A new and unseasoned company cannot expect to have its securities immediately accorded high ratings by investors, even though it follows conservative practices. It takes time for securities to become well known to investors and to build up a record of satisfactory performance. However, this does not invalidate the arguments in favor of having a conservative capitalization. If a company has been forced to resort to an unsatisfactory type of financing, it should formulate plans immediately to correct the defect in capitalization as soon as feasible. Unfortunately, there may be a tendency to put off consideration of corrective measures until difficulty is encountered. Then, it is too late. This tendency to procrastinate is due partly to the fact that some executives are prone to feel that the common stock of their company is underpriced no matter how high the quoted market price. They therefore keep putting off the sale of additional common stock. It is hard to realize that market conditions are satisfactory for stock financing until there is a break, and hindsight shows the true picture.

The importance of market demands. The demands of purchasers may influence the choice and terms of a security. For example, for a number of years, institutions were eager to purchase preferred stocks on terms quite favorable to the sellers. Later, as funds available for investment decreased, the institutions began demanding better yields and stricter protective provisions. To many executives of utility companies interested in selling preferred stocks, it seemed unorthodox to include a sinking fund in a stock issue. The executives looked upon a preferred stock as permanent capital with no maturity; a sinking fund would result in having to pay off the issue. However, in this period if a company wished to attract certain buyers for its preferred stock, it had to include a sinking fund provision in the terms of its issue.

Innovations and improvements in security features may also have a bearing on the terms of an issue. For example, at one time many completely non-callable bonds and preferred stocks were issued; today all new issues include the call feature in some form, even though the right to call for refunding purposes may have to be delayed for 5 to 10 years. New developments cannot be overlooked. Financial executives can readily see what the styles of financing are by studying terms of new security offerings during, say, seven or eight months prior to the time that the company expects to undertake its long-term financing.

The timing element—keeping the best security to the last. One of the most perplexing problems in long-term financing may be the decision as to the exact time to offer an issue. A company's cash requirements, of course, largely determine the general period when it will launch a long-term financing program. However, there may be considerable leeway as to the specific timing for the sale of individual securities.

For example, suppose that a company needs $5,000,000 immediately and another $5,000,000 in eight months, and that, after careful judgment, it decides it can raise this $10,000,000 by the sale of $5,000,000 of bonds and $5,000,000 of common stock. These questions arise: (1) Should the company sell both bonds and common stock immediately and hold the money until it is needed? (2) Should it sell $5,000,000 of the bonds now, and $5,000,000 of common stock in eight months? (3) Should it sell $5,000,000 of common stock now and $5,000,000 of bonds in eight months. If it were possible to know what the bond and stock market would do for the next eight months, the answers to the above questions could be determined by a mathematical calculation to see which method would yield the cheapest money, However, because the securities market is an uncertain element, there is no exact mathematical answer; sound judgment must be used. See for example, recent security performances (Figure 11-2).

If both the bond and stock market are ready to absorb the new issues, it would be best to sell both bonds and common stock immediately. A relatively small break in the securities market would more than offset the interest and dividends that the company would pay while some of the money is lying idle for eight months. Let us assume that the company sold 25-year 3 per cent bonds at par, and the common stock at $100 per share, which with $6.00 dividend per share, would yield 6 per cent. During the eight-months period, interest and total dividends on the $10,000,000 would amount to $300,000. Since half the money would be idle during this period, the cost of the idle money would be $150,000, assuming that none of it is invested in short-term government bonds.

If bond yields advance so that in eight months 3 per cent bonds yield 3.10 per cent to maturity, the company would only receive 98 for its 3 per cent bonds, making a total loss of $100,000 on the $5,000,000 of bonds. And if the stock fell 10 per cent in the eight months, the company could get only 90 for its stock and would lose $500,000 on the $5,000,000 of stock. From these figures, which presuppose only a small break in the market, it can be seen that when the securities markets are good, it may be foolish to wait too long before selling securities, merely to avoid interest or dividend payments on idle money.

Let us assume that the securities markets are good and that the company decides to do only $5,000,000 of financing immediately and to postpone the other $5,000,000 for eight months. Which should it sell first, bonds or stock?

Generally, the stock should be sold first. While greater savings would be realized by reversing the process, the following reasons support this decision.

1. The stock market is more volatile, and if there were a break in the securities market, stocks would probably fall more than bonds.
2. If the market has a severe setback, bonds can be sold more readily than common stock. If conditions were unfavorable in the bond market as well, the company's improved credit position might enable it to obtain a bank loan. Thus, the company, by selling stock first, would have greater assurance that it would get the $5,000,000 that would be needed in eight months. Keeping the best security to the last is a good principle to remember.

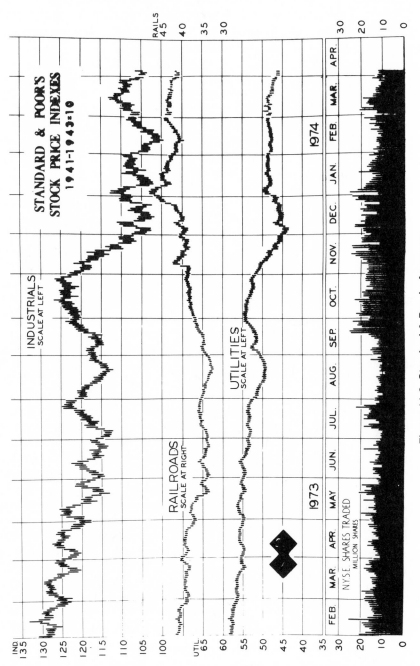

Figure 11-2. Standard & Poor's Averages.

Reproduced by permission from Standard & Poor's Corporation, New York, N.Y.

3. By selling stock first, the company keeps its capitalization ratios favorable and builds a good financial record. If debt is allowed to get out of line, the rate agencies may lower the bond rating. Even if common stock is sold as the next financing move, some time may pass before the rating agencies and the market generally recognize the corrective step.

Other problems in timing. An infinite variety of situations may arise to complicate the timing problem. Continuing with the same example, suppose the company's earnings are expected to decline for the next eight months, would it be better to postpone the sale of the common stock until earnings start up again? The answer to this question depends on the degree of the decline. If the expected decrease in earnings is not large and can be satisfactorily explained to prospective investors, and if the stock market is high, it would probably be better to take immediate action.

Decisions as to timing a sale of securities should not be based on trying to outguess the market. it may be asked how one makes a decision if the state of the market is such a determining factor and if it is so difficult to forecast its movements. The best that can be done is to consider the current level of the market in relation to the long-term average as shown by indexes of security prices. If a company needs money and market conditions are reasonably satisfactory, it is unwise to postpone permanent financing in the hope of obtaining better prices.

Pricing of securities. Investment bankers can best advise the company about the price that may be obtained for a new security. However, financial executives should have some knowledge of how the price is determined.

If a company already has securities publicly held and intends to issue more securities of the same type, the problem of determining the price for the new securities, within reasonable limits, is not difficult. The market price of the existing securities gives a good clue. However, this may turn out to be only an approximation, for the price may arise from a limited number of small transactions and may not indicate what investors will pay if a large block is thrown on the market. On the other hand, there have been times, during a strictly seller's market, when new offerings tended to be priced equally as high as, if not higher than, existing issues. Only persons thoroughly familiar with market conditions know the situation well enough to arrive at a fairly accurate price for a new issue.

If a company does not have any securities outstanding similar to the kind that are to be issued, determining the offering price is more complicated. It is arrived at by studying outstanding securities and recent offerings that are as nearly comparable as possible to the prospective offering. Part of this study consists of a statistical tabulation or so-called "stack-up." It covers a comparison of almost all the factors affecting the value of a security that can be put in terms of figures. It will include the ratios that analysts use in evaluating a security. The appropriate ratios depend on the type of security to be sold and the type of industry.

Other price factors. In discussing their financing with investment bankers, the executives of a company may be shown a statistical comparison of their proposed new issue with other existing similar securities. The ratios, however, are only the starting point. Even though a company compares favorably on a statistical basis with another company, the securities of the two companies may sell at widely different prices for two reasons. First, the ratios do not tell the whole story, and second, prejudices of investors must be taken into account. For example, if a company has never had any securities outstanding with the public and is not known among investors, it usually takes some time for its securities to become seasoned and for the market price to reflect their value. Some companies are located in areas where there are concentrations of wealth and securities of local companies may be preferred. In such cases, securities of the local companies will sell for better prices than securities of other companies equally good, but in other localities.

Treasurer's study for directors. The treasurer or principal financial officer of a company will have to make some written report on a financial proposal for other officers and directors to study. If the financial officer is not completely familiar with long-term financing, he may have to consult some of the sources of advice mentioned previously before he draws up his report for final decision by the board of directors.

The circumstances will determine the extent of the report. It should include a statement of the need for money, how the money will be raised, how the financing will affect the balance sheet and earnings, as well as other probable results. It may include a comparison of the proposed financial position of the company with other companies in the industry. An estimate of the price to be obtained for the new security issue and selling expenses should be given. In order to help the directors make their decision, it may be well to show alternate ways of accomplishing the financing, with the advantages and disadvatages of each alternative.

TYPES OF SECURITIES AND THEIR TERMS

Basic types of securities. The basic types of securities include bonds (long-term debt), preferred stock, and common stock. There are numerous variations of these types when provisions affecting income, control, and risk are considered. In the following discussion, comments are made only on those features of each of the basic types of securities that require careful consideration by the issuing company in choosing the individual securities to be issued.

Long-term debt. When a decision has been made to raise new capital by creating a long-term debt, the following questions must usually be answered.

1. Shall mortgage bonds or debentures be issued?
2. What will be the maturity?
3. What restrictive provisions must be included?
4. What kind of sinking fund provision shall be included?
5. What shall be the redemption provisions?

Additional questions may have to be considered, but the above are the most common.

Mortgage bonds versus debentures. It is possible, in many instances, to draw up an indenture for an issue of debentures, that is, unsecured bonds, that will give as complete protection to the buyer as a mortgage bond, assuming that the company has no other debt. Sophisticated investors, such as the large insurance companies, have trained experts who look at substance and not form when they are deciding about the provisions in a bond indenture. For such investors, a well protected debenture issue may be as acceptable as mortgage bonds. On the other hand, if a company contemplates selling a fixed-maturity issue to the small investor, a mortgage bond may command a better price than a debenture.

A company with properties in many states may find debentures an easier type of security to issue and live with than mortgage bonds. On the other hand, certain restrictive provisions of a debenture may be more burdensome than those for mortgage bonds. For example, a debenture issue usually contains a provision restricting future borrowing on an unsecured basis. A mortgage issue would generally not have this limitation.

Furthermore, if mortgage bonds are used for the senior obligation, then another avenue of debit financing is available—debentures. This possibility is foreclosed when debentures are the senior obligation, including, of course, the idea of a junior debenture.

Maturity. A maturity of 15, 20, 25, or 30 years is customary for a bond. An expiring franchise, wasting assets such as mines, the expiration of a contract for the supply of raw material, and the like, may be technical reasons for limiting the maturity to a certain date. A company usually prefers as long a maturity as possible. The choice of maturity date depends, among other things, upon what buyers will pay for different maturities. The longer the maturity, the higher the interest rate that is required. Generally, the issuing company must weigh the advantages of the longer maturity against the greater costs. The buyers, for reasons of their own, may not be induced to go beyond a certain maximum maturity no matter what the yield. Very long maturities, such as 100-year, or even perpetual bonds, have been issued in the past, but such bonds are no longer in vogue.

During periods of very high interest rates, when financing is difficult, a company may be forced to issue bonds with a very short maturity in order to carry out any financing. 1973 was characterized by high interest rates resulting in extraordinary competition for funds (see Figure 11-3).

Restrictive provisions. In the past, it was not usual for a company to create an issue of bonds secured by a closed first mortgage on all fixed assets of the corporation. Under this type of mortgage no additional bonds could be issued with the same lien. The closed first mortgage frequently proved burdensome to the issuing corporation, which could only finance through junior mortgage bonds or debentures while the closed first mortgage was in the way. As a result, the practice developed of issuing what is known as "open-end mortgage bonds." The mortgage authorizes the issuance of bonds in any amount under the provisions of the mortgage. In a "limited open-end mortgage" a stated amount of indebtedness may be ultimately secured by the mortgage, but this limit cannot be exceeded. Under both of these types of mortgages, the buyer is protected against the excessive issuance of debt in the future. This is done by including certain restrictive provisions in the indenture.

One type of protective feature assures that there is adequate security for the additional bonds. Thus, a typical restrictive provision states that bonds may be issued for amounts not over a certain percent of the cost of net property additions. Another type of protective feature assures that the interest on bonds already issued will not be jeopardized by demands for interest made by bondholders acquiring bonds subsequently. Thus, the provision may state that new bonds are not to be issued unless interest charges on existing bonds and bonds proposed to be issued are covered a certain number of times by net earnings.

The details of the restrictive provisions depend principally upon the character of the company. For example, dividend restrictions may be required of some companies but not of others. A company engaged in a stable industry will be given greater freedom than one in a volatile industry.

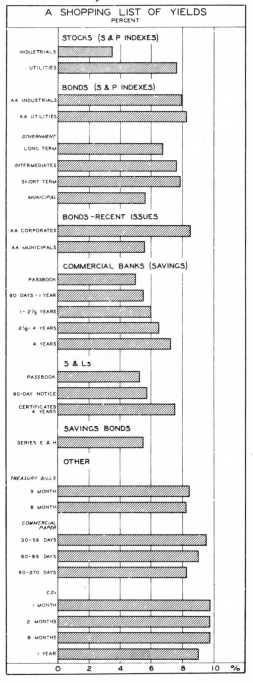

Figure 11-3. Typical 1973 yields by investment type.

Sinking fund provision. The type of company, the size of the issue, the maturity, the desires of the buyers of the bonds, the amount of earnings that a company can plow back into the business, its dividend policy, its plans for future capital expenditures, and other factors affect the sinking fund provision. The sinking fund requirements should not be so large as to jeopardize dividend payments or working capital position at any time.

For a company engaged in a business that involves a wasting asset, such as mining, the sinking fund is calculated to eliminate the debt at least by the time the reserves are expected to be exhausted. For others, the sinking fund should be so calculated as to reduce the debt to a point where the company will be able to meet the amount due at maturity out of resources or be able to refinance it even under adverse market conditions.

If a company is unable to raise funds through the sale of stock because of unfavorable market conditions and is forced to increase its debt beyond the point that it feels is proper, a sinking fund can be used to bring the debt into line over a period of years.

The importance of having a well designed and clearly worded redemption provision cannot be overemphasized, for there are many reasons, too numerous to mention, why a company might wish to retire its bonds before maturity.

A high call premium should be avoided, if possible, and the redemption rate should gradually reduce each year so that within a relatively few years the premium will be only a few points above par. Merely because the officials of a company do not anticipate, at the time of the sale of the bonds, any reason for redeeming them in the future is no excuse for not paying close attention to this provision.

Some bonds have been issued with a delayed-redemption provision. Delaying the redemption provision for a long time is unwise whenever it can be avoided. However, circumstances at the time of issue may make it advisable to provide a short delay before the redemption provision first becomes effective. For example, let us suppose that the redemption premium is low and very close to the offering price to the public. Delaying the possibility of call for 5 or 10 years may make the issue more attractive to buyers. The final decision about including a non-refundable feature for a few years will depend upon the effect on the price obtained for the bonds and the willingness of investors to purchase them. A delayed call may be particularly important in the case of convertible debentures.

Need for understanding the indenture. Every issue of long-term indebtedness involves the preparation of an instrument in which the provisions of the issue are set out in detail. This instrument, known generally as an "indenture," is usually made in favor of a corporate trustee who represents all of the respective security holders.

A modern bond indenture is voluminous, technical, dull, and extremely hard to read. Even a person well versed in finance has a difficult time digesting all of the provisions and understanding them. It is therefore of the utmost importance that the treasurer, or some other responsible top executive, thoroughly study the indenture before it is executed and know how each provision might affect the future operations of the company. A good plan in such a study is to rephrase the technical language of the instrument in simple language, for this procedure may help bring out the full significance of the clauses in the agreement. Examples of disagreements in the interpretation of important provisions years after an indenture has been issued are too numerous to mention. Frequently the disputes are resolved only after extended litigation.

The Trust Indenture Act of 1939 has helped to standardize bond indentures by requiring that they contain certain prescribed provisions and otherwise conform with the law. However, the Act applies to securities sold publicly in interstate commerce and there are many exemptions. Thus, though the Act is a step in the direction toward uniformity, it does not eliminate the need for studying and fully understanding the implications of each provision in the indenture.

Preferred stock. Some experienced financial executives contend that preferred stock is a hybrid type of security that has no place in the capital structure of the company. To their way of thinking, common stock and bonds are sufficient as media for long-term financing. They argue (1) that if a company runs into bad earnings and defaults on its preferred dividends, the financial position of the company is hurt; and (2) that if a company keeps its preferred stock so low in relation to total capitalization that the default in preferred dividends will never occur, it would be better to take advantage of the lower cost of financing with bonds. It must be admitted, however, that a company runs into far less trouble when it defers preferred dividend payments, than when it defaults in payment of bond interest.

Those who favor the use of preferred stock argue that there are many potential investors, individuals and institutions, who prefer to buy preferred stocks. As a matter of fact, some institutions with a large amount of funds available for investment cannot by law buy common stock, but can purchase preferred stock. Over the long run, by including preferred stock in capitalization, and thus broadening the source of investment funds, industry can obtain money on a cheaper basis.

Any final conclusion for or against preferred stock does not seem appropriate. The needs of the particular company must be examined to determine whether preferred stock is the most suitable financing medium at a particular time.

Preferred stock provisions. The provisions applying to an issue of preferred stock are very simple compared with those found in the average bond indenture, but they may be just as important to the welfare of the company. The provisions are found in the company's charter or by-laws. They may include restrictions as to the issuance of unsecured debt, additional preferred stock, and common dividend payments; they may offer voting rights if the preferred dividend is defaulted; and they may provide for redemption and other features. Any of these restrictions and qualifications may prove to be particularly important in the future.

Preferred stock provisions, like those in a bond indenture, should be thoroughly analyzed and understood by the financial officer of the company. For example, in the liquidation of the large holding companies under the Public Utility Holding Company Act, disputes arose over whether the preferred stockholders should receive the call price or par. Extensive litigation followed because the provisions of some preferred stocks did not make the point sufficiently clear.

The restriction as to the amount of unsecured borrowings that can be incurred may not seem important at the time the stock is issued. However, if, in the future, the company must suddenly rely heavily on bank borrowings, it may find it necessary to obtain the approval of the stockholders to amend the provision. This is a time-consuming process and may prove burdensome. Although the preferred stockholders may be entitled to some protection in this respect, the provision should not unduly hinder the company in an emergency.

Common stock. When common stock is to be issued to raise new capital, the following questions usually arise:

1. Shall it be par-value or no-par stock?
2. What price range shall be favored?
3. Should all the common be of one class with the same voting rights?
4. What will the dividend policy be?

Par versus no par. State laws and the Securities and Exchange Commission, under some acts, may require certain types of companies to have a par value for their stock. However, investors pay relatively little attention today to whether a stock has or has not par value. Under some laws, the tax on the purchase and sale of common stock favored par stock of low value. The tax on no-par stock was the same as on $100 par stock, but on stock with lower par value, the tax was reduced proportionately according to the par value. Under other laws, the tax is based on the actual value of the stock rather than on its par or face value, and is the same on both par and no-par stock. A few states still impose an organization and annual tax on no-par shares at a relatively high nominal value for the stock.

If a stock has par value, when new stock is offered it generally must be sold for par or better. Therefore, if par value is used, it should be low enough in relation to market value not to hamper future financing.

Price range. The price at which a new issue of common stock will sell is controllable to some extent by the issuing company. For example, if a new company is to raise $1,000,000 through a common stock issue, it may issue a larger or smaller number of shares and thus set the price range.

The appropriate price range for common stock is largely a result of market preferences. If a stock sells below $10.00 a share, investors tend to consider it in a class with the so-called "dogs." Also, banks prefer stocks selling at more than $10.00 per share as collateral for a loan. On the other hand, if a stock sells for a very high price, some investors feel that it is out of their price range. Although logically it should make no difference whether a person owns 100 shares of $10.00 stock or 10 shares of $100 stock, for psychological reasons it is generally considered better for a stock to sell in the range of roughly $15.00 to $80.00 per share. Due to the wide fluctuation of the stock market, and varying fortunes of individual companies, it is only possible to approximate this price range over a long period.

If outstanding common stock is selling at a very high price, and a new issue is contemplated, a stock split may be undertaken in order to bring all the outstanding shares down to the desired range. It is important in working out the split to analyze carefully the probable future price range for the stock in boom, depression, and average times, and to make the split with the long-range price fluctuation in mind.

For a stock selling at a very low figure, it is just as logical to do a reverse split and reduce the number of shares outstanding, thus increasing the value per share by getting the stockholders to take, for example, one share for two. However, management hesitates to take this step. It may be looked upon by stockholders as an admission by management of the loss in value of the stock.

Voting privilege. During the 1929 boom, many companies issued different classes of stock, essentially the same except with different voting privileges. This was done in order to preserve the voting rights for a special group of stockholders. The practice is generally not considered sound by security exchanges and regulatory bodies. Since 1926 the New York Stock Exchange has refused to list non-voting common stock. Because of this policy, and changes in previously existing non-voting stock, all common stocks now listed on the New York Stock Exchange have voting privileges. The Exchange will also refuse to list the voting stock of a company that has outstanding in the public hands a non-voting common stock.

Dividend policy. No issue of common stock can be properly planned without consideration of future dividend policy with regard to the new issue. The same factors that determined dividend policy generally must be gone over with respect to the larger amount of common stock that will be outstanding after a successful sale of the securities. If the company does not have any financing immediately under consideration, the fact should not be overlooked that investors will study dividend policy for many years back when new stock is offered. Dividend policy is discussed in Chapter 27 and therefore needs no further treatment here. However, see Figure 11-4 for the impact of aggregate dividend policy between 1935 and 1964. Note particularly, the ascending scale of payout.

Special types of issues. Although the three broad classes of securities—bonds, preferred, and common stock—are the traditional media for financing, there are other types that a company may resort to under certain circumstances. Some of them are discussed below.

Convertible issues. Bonds or preferred stock may be convertible. The conversion privilege permits the holder to exchange the bonds or preferred stock for common stock on a fixed basis during a stated period. For example, $100 par value of preferred stock may be convertible into four shares of common, or at a conversion price of $25.00. If the common stock is selling above $25.00, the conversion privilege has real value. At first glance, convertibles appear to have many advantages and no disadvantages. However, they are actually a complicated type of security with many ramifications.

There are two situations that call for using convertibles.

1. When the present financial condition is weak, but earnings prospects are favorable. The conversion feature adds speculative appeal to an issue and may make it possible to sell an issue that otherwise would not interest buyers. If such is the case, the conversion feature should be made sufficiently attractive to assure conversion taking place. The company will thus strengthen its capitalization with the greater amount of common stock.

2. When the capitalization is sound but conditions make it difficult to sell common stock. This situation arises in the following circumstances.

(a) The market is so depressed that common stock cannot be sold.

(b) The market for a particular common stock is adversely affected because a large block of stock is hanging over it.

CORPORATE INCOME AND DIVIDEND PAYMENTS IN THE UNITED STATES,
ALL INDUSTRIES, 1935–63
(In Billions of Dollars)

Year	Corporate Income before Tax	Corporate Income after Tax	Net Corporate Dividend Payments	Retained Earnings	Percentage of Income after Tax Retained
1935 . . . . 3.1	2.2	2.9	− 0.7	−32%
1936 . . . . 5.7	4.3	4.5	− 0.2	− 5
1937 . . . . 6.2	4.7	4.7	0.0	0
1938 . . . . 3.3	2.3	3.2	− 0.9	−39
1939 . . . . 6.4	5.0	3.8	1.2	24
1940 . . . . 9.3	6.5	4.0	2.4	37
1941 . . . . .17.0	9.4	4.5	4.9	52
1942 . . . . .20.9	9.5	4.3	5.2	55
1943 . . . . .24.6	10.5	4.5	6.0	57
1944 . . . . .23.3	10.4	4.7	5.7	55
1945 . . . . .19.0	8.3	4.7	3.6	43
1946 . . . . .22.6	13.4	5.8	7.7	57
1947 . . . . .29.5	18.2	6.5	11.7	64
1948 . . . . .33.0	20.5	7.2	13.3	65
1949 . . . . .26.4	16.0	7.5	8.5	53
1950 . . . . .40.6	22.8	9.2	13.6	60
1951 . . . . .42.2	19.7	9.0	10.7	54
1952 . . . . .36.7	17.2	9.0	8.3	48
1953 . . . . .38.3	18.1	9.2	8.9	49
1954 . . . . .34.1	16.8	9.8	7.0	42
1955 . . . . .44.9	23.0	11.2	11.8	51
1956 . . . . .44.7	23.5	12.1	11.3	48
1957 . . . . .43.2	22.3	12.6	9.7	43
1958 . . . . .37.4	18.8	12.4	6.4	34
1959 . . . . .47.7	24.5	13.7	10.8	44
1960 . . . . .44.3	22.0	14.5	7.5	34
1961 . . . . .44.2	21.9	15.2	6.7	31
1962 . . . . .48.2	25.0	16.5	8.5	34
1963 . . . . .51.3	26.7	18.0	8.7	33
1964 . . . . .57.6	31.8	19.8	11.9	37

SOURCES: Office of Business Economics, Department of Commerce, *U.S. Income and Output:
A Supplement to the Survey of Current Business* (Washington, D.C., 1958), Table 1–8, pp. 126–27,
for figures through 1955; *Survey of Current Business* (National Income Number), July, 1964, Table 2., p. 8, for figures for 1956–63; U.S. Bureau of the Census, *Statistical Abstract of the United
States: 1965* (Washington, D.C., 1965), p. 496, for 1964.

Figure 11-4.

(c) A company has an extensive financing program, and the market will not
absorb all the common stock that would have to be sold.

(d) Earnings of the company are expected to improve and justify a higher price for the stock. The convertible feature prevents an immediate dilution of earnings per share that would impair common dividends.

(e) The mechanical aid offered by the conversion feature of a debenture or preferred stock is needed to effect the ultimate issuance of common stock. For example, when common is selling close to par and new common stock would have to be issued at par or better, the sale of common stock might be difficult, but an issue of debentures convertible into common at par might be easy to sell. Another example of this situation arises when a company issues debt or preferred stock in a program designed to strengthen the capitalization. Conversion is relied upon to turn the debentures of preferred stock into common stock.

Determining the conversion price. Obviously, conversion will only take place if the market for the common is at least above the conversion price. Holders may then be induced to convert if the income from the common stock is more attractive than that afforded by the convertible issue, or if the company forces conversion by issuing a call for redemption. If a company's capitalization is strong, it has considerable freedom in determining at what price the issue will be convertible, for if conversion does not take place, the added burden of debt or preferred stock can be easily carried. However, if a company really needs additional common stock to keep its capitalization balanced, and sells convertible debentures for one of the reasons mentioned in the preceeding paragraph, the conversion privilege should be made sufficiently attractive to induce holders to convert. Under these circumstances, if conversion does not take place, and later the company decides to sell common stock, the convertible issue may prove to be a considerable hindrance.

Other features of convertible issues. There are many special features about convertible issues that must be tailored to the particular needs of a company. For example, the conversion privilege may be delayed for a certain period to prevent an increase in the number of shares of common stock until earnings are expected to increase. The conversion price can be stepped up at a definite date in the future. This will tend to force the holders to convert before that time. The call premium is generally low on a convertible issue to give the company greater freedom in forcing conversion by issuing a call. Convertible bonds do not generally contain a sinking fund, because it is expected that they will eventually turn into common stock. Special circumstances might, however, make a sinking fund advisable.

Equipment trust obligations. One of the important media for financing in the railroad industry has been equipment trust obligations. The poor financial condition of the railroad companies prevents many of them from using other financing methods. The obligations are secured, in effect, by a lien on the rolling stock—the locomotives, passenger cars, and freight cars. When the equipment is delivered to the railroad for use, it is, through one legal mechanism or another, prevented from accruing to the benefit of the holders of mortgage bonds. The importance of the equipment to the railroad places holders of the equipment trust obligations in a preferred position. A railroad might default on its general mortgage bonds and still pay the interest on the equipment obligations because it could not operate without the rolling stock. For this reason, investors are willing to buy the equipment trust obligations in spite of the poor financial condition of the issuing company.

Streetcar and bus companies have also used this type of obligation, as have other companies, to finance acquisition of mobile equipment. However, circumstances analogous to the railroad situation must be present in order to use equipment trust obligations. Thus, the equipment must be of reasonably general purpose and essential to the operation of the company. Also, it must be possible to keep the title out from under any general mortgage. In order to assure that the obligations are paid off before the equipment wears out, the obligations are generally of reasonably short term, 10 or 15 years, and liberal serial payments are included.

Lease arrangement. The large insurance companies provide financing for the acquisition of buildings by industrial companies through a lease arrangement. The insurance company provides the money to construct a building, retains title, and leases the property to the industrial company for an extended period. Rental payments under the lease provide the insurance company with sufficient funds of interest on the money advanced and return of its principal over the period of the lease. There is generally a provision for renewal at the expiration of the lease. The building must be suitable for general use and well located in order to interest the insurance companies, because if the industrial company defaults on its payments, the insurance company must be in a position to rent the building to another company. Stores and office buildings have been the principal types of structures financed by this means. This method of financing has some appeal for a few companies of good financial standing that do not wish to tie up their funds in fixed assets. It should be recognized that the portion of the rental payment which represents return of principal should be considered as debt when a company's capitalization ratios are computed.

A variation of this method of financing is the sale-and-lease-back arrangement which may be available as a method of financing to companies that own land and buildings. The company sells its real property and buildings to a financial institution or private investor, which simultaneously leases them back under a long-term contract, frequently with some provision for renewal.[1]

Term loans. Commercial banks are traditionally thought of as the suppliers of temporary funds for working capital. However, in periods of easy credit, commercial banks are often willing to use their excess funds to make loans as long as 10 years to provide funds for such purposes as constructing permanent plants. In some cases, banks have combined with insurance companies in purchasing serial issues. The banks have taken the series maturing in the first years, say, up to 10, and the insurance companies have taken the series with the longer maturities. Thus, commerical banks do play a part in the long-term financing picture.

In periods of easy credit the low interest rate has been one of the appealing features of term loans. It is a serious mistake, however, for a company to arrange a loan with a bank merely because of the low interest rate, if it really needs long-term debt in itscapitalization. It must make certain that the short maturities of a term loan will not be too burdensome on its cash position. Furthermore, it is well to remember that a commercial bank may be needed to supply money in an emergency. If a company has

---

[1]For a discussion of the business, legal, and tax implications of this device, see William L. Cary, "Corporate Financing Through the Sale and Lease-Back of Property: Business , Tax, and Policy Considerations," *Harvard Law Review,* Vol. LXII, No. 1, p. 1.

used up its borrowing limits by becoming heavily indebted to its bank through term loans, it may find it impossible to finance its needs for working capital by further borrowing at its commercial bank.

METHODS OF PLACING SECURITIES IN INVESTORS' HANDS

Principal distribution methods. After a decision has been reached as to the type of security to issue, and at least preliminary consideration has been given to when financing should be undertaken, the next step is to determine the method of placing the issue in investor' hands. The two principal methods are (1) private sale, and (2) public sale.

Private sale of new issues. The Securities Act of 1933 was primarily designed to protect the many small investors who are not in a position to obtain adequate information on which to judge the merits of a security. Recognizing that certain groups of well-informed investors are able to take care of themselves, the Act exempts from compliance with its provisions security "transactions . . . not involving any public offering." This is generally termed a private sale, but in an early release, the subject was discussed and the factors to consider in determining whether an offering comes under a private sale were pointed out.[2]

When this release was issued, there was still some uncertainty about the use of private sale. Since then, private sales have become quite common for certain types of transactions. An offering to a limited number of large institutional investors is generally the situation thought of when a private sale is considered. At one time, there was a rule of thumb that a private placement should not include an offering to more than 12 institutions. With the development of private placement, many deals have been arranged with a larger number of purchasers. The principal considerations are the sophistication of the officers and their access to information, the relationship between the parties, and whether the purchased securities are to be retained for permanent investment.

The type of issue best adapted to private sale is bonds of sufficiently good quality to attract the institutional investor. Preferred stocks can also be handled at private sale, but the fact that some institutions are restricted as to the amount of one issue of preferred stock that they can buy is a limiting factor. Common stocks generally do not lend themselves to private placement. Many of the large insurance companies are prevented by state law from buying common stocks.

Advantages of private sale. A company that distributes an issue of securities through private sale may gain the following advantages:

1. The deal can be arranged in a relatively short time. Generally, an indication as to price can be obtained at the start of the negotiations; the buyers try to live up to such indications. This may eliminate the possibility of losing a favorable market and prove to be of real importance in a weakening market.

2. If, in the future, the consent of the holders of the securities is required for any reason (such as changing the provisions of the security), it is easier to negotiate with

---

[2]Securities and Exchange Commission Release No. 285, January 24, 1935.

the small number of investors in a private deal than with the large number of security holders that a public sale is likely to involve.

3. The trouble and expense of registration under the Securities Act of 1933 is eliminated, and the issuer avoids disclosing information to competitors that registration might entail.

4. The issuer saves coupon-paying fees, published notices for sinking funds, and some administrative costs.

5. The investment banker's commission is eliminated. However, if an investment banker is used to aid in placing an issue a small finder's fee will be paid.

Disadvantages of private sale. The disadvantages of a private sale are:

1. There is no open market for the company's securities and if, in the future, the company wishes to retire some of the securities or to acquire them to meet regular sinking fund requirements, it must pay the call price. Thus, the company is prevented from taking advantage of adverse market conditions to purchase the securities at a discount in the open market. For example, assume that a company sells 30-year 3 per cent mortgage bonds at par, and that in five years interest rates change so that the bonds yield 5 per cent to maturity; the theoretical price for the bonds in the open market would then be 71.64. The company could not take advantage of this decline.

2. In a private sale the purchasers may be in a better bargaining position to demand the inclusion of tight restrictive provisions. For example, when a company is dealing with a small group of insurance companies to buy an issue of bonds, they may demand the inclusion of strict provisions limiting the amount of future bond issues and the amount of dividends on common stock. In a public sale, although the company must consider the purchasers' desires, it approaches a much larger group of purchasers and therefore is in a better position to name its own terms.

3. A purchaser in a private deal, knowing that a company makes some savings over a public offering, will attempt, in arriving at a final price, to obtain some of the savings for itself.

It is impossible to draw any general conclusion as to whether private sale is more or less desirable than public sale. Each situation must be analyzed individually.

Use of investment banker to negotiate a private deal. In arranging a private sale, the company can either go directly to the buyers or employ an investment banker to act as the company's agent in handling the deal. If the executives of a company are not thoroughly familiar with the market for securities and current prices for various types of securities, it will usually find it advisable to employ an investment banker. By doing so, it may obtain a sufficiently better price and terms to more than pay the investment banker's commission. Furthermore, a third party may be in a better position to negotiate for the company any differences that may arise as to restrictive provisions in the mortgage indenture, call price, sinking fund, and other features of an issue.

Public sale. If a general distribution, rather than a private sale, is contemplated, there may be the choice between public bidding and a negotiated deal with an investment banker.

Public bidding for securities has largely been used in the utility and railroad fields. It is best adapted to high-grade bonds of a standard character. There has been some criticism of competitive bidding even for this type of security, but the principal criticism has been in its use for preferred and common stocks. Certainly, if a company's executives are not experts in finance, they would be unwise to use competitive bidding, unless required to do so by law or unless there were some unusual circumstances.

Negotiating with investment bankers. How far should a company go in shopping around among investment bankers before deciding which one to use? Generally, it is best to deal with one investment banking house and to check the ideas of that institution with other sources of advice on long-term financing, such as the commercial banker. At most, a company should not talk with more than two investment banking houses. If a company shops an issue around to one house after another just to see how high a price can be obtained, the best houses may lose interest.

The principal test for deciding which underwriting house to use is the general reputation of the firm over an extended period. The company's commercial bank should be able to furnish good information on this point. If the local bank is small and unfamiliar with investment banking houses, it will undoubtedly refer the client to its large city correspondent bank.

It is important for a company to do its financing with a high grade investment banking house because (1) it helps the company's financial reputation; (2) much of the dealing in a security sale is on a verbal basis and it is important to know that the spoken word will be lived up to; (3) a high-grade investment banking firm will take a continuing interest in the financial affairs of a company; (4) the final underwriting agreement, which covers the amount of the issue and the price to be paid by the investment banker is subject to contingencies that may release the investment banker from his commitment.

Offering securities to stockholders. Up to this point, some of the problems involved in placing securities in investors' hands through private and public sale have been discussed. A somewhat different procedure is followed when stock is offered to existing stockholders. It is generally accepted legal interpretation of common stockholders' rights that each existing stockholder must be offered the right to subscribe for such proportion of any new issue of common stock as the number of shares owned by him bears to the total number of shares previously issued, unless the stockholders have surrendered this right in the charter or by subsequent vote. The existing stockholders are thus given an opportunity to protect their status, both as to control, that is, voting power, and as to economic position, that is, interest in the surplus of the company.

In simple form this is accomplished by issuing warrants to the stockholders giving them the right, during a limited period, to subscribe proportionately for new stock. Let us suppose a company has 1,000,000 shares of common stock outstanding, and that it is offering 100,000 new shares. Each stockholder would have the right to subscribe to one-tenth of a new share for each share held, or, as it is usually stated, one new share of stock for every 10 shares held.

If an existing stockholder does not wish to exercise his rights, he may dispose of them in the open market. Within reasonable limits a stockholder is thus compensated for the dilution of his position. Generally, stockholders are only given the right to subscribe for a full share, and the issuance of fractional shares of new stock is thus avoided. Stockholders can usually buy or sell additional rights to even out their holdings.

Price at which stock is offered to stockholders. In order to make an offering attractive and give value to the rights, the price at which stockholders can subscribe for the new stock must be below the market for the existing stock, and must remain below that value during the subscription period. The discount at which to offer new stock depends on such factors as (1) the nature of the existing market for the company's common stock including whether the stock is listed or not, whether it is closely held, whether it is high-grade and stable market-wise, or whether it is speculative and volatile; (2) general conditions of the security market; (3) all the circumstances surrounding the new offering including offering ratio, size of offering, length of subscription period, and methods of offering, i.e. oversubscription, underwritten or not, soliciting dealer's fees, etc.; and (4) everything that affects the quality and outlook for the particular company and its stock such as the type of business, capital structure, earnings record, dividend record, and all other related factors.

Naturally, a small issue of high-grade stock offered during a stable market with a short subscription period would call for a smaller discount than if the reverse were true.

Most of the subscriptions are made at the end of the subscription period, since it would be unwise for a stockholder to subscribe if the market for the stock fell below the subscription price. He could then obtain the stock more cheaply by purchasing directly in the open market without exercising his rights. For this reason it is important to have the subscription period relatively short to allow less time for a general break in the market to take place. On the other hand, the period should be long enough to permit stockholders to give adequate consideration to the proposal. The New York Stock Exchange is particularly careful to see that companies with stocks listed on the Exchange use a sufficiently long period. It may vary under different conditions, but the suggested period is about 16 days. This number may be reduced slightly if satisfactory arrangements are provided throughout the country for facilitating exchanges. The impact of business conditions and the percentage spreads between types of securities can have a marked effect on the cost of issuing various types of corporate paper. See Figure 11-5.

Arrangements with banking firms for offerings to stockholders. Many different types of arrangements can be made with an investment banking firm in issuing securities to existing stockholders. If business conditions are favorable, if the stock of the company is stable market-wise, and if the company is not pressed for cash, it may make an offering to existing security holders at a sufficient discount to assure success and not have the issue underwritten. On the other hand, under adverse conditions, it may be essential to have the entire offering underwritten by an investment banking firm to guarantee that the company will get its money if its own stockholders do not subscribe. In that case, the investment bankers may be paid a uniform commission for each unit of offering, or they may be paid at one rate for securities taken by the stockholders, and at a higher rate for those not taken, which the investment bankers will have to sell. In addition to this basic compensation, the investment bankers will realize additional profit from the sale of unsubscribed stock. A usual provision for utility company rights offerings is for the investment bankers to pay the company a portion of this profit.

In rare instances, investment bankers have agreed in advance to pay for the privilege of purchasing the unsubscribed portion of such issues as convertible debentures. This may occur when the offering price is so attractive that the investment bankers feel there will be little risk, that the deal will be very successful, and that they will have to dispose of only 10 or 15 per cent of the offering, which they feel they can do at a profit.

Time table for security offering. Many things must be done in connection with issuing a security from the time when the company's executives begin to think about raising funds through selling securities to the time when the company receives the money and the last details are cleared up. The various steps may differ considerably depending upon factors as the following:

1. *The type of security.* If bonds are offered, a trustee must be brought into the picture; this step is not necessary if stock is offered.

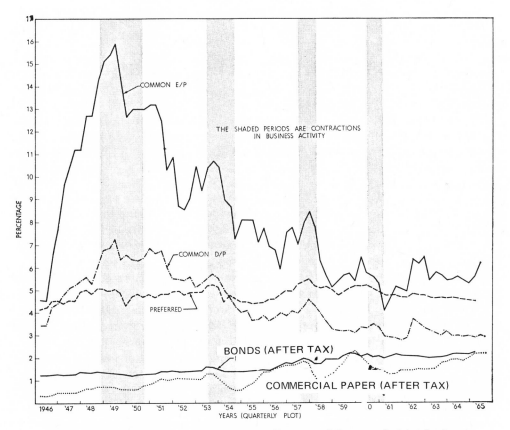

Sources of Data Used: Office of Business Economics, Department of Commerce, *Statistical Supplements to Survey of Current Business* for stock data to December, 1951; *Federal Reserve Bulletins*, for all other data.

Figure 11-5. Related Costs of Corporate Issues, 1946-65.

2. *The statutory requirements*. For example, there is wide variation in the requirements in different states as to compliance with Blue Sky laws. Many of them require an application to be filed for a permit to sell the securities in the state.

3. *The method of issuance*. Public bidding will necessitate more steps than a negotiated deal or private sale, and a public offering will generally involve the filing of a registration statement with the Securities and Exchange Commission.

4. *Requirements under special laws*. If a company is subject to some special law, such as the Public Utility Holding Company Act of 1935, meeting additional requirements will consume time.

No matter what the type of offering, preliminary planning is required. It is advisable to prepare a complete schedule with the dates when each step necessary to complete the financing should be accomplished. The schedule should be made up when the company decides to proceed with a security offering. Almost all of the steps that will have to be taken will be known in advance of the offering. Although some items and dates have to be changed, the schedule will act as a valuable tool for the treasurer or other responsible persons in seeing that everything is done on time. Company's counsel usually has most to do with preparing the schedule.

An example of a schedule is given below. It is included here to give financial executives an idea of the mass of detailed work involved in long-term financing through issuing securities, to indicate the state and federal regulations that must be complied with, and to show the sequence of required action.

Example of time table for security offering. The following time table is for a large industrial bond sold by a negotiated deal through underwriters. The bonds represent an additional issue similar to bonds already outstanding. Since there was an existing trustee and an original indenture, the schedule makes no provision for appointment of a trustee or the preparation of an original indenture.

January 19 (Monday)	(1) Registration statement, together with other documents (trustee's also T.1, T.2 if individual trustee is used, proofs of supplemental indentures of temporary bond, and so on), to be filed with registration statement and cleared for printing; all such documents to be taken to company's offices on the evening of Tuesday, January 20.
January 21 (Wednesday)	(1) Board of directors of company meets at company's office and adopts resolutions authorizing: (a) Filing of registration statement (b) Execution and delivery of Supplemental Indenture (c) Creation and issuance of new series of bonds (d) Execution of purchase contract for bonds (e) Listing and registration of bonds under Securities Exchange Act.
January 22 (Thursday)	(1) Registration statement under Securities Act of 1933 covering bonds filed with SEC.
January 26 (Monday)	(1) Blue Skying of bonds commenced.

January 28 (Wednesday)	(1) Preliminary Blue Sky memorandum and preliminary memorandum as to legality for investment delivered to investment banking firm.
January 30 (Friday)	(1) Deficiency letter received from SEC.
February 3 (Tuesday)	(1) Underwriters' meeting held.
February 4 (Wednesday)	(1) Amendment No. 1 (deficiency amendment) to registration statement filed. (2) Red-herring prospectus distributed to prospective members of selling group and other interested parties.
February 9 (Monday)	(1) Final terms as to price and related facts (interest rate, redemption prices, and so on) agreed on by company and investment bankers shortly after close of business. (2) Information as to interest rate, optional redemption prices, and sinking fund redemption prices given to bank note company with orders to pull final proof of temporary bonds and to have same ready at opening of business on Tuesday, February 10. (3) Information as to price, spread, interest rate, redemption prices, and so on telephoned to SEC and wired to State Blue Sky commissions. (4) Final amendment to registration statement printed and signed.
February 10 (Tuesday)	(1) Agreement among underwriters signed. (2) Purchase contract signed. (3) Filing final amendment to registration statement obtains final proofs of temporary bonds from bank note company at opening of business; checking the proofs as to correct insertion of interest rate, optional redemption prices, and sinking fund redemption prices; marks appropriate number of copies as Exhibit; and includes such marked copies in the final amendment to registration statement. (4) Final amendment to registration statement filed at opening of business. (5) After filing final amendment to registration statement, proofread final proof of temporary bond, and clear bank note company for final printing of the $1,000 denominations of the bonds. Await effectiveness of registration statement. (6) Registration statement effective at end of day.
February 11 (Wednesday)	(1) Supplemental Blue Sky memorandum and memorandum as to legality for investment are released to investment banking firm. (2) Public offering of bonds. (3) Information obtained from investment banking firm as to number of special temporary bonds (if any) that are to be denominations of multiples of $1,000, and as to denominations of such special bonds. Such information, if any, given to bank note company.
February 16 (Monday)	(1) Temporary bonds delivered by bank note company to signature company at opening of business.

(2) Temporary bonds assigned at signature company by company officers and authenticated by officials of trustee bank. Present trend is facsimile signatures of company officers.

February 17
(Tuesday)

(1) Supplemental indenture executed by company and by trustee and executed couterparts are mailed to local counsel and other designated parties for recording in necessary counties, with instructions to record upon wired instructions to do so.

(2) Bonds counted, packaged and sealed by underwriters. Held in safekeeping in readiness for release at closing or by telephone call from closing.

(3) Closing papers prepared in final form, executed, and put in sealed envelopes to await closing. United States documentary stamps purchased or provision made for Trustee to do so.

February 18
(Wednesday)

(1) Closing held.

(2) Local counsel instructed by wire to record Supplemental Indenture.

February 24
(Tuesday)

(1) Proceedings commenced for listing of bonds on New York Stock Exchange and registration thereof under Securities Exchange Act of 1934 (this listing and registration to be deferred until stabilization has been completed).

Special mortgage recording tax is payable in one state. Arrangements should be made substantially in advance of the recording of the Supplemental Indenture to ascertain the amount of such tax and to pay it at the appropriate time.

Cost of financing. The cost of financing may be divided into two parts. The first is generally the greater of the two (1) The compensation paid to investment banking firms. This is also referred to as the underwriters' commision or spread. (2) Other expenses, which include:

Listing fees.

Federal taxes.

State taxes and fees.

Trustee and transfer agent expenses, and so on.

Printing and engraving costs.

Legal fees.

Accountants' fees.

Engineering fees.

SEC registration fees.

Miscellaneous fees.

The cost of financing may vary greatly for different companies and even for the same company at different times. Though exceptions can be cited to disprove almost any generalization about the reasons for variation in costs, some of the factors that may cause variations are:

1. *The type of security.* Sale of a bond issue may be less expensive than the sale of preferred stock, and the latter may be less expensive than the sale of common stock.

2. *Market conditions.* Underwriters' spread is particularly affected by general security market conditions.
3. *Size of the issue.* For large issues, say, $10,000,000 or more, the cost of financing is not particularly burdensome, but for small issues costs become more important.
4. *Quality of the issue.* This factor has a bearing on the underwriters' spread.
5. *The character of the company.* This factor affects the amount of work the investment bankers must do in order to sell an issue and may also affect the expense required to prepare the offering.
6. *The terms of the underwriting agreement,* which affects the spread.
7. *Other special factors.*

The staff of the Securities and Exchange Commission has made numerous studies on the cost of financing[3]. It now issues quarterly reports showing the cost of floating securities registered under the Securities Act of 1933.

If executives of companies contemplating the sale of an issue wish to estimate the costs, a study should be made of recent sales by other companies. Exhibits to registration statements may be a good source of information. Great care must be taken to be certain that the issues are comparable in all respects.

INVESTOR RELATIONS

Need for, and advantages of, good investor relations. It is a mistake for a company to feel that it can have an investment banking house sell the company's securities and then disregard the financial fraternity and the investor until the next time it needs money. Recognizing the fallacy in this attitude, many companies with publicly held securities have embarked on a program of investor relations. The size of the company, the distribution of its securities, and its long-term financial needs are the determining factors in deciding how far to go with such a program. The advantages to be gained are:

1. In the case of common stockholders, it will help keep the real owners happy and satisfied with the management. If unsatisfactory conditions develop unavoidably, the stockholders will be less inclined to blame the management without cause.
2. It will help in raising capital in the future by broadening the investor's knowledge of the company and building up goodwill. Present security owners are, of course, future prospects for new investment.
3. If the financial community is kept informed about a company's operations, financing will be facilitated when the need for new capital arises.
4. It shortens the time required for the securities of a new company to become seasoned and for the market price to reflect their true value.
5. An informed group of security holders will tend to be a more articulate group of supporters of the private enterprise system.

---

[3]Securities and Exchange Commission, "Cost of Flotation of Corporate Securities 1951-1955."

Basic groups of security holders. Security holders may be divided into two broad groups, the uninformed and the informed. The uninformed group comprises the many small stockholders who are usually not familiar with financial matters. The informed group includes the large investors such as the insurance companies, investment trusts, college funds, charitable organizations, and other institutions with funds available for investment. Also included in this group are the members of the financial community, such as investment bankers, brokerage houses, investment service organizations, security rating agencies, and the like. The two groups must be handled in different ways in carrying on an investor relations program.

Analysis of investors in company's securities. The first step in establishing a program of investor relations is to analyze the stockholder and bondholder lists. The stockholder list is of course, always available to the company; the bondholder list may have to be built up to determine who are the holders of coupon bonds. Only if the company knows such items as the following concerning its security owners can it develop an effective investor relations program.

1. Percentage of security holders who are men and women.
2. Geographical distribution of investors.
3. How many stockholders own 1 to 10, 10 to 50, 50 to 100, and so on, shares; how many bondholders own $1,000 to $10,000, $10,000 to $50,000, $50,000 to $100,000 and so on, of bonds.
4. Who are the principal holders.
5. Length of time securities have been held.

Techniques for improving stockholder and other investor relations. Although the subject of investor relations is important enough to warrant expansive treatment, it must sufffice here to list the techniques that may be used and to make brief observations on the most important of them.

1. *Annual reports.* Although many companies still issue stereotyped, uninteresting annual reports, more and more companies are sending out annual reports that are attractive in appearance, readable, and designed to give the stockholders, as well as employees, customers, and the public, a frank and understandable account of the progress of the company, with full information about operating results and financial condition. Many surveys have been made to determine what investors want to know. Some of these appear to indicate that the uninformed investor wants a few clear, simple facts about dividends, earnings, and prospects for the company in the near future. Others, however, made among stockholders of companies that have been issuing modern reports for a number of years, show a broader interest in the company's affairs. The informed investor, of course, is more concerned with the detailed financial statements and with the completeness of the information offered than with the general attractiveness and readability of the report.

2. *Interim reports.* These reports have one principal purpose: to keep investors informed concerning the activities and business of the company during the interval between annual reports. Interim reports generally should include income statements, balance sheets, and comments about important developments since the last report. The informed investor group is particularly desirous of having complete interim statements, but it is questionable whether the uninformed investors pay very much attention to

them. The most common period for interim reports is quarterly. Some companies, however, make monthly reports without formal financial statements, except at the quarterly date.

3. *Brochures and special reports.* Many of the larger companies have prepared elaborate brochures or special reports showing detailed statistical data over a number of years. The informed investors are always appreciative of this material. One caution must be kept in mind, namely, not to issue any special reports that might be construed by the Securities and Exchange Commission as an attempt to influence the sale of an issue of securities. The Securities Act of 1933 regulates the dissemination of information in connection with a security offering; the proper place for facts concerning an issue is the registration statement and prospectus.

4. *Dividend enclosures.* This method of reaching stockholders with a message is expedient because it is carried under the same postage as the dividend check, and is effective because it is bound to be seen. Such enclosures as news letters, folders devoted to a single subject, reprints of public addresses by company officials, and announcements have been used frequently.

5. *Acquaintance with investors and others in the financial community.* Because of the importance of this method of building investor relations and because it has received less attention than some of the other techniques listed here, it is discussed more fully below.

6. *Film, radio and television versions of the annual report.*

7. *Reports on stockholder meetings.* This method of developing stockholder relations is growing in use. The practice of sending stockholders a report of what transpired at a stockholder's meeting invariably meets with stockholder approval. Various styles or types of reports on annual meetings are used. The most common include (1) a letter telling stockholders what happened at the meeting, (2) a summary of the proceedings, (3) a copy of the chairman's remarks or the president's report, (4) minutes of the meeting, and (5) a stenographic report of the full proceedings.

8. *Stockholder house organs.* Only very large companies make use of this technique.

9. *Gifts and special offers to stockholders.*

10. *Welcome and farewell letters to stockholders.* This technique requires delicate handling and cannot be used indiscriminately.

11. *Replies to letters received from stockholders.* Correspondence from stockholders should be answered promptly and should give the stockholder the information he requests, unless the questions are very unreasonable.

12. *Invitations to visit the plant.* Invitations to stockholders and the public are now common. Some of the larger companies have found it worth while to arrange for important representatives of the investing public and the financial community to make an inspection trip and tour of company plants.

Cultivating acquaintance with investors and financial community. An investor relations program should include the cultivation of the personal acquaintance of certain members of the investor community by some of the principal officers of the company. The obvious place to start is at the annual meeting of stockholders. Unfortunately, the managements of some well established companies prefer to disregard the stockholders as long as they do not make any move to oust the management. These top officials feel that if their annual meeting is attended by only a few stockholders, who do not ask any questions, the management is fortunate. The attitude is a faulty one. Management should attempt to increase attendance at stockholders' meetings and should welcome the opportunity to give a full report to the real owners. Some companies have seen the advantages to be gained through bringing the stockholders closer to management and are holding regional annual meetings in order to stimulate the interest of as many stockholders as possible in the company.

A few companies have one of their financial officers visit some of their large security holders once a year. If a company expects to have to rely heavily on outside funds, it is even advisable to visit some of the large institutional investors at regular intervals in order to keep them informed even though they do not hold any securities.

The investment bankers should not be ignored until the time comes for the sale of an issue of securities. They will be better prepared to assist in the financing when the company seeks their aid if they have been kept informed of the company's progress.

The security analysts especially should be given attention. They are the people in brokerage houses, investment banking firms, personal trust departments of banks, investment trusts, insurance companies, and other investing institutions who do the actual work of poring over the information about a company. In some of the larger cities, the analysts have organizations and hold luncheons at which the executives of a company are asked to present the story of their company. This is an excellent opportunity for a company to give wide distribution of financial information to a group that plays an important part in the financial machinery. It may be advisable for the financial executive of a company to become well acquainted with a few analysts and visit them regularly. They may be helpful in explaining how investors are reacting to a company's dividend, labor relations, and other policies. The company's investment banker or commercial banker will usually be glad to arrange a small luncheon at which the financial executives of a company can have a friendly meeting with analysts.

It is also important to keep the rating agencies completely informed concerning the company's operations and plans.

Listing on exchanges. One of the considerations in the relationship with security holders is the market that is maintained for the purchase and sale of the securities, either over-the-counter or on one or more of the security exchanges.

The best-known exchange is, of course, the New York Stock Exchange. Only the larger companies with a record of operations and an active market for their securities should consider listing their securities on this exchange. Small issues are likely to get lost in the shuffle. Some of the qualifications for listing on the New York Stock Exchange are (1) national interest in the company; (2) well demonstrated earning power under competitive conditions—net earnings after taxes should be at least $2 million annually; (3) wide distribution of its common stock—a minimum of 1 million shares distributed among at least 2,000 stockholders owning a minimum of 100 shares each. In addition to complying with all of the Exchange's requirements for listing, the issuer must agree to furnish the exchange with financial reports and other data. Also, it must register the issue with the Securities and Exchange Commission.

In addition to the New York Stock Exchange and the American Stock Exchange, there are 12 other small registered exchanges throughout the country. The advantages of listing on an exchange are fairly obvious: (1) investors can follow the market quotations with ease; (2) a uniform and concentrated market is maintained; (3) the trading is subject to regulation.

Whether to list or not depends upon the circumstances surrounding the company. When a new stock is first offered, it takes time for it to become distributed broadly and to reach the hands of the ultimate investor. This is referred to as the period required to season a stock. Dealers may be helpful during this period. One argument against listing is that security dealers tend to lose interest in listed securities, because they are restricted in the profit they can make on such issues. It takes effort on the part of the dealers to develop an interest in a security and they expect to be compensated accordingly. Over-the-counter markets are on a dealer basis with the dealer buying and selling and making his own spread between his purchase and sale price, whereas for transactions on an exchange, the commission is regulated. It is contended that dealer interest tends to make a broader market for a stock. For a small issue this may be an important point. Once a stock has become seasoned, however, the advantages of listing assume importance, particularly for a company with a large issue of common stock.

12

Duties Connected with Corporate Ownership and Funded Debt

CONTENTS

12

Duties Connected with Corporate Ownership and Funded Debt

Duties to be described. The sale of stock and the raising of funds by borrowing, other than through normal commercial bank channels, involve three types of administrative functions: (1) those that the corporation must perform itself; (2) those that the corporation may perform itself or delegate to an independent agency on a service fee basis; (3) those that must be performed by an outside agency. This chapter briefly describes each function with the purpose of showing the nature of the administrative work involved; points out factors that may help the board of directors decide whether it would be feasible and advisable for the corporation to perform the function itself; and shows what the responsible corporate officer does when the function is performed by an agency.

STOCK ISSUANCE DUTIES

Administrative steps in the issuance of stock. Whether the company is recently formed and issuing its first stock, or is an established company that is issuing additional stock, it must take the following steps.

1. *Hold a directors' meeting.* The directors must adopt resolutions at a regular directors' meeting or at a special meeting called for the purpose, authorizing the issuance of the stock. These resolutions specify the terms of the issue.

2. *Get consent of the stockholders.* If the company already has stockholders, and an increase in authorized capital stock is necessary, the stockholders entitled to vote by statute or provisions of the articles of incorporation must adopt resolutions to amend the charter. Sometimes the shares are authorized although there will be no immediate issue. The stockholders vote on this resolution either at the annual meeting of stockholders or at a special meeting or by a properly executed proxy if he cannot be present.

3. *Check the pre-emptive rights.* The holders of outstanding stock may be entitled to pre-emptive rights; that is, they may have the right to subscribe prorata to any additional shares of stock issued. The terms of the outstanding stock, as described in the charter, and the state corporation law determine whether this right exists. The issuance of stock through subscription rights is discussed in step 10.

4. *Look into requirements of the Securities and Exchange Commission.* If the company offers the issue to the public, and the issue is not an exempt one, a registration statement and prospectus must be prepared.

5. *Make arrangements for the sale of the securities.* In a very few cases, the company might market its own stock; in most cases, it will sell its securities to investment bankers and sometimes to insurance companies through a private sale. If a public offering is to be made, a group of investment banking firms, sometimes known as a syndicate, may be formed to purchase the entire issue of stock from the company and then sell the stock to the public. If, however, the company offers the securities to present stockholders through subscription rights, the company usually enters into a stand-by agreement with investment bankers to purchase the shares not subscribed for by stockholders.

6. *Arrange for listing the stock.* Most companies of substantial size prefer to have their securities listed on a stock exchange. These companies usually list on either the New York Stock Exchange or the American Stock Exchange and sometimes also on a regional exchange. There are a few large companies and several smaller companies that do not want to list their securities; most small companies do not qualify for listing on a stock exchange. The one major reason that some companies do not wish to list on an exchange is that listing requires compliance with the regulations of the Securities and Exchange Commission. These regulations demand the disclosure of some facts about the company and its officials that they do not wish to disclose.

7. *Prepare the stock certificate.* Counsel customarily prepares for the company a draft of the proposed certificate. The company must then decide whether the certificate is to be engraved, lithographed, or printed. This decision often depends upon the requirements of outside agencies, such as a stock exchange. Stock exchanges usually require certificates to be engraved, since engraving, although the most expensive process, is the most difficult to alter. Lithographing is a cheaper process. Printing, though not as cheap as lithographing, is cheaper than engraving and quite durable, but there is the danger that the printed words may be worn off after a period of time or that they can be erased from the certificate. Regardless of the method used, the base stock of the certificate must be durable and hard to tear.

When a company makes an original issue, time is often of the essence and it becomes impossible to wait for the slow process of engraving permanent certificates. A temporary certificate with an engraved border (required by the New York Stock Exchange) within which is the printed matter, can be made up in a short time so that the company or the underwriters marketing the securities can make quick delivery. The temporary certificates are comparatively inexpensive and are intended to serve only until the permanent certificates are ready, when an exchange should be made. Temporary certificates may also be used if the company is going to change the par value of its stock or make any change in the current stock certificate. The company can estimate fairly closely the number of certificates it will need and if more certificates are needed, the bank note company can print them very quickly.

Most bank note companies suggest that 100 per cent rag paper be used for both permanent and temporary stock certificates. A few companies use 100 per cent rag linen paper which is more expensive. The certificate may appear slightly more attractive but the stock exchanges do not require this more expensive paper.

The control of blank certificates is the responsibility of the officer or other person in charge of the transfer department if the company does its own transfer work. Certificates are requisitioned from this person as they are needed, usually on a weekly basis. The transfer department keeps a ledger record and enters in the ledger the number of certificates received. It posts daily the number of certificates issued; the balance should represent the number of certificates physically on hand.

When an independent agent performs these duties, it requisitions from the bank note company a supply of certificates that will last for a large company approximately three months and for a small company approximately six months. The transfer agent also maintains a control ledger.

8. *Consider appointment of a transfer agent and registrar.* The question is often asked, when is a transfer or co-transfer agent necessary? A company of small size, with little activity in the trading of its securities, has no need for a transfer or co-transfer agent. Companies of medium and large size, which have substantial stock activity, usually employ a transfer agent. It is probable that a very large company can operate its own transfer department at a lower cost and has no need for a transfer agent although there may be need for one or more co-transfer agents if the stock is particularly active in one or more sections of the country. Some companies, the stock of which is active in various sections of the country, find it necessary to have not only a main transfer agent but also one or more regional co-transfer agents. The co-transfer agent only makes the transfers of certificates and reports these to the transfer agent. The New York Stock Exchange requires that any company listed shall have a transfer agent in the financial district of New York City. A company might have its transfer agent located on the West Coast or in the Middle West and yet, to comply with the New York Stock Exchange regulation, must have a co-transfer agent in New York City.

Another question often asked is, when is a registrar or co-registrar necessary? The small unlisted company almost always serves as its own registrar. The medium and large companies, which may or may not employ an independent transfer agent, always have an independent registrar. The very large company always has an independent registrar even though it usually does its own transfer work. The function of the registrar is solely to prevent an overissue of stock, that is, an issue of shares beyond what is authorized. The registrar receives a copy of the resolution that authorizes the number of shares to be issued and must keep a careful record of all shares issued and canceled. The registrar examines each certificate issued and keeps a daily record of certificates canceled and issued so that he knows at all times that the proper number of shares is outstanding. Like the co-transfer agent, there is also in many cases a co-registrar where the company's stock has market activity in various sections of the country. The New York Stock Exchange requires of its listed companies that there be a registrar in the financial district of New York City. This requirement necessitates the appointment of a co-registrar for many companies. The co-registrar examines certificates sent to him as designated and makes a report to the registrar. The New York Stock Exchange also requires for listed companies that the registrar and transfer agent not be one and the same.

9. *Arrange for the issuance of the certificates.* The transfer agent or company issues the new certificates. The name of the owner and the date of issuance are placed on the certificate. The number of shares is stamped on the certificate unless it is a

100-share certificate, in which case the number of shares appears in the text. Most companies have one color of certificate for 100 shares and another for less than 100 shares. The certificate, after being signed by the transfer agent, is sent to the registrar who registers the certificate and returns it to the transfer agent for forwarding to the new stockholder.

10. *Arrange for the issuance of subscription rights.* If the company offers its stock through subscription rights, warrants, which evidence the right of the holder to subscribe for a certain number of shares, are sent to the stockholders of record as of a certain date. The warrant is usually prepared by a bank acting as subscription agent for the company. Rarely does the company do its own work at this point. The warrant, signed by an authorized officer of the bank, is accompanied by a prospectus and a notice to stockholders. If the stockholder wishes to sell his rights, he may do so through his bank or broker. In some cases, the bank acting as subscription agent will buy and sell rights, but this arrangement requires a special agreement between the company and its subscription agent.

In current practice, each stockholder entitled to rights receives a warrant made out for the exact number of rights to which he is entitled. Thus, if each stockholder must own five shares to subscribe to one new share, a stockholder owning twenty-two shares would receive a warrant for twenty-two rights and, if he wished to "round off" before exercising his rights, would sell two of his rights or buy three additional rights.

Many stockholders, for one reason or another, have their certificates issued in the name of a nominee, usually the nominee used by their broker or bank. The latter, acting as nominee, receives a warrant that represents the rights of all his customers using the same nominee. The bank or broker then requests the subscription agent to split up the warrant into the share amounts required. The same nominee's name is used on the individual warrants.

Guidance for preparation of registration statement and prospectus. The registration statement includes all pertinent facts about the history, business, and properties of the company, and detailed financial statements. It is accompanied by numerous exhibits, such as copies of resolutions, sample of the stock certificate or other security to be offered, copies of the by-laws and charter, and copies of agreements between the companies and other parties. Company's counsel, with the aid of the company's officers, usually prepares the registration statement in conjunction with the underwriters, their counsel, and the public accountants. It is a good idea for company's counsel to confer from time to time, either in person or over the telephone, with the Securities and Exchange Commission staff about any problems concerning the registration statement, and for the accountants who prepare the financial statements to be sure that their presentation will be acceptable to the Commission. The issuer must use the correct form. If the company is in doubt as to the form to be used, it should consult with the SEC staff.

If a company has previously filed a registration statement, the drafters will generally find it helpful to use that statement as a guide; if a first registration statement is being prepared, a recent registration statement of a similar company will be a helpful guide to language and form that have already been accepted by the Commission. It is, of course, essential that the drafters of the registration statement follow carefully the rules and regulations of the Commission and meet all of its requirements. These are set forth, explained, and kept up to date in the published loose-leaf services.

The registration statement, containing the prospectus and to be filed with the Commission, is printed in sufficient copies to supply the needs of the company, its counsel, the underwriters, their counsel, the public accountants, and the Commission.

The Commission makes a penetrating examination of the registration statement, noting any deficiencies in the information supplied. It advises the registrant by letter of the deficiencies, which must be corrected by filing amendments to the filed statement. The original registration statement with the accepted amendments is reprinted in the required number of copies. When the registration statement is entirely satisfactory, the Commission issues an order to the effect that the registration statement becomes effective as of an indicated date.

The prospectus is the major portion of the registration statement. It describes the management personnel, mentions the name of counsel, tells whether there are any interlocking directorates, gives a digest description of the securities to be issued, and presents financial statements including balance sheets, statements of income, and earned surplus. Most of these financial statements are on a comparative basis, particularly the statement of income, which covers usually the last 10 years. The prospectus also usually includes a word picture of the company's origin and development and describes the properties and operation of the company in general.

After the registration statement becomes effective the portion constituting the prospectus is printed in sufficient quantity to supply the needs of the distributors of the securities, who make them available to prospective purchasers.

Guidance in meeting other Securities and Exchange Commission requirements. A company with shares fully listed on an exchange regulated by the Securities Exchange Act of 1934 must observe the rules and regulations of the Securities and Exchange Commission with regard to (1) proxies, and (2) the filing of periodical and other reports.

Proxies and proxy statements. In preparing its proxy and proxy statement, a company should follow carefully the proxy regulations prescribed by the Commission. The secretary of the company usually prepares a draft of the proxy and proxy statement for approval by company counsel. If counsel has any doubts, he should take the matter up with the Commission. Again, it is a good idea before preparing the proxy and proxy statement to talk with the Commission if there is anything unusual. If the proxy and proxy statement are similar to those of the year before, it is a very simple matter to prepare them, always being sure to check the regulations for changes. If there is to be an amendment to the company's charter, or if a resolution is to be voted upon, it is often well to talk with the Commission to be sure that everything is in order before the proxy and statement are filed; otherwise it may result in a deficiency statement, which will delay the approval. The company should understand that the proxy regulations were devised to inform the stockholder so that he can intelligently cast his absentee vote on questions to be voted upon at the stockholders' meeting and also to provide him with pertinent information concerning the officers and directors of his company.

Periodical and other reports. Every issuer of a listed security must file an annual report with SEC and the particular exchange within 120 days after the close of its fiscal year. With a few exceptions, listed companies must also file a semi-annual financial report within 45 days after the close of the first half of the fiscal year. In addition, each issuer must file a current report within 10 days after the close of any month during which an event such as a change in the control of the issuer, changes in rights of security holders, or other enumerated changes have occurred.

It is good practice for the company to complete any required reports and have them in the Commissions's hands before the due date. It is also wise to follow carefully the information asked for on the report and to comply with it as closely as possible. It is essential to give complete figures and information asked for on these reports. They are analyzed to appraise the company and are also used to compile statistical data for all interested parties. All these reports are a matter of public information and can be cited as authority; therefore, they must be accurate. In most cases, the president of the company signs the reports. He should be sure that the information supplied is accurate and complete.

Procedures of stock issuance. Since the procedures for stock issuance come into play also upon a transfer of stock, this subject is discussed under stock transfers.

STOCK TRANSFER DUTIES

Importance of the stock transfer function. A transfer of stock takes place when the holder of a stock certificate disposes of it to a new owner. A new certificate of stock must be issued if the company's records are to show the new ownership of interest in the company. The importance of the stock transfer function, and consequently of the work involved in performing the function, is brought out in the following discussion of four basic factors.

1. *Statutory requirements.* The Uniform Stock Transfer Act or the Uniform Commercial Code governs stock transfer in every state. An increasing number of states are adopting the Code which replaces the Uniform Act's provisions on stock transfer.

2. *Stock exchange regulations.* The stock exchanges in this country have drawn up certain regulations concerning stock transfers that must be followed when a company's stock is listed upon one or more of the exchanges. Most exchanges require that the company appoint a registrar and a transfer agent. The company may act as its own transfer agent provided the exchange approves, but the exchange insists that the registrar be an independent agency. Both of these measures serve to protect the stockholder.

3. *Rights of stockholders.* Each stockholder has certain rights beyond the right to a certificate showing his ownership of shares. For example, he has the right to vote for directors (unless the stock is non-voting), to vote on other questions affecting the corporation's property as a whole, to receive dividends when they are declared, to subscribe, in proportion to his holdings, for any new issue of stock (unless denied this pre-emptive right by contract or by statute), and to share in the proceeds of dissolution. Obviously, unless the records of stock ownership are accurate and complete, so that the corporation knows who is entitled to these rights, there is danger of unwittingly denying them. The corporation must exercise reasonable care in carrying out the transfer function to avoid liability.

4. *Corporate liability.* The corporation is liable for damages to persons who are injured through the wrongful transfer of stock. The extent of corporate liability is well expressed in *Western Union Telegraph Company v. Davenport,* 97 U.S. 369 (1878). In this opinion, the Supreme Court of the United States declared that the officers of the company are custodians of its stock books, and it is their duty to see that all transfers of

shares are properly made, either by the stockholders themselves or persons having authority from them. If, upon the presentation of a certificate for transfer, the officers are at all doubtful of the identity of the party offering it, or not satisfied as to the genuineness of a power of attorney produced, they can require the identity of the party in the one case and the genuineness of the document in the other to be satisfactorily established before allowing the transfer to be made. In either case, they must act upon their own responsibility. In many instances, they may be misled without any fault of their own, just as the most careful person may sometimes be induced to purchase property from one who has no title—neither the absence of blame on the part of the officers of the company in allowing an unauthorized transfer of stock nor the good faith of the purchaser of stolen property will avail as an answer to the demand of the true owner.

Who does the transfer work? The corporation must decide whether it will do its own transfer work or employ an independent agency to do it. Some large companies have conducted cost studies to determine whether or not they should establish their own stock transfer department and have concluded that they can do their own work at a saving. Some very small companies have also found it less costly to do their own transfer work. The majority of companies, however, have found it convenient and profitable to have an agent perform the transfer services. Some companies act as their own transfer agent but have a co-transfer agent located in New York City (required if the company is listed on the New York Stock Exchange) or in some large city where there is market activity in the company's securities. Whether the corporation establishes its own stock transfer department or employs an independent agency, the stock exchange upon which the shares are listed must approve of the arrangement. If the corporation decides not to do its own transfer work, it may appoint a bank or trust company that serves as stock transfer agent for corporations through its corporate trust department, or one of the special companies that have been organized to perform this type of work for corporations. These companies provide the same services as the corporate trust departments of banks but they do not offer the facilities available only from an institution in the banking business.

Investigating the feasibility of establishing a stock transfer department. A corporation that wants to look into the feasibility of doing its own stock transfer work must expect to make a complete survey of the costs of establishing and maintaining a stock transfer department, the economies that may be effected, the difficulties, and other factors. The interested officers usually the secretary and the treasurer, must report to the board of directors on the results of the investigation and must make their recommendations. The following suggestions for preparing the report also indicate the survey procedure.

The report consists of a statement signed by the treasurer and the secretary, supported by exhibits that constitute the survey. The statement proper covers the following points.

1. The possible economies. This statement should refer to the exhibits appended to the report that show how the figures were determined.

2. The likelihood of unforeseen expenses.

3. The difficulties, such as:

(a)   The complexity of the accounts. For example, if the present capital setup shows groups of accounts that have been blocked under government regulation, accounts still holding classes of stock that have been called for redemption, or accounts still holding stock issued under a previous capital structure, many serious problems will arise in effecting transfers in and out of such accounts. These problems will require the services of highly trained personnel and it might be advisable to put off the establishment of a company transfer department until the capital setup has been simplified to the point where the work would be reduced to merely routine matters.

(b)   The prospect of recapitalization. If the company were contemplating a new recapitalization program, involving redemption of outstanding preferred stock, for example, the company might do better to continue the services of an outside transfer agent.

(c)   The necessity for assemblying a staff of employees qualified to handle all phases of stock transfer work, especially the legal phases.

(d)   The capital outlay. Establishment of a company stock transfer department requires an immediate cash outlay for equipment, supplies, and the like. The officers must know whether the capital outlay is feasible.

(e)   The space required. A proposed floor plan of a stock transfer office adequate to handle the volume of work will show how much space is required. Scaled at ¼ inch to a foot, such a plan visualizes not only the space requirement but the equipment needs as well.

(f)   The location of the office. Stock exchange regulations may require the company to have an office in the financial district, where the brokers' offices are located, at which deliveries and pick-ups can be made. In New York City, for example, some uptown companies that have their own stock transfer departments have arranged to have deliveries and pick-ups made at the offices of their registrars. The transfer agent sends a messenger to the registrar's office perhaps once or twice a day.

4. The recommendation of those signing the statement.
5. Counsel's opinion of the feasibility of the plan.

The following separate statements, which constitute the survey, should be appended to the report:

1. A list of companies that are acting as their own transfer agents.
2. A statement of the services and disbursement expenses of the outside transfer agent for the previous year.
3. An estimate of the costs that will be incurred in the current year for the services of the outside transfer agent.
4. A list of the equipment and furniture that will be required for establishing the stock transfer office and the costs if new equipment is bought as compared with investment if rebuilt machines are acquired.

5. The approximate yearly cost for maintaining the stock transfer office. This estimate would cover such items as:

> Salaries.
> Rent.
> Light.
> Stationery.
> Telephone and telegrams.
> Association fees.
> Repairs and other miscellaneous items.
> Insurance.
> Services of controller, auditor, etc.
> Non-recurring expenses, such as cost of acquiring the addressograph stencils from the present transfer agent, and the cost of correcting the supply of stock certificates on hand to show the change in the name of the transfer agent.

6. A proposed floor plan of the stock transfer office with equipment indicated.

7. A list of the personnel for the stock transfer office, showing the position, duties, and annual salary.

8. Approximate annual savings if the company maintains its own stock transfer office.

Outline of procedures in issuing certificates. The actual procedures in the issuance of stock certificates, whether handled by the corporation's own stock transfer department or by an independent agency, involve certain steps that are described below. This explanation is not intended to give the details of the various operations but is presented rather to aid in an understanding of the functions of the transfer agent.

Operations in typical stock transfer department. The following is an outline of operations performed by various personnel in a typical stock transfer department. It serves as a guide to the handling of stock transfers.

Transfer checker:

> Sorting of canceled certificates.
> Filing of canceled certificates.
> Checking old and new certificates to transfer sheet.
> Proving new certificates to blotter.
> Sending out transfer sheets.
> Sorting of certificates to deliver to clearing house and by hand.

Signer:

> Handling new certificates in signing.
> Protection and dating of new certificates.
> Sorting new certificates for checking.

Machine operator:

> Drawing new certificates.
> Canceling old certificates.
> Preparation of transfer sheets.
> Preparation of registered mail sheets.
> Miscellaneous typing.

Certificate custodian:
    Checking of transfer stops.
    Maintenance of stop file.
    Preparation of blotter.
    Allocating new certificates.
    Control and ordering of new certificates.

Teller:
    Reading material for background.
    Receiving certificates over window.
    Examination of window transfers.
    Issuance and control of window tickets.
    Comparison of signatures to file.
    Maintenance of signature file.
    Receiving mail transfers.
    Examination of mail transers.
    Sending out mail transfers.
    Handling inquiries whether or not pertinent to transfer

Clerical jobs:
    Handling correspondence.
    Investigating inquiries.
    Setting up and releasing stops.
    Preparation of dividend orders.
    Preparation of transcripts.
    Issuance of duplicate checks.
    Disposing of checks held up.
    Redeposit of checks.
    Closing accounts.
    Changes of addresses.

Supervisor:
    Review of departmental functions.
    The department as a whole.
    Coordination of jobs.
    Planning jobs.
    Training personnel.
    Reviewing methods.
    Improving operations.
    Handling of unusual jobs.
    Outline of, and coordination with, departments having immediate contact.

Preparation of a stock certificate on original or additional issue. The corporate secretary works in conjunction with the bank note company to design the stock certificates. The bank note company engraves the certificates and sends them to the transfer agent who prepares them in accordance with the corporation's instructions. A ledger record is made of the name and address of the stockholder, certificate number, and number of shares for which the certificate is issued. Each certificate is signed by the transfer agent and then processed by the registrar. The transfer agent must also notify the stock exchange or exchanges upon which the stock is listed so that they have a record of original or additional shares issued.

Inspection of old certificates surrendered. When a certificate is presented to the agent for transfer, he immediately inspects it for proper assignment to the new owner. The signature of the record owner must be properly guaranteed. Transfer agents have different requirements for guarantee. If a deceased's stock certificate is presented for transfer, the agent must examine various legal papers. He must also determine that there is no "stop" transfer on the certificate. A "stop" transfer signal is placed against the certificate number in the stock ledger for various reasons, such as the loss, destruction, or theft of certificates, the presentation of conflicting claims or proceedings involving estates, bankruptcies, receiverships, minorities, guardianships, and attachments. The transfer agent must recognize legal problems that will prevent the transfer of certificates in the cases mentioned above. The agent must designate his records properly so that "stops" can be immediately recognized when certificates are presented for transfer. A certificate that has a "stop" against it cannot be transferred until release of the "stop" is authorized to the satisfaction of the transfer agent.

Preparation and delivery of new certificate for new owner. After the agent is satisfied that the old certificate is in good order, it is then matched against a new certificate, prepared in the name of the new holder. The old certificate is then canceled. The transfer agent keeps a daily journal, known as the transfer sheet, upon which he records each transaction, showing all canceled certificates and newly issued certificates. At the end of each day, the new certificates issued must equal the old certificates canceled.

Checking. The new certificate is rechecked and sent to the registrar, who performs his function and then returns the certificate to the transfer agent. The old certificate is kept by the transfer agent for an indefinite period of time unless a definite period is prescribed by the law of the state of incorporation.

The new certificate is sent either by registered mail, first class insured mail or messenger to the broker originating the transaction or to the new holder.

Many certificates, however, are presented at the transfer counter by brokers' messengers or by stock purchasers in person. A window clerk who is familiar with the transfer requirements is stationed at the transfer counter. This window clerk examines the certificates presented to see that the assignment is properly executed, that the full number of shares has been transferred by the assignment, and that the proper transfer tax stamps have been affixed. If the certificate appears to be in order, the clerk gives a receipt (window ticket) to the messenger. The receipt specifies the date when the new certificate may be picked up at the transfer counter. The old certificate is sent to the transfer agent who performs his functions as outlined above. When the new certificate is ready, the messenger will come to the transfer counter, present his window ticket, and receive the new certificate.

Change of address. Most stockholders advise the corporation or the transfer agent when they have made a change of address. This change is entered on a special voucher for use in the transfer department. If the addressograph system is used, the stockholder's stencil is immediately corrected and the new stencil is imprinted upon the address voucher or advice to make sure that it is correct and that the old addressograph plate has been removed. The voucher is then turned over to the ledger clerk who makes the proper notation in the stockholder's ledger account. If tabulating machinery is used, a change of address voucher is given to the clerk in charge of the files. He removes the old cards and gives them, along with the voucher, to the key-punch operator who makes up new address cards. These new cards are then interpreted and are proof run to be sure they are correct before they are placed in the file. Most companies and transfer agents make it easy for a stockholder to notify them of a change in address by enclosing a change of address card in the envelope carrying dividend checks.

Taxes affecting transfer of securities. The corporation, the transfer agent, and the security holder are all concerned with certain taxes that are levied upon the transfer of securities. They are as follows: federal stamp tax, state stamp taxes, federal estate tax, and state inheritance and estate taxes. The tax laws provide that the corporation must be certain that there has been compliance with them before it or its agent can effect a transfer of securities. These tax laws are constantly undergoing changes by amendments of the statutes, administrative rulings and regulations, and court decisions. They are very technical and constant reference to a tax service is recommended to keep abreast of the changes.[1]

Stop transfer records. When a certificate of stock has been reported as lost, or when a notice has been given that the registered owner has died, or when an order to stop the transfer of stock for some other reason is given, the transfer agent must make a notation on his stop transfer records. There are two methods of keeping a stop transfer record, numerically or alphabetically. Some transfer agents keep both types of records as a double check on stop transfers. Upon receipt of notice of loss, a record card is made out that gives all the facts about the lost certificate and the replacement certificate. When a transfer agent or co-transfer agent, if any, has many stop transfers, a record is usually kept for each class of stock. Decedents' stop transfers are kept separate from stop transfers on certificates reported as lost. The transfer agent must give notice of a stop order to the registrar and co-registrar, if any, to any stock exchange on which the stock is listed, and to all parties interested in the stock and must also acknowledge receipt of the stop order from the stockholder. These notices are sent on specially designed forms. Occasionally the stockholder notifies the transfer agent that he has found his lost certificate. The transfer agent must then notify all parties concerned that the stop order has been removed.

Records kept by transfer agent. Another function of the transfer agent is to maintain records of each stockholder's account. There must be a permanent record of each stockholder's interest in the corporation and of all transfer of any part of any stockholder's interest by way of stock transfers. Every cancelled certificate and every new certificate must be properly recorded in the particular stockholder's record.

Figure 12-1 illustrates the type of account record maintained for each stockholder. This record is permanent and is filed for an indefinite period. If a new transfer agent is designated, the old transfer agent must turn over all records, including canceled certificates, to the new agent. Whether stockholder records should be destroyed or, if destroyed, photographed on microfilm, is a legal question that should always be referred to competent counsel.

Methods of issuing stock certificates and maintaining accounts. The methods used by a stock transfer office in issuing certificates and maintaining accounts are usually designed to meet the needs of the particular transfer agent. The following methods are used in large and small stock transfer offices.

---

[1]Prentice-Hall *Stock Transfers* and Prentice-Hall *Inheritance and Transfer Tax* contain all the necessary information.

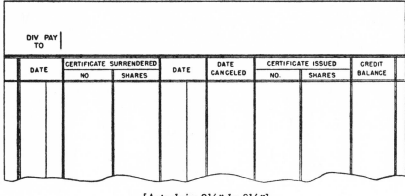

[*Actual size 9¼" by 8¼"*]

Figure 12-1. Stockholders' Ledger Sheet.

1. Some transfer agents draw stock certificates and prepare the stock transfer sheet on a typewriter. Some also post the certificates canceled and issued manually on a ledger card or sheet.
2. Some of the larger transfer agents use addressograph plates. In this system, the name and address of each stockholder, and sometimes the number of shares held, are embossed on a metal plate. These plates are enclosed in a frame and may be tabbed for the selection of information contained in the plate. The plates must be brought up to date to reflect the transactions of each day.
3. A few of the larger transfer agents use data processing machinery for maintaining stockholder accounts. This machinery is made by any of the major computer manufacturers. The basis for the process is the use of punched cards for the stockholder's record. The procedure does away with the maintenance of ledger sheets for stockholder accounts, since each stockholder's record consists of the group of cards representing the certificates registered in his name. When a certificate is sold, the appropriate certificate card is removed and placed in a closed file. The transfer sheet is prepared on a tabulating printer that lists at the close of each day the names on the certificates canceled and the names and addresses on the certificates issued, with the number of shares in each case.

Unclaimed stock certificates. The stockholder records may show at any one time that a number of stock certificates have been unclaimed and are being held by the stock transfer agent. The failure to claim a certificate may arise in the following ways:

1. In very rare cases certificates are presented in person for transfer at the office of the transfer agent and are not called for.
2. The post office returns the new certificates with advice that they are undeliverable because the address is not correct.
3. In the case of company reorganization or recapitalization plans that involve calling in old certificates and exchanging them for new ones, some of the

new certificates almost inevitably fail to reach the owners, either because they are not called for or they are sent to an incorrect address.

Methods of locating a "missing" stockholder. Enough companies have been concerned about unclaimed certificates to warrant the establishment of independent agencies that track down missing stockholders for a fee. These agencies try to locate stockholders for all sorts of reasons, including the delivery of unclaimed certificates.

The transfer agent usually follows its own routine in locating the "missing" certificate holders. It generally pursues the following steps.

1. A letter is sent to the registered holder. If the letter is not returned, and still no response is received, follow-up letters are written at various intervals.
2. If the letter is returned as undeliverable, a telephone call is made to the number last shown in the directory. Of course, this step presumes that the stockholder lives in the vicinity of the company's representative making the call.
3. If the stockholder acquired the stock through a broker, the broker is contacted to see if he knows the stockholder's address.
4. If the stockholder cannot be located, his certificate is placed in safekeeping until such time as he is located.
5. Periodic checkups are made to see if the stockholder can be located. During the period of a year, the stockholder may have contacted one of the parties mentioned above and a recheck would determine the stockholder's whereabouts.

During a reorganization or recapitalization, the stockholder often receives cash in addition to new securities. If the stockholder cannot be located, the stockholder cannot be located within a specified length of time, the company must turn the money over to the state. For example, in New York, the company has 15 years to locate the stockholder; if the company still has the money at the end of the 15 year period, the funds escheat to the State of New York.

Corporate use of daily transfer sheet. Each day the stock transfer agent sends the secretary of the corporation a copy of the stock transfer sheet showing the securities that have been transferred that day. The record shows the name of the transferor, the number of shares transferred, and the name and address of the transferee. This sheet should be examined daily by the secretary; analysis of it may reveal important information concerning changes in ownership. Management is especially interested in knowing whether shares are being purchased in small lots by individuals or in large amounts in the names of nominees and whether local or out-of-town people are among the purchasers. When the executive notices that large blocks of stock are being purchased by brokers in the names of nominees, he may want to visit the brokers to get acquainted with them. He may, but usually cannot, find out whom the nominees represent. If he finds out who actually owns the shares, he may want to visit the holders and acquaint them with the company's affairs.

One corporate secretary has built up a list of nominees and knows, in many instances, whether the nominees on the transfer sheet represent a custodian, a trust, or a large investment company. Acquaintance with the nominees may prove useful in soliciting proxies. For example, when proxies are slow in coming in and there is danger of not meeting the quorum requirements, a secretary who knows the interest behind the shares held in the names of nominees may be able to gather in the proxies of the nominees.

If a corporation has a well-rounded stockholder relations program the daily transfer sheet would be used in carrying out any portion of the program that applies particularly to new stockholders, for example, the sending of welcome letters, or the mailing of sample products as gifts. Careful records must be kept to avoid, for example, sending letters of welcome two or three times to the same stockholder because the person has traded in that stock and his name appears on the daily transfer sheets more than once.

Responsibility for stock transfer function. The secretary is usually responsible for the stock transfer function, but in some companies the treasurer or a vice-president handles the duty. The responsible officer supervises the transfer duties whether the corporation does its own work or employs an outside agent and sees that the various parts of the transfer function are properly coordinated. He should maintain close contact, through the president, with the board of directors in order to know the policies and requirements of the company regarding stock issuance and transfer and relay them to the transfer agent.

Relationships among agents. When a co-transfer agent or co-registrar is appointed, it is necessary for the transfer agent to keep in close contact with the registrar and co-transfer agent, and co-registrar. This is done through the exchange of transfer sheets, the registry of stock, notices of stop transfers and releases, and notices of dividend declarations. The transfer agent should also be in contact with any stock exchange upon which the stock is listed.

Change in transfer agent. A corporation, for various reasons, may want to change its transfer agent. To make the change the procedure outlined below must be followed.

1. The board of directors must adopt a resolution to terminate the contract with the present transfer agent.
2. The board must also adopt a new resolution to appoint the new transfer agent.
3. The old transfer agent may request that a release be executed by the proper corporation officer to relieve the old transfer agent of all liability on stock transfers made by it.
4. The old transfer agent will furnish the new transfer agent with all necessary records, with the exception of stencils. The latter may be retained by the old transfer agent; however, the new transfer agent can purchase these stencils.
5. The old transfer agent will prepare a list of stockholders of record on the day of the change and the corporation will pay for this list.

The certificates of stock outstanding are valid even though they are signed by the old transfer agent and there is no need to call in these outstanding certificates. The new transfer agent will sign all future certificates issued.

DIVIDEND PAYMENTS

Period of dividend payments. A few companies, usually closely-owned ones, pay only an annual dividend, many companies pay semi-annually, but the vast majority pay their dividends quarterly. Stockholders favor a quarterly dividend, and this practice has become fairly standard, although it is expensive because the same operation has to be performed four times during the year.

The directors include in their resolution declaring the dividend the record date as of which holders of the stock are entitled to the dividend, so that any person holding stock at the date of record (usually the close of business on a certain day) is entitled to the payment of the dividend. The resolution also includes the date of payment of the dividend. Stock exchange regulations usually require that the corporation allow at least ten days between the declaration date and the record date.

Disbursement of the dividend. As in the case of stock transfer work, the company may pay its own dividends. However, in most cases the larger companies appoint a dividend disbursement agent. Usually the transfer agent maintaining the stockholder accounts disburses the dividends because its stockholder records are used in preparing the dividend checks.

Payment of the dividend is made by check. Whether the company pays its own dividends or employs an agent to pay them, the check bears the name of the company. If the company has more than one class of stock, the dividend checks should have a distinguishing color for each class of security. The checks will also bear a number to identify and distinguish them from previous and future dividend checks. The check is signed either by an official of the company, if the company makes payment, or by an official of the dividend disbursing agent. A check signing machine is usually employed. As a record of each dividend payment, a dividend list or register is usually prepared which includes the names of the stockholders and the amount paid to each of them.

The transfer department, if the company does its own work, or the transfer agent sends a copy of the dividend register to the officer of the company in charge of this function. Most dividend checks are prepared with a stub that has an identifying number and shows the number of shares and the amount paid to the stockholder. The stub may be used for reconciliation purposes.

Simple procedure for corporation employing dividend disbursing agent. If the corporation employs a dividend disbursing agent, this agent is generally appointed by a resolution adopted by the board of directors. As mentioned above, it is common practice to appoint as dividend disbursing agent the same bank or trust company that acts as transfer agent. These agents usually furnish their own special form of resolution of appointment, and a certified copy of this resolution is kept in the corporation's files. The corporation must take the following steps before the agent disburses the dividend checks to the stockholders.

1. The board of directors of the corporation adopts a resolution declaring the dividend.
2. The corporation's secretary presents to the agent a certified copy of the resolution declaring the dividend.
3. The treasurer of the corporation deposits the necessary funds for the payment of the

dividend with the disbursing agent a few days before the dividend checks are sent out to stockholders.

4. If publication of the notice of the declaration of dividend is required either by the charter of the corporation or by a stock exchange upon which the corporation's stock is listed, the secretary of the corporation will attend to the publication.

5. The secretary of the corporation sends to the agent in sufficient time in advance of the mailing all enclosures that are to be inserted with the dividend check. It is advisable that a change of address form be included.

6. The corporation often receives notice of change of address or of lost dividend checks or of claim that no dividend has been received or that the dividend was for an incorrect amount. The corporation should forward any such notice to the dividend disbursing agent for proper action. It is good practice for the corporation to acknowledge receipt of the notice and to inform the stockholder that the matter will be handled by the dividend disbursing agent with whom the stockholder may correspond.

Procedure for dividend payment in a small corporation. In a small corporation, the by-laws usually state that the treasurer will supervise dividend payments, but the secretary, who is ordinarily in charge of the registration and transfer of securities, usually handles the details of dividend payment. The following steps are generally taken in the payment of a dividend by a small corporation.

1. The treasurer submits at a meeting of the board of directors where the declaration of the quarterly dividend is to be considered, a quarterly financial statement which includes a balance sheet and earnings statement for the period. The directors use this information as a guide to whether or not the corporation can legally declare a dividend.

2. The board of directors adopts a resolution to declare the dividend.

3. The secretary or an assistant secretary prepares from the stock record book a complete list of stockholders entitled to the dividend. This list is the dividend payment record, and the check number and amount of dividend paid to each stockholder is recorded on the list.

4. The checks are drawn in the proper amounts.

5. The checks are then totaled to see that the amount agrees with that indicated on the dividend payment record.

6. The officer responsible for handling the dividend disbursement submits to the treasurer the dividend payment record and the checks for signature.

7. The treasurer examines the dividend payment record to determine if the total shares upon which dividends are being paid agrees with the amount of stock outstanding. The treasurer then returns the dividend record and signed checks to the proper person for mailing.

Methods of drawing dividend checks. The methods of drawing checks vary as do the methods of issuing stock certificates and maintaining accounts. The usual practices are indicated below.

1. Some companies and agents use the typewriter, particularly where the number of stockholders is small. The preparation of the list of stockholders entitled to dividends and the checks are separate operations.

2. Some companies and agents use the addressograph plate system. Modern addressograph equipment provides for the selection of the basic information from the plate. Thus, the addressograph plate is used to stamp on the check the name and address and sometimes the number of shares. The amount of the check, however, must be calculated, since dividend rates may vary from time to time. As in the

above method, the dividend list and the checks must be prepared in separate operations.

3. Some companies and agents print their checks by computer equipment, using the punched cards that are a part of the stockholder accounts. The dividend amount is punched in the detailed certificate card. Forms 1099 (information returns) can be prepared at the same time. The computer equipment permits preparation of the dividend list at the same time that the checks are drawn.

Reconciliation of dividend account. An important part of the dividend disbursing job is to reconcile the checks. Whether the company or an agent pays the dividend, checks are usually drawn on a particular bank, and the company has deposited enough funds with that bank to cover the payment of the particular dividend. After the checks are returned to that bank for payment and are properly canceled and the company's account debited, they are then reconciled.

One method of reconciling checks is to stamp the check register as the checks are paid. This is usually started a month after most of the checks have been paid. The check register is then examined and a list made of all checks that have not been paid. The total amount of the checks outstanding should agree at all times with the amount still on deposit in the dividend account.

Another method of reconciling checks is to match the stubs with the checks that have been received for payment. A list is made of the stubs for which there are no checks, and the total dollar amount should agree with the funds still in the dividend account.

Unclaimed dividend payments. Unclaimed dividend payments are of two types: (1) checks that were sent out at last-known addresses and returned by the post office as undeliverable; (2) and checks that were sent out to payees and for some reason were not cashed. These checks remain outstanding. The unclaimed payments arise in the following manner.

1. A check is sent either to an incorrect address or to an old address. It cannot be delivered because no forwarding address was given by the payee.
2. The payee loses his check and does not notify the company or disbursing agent. He may forget that he has lost it or he may hope that it will turn up.
3. The payee neglects to cash the check. In certain cases he may feel that the check is too small, or he may carry it around with him for a while or put it some place for safekeeping until he gets ready to cash it.
4. The payee may die or become seriously ill and no one else may know that the check exists or, if they do know, they cannot locate it.

Methods of locating a lost payee. The following suggestions may help to locate a lost payee.

1. Look in the latest telephone directory.
2. Get in touch with the endorsers on previously paid checks.
3. Inquire of his brokers, if it is possible to ascertain who his brokers are. The broker may be located perhaps by checking canceled stock certificates in the name of the stockholder for signature guarantees.
4. The dividend disbursing agent may locate the payee through the principal corporation because he may have informed the corporation but not the dividend disbursing agent of his change in address.
5. If a check continues to be outstanding, after a reasonable period of time, send a notice to the payee asking what he has done with the check and offering to replace it

if it is lost. If the payee does not respond, and the notice is not returned as undeliverable, send similar notices from time to time in the hope that the payee will be prompted to cash the check.

Disposition of funds representing unpaid checks. As previously indicated, many large corporations deposit the total amount of a dividend in a special bank account or pay it to a fiscal agent for disbursement to the stockholders, keeping the special account and the Dividend Payable account open until the return of the checks, thus showing a liability for any checks unpresented. In the case of a dividend disbursing agent, the agent must keep the funds representing checks unpresented for a reasonable period of time and then may return them to the company. The laws differ on the retention of these funds. For example, the Commonwealth of Pennsylvania has an escheat law which requires that funds representing unclaimed dividends escheat to the state after a period of years.

BONDED INDEBTEDNESS AND INTEREST PAYMENTS

Need for a trustee. As explained in the preceding chapter companies may raise funds by issues of mortgage bonds, debentures, notes, or other evidences of indebtedness. Since the securities may be held by a considerable number of persons, it is necessary that a disinterested party serve as the representative of the holders. This party is known as a trustee and is customarily a bank or trust company. Its function is to enforce the rights, and represent the interests of, the investors who are creditors of the issuing company.

The trustee is designated by the directors of the company. In the case of a bond or debenture issue, the duties of the trustees are prescribed in an indenture. This indenture, for a mortgage bond issue, mortgages or pledges to the trustee the physical properties and any collateral securing the bonds. It contains the provisions governing the issue until maturity and is the rule book with which the company and the trustee must comply to fulfill their obligations to the security holders.

The Trust Indenture Act of 1939, which provides principally for the regulation and the sale of certain securities in interstate and foreign commerce and through the mails and for the regulation of the trust indenture under which the securities are issued, also requires the trustee to meet certain qualifications before appointment. It sets forth specific requirements to be contained in the indenture if the indenture is qualified under the Act.

Need for registrar and interest-paying agent. In addition to the trustee, there usually is, in the case of bond and debenture issues, a registrar and interest-paying agent. The function of the registrar is simply to record the names of the holders of fully registered bonds and coupon bonds registered as to principal.

In most cases, the paying agent is the same party as the trustee and registrar. Sometimes companies serve as their own interest-paying agents, but usually the paying agent is a bank or trust company. Many companies whose securities are traded in New York City or some other large city have a co-paying agent in that city for the convenience of the security holders.

Payment of interest on bonds and debentures. To meet the desires of investors, bonds and debentures are usually issued in three forms.

1. *Fully registered both as to principal and interest.* This type is very convenient for the holder. He has nothing to do except to wait for the interest payment, which is automatically sent to him on every payment date.
2. *Registered as to principal only, with coupons to be detached for interest payments.* The holder of this type has to clip a coupon prior to each payment date and send it through his bank to the paying agent.
3. *Bearer form, completely negotiable by delivery.* The holder must detach the coupons for interest payments and collect them as in 2 above.

Holders of bonds, except those registered as to interest, usually send coupons through their banks to the paying agent a few days prior to due date. The company, if it does not act as its own paying agent, sends to the paying agent prior to the payment date funds to cover the interest payment. The paying agent (other than the company) draws checks to the holders of the bonds registered as to interest and to presenters of coupons.

Supplying corporation with names of holders of bearer bonds. A company that wants to extend its investor relations activities to include its bondholders will have no difficulty in determining the names of those whose bonds are registered and may even know who most of its large bondholders are, even though not registered. The large unregistered bondholders may include institutional buyers, such as insurance companies, eleemosynary institutions, and investment companies, all of whom usually make themselves known to the company whose securities they hold. The company, however, usually has no idea who the small holders of its bearer bonds are. It may find out by requesting its coupon-paying agent to secure the names through the collecting banks that have presented the coupons for payment.

The paying agent is usually able to supply its principal with a good list of the holders of bearer bonds, obtained as follows. About a month prior to the payment date, the paying agent sends to the collecting banks a certificate of ownership form requesting information about the holders of bearer bonds of the company. The collecting banks, which have presented the coupons to the paying agent ask their correspondent banks who accepted the coupons from the holders to supply the information on the form. These banks, which first receive the coupon, either have the information in their files because the holders of the bonds deal with them or can request the information from the holders who are in their area. They then send the information to their correspondent banks, which in turn relay the information to the paying agent. The paying agent prepares the list and sends it to the company. The company then uses the list to send the holders of bearer bonds copies of the annual report, brochures, interim statements and other material of interest. If the corporation wants its investor relations official to make calls upon individual bondholders who have substantial holdings, the list shows who they are.

Cremation. The paying agent, upon payment of interest to the holders of bearer bonds, cancels the coupons, sorts them numerically, lists and stores them for a period of six months to a year after the date of the payment. At the end of this period, the coupons are once again checked against the list. If everything is in order, the coupons are cremated and the list is retained for reconciliation purposes.

Reconciliation of coupon interest payments. The paying agent must make reconciliation between unpaid interest coupons outstanding and funds deposited for payment of these coupons when there is satisfaction of the indenture. This satisfaction of the indenture may occur upon the calling of the bonds or upon maturity of the securities. How many other reconciliations, if any, are made is peculiar to the particular paying agent. Very few paying agents follow the practice of conducting a periodic reconciliation, although this forestalls the accounts' getting out of line for too long a period without being noticed. A reconciliation is made by determining from the cremation records what coupons are outstanding. These, when multiplied by the interest rate, should equal the amount in the account.

Unclaimed interest payments. In case there are unclaimed checks for the payment of interest on registered bonds, the paying agent attempts to contact the payees in the same manner as the dividend disbursing agent attempts to contact lost payees of dividend checks. The payment of interest on registered bonds is very similar to the payment of a dividend to holders of stock so that it is possible to attempt the location of the payee. However, it is quite different in the case of interest payments made to holders of bearer bonds. If the holder of a bearer bond does not send his coupon to the paying agent, it is almost impossible to get in touch with him because the agent, in many cases, does not have any record of the holders of bearer bonds. When the company requests a list of holders of bearer bonds, the paying agent makes a survey for this purpose. The list becomes inaccurate very quickly because the holder of a bearer bond might sell his bond at any time and there would be no record of the transaction. The purpose of a bearer bond is to facilitate its delivery. Consequently, few, if any, paying agents make an attempt to contact the holders of bearer bonds if the coupons have not been presented for interest payments. The paying agent holds the funds that have been deposited by the corporation for interest payments. In certain cases some of these funds are held indefinitely. In others, as provided by law, the funds are transferred after a certain period to the state, and in still other cases, the paying agent returns the funds to the corporation after a reasonable period, upon receipt of a letter of indemnification, or as provided in the indenture.

ALLIED SERVICES OFFERED BY FISCAL AGENTS

Allied services. The preceding discussion shows that the corporation may employ the services of an independent agency for stock and bond issuance and transfer, dividend payments, and interest payments. The agency used may also offer the following services.

Proxy mailing. As owners of the company, stockholders have the right to elect directors and vote on certain matters. The voting takes place at the annual meeting of stockholders, or it may happen at special meetings of stockholders. In most cases it is inconvenient for stockholders to travel great distances to attend meetings so they are afforded the privilege of casting their vote by proxy. The corporate agent addresses the proxy and mails it, along with the proxy statement, to the stockholder for execution. When the proxies are returned, the agent tabulates them. During the first few days that proxies are received by the agent, the corporation is usually notified by a form notice every third day. This notice states the number of proxies received, the shares represented and the number and percentage of shares voted for each side of the question. During the last ten days before the day of final voting, the agent notifies the corporation of the results each day, and during the last three or four days the corporation keeps in close contact by telephone with the agent to receive, in some cases, the tabulation every two to three hours. If there is a proxy solicitation agent working for the corporation, the paying agent must also keep this organization posted. In a few cases the agent handles the proxy solicitation for the corporation, but most agents prefer not to do the solicitation of proxies. They would rather work in conjunction with the proxy solicitation agent to send out follow-up proxies, it is necessary for him to keep up to date a duplicate proxy file so that the follow-up can be sent out with accuracy upon short notice.

Mailing annual reports. It is customary for the company to send an annual report to stockholders, usually prior to the annual meeting. The corporate agent addresses the envelopes, inserts the annual report and any other enclosures, and mails them. Among the other enclosures may be a proxy and proxy statement.

Annual meeting lists. A list is prepared of the stockholders and the number of shares owned by each so that the officers and directors of the company may know who is legally entitled to vote at the meeting. This list is required by statute, in many states, to be kept at the office where the meeting is to be held.

Preparing federal and state reports. The United States Treasury Department requires that it be supplied with the name and address of each stockholder who was paid $10 or more in dividends during the calendar year, on form 1099 D.I.V. This form is sent to the Treasury Department, which in turn forwards it to the office where the stockholder files his income tax return.

Some states require that their Tax Departments be advised of the stock holdings of residents or the amount that the residents were paid in dividends. The dividends paid to non-resident aliens are subject to withholding tax and this must be paid to the Treasury Department. The corporate agent files the required federal and state reports.

13

Procedures Concepts and Techniques

CONTENTS

13

Procedures Concepts and Techniques

CONCEPTS

Management's need for procedural control. Newest of the specialized responsibilities of management to emerge as a separate staff entity is the procedural control function. This activity, by definition, deals with the means whereby the work performed in administrative operations is done well and economically.

Because they are a prime instrument to carry out managerial policy, uniform procedures and their effectiveness throughout the organization are of specific interest to management. In earlier days the value of procedural manuals and related controls of forms, reports, and office equipment was thought to be confined to the lower organization levels. When the use of these instruments of communication became general, it was found that they were also providing a new control device for the higher levels. Management thus had available to it a type of information with which it could more readily evaluate people and their performance and the extent of conformity to policy. Similarly, comparison of like offices in the field became more realistic since manuals had established procedural common denominators for purposes of sound measurement.

Staff relationship of procedures function. A desirable climate for the systems function is one in which it has no authority to enforce its proposals upon the line organization. Where authority is used, resistance on the part of the beneficiaries can nullify the effect of the improvements installed. On the other hand, if the methods group possesses advisory responsibility only, recommendations are more acceptable to those they affect, and the validity of the proposals is viewed in a more impartial light. Moreover, the use of a "team approach" adds even more acceptability to suggested improvements. By the team approach is meant direct participation in the analysis by the office under study. The project then becomes a joint undertaking and the operating know-how is made available to the analysts. The response to "outside interference" is also held to a minimum. At the same time staff and line relationships are preserved. This concept will be further developed under "Organizing the Procedures Function."

Changing role of procedures activity. When the procedures development function has been active over an extended period of years, it usually evolves through three stages. In phase one, it is primarily engaged in assignments of a "brush fire" nature. Its projects at this time are unrelated and have as their aim quelling systems problems after they have become acute. In phase two, more coherence is given to what is done. Projects are related to one another through the planning of broad-brush programs devised to anticipate procedural weak spots before they break down. This approach is an organized, systematic plan covering the foreseeable future. Phase two usually results in the completion in manual form of basic administrative controls relating to organization, procedures, records, reports, and office equipment. When these essentials are consistently used throughout the organization, the procedures function is ready to pursue phase three. In this stage the methods group conducts its operations in about the same way as a firm of management consultants. Upon request of other departments in the company, their significant problems are analyzed and solutions provided for installation by the offices requesting help, rather than by the procedures organization. This becomes practical if enough key employees have been trained through participation in phase two projects so that they have a working knowledge of procedural techniques. The consulting approach, furthermore, permits ample time for the systems group to initiate other projects of major significance and of company-wide importance.

ORGANIZING THE PROCEDURES FUNCTION

Responsibility for procedures. The development, operation, and maintenance of procedures is a basic responsibility of all levels of business management. Supervisors and department executives are responsible for developing procedures necessary for the efficient conduct of their operations. General management executives are responsible for broad procedures that cut across several areas of the company.

Operating, financial, and accounting executives frequently need assistance on procedure problems. In many companies, the heads of large departments have administrative or staff assistants to handle procedures and other business management functions.

Final responsibility for procedures rests upon the chief executive officer of the business, since he is responsible for the over-all coordination and administration of the enterprise. The top official is seldom in a position to carry out this function personally since (1) the development of procedures is a specialized function requiring analysis, fact-finding, discussion, and follow-up; and (2) the chief executive does not have the time or the specialized training needed to devote to this problem. As a result, the assignment of responsibility for developing and coordinating a procedure program varies considerably from company to company, the controller's office being the most common location.

Two instances where the procedural authority lies outside the controller's jurisdiction follow.

A leading steel company describes the assignment of the responsibility for procedures as follows:

> The General Management of the parent company will be responsible for establishing all the broad, general policies of the consolidated enterprise. The heads of the several divisions and departments located at the home office of the parent company shall be responsible for writing all General Management Standard Practice Instructions.
> The Operating Division or Subsidiary Company Management shall be responsible for writing all Operating Division or Subsidiary Company Standard Practice Instructions. However, such SPI's are to be approved, prior to publication, by the individual in the home office of the parent company to whom that operating division or subsidiary company reports.

The authority for standard procedures in a textile company is assigned as follows:

The office of General Manager is responsible for all Standard Procedures. This responsibility includes the preparation and issue of all original procedures; the consideration, preparation and issue of all amendments to procedures; and the approval of all standard forms.

The actual work of writing the procedures is delegated by the General Manager to members of the organization who are best informed on the details involved. Originally procedures and amendments will bear the approval of the General Manager before they are distributed.

Where thought has been given to centering responsibility for procedures, arrangements such as the following are often found.

1. A procedures staff assists the general management executives.
2. A top management planning staff is established.

Use of central procedures staff. Many companies employ a staff of one or more procedures specialists to assist the general management executives in the development and coordination of procedures programs and activities. The following is a statement issued by the Koppers Company, Inc. defining the functions of the Central Procedures Staff:

PROCEDURE AND SYSTEM TECHNICIAN

BASIC FUNCTION:

Study of existing procedures and methods within the company and the modification or elimination of those which do not provide satisfactory operation, or which are inefficient or cause conflict of purpose.

The development of new procedures for the functioning of any division, department, section, committee, or any unit thereof.

The design of procedures to facilitate interdepartment and interdivisional relations, and the standardization of procedures of like nature to promote efficiency and control.

Preparation and publication of a Procedures Manual for the company and the constant review and revision thereof.

SCOPE:

Responsibility is delegated to this position for procedures and methods affecting any unit of the organization. Primary attention will be given to those which govern the relation of staff departments and sections with operating divisions or with each other. However, the development of methods of intradivision or intradepartment operations is an additional responsibility.

DUTIES AND RESPONSIBILITIES:

1. Development of procedures to cover all of the company's varied operations, provide efficient and readily understandable standards for particular functions, and govern interdepartment and interdivision activities.

2. Assistance and advice to all units of the organization in their problems of procedures and methods.

3. Surveys and analyses of forms and reports originating in any unit of the organization, for use within the unit or transmission to other units, for the purpose of standardizing, improving, or eliminating as may appear desirable.

4. Cooperation with Organization Technician, Control Section, in the establishment and definition of channels of information and authority.

To whom procedures staff is responsible. No common pattern exists as to where the procedures staff should be located in the organization. If this function is assigned to the controller, he should guard against an undue emphasis on the accounting and financial aspects and on details and paperwork. He would also make a special effort to develop broad administrative procedures, and to give adequate recognition to the human aspects of operating problems.

The treasurer is also assigned this activity in several companies, particularly in financial enterprises and in firms where the treasurer is responsible for all financial activities including those of the controller. Both the treasurer and the controller may supervise large numbers of personnel, such as accounting, payroll, budget, auditing, and credit and collections. For this reason, the procedures program is frequently assigned to a top executive who is independent of any of the main operations.

The office manager is often responsible for procedures coordination in companies where office work predominates, such as insurance and governmental agencies. In firms where procedures deal mainly with production or factory problems, the over-all responsibility is frequently assigned to the industrial engineering department. In financial enterprises, the treasurer or the secretary may coordinate this activity. The experience of many companies has been that one desirable location is in an independent group reporting to the top operating official such as the president, executive vice-president, or general manager.

Management planning staffs. A growing development among more progressive companies is the creation of top management planning staffs, designated by such titles as Management Control, Administration Planning, Organization Planning, and so on. Leaders in the petroleum, aircraft, motor, and chemical industries now have such units, and the number has increased substantially since World War II. The basic plan was developed in the early 1930's as a cost reduction device. This idea, modified to some extent by introduction of a "control" concept, was extended with considerable success by the armed services during World War II.

The purpose of the management planning unit is to provide staff assistance to top management on problems of policy, organization, procedures, planning, progress reporting, and other phases of administrative management. The scope of management planning activities is shown in the organization chart (Figure 13-1), from the Organization Manual of the Koppers Company, Inc.

Personnel requirements for central procedures staff. There are no hard and fast rules to determine the number of people needed to staff the central procedures group. Among the variables are (1) the size and complexity of the company, (2) the scope and nature of the procedures problem, (3) the degree to which operating personnel are made responsible for the development of procedures, and (4) the amount of change and development in the business.

Generally, a small central staff is preferable. Among the weaknesses of a large staff are (1) the tendency of operating executives to forfeit their responsibility for procedures to a staff of specialists, (2) the publication of a large number of procedures on relatively unimportant subjects, (3) the tendency for procedures to include excessive detail, and (4) a large overhead cost that is difficult to justify.

Companies that are considering a procedures program should proceed cautiously.

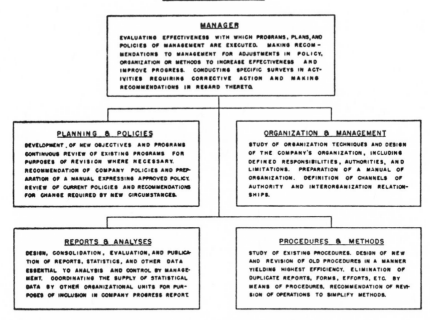

[*Actual size 8½" by 11"*]

Figure 13-1. Functions of a Management Planning Unit.

A small initial staff will, of necessity, concentrate on the more important problems requiring study. If these problems can be solved, the program itself will be more readily accepted and welcomed. This is an important asset because there is frequently resistance to any new staff activity on the part of older departments of the business. As the staff gains experience, it will be in a better position to appraise the size of the job and determine the personnel needs.

One approach which has worked well in some companies consists of enlisting participation of operating management. The procedures staff can concentrate on developing, coordinating, and guiding the over-all program and can delegate the actual preparation of individual procedures to departmental officials and their assistants. Among the advantages of this approach are that, since the operating people have first-hand information, they can produce much faster than staff people, and will have a proprietary interest in seeing that the final procedure is workable and that it is fully tested and put into operations. Difficulties to be avoided are that the operating personnel may be too close to the problem to analyze it objectively, vested interest and a desire to avoid disrupting the current operation may produce a partial solution, and lack of experience outside of the department may limit the viewpoint and scope of the analysis. The central staff should provide the general supervision and guidance to overcome these and and other difficulties.

Qualifications for central procedures staff. Procedures analysts should possess traits that may later qualify them for executive positions. As a general rule, procedures men have not been selected with this in mind, and too much emphasis has been placed on experience in only accounting, engineering or office work. As a result, men with a few years' experience in this field become "procedures specialists." Thus, they lose one of their most valuable assets as future managers—a broad business imagination and outlook.

The techniques for analysis and development of procedures can be learned by experience. It is more important for the candidate to have imagination, broad experience, inventiveness, analytical sense, ability to write, good judgment, and a cost consciousness. Underlying all these must be ability to get along with people at all levels in the organization, since the procedure must be "sold" at all stages of its development.

Experience in the main operating departments of the business is desirable. The more diversified the analyst's background, the easier it will be for him to visualize all the aspects of a procedures problem. Experience in financial or industrial engineering departments is also most appropriate. Educational training in business management and administration at broader levels is desirable but not essential.

Many large companies use the procedures department as a training ground for future executives. This activity brings a man in contact with all phases of the business and, with proper guidance and development, should provide him with a broader perspective and knowledge of the relationships between the various parts of the concern. Where this plan has been followed, the procedures "graduates" have proved to be a promising source of managerial talent. Two approaches have been used: (1) starting young new men in the procedures department, later transferring them to operating or other staff jobs; and (2) transferring experienced junior executives into the procedures department for a few years of broadening and diversification, and then assigning them to higher-level managerial jobs.

TECHNIQUES OF ANALYSIS AND DEVELOPMENT

What are procedures? Procedures, often referred to as systems, routines, standard practices, and methods, describe how the company's operations are conducted. Like product specifications, they define standards for operation and performance. Thus, there are procedures for the hiring of an employee, the loading of a truck, the addition of a new product to the line, and the like. Procedures are of two main types: (1) administrative, and (2) operating.

Administrative procedures. Administrative procedures are general instructions dealing with matters of policy, organization, and coordination. They explain how policies are to be applied and carried out and clarify organization assignments and relationships affecting several areas of the company. They are of primary interest to the management level and do not contain much detail or routine.

Subjects that might be covered by administrative procedures include (1) the financial, sales, and production aspects of inventories, (2) the research and production relationships in developing a new product, and (3) the cooperation between manufacturing and industrial engineering in setting production standards. The following is an example of an administrative procedure.

OPERATING EXPENSE BUDGETS

1. Area heads prepare budget estimates and submit them through regular chan-nels to the controller who reviews and consolidates the estimates into a proposed budget.

2. The treasurer examines the proposed budget and submits it with recommenda-tions to the management committee.

3. The management committee approves or disapproves all budgets.

4. The administrative vice-president notifies area heads of their approved budgets, with copies to the controller and the treasurer.

5. Area heads are responsible for operating within their approved budgets. The controller reports periodically to area heads on their actual performance against budgets. Special reports may also be made to the management committee.

Operating procedures. Operating procedures supplement administrative proce-dures and other general material by describing the specific steps involved in carrying out company activities and operations. Several operating procedures may stem from one broad procedure or policy. They may affect several areas of the company, such as the employment procedure; or they may be limited to one area, such as the billing entry procedure. Since they contain more of the "how," they are often longer and more detailed than administrative procedures and may refer to forms, reports, and other paper work. Operating procedures might be written on such subjects as the preparing of payrolls, the handling of cash, or the processing of orders. They range from interdivi-sional procedures to individual job instructions and may be used to define both office and plant operations.

The following excerpt from instructions on the ordering and control of printed forms illustrates a detailed operating procedure.

3. Stationery Stores, upon receipt of the sample copy or draft of the form and accompanying "Form Request Check Sheet," will:
    a.   Stamp or write date of receipt upon both form and "Check Sheet."
    b.   Review form inventory to determine:
        (1) Whether substitute form now on hand can be used;
        (2) Whether, if form is to be reprinted, present stock is exhausted. Also check past actual consumption with estimated monthly con-sumption in order to determine whether quantity requested is in-adequate, excessive, or correct. As a general rule, not less than 6 months' nor more than 12 months' supply of any form or other printed stationery item should be ordered at any given time.

Coordination of procedures. Since both administrative and operating procedures are related, they should be coordinated for best results. Administrative procedures set the broad pattern and should be written before detailed procedures are worked out. This plan is not always followed, and the result has been a bulky collection of detailed procedures that are difficult to use and understand because they have not been keyed to an over-all procedure. In many companies, administrative procedures have been neg-lected entirely.

The tie-in between procedures and policy, organization, and practices makes it difficult to distinguish between them. This distinction must be defined, however, for the proper planning and coordination of the procedures program.

A policy is a general rule indicating a line of conduct or course of action that will be taken under established circumstances. Policy statements are sometimes issued separately, but more frequently they are included in other company publications such as the employee handbook. Procedures implement policies by stating how they will be carried out. A company might have a policy to pay wages comparable to other industries in the area. The method of arriving at specific wage levels might be defined in a procedure.

Organizational planning includes the assignment of responsibility and authority to areas and personnel. These assignments are often included in function statements, management guides, organization charts, and job descriptions, and assembled in an organization manual. The responsibilities and authorities may need to be further clarified, particularly when relationships and coordination between several areas of the company are involved. Procedures provide this clarification and also the mechanics necessary for putting these assignments into operation.

Practices are operating procedures that have not been put into written form. Most practices do not need to be written since they are clearly understood and followed. Procedures are needed for practices that are complicated, that create special problems, or that offer opportunities for cost control or other benefits by being studied and put into writing.

Why procedures are needed. Procedures are a guide to approved methods of operation. They are the means by which the activities of the various departments are coordinated, the practices are analyzed, simplified, and standardized, and the personnel is kept informed. Companies that have developed standard procedures indicate that they produce lower costs, increased efficiency, better control, and a record of the forward progress of the business.

One company indicates that it issues procedures for the following reasons: "to insure that all divisions, departments, and subsidiary companies shall have a common understanding and interpretation of management policies and procedures and will carry out such policies and procedures in a uniform manner."

Some specific advantages of standard procedures are:

1. The clarification of company policies, organization, and practices.
2. The elimination of unnecessary operations and costs. In preparing a procedure, each step and operation is analyzed, and any overlapping, duplication, obsolete steps, and inefficiency are eliminated. Attention is focused on needed improvements that might otherwise go unnoticed.
3. The defining of the "best way" for getting something done. This reduces the need for snap judgment, trusting to memory, and oral instruction. Every step can be carefully thought out before it is written down. After the procedure is issued, there is less tendency for it to become cumbersome and costly as a result of personnel turnover and increase in size and complexity of the company.
4. The establishment of management and cost controls. Written procedures insure that essential steps will be taken, that work is done in proper sequence and coordination, that waste is avoided, and that assets are properly protected.

5. Assistance in personnel supervision. Procedures help in training new employees, transferring personnel between departments, standardizing and measuring employee productivity, delegating details to subordinates, and preserving valuable information held by veteran employee.

The value of written procedures is indicated in the following "Foreword" to a Procedures Manual issued by the Walt Disney studios:

> The accompanying Procedures Manual is meant to be a guide book to help us conduct the day-to-day business of the studio. Many of the rules have been in effect for years, but this is the first time an attempt has been made to collect them and put them into convenient written form.
>
> The manual is compiled by the Secretary's Office under the direction of the Management Committee. The objective is to have a set of procedures which will enable us all to do a better job with a minimum of inconvenience and red tape. To aid in attaining this goal, a tentative draft of each procedure is submitted to department managers and other supervisory employees for suggestions and criticisms. All such suggestions and criticisms are carefully studied and, if in line with over-all policy, they are incorporated in the final writing.
>
> The Management Committee seeks your whole-hearted cooperation in complying with these procedures as all of us are expected to adhere to them. However, if at any time you have a question regarding the intent of any procedure please call the Secretary's Office for information and interpretation.

Steps in arriving at a procedure. The study of any procedure involves a basic pattern. The individual problem may require greater emphasis on one step than another and will determine the amount of detail to be studied. An office procedure may call for analysis of forms, paper work, and machine operations. An administrative procedure may merely require a broad survey of interdepartmental relationships and coordination. In both cases, however, the basic steps are similar. They are:

1. Defining the problem and planning the study after securing background information.
2. Reviewing and analyzing existing practices.
3. Developing and testing the new procedure.
4. Preparing, publishing, and issuing the written instructions.
5. Installing the procedure.
6. Following-up, maintaining, and revising the procedure.

Obviously, these steps may often be combined. They are discussed below in their usual sequences to provide a guide or check-list for the analysis of any procedure.

Planning the project. The problem may originate from several sources such as a change in policy or organization, a bottleneck in the flow of work, a large number of complaints, conflicts between departments, and requests for assistance from operating executives. Three steps comprise the planning of the project.

1. *Purpose and scope of the problem.* Before starting the study, the nature of the problem and the purpose and scope of the study are defined. The study should be limited to the immediate problem in order to meet deadlines and to prevent a haphazard approach. It is helpful to visualize what the end-product will look like, who will use it, and how much detail is needed. A procedure for use by management executives should

obviously be more general than one for use by warehouse employees. Time deadlines for various phases of the study are set, allowing sufficient time for the final clearances and installation. Finally, the departments and individuals concerned with the problem are determined, and plans are made for securing their advice, assistance, and cooperation.

2. *Background information.* Necessary background information is obtained. Related material, such as policies, organization statements, procedures, reports, and memoranda, is reviewed. This information may clarify the problem and the areas concerned. The problem is discussed with the people concerned in order to obtain their ideas as to the background, approach, and needed improvements.

3. *Groundwork preparation.* The necessary groundwork is laid for the study. The executives and employees involved are informed of the study and the expected benefits and should be encouraged to participate. Frequently, department representatives are designated to assist and to provide information, ideas, and criticism.

Analyzing existing practice. After the preliminary planning, the present method of operation is studied and discussed with everyone involved. Actual work operations are examined to secure firsthand knowledge. The history and development of the present practice are reviewed. Finally, each step in the operation is critically examined to determine that it is essential. During the entire process, valuable ideas for improving the procedure occur to the analyst and the operating personnel and are recorded for later investigation. These analytical steps are:

1. *Getting acquainted.* It is desirable to spend some time in getting acquainted with the employees and executives conducting the operation since they will be the main source of information and ideas. Organization charts are studied to discover the areas and people who need to be contacted. The study is discussed with the various executives concerned. An extensive study involving contacts with many employees may need to be formally announced. Particular care should be taken to be frank with the operating personnel in discussing the purpose of the study and in soliciting ideas and suggestions.

2. *Fact-finding.* Present operations are examined and recorded. This may necessitate following, in proper sequence, the processing of work through the various stages. The analyst may perform some of the work to obtain a true picture of problems encountered. Work sheets are prepared showing the flow and volume of work. The familiar *what? who? how?* and *why?* questions should be applied to every phase of the work.

Specimen forms may be collected and work in process is examined. Records, files, and desk collections of documents are studied. Facts that seem of no value to the operating employee should be examined for possible significance.

3. *Recording the existing procedure.* During the fact-finding stage, the present procedure is recorded, preferably in chart form. This is again checked for completeness and accuracy with the people involved. The latter will often see new facts or errors when the entire procedure is presented to them. This also tests the analyst by determining whether the operating employees can understand what he has written. Along with the present procedure, significant work volume figures may be compiled for later analysis in determining possible economies or simplifications.

4. *Analyzing the existing procedure.* Analysis is required throughout the entire

study. At this stage, however, the facts that have been collected are carefully studied in order to detect changes that will produce improvements. If the procedure contains detailed steps, a procedure flow chart is prepared showing the present method. This "before chart" will help to highlight bottlenecks and other areas of possible improvement. The flow chart is a picture of the procedure in chart form to permit easier analysis and streamlining. An example of a simplified type of flow chart is provided in Figure 13-2. Usually, the procedure can be condensed considerably, and complicated and unnecessary steps can be detected through the analysis of the flow chart and related material.

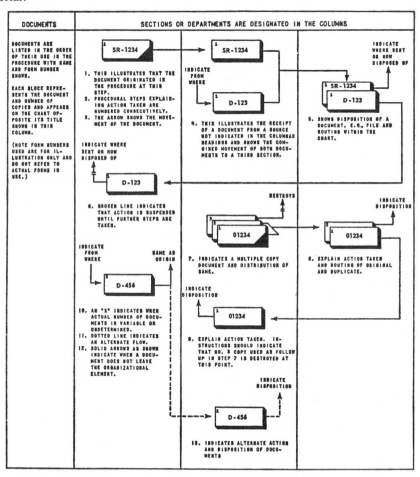

Figure 13-2. Chart Showing How to Prepare Flow Charts for Procedures.

Each step and operation is carefully scrutinized as to its essentiality. Cumbersome operations are simplified. Copies of reports, forms, and other papers may be eliminated. Numerous approvals and clearances may indicate needless duplication. Delegation of authority and decentralization of action may be needed. Backtracking of work can often be eliminated by introduction of a direct and continuous work flow.

The temptation to become involved in detailed improvements at the expense of more significant changes should be guarded against. The analyst may overemphasize the individual steps because of his limited experience with the entire problem or because of his analytical training. He must remove himself from the detail and view the board operation. One major improvement will benefit over-all profits more than many minor improvements. The analyst's ultimate value to the company depends on the number of larger improvements he can discover and work out.

Throughout the analysis, possible simplifications are discussed with people involved. "Ivory-tower" analysis often produces impractical ideas. If discussed at an early stage, they can be built up and perfected through the cooperation and experience of the operating personnel. The latter may also be stimulated and encouraged to suggest additional changes that would not occur to the analyst. Detailed changes are discussed with the lower level employees, and summarized later for discussion with executives. Changes of major importance are discussed only with the top executives.

5. *Analyzing forms.* This step is usually required in the study of administrative procedures since office procedures are built around the movement of a form or other paper work. The form is studied for possible improvements, and the value of the form itself is appraised. The preparation time is determined, and the need for each item is weighed. Redesign of the form may permit savings through elimination of items, fewer copies, easier preparation, standardization of layout, addition of more pertinent information, and consolidation or elimination of the form itself. If a form is not used at present, the design and introduction of a new form may help to standardize and simplify the operation.

6. *Summarizing existing practice and ideas for improvement.* Before developing a new procedure, it may be helpful to prepare a summary of the present procedure and the ideas and conclusions reached for improving it. If extensive change is contemplated, this may be discussed in a general way with the executives who will later decide whether or not to accept the changes. This preliminary discussion paves the way for later specific recommendations, and brings to light other developments that should be covered by the new procedure.

A procedure is often required where none previously existed, such as when a new department or function is established or a drastic change is made in operating methods. In such instances, the foregoing steps are consolidated or eliminated entirely, and the development of the new procedure is started immediately.

Developing and testing the new procedure. Based upon the facts and conclusions reached during the analysis, the new procedure is developed, cleared, and tested. At this point, the procedure is still tentative and subject to clarification and is prepared in rough form.

An "after" flow chart may be prepared where it is necessary. (See Figure 13-2.) This helps to visualize the changes being made and to sell the new plan to operating and executive personnel. Any new forms that are needed are also drafted.

The proposed procedure is then reviewed with executives whose approval must be secured. During these discussions, it is emphasized that the proposal is subject to change and refinement. Clearances are easier to obtain if the officials know that they are not approving a final product.

Rough copies of the procedure and any necessary charts are then reproduced for testing. Arrangements for the time, place, and duration of the test must be specific. The extent of the test will depend upon the nature of the procedure, the change involved, and similar factors.

An efficient ''paper'' procedure may have adverse effects on operations, and significant steps may have been overlooked. Testing also reveals further improvements made possible by the new practice.

The areas selected for testing should provide a fair appraisal of the procedure without requiring excessive costs or disturbance of operations. Responsibility for the testing should be clearly assigned to one person, such as the procedure analyst or the operating supervisor in charge of the activity affected. The person selected should be openminded and flexible enough to accept and work out suggestions for improvement.

All personnel directly concerned are notified of the date of the test, the changes to be made, materials or facilities needed, and other pertinent information. Departments indirectly affected are also notified to the extent required. Everyone is encouraged to offer suggestions based upon their experience during the test.

If several departments are affected, the test supervisor may call a meeting of key personnel in order to explain the final plans and to agree upon a definite time table. When the test begins, the supervisor personally directs the various phases but does not become too engrossed in the routine since his time will be needed to iron out bottlenecks and unforeseen problems. He observes all phases of the operation, alert for emergencies, and acts promptly to take any necessary corrective steps.

The procedure is constantly reviewed during the test, and possible simplifications are worked out. Major improvements are often possible at this stage. Suggestions are solicited from operating people. Last-minute revisions are adopted and tried out. The procedure is then ready for final preparation and issuance.

Preparing the procedure instructions. Although new procedures can be installed without written instructions, there are advantages in putting the new procedure into writing. The amount of written material needed depends largely on the specific procedure. A new administrative procedure may be described in a single broad statement. An operating procedure affecting several departments may require several detailed statements and instructions.

Several styles of procedure presentation are available. No single method is predominantly used, and advantages are claimed for each of the types. The most commonly used methods are:

1. *Narrative method.* The procedure is described in narrative style, as an informal office memorandum or instruction. Among the advantages claimed are its informality and ease of writing and understanding. This method, which is used both for broad and detailed procedures, is illustrated in the following excerpt from the ''Sales Girl's Routine'' issued by the H. L. Green Company, Inc.

> After 11:00 a.m. and throughout the lunch hours, your entire afternoon is given to waiting on customers. At your assigned lunch period, check out at designated place and if you so wish, you can obtain purse, etc. Returning from lunch, check in and leave purse, etc. at proper place. After returning to work, check the counter, filling merchandise in the bins, where necessary, from the reserve stock in the understock.

While filling in the counter, you will have with you a "stock requisition" form, upon which you will note all items that are running low in the understock. This will be turned over to the floor men. The afternoon, until an hour before closing, will be entirely devoted to waiting on customers. An hour before closing, your "requisition" will be filled and merchandise delivered to you, which must be neatly and correctly put away in the understock.

2. *Outline method.* The procedure is presented in an outline form with major and minor headings and subheadings. This method permits a more compact presentation and provides a uniform pattern for the layout and appearance of all procedures, but is simetimes felt to be too formal and difficult to understand. The following section, from a procecure for the processing of special promotional orders, illustrates this method.

Originating Department
1. Prepares PROMOTIONAL MATERIAL ORDER, showing:
    a.   Name of originating department and account to be charged.
    b.   Appropriate classification:
            (1) Chemicals,
            (2) Displays, printed matter, etc.
    c.   Total number of orders in shipment.
2. Prepares address label for each consignee.
3. Approves PROMOTIONAL MATERIAL ORDER with authorized signature in full.
4. Sends PROMOTIONAL MATERIAL ORDER to Order Department. (Shipments of more than one item to the same consignee will be grouped so that one register number can be assigned to the entire shipment.)
5. Arranges for delivery of displays, printed matter, etc. to Shipping Department along with registered PROMOTIONAL MATERIAL ORDER.

3. *Chart method.* Several charting methods are used to portray procedures. The flow chart, illustrated in Figure 13-2, is a commonly used method. Its advantage is in considering a large amount of detail in a small space and in tracing the routine of forms and paper work.

4. *Combination methods.* Several combination methods are used. The narrative and outline forms are often combined with the chart form. This permits a standardized format for all procedures.

After selecting the method of presentation, the procedure is prepared in final form for issuance, and final approvals are obtained. Preliminary approvals may have been secured during the development and testing phases. Final approval is obtained from the line executive responsible for all of the operations affected. In the case of procedures affecting several departments, approval of the general manager, the executive vice-president, or a similar coordinating official may be needed.

Publishing and issuing the procedure—formal and informal methods. Methods of publication vary, but in general they divide into formal or informal methods. The informal method, whereby the procedure is issued as a memorandum, is common in smaller companies and in those having a new or partially developed procedures program. This method has advantages in that operating employee resistance to the program may be minimized, and the issuance problem is open to experimentation before a final pattern is settled upon.

The more general practice, however, is a formal method of publication. This may involve a standard manual or format for all procedures, control over distribution of copies, a system for assigning identifying numbers or letters to each procedure and its subdivisions, a uniform type of presentation, and other practices. Among the advantages of a formal system are the following: *(a)* procedures are easily recognized and are filed in a single place, *(b)* on official format may lend authority to the document, *(c)* the procedures are easier to refer to and use, *(d)* the recipient knows whether he has a complete set of procedures, and *(e)* the problem of distribution and revision is simplified.

Procedure manuals. The procedure or standard practice manual is a formal method for the issuance of procedures. Several types exist. Some companies use a single manual for all company procedures. This may prove too bulky as the number of procedures increases. Generally, a series of manuals is issued, each tailored to the needs of selected departments or employees.

The departmental manuals vary from department to department. They may include selected material from the general manual, but mainly procedures in which the department plays a part, as well as detailed intradepartmental procedures.

The procedures for these manuals are prepared in several areas in the company, but are forwarded to a central unit for editing and publishing. This provides over-all coordination and control over the format, distribution, and presentation, and centralizes responsibility for the maintenance of the entire series of manuals in a single individual or a single department.

Authority to issue. The authority to issue the procedure should be clearly established. Since procedures are orders to employees, responsibility for issuance rests upon the line executive who has direct responsibility for all of the activities affected by the procedure. The procedures staff is not the issuing authority since it is a staff and service group with no authority over the operating departments. Its function is limited to the mechanics of publication after the procedure has been approved by the proper line executives who are responsible for the distribution of the material.

Transmittal memorandum. The formal procedure itself is often sent out with an accompanying transmittal memorandum, which may contain essential data on the background of the subject, the major points covered and information of temporary interest. The following transmittal memorandum was issued by an aircraft manufacturer:

> The attached procedure, governing the request, approval, and completion of every type of personnel action, is authorized. It does away with many previous practices, and greatly simplifies paper work and record-keeping.
> All supervisory personnel should study this new procedure carefully, as it differs in many ways from former methods.
> The following major points require your immediate attention and cooperation:
>
> 1. All personnel changes must conform with the established maximum quotas of indirect employees for each department.
> 2. The type of personnel requests that can be initiated by supervisory employees of various levels are established and only these authorized persons may place a request with the industrial relations department.
> 3. All changes affecting supervisory job classifications are to be cleared for necessity by the job classification division with the office of the divisional manager.
> 4. The job classification division shall be notified by responsible supervision

of every personnel transfer from job to job within the department, or
between departments, and any change in method, equipment or conditions
of existing jobs, which may require a change in job classification.

5.   A temporary personnel transfer or loan must not exceed a two-week period.

Introduction explaining procedure manual. The following introduction to a
procedure manual, issued by a nationally known chemical company, touches various
phases of publishing and issuing the procedure manual and is reproduced here for that
reason. The numeration scheme explained in this introduction is adaptable to any
procedure manual that includes departmental manuals.

PURPOSE AND CONTENTS OF THE MANUAL

The principal purpose of this manual is to bring together in one place for ready
reference the various rules and regulations, plans and policies, and general practices of
the Company. It also contains certain miscellaneous data and information which is
frequently used in the conduct of the Company's business.

Only such items as are of a general Company nature or are used or referred to by
several persons or groups of persons are included.

The general contents of the manual are covered in the Table of General Contents
in the front of the binder. The detailed contents of each part or section of the manual
are covered in the Table of Contents for that particular part which is inserted at the
beginning of each part.

ADMINISTRATION OF THE MANUAL

The industrial relations division of the service department has general responsibility for, and will have charge of, the administration of the manual. This division will
issue all copies of the manual and all changes or addition thereto, to the interested
persons keeping such records of same as are necessary and in general act as a clearing
house for all matters pertaining to the manual.

NUMBERING SYSTEM FOR PAGES OF THE MANUAL

The manual is first divided into 50 parts, each part being reserved for some one
broad subject or phase of the Company's business. Parts 1-10 inclusive are reserved for
general Company subjects such as organization, general policies and rules, etc. Parts
11-20 inclusive are reserved for other general department functions such as legal,
purchasing, traffic, etc. Parts 21-50 inclusive are reserved for service functions such as
personnel, industrial relations, safety, etc.

Each part is divided into 99 sections, each section covering a group of subjects or
items coming under the general subject of the part in question. For example, under the
part covering general industrial relations, we find sections devoted to continuity of
service, miscellaneous policies, etc.

Each section is further subdivided into 99 items, each item covering some particular phase or subject of the section and part in question. Each item is covered on a
separate page or group of pages which are numbered in the upper left-hand corner with
the item number. The items under each section are numbered consecutively as are the
sections under each part. The last two figures of any item number denote its consecutive number in the section and the first one or two numbers denote the consecutive
section number in the part.

DISTRIBUTION OF COPIES OF THE MANUAL

Special Fabrikoid binders marked SERVICE MANUAL have been issued and will
continue to be issued in the future to such persons as have charge of, or are required to
function in regard to, the various parts covered by the manual. These will be supplied
with index sheets and tabs to separate the various parts. The industrial relations
division of the service department will keep a record of the holders of these binders and
each person is responsible for the care of his binder and manual sheets and should

notify the service department any time it is transferred to another person because of organization changes.

Distributing, reproducing, and issuing the procedure. The method of distribution and number of copies required will depend, among other things, upon whether the entire procedure or selected portions are distributed to all recipients. The uniform distribution is easier to manage and maintain, but the recipient may receive much material in which he has no interest. There is a danger in distribution systems becoming too complicated and difficult to maintain.

The method of reproduction will depend largely upon the number of copies needed and the plan used in the publication of procedures. The easiest method when only a few copies are needed is the typewriter, but most procedures require more copies than can be made on a typewriter. The most common method appears to be mimeographing, which provides clear copies, of fairly permanent type, at a reasonable cost. As many as 5,000 clear copies can be reproduced if proper quality stencils and paper are used.

A less formal and permanent type is the Ditto process, but fewer copies are possible, and the material is not as easy to read. Other more expensive methods are available if more copies or a more professional appearance is desired. These include multilith, multigraph, and printing. The merits of these methods are discussed in material published by duplicating machine houses. The reproduction should be done within the company if possible in order to provide needed flexibility and speed in making last-minute changes, securing extra copies, and so on. Reproduction of charts and specimen forms may raise special problems requiring outside assistance.

All text and illustrations should be finally checked and a clear copy should be used for reproduction. The analyst should discuss with the printer any problems of layout and arrangement and should be available to advise on other problems that may arise.

The issuance and distribution should be carefully scheduled and planned. Before the copies are released, arrangements should be made for the timing of the installation, and agreement should be reached regarding the initial operation. The effective date and any other special instructions should be contained in the procedure itself or in an accompanying memorandum.

Installing the procedure. Minor changes and simplifications are installed at various stages of the study. This can often be done without disrupting operations, and the benefits can be realized at once. New procedures and those containing drastic changes often need to be installed at one time. In such cases the installation must be carefully planned and executed. The steps to be taken include:

1. *Assigning responsibility for the installation.* In general, the operating executive directs the installation, with guidance and assistance from the analyst.
2. *Scheduling the installation.* An installation time table is developed and given to everyone concerned, after consulting with key personnel.
3. *Preparing necessary instructions.* In addition to the procedure itself, written instructions and orders to operating personnel are often necessary and are prepared for issuance by the proper line executives.
4. *Directing the installation.* Constant supervision over the installation and

operation is needed in the early stages. Problems arise and call for prompt solution since employees need guidance and instruction.

5. *Periodic checking of the operation.* The analyst gradually removes himself from the picture but periodically reviews the effectiveness of the operation.

Although the procedure may be operating satisfactorily, supplementary instructions may be needed. Operating supervisors are encouraged and stimulated to develop these. The analyst advises in the preparation of supplementary instructions and reviews them before issuance to ensure that they conform to the over-all procedure.

If the new procedure involves major improvements, it may be desirable to complete the project by preparing a summary for all interested operating and management executives. This report may indicate the action and changes taken, the benefits resulting, the progress to date, and recommendations of future action.

Maintaining and revising the procedure. Procedures must be promptly and constantly revised to reflect changes in method of operation. The method of revision may be included in the "procedure for procedures," in the introduction to the procedure manual, or in some other document that is readily available.

There is a continuing need for follow-up and auditing of procedures. The operating executives are primarily responsible for complying with established procedures. A regular independent review is necessary to check compliance and to initiate revisions where necessary.

The periodic review may be assigned to one of several areas. The controller often has this function, the actual work being done by his internal auditing staff. Less frequently, this task is given to the procedures staff, or the job evaluation group. In addition to the narrow question of compliance, the auditor must consider proper corrective action, whether it be revision of the procedure, change in operating methods, clarification of underlying organization or policy matters, the re-assignment of personnel, or other steps which will achieve the ultimate purpose of procedures—to assist and facilitate the natural course of operations.

Summary. In analyzing and developing any procedure, the main objective is simplicity and clarity. This in turn will promote efficient, economical, and smooth operation. These are goals of vital concern to the controller and the treasurer, and whether or not these officials are responsible for the procedures program, they should see that the objectives are kept constantly in view and are being fulfilled.

In order to develop procedures that meet this purpose, a simple approach must be followed. As indicated earlier, many of the steps enumerated above can be combined or eliminated entirely in the study of specific problems. A constant effort must be made to avoid becoming bogged down in the details. The routine operations of a business have a way of going on from day to day without constant guidance. Minor inefficiencies may creep in from time to time, but they do not usually add up to major problems. The ironing out of these small and scattered weaknesses must be delegated to all levels of supervision. They may need to be stimulated and guided in this work, but an organized program of work simplification can produce substantial results in a short time. Improvements are often possible without the need for written procedures.

The areas affording the greatest opportunities for procedure improvement are the broad problems of interdepartmental relationships, coordination, and administration.

These problems are often beyond the scope of the operating executive and require objective and independent study. The problems are broad and often nebulous and cannot be properly visualized and clarified without being put into writing. Because they are indefinite and may involve conflicts between top executives, they are allowed to continue and a firm decision is often delayed. The danger of such a practice is that these difficulties, though seemingly unimportant in themselves, may have chain reactions that filter out to many areas of the company. The cumulative cost may be substantial.

The procedure program should concentrate on these broad problems. Clarification of a single one may have more lasting benefit than many minor improvements in routine. The analysis must be searching and on a broad and fairly high level. The resulting procedure should likewise be of the type that will interest and help the top level of management. After the problem is ironed out, several operating procedures may need to be restudied and revised. The operating levels of management should be encouraged to do this phase of the job, and the central procedures staff can be most effective in stimulating, guiding, and coordinating this work. Before the operating procedures are issued, the central staff should review them to be certain that they conform to the intent and substance of the over-all procedure.

PLAN FOR DEVELOPING BUSINESS ELECTRONICS PROGRAM

Procedure analysis techniques used. With the advent of electronic office equipment, it has been confirmed that problem identification and analysis and machine programming are well within the field of methods work. Many companies have recognized that systems analysts may be quickly adapted to solving the problems involved in setting up a data processing center for business applications. Opinion is divided, however, as to the economices of the applications, but the worth of the machines for many scientific and engineering problems is unchallenged.

For the methods analyst to develop an electronic data processing program for conversion of manual or punched card procedures to computers, he will resort to fundamental techniques similar to those previously described. This will be noted in the following plan for action which any company, regardless of size, can put into effect with relatively little cost. This plan provides a sound basis for management to judge to what extent, if any, electronic computing machines properly fit into company operations.

Phases of the plan. The plan consists of six phases. They are (1) establishing clear-cut goals for the program, (2) organizing properly so that the objectives may be achieved readily, (3) gathering the pertinent facts bearing on the subject (4) developing electronic applications for immediate or future actions, (5) testing the applications for immediate or future actions, (5) testing the applications, and (6) installing new equipment and procedures if the situation warrants. No one of the six phases carries a greater import than any other.

Conducting the program. Starting with *phase 1*, the goals of the program, or essentially what management wants to know, the first determination is whether or not the company should buy or rent electronic computing equipment. Second, if it should, which machine or system should be selected. And, third, once the equipment has been chosen, what plan should be followed for its use. These are three basic objectives.

Once the goals are set, the *second phase* of the program is to determine who is to be responsible for carrying it out. Of primary importance is the assignment of a full-time coordinator, either the procedures director or one of his staff.

The *fact-gathering phase* is broken down into four areas of research: (1) the concept of electronic data processing and the techniques that are used; (2) the equipment itself and what it will and will not do; (3) proven and planned applications of other companies; and (4) procedures and computations that the company itself believes might be better accomplished electronically.

The coordinator will wish to familiarize himself with the growing body of not too technical literature in the field; he also has available to him a variety of semi-technical courses of brief duration which some of the manufacturers of equipment provide for this purpose. At the same time, he will be covering the second area of interest from which he will learn the attributes and limitations of equipment on the market and on the drawing board as well. From this information there should evolve an inventory of the various items of equipment and their significant characteristics, such as slow, medium, fast, and specialized, depending upon the speed and other characteristics of the several components. Close contact should be maintained with the manufacturers of equipment.

After this information has been gathered, it is time to turn to the experience of other companies in all industries who have obtained experience in this field. In many cases, it will be found that these concerns have followed a similar over-all program. This research will cover the pertinent details of all other companies' applications from which can be started the preparation of recommendations for management consideration.

The final step in the fact-gathering phase is the preparation of a descriptive listing of all major paper work procedures performed throughout the company, the present method of handling, volume of transactions and costs. From this listing it should be evident in what areas electronics will prove beneficial. If the procedures are being handled on a manual or punched card basis and are proven unwieldy and costly, consideration of an electronic data processing system is warranted.

Upon completion of these aspects of fact finding, the *fourth, or development, phase* begins. How long after the start of the program this point will arrive depends to a large extent upon the variety of company activities which must be reviewed. If the study is to be thorough, the fact finding should not be rushed. Conversely, the development of conclusions should not be too difficult in the light of the completeness of the facts that are at hand at this time. It may be that the costs alone of changing systems will at once indicate that now is not the appropriate moment to switch from manual to electronic methods. If this is the situation, the program can be called off. Should the reverse situation be true, and should costs and other pertinent consideration point up appreciable savings or operational improvements by the use of electronics, the selected applications may then be adopted for electronic processing with the appropriate equipment.

Even if the equipment chosen is a machine to be used as a component part of a punched card unit, there will still be necessary appreciable programming time to obtain the desired results. If the situation indicates the use of the larger type electronic data processing system, then the programming (or translation of the process into machine "language") of the particular application to fit the chosen system can become a sizeable job. Because of the technical requirements of programming, the company that lacks procedure manuals or comparable detailed instructions covering the present way things are done will find it hard to convert to electronic data processing systems. Each step in a procedure, both arithmetical and clerical must be set down in logical sequence and coded to fit the computer's operation. This can run into thousands of program steps. The time and costs involved in the initial programming of procedures for electronic data processing equipment are usually high. After the initial programs are prepared and recorded in permanent form, however, operations can be performed repeatedly by the equipment with little or no human intervention, and therein lies the great advantage of electronic data processing.

The *last two phases* of the program for action, testing and installation, are self-explanatory. Applications selected for the electronic equipment should be thoroughly tested to work out the "bugs" prior to installation. The change-over should be made with care lest a last minute slip-up condemn the new method.

Although business applications may not by themselves economically justify one or more computers, if technical applications have already done so, accounting and clerical procedures may be absorbed by available machine time. Under these conditions some economic justification is added as well as is improvement in nontechnical data processing.

SUMMARY

Concepts. Improved and uniform procedures constitute a significant control for management by permitting more accurate evaluation of the performance of the various organizational groups and the extent of conformance to established major policies.

Organization. As a staff function, using the team approach with representatives of the affected offices, the procedures activity should report to a senior management level for best results.

Techniques. Analysis and developing procedures in a systematic way require pre-planning and carrying out the following steps: (1) Define the problem and plan the study after securing background information; (2) review and analyze existing practices; (3) develop and test the new procedure; (4) prepare, publish and issue the written instructions; (5) install the procedure; (6) follow up, maintain and revise the procedure.

Electronics. The procedures organization is the logical group to plan the adaptation of existing procedures to electronic machines. By using techniques with which they are already familiar, methods analysts can readily develop information which management needs to decide the extent to which it would undertake an electronic program for business applications.

14

Setting Up and Maintaining

Inventory Control Records

CONTENTS

14

Setting Up and Maintaining Inventory Control Records

INVENTORY CONTROL PLANNING

Definitions. The setting up and maintaining of inventory control records is of interest to all businesses that own a stock of goods intended, eventually, for sale. It is of special importance to companies that purchase raw materials, process them into finished goods, and hold these goods for sale in the ordinary course of trade.

In a statement of the American Institute of Certified Public Accountants the following definition of inventory is given:

> The term "inventory" . . . designate[s] the aggregate of those items of tangible personal property which (1) are held for sale in the ordinary course of business, (2) are in the process of production for sale, or (3) are to be currently consumed in the production of goods or services to be available for sale.[1]

In this chapter, the terms "physical inventory" and "perpetual inventory" will appear. *Physical inventory* represents the actual count and valuation in money of tangible personal property held for sale or processing in production of goods or services for sale. The practices in taking physical inventory and the methods of valuing the inventory are described in the following chapter. *Perpetual inventory* is actually a misnomer since it merely refers to a method of keeping a continuing record of an inventory of tangible personal property. This record supplies accurate internal control of the receipts, disbursements, and current balance of the goods or property. It originates with, or from, a physical inventory.

In addition to the above inventory terms, there are various types of inventories with which one should be familiar.

Raw materials inventory represents tangible personal property, held for processing or production, on which no productive labor has been used to change it from the original form in which it was acquired by a manufacturer.

Work-in-process inventory represents materials partially changed from their original form by the application of labor or machine process, but not yet finally converted into a manufactured article ready for sale.

---

[1]Committee on Accounting Procedure, American Institute of Certified Public Accountants, *Accounting Research Bulletin* No. 29, p. 235.

Finished product inventory represents completed goods or merchandise ready for sale.

Supplies inventory refers to materials or supplies (other than those classed as raw materials) required to operate the business and keep it in a safe and efficient condition.

Consigned stock inventory represents materials or merchandise transferred from a manufacturer or consignor to a consignee, agent, or factor for sale. The title to the material or merchandise remains with the manufacturer or consignor until paid for and therefore should be reflected in his inventory.

Branch warehouse inventory represents materials or merchandise owned or controlled by the manufacturer but housed at a branch or distribution point.

In transit items, when included in inventory, represent material that has left a supplier's place of business, just prior to an inventory "cut off" date, but has not arrived at destination prior to inventory taking. They enter into inventory even though the materials will not actually be received until after inventory has been taken, because title has passed, or because the invoice has been prepaid to earn a cash discount or for some other reason.

Goods in a bonded warehouse are inventories. Materials that are stored in a bonded warehouse generally represent items on which a customs duty, tax, or levy is due and has not been paid. Release of the material cannot be obtained until the amount due on the materials to be withdrawn has been paid to the government. Ownership and inventory of the materials is generally reflected by a properly signed warehouse receipt.

All types of inventories are susceptible to inventory control. That term implies that management has established an inventory policy and limits within which the inventory is to be kept; it means that methods and devices have been created, which, if properly maintained, give warning to prevent inventory from going below or above certain minimum and maximum quantities, and that accurate records are kept from which data may be accumulated to show actual conditions and trends.

Need for inventory control. The average organization can be divided into three main divisions: (1) financial, (2) production, and (3) sales. In each of these divisions there is need for inventory information and control.

Financial interest. The directors and other financial executives are concerned with the dollar value of the inventory because it represents a vital part of the working capital of a company. Excessive inventories place a heavy drain on a company's cash resources. Management therefore is interested in keeping total inventories at a minimum consistent with serving the needs of customers. In an uncertain cycle, when prices are falling, excessive inventories can mean heavy losses. In a rising market, a shortage of inventory can mean losses due to high replacement costs, especially where merchandise has been sold on the basis of previous material prices. Obsolescence, style changes, changes in production methods, or changes in method of doing business can also result in very heavy inventory losses to a company that does not have complete control of its inventories.

Complete inventory control enables management to decide the policy to be followed when the need for borrowing arises, particularly as to the amount and the length of time during which the loan will be required.

Banks scrutinize inventory figures particularly from the standpoint of valuation and marketability of the asset. A company with a large inventory that does not have a ready sale, regardless of how inviting the price may be cannot expect as favorable a loan as another company with an inventory that could be sold readily in an emergency. This statement, of course, does not infer that a bank bases its judgment in the making of a loan primarily upon the value of a company's inventory. Other factors, such as total net quick assets, profit history, integrity of the management, and the like are considered by a bank in making loans.

Production interest. Production executives are always concerned with the amount of materials and supplies on hand, to assure continuous output. For economical scheduling of operations and to be sure of having the right material for the right job, they must know the inventory situation at any time.

Sales interest. Sales executives are vitally concerned with finished goods inventories and scheduled production in order to plan and carry out their sales strategy and to avoid slow-moving stock.

All of these divisions are interested in having neither too much nor too little inventory on hand. Inventory control, with its limits as to minimum and maximum quantities, is designed to satisfy the needs of the three divisions.

Survey to show type of inventory control records needed. The installation of a system of controlling inventory should never be approached in a haphazard fashion. To become an important management tool in the hands of the people who will use the figures most, the inventory control system must be carefully thought out and planned. This process entails making a survey of the needs of the business. The survey should have in mind the objective of providing all the information, with a minimum of clerical effort and paper work, necessary to guide the responsible executives and to safeguard the business.

In a manufacturing establishment, the inventory would be divided into three chief groups: (1) raw materials; (2) work in process; and (3) finished goods. In this type of business, aside from top management, the purchasing director or agent is the person for whom inventory information is primarily required. The records must establish guides for him as to turnover, quantity of material consumed within a given period of time, the length of time required for transportation and delivery of replacement material and supplies, and other data. The records help him carry out his function of seeing that material and supplies are on hand when needed for protection. After materials have been procured, their flow through the production processes must be carefully followed by means of inventory controls.

In a merchandising, wholesaling, or jobbing business, the merchandise handled is finished goods. Therefore all the detail mentioned for a manufacturing establishment is not required, although the objectives of the records are the same. In the merchandising business, inventory turnover is very important; the method of control must be built around this factor.

Top management's principal use of inventory controls is in seeing that a minimum cash investment is required. This again means watching turnover. Top management is also interested in seeing that inventories are protected against losses through theft and the like.

As a guide in determining management policies, the inventory must be correctly stated because of the effect it has upon the financial statements. A final inventory that is understated through improper pricing or count will result in an understatement of the net earnings and may even result in showing a loss on operations for the period. An overstated or inflated final inventory will result in an overstatement of the net earnings for the period of operations and may result in showing net profits when, in fact, the company has operated at a loss.

The survey should also disclose the need for current and timely reports. In a merchandising business, it is of little value to ascertain in late spring or early summer that there is still a quantity of winter overcoats on hand. Similarly, in a manufacturing organization it may be disastrous to discover too late that dead parts or obsolete items are "eating up" a lot of working capital.

RECORDS NEEDED FOR INVENTORY CONTROL

Responsibilities and flow of materials. In the flow cycle of materials each of the following six major steps affects inventory control.

1. The issuance of a purchase order to a vendor.
2. Delivery of the materials by the vendor to the receiving department.
3. Inspection and count of the materials.
4. Delivery to a storeroom or warehouse.
5. Issuance to a productive department.
6. Delivery from productive department to finished stores.

Each of these steps must be under the direct supervision of a responsible individual within the organization.

Types of records needed for controls. As materials flow through the six steps, six essential records are required for minimum inventory control. In addition, five supplementary records are required to keep the system operating smoothly. The essential records include:

1. *Purchase requisition.* This record authorizes the purchasing department to purchase indicated materials.
2. *Purchase order.* This is a formal notice to a vendor to ship the merchandise listed on the order.
3. *Receiving report.* This report records the receipt of material ordered.
4. *Stores or stock ledger.* In this ledger a record is kept of materials and supplies on hand, generally by quantities.
5. *Stores requisition.* This is a request by a production department for materials or supplies.
6. *Perpetual inventory record.* This record contains all pertinent data as to quantity and value of the purchase, receipt, disbursement, and balance on hand of material and supplies.

The supplementary records include:

1. *Change notice of purchase requisition.* Through this record the purchasing department is notified of changes in the original requisition.
2. *Change notice of purchase order.* This is a formal notice to a vendor of changes in the original purchase order.

3. *Purchase order shipping release*. This record supplies a vendor with a schedule showing required shipping dates.
4. *Material returned to stores*. The use of this record is obvious from the title.
5. *Report of obsolete or slow-moving items*. This record helps minimize inventory losses.

Each of the above records is discussed below in the order in which they come into use.

Location of inventory control records. The accounting department should be the focal point of inventory control records, because of the important part they play in the preparation of financial statements and operating reports.

It is advisable that the stock ledger described below, be kept in the storeroom. The storeroom then becomes a central source of all information as to inventory quantities, regardless of where they may be located. In organizations where substorerooms are maintained at various points throughout the plant, it is advisable that each substoreroom keep a stock ledger for its own materials. In this way definite responsibilities can be placed for the accuracy of the count and record of material.

The purchase requisition. The purchase requisition generally originates in the storeroom. In that case, it is made out by the stock clerk and approved by the supervisor. Or it may come direct to the purchasing department from a production supervisor.

The requisition form should contain the following minimum data:

Number (the forms should be prenumbered).
Date.
Person addressed (purchasing agent or person arranging purchase).
Quantity.
Description of material.
Where material is to be delivered.
How to be shipped.
Date material needed.
Authorized signature.
Approval.

The number of copies to be made is a matter of organizational policy. For all practical purposes, only two copies are necessary, an original and duplicate. The original goes to the purchasing department as authority to purchase and the duplicate remains in the storeroom or other originating point for filing and recording purposes.

The quantity should be expressed on the requisition in common terms of usage of the material. For example, if production processes specify pounds, then pounds should be requisitioned, not boxes or barrels. The correct expression of quantity terms is important for inventory control purposes. Equally important is the correct description of the materials required. Uniformity and proper nomenclature prevent costly misunderstanding.

Some companies insist that separate purchase requisitions be issued for direct materials used in production and for indirect materials or supplies used for maintenance and the like. There is considerable merit in this plan, for it reduces to a minimum the possibility of overlooking the ordering of an item on a requisition because the two classes of materials are ordered from different vendors. Others go to the extreme of listing only one item on a requisition, for the same reason, but this is not ordinarily advisable.

Change notice of purchase requisition. After a purchase requisition has been issued, it may be found necessary to change the quantity, type of material, or other essential data. These changes should never be made verbally. A written form, as illustrated in Figure 14-1, definitely places the responsibilities for changes made in the original requisition. The change notice is made out in as many copies as the original purchase requisition and distributed in the same way. When it is received by the purchasing agent, it is fastened to the original requisition.

CHANGE NOTICE OF PURCHASE REQUISITION

A-Y AND Z MANUFACTURING CO.

TO
PURCHASING AGENT

C.N. NO ____________
DATE ____________

REFER TO THE FOLLOWING PURCHASE REQUISITION NOW IN YOUR FILE:

REQ. NO.: ____________ DATE: ____________

AND CHANGE THE FOLLOWING INFORMATION:

TO READ:

____
SIGNED

[*Actual size 8½" by 7"*]

Figure 14-1. Change Notice of Purchase Requisition.

Purchase order. The authority for the issuance of a purchase order is the purchase requisition.

The style and size of purchase order forms will vary with each company, but the following data should be included on all such forms:

Number (the forms should be prenumbered.
Purchase requisition number.
Date.
Destination and route.
Price and terms.

Name and address of vendor.
Quantity.
Description of material.
Signature.

The purchase order may include certain clauses setting forth the conditions of purchase. Thus, there may be clauses relating to invoice instructions, acknowledgment, changes in terms of purchase by the seller, special package markings, charges for packing and cartage, routing and shipping, the right to cancellation, quality and quantity, rejected material, inspection, price change, payment, compliance with state and federal laws, and other conditions.

In a medium-sized organization that operates under a budget system, at least six copies are necessary. Each should be on a different colored paper and should indicate its destination. The copies are distributed as follows:

1. Vendor
2. Purchasing department file copy.
3. Accounting department.
4. Budget department.
5. Receiving department.
6. Storeroom.

On copies five and six it may be advisable to leave blank, or "black out" the price and quantity of the materials. This is done to make certain that the receiving and stores clerks actually count the material received.

The practice of sending two copies of the purchase order to the vendor is becoming common. The extra copy is signed and returned to the purchaser. It thus acts as an acknowledgment and acceptance of the terms and conditions of the order.

Change notice of purchase order. Figure 14-2 is a companion to the "change notice of purchase requisition," Figure 14-1. It is made out in as many copies as the original purchase order. In view of possible legal entanglements with vendors, as well as added charges, it is very important that all changes be as specific as possible to avoid misunderstandings and that they be specific in writing.

When the notice of change of purchase order has been made out and copies routed to the proper parties for filing and reference purposes, a copy is attached to the original order that it changes.

Make-and-hold or blanket orders. This type of order is used when a manufacturer orders material that is to be delivered over a period of months. It gives the manufacturer the advantage of a quantity price and the vendor the opportunity of taking advantage of idle machine time to produce the merchandise. When the merchandise is required, a notice or shipping release is sent to the vendor, showing the actual dates and quantity of the material that should be shipped.

Receiving report. The receiving report should contain the following essential data:

Number (the forms should be prenumbered).
Purchase order number, related to material received.

```
┌──────────────────────────────────────────────────────────────┐
│                                                                │
│              A-Y AND Z  MANUFACTURING CO.                      │
│                                                                │
├──────────────────────────────────────────────────────────────┤
│                          IMPORTANT                             │
│                 CHANGE NOTICE OF PURCHASE ORDER                │
├──────────────────────────────────────────────────────────────┤
│  TO: _____        DATE _____       │
│      _____                                  │
│                                                                │
├──────────────────────────────────────────────────────────────┤
│  PLEASE REFER TO THE FOLLOWING PURCHASE ORDER:                 │
│       ORDER NO. _____      DATE _____       │
│                                                                │
│  AND REVISE THE FOLLOWING:                                     │
│                                                                │
│                                                                │
│                                                                │
│                                                                │
│  TO READ:                                                      │
│                                                                │
│                                                                │
│                                                                │
│                                            _____  │
│                                            PURCHASING  AGENT   │
└──────────────────────────────────────────────────────────────┘
```

[*Actual size 8½" by 7"*]

Figure 14-2. Change Notice of Purchase Order.

Date.
From whom merchandise was received.
Via (method of shipment) (car number if by rail).
Transportation charges prepaid, or if collect, the amount paid.
Description of material (to agree with purchase order) and count.
Where delivered for storage.
Signature.

The number of copies to be made of this report will depend on the company's requirements. The minimum, however, is three, to be distributed as follows:

1. Purchasing department.
2. Accounting department.
3. Receiving department, to be attached to the copy of the purchase order covering the material.

Stores or stock ledger. The types or style of stores ledger form to be used depends on such factors as management policy, type of accounting machine available, and where the records are to be maintained. The primary purpose of the ledger is to indicate the inventory status of any given article at any time.

Three types of stores ledger are in general use.

1. *Book.* This is generally a loose-leaf or visible binder record.
2. *Filing card.* The size is usually 5″ x 8″ and may be designed for a vertical tray, desk tray, visible drawer, or wheel-type holder.
3. *Ledger sheet.* The size will vary in different organizations, but the style is similar to the record that is used for machine posting of accounts receivable. This form differs from previous two types in that the posting operation is done by an accounting machine.

Another method of storekeeping used principally by large companies makes use of punched cards and a tabulating machine. This method calls for a manually written card, a part of which may be preprinted as to subject matter, which is given to a key-punch operator. Following a designated code, the operator perforates the card in the proper places. The cards are then placed in a printer and tabulator, which makes the computations and prints the information on a specially ruled sheet.

Regardless of the type of record sheet, space for the following minimum data should be provided in the heading or top section of the record:

Name of item.
Description, size or stock number.
Storage location.
Minimum stock quantity.
Maximum stock quantity.

The section of the record should be divided into the following three main sections:

1. Ordered, subdivided into:
   Date.
   Purchase order number.
   Quantity ordered.
2. Received, subdivided into:
   Date.
   Receiving slip number.
   Quantity received.
3. Disbursed, subdivided into:
   Date.
   Stores requisition number.
   Quantity issued.
   Balance on hand.

Stores requisition. The authority to make out a stores requisition is generally limited to production supervisors or department heads. In some organizations the form originates in the production control or planning department. The essential data required on a stores requisition is as follows:

Number.
Date.

Person addressed (specific storekeeper, etc.)
Quantity.
Stock or part number.
Description of article.
Unit price.
Amount.
Signature.

In addition, space can be provided for such information as:

Charge to job number.
Charge to department.
Entered in stock control legder, and other similar data that would be required in the accounting system.

The stores requisition is generally made out in duplicate or triplicate. If made in duplicate, one copy remains on file in the originating department and the other is delivered to the storekeeper and then to the accounting department. If made in triplicate, the storekeeper retains his copy and a separate one is sent to the accounting department.

Material returned to stores. This form is essential for proper inventory control, as it identifies the material that is returned to stock and gives the proper department or account credit for the return. No material should be received in the storeroom without an accompanying report of some kind.

Although the form has a printed heading, it is a simple receipt to notify the storekeeper which department should receive credit for the material. (See Figure 14-3.)

RETURNED GOODS

FROM DEPT NO. ____________ DATE ________
REASON:

QUANTITY	STOCK NO.	DESCRIPTION	PRICE	AMOUNT

DISPOSITION

STOREKEEPER ____________ DEPT HEAD ____________

[*Actual size 5½" by 8½"*]

Figure 14-3. Material Returned to Stores.

Perpetual inventory record. This form is designed to show inventory amounts and values on hand at any time, without the need of physical inventory. It follows along the general lines of the stock ledger card but carries more detail and also money values. The amount of detail that is recorded on the perpetual inventory record is decided by the needs of operating executives as well as the size of the organization. The average perpetual inventory record carries the following data in the upper section of the card:

Name of item.
Description, size, or stock number.
Storage location.
Minimum stock quantity.
Maximum stock quantity.

The lower section of the record is generally divided into the following three main sections:

1. Ordered, subdivided into:
    Date.
    Purchase order number.
    Quantity ordered.
2. Received, subdivided into:
    Date.
    Receiving slip number.
    Quantity received.
    Unit price.
    Total value.
3. Disbursed, subdivided into:
    Date.
    Stores requisition number.
    Quantity issued.
    Balance on hand.

Report on obsolete or slow-moving items. This report does not enter directly into any system of control of inventories. However, it is tied in with management's purpose in maintaining proper inventory control. The chief purpose of the form is to call management's attention to inventory that is not moving and that requires executive attention to reduce the idle working capital represented in the items.

A report of this type must be designed to meet the particular company's needs. The form might provide space for the following basic data:

Heading.
Date.
Description of material, size, stock number, etc.
What used for.
Quantity on hand.
Unit cost.

Value.
Date of last issue and amount.
Last date placed in stock.

The number of copies depends on organization requirements. Copies may be routed to the sales manager, purchasing agent, production manager, and the company's top executive in charge of inventories.

INVENTORY CONTROL PROCEDURES

The departments concerned. From the description of the forms in the preceding section, it is obvious that procedures involving their use and disposition must be developed in the following four departments:

1. Purchasing.
2. Receiving.
3. Storeroom.
4. Accounting.

The inventory control function of each of these departments is described below.

Purchasing department. To plan properly the inventory control procedure in the purchasing department it is necessary to be familiar with the organization of the department. In many large companies, purchasing is broken down and the purchase of a limited number of items is assigned to individuals who become specialists in those items. This plan results in developing numerous sources of supply, which may make it easier to buy at the right price. A purchasing agent, whether a specialist or not, must have a thorough knowledge of the use to which the materials he purchases will be put. He must be able to weigh the price of an article against the quality for very often a lower price means inferior merchandise and frequent breakdowns in production operations.

Organizations with numerous plants find definite advantages in centralizing their purchasing. Some of these advantages are:

1. Responsibility for all purchases is definitely fixed, and there is less confusion of authority.
2. Buying power is aggregated and lower prices can be obtained through quantity purchases. At the same time clerical cost is reduced.
3. Standardization of purchases is made easier and the variety of materials carried in stock is reduced to a minimum. This is one of the best means of effecting economies.
4. Better control of inventories is effected.

Because the purchasing department is closely associated with manufacturing operations, the scope of its activities and responsibilities should be clearly defined and understood within the organization.

Inventory control records in the purchasing department. Of the records described earlier, the following concern the purchasing department:

1. *The purchase requisition and change notice*. When these forms have served

their purpose, they are filed away in the purchasing department to be referred to when necessary.

2. *The purchase order and receiving report.* The copy of the purchase order retained by the purchasing department is first used as the posting medium to the purchase record maintained in the department. It is then placed in a tickler file under the vendor's name to be used for follow-up purposes. Copies of the receiving reports covering the order are first recorded in the purchase record and then filed with the copy of the order. When the vendor's invoice is received covering the entire order, the copies of the order and receiving report are withdrawn from the file, attached to the invoice, and sent to the accounting department for payment. If the invoice is only for a partial shipment, a notation of the date, amount of invoice, and quantity is made on the order. The invoice is marked "part shipment" and is sent with the receiving report to the accounting department for payment.

Receiving department. The receipt of all materials into a plant should be through one central point for effective inventory control and efficient management. Centralization of the receipt of materials does not mean that all materials must necessarily pass through one location. This is impractical in the case of carload shipments of stockpile items, such as coal, ore, wheat, and the like. It merely means that the paper work involved passes through one source, whether there are several receiving rooms or stations throughout a plant, or just one receiving location.

Location of receiving office. In the average plant the receiving department office is situated adjacent to the principal receiving platform, truck or rail. This affords the person in charge an opportunity to keep a watchful eye on all movements and merchandise received. When railroad box car unloading platforms are inside the building proper, the same precautions are not necessary. Each management must decide for itself the degree of precaution needed.

Floor space to be set aside for the receiving department need be only large enough to handle and route incoming merchandise. This will avoid accumulation of material within the area and will expedite the movement of material to the storeroom or designated point. It also reduces the opportunity for pilferage or theft. However, materials should never leave the receiving department until they have been checked as to proper weight or count and the complete information has been listed on the receiving report.

The receiving clerk in charge of this department must be instructed never to accept a vendor's packing list without checking. Too often, owing to negligence of a vendor's employees, shipments are short or in excess of the packing slip. The correct recording of the receipt of materials is one of the first steps in inventory control. However, a receiving clerk need not go to extremes to check the accuracy of materials received. He must be trained to test-check in order to save time. For example, if he test-checks a certain sized package and finds that it contains a certain count, he can be satisfied that the count in another package of the same size will be the same. He is then justified in assuming that the count shown on the packing slip is correct if the number of packages indicated have been received. A good receiving man will find many ways to test-check the accuracy of count or weight of materials received.

If the material is to be tested and inspected, a sample or notice is sent to the inspection department with all of the required data. The material is delivered to an inspecting point until approved. If no inspection is required, it is forwarded to the storeroom or direct to a consuming department.

Inventory records in the receiving department. The receiving department is concerned only with the receiving report. Its use and disposition have already been described.

Storeroom. Many organizations have two types of storerooms, one for raw materials and supplies and another for finished goods. Even though they handle different materials, their methods of operation are the same.

A storekeeper is in charge of the stockroom. He should be under the supervision of the purchasing agent or someone other than a production official. The reason for excluding a production person as the supervisor of the storekeeper is that production executives tend to provide too great a margin of safety in quantity of materials on hand in order to avoid any possible production delays. This practice not only ties up an excessive amount of working capital but may also impede style changes required to meet competition.

The storekeeper should be thoroughly familiar with all of the production processes and the parts and supplies used in the plant.

Location of storeroom. The storeroom should be located where it will provide a free and even flow of incoming and outgoing materials, and will be readily accessible to the production department. It should be designed to protect materials against deterioration, theft, and removal by unauthorized persons. In larger plants, it has been found economical to have subsidiary storerooms adjoining production centers in which a working supply of materials, obtained by requisition from the central storeroom when needed, is maintained. The records for controlling the inventory in the substorerooms are similar to those employed in controlling inventory in the central storeroom, as will be shown later.

Size and arrangement of storeroom. The size of an original storeroom is very difficult to establish because future expansion must be anticipated. Management must estimate the floor space required to store materials, on the basis of what it judges the volume will be. Once the floor space has been established and assigned, the arrangement of the storeroom can be planned.

The first point to be considered in designing and arranging the storeroom is the type of material to be stored. Bulky materials generally require no shelves and frequently may be stored in the open. Oil and other combustible materials must be stored in a fireproof building or in accordance with local ordinances. Other materials must be protected against dampness and deterioration. Aside from these considerations, the storeroom arrangement should provide ready access to all materials and a method of identifying their location. Related items should be grouped in one section. The heavier items should always be stored near the floor. Material should be so placed that "old stock" is used first and is not allowed to deteriorate. Space should be provided for assembling materials requisitioned so that they will be ready when needed. Some companies use the storeroom as an assembly department for preparing chemicals or other ingredients according to formula and prior to mixing. Provisions must be made for the prevention of theft of expensive items by having a section of the storeroom with self-locking and self-closing doors to which entry can be made only by use of a key kept by the proper personnel. The aisles should be lettered and the shelves numbered by a system that is consistent and easily identifiable.

The shelves can be partitioned off as required. The shelves above a certain height from the floor should be set back so that a counter or ledge is formed on which a person can stand to reach the upper shelves.

Storeroom equipment. Proper equipment in a storeroom is essential for economy in handling goods. Wood shelves and bins may be cheaper than steel in initial cost, but they are not as flexible as steel, nor as durable. Many companies store certain items in small movable bins or boxes that hold an ordering unit of a part. This arrangement saves labor in filling and assembling stock requisitions. Sliding ladders are useful in a storeroom, as are conveyor baskets or belts that work on a trolley arrangement. Pallets and lift trucks have become important items in materials handling. Many dollars can be saved if a company's raw materials or products lend themselves to pallet or skid handling and storing.

Ordering point. When the inventory of an article reaches a point where it requires replenishment, it is at the ''ordering point.'' In some companies, the storekeeper knows that he must re-order when a reserve supply, tied with a ribbon, or packaged and bagged, must be broken into to fill a requisition.

When material must be ordered, the stockman fills out the required number of copies of a purchase requisition, making sure that all of the information is properly indicated.

Minimum and maximum quantities. The ordering point is also known as the minimum inventory requirement. This quantity is arrived at by taking into consideration time for the vendor to manufacture, transportation, and a safety factor, based on production requirements. The maximum inventory quantity is sometimes based on storage space available, although the general practice is to use production requirements for a given period of time, such as three months. The minimum and maximum quantities cannot remain fixed but must be constantly checked and changed in accordance with production needs. This is a very important part of a storekeeper's functions.

Inventory records in the storeroom. The storeroom maintains the stock record. To keep this record up to date, the storeroom receives copies of the following records.

1. Purchase requisition.
2. Purchase order.
3. Receiving report.
4. Stores requisition.

It also makes a report on obsolete and slow-moving items. The operations involved in keeping its records are described below.

The stock record. The real function of a stores department is to have custody of materials and account for them. The stock record card is the medium used by the storekeeper to account for the materials given into his custody. A record card is maintained for each item in stock.

All items in the stockroom should be coded with a series of digits and letters if necessary, and catalogued with their proper or technical names. Nicknames or ''gimmick terms'' should not be used. The description of the material should include its metal or chemical content so that the interchangeability with other similar materials can be readily determined. The location should indicate the aisle, shelf, and bin number. The minimum (ordering point) and maximum stock quantities should be recorded.

Maintaining the stock record. As described earlier, the stock record consists of three sections. The procedure for entering the record is as follows.

Ordered section. The information for posting to the ordered section of the stock record card comes from the copy of the purchase order that is routed to the storeroom.

Received section. When materials are delivered to the storeroom from the receiving department with the receiving report, they are checked against the purchase requisition. The receipt of the material is posted to the stock record from the receiving report. If the shipment is complete, the requisition is taken from the active file and placed in a completed file. If only a partial shipment is received, the information as to date and quantity is written on the back of the requisition and this information is posted to the stock card. The requisition is then returned to the active file.

If no extra copy of the receiving report was made for the stockroom, the copy which the storeroom received with the material is sent to the accounting department after posting to the stock record.

When the production department returns materials to the stockroom, the material is accompanied by a form, (Figure 14-3). Receipts are posted on the stock record from this form. After posting, the form is sent to the accounting department.

Disbursed section. Materials are issued from the storeroom upon the authority of a stores requisition properly signed by an authorized person. When the material called for has been issued, the information is posted in the proper section of the stock card, and the remaining balance of materials is calculated and placed in the balance column. The stores requisition form is then sent to the accounting department.

The balance column is calculated each time a receipt or withdrawal is posted to the card. The balance should be checked at least twice a year by a physical inventory made by persons other than the stockroom personnel.

Finished goods storeroom. The finished goods storeroom is operated in the same way as a raw material storeroom. Management, however, places greater emphasis on the accuracy of the finished goods inventory. Important decisions—all based on inventory—are affected, such as style change determinations, new models, and selling price structure, if merchandise is not moving into consumer's hands.

The procedure for inventory control of finished goods differs slightly from materials and supplies in that when the minimum stock or ordering point is reached, a production order is issued to the proper scheduling, control, or production department to replenish the stock. In some organizations, the control of finished goods inventory and the placing of production orders is under the supervision of the sales department.

The in-and-out movement of finished merchandise is recorded on a stock card. The withdrawals from the stock are authorized by a shipping notice, designed to meet the organization's needs. A typical example is shown in Figure 14-4. Sometimes a copy of an invoice will be the authority for shipment.

Defective, spoiled, and obsolete materials. Regardless of how efficiently a company is operated and organized, there will be spoiled and obsolete materials. A proper organizational setup must be maintained to turn this expense factor into a profitable operation or at least to minimize its losses. Two general types of materials come under this heading, one resulting from manufacturing operations and the other from slow-moving finished goods.

Organizing for salvage. The salvage or disposition of spoiled or obsolete material should be assigned to one individual or a department. It is preferable that the

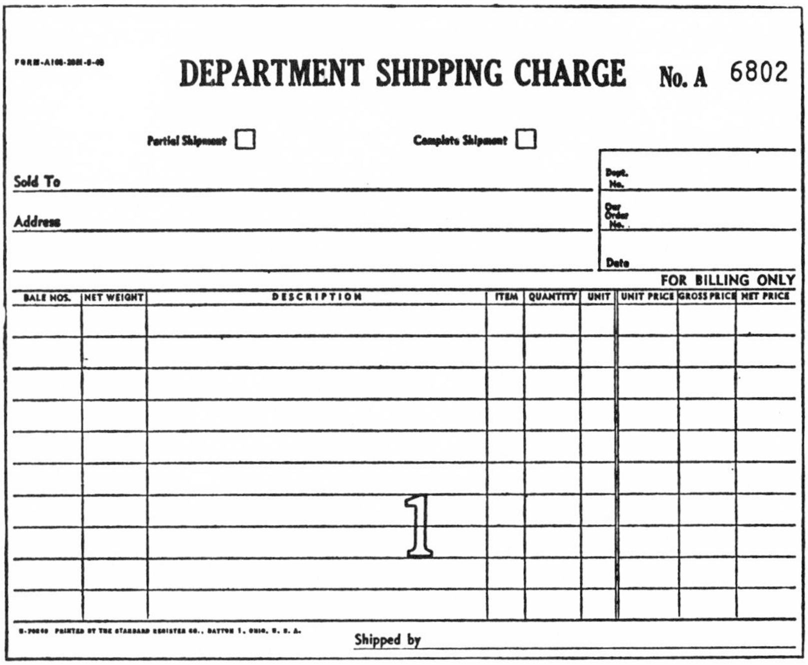

FORM-A108-20M-8-48

DEPARTMENT SHIPPING CHARGE No. A 6802

Partial Shipment ☐ Complete Shipment ☐

Sold To

Address

Dept. No.

Our Order No.

Date

FOR BILLING ONLY

BALE NOS.	NET WEIGHT	DESCRIPTION	ITEM	QUANTITY	UNIT	UNIT PRICE	GROSS PRICE	NET PRICE
		1						

PRINTED BY THE STANDARD REGISTER CO., DAYTON 1, OHIO, U. S. A.

Shipped by

[*Actual size 8½" by 6½"*]

Figure 14-4. Shipping Notice.

responsible individual or department not be under the jurisdiction of the production department because spoiled work is a reflection on efficient shop operation and production men may be inclined to overlook some items. It has been found advantageous to assign the responsibility for salvage and waste disposition to the storekeeper, under the jurisdiction of the purchasing department. The storekeeper, by training and experience, must be alert to see that he keeps the "dead" or slow-moving stock in his storeroom at a minimum. The purchasing department is generally in a better position than any other department to market and sell scrap and obsolete material. It has the knowledge of price trends and market conditions and has contacts with salesmen who can provide information as to possible outlets for the material.

Slow-moving finished goods. In many organizations, the disposition of slow-moving finished goods is placed in the hands of the sales department. The primary reason is that the merchandise must be disposed of in such a way that it will not compete with the company's regular product that is sold through regular channels. The method of merchandising slow-moving goods will depend in a large measure on company policy as well as on the type of merchandise that is to be disposed of.

Procedure for disposing of scrap and obsolete items. There are many ways in which an organization can increase its return from scrap and obsolete items. Care and proper classification of scrap pay big dividends through higher prices. Reconversion or reclaiming of by-products generally opens a new market or outlet for this material. One method that is practiced considerably is to circularize possible users, asking for bids on the material to be sold. Employee suggestions and awards of prizes frequently result in ideas for cutting down on scrap and for disposing of scrap and obsolete items.

To determine which are the slow-moving or obsolete items, the storeroom clerk reviews his inventory cards each month, listing the items that show no movement over a predetermined period. This period may be a week, a month, or several months, depending on the merchandise and organization policy. The items are listed on a report similar to the one described previously. The report is sent to the perpetual inventory clerk in the accounting department who checks the quantity with his card record and applies the unit cost and value. The report, when completed, goes to the top executive in charge of inventory for his approval and then to the purchasing or sales department to proceed with disposal in line with general company policy.

If the material is to be junked, the stock clerk is so notified and he immediately removes the merchandise from his storeroom to the "junk-pile." His authority for removal to the junk pile is his authority to credit his stock record for the removal of the merchandise from his jurisdiction.

Inventory control records in the accounting department. The accounting department maintains the perpetual inventory record. To keep this record up to date, the accounting department receives copies of the following records.

1. The purchase order and change notice.
2. The receiving report.
3. The stores requisition.
4. The material returned to stores.

Operation of the perpetual inventory record. The top section of the perpetual inventory record is identical with the stock record form. The information to be centered in this section is obtained from the storekeeper who supplies the data required for a new stock item with the receiving report that he sends to the accounting department.

In an original installation, a copy of the information supplied to the storekeeper for this section of his card is also supplied to the accounting department for the perpetual inventory record. Consequently, when new items are added to the inventory, the data referred to above is reported to the accounting department on a memorandum form that may be headed "New Item Added To Stock."

Ordered section. The data for the ordered section of the card are obtained from the copies of the purchase orders and change notices that are received by the accounting department. Each copy of the order is filed by vendor and is referred to for crediting and control purposes.

Received section. The data for this section come from two sources, the receiving report and vendor's invoice. The first three columns—date, receiving report number, and quantity—are posted from the copy of the receiving report. The report is then attached to the accounting department's copy of the purchase order to which it refers. The unit price and total value come from the vendor's invoice. The unit price should include freight or transportation charges, if any, required to bring the material to the plant. At the time that the unit price and value are posted, the clerk should check to see that the quantity on the invoice agrees with the amount reported received. Any discrepancies should be reported to the proper authorities immediately.

In some organizations, the data posted in the received section is obtained from a copy of the vendor's invoice. In such cases, the procedure is as follows: When an invoice for materials or supplies has been received and approved by the purchasing department, the invoice with a copy of the receiving report and a copy of the purchase order attached is sent either to the accounts payable or perpetual inventory section of the accounting department. It is usually preferable that the papers go first to the accounts payable section for vouchering or payment to avoid loss of discount and then to the perpetual inventory section. This method saves the necessity for an extra copy of the receiving report and an extra copy of the purchase order for the accounting department prior to the receipt of vendor's invoice. It also entails only one posting to the perpetual inventory record (and therefore only one handling of the card) to record the quantity, unit price, and value of the merchandise received.

Entry must be made for materials returned to stores. This information is obtained from the report of materials returned to stores that is forwarded from the storeroom.

Disbursed section. The information to be entered in the disbursed section is obtained from the copies of the stores requisitions that are sent to the accounting department by the stock record clerk.

The balance column is carried in quantities only in order to reduce clerical effort and detail. Some organizations show values for every disbursement as well as values for each balance quantity posted by having all stores requisitions priced and extended before posting to the perpetual inventory record. This is not essential because the dollar value of the quantity balance can be very rapidly determined whenever it is required. At the close of accounting periods, the value is calculated and shown in the balance column in colored pencil. This method saves considerable clerical effort.

If the company maintains a standard cost system, the method described above for pricing on the perpetual inventory record will not apply. Instead, the material will be entered as received and priced at the established standard cost price. The same price will apply when materials are charged out and for the balance on hand.

Should the accounting procedure call for inventories to be computed on Lifo, Fifo, or some of the other inventory pricing methods described in the next chapter, the selected methods must be adapted for pricing the quantity of inventory at the end of any accounting period.

15

Practices in Taking and

Valuing Inventories

CONTENTS

15

Practices in Taking and Valuing Inventories

PLANNING AND PREPARATION

Purpose of physical inventory. The taking of periodic physical inventories is an essential part of the accounting control of any business that deals in tangible goods. No matter how efficient an inventory control system may be, management should insist upon the confirmation of book amounts at regular intervals through actual count, weight, or measure. A good inventory control system provides vital information and adequate control of materials and supplies only if it is accurate, and even the best system is susceptible to error and should be checked at intervals.

This checking of quantities may be accomplished by a complete count at one time or by staggered or cyclical counts of portions of the inventory so that all of the inventory is taken at least once a year. This is sometimes accompanied by a segregation of the inventory into group components or stock classes that will permit the taking of some of the inventory each month. This procedure is advantageous in that it is not necessary to suspend operations for inventory taking. The counting is done by persons familiar with the stock; errors and discrepancies are often revealed more promptly; and the procedure may be less expensive than a complete one-time count. On the other hand, perpetual inventory records must be complete and up to date to permit checking with cycle counts; establishment of cut-offs is sometimes difficult; portions of the same item of stock may be widely separated; inventory taking in the midst of fast-moving operations is often difficult; and the procedure should ordinarily be supplemented by a complete inventory every three to five years. Careful studies may be necessary to compare the relative advantages of the two methods.

If performed properly, a physical inventory does considerably more than merely check the accuracy of the book records. It should include (1) a review of stock storage and housekeeping procedures; (2) a proper arrangement of stock for most expedient handling; (3) a segregation of obsolete, discontinued, and damaged merchandise; (4) a general review of the procedures involved in stock purchasing, receiving, storing, and issuing; and (5) a review of the balances in the stock accounts to detect any laxity in the purchasing or the control of quantities on hand.

Many small business concerns have no inventory control system and their only accounting for stock on hand occurs on the dates when complete physical inventories are taken, usually annually. When such a situation exists, the periodic physical inventory is the only means of determining the financial condition of the business or its operating results. Close attention must therefore be given to the physical inventory procedures.

Preliminary arrangements. A successful physical inventory program requires that certain preliminary arrangements be made well in advance of the time set for taking the inventory. These arrangements include:

1. Selection of the inventory date.
2. Selection of inventory crews.
3. Organization of inventory personnel.
4. Development of program and instructions.
5. Development of counting procedures.
6. Use of forms.
7. Preparation of stock for counts.
8. Establishment of controls and supervision.
9. Consultation with independent auditors.

As in all other phases of business operation, planning is important to produce an effective result at lowest cost.

Selection of the inventory date. In most cases, inventory-taking and full-scale operations cannot successfully be carried on at the same time. The use of operating personnel for count purposes and the interruption of the flow of materials necessary to insure accurate counts interfere seriously with production. Likewise, even restricted operating activity makes the task of the inventory crew more difficult. Some concerns close down completely for inventory purposes or coordinate the inventory with company-wide vacations; others curtail activities to the point where only limited work is carried on. Many concerns take inventory over a weekend or holiday so as to interfere with operations as little as possible.

It is by no means necessary that the physical inventory be taken as of the last day of the fiscal year. It is usually desirable, of course, that the inventory be taken relatively close to the year-end, but other factors may be considered. The time at which inventory quantities are at their lowest is obviously an advantageous one. This is an important argument in favor of adoption of a fiscal year that represents a "natural business year." However, irrespective of the close of the financial year, alternative inventory dates are acceptable and may well be desirable when the continuing inventory records are sufficiently complete and accurate to permit ready computation of the inventory amounts at the year-end. A concern on a calendar year basis with good inventory control records and its lowest inventory point at September 30 would do well to take inventory at that time and rely upon its control records, adjusted to the September 30 physical inventory and carried on to December 31 in the usual way, for its year-end figures.

Selection of inventory crews. In many instances, especially if inventories are not taken on a cycle basis, it is necessary to expand the stockroom staff by adding members from operating and office departments. All such employees should be thoroughly indoctrinated as to the importance of good inventory taking and they should not look upon it as some incidental job to be taken lightly. This is one of the reasons why inventory-taking, if possible, should be carried on during a time of slack or suspended operating activity. The nature of the work to be done should be kept in mind in determining which individuals should be brought in from other departments. Physical inventory-taking involves identification and count, weight, or other measure of all items of merchandise or materials, supplies, work in process, and finished goods. Office workers with no production experience may be of little value in identifying special stock items or the status of work in process. On the other hand, products that are packaged and labeled may. be counted as accurately by office employees quite unfamiliar with operations as by regular stockroom employees. The necessity of moving heavy materials, of reaching positions difficult to accessibility, and other peculiar working conditions must be also kept in mind in assigning employees to the inventory crew.

Consideration must also be given to the desirability of having the physical inventory counts made by someone other than the individual regularly charged with responsibility for the quantity in question. The man in charge of a given section of the storeroom might well be the man best qualified to count the items in that section. From the standpoint of checking the amounts for which he is responsible, however, it is generally a good policy to have someone else count those items. The fresh attitude of a person unfamiliar with the material and storing facilities usually more than offsets the experience of the regular employee in so far as obtaining an accurate count is concerned.

Organization of inventory personnel. The inventory personnel should be organized with definite lines of responsibility and specific assignments. One such organization is charted in Figure 15-1. The chief inventory officer should be of executive rank, generally the controller, treasurer, or chief accounting officer. It is more important that the inventory officer be completely familiar with the inventory methods and procedures than with the details of the stock to be counted. His chief function is to assure an accurate and efficient inventory by establishing sound procedures and instructing personnel in advance of the physical counting.

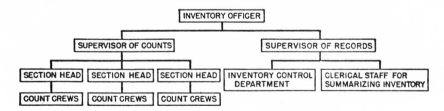

Figure 15-1. Organization of Inventory Personnel.

The inventory officer ordinarily should have two supervisors as assistants, one in charge of making counts and one in charge of the records involved. The former should aid in programming the inventory work and in assigning personnel, to insure that facilities and stock are suitably prepared for inventory-taking, and to be on hand during the counting process to meet problems as they occur. The supervisor in charge of records is usually a member of the accounting department, if possible the head of the inventory records section. Much of his work follows the physical counts, but he must also see to it that all book records are in balance and up to date as of the date of the inventory, that the proper forms and supplies are available, and that certain controls are applied while counts are in progress.

Section heads should be selected to serve under the supervisor in charge of counts. These men should be completely familiar with the items in their respective departments both as to technical description and location. They should circulate throughout their departments while counts are in progress to insure that instructions are properly followed, to see that the various crews are on schedule, and to answer any questions raised by the individuals making the counts. Problems that cannot be solved by the section head concerned should immediately be brought to the attention of the supervisor in charge. Men selected as section heads should be employees normally assigned to the department concerned so that they are able to answer the questions that arise.

Count crews, normally of two men each, do the actual work of counting under the immediate control of the section head. At least one member of each count crew must have a working knowledge of the materials to be counted. Where sufficient experienced operating personnel is not available, office workers can be briefed ahead of time to give them a satisfactory acquaintance with the stock. A good policy is to include one office worker and one person familiar with the material on each two-man count crew in order to obtain a combination of technical knowledge, respect for clerical detail, and a measure of internal control.

Each member of the inventory crew should be well briefed in advance of the inventory date so that there are no questions about duties or procedures during the counting process.

Development of program and instructions. Written instructions covering the entire inventory procedure, prepared well in advance of the inventory date, are a necessity. Instructions should be prepared in detail with step-by-step directions for completion of each phase of the procedure. The following subjects should be covered.

1. Period during which counts are to be made. (This should include time schedules for specific departments or areas.)
2. Personnel to be employed and their responsibilities.
3. Preparation of stockrooms, assembly lines, and receiving and shipping departments prior to counting. (Any departments requiring special treatment should be discussed in detail.)
4. Specific mention of the unit of measure (pieces, pounds, gallons, linear feet, board feet, and so on) to be used for each type of material to be counted.
5. Procedures to be followed in determining inventory quantities with specific mention of exceptions, if any.
6. Copies of all forms to be used, with complete instructions as to their use, including sample forms filled in.
7. Procedures for releasing the departments or plant divisions when and as all inventory requirements are completed.

8. Description of general controls to be maintained.

Each member of the inventory crew should be provided with a copy of the instructions, or at least with those instructions that apply to his work, sufficiently far ahead to give him an opportunity to ask any questions well in advance of the inventory date. Throughout the preliminary preparations, all parties concerned should be constantly alert to discover and eliminate any possible difficulties that might interfere with a successful inventory.

Development of counting procedures. Together with the inventory instructions, a program for counting should be prepared. This program should include all departments and sections in which stock must be counted and should show the time first counts are to be started,the men assigned to the department, and an estimated time of completion. Any departments requiring special procedures should be noted and provided for. Throughout the counting process, the progress of all counting crews should be carefully followed and checked against the program in order that crews from a department that is ahead of schedule may be transferred to departments that are lagging.

Use of forms. Either lists or tags may be used to record counts as they are made, but the advantages of tags are so many and so important that lists are now used only infrequently and then in specialized circumstances. Various types of inventory tags are used. Examples are given in Figures 15-2 and 15-3. In general, they are designed to be affixed to the material counted and contain space for all pertinent information as to date, description of the item counted, quantity, and the initials of the counter. For work in process, a means of indicating the stage of completion should also be provided. In

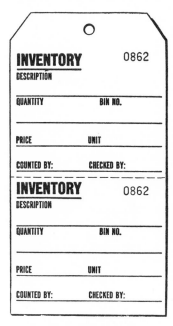

[*Actual size* 3⅛″ *by* 6¼″]

Figure 15-2. Two-Part Inventory Tag.

INVENTORY, 19—

N° 6001

Part No._____

Description_____

Quantity_____   _____

Completed To.   Used
Operation No._____   On_____

Plain   _____
Enameled   _____   Counted By _____
Painted   _____   Checked By _____
Japanned   _____
Aluminized _____   Posted By   _____

INVENTORY, 19—

N° 6001

Part No._____

Description_____

Quantity_____

Completed To   Used
Operation No._____   On_____

Plain   _____
Enameled   _____   Counted By _____
Painted   _____   Checked By _____
Japanned   _____
Aluminized _____   Posted By   _____

[Actual size 5″ by 8″]

Figure 15-3. Two-Part Inventory Tag for Work in Process.

some cases space is provided to record amounts received and issued for a time after the count is completed in order to facilitate recounts if the first quantity determined does not agree with the book records. If the inventory is to be a one-day affair with immediate comparison of counted quantities and book quantities, or if the procedure provides for double counts, relatively simple tags are satisfactory.

Tags should be consecutively numbered to provide a check on ommissions. Various colors can be used to indicate different departments or lines of product.

If it is necessary to sort inventory tags in a variety of ways for statistical or reporting purposes, a three-part tag with a carbon may be designed to provide an extra copy for sorting and tabulating purposes.

Inventory sheets are used in some cases for final accumulation of quantities counted. An example is given in Figure 15-4. They should provice space for date, department or line of material, tag number, description, price, and extension, with additional space for the initials of all individuals whose work appears on the sheet. These forms may also be used for recording counts as made if tags are not used.

A form designed specifically for a department store inventory is shown in Figure 15-5. A code letter for each item is entered in the "season" column, and totals by season classifications are accumulated and entered on the strip to the right of the perforation. The strip is then removed. On the main portion of the form all items are then extended in detail, and if the total of the extension column agrees with the previously detached strip, the extensions and footing of the page are considered correct. As a matter of fact this comparison of totals is often done in "batches" or by departments and is much faster than a detailed checking of extensions and footings.

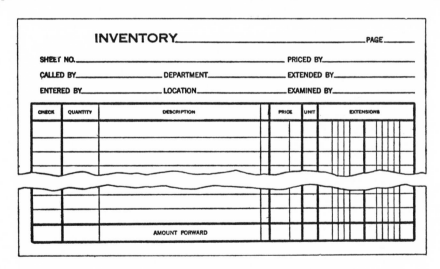

[*Actual size 9½" by 12"*]

Figure 15-4. Sheet to Be Used for Inventory Tabulation.

The form may be used with a carbon copy which is the same as the original, except for the portion to the right of the unit price column (see Figure 15-6).

The carbon copy is used by store or department managers to record subsequent conditions with respect to each item of merchandise that was "old" at the time of the inventory. At the end of each 4-week period subsequent to the inventory, the quantity on hand is entered above the diagonal line and any additional markdowns are entered

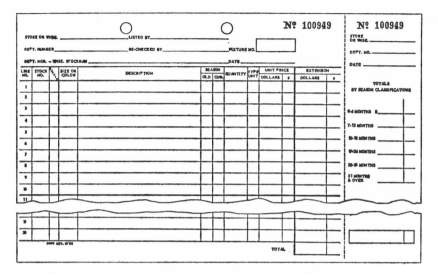

Figure 15-5. Sheet for Department Store Inventory.

below the line. A pasteover strip may be added for the 7th through 13th periods of the fiscal year.

The carbon copy, Figure 15-6, of the portion to the right of the unit price column carries the following instructions.

ENTER COUNTS OF OLD AGE MDSE. ABOVE LINE

ENTER PRICE CHANGES UNDER LINE

COUNTS OF OLD AGE MDSE. TO BE MADE AND THE BOOK
SUBMITTED TO THE MDSE. SUPT., FRIDAY, THE 4TH WEEK
OF EACH PERIOD

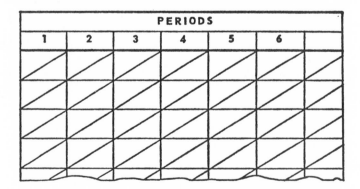

Figure 15-6. Carbon Copy, Inventory Sheet.

Preparation of stock for counts. Prior to the inventory date, all possible steps should be taken to facilitate the counting of stock. Material should be re-stacked where necessary so that sizes and quality are uniform. Aisles should be cleared. Like items should be brought together. Broken cases or lots should be combined to reduce fractional counts. The ready material at machines or on the assembly line should be used up to the extent possible, or returned to stores. Job lots should be collected and identified. In many instances, raw materials necessary to complete specific orders in processes are requisitioned from stores and placed at the in-process site.

Obsolete, damaged, or otherwise unsatisfactory stock should be carefully studied for appropriate action. This should include a thorough review of all material on hand to determine if slow-moving items are still used or have become obsolete. Such a review of stock status is essential to a sound inventory and is beneficial in that it helps to focus attention on materials which, although occupying valuable stockroom space, are no longer important to operations. Waste and scrap material should be sold or otherwise disposed of, in so far as possible.

All purchased material to be returned should be shipped to the vendor before the inventory date. The receiving department should be cleared out as completely as possible, as should the shipping department. Goods packed but not shipped should be segregated to be inventoried or not, depending on whether billed. Any efforts of this type, which do not seriously interfere with production and which contribute to an accurate inventory, should be considered. A general tidying up of storerooms and plants is very helpful.

In retail establishments, stocks should be inspected for missing price tags, customer returns should be re-marked, drawers and shelves should be inspected for soiled or damaged merchandise, and all stock should be properly arranged and classified to the extent possible. In department stores it is customary to prepare floor plans for the "forward stock," showing numbers for each fixture, drawer, or shelf. After the plans have been approved, inventory sheets are issued on a controlled basis and are placed with the merchandise just prior to the inventory taking. Each bin, shelf, or drawer has a separate inventory sheet so that when the sheets have been "lifted" after inventory a quick check can be made to see that all inventory has been taken.

Establishment of controls and supervision. The inventory program should be used to check in all members of the crew before counts begin and to follow their progress throughout the counting period. At regular intervals and as each section or department is completed, progress reports should be obtained. It is essential that each department be released as soon as possible but not before inventory within the department has been completed.

Loss of a group of inventory tags or even of a single tag may result in a considerable error in the final inventory. An indispensable component of inventory control is complete accounting for all tags issued. Inventory tags should be numbered consecutively and a control sheet maintained showing tags issued to each department and to each individual. Instructions should specify that no tags are to be destroyed or thrown away. If errors are made on tags, or if they are torn or otherwise damaged, new ones should be made out and the replaced tags voided but retained and turned in to the supervisor. As counts are completed, the tags should be turned in to the supervisor and checked off on the control sheet.

Each individual in a supervisory capacity must take a close interest in the work. His supervision should be constant and active. Throughout the period of counting, he should be in contact with the individuals working under him, not only to answer their questions,but also to review their work as it is performed and thus insure that instructions are properly followed. Slipshod methods should not be tolerated; it is the duty of the supervisors at every level to insure that old and new employees alike do their best to obtain accurate counts.

Consultation with independent auditors. The accounts of a vast number of business concerns are regularly examined by independent certified public accountants. In such cases, in order to satisfy himself that the taking of the inventories was done carefully and accurately, and also to gain general familiarity with them, the CPA is required by generally accepted auditing practice to be present at the inventory taking to observe the effectiveness of the procedures when it is practicable and reasonable to do so and if the amount of the inventories is significant. Although the CPA may review and approve the instructions for taking the inventories and may test some items, it is the company's responsibility to take the inventory satisfactorily. The CPA's purpose in observing the inventory taking is to satisfy himself that the company is discharging its responsibility.

The CPA's procedures are designed to satisfy him that the amounts set forth by the company as inventory represent actual inventory, that they are presented with reasonable accuracy and in accordance with generally accepted accounting principles consistently applied, and that the bases of stating the inventory, as well as the pledge or assignment of any inventory, are properly disclosed. These objectives require the CPA to investigate the care and accuracy with which the company has counted the inventory, the methods and bases adopted by the company in pricing it, and the substantial correctness of the company's mathematical computations.

For these reasons it is important that there be close cooperation between the inventory officer and the CPA in both the planning and in the carrying out of the inventory work.

TAKING THE INVENTORY

Counting and summarizing. Once all phases of planning and preparation have been completed, the task of actual inventory-taking will be greatly simplified. In this discussion, the word "count" is used in a broad sense and is intended to mean the determination of unit quantities on hand, whether by weight, count, or measurement.

Methods of counting. The purpose of every count is to ascertain the number of units physically on hand on the inventory date. This requires proper identification of the material, followed by a count of the individual unit. The problems involved are numerous, but if the essential purpose of the count is kept in mind, satisfactory solutions can always be found.

Material uniformly packaged and stacked makes for easy count. The crew must determine, however, that the stack is solid, that all rows or tiers are of equal size (or counted in detail), and that only material of the same grade and size is included. Units in broken cases or lots should be counted individually. Piles or lots of odd sizes require special attention. Measuring devices should be provided where necessary.

Before the head crews enter a department or section, the section head or some other competent individual should work through the area placing inventory tags on the various groups and piles of merchandise to be counted. A separate tag should be used for each stack or group of items. If separated piles of the same material exist, they should have a tag. Some order should be followed in spotting the tags, generally by following the physical arrangement of the stock within the area. Tags should be effectively secured to the stock and before the count crews are permitted to begin their work, the department should be reviewed to ascertain that all stock is tagged.

In some cases, it is advisable to have the inventory control department write up descriptions on the tags ahead of time. When this is done, it is essential that a man fully acquainted with the stock place all tags and that the count crews check the description on the tag carefully before making the counts.

The actual counting should almost always be a two-man operation with one counting and the other observing and completing the tag. Some inventory procedures provide for two successive counts with a recount to clear any differences.

When all counts have been completed, the section head should survey the area to check that all stock has been counted. The tags can then be collected and forwarded to the inventory office for pricing and extending. When a two-part perforated inventory tag has been used, one part of it is detached and collected; the second part, or stub, remains with the goods for ready identification in rechecking or recounting.

Recounts, if not already cared for under a program of double counts, may follow from comparison of the physical inventory count with the inventory control record. If only a single count has been made, a difference may result from either an error in the records or in the count; a recount is in order before the records are corrected. If two counts have been made, however, and differences in count eliminated, then it is a reasonable assumption that differences represent errors in the records, and adjustments should be made accordingly.

Descriptions of material. A problem that must be carefully considered is that of getting on the inventory tag a correct description or identification. Material that has a specific catalogue description and code number for inventory control purposes may be popularly known by some abbreviation or unofficial term. Use of the latter title on an inventory tag may give the accounting department considerable difficulty in identifying the item counted. Omission of part numbers, size, quality code, stage of completion, and the like may likewise cause excessive loss of time in later pricing of physical counts.

One method of eliminating the confusion brought on by this difficulty is to prepare tags in the accounting department in advance of the inventory date. This should include inserting the proper description, an indication of the unit of measure to be used in counting, and, if possible, an indication of any standard locations. The inventory tags are then held until the inventory date when they are distributed to the section heads for "spotting."

Special types of count. Certain types of material do not lend themselves to physical count. Large piles of coal or scrap metal, partially filled tanks and vats, and large quantities of small and inexpensive items such as bolts and metal or plastic parts, all require special treatment if an accurate inventory is to be obtained. Piles of coal or scrap may require estimation by competent engineers; quantities in large containers can be computed with considerable accuracy from the known capacity of the container and a measurement of its contents; stocks of small parts can be weighed and the total computed. Regardless of the need for an accurate inventory, it is foolish for someone to count laboriously by hand hundreds of small, low-value items when more expeditious methods will yield satisfactory results. Proper planning for special classes of material is of primary importance in obtaining prompt and accurate counting. It is essential that the temptation to accept book quantities for items difficult to count be resisted. A true physical inventory requires that the quantities of all materials, supplies, and product be determined independently of the records and as accurately as possible.

Obsolete and damaged material. As previously indicated, one phase of preparing for inventory is to segregate all obsolete, damaged, or otherwise unsatisfactory stock and to dispose of as much of it as possible. Obsolete or damaged material that is not disposed of should be segregated and clearly marked. A distinguishing color or other code should be used to identify the inventory tags, and special sheets should be provided in the summary for such items, so that they can be properly evaluated in pricing.

Summarization of inventory. After the counts have been completed, the inventory tags pulled, and all tags accounted for, the task of summarizing the inventory begins. This includes the following:

1. Comparison with inventory control records.
2. Listing or summarizing.
3. Pricing.
4. Extending and footing.

Where no inventory control records are available for comparison, the inventory result is necessarily obtained from the other three steps.

Comparison with inventory control records. Before taking off the information included on each inventory tag, it is desirable to compare the information on the tag with the corresponding inventory control card. This may require a resorting of all tags but as any compilation of physical and perpetual inventories should be in a systematic order, the sorting is usually necessary in any event. It should, of course, include bringing together all tags for a given item in cases where a dividend supply has required two or more tags. Comparison with the inventory records should include both a review of the description, to detect any tags mismarked or out of place, and a comparison of the quantities.

Some definite plan should be established for dealing with differences between physical counts and recorded quantities. If the counting procedure did not provide for two reconciled independent counts of the inventory in the first instance, any differences between the physical listings and book records should be listed on worksheets and verified by re-count. In either case, the book records should then be adjusted to the actual count, in such a way that the nature and date of the adjustments are set out clearly.

Alternatively, it may be desirable to set up limits within which automatic adjustment of the book records will be made.

A record should be kept which tabulates all adjustments to the book records and arrives at a total difference or adjustment from book inventory to physical. This summary should be carefully scanned by the inventory officer and the chief accounting officer for any indication that the inventory control system is unsatisfactory or inaccurate.

Listing or summarizing. In copying from tags to inventory sheets or in converting the data to punched cards or other means of listing and summarizing, certain precautions must be taken to insure that:

1. Tags are properly grouped and in the desired sequence before the work is commenced.
2. Points at which subtotals are required are properly indicated so that new listings may be started with a new sequence of tags.
3. Clerks are properly impressed with the necessity for accuracy.
4. All data transcribed, especially amounts, are either read back or checked in some other way.

Pricing, extending, and footing. The subject of pricing the various items making up the inventory is discussed at some length in the latter part of this chapter. Once quantities and prices have been entered on inventory sheets, completion of the inventory by multiplying units by unit prices and totaling the extended columns is a mechanical procedure. This can frequently be performed by comptometer operators in a relatively short time. All such work should be checked either by independent computation or, in the case of inexpensive merchandise, by sight-testing the inventory sheets.

Merchandise in transit. The inventory must include only property owned as of the inventory date; a definite "cut-off" of merchandise shipments and receipts must be effected. This requires that special attention be given to shipments and receipts during the inventory period and to any merchandise in transit.

Goods sold and properly billed to customers are not included in the inventory. Merchandise that has been segregated and crated but not yet shipped and therefore not billed should be included. It is well to keep a careful record of any shipments during the inventory period so that a check can be made to insure that goods shipped and included in billings as of the inventory date are not likewise included in inventory and that goods excluded from inventory have been included in accounts receivable.

As previously indicated, the receiving room should be cleared in advance of the inventory date. Again a record should be kept of activity during the inventory date. All shipments received should be listed and later checked against the appropriate accounting records to insure that all items inventoried were included in accounts payable and that shipments received during intentory-taking but not entered in accounts payable were not included in inventory. The rule generally followed in respect to shipments received is to include all those for which title has been acquired at the inventory date and to record the liability accordingly. Rubber stamps, indicating "before inventory" and "after inventory," are frequently used on receiving and shipping documents shortly before and shortly after the cut-off.

Merchandise at branches or warehouses. Provision should be made for counting all merchandise wherever stored, whether at branches or in warehouses. If the amounts involved are substantial, it may be desirable to appoint an inventory officer with assistants for the branch inventory.

If it is not feasible to take inventory at all points on the same date, different dates may be selected for the various locations, provided the records are such as to permit appropriate computations of such inventories at the uniform final accounting date. This is frequently helpful in order to permit one or two inventory officers to be present during the taking of inventories at all locations.

Intracompany shipments always require care to prevent inclusion of the same merchandise in more than one inventory.

Consigned merchandise. Goods shipped on consignment should be included in the inventory of the consignor and excluded from the inventory of the consignee. If the quantity involved is material, provision should be made for obtaining physical counts in accordance with the inventory instructions. The checking of such inventories by correspondence with the consignee is usually an important step in establishing that the accountability for such items is properly maintained and that there is no confusion between consignee stock on hand and that owned.

Work in process. The counting of work in process presents one of the most difficult aspects of the physical inventory. The peculiar problem involved varies somewhat with the nature of the cost accounting system employed. In a job-lot system it is necessary that the count crew be thoroughly familiar with the details of plant operations as well as with the product. Job records may be used to determine the status of the work, but the count crew should be impressed with the necessity for making an independent observation of the degree of completion. To assure that all jobs in process are included in the count, inventory tags may be prepared in advance from the work-in-process records, and the count crews required to account for every tag. Inventory tags to be used for work in process must include some space or other provision for indicating the last operation completed.

A process cost system does not offer the assistance of job-lot records. The count crew must determine (1) the number of units of each size or grade within each process, and (2) the stage of completion of each unit or, alternatively, the average stage of completion of all like units within the process. Of these, the second is by far the most difficult, requiring a thorough knowledge of the process.

Inventory time schedule. To insure that all phases of the inventory program, preliminary and subsequent procedures as well as the counting process, are carried out on schedule, the inventory officer may find it helpful to set up a schedule indicating each step in the entire program. Then, as the various individuals responsible complete their duties a notation may be made on the schedule, thus indicating any work yet to be done. The schedule might appear as in Figure 15-7.

Use of tabulating equipment. With adequate arrangements in advance of the inventory date, it is frequently desirable to make use of tabulating equipment in inventory listing, extending, and footing. A company with its own installation may use the machines it has, or the work may be sent out to a service bureau for processing.

Inventory tags can be designed on punched card forms that may be either mark-sensed for automatic punching or handled in the ordinary manner by a key-punch operator. After the necessary information is punched into the card, extensions, sorting,

INVENTORY TIME SCHEDULE			
Assignment	*Assigned to*	*Date Required*	*Date Completed*
Draft inventory instructions	J. Dodds	12/1	
Assign inventory crews	J. Dodds	12/20	
Obtain inventory tags, sheets, and other supplies	P. Green	12/15	
Prepare program for counting	T. Otis	12/20	
Prepare tag control	P. Green	12/20	
Mimeograph instructions for distribution	M. Nickel	12/20	
Distribute inventory instructions	M. Nickel	12/27	
Enter stock descriptions on inventory tags	P. Green	12/27	
Meet inventory crew for briefing	J. Dodds	12/27	
Start counts	Crews	12/31	
Complete counts	Crews	1/2	
Check counts against control records	M. Little	1/5	
Complete pricing	J. Jones	1/12	
Complete extensions and footings	P. Green	1/16	
Review errors in inventory control record disclosed by physical	M. Little	1/20	
Submit suggestions for improvement in inventory procedure	P. Green T. Otis Dept. heads	1/20 1/20 1/20	

Figure 15-7. Inventory Time Schedule.

listing, and footing are automatically completed. Considerable savings of time can frequently be obtained by pre-punching information common to all or large groups of cards. A tabulating card designed for use as an inventory tag is shown in Figure 15-8.

Use of electronic data processing machines. If the inventories are sufficiently extensive to justify the use of electronic data processing machines in the control and management of stock and for processing the accounting data in connection with receipt, sale, and withdrawal of stock as well as price changes and other adjustments, the following outline summarizes the steps that might be taken in connection with physical verification of inventory balances.

It is assumed that all significant data in connection with inventory balances, including stock number, quantity, and price, are on magnetic tape in stock sequence number. It is assumed also that verification is to be made of segments of the inventory on a cycle basis. No adjustment is to be made if the amount of the difference in value is not more than $10.00 unless the difference in quantity is more than 10 per cent. (Obviously, any other criteria could be established as limits below which no adjustments would be made.)

The following steps are illustrative of those that might be followed in one of the cycle tests, using punched cards and related machines in conjunction with an electronic computer and tape units.

1. Select the block of stock numbers to be tested.
2. Prepare inventory count cards in punched-card form, arrange in whatever sequence will most greatly facilitate location of stock for counting, number the cards serially, and interpret.

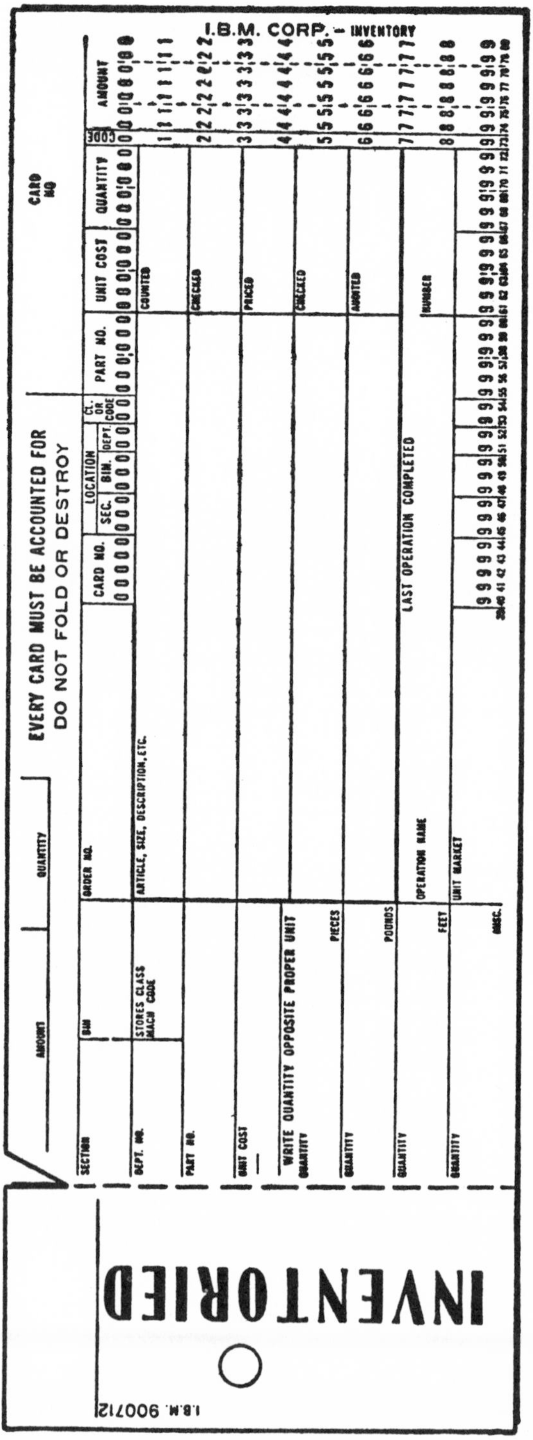

[*Actual size 3¼" by 9"*]

Figure 15-8. Tabulating Card Designed for Use as Inventory Tag.

3. Distribute cards to counting crews and record on a listing for card control.
4. Make inventory counts.
5. Check off return of all cards after inventory crews have completed the counting.
6. Key punch inventory counts into the cards. (If counts have been made by means of mark sensing, reproduce quantities into cards by use of a reproducing punch.)
7. Sort count cards into stock number sequence. (If any emergency activity has taken place with respect to the stock numbers that have been "frozen" for inventory, merge in these activity cards with the count cards.)
8. Compare in a computer pass the cards in Step 7 with the quantities on the tapes.
   - (a) If quantities agree, set up to punch balance cards for summarization.
   - (b) If quantities do not agree, check difference for variance of 10% or less. If variance is within the 10% leeway, multiply quantity variation by price. If variation is $10.00 or less, follow Step 8a.
   - (c) If variations do not meet the criteria of Step 8b, set up to punch cards showing stock number. These cards will be collated with inventory count cards, and new count cards will be prepared for recounts. Processes will be repeated, using the new cards, when recounts have been completed.
   - (d) If there is a balance on the tape but no inventory count card, set up to punch data relating to that item as shown on the tape.
9. Match-merge agreement balance cards with inventory count cards (Step 8a) and prepare reconciliation listing #1.
10. Match-merge leeway cards (Step 8b) and prepare reconciliation listing #2.
11. In connection with recount cards, follow essentially the same steps as in the case of the initial counts, using, if possible, teams other than those making the initial counts.
12. Match-merge recount cards with balance cards (Step 8c) and prepare reconciliation listing #3.
13. List cards in Step 8d as listing #4.
14. List manually-prepared count cards (items not on tape) as listing #5.
15. Investigate discrepancies.
16. Prepare adjustment transaction cards and up-date tape records to correct balances as necessary.

The foregoing steps are necessarily oversimplified but are indicative of the fact that an electronic computer, by means of its rapid "comparison capabilities" (i.e. ability to select among alternative sequences of action, depending on whether one quantity is equal to, greater than or less than another quantity) can be put to good use in reconciling physical inventories with "book inventories," assuming that "book inventories" are kept on magnetic tape.

Possible variations of inventory reconciliation procedures in an electronic computer installation are endless. For example, a card-to-tape converter might be used to record data from the count cards on magnetic tape. Then tape comparisons could be made, comparing quantities per physical count with quantities per perpetual records. Exceptions could be written out on an output tape, and while printing from the tape, items could be coded to indicate need for further investigation.

Programming the steps in such an inventory reconciliation procedure is a job for trained technicians, but if the perpetual inventory records are maintained on magnetic tape, then those who program the basic system will certainly want to program an expeditious method for making periodic reconciliations with physical counts and for effecting any necessary corrections in the running balances.

VALUATION OF INVENTORIES

Basic principle. The pricing of an inventory is not in any sense a simple matter of arithmetic, but a very important task which should not be undertaken without full consideration of the basic objective of inventory determination and the importance of the result in business accounting. The ascertainment of total value of the stock on hand, though significant as a factor in establishing the financial condition of an enterprise at a given date, is now considered to be of much greater importance because of its effect upon the computation of net income of the business for separate fiscal periods of its history. The mechanics of pricing, therefore, are secondary to an understanding of the basic principle.

A business that buys (or manufactures) and sells goods for profit incurs many expenditures and costs in the process. Some of these are to acquire tangible inventory items, in one form or another, or to add to the value of such tangible items as they go through stages of handling or fabrication. Some add nothing to tangible values but are instead related to the selling or disposition of the items after they are completed. The expenditures and costs that create or add to physical values, directly or indirectly, are those which are, in the broad sense, the costs of acquiring inventory and are sometimes known as ''product'' costs; all others are ''period'' costs and are accounted for as current business expenses without direct relationship to the physical flow of goods into sales.

As sales of goods are made and revenues produced thereby, it is necessary in accounting to match against such revenues for a given period the product costs properly chargeable thereto. The function of the periodic inventory in this process is described as follows in an authoritative statement of the American Institute of Certified Public Accounts:[1]

> . . . In accounting for the goods in the inventory at any point of time, the major objective is the matching of appropriate costs against revenues in order that there may be a proper determination of the realized income. Thus, the inventory at any given date is the balance of costs applicable to goods on hand remaining after the matching of absorbed costs with concurrent revenues. This balance is appropriately carried to future periods provided it does not exceed an amount properly chargeable against the revenues expected to be obtained from ultimate disposition of the goods carried forward. In practice, this balance is determined by the process of pricing the articles comprised in the inventory.

On this premise, it is now possible to consider some of the general precepts of inventory pricing.

The cost premise. Basically, inventories should be priced at cost. As applied to inventories, cost means the sum of the applicable expenditures and charges directly or indirectly incurred in bringing an article to its current condition and location. This means that, ordinarily, all incurred costs should be included in the inventory price.

In recent years some accountants have displayed interest in a procedure known as ''direct costing.'' This is a method of costing whereby inventories are charged with only such overhead items as vary with production, fixed overhead being charged off as

---

[1]Committee on Accounting Procedure, American Institute of Certified Public Accountants, *Accounting Reasearch Bulletin*, No. 43, Chapter 4, p. 28.

incurred and excluded from the cost of the product. This method of costing may have some merit for interim reports to management and for the handling of internal managerial problems, but its use as a method of valuing inventories in financial statements and for the matching of costs with revenues cannot be considered as generally accepted.

Clearly, overhead costs of manufacturing departments are as essential to the completed product as either raw materials or direct labor. Proper pricing policies require the inclusion of all cost elements, and burden should be included with the rest. Understatement of inventory is as serious an error as overstatement.

The basic premise of pricing at cost requires one important modification. A downward departure from cost is required when the usefulness of the goods is no longer as great as cost. This limitation expresses a concept which is sometimes described by accountants as "useful cost," in which sense it, of itself, contains the sole criterion for inventory pricing. This is readily illustrated. Obsolete or damaged merchandise is not to be priced at cost if there is reasonable evidence that the material will not return its cost when sold. Such items have lost some or all of the usefulness for which they were originally purchased and should be priced accordingly. Similarly, a change in price level may indicate that merchandise has lost some of its usefulness. Goods purchased at $10.00 a unit which now are worth only $8.00 have lost economic usefulness, and this must be considered in pricing them in the inventory. Whenever there is evidence that the utility of goods in their disposal in the ordinary course of business will be less than cost, whether because of physical deterioration, obsolescence, changes in price levels, or other causes, the difference is a current loss and is excluded from the inventory price.

The proposition of pricing inventory items at retained usefulness is applied in practice through the rule of "cost or market, whichever is lower." Under this phase the term "market," when lower than cost, is synonymous with useful cost; its use and limitations are described later.

As pointed out in the preceding paragraphs, the physical inventory procedure should include a thorough review of all inventory items. This provides for the segregation of damaged stock, discontinued liens, or any other material the usefulness of which has decreased. A review of the entire inventory for items subject to declining prices is also in order. All items of this general nature (decreased economic usefulness) should be given special pricing consideration so that no item will be included in the final inventory tabulation at an amount in excess of its market, as thus defined.

Meaning of cost. For purchased merchandise, cost under this rule is taken to include all expenditures and changes in acquiring material, including invoice price, transportation, necessary handling, and any general overhead directly applicable to the acquisition of the material in its location for sale. In the case of manufactured goods, cost includes all such costs of materials purchased plus direct labor and an appropriate portion of factory overhead.

Selling expenses constitute no part of inventory costs. Also, except for the portion of general and administrative expenses that may be clearly related to production, such items are treated as period changes and not as inventoriable product costs.

Further definition of the term "cost" as applied to inventory pricing involves many intricate aspects of cost accounting that are not within the scope of this chapter. For example, under some circumstances, items such as idle facility expense, excessive spoilage, double freight, and rehandling costs may be so abnormal as to be properly treated as current period changes rather than as a portion of the inventory costs. Many other considerations may arise and all should be dealt with in accordance with consistent cost-finding principles. Standard costs, if adjusted at reasonable intervals to reflect current conditions, are acceptable.

Meaning of market. The application of the term "market" as used in the "lower of cost or market" rule has been clarified by the Committee on Accounting Procedure of the American Institute of Certified Public Accountants as follows:[2]

> As used in the phrase *lower of cost or market*, the term *market* means current replacement cost (by purchase or by reproduction, as the case may be) except that:
> (1)   Market should not exceed the net realizable value (i.e., estimating selling price in the ordinary course of business less reasonably predictable costs of completion and disposal); and
> (2)   Market should not be less than net realizable value reduced by an allowance for an approximately normal profit margin.

Thus market price, which is to be used only when it is lower than cost, means the cost to replace the given item, except that it must not be greater than the net amount to be realized nor less than an amount which provides the normal rate of profit when the item is sold.

Replacement cost is the initial amount because it represents the *prima facie* measure of usefulness of the goods on hand in the ordinary course of business. The modifying ceiling, the amount realizable for the actual goods on hand, is a logical one and takes account of all factors of deterioration in value. The modifying floor, the amount which will realize a normal margin of profit, is designed to prevent the shifting of profit from one year to the next; no write-down from cost to replacement is required when a normal profit can be realized on cost in the ordinary course of events.

The appropriate inventory price thus to be used under a variety of possible situations may be illustrated in an oversimplified example. The X Company manufactures an article which it consistently sells *at a standard price* of $1.00 and upon which, during the preceding five years, the company has realized an average net profit of $.09. In the seven assumed situations below, the amounts beside which an asterisk appears represent the appropriate amounts to be used for inventory pricing purposes. Of course, very few inventory situations lend themselves to so easy a solution, but the principles illustrated are those now recognized as best accounting practice.

	A	B	C	D	E	F	G
Actual Cost	$.72*	$.76	$.77	$.84	$.85	$.85	$.68*
Cost to replace at inventory date	.76	.70	.75*	.83	.70	.80*	.65
Selling price less estimated cost to complete and sell	.82	.82	.82	.82*	.82	.82	.82
Selling price less estimated cost to complete and sell and average profit margin	.73	.73*	.73	.73	.73*	.73	.73

---

[2]American Institute of Certified Public Accountants, *op. cit.*, p. 31.

Application of the cost or market rule. It has long been the practice, perhaps largely because of the requirements of the income tax regulations, to apply the "lower of cost or market rule" separately to each item in the inventory. It is now recognized that this practice is no longer always desirable, especially in view of the "useful cost" theory explained above. The alternatives are considered in detail in the statement of the American Institute of Certified Public Accountants' Committee on Accounting Procedure:[3]

> . . . The most common practice is to apply the *lower of cost or market* rule separately to each item of the inventory. However, if there is only one end-product category, the cost utility of the total stock—the inventory in its entirety—may have the greatest significance for accounting purposes. Accordingly, the reduction of individual items to *market* may not always lead to the most useful result if the utility of the total inventory to the business is not below its cost. This might be the case if selling prices are not affected by temporary or small fluctuations in current costs of purchase or manufacture. Similarly, where more than one major product or operational category exists, the application of the *cost or market, whichever is lower* rule to the total of the items included in such major categories may result in the most useful determination of income.
>
> When no loss of income is expected to take place as a result of a reduction of cost prices of certain goods because others forming components of the same general categories of finished products have a market equally in excess of cost, such components need not be adjusted to market to the extent that they are in balanced quantities. Thus, in such cases, the rule of *cost or market, whichever is lower* may be applied directly to the totals of the entire inventory, rather than to the individual inventory items, if they enter into the same category of finished product and if they are in balanced quantities, provided the procedure is applied consistently from year to year.
>
> To the extent, however, that the stocks of particular materials or components are excessive in relation to others, the more widely recognized procedure of applying the *lower of cost or market* to the individual items comprising the excess should be followed. This would also apply in cases in which the items enter into the production of unrelated products or products having a material variation in the rate of turnover. Unless an effective method of classifying categories is practicable, the rule should be applied to each item in the inventory.

Flow of cost. Included in the problem of pricing inventory is a decision as to the flow of costs to be assumed in applying the cost or market rule. This may be illustrated with the following hypothetical inventory item:

	Received		Issued	Balance
Date	Units	Price	Units	Units
1/1	200	$2.00		200
3/1	100	3.00		300
6/1			150	150
9/1	200	2.50		350
12/1			100	250

To arrive at the inventory valuation for this material it is necessary to decide whether the 250 units on hand at the end of the year were:

---

[3]*Ibid.,* p. 32.

1. The first units purchased (that is, 200 purchased January 1 plus 50 of the 100 units purchased March 1).
2. The last units purchased (that is, 200 purchased September 1 plus 50 of the 100 units purchased March 1), or
3. A proportionate share of all units purchased during the period.
4. Certain specific units which can be identified.

Some assumption must be made as to the flow of units of merchandise (and of cost) through the business. If the first units purchased are the first units sold (first-in, first-out), then the inventory must be made up of the last units purchased. If the first units purchased are stockpiled and the last units acquired are the ones issued first (last-in, first-out), then the inventory consists of the first units purchased. Again, the item may be of such nature that units cannot be segregated by purchases but become intermingled so that it is impossible to tell whether the units in the inventory were included in the oldest or latest purchase. Finally, it may be possible to identify the specific units sold and on hand so that the individual costs of the units remaining on hand can be determined.

The most commonly used concepts of cost flow in inventory pricing, therefore, are (1) specific identification, (2) average cost, (3) first-in, first-out (Fifo), and (4) last-in, first-out (Lifo). There are other variants of these cost approaches, including the "base stock" method, but these are of extremely limited use. The four principal methods of costing are described below.

Specific identification. This method contemplates the application of the specific costs of the identified items on hand. It is appropriate for distinctive, high-priced articles such as jewelry, *objets d'art*, and the like. In almost all other cases, it is impractical to apply because the goods lose individuality in the process of production and sale. In usual manufacturing or trading operations, the method is seldom used, even when it is theoretically possible to establish identified unit costs of individual pieces on hand, because of the unjustified amount of work that the method would involve.

Average cost method. The arithmetical average cost of all similar units acquired during the fiscal period, including those carried over in the previous inventory, is applied to the units on hand. This method is seldom used in retail establishments, but is occasionally applied in pricing raw materials, work in process, or even finished goods of manufacturers. Because it fails to recognize fully either the physical turnover of goods or the effect of price changes within the fiscal period, it is generally considered less satisfactory than the "first-in, first-out" method or the "last-in, first-out" method.

First-in, first-out method. This method assumes that the goods first acquired are the goods first sold, in typical grocery store style. It is the method in most common use, largely because it conforms most nearly to the physical flow of the goods. By pricing inventory at the cost of the most recent acquisitions equal to the quantity on hand, this method puts the oldest costs into the cost of sales of the period. When goods are continually turned over and replaced, as in the usual business, this tends to increase inventory values in periods of rising prices, even though there may be no material change in the relative composition or quantity of the entire inventory.

Last-in, first-out method. This method is the inverse of the first-in, first-out method and assumes that the units sold are those more recently acquired and that the units on hand are those first acquired. In most cases in actual practice, this is a fiction that attempts to accomplish a measurement of economic income by assuming that, especially in a period of changing prices, the real income to the business is measured by the difference between current cost (or most recent cost) and selling price. This method produces less profit than the first-in, first-out method in periods of rising prices and more profit in periods of declining prices.

Lifo pricing may be applied on a so-called unit method or a dollar value method. The former involves a segregation of the inventory into groups or pools according to the type of merchandise purchased or, in the case of manufacturing concerns, according to such recognizable factors as manufacturing processes or raw material. Pricing is done separately for each group or pool. The inventory at the beginning of the year for which Lifo is adopted is priced at cost and when the total for each group is divided by quantities on hand, the result is the beginning or base unit price. This base unit price is used in valuing the inventory at the end of the year to the extent that quantities on hand do not exceed those on hand at the beginning of the year. Additional quantities are priced at either earliest, latest or average costs incurred during the year, depending on the procedure selected which, of course, should be consistent from year to year. Increments in quantities thus form "layers" for each year. Reduced quantities at the end of subsequent years have the effect of eliminating the most recent layers first, in accordance with the last-in first-out theory.

Under the dollar value method, manufacturing concerns use inventory components, such as material, labor and overhead; and retail establishments use the inventories regularly priced under the retail method as a basis for Lifo pricing. The inventory at the end of a year is recomputed at beginning-of-the-year prices, either in detail or by applying an index number, and any increment for that year is priced by the use of an index number based on the earliest, latest or average purchase prices of that year, depending on which procedure has been selected. Computations at the end of subsequent years are made, usually by cumulative index numbers, in relation to the initial Lifo inventory. As in the case of the unit method, net reductions in inventories during the year (determined after eliminating the effect of price changes during that year) have the effect of eliminating the latest increments first.

Selecting the method of pricing. Any one of the methods of pricing described above is acceptable. Actually, the use of any (except the specific identification method, when it is practical) is likely to be at variance with the exact physical flow of goods. As a matter of fact, accountants now generally consider these to be different ways of recognizing the flow of "cost factors" (rather than of the actual movement of the goods), thereby attaching economic significance to the choice of method.

It is recognized that the major objective in selecting a method should be to choose the one which, under the circumstances, most clearly reflects periodic income. This suggests that these tests be applied:

1. Where sales prices are promptly influenced by changes in reproductive costs, an assumption of the Lifo (or base stock) flow of costs may be the more appropriate.

2. Where no such cost price relationship exists, the Fifo or an "average" cost method may be more properly utilized.

In some cases, the business operations may be such as to make it desirable to apply one of the acceptable methods of determining cost to one portion of the inventory and another of the acceptable methods to other portions of the inventory.

The method selected cannot be varied with fluctuations in the business cycle. Once adopted, the pricing method must be followed consistently year after year. Hence considerable care should be exercised in selecting the most desirable method.

Retail method. The retail method of inventory pricing is a procedure for determining inventories at cost[4] based upon current retail prices and calculated percentages of markup or "mark-on." The method is quite generally used in department stores and other retail establishments where each item of stock is tagged at its retail selling price and where the average markup does not vary appreciably within a given department, section, or line of merchandise.[5]

Purchase records for specific departments will ordinarily show the following type of information:

	Cost	Retail
Purchases	$3,450	$4,950
Transfers in (from other depts.)	20	30
Inward transportation costs	30	——
Additional markups or markup cancellations (such as errors in original markups)	——	20
Returns to vendor	——	——
Transfers out (to other depts.)	——	——
Net additions to stock	$3,500	$5,000

Markon — 30%

Obviously the markon percentage relating to the net additions for an interim period should not be used in determining the "cost inventory" at the end of the period; rather, the "cumulative markon" should be used which gives effect to the beginning inventory and to all year-to-date or season-to-date net additions to stock.

Departmental records will also be maintained to show net retail deductions, such as:

Markdown.

Markdown cancellations.

Employee discounts (usually included with markdowns).

Provision for inventory shrinkage (current period anticipations or accruals of year-end shrinkage, to be finally determined on the basis of physical inventories).

Sales.

Customer returns.

When the cumulative net retail deductions are subtracted from the cumulative net additions at retail, the result is the ending inventory at retail. This amount is multiplied

[4]As used in this discussion, and as generally applied in the retail inventory method, the term cost means "inventoriable cost" and may be considered to represent the lower of cost or market.

[5]See "The Retail Inventory Method in Practical Operation," published by the Controllers' Congress, National Retail Merchants Association, 100 West 31st Street, New York 1, N. Y.

by the complement of the cumulative markon percentage to arrive at the ending inventory at cost.

These calculations, for the first two periods of a fiscal year, may be illustrated in the accompanying table.

Line No.		Period 1 Cost	Period 1 Retail	Period 2 Cost	Period 2 Retail
1.	Inventory at beginning of period	$68,000	$100,000	$ 70,520	$104,475
2.	Cumulative additions to beginning of period	68,000	100,000	98,200	145,475
3.	Purchases (net of returns)	30,000	45,400	42,600	64,000
4.	Inward transportation costs	250	——	425	——
5.	Additional markups, less markup cancellations ..	——	150	——	525
6.	Transfers in (or out)	(50)	(75)	——	——
7.	Total additions (sum of lines 2 to 6)	$98,200	$145,475	$141,225	$210,000
8.	Markon %	32.50%		32.75%	
9.	Net sales		40,000		52,000
10.	Markdowns (and employee discounts) less markdown cancellations		800		940
11.	Shrinkage		200		260
12.	Total deductions — this period		41,000		53,200
13.	Total deduction — year to date		41,000		94,200
14.	Retail inventory (line 7 minus line 13)		$104,475		$115,800
15.	Complement of markon %	67.50%		67.25%	
16.	Cost inventory	$70,520		$ 77,875	

It should be noted that markdowns are considered as "retail deductions" and are not offset against the net additions used in determining the markon percentage. This gives effect to the cost-or-market rule and provides for the taking of losses in the period in which they are recognized. Furthermore, additional markups are not offset against markdowns. To do so would permit corrections or adjustments of regular markups to offset period losses occasioned by markdowns. It would result in a higher ending inventory by decreasing the markon percentage and thereby increasing the complement which is applied to the ending inventory at retail to arrive at the ending inventory at cost.

Special pricing problems. The previous sections of this chapter have been concerned with the problem of pricing inventory in general. In addition, there are special pricing problems for such items as:

1. Obsolete and damaged stock.
2. Repossessed merchandise.
3. Joint and by-products.
4. Special merchandise priced above cost.

These problems, together with those involved in inventory reserves and in income tax requirements, are dealt with in the remaining paragraphs.

Obsolete and damaged stock. The "lower of cost or market" rule, satisfactorily applies to obsolete and damaged stock. Once material is classed as obsolete or damaged, its initial cost is no longer applicable for inventory valuation purposes. The inventory valuation must be determined by estimating or otherwise arriving at the probable sales price and subtracting therefrom the expected expenses of sale, if any. The result is the net realizable value and in such case represents "market."

Repossessed merchandise. Repossessed merchandise may present a somewhat different problem. If the condition of the merchandise is such that it can probably be disposed of in the ordinary course of business, it should be priced for inventory purposes at the lower of cost or market in the same manner as other merchandise. If the amount involved is significant, the inventory price selected should represent estimated selling price less all expenses of reconditioning and less a reasonable profit on sale. This is especially true where repossessions are a regular recurring part of operations and are in substantial volume. Incidental repossessions of merchandise, on the other hand, may properly be priced at net realizable value. Repossessed items which cannot be resold should be classed with obsolete and damaged stock and priced accordingly.

Joint costs. Joint costs and by-product costs present yet another pricing problem. The problem is one of dividing cost among two or more products so that each may be priced under the "lower of cost or market" rule. In the absence of a more accurate basis for prorating costs over two or more products, the relative sales price of the products is usually used to work out a proportion for allocating joint costs. For example, assume products *A* and *B* are made from a single item of raw material and that processing costs include work done on the raw material both before and after *A* and *B* become separately identifiable. Joint material cost is $40.00 per unit and joint processing costs are $30.00 per unit. Direct costs and sales prices are as follows:

Product	Direct Costs	Anticipated Sales Price	Ratio
A	$15.00	$ 60.00	40.00%
B	25.00	90.00	60.00
		$150.00	100.00%

The cost allocation on the basis of sales price is shown in the following summary:

	A	B
Joint (A—40%; B—60%)		
Raw materials	$16.00	$24.00
Processing	12.00	18.00
Direct	15.00	25.00
Total cost	$43.00	$67.00

In some cases, the costs that can be directly charged to the individual products are by far the largest of all costs and may be in different proportions than are the sales prices. If this is true, it may be desirable to base the proportion for allocating the joint costs on the relative sales prices after deducting separable expenses.

Pricing above cost. The general rule for inventory pricing makes no provision for pricing above cost, and exceptional circumstances are required to justify such pricing. Any instance of pricing above cost must fulfill the following requirements to establish the propriety of deviating from the cost or market rule.

1. Costs must be impossible or difficult of determination.
2. A ready and constant market with quoted prices must exist.
3. Units making up the inventory should be fungible.

Very few cases meet these requirements, and the only items now generally priced above cost are those having a fixed monetary value, such as gold or silver.

Inventory reserves. Inventory reserves are sometimes considered to mean reserves created either (1) to provide a reduction of an initial inventory valuation to the appropriate lower of cost or market figure; or (2) to provide for anticipated future losses due to price declines, overstocking, and the like.

In general, there is little reason to establish a reserve to reduce an inventory to the lower of cost or market. Proper application of the pricing rules should locate either the specific items or groups of items which require reduction. The price of these items can then be decreased directly to effect the desired valuation. Little can be said in favor of a general reserve to accomplish what can be as well done by specific adjustments, especially since over-all or general reductions of inventories are not recognized as deductions for tax purposes.

Whether the write-down of inventory to the lower of cost or market is accomplished directly or by establishing a reserve, the offsetting debit represents a cost of doing business in the period of write-down occurs and must be recognized as an expense (or loss) in the statement of income. If the amount involved is material, proper disclosure requires that it be stated as a special item, apart from the "cost of sales" figure.

Reserves to provide for future inventory declines represent a segregation of surplus to provide for future contingencies. They are not provisions for losses incurred, and therefore the charge offsetting the reserve credit cannot be included in the computation of net income. Enlightened accounting views such inventory reserves as undesirable and imposes restrictions on their use to an extent that makes them generally meaningless.[6] Disclosure of any possible future decline, if considered important, can be made by footnote or parenthetical explanation, and the surplus reservation is of little significance.

Federal income tax requirements. The Internal Revenue Code, Sec. 471 provides:

> Whenever in the opinion of the Secretary or his delegate the use of inventories is necessary in order clearly to determine the income of any taxpayer, inventories shall be taken by such taxpayer on such basis as the Secretary or his delegate may prescribe as conforming as nearly as may be to the best accounting practice in the trade or business and as most clearly reflecting the income.

Inventory practice may vary with the nature of the business but the rules followed within a given trade or business are thus expected to be reasonably uniform. Further, it is essential that each taxpayer be consistent from one year to the next in his own inventory procedure and pricing.

Either cost or the lower of cost or market is accepted for tax purposes, and one of these two bases must be applied with reasonable consistency to the entire inventory, except for goods inventories under a so-called "elective" (last-in, first-out) method. When the lower of cost or market is used, each article in the inventory is to be separately priced for tax purposes; it is not permissible to price the entire inventory at cost and again at market and take the lower total (Sec. 1.471-4).

The regulations define "market" for inventory purposes, under ordinary circumstances and for normal goods, to be the current bid price prevailing at the date of the inventory for the particular merchandise in the volume in which usually purchased by the taxpayer. In the case of work in process or other goods for which no open market exists, "market" is taken to be reproductive cost as of the inventory date (GCM 9401, CB X-1, 102).

Goods that are unsalable at normal prices or unusable in the normal way, because of damage or imperfections, should be valued at bona fide selling prices less direct cost of disposition. If such goods consist of raw materials or partly finished goods held for use or consumption, they should be valued upon a reasonable basis, taking into consideration the usability and condition of the goods, but in no case shall such value be less than the scrap value. Bona fide selling price means actual offering of goods during a period ending no later than 30 days after inventory date. The taxpayer has the burden of proof as to the deviation from normal value.

The retail method of pricing is acceptable for retail merchants providing certain conditions are met (Sec. 1.471-8). In general, it is assumed that the first-in, first-out method of pricing will be applied but Section 472 of the Internal Revenue Code specifically provides for use of the last-in first-out method by any taxpayer under

---

[6]Committee on Accounting Procedure, American Institute of Certified Public Accountants, Accounting Research Bulletin, No. 43, Chapter 6.

specified conditions. Among other requirements, a taxpayer using the Lifo method for tax purposes must also use that method in his accounts and financial statements.

The essential requirements for the adoption and use of the last-in first-out inventory method are set out in Section 1.472-2 of Regulations. The taxpayer must first file an application for permission to use the method. Once the method is established, valuation of inventory thereafter is to be on the basis of cost, regardless of market value. Further rules are prescribed for essentiaally two classes of taxpayers: (1) Those engaged in the purchase and sale of merchandise or in the initial production of merchandise and its sale without further processing; and (2) those engaged in manufacturing, fabricating, processing, or otherwise producing merchandise.

The federal income tax requirements mentioned are necessarily general in nature. To avoid the possibility of penalty, it is essential that all requirements be thoroughly understood. Reference should be made to the applicable sections of the Internal Revenue Code, the Regulations, and a good interpretive tax service or tax consultant to obtain a sound understanding of this and other problems affecting inventory pricing for federal income tax purposes.

16

Systems and Practices for
Control of Accounts Receivable

CONTENTS

16

Systems and Practices for
Control of Accounts Receivable

Basis for time-saving procedures. The procedures discussed in this chapter relate generally to operations involving a substantial volume of clerical work for most companies. In analyzing the best procedure to use in any particular instance, it is necessary to keep in mind the fundamentals of system design that tend to minimize clerical effort. and the following recommendations.

1. Use one writing, or as few writings as possible, of each piece of information to serve the needs of those who must use it.
2. Limit the amount of writing and the number or extent of clerical operations.
3. Limit the number of pieces of paper or reports to the minimum required for necessary functions.
4. Use appropriate mechanical equipment, forms, sorting, and filing devices.

Although the saving in clerical effort for any one operation may be minute, the fact that each operation must be continually repeated means that the aggregate savings may be substantial if appropriate attention is directed to each detail.

ORDER ENTRY

Documents related to order entry—manufacturers. The more important documents related to entry of an order by a manufacturer may be summarized as follows.

1. Letters or other communications received from customers which detail the items ordered.

2. Contracts representing a formal agreement as to deliveries to a customer. These are more commonly encountered where the manufacturer is essentially a subcontractor of the customer and the agreement covers continuing deliveries of product over an extended period of time.

3. Purchase orders received from customers. These are probably the most common media by which manufacturers receive notice of orders from customers.

4. Salesmen's order forms prepared by the manufacturer's salesmen. These are usually signed by the customer.

5. Sales order form prepared by the manufacturer. This document is usually prepared by the sales department in connection with every order, even though one or more of the other documents previously listed are available. Copies of the sales order form may serve several purposes, including:

(a) Acknowledgment to the customer that the order has been received and accepted. The prices and other terms on which the order has been accepted are usually indicated, as well as expected delivery dates.

(b) Advice to other departments that the order has been accepted. The departments receiving copies will depend upon the assignment of functions and responsibilities within the manufacturing organization. The departments that commonly receive copies are production scheduling, accounting, and shipping.

(c) Packing slip to accompany shipment.

(d) "Shipper" copies serving as internal notice that a shipment has been made. These copies frequently go to such departments as sales, production scheduling, and accounting.

(e) Invoice copies to be sent to customer when an order is shipped.

(f) Invoice copies to be retained for internal use, particularly in the accounting department. Copies are often forwarded to salesmen as an advice that the order has been filled.

When a sales order is prepared in a form suitable for multiple-purpose use such as is outlined above, it is frequently described as a "combination sales order-shipper-invoice form." An example of this type of form is shown in Figure 16-1. The various copies are identified as follows at the bottom of the form:

1. Invoice.
2. Invoice copy.
3. Accounting—chronological.
4. Accounting—geographical.
5. Accounting—alphabetical.
6. Acknowledgment.
7. Shipper.
8. Packing list.
9. Accounting—numerical.
10. Originating department.

It should be noted that though portions of each copy in the set are prepared as a carbon copy of either the top or subsequent copies, not all of the writing on one copy necessarily appears on the other copies.

Figure 16-2 illustrates the typical steps in the preparation and use of a combination sales order-shipper-invoice form.

Documents related to order entry—distributors. The order entry forms used by distributors are usually similar to those used by a manufacturer, although formal contracts or agreements are not so frequently encountered. It may be necessary for the procedures to accommodate one or more of the following situations sometimes peculiar to distributors.

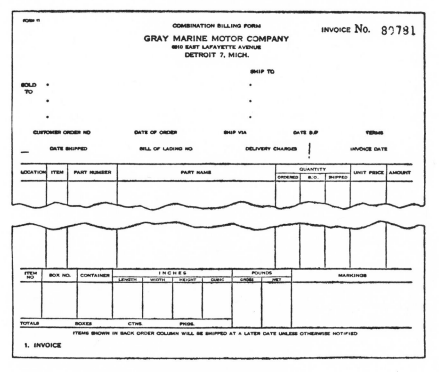

[*Actual size 8⅜″ by 11¾″*]

**Figure 16-1. Combination Sales Order-Shipper-Invoice Form
Making Use of One-Time Carbon.**

1. Filling orders from warehouse stock.
2. Back order of all or portion of the order and future shipment when stock is available.
3. Placing of purchase order with manufacturer for each order received from customers, because items ordered by customer are not carried in stock.

Variations of the combination sales order-shipper-invoice form are frequently used by distributors to provide for these special problems with minimum rewriting of the necessary information.

Documents related to order entry—retail stores. Retail stores do not usually receive written orders from their customers,and therefore any documents relating to order entry are internal in character. These may be summarized as follows.

Documents, a copy of which is given to customer:

1. Sales slip.
   (a) Bound books provided for each sales clerk, or
   (b) Some mechanical device (such as Autographic Register, Uarco, and others) in which the sales invoices and necessary copies are printed in perforated rolls or strips with one-time carbon interleaving. These mechanical devices usually provide for one copy of the sales slip to remain locked in the device. Removal of this copy is

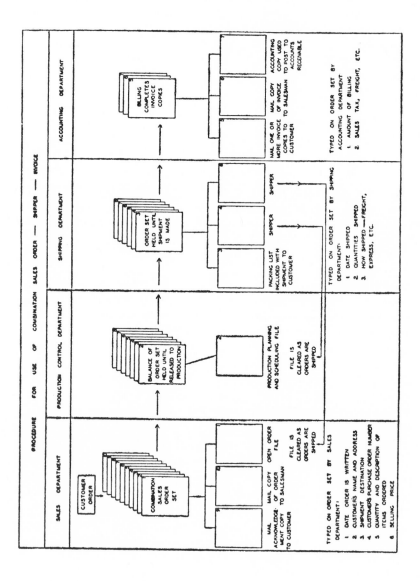

Figure 16-2. Chart Illustrating Preparation and Use of a Combination Sales Order-Shipper-Invoice.

then limited to one or more authorized individuals provided with a key to the device. This feature prevents alteration of the retained copy to reflect details of a sale different from the customer's receipt copy.

2. Cash register receipt recording amount of sale. The cash register usually records information on each sale and daily totals on a tape locked in the machine.

3. Adding machine tape listing each item purchased and the total amount of the sale. This tape may be produced by a cash register or an ordinary adding machine and is handed to the customer as a record of the transaction. This procedure is commonly used by chain grocery stores.

Documents retained for internal use:

1. Copies of sales slips.
2. Cash register tapes.
3. Reports of cash register readings.

Documents related to order entry—mail order houses. Mail order houses generally use the order form sent in by the customer to fill the order from stock (some portions or all of the order may be rewritten for internal convenience) and then return all the documents related to the order to the customer with the merchandise.

This technique provides the customer with a written record of what he ordered and what he receives, at the same time requiring only a minimum of rewriting by the mail order house. The record of details of the transaction retained by the mail order house may be very limited or even nonexistent.

Credit approval prior to acceptance of an order. It is necessary for any seller, whether manufacturer, distributor, or retailer, to consider the problem of credit approval before accepting an order on credit. This is most commonly done by routing the customer's order, or the sales order prepared by the seller, to an individual or department charged with the function of approving credit. Normally a separate approval is given each order, necessitating submission of a copy of each document needed for requesting credit approval. It is not customary to send the customer an acknowledgment of the acceptance of the order until credit has been approved.

Back order procedures. In preparing the sales order, it may not be possible to determine whether shipment of the entire quantity covered by the sales order is possible at one time. This problem is accentuated when the sales order represents a listing of several items, with shipment eventually possible on some items, or for portions of the quantities, without full completion of the order. Some kind of paper work is required to carry forward the remaining portion of the order. To meet the problem, three quantity columns are usually provided on the combination sales order-shipper-invoice form. The first provides space for entry of quantities ordered at the time the sales order is written. The second column is used for entry of the quantity actually shipped. The entry is completed by the shipping department or stockroom making the shipment, so that the quantities shipped appear on shipping and invoice copies. The difference between the first and second quantity columns is then extended in a third quanity column representing the balance on order. A new combination sales order-shipper-invoice form may then be originated listing only the unshipped balances.

Many variations of this procedure exist to fit conditions peculiar to individual situations. A complete rewriting of much of the sales order information on back-order copies can be effected by use of spirit duplicating equipment (Ditto, Standard Duplicating, and so on). This method permits the original master copy of the sales order to be used in preparing additional order sets for the back-ordered items. The procedure may involve blanking out portions of the previous order or the preparation of an "insert or variable master" form containing writing different from the original master form. Proper development of these procedures permits the necessary flow of paper work for back orders with a minimum of clerical time required for rewriting essential information.

Caution in handling large backlogs of open orders. When there is a large backlog of unfilled orders, and shipment cannot be made for several months, one of the problems confronting management is the question of just how firm the orders really are—particularly if conditions change. The problem is of considerable importance if the procedure is such that the backlog of open orders from customers results in a more or less automatic placing of purchase orders for the goods or for materials and parts to manufacture the goods. This may result in a situation where, as a practical matter, the customers cannot be made to accept shipment on their orders, whereas, on the other hand, the purchase commitments are firm and cannot be canceled without substantial loss.

The answer to this problem is as much a question of management judgment as it is a problem of mechanical procedure. Avoidance of substantial purchase commitments may not be a solution, because the customers may insist on shipment of their order at firm prices. On the other hand, the customer may refuse to accept delivery and as a practical matter little can be done about it.

From the procedural viewpoint, the following questions must be answered:

1. Do the conditions of acceptance of the order and the legal form of the order afford maximum protection to the seller?
2. Is the procedure for translating customer's orders into purchase commitments a deliberate and planned one whereby the hazards are known and measured as a business risk, or is the procedure a mechanical one executed without adequate consideration of all the factors involved?

Open order analysis. Punched card procedures facilitate the analysis of open orders. A typical report prepared by use of punched cards is shown in Figure 16-3.

Requirements for effective internal control over order entry and open orders. Effective internal control procedures must be directed toward the following points.

1. Assurance that the selling prices entered on the sales order and acknowledged to the customer are correct. This is important both because of the commitment made to the customer and because the prices indicated on the sales order are usually the basis for billing shipments as they are made. Maintenance of accuracy in entering prices on sales orders is aided by:

(a) Positive identification, often facilitated by use of catalogue or part numbers.

(b) Simple methods of specifying extras or accessories (the use of accessory group code number or letters by the automobile industry is a case in point).

(c) Carefully organized price catalogues and understandable price lists or price records.

District	COMMODITY		SCHEDULED DELIVERY			QUANTITY SCHEDULED	SALES AMOUNT
	CODE	DESCRIPTION	LESS THAN 10 DAYS	10 TO 20 DAYS	OVER 20 DAYS		
1	0301	BEAUTY SOAP REGULAR	500	500	297	1297	2594.00
1	0302	BEAUTY SOAP GUEST	300	144		444	932.40
1	0303	BEAUTY SOAP BATH	500	500	88	1088	2448.00
						2829	5974.40*
1	1311	COOL SHAVE SMALL	750	570		1320	2640.00
1	1312	COOL SHAVE LARGE	750	750	738	2238	5035.50
1	1313	SHAVE SOAP SMALL	750	619		1369	2601.10
1	1314	SHAVE SOAP LARGE	300	238		538	1560.20
1	1315	SHAVE SOAP GIANT	300	300	60	660	2046.00
						6125	13882.80*
1	1351	BRUSHLESS CREAM SML	400	400	350	1150	2300.00
1	1352	BRUSHLESS CREAM LRG	400	400	100	900	2250.00
1	1353	BRUSHLESS COOL SML	400	144		544	1088.00
1	1354	BRUSHLESS COOL LRG	200	200	200	600	1350.00
						3194	6988.00*

Caption above table: ORDERS ON HAND BY COMMODITY — BY DISTRICT

[*Actual size 4¾″ by 9½″*]

Figure 16-3. Order Analysis Making Use of Punched Card Equipment.
(Courtesy of International Business Machines Corporation)

(d) Rechecking of selling prices by an individual or department independent of the initial pricer—perhaps on a selective or test basis.

2. Control of orders written to insure that they do not become misplaced, frequently by the use of prenumbered forms, so that all numbers can be eventually accounted for.

3. Control of credit authorization to insure that orders are not accepted without proper credit approval.

4. Control of periodical analysis and reporting of open orders so that:

(a) Reports of unfilled orders are accurate.

(b) Orders filled are properly cleared from the open order files.

(c) Cancellations or modifications of open orders are reflected in the records.

(d) Only approved new orders are picked up in the records.

BILLING PROCEDURES FOR A MANUFACTURER OR DISTRIBUTOR

Authorization to ship. Any billing procedure must start with the shipment of product or merchandise. In order to make the shipment, the shipping department must either have records of open orders, which it reviews to determine where shipments are to be made, or, as is more commonly the case, must receive an authorization to ship from some other department—usually the sales department or the production control department.

This authorization to ship must convey the following information.

1. To whom the shipment is to be made.
2. The customer's purchase order number.
3. The shipper's sales order number.

4. What is to be shipped.
5. The quantities to be shipped.
6. How the shipment is to be made—parcel post, rail freight, express or truck. The authorization may read "ship best way," leaving the method to the discretion of the shipping department.

The authorization may be a special form, but more commonly one copy or a portion of a set of the combination sales order-shipper-invoice form serves this purpose.

Advice of completed shipment. Two notifications are normally required from the shipping department.

1. The packing list—to accompany the shipment to the customer telling him among other things (*a*) what the shipment consists of—quantities and description; (*b*) the customer's purchase order number.
2. The shipper—an internal document advising other departments that the shipment has been made. This advice is necessary for the billing or accounting department to prepare an invoice and the sales or order department to clear their open order file.

These two documents are usually prepared in one writing and may be part of the combination sales order-shipper-invoice form.

Billing—pricing. An essential step in the billing of each shipment is the determination and entry of the selling price on the invoice. This may be done by writing the selling prices on the shipper form and then using the priced shipper as the source of information from which the invoice is typed. When the combination sales order-shipper-invoice form is used, the selling price and all terms of payment usually appear on the order set when the invoicing operation is commenced.

If the selling price must be entered at this point from an independent source, it may be done from catalogues, price lists, special records set up to record selling prices, or from copies of the sales order that show the selling price.

Billing—extension and invoice writing. The quantity shipped, the description of product or merchandise shipped, and the unit selling prices, now being available, the next step is to extend the quantity shipped and the selling price to obtain the amount of the billing and complete the invoice. There are three common methods of performing this operation.

1. By some type of calculating machine for making the extension and footing, and a separate typewriter for the invoice writing.
2. By a billing machine which combines a calculating machine with a typewriter.
3. By punched card accounting equipment to write the essential information, extend quantities, and total the extensions.

Comparison of billing methods. Each of the methods mentioned above has advantages and disadvantages depending upon the nature of the particular situation, the volume of billings, and the manner in which the procedure must be performed.

If separate calculating machines are used, it is often helpful if they have both "upper" and "lower" registers so that extensions can be made in the lower register for each item in the shipment listed on the invoice, with extension being accumulated in the upper register to determine the total amount of each invoice. This also facilitates extension and accumulation of list prices and the application of discounts to totals so accumulated.

If a large number of invoice copies must be written at one time, the use of properly selected paper stock and carbons is essential to secure clear copies. Electric typewriters aid in securing good copies, as well as uniform type impression, speed, minimization of operator fatigue, and other advantages offered by these machines.

The billing machines combining a calculating device and a typewriter have been very popular. It is possible to perform the entire invoicing operation on these machines with excellent results. Many favor the use of separate calculating machines and electric typewriters on the grounds that they are faster.

Punched card and electronic equipment also have many advantages where the volume is substantial. Typical invoices prepared by use of punched card equipment are shown in Figure 16-4 and Figure 16-5. This technique offers the following special timesaving features and advantages.

THE BREWING COMPANY
CITY, STATE

ROUTE 214 ANDREWS BROTHERS
STOP NO. 57 124 MARKET STREET
ROCKFORD ILLINOIS

DATE 2 1 8 INVOICE NO. 21037 CUSTOMER'S ORDER NO. 76385

QUANTITY	PACKAGE	PRODUCT	BEVERAGE PRICE	CONTAINER DEPOSIT	TOTAL AMOUNT
25	HLVS	MERIT BEER	7 75	6 00	343 75
5	HLVS	RICHTERS ALE	8 50	6 00	72 50
40	CS ST	MERIT BEER	1 75	70	98 00
20	CS EX	MERIT BEER	1 75	70	49 00
		LESS RETURNS			
30	HLVS	EMPTY CONTAINERS		6 00	180 00 CR
35	CS ST	12 OZ BOTTLES		70	24 50 CR
5	CASES	EMPTY CASES 12 OZ		22	1 10 CR
2	CS QT	32 OZ BOTTLES		70	1 40 CR
					* 356 25

CONTAINERS ON THIS ORDER, WHEN EMPTY, SHOULD BE RETURNED FOR CREDIT. PAY LAST AMOUNT IN THIS COLUMN.

[*Actual size 5½" by 8½"*]

Figure 16-4. Invoice Prepared by use of Punched Card Equipment.
(Courtesy of International Business Machines Corporation.)

1. Address cards can be prepared in quantity in advance for each customer and pulled from a tub file as each shipment is made, instead of requiring a separate typing or key-punching operation for each order or invoice when writing the address.

2. Description cards of items shipped may be prepared in advance in a manner similar to that above. These description card files sometimes include prepunched quantites for typical shipment lot sizes, and this feature may then be used as a perpetual inventory control; that is, the description cards in the tub file can be made to represent the quantities in inventory available for shipment.

3. The extension and footing of each invoice is done rapidly and automatically by machine.

4. The cards used in the invoicing operation can also be used in connection with

REPRESENTATIVE COMPANY

INVOICE

Sold To	ACE DRUG CO 1412 STATE ST LUDINGTON MICH
Ship To	ACE DRUG CO 811 MAIN ST MUSKEGON MICH
Via	ACME TRUCK PREPAID
Terms	2% 10 DAYS NET 30

			BRANCH	CUSTOMER
			1 3	6 7

SALESMAN	ORDER NUMBER	ORDER DATE	REF. NO.	INVOICE	INVOICE DATE
G DRISCOLL	AM 8462	0 6 0 7	7 1 4 2 0	1 3 4 2 0	0 6 2 0

COMMODITY		UNIT PRICE	QUANTITY		AMOUNT
CODE	DESCRIPTION		NUMBER	UNIT	
0 3 0 1	BEAUTY SOAP REGULAR	2 0 0	1 2	DZ	2 4 0 0
0 3 0 2	BEAUTY SOAP GUEST	2 1 0	1 2	DZ	2 5 2 0
1 3 1 4	SHAVE SOAP LARGE	2 9 0	2 4	DZ	6 9 6 0
1 4 1 1	OIL SHAMPOO MEDIUM	3 0 0	5 0	DZ	1 5 0 0 0
1 4 2 1	REG SHAMPOO SMALL	1 1 0	2 4	DZ	2 6 4 0
3 2 4 2	SUPER PASTE MEDIUM	1 8 5	6	DZ	1 1 1 0
	BACK ORDERED				
0 3 0 2	BEAUTY SOAP GUEST	2 1 0	1 2	DZ	
5 4 1 0	LAUNDRY SOAP BAR	2 4 0	2 4	DZ	
5 4 2 0	LAUNDRY SOAP CHIP	2 5 0	1 2	DZ	
	FREIGHT				2 4 3
					3 0 8 7 3 ✱

[Actual size 8¼″ by 8½″]

Figure 16-5. Invoice Prepared by Use of Punched Card Equipment.
(Courtesy of International Business Machines Corporation.)

punched card records for open orders and for accounts receivable without much additional manual effort.

5. The cards used in the invoicing operation can also be used to produce a sales distribution or analysis without much effort.

Electronic data processing equipment offers all the advantages of punched card equipment: it operates with greater speed and accuracy and with very little manual intervention. Electronic equipment is capable of currently accumulating, classifying, and editing data that are available by alternate methods only with considerable clerical effort or perhaps after the data have lost their usefulness. The cost of the equipment is sufficiently high to justify its use economically only where its unusual capacities offset its cost. Most invoicing and accounts receivable applications are sufficiently routine to warrant conversion to electronic equipment only to integrate them with inventory and production control, sales forecasting, and similar routines.

Mention has been made previously of the use of spirit duplicating equipment to produce a combination sales order-shipper-invoice form. This plan is widely used in combination with the types of mechanical equipment mentioned above.

Billing—mailing of invoices. Considerable clerical effort in addressing envelopes for mailing can be eliminated by having invoices designed to be used in a "window" envelopes. This also avoids errors and mix-ups that occur in addressing envelopes separately and enclosing the invoices in them.

Sales journals and accounting distribution. Having prepared invoices to customers, it is necessary to summarize the bills for accounting purposes. Usually it is also necessary to analyze the totals by types of product, territories, salesmen, and so on.

A simple method of accomplishing this result is to file the invoices in a post binder by accounting periods and run adding machine tapes to obtain totals of each desired classification. These adding machine tapes may then be fastened to a sheet in the binder to form a permanent record. The post binder of invoice copies and adding machine tapes thus serves as a sales journal and a sales distribution.

Columnar sales journals are also widely used to list invoices and obtain an analysis of the sales. These may be a pen and ink record, or they can be prepared by use of a bookkeeping machine. In the latter instance, it is customary to make the posting to the accounts receivable ledger card as part of the same operation.

Punched card accounting is particularly suited to analysis of sales invoices, even though the invoice itself may not be written from the cards. The essential data is key-punched into each card, automatically sorted for each desired classification of sales, and totals accumulated for each classification by automatic machines. An example is shown in Figure 16-6.

TRADING AREA ANALYSIS							
TRADING AREA AND CUSTOMER NAME	TRADING AREA NUMBER	NO. OF LAST PURCHASE	PROD- UCT CLASS	BOUGHT THIS MONTH	TO DATE THIS YEAR	SAME MONTHS LAST YEAR	12 MONTHS LAST YEAR
ATLANTA GA	112						
ATLANTA CANDY CO	112	3	1	156	427	318	1267
		3	2	82	259	206	943
		3	3	98	310	295	1229
				336●	996●	819●	3439●
GILLETT BROS MACON	112	3	1	25	84	76	310
		3	2	42	128	115	427
		3	3	37	126	109	436
				104●	338●	300●	1173●
WAGNER CANDY CO	112	3	1	260	673	531	2046
		1	2		125	526	1932
		3	3	212	704	760	2765
				472●	1502●	1817●	6743●
		●		912	● 2836	● 2936	●11355
SAVANNAH GA	137						
BERTRAM THOS	137	3	1	154	454	327	1327
		12	2			364	942
		3	3	96	272	259	1126
				250●	726●	950●	3395●
HANSON DRUGS CLAXTON	137	3	1	75	239	216	837
		3	2	42	136	98	406
		3	3	36	104	86	394
				153●	479●	400●	1637●

Figure 16-6. Sales Analysis Making Use of Punched Card Equipment.
(Courtesy of International Business Machines Corporation.)

Another useful device for the preparation of a distribution of sales invoices makes use of printed strip statements for each day or week. These forms have holes punched at the top for mounting on a peg board or strip. Each printed horizontal line represents a desired classification. The totals of each classification are obtained by daily analysis of the sales invoices. These are entered on an exposed margin of the strip form. The strips for a week or month are then cross-added to secure totals which are entered on a similar form inserted on the pegs. This printed form may also be used as a management report.

The patented device "Keysort" is also useful for sales analysis. Either a copy of the invoice is made on a Keysort card and this copy is punched, or the essential data are key-punched from a copy of the invoice into a Keysort card. Sorting is then done with a specially designed needle. The cost of the cards and related equipment is not substantial, and if the information must be sorted and classified several different ways, the saving in sorting time is worth while. Keysort is simply a sorting device, and the cards or other media sorted by use of the needle must be totaled by calculating or adding machines.

Special billing problems. The following practices create special billing problems that are discussed below.

1. Returned goods and allowances.
2. Trade discounts.
3. Cash discounts.
4. Chain discounts.
5. Sales commissions.

Returned goods and allowances. When merchandise or product is returned to the seller or allowances must be made to the customer, a credit memo is prepared for accounting purposes. It is customary for the seller to insist that his advance approval be secured before the customer is permitted to return the merchandise, although the arrival of the merchandise on the receiving dock may be the first notice of its return. A receiving report is ordinarily prepared, and after appropriate approval by the sales department or some other department authorized to approve such returns, the accounting department prepares the credit memo. Copies are mailed to the customer like an invoice, and an accounting distribution of the credit memo is compiled. The credit memos may be intermingled and netted in the totals with invoices. The charges for sales returns and allowances are usually made to separate accounts that are deducted from sales in the operating statements.

Trade discounts. Selling prices are often quoted on a list price basis, with deduction of a discount permitted depending upon the quantity sold, the class of purchaser, or the distance from the seller when items are shipped with transportation prepaid. Consideration must be given to laws, such as the Robinson-Patman Act, limiting the use of varying selling prices to different customers without corresponding variation in the cost of doing business with the customers.

For accounting purposes, trade discounts are ordinarily deducted directly on the sales invoices, and only the list price less discount is considered in building up the sales distribution. Trade discounts, as distinguished from cash discounts, are not usually dependent upon prompt payment for the transaction. It is generally customary to treat all discounts in excess of 2 per cent as trade discounts for accounting purposes, even though they are described as cash discounts and are related to timely payment of the transaction.

Cash discounts. Cash discounts are given as a premium for timely payment for a transaction. They are often shown on an invoice as "2 per cent 10 days, net 30 days," meaning that 2 per cent discount is allowed if the invoice is paid within 10 days of the date of the invoice, and payment without deduction for the discount is permitted any time within 30 days from the date of the invoice.

Cash discounts in connection with sales invoices are usually described on the accounting records as "Discounts allowed on sales" or in similar terminology. They are ordinarily reflected in separate accounts, even though almost all invoices may be paid on a net basis after deduction of the discount. The charge to accounts receivable and the sales distribution are usually made on a gross basis without consideration of the discount by the seller. When the payment is received from the customer on a net basis, the discount having been deducted from the invoice, the discount is entered separately in the record of cash receipts, and the credit to accounts receivable is made on a gross basis to clear the charge originally made.

Chain discounts. Trade discounts are frequently stated as a series of discount rates such as "20/10/5%." This type of discount is known as a "chain discount." The following illustrates the meaning of a chain discount of 20/10/5%, assuming it is to be applied to a list price of $100:

List price	$100.00
Less 20% discount	20.00
Balance	$ 80.00
Less 10% discount on balance	8.00
Balance	$ 72.00
Less 5% discount on balance	3.60
Net Price	$ 68.40

The amount of the "20/10/5%" chain discount is thus $20.00 plus $8.00 plus $3.60, or $31.60.

Chain discounts obviously complicate the extension of net selling prices on a sales invoice and require more clerical work. A similar problem is encountered with punched card accounting, since three multiplying operations are involved.

One solution to reduce the amount of clerical work is the use of a table of chain discount equivalents; for example "20/10/5%" is the equivalent of a trade discount of 31.6 per cent. See Table 1.

Payment terms. The terms of payment are almost invariably shown on invoices. Abbreviations are common, such as the following:

Net 30 days	Payment due on or before 30 days after date of invoice.
Net 10th and 25th prox.	Payment of invoices dated 16th to end of month due on 10th of following month; invoices dated beginning of month to 15th of month due on 25th of month. (Prox. = proximo, meaning the next or coming period.)

Special charges on the sales invoices. Frequently special charges are made on invoices for sales taxes, excise taxes, transportation, and the like. These also complicate the billing operation since the amount of the charge must be computed, and sometimes the sales or excise taxes do not apply to all items listed. Usually it is also necessary to secure separate totals of these items for the accounting distribution of sales invoices.

Sales commissions. Salesmen are often paid on a commission basis, sometimes when the order is accepted, but more commonly when the shipment is made and the

TABLE I

DECIMAL EQUIVALENTS OF CHAIN DISCOUNTS

Primary Discount

Secondary Discount	5	7½	10	12½	15	16⅔	20	22½	25	27½	30	32½	33⅓	35	37½
2	.93100	.90650	.88200	.85750	.83300	.81667	.78400	.75950	.73500	.71050	.68600	.66150	.65333	.63700	.61250
2½	.92625	.90188	.87750	.85313	.82875	.81250	.78000	.75562	.73125	.70688	.68250	.65813	.65000	.63375	.60938
5	.90250	.87875	.85500	.83125	.80750	.79166	.76000	.73625	.71250	.68875	.66500	.64125	.63333	.61750	.59375
5 2½	.87994	.85678	.83363	.81047	.78731	.77187	.74100	.71784	.69469	.67153	.64838	.62522	.61750	.60206	.57891
5 5	.85738	.83481	.81225	.78969	.76713	.75208	.72200	.69943	.67688	.65431	.63175	.60919	.60167	.58663	.56406
5 5 2½	.83594	.81394	.79194	.76994	.74795	.73328	.70395	.68195	.65995	.63795	.61596	.59396	.58663	.57196	.54996
7½	.87875	.85563	.83250	.80938	.78625	.77083	.74000	.71688	.69375	.67063	.64750	.62438	.61667	.60125	.57813
7½ 2½	.85678	.83423	.81169	.78914	.76659	.75156	.72150	.69895	.67641	.65386	.63131	.60877	.60125	.58622	.56367
7½ 5	.83481	.81284	.79088	.76891	.74694	.73229	.70300	.68103	.65906	.63709	.61513	.59316	.58583	.57119	.54922
10	.85500	.83250	.81000	.78750	.76500	.75000	.72000	.69750	.67500	.65250	.63000	.60750	.60000	.58500	.56250
10 2½	.83363	.81169	.78975	.76781	.74588	.73125	.70200	.68006	.65813	.63619	.61425	.59231	.58500	.57038	.54844
10 5	.81225	.79088	.76950	.74811	.72675	.71250	.68400	.66263	.64125	.61988	.59850	.57713	.57000	.55575	.53438
10 5 2½	.79194	.77111	.75026	.72944	.70858	.69469	.66690	.64606	.62522	.60438	.58354	.56270	.55575	.54186	.52102
10 7½	.79088	.77006	.74925	.72844	.70763	.69375	.66600	.64519	.62438	.60356	.58275	.56194	.55500	.54113	.52031
10 10	.76950	.74925	.72900	.70875	.68850	.67500	.64800	.62775	.60750	.58725	.56700	.54675	.54000	.52650	.50625
10 10 2½	.75026	.73052	.71078	.69103	.67129	.65812	.63180	.61206	.59231	.57257	.55283	.53308	.52650	.51334	.49359
10 10 5	.73103	.71179	.69255	.67331	.65408	.64125	.61560	.59636	.57713	.55789	.53865	.51941	.51300	.50018	.48094
12½	.83125	.80938	.78750	.76563	.74375	.72917	.70000	.67813	.65625	.63438	.61250	.59063	.58333	.56875	.54688
12½ 2½	.81047	.78914	.76781	.74648	.72516	.71094	.68250	.66117	.63984	.61852	.59719	.57586	.56875	.55453	.53320
12½ 5	.78969	.76891	.74813	.72735	.70656	.69271	.66500	.64422	.62344	.60266	.58188	.56110	.55417	.54031	.51954
12½ 7½	.76891	.74868	.72844	.70821	.68797	.67454	.64750	.62727	.60703	.58680	.56656	.54633	.53958	.52609	.50586
12½ 10	.74813	.72844	.70875	.68907	.66938	.65625	.63000	.61032	.59063	.57094	.55125	.53157	.52500	.51188	.49219
12½ 10 5	.71072	.69202	.67331	.65462	.63591	.62344	.59850	.57980	.56109	.54239	.52369	.50499	.49826	.48629	.46758
12½ 10 5 2½	.69295	.67472	.65648	.63826	.62001	.60791	.58354	.56531	.54707	.52883	.51060	.49237	.48580	.47413	.45589
12½ 10 7½	.69202	.67381	.65559	.63739	.61918	.60709	.58275	.56455	.54633	.52812	.50991	.49170	.48514	.47349	.45528
12½ 10 10	.67331	.65559	.63788	.62016	.60244	.59068	.56700	.54929	.53157	.51385	.49613	.47841	.47203	.46069	.44297
15	.80750	.78625	.76500	.74375	.72250	.70833	.68000	.65875	.63750	.61625	.59500	.57375	.56667	.55250	.53125
15 2½	.78732	.76660	.74588	.72516	.70444	.69062	.66300	.64229	.62157	.60084	.58013	.55941	.55251	.53869	.51797
15 5	.76713	.74694	.72675	.70656	.68638	.67292	.64600	.62581	.60563	.58544	.56525	.54506	.53833	.52488	.50469
20	.76000	.74000	.72000	.70000	.68000	.66667	.64000	.62000	.60000	.58000	.56000	.54000	.53333	.52000	.50000

2 Reproduced by courtesy of Lefax, Inc., Philadelphia, Pa., from "Business Data Sheet No. 5-167."

TABLE I (continued)

Secondary Discount	Primary Discount														
	40	42½	45	47½	50	52½	55	57½	60	62½	65	66⅔	70	72½	75
2	.58800	.56350	.53900	.51450	.4900	.46550	.44100	.41650	.39200	.36750	.34300	.32667	.29400	.26950	.24500
2½	.585	.56063	.53625	.51188	.4875	.46313	.43875	.41438	.39	.36563	.34125	.325	.2925	.26813	.24375
5	.57	.54625	.5225	.49875	.475	.45125	.4275	.40375	.38	.35625	.3325	.31667	.285	.26125	.2375
5 2½	.55575	.53259	.50944	.48628	.46313	.43997	.41681	.39366	.3705	.34374	.32419	.30875	.27788	.25472	.23156
5 5	.5415	.51894	.49638	.47381	.45125	.42869	.40613	.38356	.361	.33844	.31588	.30083	.27075	.24819	.22563
5 5 2½	.52796	.50596	.48397	.46194	.43997	.41797	.39557	.37397	.35198	.32998	.30798	.29331	.26398	.24198	.21998
7½ 5	.555	.53188	.50875	.48563	.4625	.43938	.41625	.39313	.37	.34688	.32375	.30833	.2775	.25438	.23125
7½ 5 2½	.54113	.51858	.49603	.47348	.45094	.42839	.40584	.3833	.36075	.3382	.31566	.30063	.27056	.24802	.22547
7½ 5	.52725	.50529	.48331	.46135	.43938	.41741	.39544	.37347	.3515	.32954	.30756	.29292	.26363	.24166	.21969
10	.54	.5175	.495	.4725	.45	.4275	.405	.3825	.36	.3375	.315	.2925	.27	.2475	.225
10 2½	.513	.50456	.48263	.46069	.43875	.41681	.39488	.37294	.351	.32906	.30713	.285	.26325	.24131	.21938
10 5	.50018	.49163	.47025	.44888	.4275	.40613	.38475	.36338	.342	.32063	.29925	.27788	.2565	.23513	.21375
10 5 2½	.4995	.47933	.45849	.43765	.41681	.39597	.37513	.35429	.33345	.31261	.29177	.2775	.25009	.22925	.20841
10 7½	.47453	.47869	.45788	.43706	.41625	.39544	.37463	.35381	.333	.31219	.29138	.26363	.24975	.22894	.20183
10 7½ 5	.486	.45472	.43499	.41521	.39544	.37567	.3559	.33612	.31635	.29658	.27681	.27	.23726	.21749	.19772
10 10	.47385	.46575	.4455	.42525	.405	.38475	.3645	.34425	.324	.30375	.2835	.26325	.243	.22275	.2025
10 10 2½	.4617	.45411	.43436	.41462	.39488	.37514	.35539	.33564	.3159	.29616	.27641	.2565	.23693	.21718	.19744
10 10 5	.45016	.44246	.42323	.40399	.38475	.36551	.34628	.32704	.3078	.28856	.26933	.25009	.23085	.21161	.19238
10 10 5 2½	.4374	.4314	.41264	.39389	.37513	.35637	.33762	.31886	.3001	.28135	.26259	.243	.22508	.20632	.18757
10 10 10	.525	.41918	.40095	.38273	.3645	.34628	.32805	.30983	.2916	.27338	.25515	.29138	.2187	.20048	.18225
12½	.51188	.50313	.48125	.45938	.4375	.41663	.39375	.37188	.35	.32813	.30625	.2841	.2625	.24063	.21875
12½ 2½	.49875	.49055	.46922	.4479	.42656	.40622	.38391	.36258	.34125	.31993	.29859	.27681	.25594	.23462	.21328
12½ 5	.48563	.47797	.45719	.43641	.41563	.3958	.37406	.35329	.3325	.31172	.29094	.26953	.24938	.2286	.20781
12½ 7½	.4725	.4654	.44516	.42493	.40469	.38538	.36422	.34399	.32375	.30352	.28328	.26224	.24281	.22258	.20234
12½ 10	.44888	.45282	.43313	.41344	.39375	.37497	.35438	.33469	.315	.29532	.27563	.24913	.23625	.21657	.19688
12½ 10 5	.43766	.43018	.41147	.39277	.37406	.35622	.33666	.31796	.29925	.28055	.26185	.2429	.22444	.20574	.18704
12½ 10 5 2½	.43706	.41943	.40118	.38295	.36471	.34732	.32824	.31001	.29177	.27354	.2553	.24257	.21883	.2006	.18236
12½ 10 7½	.42525	.41886	.40065	.38243	.36422	.34685	.32780	.30959	.29138	.27317	.25496	.23602	.21853	.20033	.18211
12½ 10 10	.51	.40754	.38982	.3721	.35438	.33747	.31894	.30122	.2835	.26579	.24807	.28333	.21263	.19491	.17719
15	.49725	.48875	.4675	.44625	.425	.40375	.3825	.36125	.34	.31875	.2975	.27625	.255	.23375	.2125
15 2½	.48	.47653	.45582	.43510	.4144	.39366	.3730	.35222	.3315	.31097	.29007	.26667	.24863	.22791	.20719
20	.48	.46	.44	.42	.40	.38	.36	.34	.32	.30	.28	.26667	.24	.22	.20

customer is billed. Sometimes the salesman's commission is dependent upon payment of the invoice by the customer. In any of these instances, clerical work is increased in the sales order or billing routine, represented by the extension of sales dollars at the commission rates and accumulation of the totals for each salesman.

Simplification of the clerical work depends upon the particular problem involved. Some of the methods include use of:

1. Copies of the sales order or copies of the sales invoice, which are sorted by salesmen. The items for each salesman are then totaled, and commissions computed by application of commisison rates to totals for a day, week, or month.
2. Separate columns in the sales journal to compute or accumulate commissions based upon billings.
3. Separate columns in the cash receipts record to compute or accumulate commissions based upon cash collections.
4. Punched card accounting or Keysort to compute and accumulate salesmen's commissions.

Preprinted sales invoices. Many situations arise where it is practicable to have the quantities and descriptions of items to be billed printed on the sales invoice form with appropriate extensions, tax or transportation charges, and totals. This technique is widely used by monthly book clubs, professional testing companies, and others who have many identical billings. It is then only necessary to type in the customer's name and address on the invoice.

ACCOUNTS RECEIVABLE RECORDS

Choice of accounts receivable records. A wide choice of methods exists in the field of accounts receivable records. The decision in any particular instance should consider the following.

1. Volume of transactions.
2. Amount of detail to be posted to the record.
3. Payment by customer of individual charges as contrasted with payment of groups of charges or the monthly account balance.
4. Frequency of partial payment of individual charges.
5. Necessity of furnishing customers with statements of their accounts.
6. Reduction of clerical cost by use of manual devices or mechanical equipment.
7. Adequate internal control.

Manually posted accounts receivable records. The most common accounts receivable record used by small businesses consists of a simple pen-posted ledger sheet, provided with debit, credit, and balance columns. This may be filed alphabetically by customer in a post or spring-back binder. Although requiring only a nominal investment in forms or equipment, this procedure also involves a separate writing of a sales journal and cash receipts record—or their equivalent. Any statements of accounting or listing of unpaid items also requires a separate operation. This method is not economical except in the simplest situations.

A manual procedure that is fairly common makes use of a file of copies of invoices which represent the accounts receivable record. As items are paid, they are withdrawn from this file and transferred to a paid file. Partial payments are posted to the invoice to which they apply. Statements of unpaid items are prepared by listing the invoices in the open file. This procedure substitutes a sorting and filing operation for the posting of charges to the conventional ledger record. Post or spring-back binders can be used to file the invoice copies, and separate files can be used for each subdivision of accounts or each accounts receivable control. This method has been successful, even where the volume of transactions is substanial, although it has certain disadvantages. The preparation of statements requires a separate writing for each charge. Some difficulty may be experienced in balancing unpaid items with the control accounts, particularly when payments on account or partial payments on individual invoices frequently occur.

Numerous mechanical aids can be used in connection with manually posted accounts receivable records. The accounts receivable ledger sheets may be mounted on their left-hand side in a multiple-ring binder permitting the exposure of one line at the top or bottom of each ledger sheet where the customer's name is visible. Indexed dividers are used with each set of sheets, facilitating the rapid location of each account for manual posting. A form used in this type of record is shown in Figure 16-7.

Another simple device makes use of a peg board on which is mounted a cash receipts journal or a sales journal. The accounts receivable ledger cards are placed on this peg board as each entry is made, permitting the preparation of the books or original entry at the same time the posting is made to the accounts receivable ledger card. This is accomplished in one writing by using carbon paper. Since both entries are made in one writing, the possibility of posting errors is minimized. Standard forms are available for regular and installment accounts. The device is illustrated in Figure 16-8.

Any of the mechanical devices for filing cards such as Kardex, Cardineer, VIS-Irecord, Hadley, Vertical-Visible Record, or Acme visible record can be used to advantage in connection with manually posted accounts receivable records.

Use of bookkeeping machines for accounts receivable. Bookkeeping machines are of two basic types—numerical and alphabetical. The numerical machines have keys that permit the printing of dates, certain symbols, and a numerical reference for each debit or credit entry, but have no typewriter keyboard. The alphabetical machines include a full typewriter keyboard. Both of these types of machines have one or more registers for adding and subtracting items posted. They are normally used to prepare sales journals, cash receipts journals, and statements of account at the same time that postings are made to the accounts receivable ledger sheets. Some of these machines can also be used to accumulate distributions internally in registers or to prepare a columnar distribution sheet or distribution tickets to obtain the accounting distribution of sales invoices and cash receipts. An example is shown in Figure 16-9.

Although the alphabetical type of machine is more flexible (the typewriter

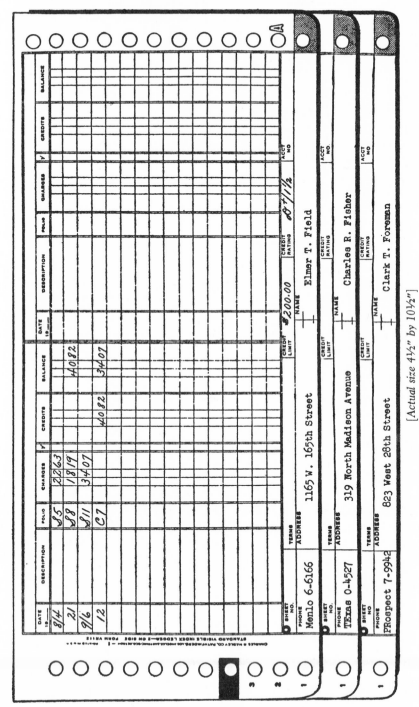

Figure 16-7. Accounts Receivable Record for Filing in Multiple-Ring Binder.
(Courtesy of Charles R. Hadley Company.)

[Actual size 4½" by 10½"]

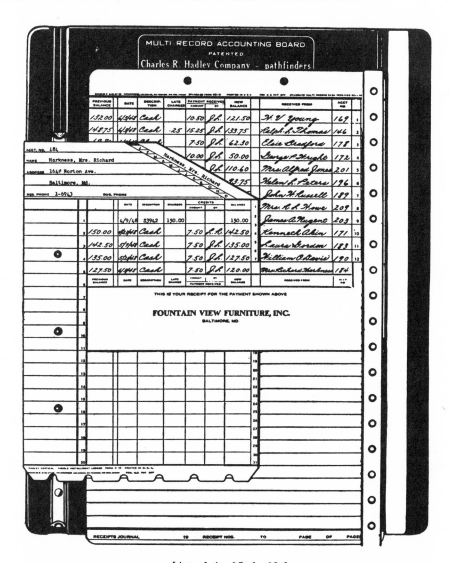

[Actual size 15" by 12"]

Figure 16-8. Manually Posted Accounts Receivable Record Making Use of Writing Board. A sheet of carbon paper would cover the receipts journal. It was omitted from this illustration to show the entries.
(Courtesy of Charles R. Hadley Company.)

keyboard is available for writing any necessary information), the numerical bookkeeping machines of most manufacturers have certain automatic mechanical features that result in faster posting.

With a numerical machine, the customer's name and address are entered on ledger cards and statements by use of a separate typewriter or addressing machine.

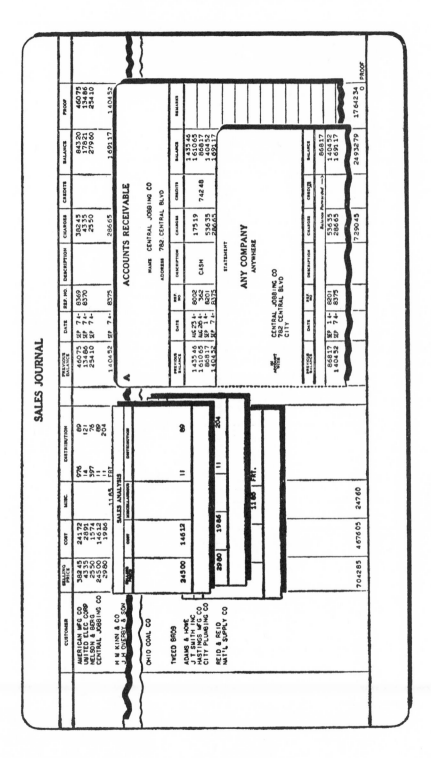

Figure 16-9. Accounts Receivable Record with Provision for Sales Analysis.

(Courtesy of Burroughs Corporation.)

Bookkeeping machines for accounts receivable records are ordinarily more economical than manual systems whenever a substantial volume of transactions must be recorded. The reduction in clerical time results in part from the preparation of several documents with one writing, the accumulation of totals in the registers, which are a part of the machines and the ease of balancing the detail records with control accounts.

Punched card and electronic systems for accounts receivable. Punched card and electronic equipment, such as that manufactured by International Business Machines Corporation, for example, have many features that make them desirable in connection with accounts receivable records for volume transactions. The cost of using this equipment for accounts receivable is reduced when it is integrated with other operations such as order entry, order analysis, billing, and sales analysis. Punched card and electronic equipment can be used to record all receivable transactions and prepare statements of account listing all transactions or only the unpaid items. They can also be used to prepare aged anlayses of the receivables.

Preparation of statements of account. Mention has previously been made of some of the methods of preparing statements of account for mailing to customers——usually once a month. Most of the mechanical accounts receivable systems result in the preparation of such a statement for every customer as a matter of routine. When the statements must be prepared as separate operation, the items listed are usually only the unpaid items, and often only the past due items. A statement prepared in connection with punched card procedures is shown in Figure 16-10.

STATEMENT
THE CONFECTIONERY COMPANY CITY, STATE

MAKERS OF FINE CANDIES

IN ACCOUNT WITH
ATLANTA CANDY COMPANY
829 CONKLYN AVENUE
ATLANTA 12 GEORGIA

4 MO. | 1 DAY | YR.

PAST DUE CHARGES

DATE			INVOICE NO. OR TYPE OF ENTRY	AMOUNT	CURRENT MONTH	31 TO 60 DAYS	61 TO 90 DAYS	OVER 90 DAYS
MO.	DAY	YR.						
1	2 5		1 0 2 1 2	2 4 5 1 0			2 4 5 1 0	
1	2 8		CASH	2 0 0 0 0 CR			2 0 0 0 0 CR	
2	1 5		1 5 4 0 6	1 9 7 4 0		1 9 7 4 0		
3	0 5		1 8 3 2 7	1 8 4 6 0	1 8 4 6 0			
3	2 1		2 0 1 3 4	1 5 2 1 0	1 5 2 1 0			
				5 7 9 2 0	3 3 6 7 0	1 9 7 4 0	4 5 1 0	

PAY LAST AMOUNT IN THIS COLUMN↗

Figure 16-10. Accounts Receivable Statement Prepared by Use of Punched Card Equipment.
(Courtesy of International Business Machines Corporation.)

It is questionable in some instances whether it is worth while to mail to commercial customers statements of account that list items that are not past due where there is reasonable expectation that they will be paid in accordance with the specified terms as a matter of routine. This question is particularly important when the statement is not available as a by-product of the accounts receivable record and must be prepared each month as a separate operation.

In order to stagger the clerical work needed to balance receivable ledgers against control accounts and mail statements to customers more evenly throughout each month, one technique often used is to establish separate cut-off dates during each month for sections of the accounts receivable records. Most industrial customers, however, prefer to receive a statement terminating as of the end of each month to aid them in checking their accounts payable operation.

Many retail organizations have adopted a technique known as "cycle billing." There are variations in the details of the procedure, but generally the original sales slips, or copies thereof, are sorted by customer and placed in an alphabetical file. Once each month, on a staggered basis for groups of letters in the alphabet, the sales slips are listed on a statement form and mailed to the customer. Typical forms for cycle billing are shown in Figure 16-11.

When the original sales slip is mailed to the customer, the store usually retains a microfilm record. This procedure eliminates the necessity of describing each item on the statement, and when the description is abbreviated, the customer is frequently puzzled as to its meaning. Cycle billing not only spreads the work of posting, balancing, and statement prepapration over each month, but also affects the work related to cash receipts. Because many retail customers pay their bills shortly after the beginning of each month, the procedure can have the effect of somewhat delaying collections. This factor, however, has not been found to be too serious, but might prove a disadvantage in certain lines.

Filing accounts receivable records. The order of filing accounts receivable is generally dependent upon the mechanics of collection. The more common methods are:

1. *Alphabetical* (the usual method).
2. *Numerical*, by a number assigned to each customer (often used with punched card accounting or whenever customers are assigned a number for other reasons).
3. *By salesmen*, and then alphabetical (more convenient if the salesmen make collections).
4. *Territorial*, and then alphabetical (useful when collection responsibility is assigned on a territorial basis).
5. *By store or plant*, and then alphabetical (more common when accounts receivable records are maintained at a central point for several stores or plants).

Use of control accounts. It is customary to provide control accounts for groups of accounts receivable records whenever the number of accounts is substantial. This permits delegation of responsibility to more than one individual and is essential when the accounts are numerous in order to localize posting or other errors. Only one

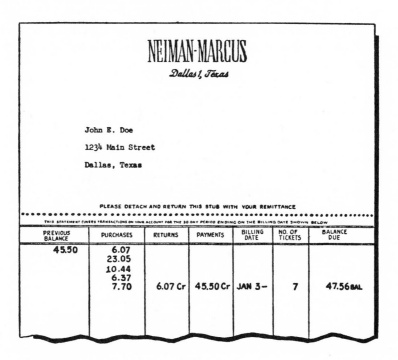

Figure 16-11. Statement and Credit History Ledger Prepared on Cycle Billing Machine.
(Courtesy of Burroughs Corporation.)

accounts receivable control is usually established in the general ledger, but subcontrols are maintained in the underlying records.

The number of accounts assigned to each control depends upon the system or equipment in use and the volume of transactions. When posting is done manually, about 400 accounts are considered as the maximum for each control. The number of accounts may be increased with bookkeeping machines or punched card accounting, although 1,000 is probably a practical limit in most situations unless activity is low.

Aids to posting accounts receivable ledgers. Consideration should be given to the sequence of the posting media (usually a copy of an invoice or a cash remittance advice). When the posting media have not been sorted in the same order or sequence as the ledger cards, the posting time is increased.

It is helpful to "stuff the ledgers" or intersort the posting media with the ledger accounts so that the posting clerk or the machine operator has the posting media and the ledger account together before the posting operation is commenced.

Proper selection of equipment for housing or filing accounts receivable records will aid in reducing clerical time. The accounts should be carefully indexed, and ledger trays should not be crowded. If the sequence of posting must be in more or less random order, or when the items to be posted affect only a small percentage of the open accounts, vertical filing devices that permit the operator to scan the names of a number of accounts at one time are worth while. A form for use with such a filing system is shown in Figure 16-12.

Installment accounts. Although any of the types of accounts receivable records previously discussed can be used with installment accounts, the type of record shown in Figure 16-13 was especially designed for this purpose.

The record is filed in a vertical file in which the right-hand column is exposed. When an account is first opened, the usual data are inserted in the heading. All payments to be received are then scheduled in the Payments Due section. The date the payment is due, the amount of the payment, and the balance resulting are all shown. By prescheduling payments and new balances, the process of posting actual collections is reduced to the simple act of stamping the ledger card. A rubber date stamp with a straight line long enough to cancel out an amount in the balance column is used. The stamp makes an impression thus:

————————————————Jan. 10, 19 . . . .

This one operation prints the date of payment in the Date Paid column and cancels out the previous balance in the Balance column.

Follow-up of past due accounts is then accomplished by scanning the exposed Date Paid column of each section of cards in the vertical file. Cards on past due accounts can be removed from the tray or a list can be made and delivered to the collection department. Fewer past due accounts are missed since a break in the line of dates across each file is immediately apparent. Bookkeeping machines are available for this type of operation.

Another variety of installment ledger card is shown in Figure 16-14.

Use of photography. The use of microfilm copies of records is increasing. It is usually much cheaper to microfilm a document than it is to prepare an extra copy. Microfilming is particularly suited to any situation where only one copy of a document is available which must serve several purposes—for instance, when a retail store mails

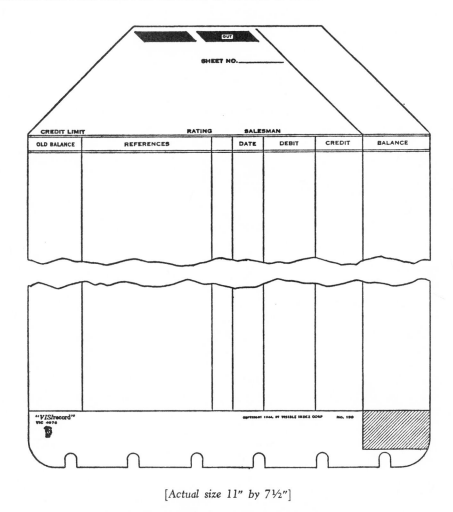

[Actual size 11″ by 7½″]

Figure 16-12. Machine-Posted Accounts Receivable Record for Use with Vertical Filing Equipment. *(Courtesy of Visible Index Corporation.)*

its sales checks to a customer instead of detailing the items on a statement. The technique also permits the destruction of bulky records and reduces the expense of storage or filing. Banks frequently microfilm all checks that clear through their records. The microfilm requires very little storage space, and with proper indexing and cataloguing, a copy of any document included in such a file can readily be located.

Aging accounts receivable. One of the internal control procedures that serves as a check on collection activities and policies is the periodical analysis of all open accounts by period of charge. This may be done by listing the balances on columnar sheets and providing columns for each period desired. It is then possible to summarize the analysis in the form shown below as a management report.

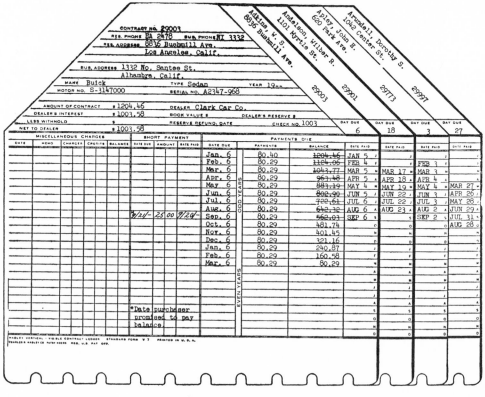

[*Actual size 8″ by 8″*]

Figure 16-13. Installment Ledger Card for Use with Vertical Filing Equipment.
(Courtesy of Charles R. Hadley Company.)

ANALYSIS OF ACCOUNTS RECEIVABLE BY BILLING DATES
AS OF DECEMBER 31, 19—   AS OF DECEMBER 31, 19—

Age of Billing	Amount	Per Cent to Total	Amount	Per Cent to Total
30 days or prior	$1,467,391	84.1%	$1,160,410	76.0%
30 to 60 days	204,310	11.7	260,190	17.1
60 to 90 days d.	60,509	3.5	84,300	5.5
Over 90 days	10,103	.7	21,604	1.4
Total accounts receivable ..	$1,742,313	100.0%	$1,526,504	100.0%

An aged trial balance prepared by use of punched card procedures is shown in Figure 16-15.

Determination of open or unpaid items. When the customer does not pay the account balance as shown by a statement of his account but has made payment of

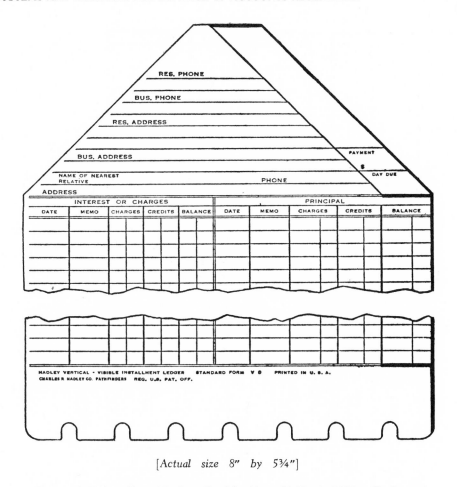

[*Actual size 8″ by 5¾″*]

Figure 16-14. Installment Ledger Card for Use with Vertical Filing Equipment.
(Courtesy of Charles R. Hadley Company.)

selected items, it is desirable to provide some means of keying or identifying the unpaid items on the accounts receivable record. This can be done by assigning a number or letter to each payment credited to an account and entering the same number or letter near each item paid by the remittance. The items not coded should then make up the account balance.

Authorization for write-off of bad debts. The authority for approving the write-off of uncollectible accounts should be assigned to a responsible executive who does not have access to incoming cash receipts or to the accounts receivable ledgers. The usual procedure is to have the collection department prepare lists of the items deemed uncollectible, indicating the period during which the debt was incurred, debtor's name, and the amount of loss, together with a summary of the reasons why collection cannot be made and the extent of collection efforts. In smaller organizations, it is customary to have these reviewed by the top operating executive. In larger

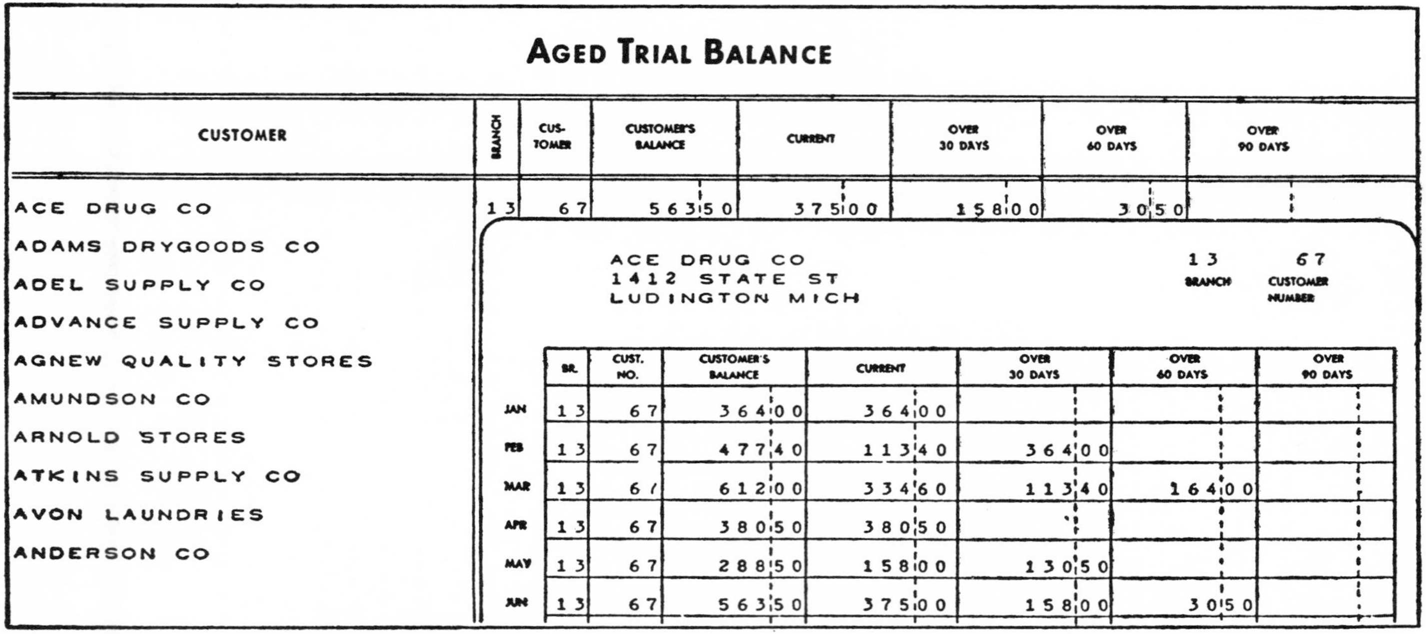

AGED TRIAL BALANCE

CUSTOMER	BRANCH	CUS-TOMER	CUSTOMER'S BALANCE	CURRENT	OVER 30 DAYS	OVER 60 DAYS	OVER 90 DAYS
ACE DRUG CO	13	67	563 50	375 00	158 00	30 50	-
ADAMS DRYGOODS CO							
ADEL SUPPLY CO							
ADVANCE SUPPLY CO							
AGNEW QUALITY STORES							
AMUNDSON CO							
ARNOLD STORES							
ATKINS SUPPLY CO							
AVON LAUNDRIES							
ANDERSON CO							

ACE DRUG CO
1412 STATE ST
LUDINGTON MICH

BRANCH 13   CUSTOMER NUMBER 67

	BR.	CUST. NO.	CUSTOMER'S BALANCE	CURRENT	OVER 30 DAYS	OVER 60 DAYS	OVER 90 DAYS
JAN	13	67	364 00	364 00			
FEB	13	67	477 40	113 40	364 00		
MAR	13	67	612 00	334 60	113 40	164 00	
APR	13	67	380 50	380 50			-
MAY	13	67	288 50	158 00	130 50		
JUN	13	67	563 50	375 00	158 00	30 50	-

Figure 16-15. Aging of Accounts Receivable Making Use of Punched Card Equipment.
(Courtesy of International Business Machines Corporation)

organizations, the approval for write-off is given by the chief financial executive unless the amounts are particularly significant.

Provision for doubtful accounts. Good accounting practice requires the recognition of probable losses in connection with accounts receivable in the preparation of a balance sheet and in the statement of earnings for a period. This provision was formerly described as a "reserve" in balance sheet presentation, but this terminology has now been generally abandoned. The amount of the estimated loss is shown in the balance sheet as "Provision for doubtful accounts" or similar terms. There are two common methods of establishing a provision for doubtful accounts.

1. As a percentage of sales. Under this plan, a relationship is established between sales and bad debt losses by analysis of historical data. This percentage is then applied to current sales to determine the current additions to the provision for doubtful accounts.
2. By analysis of receivables to determine specific items where losses are likely to be incurred.

It is desirable to check the general adequacy of the provision for doubtful accounts established by the "percentage of sales" method by a periodic review of the specific items that are doubtful of collection. This makes it possible to revise the percentage factor as experience or changed conditions require.

The provision for doubtful accounts should include an amount sufficient to cover the estimated costs or expenses incident to the collection of delinquent accounts if the amount is significant.

Installment accounts and deferment of income. The income or profit resulting from the sale of a product or merchandise is ordinarily recognized as accruing at the time the sale is made and title passes to the buyer. The federal income tax law permits a taxpayer, at his option and subject to certain conditions, to report the profits over the period of years covered by installment payments based upon the profit realized from each such payment. This method has the effect of deferring taxable income until collections are made, even though the taxpayer is reporting other transactions on an accrual basis. The treatment of income from installment sales for bookkeeping purposes and for the preparation of financial statements does not necessarily have to be on the same basis as that used for tax purposes.

Essential elements of internal control in connection with accounts receivable. Adequate internal control related to accounts receivable must give consideration to the following points:

1. Division of duties. The individuals responsible for maintenance of accounts receivable records should not have access to cash receipts whether in the form of currency or checks.
2. Sending statements to customers. There should be some independent check or control to ascertain that statements of account mailed to customers are in agreement with the receivable records.
3. Authority for bad debt write-offs.
4. Authority for cash and trade discounts, returned goods, and allowances.
5. Approval of credit, including terms and limits.
6. Periodic review of delinquent accounts by a responsible executive.
7. Regular balancing of detail accounts with controls.

8. Adequate physical control of receivable records, including protection against fire or other damage.

CASH REMITTANCES

Division of duties. It is essential that there be a clear-cut division of duties between individuals responsible for the handling of cash receipts and preparation of bank deposits and those responsible for maintenance of accounts receivable or general ledgers. The fact that all remittances are in the form of checks from customers does not provide adequate protection as evidenced by the numerous defalcations that have occurred under these conditions.

Remittance advices. Most companies now use some form of voucher check, a portion of which lists the invoices paid, the deductions for cash discounts and other items, and the net amount of the payment. This remittance advice is usually detached from the check by the cashier and forwarded to the accounts receivable section for use as the posting media. A separate writing of a cash remittance notice or listing for internal use is therefore unnecessary. A typical remittance advice is shown in Figure 16-16.

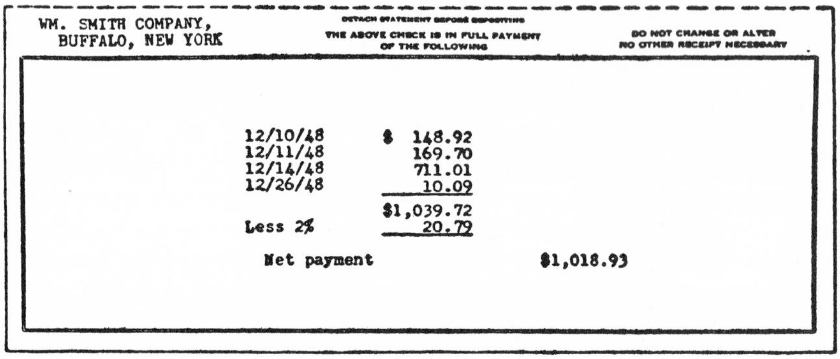

WM. SMITH COMPANY, BUFFALO, NEW YORK	DETACH STATEMENT BEFORE DEPOSITING THE ABOVE CHECK IS IN FULL PAYMENT OF THE FOLLOWING	DO NOT CHANGE OR ALTER NO OTHER RECEIPT NECESSARY

```
            12/10/48      $   148.92
            12/11/48          169.70
            12/14/48          711.01
            12/26/48           10.09
                          $1,039.72
            Less 2%            20.79

            Net payment                  $1,018.93
```

[*Actual size 3½″ by 8¼″*]

Figure 16-16. Remittance Advice Received from Customer Used as Posting Media in Connection with Accounts Receivable Record.

Giving customer a receipt. When the customer pays by check, the canceled check serves as a receipt. This procedure is typical of manufacturing companies and others dealing with business organizations rather than individuals. A separate receipt is desirable and necessary, however, for most retail and financial transactions where the payments may be either in cash or by check.

Using prenumbered receipts and retaining a carbon copy for internal use afford some protection in properly accounting for all collections.

A copy of the receipt can also serve as a posting medium for cash and receivable records without rewriting. Some of the systems previously discussed in this chapter make use of the receipt to post to cash and receivable records in one operation.

Prelisting of receipts. In order to strengthen internal control over cash receipts, many companies provide for a separate listing of all remittances by the individual who opens the mail, or some other remittances independent of the cashier and accounts receivable bookkeepers. These listings are then compared with recorded receipts and bank deposits and any discrepancies are investigated.

Centralization versus decentralization. Companies with several plants and several stores have no organizational and procedural problem with respect to whether billing, accounts receivable, or collections should be centralized or decentralized. The advantages and disadvantages of these functions may be summarized as follows.

Advantages of centralization:

1. More effective use of mechanical equipment.
2. Possibility of more competent supervision.
3. Better control of procedures followed. Internal control over the handling of cash and collections may be improved.
4. Possibility of greater economy because of volume operation and other factors listed above.

Disadvantages of centralization:

1. Decentralization permits the delegation of responsibility for all phases of the business to one local administrative head.
2. There is a time lag in transmitting documents.
3. Individuals responsible for recording details of transaction do not have close contact with the facts.
4. Rates of pay for clerical workers may be lower at decentralized locations.
5. Maximum savings may not be realized from centralization if branches are required to continue the following processing, also done centrally:
   a. Prepare shipping lists containing most of the information on centrally prepared invoices.
   b. Compute the total value of shipments for insurance, special discounts, credit, and the like.
   c. Require current data on accounts receivable for credit and collection information on customers' inquiries.

DATE DUE

30 505 JOSTEN'S